THE HUMAN DIMENSION OF
INTERNATIONAL LAW

The Human Dimension of International Law

Selected Papers

ANTONIO CASSESE

OXFORD
UNIVERSITY PRESS

OXFORD
UNIVERSITY PRESS

Great Clarendon Street, Oxford OX2 6DP

Oxford University Press is a department of the University of Oxford.
It furthers the University's objective of excellence in research, scholarship,
and education by publishing worldwide in

Oxford New York

Auckland Cape Town Dar es Salaam Hong Kong Karachi
Kuala Lumpur Madrid Melbourne Mexico City Nairobi
New Delhi Shanghai Taipei Toronto

With offices in

Argentina Austria Brazil Chile Czech Republic France Greece
Guatemala Hungary Italy Japan Poland Portugal Singapore
South Korea Switzerland Thailand Turkey Ukraine Vietnam

Oxford is a registered trade mark of Oxford University Press
in the UK and in certain other countries

Published in the United States
by Oxford University Press Inc., New York

© Oxford University Press 2008

The moral rights of the author have been asserted

Crown copyright material is reproduced under Class Licence
Number C01P0000148 with the permission of OPSI
and the Queen's Printer for Scotland

Database right Oxford University Press (maker)

First published 2008

British Library Cataloguing in Publication Data

Data available

Library of Congress Cataloging-in-Publication Data

The human dimension of international law : selected papers / Antonio Cassese.
p. cm.
Includes bibliographical references and index.
ISBN 978–0–19–923291–8 (hardback : alk. paper) 1. International law.
2. Cassese, Antonio. 3. Law teachers—Italy—Biography.
I. Cassese, Antonio
KZ3395.C25.A2 2008
341—dc22   2008004180

Typeset by Newgen Imaging Systems (P) Ltd., Chennai, India
Printed in Great Britain
on acid-free paper by
CPI Antony Rowe, Chippenham, Wiltshire

ISBN 978–0–19–923291–8

1 3 5 7 9 10 8 6 4 2

Preface

This book is a collection of writings of Antonio Cassese on international humanitarian law, human rights law, and international criminal law. It aims to shed light on the intellectual approach to these branches of international law taken by one of the most original and creative lawyers of his generation.

As is customary in many countries all over Europe, as Professor Cassese turned seventy we, a group of pupils and friends, came to think of what we could do to 'celebrate' our beloved maestro. In discussion, among the many ideas which arose was that of compiling all the articles he had written during the course of his illustrious academic career. Unfortunately, our maestro had written so much that we could easily have filled half a dozen volumes with his articles. We thus thought that we could, although rather arbitrarily, try to select his 'best' articles. We had scarcely started this project when we realized that we were being faced with very difficult choices. Suddenly, however, it appeared obvious that there was indeed a solid and unitary underlying idea in the books, articles, and activities undertaken by Antonio Cassese ('Nino' to all his friends): 'humanity' was at the core of his academic and professional interests, and we felt that this would indeed be an appropriate theme to tie together the selections for this book. We then decided to select mainly articles which were published a long time ago, or had appeared in publications that are difficult to find today. There are a few articles included here which are very well known, but we thought they would fit extremely well within the scope of the book.

This book also contains a set of portraits by distinguished personalities in different fields, who have interacted with Nino in many different roles in his and their professional lives. The aim of these portraits is to offer the reader an insight into Nino's personality. Readers will also find a new paper by Professor Cassese himself, in which he tries to take stock of his professional life and his approach to international law through four decades of teaching, writing, and practising law in international settings.

This selection of essays clearly show that Antonio Cassese knows that the international community remains solidly based on state sovereignty, self-interest, and power politics. This selection of essays, however, also shows that he firmly believes that states can come to be bound little by little to respect individuals. That is why he likes to describe the modern state as Gulliver tied down by the Lilliputians with a multitude of little laces that make it difficult for him to move. With unbeatable energy Antonio Cassese has always seen international law as this multitude of laces, as a means to force states to face the needs of the Lilliputians, and of humanity. For him, law is a tool to regulate society, but it is not a neutral tool. For him, law, including international law, must have a direction. There are values which are intrinsic to society that ought to be protected. All his writings indicate that, consciously or unconsciously, this idea has always underpinned Nino's academic work. The constant effort to couple this ideal source of inspiration with a parallel tension towards rigorous legal analysis and stringent reasoning makes him a great example of a 'utopian positivist'.

Working with Nino is a privilege and a fascinating experience. All those who know him are aware that he never stops working; how he is full of new ideas and new projects. Sometimes you think you should try to follow his rhythms, and you realize you will never make it. Sometimes you feel useless and are tempted to give up. However, if you stop to reflect for one second you realize how enriching is to be associated with him and how he gives you a sense of contributing in some way to strengthening the common ideals of a better world. Then you feel rewarded and find new energy to keep running, trying not to lose sight of the maestro, who has almost certainly already launched a new endeavour.

Special thanks go to Louise Arbour, Andrew Clapham, Luigi Condorelli, Claude Jorda, and Antonio Tabucchi for agreeing to write the 'portraits'. And thank you, Nino, for being our *roveto ardente*.

The Editors*

* Paola Gaeta and Salvatore Zappalà. With many thanks to the members of the Editorial Committee: Micaela Frulli, Luisa Vierucci, and Urmila De.

List of Acknowledgements

The editors and publishers would like to thank the following for permission to reproduce in this book material which has previously been published elsewhere:

American Society of International Law for 'A New Approach to Human Rights: The European Convention for the Prevention of Torture', from *American Journal of International Law* (1989).

Editoriale Scientifica for 'Means of Warfare: the Traditional and the New Law', from A. Cassese (ed.), *The New Humanitarian Law of Armed Conflict* (Napoli: Editoriale Scientifica, 1979).

Giuffrè for 'Current Trends in the Development of the Law of Armed Conflict', from *Rivista Trimestrale di Diritto Pubblico* (1974).

Giuffrè for 'Remarks on the Present Legal Regulation of Crimes of States', from *Essays in Honour of Roberto Ago*, vol. III (Milano: Giuffrè, 1987).

Giuffrè for 'The International Community, Terrorism and Human Rights', from *Studi in onore di Giuseppe Sperduti* (Milano: Giuffrè, 1984).

Giuffrè for 'The Spanish Civil War and the Development of Customary Law Concerning Internal Armed Conflicts', from A. Cassese (ed.), *Current Problems of International Law* (Milano: Giuffrè, 1975).

Giuffrè for 'Weapons Causing Unnecessary Suffering: Are They Prohibited?', from *Rivi sta di diritto internazionale* (1975).

Koninklijke BRILL N.V. for 'Crimes against Humanity: Comments on Some Problematical Aspects', from L. Boisson de Chazournes and V. Gowlland Deabbas (eds), *The International Legal System in Quest of Equity and Universality, Liber Amicorum G. Abi-Saab* (The Hague: Martinus Nijhoff, 2001).

Koninklijke BRILL N.V. for 'Legal Considerations on the International Status of Jerusalem', from *The Palestine Yearbook of International Law* (1986).

Koninklijke BRILL N.V. for 'The European Committee for the Prevention of Torture and Inhuman or Degrading Treatment Comes of Age', from N. Blokker & S. Muller (eds), *Towards More Effective Supervision by International Organizations* (The Hague: Martinus Nijhoff, 1994).

Koninklijke BRILL N.V. for 'Wars of National Liberation and Humanitarian Law', from C. Swinarski (ed.), *Studies and Essays on International Humanitarian Law and Red Cross Principles* (The Hague: Martinus Nijhoff, 1984).

Pedone for 'La diffusion des idées révolutionnaires et l'évolution du droit international', from *Révolution et droit international*, SFDI, Colloque de Dijon (Paris: Pedone, 1990) (translated from French into English and published here as 'Revolution and International Law').

Pedone for 'La guerre civile et le droit international', from *Revue générale de droit international public* (1986) (translated from French into English and published here as 'Civil War and International Law').

Polity Press for 'A "Contribution" of the West to the Struggle against Hunger: the Nestlé affair', from A. Cassese, *Human Rights in a Changing World* (Oxford: Polity, 1990).

Polity Press for 'Abraham and Antigone. Two Conflicting Imperatives', from A. Cassese, *Violence and Law in the Modern Age* (Oxford: Polity, 1988).

Springer for the 'Prohibition of Torture and Inhuman or Degrading Treatment or Punishment', from R. St. J. MacDonald et al. (eds), *The European System for the Protection of Human Rights* (The Hague: Kluwer, 1993).

Texas International Law Journal for 'Foreign Economic Assistance and Respect for Civil and Political Rights: Chile—A Case Study' (1979).

Wolters Kluwer Law and Business for 'The Prohibition of Indiscriminate Means of Warfare', from R.J. Akkermann et al. (eds), *Declarations on Principles. A Quest for Universal Peace* (Leyden: Sijthoff, 1977).

Contents

Portraits of Antonio Cassese

Soliloquy   lix

Antonio Cassese

I. THE HUMAN DIMENSION OF WARS

A. General   3

B. Classes of Wars and Belligerents   99

Tables of Cases

FRANCE

GERMANY

INTERNATIONAL ARBITRATIONS

INTERNATIONAL COURT OF JUSTICE

INTERNATIONAL CRIMINAL TRIBUNAL FOR RWANDA

INTERNATIONAL CRIMINAL TRIBUNAL FOR THE FORMER YUGOSLAVIA (ICTY)

INTERNATIONAL MILITARY TRIBUNAL

ISRAEL

ITALY

JAPAN

NETHERLANDS

NORWAY

PERMANENT COURT OF INTERNATIONAL JUSTICE

SINGAPORE

SPAIN

Tables of Legislation

FRANCE

JAPAN

NORWAY

SPAIN

SWITZERLAND

UNITED STATES OF AMERICA

USSR

List of Main Publications of Antonio Cassese

TEXTBOOKS

International Law and Politics in a Divided World (Oxford: Oxford University Press, 1984).
International Law (Oxford: Oxford University Press, 2001).
International Criminal Law (Oxford: Oxford University Press, 2003).
International Law, 2nd edn (Oxford: Oxford University Press, 2005).
International Criminal Law, 2nd edn (Oxford: Oxford University Press, 2008).

BOOKS AND ESSAYS

Il diritto interno nel processo internazionale (Padova: Cedam, 1962).
Il controllo internazionale (Milano: Giuffrè, 1972).
Il diritto internazionale bellico moderno. Testi e documenti (Pisa: Libreria Sc. Giordano Pellegrini, 1973).
'Modern Constitutions and International Law', in 192 *Recueil des cours de l'Académie de droit international de la Haye* (1985) 331.
Violence and Law in the Modern Age (Cambridge: Polity Press, 1988).
I rapporti Nord-Sud. Testi e documenti di politica internazionale dal 1945 ad oggi (Roma: Editori riuniti, 1989).
Terrorism, Politics and Law: the Achille Lauro Affair (Cambridge: Polity Press, 1989).
Human Rights in a Changing World (Cambridge: Polity Press, 1990).
B.V.A. Röling—The Tokyo Trial and Beyond (Cambridge: Polity Press, 1993).
Self-determination of Peoples. A Legal Reappraisal (Cambridge: Cambridge University Press, 1995).
Inhuman States. Imprisonment, Detention and Torture in Europe Today (Cambridge: Polity Press, 1996).
I diritti umani oggi (Bari-Roma: Laterza, 2005).

COLLECTIVE WORKS EDITED BY A. CASSESE

Current Problems of International Law (Milano: Giuffrè, 1975).
Pour un droit des peuples—Essais sur la Declaration d'Alger (co-ed.) (Paris: Berger et Levrault, 1978).
United Nations Peace-Keeping Operations—Legan Essays (Leiden: Sijthoff, 1978).
Fundamental Rights—United Nations Law: Two Topics in International Law (Alpheen aan den Rijn: Sijthoff and Noordhoff, 1979).
The New Humanitarian Law of Armed Conflict, vol. I (Napoli: Editoriale Scientifica, 1979).
The New Humanitarian Law of Armed Conflict, vol. II (Napoli: Editoriale Scientifica, 1980).
Parliamentary Control Over Foreign Policy (Alpheen aan den Rijn: Sijthoff and Noorhoff, 1980).
Control of Foreign Policy in Western Democracies—A Comparative Study of Parliamentary Foreign Affairs Committees, 3 vols (Padua, New York: Cedam and Oceana Pub., 1982).
The Current Legal Regulation of the Use of Force (Dordrecht: M. Nijhoff, 1986).
Change and Stability in International Law Making (co-ed.) (New York, Berlin: Walter de Gruyter, 1989).
International Crimes of States (co-ed.) (New York, Berlin: Walter de Gruyter, 1989).

Transfrontalier Television in Europe: the Human Rights Dimension / La télévision transfrontalière en Europe dans la perspective des droits de l'homme (co-ed.) (Baden-Baden: Nomos Verlag Ges., 1990).
Human Rights and the European Community: Methods of Protection (co-ed.) (Baden-Baden: Nomos Verlag Ges., 1991).
Human Rights and the European Community: the Substantive Law (co-ed.) (Baden-Baden: Nomos Verlag Ges., 1991).
The International Fight Against Torture/La lutte internationale contre la torture (Baden-Baden: Nomos Verlag Ges., 1991).
The Rome Statute of the International Criminal Court: A Commentary (co-ed.) (Oxford: Oxford University Press, 2002).
Crimes internationaux et juridictions internationales (co-ed.) (Paris: Presses universitaires de France, 2002).
Juridictions nationales et crimes internationaux (co-ed.) (Paris: Presses Universitaires de France, 2002).
Problemi attuali della giustizia penale internazionale (co-ed.) (Torino: Giappichelli, 2005).

ARTICLES

United Nations, Peace-Keeping, and the Use of Force

'Wars Forbidden and Wars Allowed by the Italian Constitution', in *Studi in onore di Balladore Pallieri*, vol. II (Milano: Giuffrè, 1978) 131.
'Recent Trends in the Attitude of Superpowers Towards Peace-keeping', in A. Cassese (ed.), *United Nations Peace-Keeping Operations—Legal Essays* (Leiden: Sijthoff, 1978) 223.
'How Could Nongovernmental Organisations Use U.N. Bodies More Effectively?', in 4 *Universal Human Rights* (1979) 73.
'Commentaires aux Articles 1, alinéa 2, et 51 de la Charte des Nations Unies', in J.-P. Cot, A. Pellet (eds), *Commentaire de la Charte des Nations Unies* (Paris: Economica, 1985) 769.
'Commentaire à l'article 51', in J.-P. Cot, A. Pellet (eds), *La Charte des Nations Unies, Commentaire article par article*, vol. I, 3rd edition (Paris: Economica, 2005), 1329.
'The General Assembly: Historical Perspective, 1945–1989', in P. Alston (ed.), *The United Nations and Human Rights* (Oxford: Clarendon Press, 1992) 25.
'Ex Iniuria Ius Oritur: Are We Moving Towards International Legitimation of Forcible Humanitarian Countermeasures in the World Community?', in 10 *European Journal of International Law* (1999) 23.
'A Follow-up: Forcible Humanitarian Countermeasures and Opinio Necessitatis', in 10 *European Journal of International Law* (1999) 791.
'Una modesta proposta sulla legittima difesa preventiva', in M. Spinedi et al. (eds), *La codificazione della responsabilità internazionale degli Stati alla prova dei fatti: problemi e spunti di riflessione* (Milano: Giuffrè, 2006) 189.

Human Rights

'Il controllo internazionale sul rispetto della libertà sindacale nel quadro delle attuali tendenze in material di protezione internazionale dei diritti dell'uomo', in XII *Comunicazioni e studi* (1966) 289.
'L'efficacia delle norme italiane di adattamento alla Convenzione europea dei diritti dell'uomo', in 5 *Rivista di diritto internazionale privato e processuale* (1969) 938.
'The Admissibility of Communications to the U.N. on Human Rights Violations', in 5 *Human Rights Journal* (1972) 375.
'Le droit de recours individuel devant la Commission européenne des droits de l'homme', in *Les clauses facultatives de la Convention européenne des droits de l'homme* (Bari: Levante, 1974) 45.

'The New U.N. Procedure for Handling Gross Violations of Human Rights', in 30 *La Comunità internazionale* (1975) 49.

'International Protection of the Right to Leave and to Return', in *Studi in onore di Manlio Udina*, vol. I (Milano: Giuffrè, 1975) 219.

'The Helsinki Declaration and Self-determination', in T. Buergenthal (ed.), *Human Rights, International Law and the Helsinki Accord* (Montclair, NJ: Allenheld, Osmun & Co., 1977) 83.

'Progressive Transnational Promotion of Human Rights', in B. Ramcharan (ed.), *Human Rights: Thirty Years after the Universal Declaration* (The Hague: Nijhoff, 1979) 249.

'Foreign Economic Assistance and Respect for Civil and Political Rights—A Case Study', in 14 *Texas International Law Journal* (1979), 251.

'Foreign Economic Assistance and Human Rights: Two Different Approaches', in 4 *Human Rights Review* (1979) 41.

'Political Self-determination—Old Concepts and New Developments', in A. Cassese (ed.), *Fundamental Rights—United Nations Law: Two Topics in International Law* (Alpheen aan den Rijn: Sijthoff and Noordhoff, 1979) 73.

'The Approach of the Helsinki Declaration to Human Rights', in L. Henkin (ed.), *The International Bill of Rights—The U.N. Covenant on Civil and Political Rights* (New York: Columbia University Press, 1981) 92.

'Enquires into the Impact of Foreign Economic Assistance on Human Rights. Some Problems of Method', in *Gedächtnisschrift für Ch. Sasse*, vol. II (Kehl am Rhein, Strasbourg: Engel Verlag, 1981) 611.

'Le droit des peuples à l'autodétermination: de la Charte de l'Onu à la Déclaration d'Alger de 1976', in *Le mois en Afrique, Etudes politiques, économiques et sociologiques africaines* (1981) 99.

'A New Approach to Human Rights: the European Convention for the Prevention of Torture', in 83 *American Journal of International Law* (1989) 128 (also in French: 'Une nouvelle approach des droits de l'homme: la Convention européenne pour la prévention de la torture', in 93 *Revue générale de droit international public* (1989) 6).

'Les individus', in M. Bedjaoui (ed.), *Droit international*, vol. I (Paris: Pedone, 1991) 119.

'The Israel-PLO Agreement and Self-determination', in 3 *European Journal of International Law* (1993) 564.

'Prohibition of Torture and Inhuman and Degrading Treatment or Punishment', in R. St. J. Macdonald et al. (eds), *The European System for the Protection of Human Rights* (Dordrecht, Boston, London: M. Nijhoff, 1993) 225.

'The European Committee for the Prevention of Torture and Inhuman or Degrading Treatment or Punishment Comes of Age', in N. Blokker et al. (eds), *Towards More Effective Supervision by International Organizations. Essays in Honour of Henry G. Schermers* (Dordrecht: Martinus Nijhoff, 1994) 115.

'Self-determination of Peoples and the Recent Break-up of USSR and Yugoslavia', in R. St. J. MacDonald (ed.), *Essays in Honour of Wang Tieya* (Dordrecht: Martinus Nijhoff, 1994) 131.

'Self-determination Revisited', in M. Rama Montaldo (ed.), *El derecho internacional en un mundo en transformación* (Montevideo: FCU, 1994) 229.

'The International Court of Justice and the Right of Peoples to Self-determination', in V. Lowe et al. (eds) *Fifty Years of the International Court of Justice: Essays in Honour of Sir Robert Jennings* (Cambridge: Cambridge University Press, 1996) 351.

'Are Human Rights Truly Universal?', in O. Savic (ed.), *The Politics of Human Rights* (London and New York: Verso, 1999) 149.

'The Impact of the European Convention on Human Rights on the International Criminal Tribunal for the Former Yugoslavia', in *Protection des droits de l'homme: la perspective européenne: mélanges à la mémoire de Rolv Ryssdal/Protecting human rights: the european perspective: studies in memory of Rolv Ryssdal* (Cologne: Carl Heymanns Verlag KG, 2000) 213.

la perspective européenne: the European perspective: /studies in memory of Rolv Ryssdal (Cologne: Carl Heymanns Verlag KG, 2000) 213.
'Are International Human Rights Treaties and Customary Rules on Torture Binding Upon US Troops in Iraq?', in 2 *Journal of International Criminal Justice* (2004) 872.
'Balancing the Prosecution of Crimes against Humanity and Non-Retroactivity of Criminal Law: the *Kolk and Kislyiy v. Estonia* case before the ECHR', in 4 *Journal of International Criminal Justice* (2006) 410.

International Humanitarian Law

'Current Trends in the Development of the Law of Armed Conflict', in 24 *Rivistra trimestrale di diritto pubblico* (1974) 1407.
'Weapons Causing Unnecessary Suffering: Are They Prohibited?', in 58 *Rivista di diritto internazionale* (1975) 12.
'The Spanish Civil War and the Development of Customary Law Concerning Internal Armed Conflicts', in A. Cassese (ed.) *Current Problems of International Law* (Milano: Giuffrè, 1975) 287.
'The Prohibition of Indiscriminate Means of Warfare', in R.J. Akkerman et al. (eds), *Declarations on Principles: a Quest for Universal Peace.* (Leiden: Sijthoff, 1977) 171.
'The Contribution of Italy at the Diplomatic Conference on the Development of International Humanitarian Law of Armed Conflicts (1974–77)', in 3 *Italian Yearbook of International Law* (1977) 217.
'Means of Warfare: the Traditional and the New Law', in A. Cassese (ed.), *The New Humanitarian Law of Armed Conflict*, vol.. I (Napoli: Editoriale Scientifica, 1979) 161.
'A Tentative Appraisal of the Old and the New Humanitarian Law of Armed Conflict', in A. Cassese (ed.), The New Humanitarian Law of Armed Conflict, vol. I (Napoli: Editoriale Scientifica, 1979) 461.
'Mercenaries: Lawful Combatants or War Criminals?', in 40 *Zeitschrift für ausländisches öffentliches Recht und Völkerrecht* (1980) 1.
'The Status of Rebels Under the 1977 Geneva Protocol on Non-international Armed Conflicts', in 30 *International and Comparative Law Quarterly* (1981) 416.
'The Geneva Protocols of 1977 on the Humanitarian Law of Armed Conflict and Customary International Law', in 3 *UCLA Pacific Basin Law Journal* (1984) 55.
'Wars of National Liberation and Humanitarian Law', in C. Swinarski (ed.), *Etudes et essais en l'honneur de Jean Pictet* (Geneva, The Hague: M. Nijhoff, 1984) 313.
'La guerre civile et le droit international', in 90 *Revue générale de droit international public* (1986) 553.
'Legal Considerations on the International Status of Jerusalem', in 3 *The Palestine Yearbook of International Law* (1986) 13.
'La diffusion des idées révolutionnaires et l'évolution du droit international', in *SFDI Révolution et droit international* (Paris: Pedone, 1990) 295.
'Power and Duties of an Occupant in Relation to Land and Natural Resources', in E. Playfair (ed.), *International Law and the Administration of Occupied Territories* (Oxford: Clarendon Press,1992) 419.
'The International Tribunal for the Former Yugoslavia and the Implementation of International Humanitarian Law', in L. Condorelli et al. (eds) *Les Nations Unies et le droit international humanitaire: actes du Colloque international à l'occasion du cinquantième anniversaire de l'ONU* (Genève—19, 20 et 21 octobre 1995) (Paris: Pedone, 1996) 229.
'The Martens Clause: Half a Loaf or Simply pie in the Sky?', in 11 *European Journal of International Law* (2000) 187.
'Community Action to Prompt Implementation of the Geneva Conventions: A Plea for Bolstering the ICRC's Role', in *Soberanía del Estado y Derecho internacional: homenaje al profesor Juan Antonio Carrillo Salcedo*, vol. 1 (Sevilla: Universidad de Sevilla, Secretariado de Publicaciones, 2005) 361.

'On Some Merits of the Israeli Judgment on Targeted Killings', in 5 *Journal of International Criminal Justice* (2007) 339.

Terrorism

'Terrorism and Human Rights', in 32 *American University Law Review* (1982) 945.

'The International Community, Terrorism and Human Rights', in *Studi in onore di G. Sperduti* (Milano: Giuffrè, 1984) 477.

'The International Community's Legal Response to Terrorism', in 37 *International and Comparative Law Quarterly* (1988) 589.

'Terrorism is Also Disrupting Some Crucial Legal Categories of International Law', in 12 *European Journal of International Law* (2001) 993.

'Terrorism as an International Crime', in A. Bianchi (ed.), *Enforcing International Law Norms against Terrorism* (Oxford: Hart Publishing, 2004) 213.

'The Multifaceted Criminal Notion of Terrorism in International Law', in 4 *Journal of International Criminal Justice* (2006) 933.

International Criminal Law

'La communauté internationale et le génocide', in *Le droit international au service de la paix, de la justice et du développement: Mélanges Michel Virally* (Paris: Pedone, 1991) 183.

'The International Criminal Tribunal for the Former Yugoslavia: Some General Remarks', in *Studi in ricordo di Antonio Filippo Panzera* (Bari: Cacucci, 1995) 235.

'Il Tribunale penale per la Iugoslavia: bilancio di due anni di attività', in *Dai tribunali penali internazionali ad hoc a una corte permanente: atti del Convegno*, Roma 15–16 dicembre 1995 (Napoli: Editoriale Scientifica, 1996) 177.

'Reflections on Some of the Novel Features of the International Criminal Tribunal for the Former Yugoslavia', in 43 *Jugoslovenska revija za medunarodno pravo: organ Jugoslovenskog udruzenja za medunarodno pravo* (1996) 111.

'The International Criminal Tribunal for the Former Yugoslavia and Human Rights', in 2 *European Human Rights Law Review* (1997) 329.

'Reflections on International Criminal Prosecution and Punishment of Violations of Humanitarian Law', in J. Charney et al. (eds), *Politics, Values and Functions. International Law in the 21st Century. Essays in Honour of Professor Louis Henkin* (The Hague: Nijhoff, 1997) 261.

'Reflections on International Criminal Justice', in 61 *The Modern Law Review* (1998) 1.

'On the Current Trends Towards Criminal Prosecution and Punishment of Breaches of International Humanitarian Law', in 9 *European Journal of International Law* (1998) 2.

'The Statute of the International Criminal Court: Some Preliminary Reflections', in 10 *European Journal of International Law* (1999) 144.

'Crimes against Humanity: Comments on Some Problematic Aspects', in L. Boissou de Chazournes and V. Gowlland-Debbas (eds), *The International Legal System in Quest of Equity and Universality. Liber Amicorum Georges Abi-Saab* (The Hague: Nijhoff, 2001) 429.

'The Contribution of the International Criminal Tribunal for the Former Yugoslavia to the Ascertainment of General Principles of Law Recognized by the Community of Nations', in S. Yee et al. (eds), *International Law in the Post-Cold War World: Essays in Memory of Li Haopei* (London: Routledge, 2001) 43.

'Crimes Against Humanity', in A. Cassese et al. (eds), *The Rome Statute of the International Criminal Court: A Commentary*, vol. I (Oxford: Oxford University Press, 2002) 353.

'From Nuremberg to Rome: International Military Tribunals to the International Criminal Court', in A. Cassese et al. (eds), *The Rome Statute of the International Criminal Court: A Commentary*, vol. I (Oxford: Oxford University Press, 2002) 3.

'Genocide', in A. Cassese et al. (eds), *The Rome Statute of the International Criminal Court: A Commentary*, vol. I (Oxford: Oxford University Press, 2002) 335.

'Justifications and Excuses in International Criminal Law', in A. Cassese et al. (eds), *The Rome Statute of the International Criminal Court: A Commentary*, vol. I (Oxford: Oxford University Press, 2002) 951.

'L'influence de la CEDH sur l'activité des Tribunaux pénaux internationaux', in A. Cassese et al. (eds), *Crimes internationaux et juridictions internationales* (Paris: Presses universitaires de France, 2002) 143.

'Y'a-t-il un conflit insurmontable entre souveraineté des États et justice pénale internationale?' in A. Cassese et al. (eds) *Crimes internationaux et juridictions internationales* (Paris: Presses universitaires de France, 2002) 13.

'Peut-on poursuivre des hauts dirigeants des États pour des crimes internationaux?: à propos de l'affaire Congo c/ Belgique (C.I.J.)', in 57 *Revue de science criminelle et de droit pénal comparé* (2002) 479.

'When May Senior State Officials be Tried for International Crimes? Some Comments on the *Congo v. Belgium* Case', in 13 *European Journal of International Law* (2002) 853.

'State Sovereignty v. International Criminal Justice', in *Studi di diritto internazionale in onore di Gaetano Arangio-Ruiz*, vol. 1 (Napoli: Ed. Scientifica, 2003) 25.

'The Belgian Court of Cassation vs. the International Court of Justice: the "Sharon and others case"', in 1 *Journal of International Criminal Justice* (2003) 437.

'Is the Bell Tolling for Universality?: A Plea for a Sensible Notion of Universal Jurisdiction', in 1 *Journal of International Criminal Justice* (2003) 589.

'Quelques réflexions sur la justice pénale internationale', in *La justice pénale internationale dans les décisions des tribunaux ad hoc: études des Law Clinics en droit pénal international* (Milano: Giuffrè, 2003) 283.

'The Role of Internationalized Courts and Tribunals in the Fight against International Criminality', in Cesare P.R. Romano et al. (eds), *Internationalized Criminal Courts and Tribunals: Sierra Leone, East Timor, Kosovo, and Cambodia* (Oxford: Oxford University Press, 2004) 3.

'The Special Court and International Law: The Decision Concerning the Lomé Agreement Amnesty', in 2 *Journal of International Criminal Justice* (2004) 1130.

'Black Letter Lawyering v. Constructive Interpretation: The *Vasiljevic* case', in 2 *Journal of International Criminal Justice* (2004) 265.

'La prise en compte de la jurisprudence de Strasbourg par les juridictions pénales internationales', in G. Cohen Jonathan et al. (eds), *Le rayonnement international de la jurisprudence de la Cour européenne des droits de l'homme* (Bruxelles: Bruylant, 2005) 28.

'The Proper Limits of Individual Responsibility Under the Doctrine of Joint Criminal Enterprise', in 5 *Journal of International Criminal Justice* (2007) 109.

'Is the ICC Still Having Teething Problems?', in 4 *Journal of International Criminal Justice* (2006) 434.

National Constitutions and International Law

'Art. 10 Cost', in G. Branca (ed.), *Commentario alla Costituzione, Artt. 1–12, Principi fondamentali*, Tomo I (Bologna-Roma, Zanichelli-Societa' Editrice del Foro Italiano, 1975) 461.

'Art. 11 Cost.' in G. Branca (ed.), *Commentario alla Costituzione, Artt. 1–12, Principi fondamentali*, Tomo I (Bologna-Roma, Zanichelli-Societa' Editrice del Foro Italiano, 1975) 565.

'The Non Extradition of Foreigners for Political Offences in the Italian Constitution', in 1 *Italian Yearbook of International Law* (1975) 173.

'Art. 80 Cost.', in G. Branca (ed.), *Commentario alla Costituzione, Articoli 76–82, La formazione delle leggi*, Tomo II (Bologna-Roma, Zanichelli-Societa' Editrice del Foro Italiano, 1979), 150.

'IX comma dell' Art. 87, seconda parte' in G. Branca (ed.), *Articoli Commentario alla Costituzione, 83–87, Il Presidente della Repubblica*, Tomo I (Bologna-Roma, Zanichelli-Societa' Editrice del Foro Italiano, 1978) 270.

Parliaments and Foreign Policy

'Parliamentary Control of Treaty-Making in Italy', in 2 *Italian Yearbook of International Law* (1976) 165.

'The Role of Foreign Affairs Committees in Treaty-Making in Italy', in A. Cassese (ed.), *Control of Foreign Policy in Western Democracies: A Comparative Study of Parliamentary Foreign Affairs Committees*, vol. II (Padua, New York: Cedam and Oceana Publications, 1982) 227.

'The Role of Legal Advisers in Ensuring that Foreign Policy Conforms to International Legal Standards', in 14 *Michigan Journal of International Law* (1992–3) 139.

Miscellanea

'Sovereignty Within the Law in Italy', in A. Larson, C.W. Jenks (eds), *Sovereignty Within the Law* (Dobbs Ferry: Oceana, 1965) 60.

'A New Reservation Clause (Art. 20 of the U.N. Convention on the Elimination of All Forms of Racial Discrimination)', in *Recueil d'études de droit international en hommage à P. Guggenheim* (Genève: Tribune, 1968) 266.

'Consensus and Some of its Pitfalls', in 58 *Rivista di diritto internazionale* (1975) 754.

'The Concept of "Legal Dispute" in the Jurisprudence of the International Court of Justice', in *Studi in onore di G. Morelli* (Milano: Giuffrè, 1975) 173.

'Legal Services in Italy for Deprived Persons, Particularly in Urban Areas', in *Council of Europe, Proceedings of the Sixth Colloquy on European Law* (Strasbourg: Council of Europe, 1976) 37.

'The Concept of Law Upheld by Western, Socialist and Developing Countries', in R.-J. Dupuy (ed.), *The Future of International Law in a Multicultural World* (The Hague: M.Nijhoff, 1984) 317.

'L'immunité de juridiction civile des Organisations internationales dans la jurisprudence italienne', 30 in *Annuaire français de droit international* (1984) 556.

'Le droit international et la question de l'assistance aux mouvements de libération nationale', in 19 *Revue belge de droit international* (1986) 307.

'La lotta per il nuovo diritto. Ricordo di B.V.A. Röling', in *Politica e diritto* (1987) 275.

'Remarks on the Present Legal Regulations of Crimes of States', in A. Cassese (co-ed.), *International Crimes of State* (New York, Berlin: Walter de Gruyter, 1989) 200.

'Remarks on Scelle's Theory of "Role Splitting" (dédoublement fonctionnnel) in international law', in 1 *European Journal of International Law* (1990) 210.

'Realism v. Artificial Constructs: Remarks on Anzilotti's Theory of War', in 3 *European Journal of International Law* (1992) 149.

L'inaccessible étoile

Louise Arbour

My very first encounter with Nino Cassese was, as anyone who knows him can imagine, immensely scary. I had been approached, in a most secretive manner, to replace Richard Goldstone as chief prosecutor of ICTY and ICTR. I was mildly stressed out, in part because of my then position in the Canadian judiciary, and because of the uncertainty of what might be ahead for me. As is only natural in times of stress, I went for a haircut. While at the hairdresser, I received a call that the President of ICTY wanted to speak to me. After some pleasantries, which lasted all of two or three seconds, he got to the point: what did I know about crimes against humanity? He was aware of the decisions of the Canadian courts in *R v. Finta*, and that I participated in the majority opinion in that case in the Ontario Court of Appeal. As far as I was concerned, that showed knowing more about crimes against humanity than most judges operating in a national court system in 1996.

I couldn't quite put it to him that way since he had already moved to the next topic: what did I know about investigating and prosecuting? By then I had lost interest in my haircut. Who is this guy? Does he own the place? He kept referring to ICTY as 'our tribunal'. In retrospect it is clear to me that he was only acting out his own anxieties. He was simply not going to allow 'our tribunal' to fail. The prospect scared him, so if he could scare me instead, or in addition, then good: it would not fail.

And this is how began one of the most intriguing, and most challenging, professional encounters of my entire career. We had both been reincarnated into the characters of a very complex play, the script of which we were writing as we went along. Contrary to most people in that business, Nino did not hold academics in contempt. Just as well for both of us. He was a much better, much more established, and much more confident academic than I had ever been, but I was a much more experienced judge than he was. In many ways, he should have been the prosecutor and I the judge. In fact, left to his own device, he would have happily been all: the prosecutor, the registrar, and the judge, just to make sure that no one allowed 'our tribunal' to fail.

We were, still are, both of us, passionate about the law. But if I may be pardoned a cliché, criminal lawyers are from Mars, international lawyers are from Venus. I never believed in the clash of civilizations between civil law and common law trained lawyers. The great divide, exemplified by the profound intellectual tensions between Nino and me, came from our backgrounds in international

and criminal law respectively. Criminal law is authoritative, rule-based, rigour-
ous, and designed in part to keep in check the immense powers of the state.
International law is consensual, norm-based, fluid, and immensely deferential to
states. If Nino and I could ever come to see the world through a jointly-made lens,
then there was a future for international criminal law. In the end I think we did.
And that discipline has a remarkable past, a very honourable present, and a most
promising future. And a lot of that is due to the remarkable tenacity of this most
annoying man.

I don't mean annoying all the time. It is just the unrelenting, unyielding search
for something out there, something better than what was there before, a lot better, something that will come from working harder, trying out new ideas, but
only good ones, bumping into those who are still trying to figure out yesterday's
news. *L'inaccessible étoile*. Maybe this is what he is after.

Then I left. I hope he was sorry to see me go. He almost made an international
lawyer out of me. And as for his mastery of the beauty of criminal law theory, he
figured it out all by himself.

The Generous Cosmopolitan Taskmaster

Andrew Clapham

The year is 1986, my progress in the PhD programme is being held up by a new arrival at the European University Institute (EUI) in Florence. The Head of the Law Department tells me that the new man, Professor Antonio Cassese, wants to see me to discuss my thesis proposal. My encounter with Professor Cassese is confusing. He tells me that there are a number of articles related to my topic to be taken into consideration and tasks me with reading them for our next meeting; he then says he has no time to discuss this further, but that I am invited to drive out to see him for lunch at his country house on Sunday. The intensity of the encounter leaves me reeling. The professor is generous with his time that Sunday, I meet and enjoy the company of Sylvia and their children, I learn about: international relations, which key scholars I should be reading, how to make a pasta primavera, and the predictions for the olive crop. Over the next few weeks I work around the clock to produce drafts to satisfy my new taskmaster. Around this time my teacher imparts to me a Kantian sense that how people treat each other has to have limits, and those that transgress that line should be made accountable.

Antonio Cassese has succoured a generation of students who are immensely proud to identify with him. Our experiences may well differ in the detail but probably follow similar paths. Cassese cajoled us, and shaped our approaches in ways that are deeply appreciated, but hard to emulate. The energy, dogged determination, and lust for learning combine into a potent cocktail. This enthusiasm is not confined to the world of academia. Many witnessed Cassese channelling his capacity for graft into the newly formed European Committee for the Prevention of Torture, which he presided over in its early days. His appetite for meetings, methodology, and missions catapulted the Committee into action and ensured that governments give way on crucial points allowing this new mechanism to become one of the most successful inter-governmental initiatives for the prevention of ill-treatment in detention. His admitted 'cunning' meant he was able to unearth hidden detention areas and the practice of torture.[1] With the later election to the International Tribunal for the former Yugoslavia, again as the President at the start, we again find an absolute determination to turn this new entity into an effective institution, which in turn leaves a lasting contribution to the emerging new field of international criminal law. Cassese was not, however, content to develop this from the bench; I well remember the impact he had on

---

[1] Some of the details are outlined in the papers which appear in the present volume.

his trips to UN Headquarters in New York, on the occasion of his speeches to the General Assembly and Security Council on behalf of the International Tribunal for the former Yugoslavia.

At times the ambitions and determination to make things work can overwhelm those in contact with the human whirlwind; but remarkably one can assume that many of the ideas and initiatives are far from impetuous. Moreover the capacity for culture has left with me with a couple of abiding memories. I remember a shopping trip in Brussels. We had finished with the round of meetings at the European Parliament and Cassese announced that we had time for some shopping. We arrived at the FNAC, not sure what to expect. We separated and returned to the cash desk, with a twelve inch remix of Lambada (information for those worried about the chronology) and the professor, with four volumes of *Kierkegaard's Writings*. I cannot think of anything more intimidating at that particular moment (except perhaps if these incredibly serious looking books had been in Danish). In the evening, I recall all of us in the team being treated to the theatre, something entertaining by Sartre. All the time we were working to keep up with an insatiable appetite for deepening an understanding of human behaviour and existence; all the time we were treated with incredible largesse.

Most recently, at the end of 2004, Cassese was back in Geneva as the Chairperson of the UN International Commission of Inquiry on Darfur established by the Secretary-General at the request of the Security Council. He again brought this bighearted mixture of industriousness and generosity to bear, taking Commissioners and others out for dinner while insisting that the work continue through Christmas. No one could be in any doubt that he was determined to get to the bottom of the atrocities in Darfur, and one sees again the depth of his commitment to ensuring that the international community develop a cosmopolitan law which places the duties and rights of individuals centre stage. It is this idea that Cassese has continued to champion as instrumental to achieving a better world. In his words: 'peace may also be achieved by imposing international accountability upon the alleged perpetrators of horrific crimes that threaten stability and peaceful relations'.[2]

---

[2] A. Cassese, 'Is the ICC Still Having Teething Problems?', 4 *J Int Criminal Justice*, 434–41, at 436.

Nino Cassese and the Sparrow's Feet

Luigi Condorelli

I have known Nino Cassese for over forty years, since the very beginning of our academic careers. These took shape in parallel over more or less the same time span, starting in the late fifties of the last century for him and in the very early sixties for me. Nino, at the University of Pisa, and I at Florence, were both assistants to unforgettable teachers (Giuseppe Sperduti and Giuseppe Barile, respectively), who were very close to each other and both pupils of that other great figure, the late Tomaso Perassi. And, as academic genealogies in Italy were extremely important (and still are, for better or—alas!—often for worse), we have always regarded ourselves as 'academic cousins'. But very soon, this professional and generational relationship, nourished also by a great closeness of cultural interests, was enriched by a strong bond of friendship. Tried and tested in Florence, it was never to fail, even when the ups and downs of life and career separated us, and for long periods, geographically. In short, we two know each other well, maybe even too well. We each know everything—well, nearly everything—about the other: virtues and defects, strong points and weaknesses, likes and dislikes, merits and shortcomings . . .

The foregoing should explain why I felt it somewhat difficult when his pupils, who are promoting this fine project to present him with a token of our respectful affection on the occasion of his seventieth birthday, asked me to write a few lines about him. Obviously I couldn't simply turn around and say no. And yet, I feel that a testimonial (especially if one wishes to tell the public something more than what they already know about such a well-known and complex figure as Nino Cassese), while it should certainly be sincere, ought also (in fact, especially) be truthful. So how was I to avoid letting such a great friendship as the one between us make my portrait biased and therefore to some extent untruthful?

After some pondering, I had an idea, perhaps a slightly vengeful one: to put the ball, so to speak, in their court, and bring the same difficulty to Nino's pupils by asking them to give me a brief portrait of their teacher, bringing out his essential features. That would let me compare their view of Nino Cassese with my own and thus—hopefully—confirm it as well-founded.

I was very satisfied with the results, even though the portrayals of Nino I was sent showed sometimes considerable differences. Yet there were none on the essential point: whether it is as his colleague and friend or as his pupil that one looks at Nino, his exceptional qualities emerge identically. His immense capacity for work, which makes him a 'monster' (in the Latin meaning of 'monstrum', a unique being) of productivity in terms of both scientific research and practical action, reflects and expresses a great moral tension and an absolute commitment; and these two expressions pervade, animate, and sustain him in every aspect of his activities. For him, anyone doing academic teaching and research must obviously seek and reveal the truth in its deepest, most hidden core, beyond external appearances, rhetorical show, platitudes, and political or ideological shields. But this critical research cannot and must not be an end in itself. Understanding is not enough: knowledge must be continued and completed in action, must be the instrument used to improve the world, the fate of man and society. Does disenchanted, ruthless analysis impel us to pessimism and suggest that the goal is remote and impossible to reach, that the enemy to be beaten is a giant with a thousand arms and a thousand legs, that the forces available to deploy against it to defeat it are too slight, that the obstacles to overcome are mountains as high as the Himalayas? No matter! We still have to try, to invent original solutions, to blaze new trails, in short, to put our all into it, in order to reach through our action, perhaps not the maximum that may be desirable, but at least something of use. For even very little is better than nothing, if that little carries a seed of hope and marks an advance for mankind. Moreover, we must involve others in the fight: pupils, collaborators, and fellow travellers who must share the same secular religion and commit themselves with all their strength from the outset, for there's no time to lose! Needless to say, the setbacks, disappointments, insults, and injuries we are bound to suffer when striving in such a spirit must, rather than discourage us, embolden us to resume the uphill struggle with renewed vigour, after at most a brief (very brief!) pause, barely enough to let us lick our wounds.

Nino Cassese puts into practice, with absolute dedication and with all the energy he is capable of (which, as anyone acquainted with him well knows, is stupefying), Gramsci's slogan that the pessimism of the reason must go hand in hand with the optimism of the will. And looking back at the path he has followed thus far, one cannot but be impressed at the resulting proof that . . . Gramsci was right! Nino's imprint on international human rights law in force or on contemporary international criminal law is highly visible. Nino has influenced these areas of law profoundly, shaping and improving them through his studies, but even more through his actions: for instance, first as president of the European Committee on the Prevention of Torture, then as judge and president of the International Criminal Tribunal for the former Yugoslavia. The examples just mentioned are only the best known. I could cite hundreds of other less conspicuous ones. I shall refrain from doing so, in order not to overburden this article. But I feel it important to underline how consistent with Nino's overall commitment is his continuous effort to inform the non-expert public by his press writings of whatever may endanger or threaten to compromise human rights. The popularization of the truth is another kind of action!

Nino Cassese loves funny stories, jokes, and anecdotes, which we often swap in carefree moments (I was almost forgetting to say that Nino is a highly erudite and very amusing companion, with whom one can spend many an extremely enjoyable, and enriching, hour). Among all those stories, there is one he likes more than others, and—I believe—not by chance, for I've heard him tell it several times. It's about a medieval knight (let's call him 'Agilulf') fully equipped with lance, helmet, armour, and white charger, who, after great derring-do, returns to his castle, and just as he enters his domain, notices a tiny sparrow lying on its back right in the middle of the road, with its little claws pointing upwards. 'What are you doing?' he asks. And the little bird tells him he has heard that the sky is going to fall that very day, so he's ready to hold it up and protect his liege lord's possessions. The nobleman is rather touched by his minuscule subject's loyalty, but cannot help laughing. If the sky really were to fall, what could such a small creature with his scrawny little feet ever do? And the sparrow somewhat resentfully replies: 'Everyone does what he can!'

Thank you, Nino, for everything you have done so far, and are bound to go on doing from this day onward, for your, for all of our, Agilulf—whose real name is 'Social Justice'.

A Tribute to Professor Nino Cassese

Claude Jorda

The first time I met Nino Cassese was on the telephone. And calling it 'meeting on the telephone' isn't just giving vent to an excessive taste for paradox. For at the time of that phone call, in late December 1993, I was in a very difficult situation, from all points of view and in every sense of the word. Yet this man, whose personal charm I did not yet know, still less his intellectual charisma, managed through this simple contact at a distance to make me share his enthusiasm for the lifelong fight he was pursuing. In a few minutes, my fate was sealed.

I had just, very reluctantly, left the prestigious post, and very great responsibilities, of Chief Prosecutor of Paris. Rather than join the Court of Cassation—known in short to initiates as 'la casse', which one might translate as 'the trouble'—I chose, over the ambiguous retirement of every senior French judge, a sort of geographical and intellectual exile. I knew nothing about the field. In fact France was choosing me mostly to 'clear its debt', as it were, in relation to a senior magistrate who could not be reproached with anything other than blocking up the judicial hierarchy, and, perhaps especially, not leaning towards the dominant mode of thought.

In a word, I was not choosing anything.

And Nino Cassese's great skill lay in giving me the impression 'I' had been 'chosen' for my worth, although that was something still very much hypothetical, indeed virtual.

From our very first meetings at Churchillplein (where he had managed in only a few weeks to find some rather magnificent premises—in what had been an insurance company, and what could be more symbolic than that?—that I continue to regard as much more functional than those of the present International Criminal Court) I nonetheless made him understand that I had no background for being a 'good international judge'; that my career had been more as Prosecutor than as Judge; that I had no particular knowledge of the field; that all I could manage of English were some stammerings or grunts.

Nino Cassese had an answer for everything. Your experience in the Prosecutors' Office? Very valuable for the early stages of the Court, in relation to the prosecutor's penal policy. Your knowledge of criminal and humanitarian international law? We are all here to build it after the void left since Nuremberg and Tokyo. Your English? No problem. Moreover, on top of French being a working language of the Tribunal, we shall be needing some French legal culture, especially the contributions from civil law.

How could one possibly resist such a communicative type of enthusiasm?

But do not imagine that this enthusiasm was always manifest and conveyed in pleasure.

As from Christmas 1993, each of us was assigned a very specific job on working out the Rules of Procedure and Rules of Evidence: an essential tool in enabling us to embark on any judicial activity. And it was here that I met with the greatest amiability and trustfulness on the part of Nino Cassese. I was still caught up in my responsibilities as Chief Prosecutor of Paris and had to finish off some very delicate cases, relating in particular to terrorism. But at the same time Nino wanted to show me the path this new career had taken. The whole of Nino is in these sentences: 'Of course, you do what you can manage. BUT it would be so nice to have the benefit of your experience. Perhaps you could come up with something for when we come back again in January.' And like all the rest of my new colleagues I did what I had been asked to.

Nowadays, especially since new international criminal courts have been set up, it seems to be all a matter of course to get academics and practitioners coming from every continent to work together, with their often different practices, sometimes surprising habits, and specific knowledge, frequently hard to verify. But if we look back at 1994, we can well imagine what a job it was to create this sort of collaboration *ab ovo*. For instance, how were the Chambers to be made up? How should one treat the chief legal systems, when the situation referred by the Security Council concerned countries of the civil law tradition but many of the Judges, and the Prosecutor, belonged to the common law tradition? And other examples could be cited.

In my view it shows all of Nino Cassese's skill that this work of bringing together different worlds was accomplished, and in record time too. I shall always remember the eleventh of February 1994, when from an improvised stage in the room that is now the courtroom, our President delivered to the world our Rules of evidence and of procedure. Of course, those Rules were not to prove perfect, and have had to be amended dozens of times since. But the message President Cassese was delivering, both to the Prosecutor and to the countries of the region, as well as to the Security Council and the international community, was clear: 'From now on you are going to have to reckon with this entirely new institution', and especially, 'We are not some sort of alibi jurisdiction for the world's good conscience!'

This message, had, of course, to be followed up by clear actions. Here again, it was Nino Cassese's merit literally to take on the promotion of the Tribunal. Turning himself into a subtle diplomat (and here one should not forget his connections with the Florence of Machiavelli), President Cassese brought to bear all his fame as a great professor of international criminal law and international humanitarian law to make sure this totally new court could begin its judicial work without delay. Sparing neither time nor effort, he soon got results. Even while the countries in the region were still at war, the first accused was brought before the Tribunal. One day we shall perhaps know exactly what part President Cassese took in this 'premiere' for international criminal justice. To be sure, this first accused was not the top leader one might have expected. But what a relief it was to be able to present ourselves before the world and before the Security Council and say: 'Look, the justice system you created is up and running, and you can be sure we are determined to make it work.'

Such exhilarating times must not be allowed to let us forget all the human aspects that made our President both an exacting and rigorous leader, and at the same time a man in the full sense of the word, namely a warm humanist.

His faults? Of course, our friend Cassese had some. But were they not the defects of his qualities? Dancing with rage because a note wasn't written as quickly as he himself would have, for example; impatience; criticisms always well formulated but pointed, and therefore all the more resented by their addressee. And a few I shall gloss over. But what need is there to recall these minor flaws, seen against all the immense labours our captain accomplished to sail the ship and bring it safely home to port?

I should be less than complete, though, were I to omit all the things the first companions on that voyage cannot forget about the man: his simplicity, his hospitality at his home, his culinary gifts, the delights of his pasta washed down with some Tuscan wine, or sometimes even, to please me, some claret from Bordeaux.

Those were heady times, and, thanks to you, Nino, an exciting adventure. All those who shared in it will be eternally grateful to you for it.

But what, ultimately, would our feelings and the satisfaction of our desires amount to were they only the expression of our personal impulses and emotions? I believe the thing that truly has to be hailed in this immense enterprise and in its success is the fact that without our first President nothing thereafter could have been accomplished the same way nor with the same happy outcome.

Who managed to set going this very first international court since Nuremberg? President Cassese.

Who supplied the inputs in terms of precedents throughout the whole of the first case, *Tadić*? Professor Cassese.

Who was able to create the humanist but uncompromising moral climate that brought each of the comrades in this adventure to strive to give their very best? Our friend Nino Cassese.

For all of that, Nino, please accept the sincere thanks of someone who is proud to be counted among your friends.

An Attempt to Explain a Friendship

Antonio Tabucchi

Contrary to the opinion of discerning critics according to whom my narrative style (and hence my worldview, because if someone writes 'like that' it means that he is 'like that', they surmise) inhabits a universe of doubt, uncertainty, and scepticism to the point that they would have me belong to that extra-temporal category they define as Postmodernity, a quasi limbo to which they condemn writers who have faith in nothing and who Dante didn't have the time to put in the place they deserved; contrary to all this, I was saying, the older I get the more certainties I have. And the certainty I am most certain of, and to which I admit with all the frankness of a patient describing his dietary failings to the doctor who is palpating his liver, is as follows: I have a steadily growing faith in Heisenberg's Principle, more commonly known as the Uncertainty Principle.

Before Werner Heisenberg (1901–1976), the illustrious scientist who defined this principle as it deserved and who by tackling mathematics head-on had the courage to plunge into the maelstrom of numbers (which as we know is infinite), the abovementioned principle, for lack of a better alternative, had been dubbed by ordinary mortals with the banal name of Chance or even Fate. From its lowly position as Fate, which has produced Greek tragedy and other literature in abundance, it went on to become the Principle underpinning the calculation of probabilities. And later of quantum mechanics, a science the mere mention of which gives one the shivers. Given my scientific incompetence it would be impossible for me to explain it, and, as the man of letters that I am, I must fall back on an example provided by a truly great writer, Carlo Emilio Gadda, who was an engineer and hence had what it takes to talk about numbers. Talking of a case that concerned him, Gadda said: 'It is a question, as anyone will understand, of a combinatory incident governed by the Principle known as the Uncertainty Principle or Heisenberg's Principle. As when two gamblers, playing at dice, both throw a five and a three'.

The first combinatory incident: Florence, understood here as a gaming table on which people play dice and, obviously, I crave the indulgence of the illustrious city of art if I use it as a metaphor better suited to a casino. The fact is that the two presumed players, I mean to say Antonio Cassese and myself, chanced to throw their dice on the green baize of Florence. The curious thing is that they had all the time they needed (a really long time, fifteen years or so at least) to throw them in another city, also a city of art albeit a rather less famous one; in other words Pisa, where both of them had lived for all those years, what's more with mutual friends who might have witnessed the reciprocal cast of the dice: Cassese because he was Professor of

International Law at Pisa University and previously a pupil at the Scuola Normale Superiore, which Tabucchi had once attended on a scholarship, even though a bit later; and Tabucchi because he is a Pisan born and bred. But no, they never met because of that 'combinatory incident' of the dice upon which Heisenberg's Principle is based. Why? The answer belongs to the mystery of mathematics.

Moreover, and here the Heisenberg Principle gets even more complicated, the dice were not thrown by their own hands, but by those of their wives. Or perhaps by their children, they too obviously innocent regarding the combinations of the table upon which the dice of life meet, once they have been cast, even though no one knows who really cast them. Let's just say that that's how it went, in literal obedience to the story that is Reality, which by simply being what it is strikes me as more mysterious than mathematics. Because it just so happens that both men, families included, went to live in Florence, each for his own reasons, which do not concern us here, and both had sons and daughters of the same age, another numerical fact, mark you. And both had put their children in the same high school. Further, in that school, as in every other school in the country, they held monthly parent-teacher meetings, dreamed up by the Education Minister of those days to 'open up a dialogue' between the state and the citizenry, a dialogue that continues to this day. Usually, these discussions were held with the mothers of the pupils, for Italian fathers, as Leopardi says in the *Zibaldone*, tend to deal with far more important matters than the education of their offspring.

The fact is that one day my wife Maria José came home and told me that at the parent-teacher meeting she had met the mother of a girl in our son's class and that they had taken to each other right from the word go. Actually the word Maria José used was empathy, for at that time her bedside companion was Goethe's *Elective Affinities*, because we all have our weaknesses and these must be respected. I met an extraordinary woman, she told me at dinner, a person 'of rank' (this being her idiolect), and tomorrow I'm going to take coffee at her house.

My friendship with Antonio Cassese came after that coffee, I ought to add. I don't know if this is a consequence, as would seem presumable, but it certainly came afterwards, just as three comes after two, given that I began my discourse in mathematical terms. And, given that the 'after' is basically fairly well known, it strikes me as quasi tautological to speak of this friendship, which ought to be the reason for these pages. There are witnesses, and even objective proof: for example the printed dedication in the novel *The Lost Head of Damasceno Monteiro*, 'to Antonio Cassese', which is there to demonstrate—even to those who do not believe it—that that book was in fact dedicated to Antonio Cassese.

But what's the use of testifying to the 'after'? The 'after' is no more than a matter of record. It may be of use to courts or tribunals, when things have already happened, and the fact has been acknowledged. I would like to understand the 'before', how certain things come together that then, by coming together, cause the things that happen to happen: I think this is where we may find the secret that gives us an awareness of the things that happen. But this 'before' is off limits even to scientists like Heisenberg, who, in the infinity of possible combinations, are extraordinarily good at calculating the 'after'; in other words the moment in which the two dice players both throw a five and a three. I don't know if you have noticed the limitation of the magnificent calculation of probabilities. It is that such a calculation allows you to calculate one probability in millions, but to have the elements with which to calculate, you must first have played many times, cast many dice. And how those games came out no one knows.

Regarding my 'after', that's to say my friendship with Antonio Cassese, I have little to add, because this too is a matter of record. What I can say, if this has any importance, is that in those years I felt a little disoriented. At that time an American historian was assuring us that History had ended, in the sense that a certain little wall having collapsed, humanity was about to enjoy eternal peace and justice. In the meantime, all around us, the most atrocious things were happening, and to some it might have seemed that the world was going to rack and ruin. A rack and ruin of such dimensions that even a sceptic like me, perhaps already pre-postmodern, felt a need of reassurance, a wish that someone would talk to him about possible earthly justice, given that the divine variety seemed to be dragging its feet. And who perhaps wished to be reassured about the dangers faced by our bodies, the sacred nature of our bodies, their inviolability, given that—as Wislawa Szymborska put it—the soul is sometimes present and sometimes less so; it all depends on the historical period and the degree of belief in this ineffable thing. 'But the body is there, is there, is there/and cannot find shelter'.

Of Antonio Cassese's works, I have read *Umano-Disumano* (Inhuman States), an account of his experience as a human rights commissioner concerned with places of detention (prisons, police stations, etc.) where torture is still cheerfully practised, or where inhuman and degrading treatment is meted out. When it comes to maltreatment, moreover, the situation in Italy is not exactly wonderful, as emerges from the report issued by the Commission led by Cassese, a report that the Italian Home Office has never published.

I set to listening animatedly (no mistake: listening animatedly) to all that Antonio, either alone or together with a friend, the jurist Danilo Zolo, had to teach me about international law, which was practically everything, and human rights (about which I already knew something), and on the possibility of defending our poor bodies from the villains who sometimes decide the fate of the world. By the way, on listening to him I discovered that he liked literature. And that he knew a lot about it. And that he had even written on Kafka, but that was something he had told nobody about, something that for two pins I'd talk about here, for friendship also admits of 'grassing' provided the informer is doing so in a good cause. And basically that's it, or almost. But, in this account of mine, after having tackled the 'before' and the 'after', and perhaps after getting lost in cogitations about Heisenberg's Principle, I fear I have forgotten the most important thing that the calculation of probabilities does not take into account: simultaneity. Why is it, as a result of an inscrutable calculation that not even quantum mechanics can unravel, and over and above the fact that the players both throw a three and a five, are those same players permitted to throw the dice simultaneously in the same segment of time of this immense Time that belongs to Forever? And so, I am reminded of a kind of salutation that Hermann Hesse wrote in a letter to his friend Thomas Mann during the hard times that both men had to get through. 'Dear Thomas Mann', wrote Hesse, 'I thank you for being my contemporary'. It is with this same phrase that I would like to greet, with this letter that isn't a letter, my friend Antonio Cassese.

Soliloquy

1. My Early Years: Hesitating between Law and Humanities

I read law only because urged to do so by my father, a somewhat impecunious historian who worked as a civil servant (he was director of the local Public Record Office). I wanted to study philosophy or humanities. We lived in a poor region of southern Italy (Campania), which was plagued by unemployment, and my father's advice was that I should choose a field that would ensure a secure professional future. I eventually enrolled at the University of Pisa, primarily because in that central Italian town there was a chance to enter a 'Juridical College' (associated, in those years, with the celebrated *Scuola Normale Superiore*) that not only provided free board and lodging, but also high-level training in addition to that imparted by the Pisa Law School. Studying law proved tough for someone whose mind was set rather on philosophy or sociology. But I learned the hard discipline of law. Almost all the teachers were excellent, their method that of strict positivism. I thus absorbed the rigorous logical and systematic approach of that method along with all the attendant technical tools of legal interpretation. Still, I gradually came to feel attracted only to constitutional and international law, for they were less distant from political and social reality than, say, torts, evidence, or commercial law. In the end, on personal grounds (the professor of constitutional law was moving to Turin University and a new professor of international law, Giuseppe Sperduti, had just been appointed), I opted for international law. But there, again, I picked a rather unsophisticated topic when it came to choosing a topic for my LLM dissertation: the self-determination of peoples. In addition, I asked permission to study in Germany, at Frankfurt am Main, and I spent a semester there, ostensibly to research my thesis but in reality to attend lectures held by two leading sociologists, Theodor Wiesengrund Adorno and Max Horkheimer, both of whom belonged to the famous Frankfurt Institute for Social Research (*Institut für Sozialforschung*). As things turned out, those lectures did not prove very useful to me: Adorno was obscure; his lectures were fashionable gatherings of elegant girls and sophisticated members of the intelligentsia who flocked to listen to a philosopher who most of them—I surmise—did not understand. Horkheimer was intellectually more accessible; he was also affable (he once asked me and a couple of German students to lunch and I was much surprised by the fact that he had a chauffeur and took us to an expensive restaurant, a fact that to my naïve and youthful mind was in strident contrast with his profession of—modern and updated—Marxism).

My wavering between strict methods of legal inquiry and recurrent forays into other disciplines came to the fore when, after graduation and on immediately becoming a research assistant, I tended to be a strict legalist in my supervision of LLM theses, repressing my own desires and tendencies. For example, this happened with one of my supervisees, Tiziano Terzani, who later became a famous reporter and writer on social and religious matters. A couple of years ago I met him again, after he had given a fascinating speech. Once the loud applause subsided, I told him how much I admired his narratory skills. He confided in a low voice that his decision to become a reporter and a writer was due to me. Faced with my astonishment, he reminded me that when in the summer of 1961 I had sent him back his thesis together with my comments, in order to sum up my criticisms of his flowery language and frequent meta-legal digressions, on the front page I had written, as a sort of warning, a phrase from Kant: '*Die Wissenschaft soll trocken sein*' (science must be dry). This, he claimed, had prompted him to abandon all hopes of an academic legal career and to opt instead for journalism.

2. Torn Between Positivism and Socially-Oriented Study of Law

One of the reasons for my doubts about the path to take was also linked to the legal method that at the time (and perhaps still now) prevailed in continental Europe: strict positivism. It is based on a rigid distinction between *lex lata* (the law in force) and *lex ferenda* (the law as it might be changed), and insists that lawyers should deal only with the former, and not with the question of whether law ought to be changed and how. In addition, lawyers should not meddle with social, historical, or sociological inquiries into the birth of *lex lata*. This approach, which concerned in particular the study of public law (private law, harking back to an old tradition, had remained immune from 'contamination' with other meta-legal disciplines), emerged in the late nineteenth century and was consolidated first in Germany and then in most European countries. In Italy it had been powerfully propounded by two distinguished publicists: Vittorio Emanuele Orlando (1860–1952) and Santi Romano (1875–1947), who both ended up as professors of public law at Rome University.

In the area of international law, one of the strongest advocates of the adoption of this method, a man whose stance tended to be more formal and positivist than that of Dionisio Anzilotti (1867–1950), was Tomaso Perassi (1886–1960), professor in Rome from 1928 to 1955. He was a highly respected and most influential scholar in Italy in his lifetime. I had the chance to meet him in his office at the Italian Constitutional Court, of which he was then vice-president. As a third-year law student, I had written a detailed review of the latest edition of a masterly textbook of international law by the leading Austrian scholar Alfred Verdross

(1890–1980).[1] My professor had carefully edited the review (I still have my type-script with his corrections) and then asked me personally to hand the revised text to Perassi, who also was the editor-in-chief of the leading Italian journal on international law (*Rivista di diritto internazionale*). Sperduti insisted that I should meet Perassi, who after all was my 'academic grandfather' (Sperduti being one of his disciples). I thus went to Rome full of trepidation, to make the acquaint-ance of the great academic and judge. Unexpectedly I found a very urbane old gentleman, who treated me, a young man of twenty, almost as a fellow scholar. He smiled with great benevolence, through two slits from which filtered a pene-trating and—it seemed to me—sly glance, and did not say a word. Overwhelmed with awe and embarrassment, I talked and talked for about half an hour of my plans for the future, of Pisa University, of my predilection for international law, then, on seeing that he had not uttered a single word, I abruptly stopped, stood up, said goodbye and left. Only later, when I told one of Perassi's numerous senior disciples about my traumatic meeting with him, did I learn that he was fam-ous for being a man of few words; for instance, he would ask those who went to submit papers for publication to sit and read them aloud, after which he would say a couple of words either of rejection or of acceptance. Perassi was also the author of a remarkable booklet on legal methodology, where he concisely set out the fundamentals of the strictly positivist approach.[2] This approach led him to write papers on the Covenant of the League of Nations and—later—on the UN Charter that are notable for a dry and formalistic legal analysis that, while superb in its delineation (marked by great legal rigour and exemplary lucidity) of the for-mal features of the two institutions, fails to explain the role and the significance of these institutions in the world community.[3] On reading these two essays I was struck by how that legal method was incapable of delving beneath the legal surface of major political bodies of the international community. Those essays, as well as other writings by Perassi that appeared in the 1930s and 1940s, all per-fectly technical and abstract, reminded me of a well-known poem by Fernando Pessoa (*Ouivi contar que outrora, quando a Pérsia*). The poem talks about two chess players in Persia who, unperturbed, carry on playing with great acumen and skill amidst the raging of an implacable war, their gaze fixed on the chess-board, bent only on thinking up the best move, while all around them houses are burning or are pillaged, women are being raped and children killed.[4]

[1] The book was A. Verdross, *Völkerrecht*, 3rd edn (Wien: Springer Verlag, 1955). The review was published in 40 *Rivista di diritto internazionale*, 1957, 653–6.
[2] *Introduzione alle scienze giuridiche* (Roma: ed Forato italiano, 1938), reprinted in T. Perassi, *Scritti giuridici*, I (Milano: Giuffrè, 1858), 3–52.
[3] 'L'ordinamento della Società delle Nazioni' in *La vita italiana*, 1920, 411–29, reprinted in *Scritti giuridici*, cit., 307–325; *L'ordinamento delle Nazioni Unite* (Padova: Cedam, 1950), reprinted in *Scritti giuridici* cit., 339–85.
[4] This also applies to those papers by the eminent international lawyer, devoted to topical issues, always dissected in a dry and legalistic manner. See for instance the essay on the Spanish constitu-tion of 1931, where the great novelties of that Constitution are either missing or not discussed ('La

Later on, however, I realized that this abstract positivist approach was important in at least two respects: it did away with the confusion between legal and historical or political inquiries, which had plagued many legal works in the nineteeth and early twentieth centuries; it enabled lawyers to keep politics at bay thereby avoiding smuggling political or ideological leanings into scholarly inquiries. Still, this dry investigation of legal institutions—devoid of any consideration of their social context as well as hindering any move from the study of existing law to a proponent approach—did not satisfy me at all. I was later to discover the limitations of this approach, when I read in the diaries of the Italian Foreign Minister Galeazzo Ciano some derogatory remarks about Perassi, who for many years during the fascist era had been first (from 1931–1936) one of the legal advisers and then (between 1937–1943) the chief legal adviser to the Italian Foreign Ministry[5] (without however ever sharing the political views of fascist leaders or reflecting them in his legal writings—thanks to his positivism). Ciano noted on 9 April 1939 that he had to draft a document on the union between Italy and Albania (which, upon being attacked by Italian troops, had just capitulated); he then adds that he will have to consult with some 'professional pettifoggers' (*professionisti del cavillo*) at the Ministry (T. Perassi and two diplomats).[6] To my mind, this passage from Ciano's diaries confirmed the notion that, once he has embraced a strictly positivist approach, a lawyer may easily risk becoming a Servant of the Prince, although he can claim he is merely a 'technical expert'.

In the following years I also discovered another side of positivism: its role as a powerful shield of state sovereignty. Insistence on positivism played such a role, for instance, in Paris in 1919, when the two US members of the 'Commission on the Responsibility of the Authors of the War and on the Enforcement of the Penalties' set up at the Peace Conference strongly objected to introducing the notion of 'offences against the laws of humanity' in future trials against war criminals, because 'the laws and principles of humanity are not certain, varying with time, place and circumstances, and according, it may be, to the conscience of the

nuova Costituzione spagnola ed il diritto internazionale', in *Rivista di diritto internazionale* (1932), 453–6, reprinted in *Scritti giuridici*, cit., I, 411–14). However, most of his writings that appeared in those years were instead devoted to technical issues. See for instance 'Le assicurazioni sociali nel diritto internazionale' (1931) in *Scritti II*, 129–50; 'Consoli ed agenti diplomatici; Immunità in material penale'(1932), *ibid.*, 3–5; 'Su l'esenzione degli agenti diplomatici dalla giurisdizione' (1932), *ibid.*, 9–13; 'I caratteri formali della clausola facoltativa sulla giurisdizione obbligatoria della Corte Permanente di Giustizia internazionale' (1932), *ibid.*, 25–30; 'Sull'articolo 22 del trattato del Laterano' (1937), *ibid.*, 453–4. Numerous other papers dealt with issues of private international law.

[5] G. Morelli ('Tomaso Perassi', in 45 *Rivista di diritto internazionale* (1962), 3–14) hints at this activity (at 5). Detailed information is provided by F. Salerno ('La *Rivista* e gli studi di diritto internazionale nel periodo 1906–1943', in 90 *Rivista di diritto internazionale* (2007), at 310, note 22). No mention is made by C. Mortati ('L'opera di Tomaso Perassi', in 45 *Rivista di diritto internazionale* (1962), 204–16).

[6] G. Ciano, *Diario*, vol. I (1939–1940), 6th edn (Milano: Rizzoli, 1950), at 78. The two diplomats were Gino Buti (1888–1972), later ambassador to the Vichy Government, and Leonardo Vitetti (1895–1973), Director-General of General Affairs at the Foreign Ministry.

individual judge. There is no fixed and universal standard of humanity'.[7] (It is striking that these considerations were not reiterated in 1945 by the US delegation to the London Conference that drafted the Charter of the International Military Tribunal at Nuremberg, which included in Article 6 the notion of 'crimes against humanity' thereby accepting that the laws of humanity were applicable in international law.) Similarly, by insisting on positivist considerations, the US, British and Italian members of the Advisory Committee of Jurists (appointed by the Council of the League of Nations in 1921 to draft the Statute of the Permanent Court of International Justice), opposed a provision entrusting the future Court with the task of applying 'principles of objective justice'. Indeed, as the US member Root noted, 'nations will submit to positive law, but will not submit to such principles as have not been developed into positive rules supported by an accord between all States'.[8] True, the 'principles of objective justice' are undefined. But what is even more important is that the 'laws and principles of humanity' were hazy in those days and could not be used as criminal legal standards to prosecute individuals. Perhaps, however, if in 1919, compliance with the 'laws of humanity' had been proclaimed as a legal imperative binding on all states, in 1939–45 the political and military leaders of some European states would have thought twice before trampling upon the most elementary principles of human dignity. More generally, I wonder whether one ought not to move beyond the strict legal parameters agreed upon by states, at least whenever the need to oppose glaring injustice would oblige one to do so. This concept—i.e., that one can exceptionally depart from positivism—was proclaimed in 1946 at Nuremberg by the International Military Tribunal, when it justified non-compliance with the *nullum crimen sine lege* principle for the crime of aggression (as well as, implicitly, for crimes against humanity). Indeed, the Tribunal not only stated that in international law 'the maxim *nullum crimen sine lege* is not a limitation of sovereignty, but is in general a principle of justice' (a proposition true at the time, no longer valid today); but, more importantly, it also said 'To assert that it is unjust to punish those who in defiance of treaties and assurances have attacked neighbouring states without warning is obviously untrue, for in such circumstances the attacker must know that he is doing wrong, *and so far from it being unjust to punish him, it would be unjust if his wrong were allowed to go unpunished*'.[9]

---

[7] See 'Report Presented to the Preliminary Peace Conference by the Commission on the Responsibility of the Authors of War and on the Enforcement of Penalties', in *Violations of the Laws and Customs of War, Report of Majority and Dissenting Reports of American and Japanese Members of the Commission of Responsibilities, Conference of Paris 1919* (Oxford: Clarendon Press, 1919), at 73.

[8] League of Nations, PCIJ, Advisory Committee of Jurists, *Procès-verbaux of the Proceedings of the Committee* (The Hague: Van Langenhuysen Brothers, 1920), at 287.

[9] *Trial of the Major War Criminals Before the International Military Tribunal—Nuremberg 14 November 1945–1 October 1946* (Nuremberg: International Military Tribunal, 1947), at 219 (emphasis added).

In any event, the two contradictory mindsets continued to coexist in me. A German friend from Frankfurt would scoff at my wavering between the two by quoting the well-known verses from Goethe about the two 'souls' living together in Faust, one of which wished to depart from the other.[10] I adopted a sort of scholarly 'Dr. Jekyll and Mr. Hyde' attitude. My first books and other writings were dry pieces of legal scholarship,[11] I would say today of average value. After getting a professorship and thus feeling freer to choose not only the subjects of my research but also the way to deal with them, I began to inquire into legal problems that had a strong human and social dimension: human rights and the humanitarian law of armed conflict. However, I tackled those problems from a strictly legal viewpoint, producing writings that perhaps might still be of interest—but only to scholars.

Nonetheless, I was not happy and kept grappling with the problem. I felt a lingering unease with traditional legal methods. A notion was haunting me. In a letter of 25 December 1896, an Italian philosopher, Antonio Labriola, who had eventually embraced socialism in politics and the method of 'historical materialism' in his scholarly inquiries, wittily attacked the younger Italian philosopher Benedetto Croce for his post-Hegelian idealist views. He pointed out that philosophical idealism made him think of a schoolteacher in Naples who explained Plato's ideas by saying to his pupils that they were like caciocavallo (a kind of gourd-shaped cheese that in southern Italy is kept hanging from the ceiling so that it matures better).[12] In my imagination, the legal rules and the abstract, in-a-vacuum inquiries made into them by my fellow professors of law turned into those hanging pieces of cheese.

Then in the 1980s I gradually began to write for a larger audience. I had received a big push in this new direction from a few friendly after-dinner conversations in Oxford, in 1980, with the celebrated historian Arnaldo Momigliano (1908–1987), then fellow at All Souls College, where I was spending a year as a visiting fellow. In long walks, where I would keenly listen to his words while carefully avoiding the puddles all around us, he introduced me to the books and ideas of Moses Finley (1912–1986), the great American historian of antiquity. Finley's ability to combine rigorous historical method with the capacity to expound the results of his research in plain language, highly attractive even to the layman,

---

[10] *Zwei Seelen wohnen, ach! in meiner Brust, Die eine will sich von der andern trennen; Die eine hält, in derber Liebeslust, Sich an die Welt mit klammernden Organen; Die andere hebt gewaltsam sich vom Dust Zu den Gefilden hoher Ahnen.* (Faust I, 1112–1117).

[11] *Il diritto interno davanti al giudice internazionale* (Padova: Cedam, 1962); *Il controllo internazionale* (Milano: Giuffrè, 1972).

[12] Extracts from the letter are cited by B. Croce in his essay 'Come nacque e come morì il marxismo teorico in Italia (1895–1900): da lettere e ricordi personali', published as an annex in A. Labriola, *La concezione materialistica della storia*, 2nd edn (Bari: Laterza, 1946), 265–312, at 296 (this is what Labriola wrote: 'A proposito. Sai come un professore di Liceo del Salvatore (prima del '60)—prete di mestiere e frequentatore del botteghino del Corpo di Napoli, dove dava ai passanti i numeri del lotto—definiva le idee di Platone agli scolari: *Figurateve tante casecavalle appise.*').

struck me as an exemplary way to tackle scholarly problems. I thus published a string of books on topical issues discussed with an eye to the layman.[13] I now feel that, in the end, they did not attract either legal experts (who disparaged them as being merely intended to popularize legal topics) nor the wider audience they had targeted at.

This fluctuation between two poles has not stopped, I fear, as is shown from the various editions of a book of mine on the law of the international community.[14]

What is the ideal way of harmonizing the two tendencies? I believe that a lawyer should be able to inquire into a legal institution, a cluster of legal issues or a legal provision both by applying a strict and rigorous legal method and also by inquiring into *why* the institution, the cluster of issues or the provision have been formed the way they have; or in other words, what political, social or economic motivations have led to their present configuration. Furthermore, a lawyer should not shy away from suggesting how the institution, the issues or the rules might be improved better to take account of social needs. I am aware that, once it is so formulated, this scientific programme appears to be an easy task. I do not know to what extent I have proved up to this challenge in my endeavours. I did try to embrace this approach in a revisitation of my old theme of self-determination, but feel now that I failed.[15]

3. From Contemplation to Action

This has not been the only contradiction in my thinking and intellectual leanings. I have also been constantly torn between research and action. There was, on the one side, the desire to undertake research work in a rarefied place, far from the hubbub of daily life: the ideal place is an old library, such as the Codrington library at Oxford, or even a modern one, such as the law library of the Columbia Law School in New York, but then only on Sundays or late in certain evenings, when there are fewer people about. There I am at ease and at peace with myself, particularly if I have to peruse old textbooks or dusty collections of diplomatic documents or judicial cases. Being a bookworm is comfortable. Life is complex and thorny; it is sometimes less painful to look upon it from afar. Many will remember Lucretius' image of the man safely resting on the beach while a

---

[13] *Violence and Law in the Modern Age* (Oxford: Polity Press, 1988); *Terrorism, Politics and Law—The Achille Lauro Affair* (Oxford: Polity Press, 1989); *Human Rights in a Changing World* (Oxford: Polity Press, 1990); B.V.A. Röling, *The Tokyo Trial and Beyond—Reflections of a Peace-Monger* (edited by A. Cassese) (Oxford: Polity Press, 1993); *Inhuman States—Imprisonment, Detention and Torture in Europe Today* (Oxford: Polity Press, 1996).

[14] See *International Law in a Divided World* (Oxford: Clarendon Press, 1986); *International Law* (Oxford: Oxford University Press, 2001); see also the 2nd edn (*ibid.*, 2005).

[15] *Self-determination of Peoples—A Legal Reappraisal* (Cambridge: Cambridge University Press, 1995).

devastating storm is raging at sea,[16] where sailors in a ship are desperate to find
shelter; or Montaigne's rather less cowardly observation that one should always
have a 'back shop' (*une arrière-boutique*) available, where one can take refuge
from the wearing chores of the day.[17] For all its attractions and advantages, I
have always felt dissatisfied with this mindset. After a while, reality proves irre-
sistible. I have thus made many attempts to move from 'paper life' to real life.
This of course I could do only in a narrow area close to my professional competence. Thus, I started off as a 'para-diplomat' attending various international
meetings held by organizations such as the United Nations and the Council of
Europe. There you come in touch with diplomats, judges, politicians, and international civil servants. Attending the works of such bodies (the UN Commission
on Human Rights, as it then was, or the Sub-Commission on Minorities, or the
Council of Europe bodies on human rights) as a delegate or a member is a useful
way to understand the actual operation of international dealings. What proved
more insightful, however, was the experience gained in other bodies.

First came the Diplomatic Conference on the updating of the 1949 Geneva
Conventions (1974–1977, preceded by two sessions of a Conference of Experts,
1971–1972). There, acting as a member of the Italian Government delegation, I
managed to see how international treaties are hammered out and how much time
delegations sometimes spend on wordings that are seemingly harmless but in fact
conceal conflicting state interests. Perhaps on one or two occasions I also made
a tiny contribution to enhancing the humanitarian scope of the laws of warfare,
of course within the limited confines possible for a delegation that was bound to
stick to NATO coordination and directives.[18]

---

[16] Lucretius, *De Rerum Natura*, I, 1–6 '*Suave, mari magno turbantibus aequora ventis,/e terra
magnum alterius spectare laborem/non quia vexari quemquamst iucunda voluptas,/sed quibus ipse
malis careas quia cernere suave est/Suave etiam belli certamina magna tueri/per campos instructa tua
sine parte pericli*'. ('What joy it is, when out at sea the stormwinds are lashing the waters, to gaze
from the shore at the heavy stress some other man is enduring! Not that anyone's afflictions are in
themselves a source of delight; but to realize from what troubles you yourself are free is joy indeed.
What joy, again, to watch opposing hosts marshalled on the field of battle when you have yourself no part in their peril!', Lucretius, *On the Nature of the Universe* trans. R.E. Latham (Penguin
Books, 1979) at 60).
[17] Montaigne, *Les Essais* (1595), I, XXXVIII '*Il se faut réserver une arrière-boutique, toute nôtre,
toute franche [i.e. libre], en laquelle nous établissons notre vraie liberté et principale retraite et soli-
tude. En cette-ci faut-il prendre notre ordinaire entretien, de nous à nous-mêmes, et si privé, que nulle
accointance ou communication de chose étrangère y trouve place.*' Michel Seigneur de Montaigne, *Les
Essais* (éd 1595) (Librairie Générale Française, 2001) at 372–3.
[18] As a result of my participation in and observation of the Geneva Diplomatic Conference, I
wrote two papers that perhaps are still worth some attention: 'The Prohibition of Indiscriminate
Means of Warfare', in R. J. Akkerman, P. J. van Krieken, C. O. Pannenborg (eds), *Declarations on
Principles—A Quest for International Peace* (Leyden: Sijthoff, 1977), 171–94; 'Means of Warfare:
the Traditional and the New Law', in A. Cassese (ed.), *The New Humanitarian Law of Armed
Conflict* (Napoli: Editoriale Scientifica, 1979), 162–98. I also wrote 'A Tentative Appraisal of the
Old and the New Humanitarian Law of Armed Conflict (*ibid.*, 461–501), 'Mercenaries: Lawful
Combatants or War Criminals?', in *Zeitschrift für ausländisches öffentliches Recht und Völkerrecht*
(1980) 1 ff; 'The Status of Rebels Under the 1977 Geneva Protocol on Non-International Armed
Conflict', *International and Comparative Law Quarterly* (1981) 416 ff; 'Wars of National Liberation

A second experience that proved even more instructive was that as a member and chairman of the Council of Europe Committee against Torture. These were four years of gruelling work, visiting police stations, prisons and other places of detention throughout Europe, and then drafting reports with recommendations. However, these were years where for the first time in my life I moved from a relatively leisurely activity (studying, discussing, writing and lecturing) to stark confrontation with harsh realities: inspecting places where human beings were being detained and frequently ill-treated. I also gradually realized how important it is to be uncompromising when facing a reluctant state official who intends to deny you access to a police station or to a cell, or refuses to disclose information. In many instances, having received information that some special detainees were being hidden in certain cells, I demanded to visit them. Whenever I was found wrong, I apologized to the authorities. In many other cases, however, I was not wrong, and duly reported our findings. At the expiry of the first four-year term I resigned: I was burnt out and needed to recover from seeing so much evil. I also recovered by writing a small book, a sort of memoir, which to my regret had a weaker impact than I had hoped.[19] One of the lessons I learned in my visits to prisons, police stations, psychiatric asylums, detention centres for foreigners, and other places where persons are deprived of their liberty, is that inhumanity is inextricably intertwined with our humanity; it is indeed part of our humanity. It is something that a French writer, Romain Gary, had already noted in one of his novels.[20]

A third and even more challenging experience was that of international criminal judge. In 1993 the UN General Assembly elected me as a judge with the International Criminal Tribunal for the former Yugoslavia. Soon after we were sworn in, I was elected President. In a matter of a few days I became engrossed in that task, which among other things obliged me to learn a great deal about areas that hitherto I had neglected, chiefly criminal and comparative law. I worked very hard to get the new judicial body off the ground. I think I managed to turn an organ that, when it was first established, almost everybody considered doomed to failure, into an effective and indeed vibrant judicial institution. Sitting in judgement on criminal cases proved very demanding. I think that nevertheless I made a quite innovative if controversial contribution to the development of its case law. These, however, were trying days. I still remember an evening in November 2005, in New York. I had just reported to the General Assembly on the problems

and Humanitarian Law', in C. Swinarski (ed.), *Etudes et essais en l'honneur de J. Pictet* (Geneva–The Hague, M Nijhoff, 1984), 313 ff.

[19] *Inhuman States—Imprisonment, Detention and Torture in Europe Today* (Oxford: Polity Press, 1996).

[20] In his novel *Les Cerfs-volants* (Paris: Gallimard, 1980) after stressing that what was terrible about Nazism was its 'inhuman side', he added that 'il faut bien se rendre à l'évidence: ce côté inhumain fait partie de l'humain. Tant qu'on ne reconnaîtra que l'inhumanité est chose humaine, on restera dans le mensonge pieux' (at 265).

besetting the Tribunal and our endeavours to surmount them. There was a dinner with various diplomats, most of whom were French-speaking (which led all the others to switch to that language, out of courtesy). One of them asked me whether I thought that the Tribunal could become the momentous institution I was hoping for. I said that we were at a crucial point, a real turning point, a moment that could be described as 'make or break' (*ça passe ou ça casse*, I said). The Dutch Ambassador to the UN joined in saying that he was sure we would make it (*Ça passe, ça passe, car vous vous appelez 'Passese'*). I thought this was a witty reward for my dogged efforts. However, there again, after six years of working with unsparing energy, I had to give up, and reluctantly resigned, in order to stave off a breakdown. It later dawned on me that one of my numerous defects was that of plunging into action, without occasionally retiring into that comfortable 'back shop' extolled by Montaigne.

Finally, in visiting the Sudan and in particular Darfur as the chairman of the UN Commission of Inquiry on Darfur in 2004–2005, I was able to draw upon both my experience as an inspector and my time spent as a judge. Conducting an in-depth inquiry in a brief time span was again exacting physically and psychologically; but I feel it was worth going through that ordeal.

In retrospect, I consider myself very fortunate for having made these forays into real life. They enabled me to escape the danger of the 'intellectual' who, as Albert Einstein once noted, 'has no direct contact with life in the raw, but encounters it in its easiest, synthetic form—upon the printed page.'[21]

4. Confronting Evil

In my forays into real life, I have had many opportunities to meet not only unsavoury characters but also some truly striking representatives of the dark side of human nature. I vividly remember their faces.

One was the face of the young, short Turkish police officer who had beaten up and then raped a Kurdish girl (I met her, by mere chance, the next day: she was lying in her bunk in a prison cell, as pale as death, and it was only at the insistence of her cell mate that in the end she recounted her ordeal, describing her tormentor so minutely that I could not fail to recognize him in the police officer with whom I had talked at length the day before. He had struck me, for he was so nervous, agitated and aggressive; when we shook hands at the end of the long interview in the police station, his hands were moist with sweat).

Another was the face of the tall and elegant chief of police in Ankara, who would smile at most of our questions and blatantly lie about facts as well as persons in detention, or arrogantly dismiss any cautious criticism we might make.

---

[21] A. Einstein, in A. Einstein and S. Freud, *Why War?* (Paris: International Institute of International Cooperation–League of Nations, 1933), at 19.

Then there was the face of some of the defendants in the dock at The Hague—former military personnel, but also political leaders or simple civilians—who, although accused of appalling deeds, brazenly denied everything even when confronted with compelling testimony, and never showed even a scintilla of repentance.

It is, however, easier to spot the traces of Evil in the faces of the victims: their suffering can less easily be erased or concealed than the wickedness of their persecutors. I saw much suffering on the faces of the hundreds of detainees I met and interviewed in European prisons over four years; I saw sadness and suffering on the face of the Kurdish girl I mentioned above; I saw indelible suffering in so many witnesses we heard in court (their testimony was often so heart-rending that occasionally even the coldest and emotionally hardened judge could not avoid being deeply moved).

It should come as no surprise that all these encounters, even more than my scholarly or quasi-diplomatic dealing with human rights, constantly posed to me the age-old question of how it is possible for a human being to behave so inhumanely towards another human being. Perhaps philosophers or psychologists have found an answer, if only a tentative one. I have not. It is an agonizing question. It is the foundation of *If this is a man* by Primo Levi. And the main reason why that book is so troubling: it is not only a book on Auschwitz; it is essentially a book where on each page the author asks himself: how was it possible for human beings to behave that way? And he leaves us with this harrowing question.

A modern philosopher, Benedetto Croce, once wrote that were inhumanity not part of us, we could not understand Oedipus Rex, Macbeth or Othello. This remark is not sufficient, however. I have found some sense of orientation in the reflections of Martin Buber in *Good and Evil* (a work that, albeit based on theological thinking and inspired by deep religiosity, can also persuade a secularist like me). In this work, Buber notes that man has two innate urges: a 'good' one and an 'evil' one. 'In the creation of man'—says Buber—'the two urges are set in opposition to each other. The Creator gives them to man as his two servants which, however, can only accomplish their service in genuine collaboration. The "evil urge" is no less necessary than its companion, indeed even more necessary than it, for without it man would woo no woman and beget no children, build no house and engage in no economic activity, for it is true that "all travail and all skill in work is the rivalry of a man with his neighbour" (Ecclesiastes 4:4). Hence this urge is called "the yeast in the dough", the ferment placed in the soul by God, without which the human dough does not rise. [...] of the two, it is the evil urge which is fundamental'. Buber adds that 'Man's task [...] is not to extirpate the evil urge, but to reunite it with the good'. More generally he notes that 'This important doctrine cannot be understood as long as good and evil are conceived, as they usually are, as two diametrically opposite forces or directions. Its meaning is not revealed to us until we recognize them as similar in nature; the "evil" urge as passion, that is, the power peculiar to man, without which he can neither beget nor bring forth, but which, left to itself, remains without direction and leads astray; and the "good" urge as pure direction, in other words, as an unconditional direction, that towards God. To unite the two urges implies: to equip the absolute potency of passion with the one direction that renders it capable of great love and of great service. Thus and not otherwise can man become whole'.[22]

These thoughts have shed some light on my personal experience with Evil. I do not know, however, how well-founded they are. And, at any rate, they cannot set to rest our disquiet about what daily occurs around us and also within us. What should perhaps help us to attenuate our pessimism (and its inner equivalent, depression), so as to allow us to continue in our daily exertions, is the awareness that there are, however, so many persons who channel their aggressive drive towards socially useful action. Also knowing that generosity, compassion and care for the others are so widespread, helps immensely. Elie Wiesel recounts in *La Nuit* that, upon arrival in 1944 at Auschwitz-Birkenau, one of those hopeless and wretched inmates furtively approached him and whispered not to say to the SS that would interrogate all the new 'arrivals', that he was fifteen and his father fifty ('tell them that you are 18 and your father 40').[23] That unknown detainee, moved only by genuine compassion, thus saved them from immediate gasification.

5. Major Areas of Scholarly Interest

If I now take a look at the subjects in which I have been interested and on which I have toiled so hard in my scholarly activity, it appears to me that they boil down to a very few areas, and always the same ones: human rights, the self-determination of peoples, the humanitarian laws regulating armed conflicts, the use of force by states, and more generally legal restraints on violence in the world community; and international criminal law. Probably it was the desire to understand both what motivates states to use violence, and what we individuals can do to mitigate violence, that prompted me to explore these areas of international law. These are areas where the relation between force and legal standards aiming at restraining force is more problematic; areas where the legal network thins and is full of holes, and therefore the observer may better grasp the power relations that exist between the primary actors on the international scene: the sovereign states. Not unwittingly, I was moved by the old maxim of Roman wisdom: *hominum causa omne jus constitutum est* (any rule of law is ultimately made on account of human beings). This maxim had been instilled in me by the teachings of my professor at Pisa, Giuseppe Sperduti (1912–1993). He was a profound and acute scholar, whose writings were unfortunately marred by obscurity and an overindulgence

---

[22] M. Buber, *Good and Evil—Two Interpretations* (Upper Saddle River, NJ: Prentice Hall, n.d.), at 94, 95, and 97.
[23] E. Wiesel, *La Nuit* (1958) (Paris: Les Éditions de Minuit, 2007), at 72.

in logical or theoretical musings. Also, like most lawyers of his generation of the 1930s and 1940s in Germany and Italy, he was obsessed with originality: he was always quick to stress that he had been the first to propound certain views. More generally he was constantly asking himself who had been the first to say what, as if views and ideas were physical objects that one possesses and hence can lend or sell but of which one may always claim ownership, and not unstable and evanescent phantasms, often generated in many persons' minds and soon to be found in general circulation. He started off as a positivist academic politically close to fascism, then, in the aftermath of the Second World War, he gradually rediscovered his Catholic ideological origins and became increasingly attracted to human rights. He ended up a staunch and indeed formidable supporter of human rights, far from the state idolatry of his early positivism. As a member of the European Commission of Human Rights for many years (1960–1992), he played an important role in pushing through an expansive interpretation of many provisions of the European Convention on Human Rights. It was he who so much insisted on the need for international law to be oriented towards human beings.[24] When working as a judge at The Hague, I managed to have that Latin maxim I cited above accepted by my fellow judges. I put it into a judgment on which I had spent much labour, *Tadić (Interlocutory appeal).*[25]

I still believe that only those problems that dramatically affect the daily life of human beings are worth studying. I still believe that it is the cluster of legal rules and institutions that may have a dramatic impact on the life and suffering of human beings that should constitute the main focus of our attention as scholars.

6. A Decisive Encounter

One of the advantages of my profession has been the chance to meet so many notable persons: scholars, diplomats, judges, and military experts. In my private life I have also had the fortune to meet various writers and philosophers, some of whom I have come to know fairly well. I have always endeavoured to distil as much as possible from these encounters, in terms of knowledge, human experience and vision. I unconsciously heeded the repeated advice of my parents (advice that harked back to the fundamental wisdom of the oral cultural tradition of poor areas): 'always seek the company of those who are better than you and also pay for their expenses'.

---

[24] I tried to outline the major contribution made by Giuseppe Sperduti to international law in a paper written after his death ('Note sull'opera di Giuseppe Sperduti', in 77 *Rivista di diritto internazionale* (1994), 313–25). There I stressed that to 'commemorate' Sperduti would mean to do him a disservice: he was a man with a strong critical mind, always eager to critically appraise ideas, views and persons. To write about him without assessing his scientific merits but also his scholarly weaknesses would mean to betray his intellectual and moral legacy.

[25] ICTY, Appeals Chamber, *Decision on the Defence Motions for Interlocutory Appeal on Jurisdiction*, 2 October 1995 (case no IT-94-1-AR72), § 97.

Of these many encounters, the one that had the greatest influence on me was that with B.V.A. Röling. He was a Dutch criminal lawyer who, when still fairly young, had been a judge in the Tokyo trial of the major Japanese war criminals in 1946–47. Then, back in his own country, he had turned to international law. I first met him in Strasbourg in 1973, when he, Pierre Boissier (a Swiss expert in humanitarian law), and I had been invited to give lectures on the laws of warfare. Röling and I became friends and frequently met until his death in 1985. He was impressive: tall, with sharp blue eyes, snow-white hair and, what impressed most, a soft yet deeply persuasive voice. He would never raise his voice, never get angry. What struck the listener was his enormous human experience coupled with his command of various fields of knowledge (law, peace research, history, political science, sociology). In 1958 he had fallen out with the Dutch Ministry of Foreign Affairs (which had until then sent him as a Dutch delegate to the UN General Assembly), because in December 1957, on his journey back from New York, taking advantage of the leisure time offered by the ship, he had written a little book in which he stressed the urgent need for the Netherlands to grant independence to Irian (Western Guinea), then a Dutch colony.[26] He was immediately struck off the list of Dutch delegates to the U.N. He never complained about this personal setback. Similarly, he never complained about not being appointed professor at the most prestigious Dutch University, that of Leyden, because of his unorthodox stance. It is only from some of his disciples that I later learned of these personal disappointments. Unlike most of us, he succeeded in reconciling himself with academic life, and never bore a grudge.

Röling was not a profound scholar; nor did he ever write one of those magnificent books where you feel that the author, in addition to opening new vistas, offers a refined and fully elaborated text. His major and most enduring scholarly work is a booklet he wrote in 1960: *International Law in an Expanded World*. A work that was not notable for the rigour of the argumentation or the elegance of the exposition, but a powerful book that departed from traditional legal scholarship and, by drawing upon history, sociology and international relations, it had two great merits: first, it presented an extremely original and challenging view of the history of the international community, its composition and its tensions; second, it took a 'progressive' stance, siding with what he used to call the 'underdogs', the 'have-nots', in short, the developing countries, and calling to action all those who, tired of a Eurocentric or Western-centric outlook, were bent on changing international relations. This was not at all a traditional, 'objective' law book; it was a 'livre de bataille' that shrewdly used and amalgamated various disciplines

---

[26] B.V.A. Röling, *Nieuw Guinea als Wereldprobleem* (Assen: van Gorcum and Co., 1958). After critically outlining the debates on New Guinea (Irian) in the UN General Assembly (at 45–78) Röling put forward his own views about the need for The Netherlands to relinquish its authority over the colony, setting forth two alternatives: either the colony was to be handed over to Indonesia, or the Netherlands was to entrust the UN with the task of deciding on the matter (at 79–104).

to take a fresh and insightful look at international relations. It was a book that stood squarely on the side of the underprivileged.

Röling taught me a lot. He had a fascinating capacity to talk about the many episodes culled from his vast experience. I remember that once, at a conference, he gently but firmly attacked me. I had presented a paper on the prohibition of weapons causing unnecessary suffering. Having investigated state practice in depth, I had concluded that that prohibition was pointless, for states had never complied with it. Thus, I said, the prohibition was to be held devoid of any legal force. He took the floor and fiercely dissented. He noted that international principles may serve as legal standards even when they are unheeded, be it for a short time or for a much longer time. And he stressed that if a scholar adds his own scepticism to the inherent fragility of legal tenets restraining the use of violence, eventually—if unwittingly—he plays a negative role, helping to hamstring the reign of law. International principles, he added, may lie dormant for a time; but they are there and sooner or later they may be used by one or more international actors to curb violence.

7. The Evolution of the International Community

I have now come to a point in life where I ought to prepare for the Return to Darkness. It is a time for pause and reflection.

I may thus perhaps venture some general reflections on the international community and say how I appraise both the developments that in my lifetime have occurred in that community and the general outlook for the legal standards governing international dealings.

In my lifetime I have witnessed the evolution of three stages of the world community: when it was a community militarily and politically divided into two blocs and ideologically split into western, socialist, and developing countries (1950–1989); when, with the collapse of the Soviet bloc, it became a community dominated by one superpower, which however was not mighty enough to rule over all the members of the community and had to compromise on many issues with other major powers (1990–2000); and when the community, whilst remaining structured as before, has been overwhelmed by the threat of terrorism, so much so that most dealings of the major international actors are now influenced by the question of how to stem or destroy terrorism (2001 to the present). This is a period that some have termed the Fourth World War (the third being the Cold War).

In the first of these three stages, the military and political authority of the Soviet bloc was underpinned by a strong ideology that also permeated those states' attitude towards the international community. The fundamental principles advocated by that group of states were: protection of each State's sovereignty; the fight against western economic penetration and colonialism; and ideological, political and military expansion in other areas of the world. Everything was subordinated to those tenets. Even the self-determination of peoples was proclaimed only as a device for disrupting colonialism, racial segregation of the majority by a white minority (apartheid), as well as, after 1967, as a means of restraining Israel's occupation of the West Bank and the Gaza Strip. Self-determination understood as the free and unhindered choice by the people of their rulers through a multi-party system reflecting the various groupings in society, was anathema to them. Similarly, human rights were only proclaimed to attack the West. International scrutiny of the way in which human rights were implemented in those states was out of the question. Nevertheless, it was thanks to this strong anti-western position on the part of socialist states that developing countries were able to set forth their own ideology based on the same tenets plus an emphasis on economic development, and therefore to propound a restructuring of international economic relations. All this was accompanied, in developing countries, by a naïve belief in the magical power of words and of the force of resolutions adopted by the UN General Assembly. Western states essentially remained on the defensive, clinging to traditional principles and trying to maintain the existing order as much as possible, even though the unravelling of colonialism was ineluctable. Their legal experts, however, were manifestly more sophisticated and argued their points with a better logic than those representing the other two groupings. Whatever the merits of each of the three blocs, it is a fact that international legal standards could only emerge if they mustered a large measure of support in all three. Hence, when drawing up new legal rules, an effort to understand and accept the viewpoint of other groups was always necessary. This process rendered negotiations on international legal standards difficult from a practical viewpoint, but it also made them intellectually fascinating. The drafting, between 1962 and 1970, and the adoption, in 1970, of the famous 'Declaration on Friendly Relations' (General Assembly resolution 2625-XXV, of 24 October 1970) was the culmination of this long process.

Owing to the clash of opposing ideologies, this was the period when new concepts were formulated and introduced into the legal network regulating the world community. Chief among them were the notions of obligations *erga omnes* and of *jus cogens*, as well as the duty of cooperation. They were generous attempts to accomplish two major objectives. First, to insert new values, endowed with universal force and binding on all people regardless of their conduct, within a legal structure traditionally based on self-interest, of the formal equality of all members and strict reciprocity of obligations. Second, to establish a hierarchy of values, where the new values must be overriding and all-embracing.

The downfall of socialism among other things entailed not only the disappearance of a strong front of socialist states but also the gradual demise of the ideological arsenal that developing countries had been using. Today this group substantially concentrates on economic claims linked to its underdevelopment. These states no longer propound principles or standards that in some way underpin or buttress a general outlook. The *ideological absence* of these states has divided the world community into two camps, lined up no longer along political or ideological principles, but rather along considerations of economic and military power. International legal discourse has thus become relatively less variegated than before. Probably the only major achievement of this period is the astounding success of the ideal of international criminal justice, which has led to a proliferation of international criminal courts and tribunals. Another sign of progress can perhaps be seen in the expanding force of the doctrine of human rights, which is no longer marred by ideological manipulation and abuse. As a result the only weapon still in the hands of the, alas, numerous authoritarian states is the doctrine of domestic jurisdiction, which has consequently gone through a revival (particularly at the hands of China).

After September 2001 the social structure of the world community has remained substantially unchanged, subject to two exceptions. First, new actors have emerged and asserted their presence with the greatest vigour: notably non-state militarily organized groups, mostly with terrorist leanings. Secondly, some developing states (China, India, Pakistan, Brazil, South Africa) have become major powers, and some of them are also endowed with nuclear weapons. What has dramatically changed, however, is the political philosophy embraced by states. There is now a huge divide between states and non-state organizations espousing a terrorist outlook, and states threatened by and hence opposed to terrorism. In sum, terrorism and its philosophy have become the major divide in the world community. The new aspect is that terrorism is also increasingly associated with Islam, all the more so because one of the favourite and most lethal methods of terrorist combat is self-sacrifice (suicide bombers).

At present the world community is thus split into two camps: in one there are persons, organizations and states bent on destroying western civilization by any means, no matter how cruel they have to be and no matter who the victims might be; the other camp is under the sway of those only eager to fight back by dint of the overwhelming force of weapons. There is no dialogue and no attempt in either camp to understand the motivations and aspirations of the adversary. Armed conflicts have thus spread at a staggering pace; sometimes no distinction can be made between international and internal armed conflicts, as mixed conflicts are becoming more and more frequent and, even more dramatically, more asymmetrical. By the same token, the body of law designed to regulate and restrain armed violence, that is, international humanitarian law, has acquired enormous importance; however, as I will note below, at the same time its basic failings have conspicuously come to light. On top of that, we are still faced with a striking contradiction: the Five Permanent Members of the Security Council, who make up the 'board of directors' of the international community[27] and

---

[27] H. Kissinger, *Diplomacy* (New York–London: Simon and Schuster, 1995) spoke first of President F.D. Roosevelt envisioning 'a postwar order in which the three victors, along with China, would act as a board of directors of the world' (at 395).

under the UN Charter should be responsible for ensuring peace and stability, are the biggest manufacturers and exporters of weapons, which they primarily export to developing countries.

8. The Hallmarks of the Present World Community

If I take a look at the legal standards and the legal institutions of the world community as they have evolved in the last twenty or thirty years, I cannot help feeling dispirited. The great promises heralded in the 1960s and 1970s—the upholding of forward-looking notions such as obligations *erga omnes*, 'obligations owed to the international community as a whole',[28] *jus cogens*, the aggravated responsibility of states, the common heritage of mankind, the right to development—have remained unfulfilled. Thirty or forty years later, these notions have still not been acted upon by states or judicial organs. They still do not have the strength to guide the day-to-day activities of the primary actors on the world stage. Furthermore, the body of law designed to restrain states from resorting to military force has remained full of loopholes: neither the doctrine of anticipatory self-defence nor that of resort to force on humanitarian grounds has been clarified by states or the United Nations. The two major flaws of international humanitarian law, that is: the failure to restrain the conduct of hostilities through the enactment of detailed and precise legal standards designed to protect civilians more effectively, and the failure to ensure impartial and constant monitoring of breaches of the law on the part of the combatants, have not been remedied. Human rights law, the most significant hallmark of the new international community reborn in the aftermath of the Second World War, has not made much headway. The gap between standard-setting and implementation remains conspicuous. The replacement of the UN Human Rights Commission with the Human Rights Council has not involved any major change: that body still remains in the hands of sovereign states, bent on playing politics more than ensuring respect for human dignity. The law of the sea has been stripped of its most progressive concept, that of 'common heritage of mankind', thus returning to traditional notions based on reciprocity and joint interests. The law and institutions of development, of trade, in particular the WTO, as well as the law of the environment are plodding along, strained by the effort to keep up with the mushrooming of the often intractable problems of poverty, underdevelopment, large-scale pollution, and global warming.

In addition, some concepts generously propounded in the aftermath of the Second World War, in particular that of the self-determination of peoples, have failed to be realized. It is a sad fact that neither in Palestine (since 1967 at least) nor in Western Sahara (since 1975 or at least 1991) has this concept proved efficacious

---

[28] Now proposed in Article 42 of the International Law Commission's Articles on State Responsibility.

as a tool for liberating those peoples. True, the problems are exceedingly complex and the political and military implications of any solution stand in the way of a rapid settlement. The problems are however left to fester and states do not see any incentive in a principle that instead should serve as one of their major guiding lights.

In short, the traditional 'soul' of the world community has continued to march on unperturbed. Only its surface has been lightly scratched by those new values and legal standards. The world community continues to be dominated by sovereign states, each of which is primarily bent on the pursuit of its own short- or medium-term interests.

On top of that, fundamentalist ideologies are pervading the world: some in favour of violent subversion and terror, others—admittedly not dangerous, albeit very worrisome—in favour of the exportation of western democracy to the whole world, if need be by force of arms. These ideologies, whatever their implications, are a far cry from the ideals enshrined in the UN Charter: peace, respect for human rights (that is, toleration and understanding) and the self-determination of peoples (that is, the freedom of peoples from the oppression of foreign countries).

What compounds this rather gloomy picture is the dearth of great leaders capable of taking to heart, and putting their minds at the service of, the world community. The only great living visionary, Nelson Mandela, has retired on age and health grounds. There is no Franklin Delano Roosevelt, Churchill, or de Gaulle around. In his *Philosophy of History* (1823–31) Hegel defined this category of persons *Welt-Historische Individuen*, world-historical individuals, 'soul leaders' (*Seelenführer*), 'men who [have] an insight into the requirements of the time—what [is] ripe for development', men who 'will and do accomplish something great'.[29] If one of those men were with us, he could perhaps inject new ideas into the fabric of the world community and push through solutions to some of the festering problems currently polluting that community: for instance the Palestinian question, the problem of Western Sahara, the numerous armed conflicts with all the attendant atrocities in Africa, the plight of the populations in many developing countries that find it hard to build modern and democratic state structures, or the question of global warming.

As a consequence, there seems to be no more room for innovative concepts such as those that emerged in the first of the various stages of development of the world community. Except for international criminal justice and the vigorous life of regional judicial bodies protecting human rights (in Europe and Latin America) there is a dearth of international actors pursuing ideals and concerns not subordinated to self-interest.

In sum, the world community is still bedevilled by the huge gap between generous and visionary legal rhetoric and the harsh reality of states each substantially

[29] G.W.F. Hegel, *Vorlesungen über die Philosophie der Weltgeschichte* (text of 1840 edn by G. Lasson, 2nd edn, Hamburg: F. Meinert, 1920, at 77–8).

pursuing its own national interests. The generous promises and projects made in the 1960s and 1970s have not materialized. It is as if states, after much discussion and interminable polemics on its placement and configuration, had built a magnificent skyscraper, provided it with an entrance, floors, stairs, lifts, fully furnished rooms, and even vases full of freshly cut flowers, and then left the building empty, for nobody dares to enter and live there.

The outlook is grim. The lawyer, faced with what seems a partial eclipse of reason, more and more often feels like a person painting 'still lifes' on the walls of a sinking ship.

9. Does an International Community Proper Exist?

The crucial issue is whether an international community proper exists. No doubt it does exist as a myth, and this myth was explored in a masterly way by René Jean Dupuy.[30] But does it also exist as a living reality? The question was raised in lucid terms in 1936 by a leading British scholar, James Brierly.[31] His answer, written in dark times when a world war and its attendant devastation were looming large, was very nuanced.

Today, some of the trappings of a community proper are visible. There are legal standards regulating the conduct of all the members of the community, whatever their size, status, development, and military and economic power. There are legal institutions embracing all the states: the United Nations and the UN family of specialized agencies. There is a sort of constitution, the UN Charter, which sets out the goals that international institutions ought to pursue and also lays down the general principles by which states should abide: peace, friendly relations, interstate co-operation, respect for human rights, the self-determination of peoples. There also exist legal standards that restrain the previously absolute liberty of states to regulate their own actions and dealings: these are the peremptory norms to which I referred a moment ago, the so-called *jus cogens*.

What however is lacking is a '*community sentiment*', the feeling in each member state that it is a part of the whole and must pursue common goals; a shared conviction that each member not only must comply with existing legal and moral standards, but is also bound to call upon and even demand that other members do likewise in the interest of the whole community. In each national system there exist both strong bonds within the community and also public

---

[30] See in particular *Communauté internationale et disparités de développement*, in 165 *Hague Recueil*, 1979-IV, 9–232; *La communauté internationale entre le mythe et l'histoire* (Paris: Economica, 1986). The same topic is also discussed in *L'Humanité dans l'imaginaire des nations* (Paris: Julliard, 1991), but in philosophical and literary terms.

[31] 'The Rule of Law in International Society' (1936), reprinted in J.L. Brierly, *The Basis of Obligation in International Law and Other Papers*, selected and edited by H. Lauterpacht and C.H.M. Waldock (Oxford: Clarendon Press, 1958), 250–64.

institutions that in a way cement or replace those bonds. True, all too often in modern cities passers-by look the other way when they see a person lying wounded on a street or otherwise in need of aid. But then, public institutions (police officers, hospital officials, and so on) or private organizations (charities, and other non-profit bodies) step in to provide relief; their action is a surrogate for the sense of humanity lacking in single individuals. In the world community members are instead still self-oriented, and adequate public institutions are lacking. True, there are public bodies that should incarnate this community sentiment and speak out on behalf of the whole community when one or more members grossly deviate from accepted standards in matters that should be of major concern for everyone. But they are either silent or timid, or their voice is not loud enough. Ethiopia and Eritrea, two very poor countries that would need to promote economic development and education, and eradicate widespread poverty, were engaged instead in an all-out war (1998–2000). Other states have done very little to stop this aberration. The fundamental human rights of their own citizens are violated by Governments on a daily basis in dozens of countries: from Myanmar Burma to China, to the Democratic Republic of Congo, to the Sudan, and to many former Soviet republics. Third states look on, and make appeals at the most. Some UN bodies adopt resolutions or send 'rapporteurs' to draw up reports to which very few pay attention. When the United States touted the existence of a third category between lawful combatants and civilians, that of 'unlawful combatants' (deprived of the rights and immunities of civilians as well as the immunity from prosecution for legitimate acts of war, which accrues to belligerents), one would have expected that the ICRC, as the guardian of international humanitarian law, as well as other states would vigorously reject this category as contrary to existing law. Nothing happened. The ICRC visited Guantánamo, producing confidential reports on the treatment of unlawful combatants there, and issued general statements on the various categories of persons involved in armed hostilities. Similarly, when the United States engaged in ill-treating detainees in Iraq, no state protested or demanded respect for international standards against torture and inhumane and degrading treatment. The UN Committee Against Torture passed a report calling upon the US to abide by the 1984 Convention on Torture. Is that enough? Similarly, no firm protest accompanied by a demand for the cessation of its repeated breaches of law has been made to Russia for its action in Chechnya. Only the European Court of Human Rights has on a few occasions found Russia in breach of the European Convention. Furthermore, the international community, through the United Nations, has consistently expressed its concern over the situation in Darfur, the civil war raging in the Democratic Republic of Congo and other African states, as well as the intolerable breaches of human rights in Zimbabwe and Myanmar (Burma). However, the gap between the action taken and the suffering—as well as the needs—of the population there, is enormous: the plight of the individuals in those countries wholly dwarfs international action.

In short: can we consider that these faint voices express the community sentiment I was evoking above?

10. The Outlook for the World Community

The 'cosmopolitan society' dreamed of by Kant, a federation of free states that
absolutely ban war and live in a condition of 'good neighbourliness', is still far
off. The world community is destined to remain dominated by self-interested and
therefore permanently clashing sovereign states for many years. The 'evil nature
of man, which can be observed clearly in the free relations between nations', to
take up Kant's words,[32] will continue to plague the world community for a long
time.

The idea of a world government must *a fortiori* be ruled out, unless a natural
catastrophe of immense proportions or a new world conflagration resulting from
an increase in friction between the Great Powers brings about such a change that
a reborn world community is transformed into a *world state*.

The more plausible prospect is that of a gradual strengthening of *regional
bonds*. In twenty or thirty years this development could lead to the formation of
regional organized groups centrally running regional affairs and ensuring relative
peace within each group. Judicial or executive regional agencies could be set up
to ensure that shared values are applied within each group. Such groups might
also establish enforcement agencies capable not only of looking after regional
concerns but also of acting on behalf of the world community (say, in contact
with and upon the authorization of the UN Security Council) to impose peace,
law and order in other areas of the world by the use of force.

Thus, although an international community proper would not yet exist, at
least some building blocks would be put in place for the eventual restructuring of
society and a better distribution of power.

11. Let us Heed our Daimon

With hindsight, I feel that while perhaps my 'practical' action has been somehow
helpful, I have not contributed much to legal scholarship. However, from the
outset I have been sceptical about writing books. One writes a book with ardour
and hope and tries to inject into it as many new ideas and views and scholarship
as possible; while one is writing a book, everything else wanes in importance,
as if that book were the linchpin of the world. I have never forgotten, however,
some thoughts by Arthur Schopenhauer I read many years ago. He wrote that,

---

[32] *Eternal Peace* (1795), in I. Kant, *Moral and Political Writings*, ed. by C.J. Friedrich (New
York: The Modern Library, 1977), at 442.

according to Herodotus, Xerxes wept at the sight of his enormous army, made up of so many lusty and valiant warriors, thinking that, of all these men, none would be alive in a hundred years' time. 'So', added the philosopher, 'who cannot but weep at the sight of the thick fair catalogue to think that, of all these books, not one will be alive in ten year's time'.[33] I am afraid that most of our books have an even shorter life span. This, however, is not grounds for weeping. There are other, more serious grounds.

Philosophers teach us that, whatever the general circumstances of life, one ought to heed one's own *daimon* and accomplish the task of the day, however modest and tiny one's performance may be. It would be pusillanimous to stop striving for something higher than our day-to-day, life-sustaining job, only because the times are very gloomy indeed. Let us therefore march on and engage in our daily exertions—whatever their value—on the socio-legal problems that affect human beings. The hope that we may be able to pass on something intellectually and emotionally valuable to our children and grandchildren is an abiding solace. An academic also has another great joy: the hope that he or she has taught a way of thinking to a goodly number of young persons. I am overjoyed to see that some of those to whom I have tried to teach the use of the intellectual tools of our job are now faring so well and have surpassed me by far in the quality of their thinking.

When the ineluctable hour comes, it will neither find us dismayed nor slothful.

Antonio Cassese

[33] A. Schopenhauer, *Essays and Aphorisms*, edited by R.J. Hollingdale (Penguin Books, 1970), at 209.

PART I

THE HUMAN
DIMENSION OF WARS

A. General

1. Current Trends in the Development of the Law of Armed Conflict*

1. Introduction

An increasing number of States are becoming aware of the obsolescence of the laws of war. On the initiative of both the United Nations (UN) and the International Committee of the Red Cross (ICRC), a number of studies have been made and international conferences convened for the purpose of preparing the ground for the drafting of two Additional Protocols to the 1949 Geneva Conventions on the Protection of War Victims. A first session of a Diplomatic Conference of all States parties to the Geneva Conventions was held this year. It is expected that the Protocols will be completed in the course of the second session of the Conference, due to take place next year at Geneva.

The titles of the Protocols do not entirely suggest what is actually under way. What is aimed at is an extensive updating and supplementing of whole sections of the laws of warfare, both of the so-called Law of the Hague (concerning primarily the conduct of hostilities) and of the Law of Geneva (regarding war victims, as well as internal armed conflicts). It is not difficult, therefore, to grasp the great importance of the whole exercise.

In addition to the breadth of the vital subject they affect, the legislative efforts under way derive great value and significance from the fact that large segments of the international society, which previously either did not exist or played a relatively minor role in the matter at issue, are now participating decisively in framing the laws of war. I refer of course to the Afro-Asian and socialist countries. To realize the importance of this increased international involvement, it may suffice to recall that only 13 States, all of them European, took part in the first

* This article is adapted from a lecture delivered at the *Institut Henry-Dunant*, Geneva, on September 12, 1974. Originally published in 24 *Rivista trimestrale di diritto pubblico* (1974) 1407.

Although the writer was a member of the Italian Delegation to the 1971 and 1972 Geneva Conferences of Government Experts of the Reaffirmation and Development of International Humanitarian Law Applicable in Armed Conflicts, as well as to the 1974 Geneva Diplomatic Conference on the same subject, the views expressed here are my own and do not reflect those of any Government agency.

general Diplomatic Conference on the laws of war—the Brussels Conference of 1874. There was greater participation in the Hague Conferences of 1899 and 1907: respectively 26 and 44 States, while some extra-European States joined in, such as the United States, Persia, China, Japan, and a growing number of Latin American countries. In 1907 the majority was strongly in the hands of European and Latin American countries. In the 1949 Geneva Conference out of 59 countries there were for the first time a group of eight socialist countries, plus two African States.[1] While it could be stated that the 1949 Geneva Conventions 'were a product of European experience and history',[2] in contrast 125 States took part in the first session of the 1974 Diplomatic Conference; one half of the countries participating in this conference had not taken part in the drafting of the 1949 Conventions.[3] In 1974 the Afro-Asian States were able to command a comfortable majority; acting in concert with either the socialist or Latin American States they could muster a two-thirds majority. The Western European States, the United States, and Latin American States, which had left their mark on the current international law of war, proved to be no longer the dominating figures.

Given the complexity and the magnitude of the legislative activity now in progress, it is rather difficult to be able to pin-point all the developments presently emerging. I shall therefore confine myself to dealing with six main areas where the law of armed conflicts is most glaringly in need to be updated because of fresh and multifarious developments in warfare.

First, we will consider the dividing line between international and internal armed conflicts. The emergence of wars of national liberation has placed great strains on this classification, because many States claim that such wars must be labelled 'international conflicts' even though they do not take place between States. Secondly, there is the problem of which categories of combatants can be treated as legitimate belligerents and consequently qualify on capture for

---

[1] Egypt and Ethiopia. See *Final Record of the Diplomatic Conference of Geneva of 1949*, vol. 1, pp. 158–170. Five other States took part in the Conference with the status of 'observers' (*ibid.*, p. 171). The plenipotentiaries of 64 States (some of which had not participated in any way in the Diplomatic Conference, but were parties to previous international instruments on the protection of war victims) signed the Conventions and the Final Act (*ibid.*, pp. 173–178).

Liberia, which according to some delegates to the 1974 Geneva Diplomatic Conference (see e.g. Egypt, Diplomatic Conference on the Reaffirmation and Development of International Humanitarian Law Applicable in Armed Conflicts, *Provisional Summary Records*, CDDH/SR. 10, p. 4; Burundi, *ibid.*, SR. 11, p. 22) was one of the three African States representing Africa in 1949, in fact neither took part in the 1949 Conference nor signed the Conventions and the Final Act.

[2] See the statement made by the representative of Nigeria in the 1974 Geneva Conference: Diplomatic Conference on the Reaffirmation and Development of International Humanitarian Law Applicable in Armed Conflicts, *Provisional Summary Records*, CDDH/SR. 12, p. 3 (hereafter cited only by their symbol). The final edition of the *Summary Records* was only made available to me after the writing of this paper. I had, however, the opportunity to check all the quotations which I had made using the provisional *Summary Records*. Wherever changes had been made in the final edition, I used this edition, and in these cases reference has been made in the footnotes to both the provisional and the final edition.

[3] Cp. *ibid.*

prisoner-of-war status. The spreading of guerrilla warfare has given rise to the question of whether, and on what conditions, guerrilla fighters fall within those categories. Thirdly, there is the question of the introduction into warfare of new and very cruel weapons. It is imperative to establish whether the use of such weapons is, or should be, legally banned. Fourthly, the protection of civilians in light of new methods of combat needs attention. Aerial bombardment, especially target area bombing, saturation bombing etc., and electronic warfare, as well as guerrilla warfare, expose civilians to increased dangers, against which present international law offers no adequate protection. Fifthly, we will consider ways and means of ensuring the implementation of the law of armed conflict. There is a growing disregard for this law, which the existing implementation devices are not capable of remedying. Sixthly, and lastly, we will focus on the legal regulation of internal armed conflicts. At present such conflicts spread with increasing frequency; yet, their international regulation is still deficient in far too many respects.

In order to provide the general background against which the growth of new law must be evaluated and thereby to allow a better assessment of fresh developments, I shall first make a very sketchy survey of the existing law before dealing with each of the six problem areas. I shall then point to the strains that current developments in modern warfare are putting on that law and focus on the main trends which are at present emerging among States toward updating and improving the law.

2. Wars of National Liberation

The first topic to be considered is *the general subdivision of armed conflicts into two categories*: international conflicts and non-international conflicts. This dichotomy, which is deeply rooted in international law, is still generally accepted. Under strong criticism and likely to be modified are the contents of the distinction, namely the classes of conflicts to be grouped under either heading.

Thus far the international law of warfare has been based on the assumption that a basic difference exists between *international* wars, that is to say armed conflicts between two or more States, and *non-international armed conflicts,* namely conflicts breaking out in the territory of a State between rebels and the central authority. The distinction between these two classes of conflicts is not only a matter of logic; it has a great practical impact. For *the whole of the law of warfare* applies to international conflicts only. Internal conflicts, instead, are governed by very few international rules, namely some general principles of customary law relating to the protection of civilians, and by Article 3, common to the four 1949 Geneva Conventions. The reason for this discriminatory treatment is self-evident. States are interested in having wars with other States mitigated as much as possible by international rules. This is called for by *reciprocity*: any State benefits from its combatants being treated as prisoners of war, its sick, wounded, and shipwrecked being cared for, and its civilians being spared the evils of war. On the contrary, Governments are much less, if at all, interested in having rebellions within their territory governed by international law. Their main concern is to retain enough freedom to crush promptly any form of insurrection. Their sovereignty and territorial integrity cannot but oppose any sweeping encroachment by international law. This is why so few international rules govern internal conflicts. In addition, these rules have a humanitarian scope in that they are primarily aimed at protecting the victims of internal conflicts. They do not confer any special status on rebels, who therefore retain, even from the standpoint of international law, the legal qualification impressed on them by municipal law—that of criminals.

This state of affairs is going to change, at least with respect to a special category of armed conflicts. Wars of national liberation, though they break out in the territory of a given State and occur between rebels on one side and the central authorities on the other side, are to be considered international conflicts in the opinion of a large majority of States, namely Afro-Asian and socialist countries, as well as some Latin American States. These States have succeeded in passing a number of resolutions on the matter in the United Nations General Assembly. What is more important is that they have secured the adoption of a similar provision by one of the Committees of the 1974 Diplomatic Conference on Humanitarian Law of War. Under this provision, which was approved by 70 votes to 21, with 13 abstentions,[4] the Additional Protocol I to the 1949 Geneva Conventions, which covers international armed conflicts, shall also apply to 'armed conflicts in which peoples are fighting against colonial domination and alien occupation and against racist regimes in the exercise of their rights of self-determination, as enshrined in the Charter of the United Nations and the Declaration on Principles of International Law concerning Friendly Relations and Co-operation among States in accordance with the Charter of the United Nations'. This provision is very likely to be adopted next year by the Plenary of the second Session of the Diplomatic Conference, thereby becoming Article 1 of Protocol I.

The political purpose and the legal implications of this provision are clear: its framers intend to apply to wars of national liberation the whole body of the laws of warfare. What are the political and legal motivations of this stand? The records of the United Nations General Assembly and the 1974 Geneva Diplomatic Conference disclose that the majority stand was prompted by two different motivations which, however, are not mutually exclusive.

According to one, more extreme motivation, wars fall into two categories— just and unjust. Unjust wars are those of aggression; into this class would fall

---

[4] Out of the 70 States that voted for this provision, 49 were Afro-Asian, 12 were socialist (Eastern European countries, plus Albania and the People's Republic of China), 7 were Latin American (including Cuba), and 2 were Western countries (Finland and Norway). Most of the States which cast a negative vote were Western countries. See Diplomatic Conference, etc., *Report of Committee I.* CDDH/48, p. 6.

wars waged by colonialist powers against peoples fighting for their liberation. Anti-colonial wars and wars against foreign domination are, on the contrary, 'just' wars. Consequently, peoples waging such wars should enjoy the status of legitimate belligerents. As the delegate of the People's Republic of China put it at the 1974 Diplomatic Conference: 'It is utterly inconceivable that the combatants and civilians fighting against aggression, for national liberation and independence, should not benefit from a humanitarian treatment whereas those taking part in a war of aggression are treated humanely upon capture'.[5] The delegate of Albania, in his turn, stated that 'the national liberation struggles waged by oppressed peoples were legitimate and represented the only certain road towards freedom and independence. That should be expressly stated in Protocol I because freedom fighters, who were subjected to savage repression by the imperialist Powers, had the right to effective protection. Those who waged an unjust war against those combatants should bear the responsibility for their crimes'.[5-bis]

This motivation, it is plain, is fundamentally based on ideological considerations. It essentially rests on a value-judgement, namely that wars of national liberation are 'right'. The consequence drawn from this assumption is that those wars are international in character. It does not seem, instead, that another implication of the concept of 'just wars', namely the principle of inequality of treatment between combatants is advocated, at least in express terms, by the proponents of the motivation under consideration. Under this principle those who fight for a just war should enjoy better legal protection than those engaged in a unjust war, whom one could even deprive of any legal safeguards.

[5] See the full text of the statement made in Plenary by the Chinese delegate, *Intervention de Pi Ki-Long, Chef de la délégation chinoise à la Conférence diplomatique de Genève*, p. 4. The Chinese delegate said the following: 'Le statut légitime de la guerre de libération nationale a déjà été confirmé par les buts et principes de la Charte des Nations Unies ainsi que par les résolutions pertinentes de l'Assemblée générale de l'O.N.U. . . . Certains s'opposent toujours, et par mille et un moyens, à ce que le protocole définisse le statut légitime de la guerre de libération nationale. Selon eux, n'est "régulière" et "légale" que la guerre d'agression tandis que la guerre de libération nationale est "illégale". N'est-ce pas là une logique impérialiste sans fard? D'autre part, il est absolument inconcevable que les combattants et les civils qui luttent contre l'agression, pour la libération et l'indépendance nationales, ne bénéficient pas du traitement humanitaire alors que ceux qui ont pris part à une guerre d'agression sont traités avec humanité en cas de capture'. The statement is summarized in CDDH/SR. 12, pp. 5–7.

In Committee I the delegate of the People's Republic of China stated that 'the wars of national liberation were just wars waged against imperialist and colonialist domination. The United Nations General Assembly at its twenty-eighth session had proclaimed that the struggles of peoples against colonial and alien domination and racist regimes were to be regarded as international armed conflicts in the sense of the 1949 Geneva Conventions (Res. 3103-XXVIII)' (CDDH/I/SR. 4, p. 5). As to the stand taken in the United Nations by the same country on 'just and unjust wars', see the statement made in 1973, in the UN General Assembly (A/C.I/PV. 1968, p. 61).

A view very close to that of China was taken at the Geneva Diplomatic Conference by Albania (*ibid.*, I/SR. 5, p. 5). Cp. also the statement by Madagascar ('the field of application of Art. 1 of Draft Protocol I should be extended to cover the just struggles being waged by national liberation movements'; *ibid.*, I/SR. 2, p. 16), and those made in the general debate, in plenary, by Mauritania (CDDH/SR. 17, p. 6), and Zaire (*ibid.*, SR. 19, p. 3).

[5-bis] CDDH/SR. 14, p. 9.

The other motivation, which is by far more widespread, being supported by all Eastern European countries,[6] most Afro-Asian States,[7] some Latin American States,[8] a few Western countries,[9] as well as the Organization of African Unity[10] and several liberation movements,[11] stresses instead the legal side. The reasoning is very simple. The United Nations Charter proclaims the right of peoples to self-determination. This right has been further developed and elaborated by a stream of resolutions adopted by important United Nations bodies; prominent among them are the 1960 Declaration on the Granting of Independence to Colonial Countries and Peoples and the 1970 Declaration on Principles of International Law Concerning Friendly Relations and Co-operation among States. As a result of all these authoritative pronouncements a rule of general international law has gradually emerged and is now generally accepted. By virtue of such a rule, peoples of colonies or non-autonomous territories which have not yet achieved independence, have a legal status independent of the metropolitan power. In addition, such peoples, as well as all peoples under alien domination or racist régime have an international right to self-determination. They are, therefore, subjects of international law. It follows that wars waged by such peoples against colonial, alien, or racist régimes are wars between members of the international society and are therefore international in character. The obvious consequence of this line of reasoning is that a rule stipulating that wars of national liberation are international armed conflicts would simply codify international law already in force.[12]

Which are the arguments put forward by most Western States to oppose the labelling of wars of national liberation as international conflicts? It is apparent from the debates at the Geneva Conference that the main target of Western criticisms has been the moderate, legally-oriented motivation of such labelling. There

---

[6] See e.g. the statements by the representatives of Romania (CDDH/I/SR. 2, pp. 4–5), Yugoslavia (*ibid.*, p. 5 and CDDH/SR. 11, p. 7), German Democratic Republic (*ibid.*, pp. 10–11), USSR (*ibid.*, SR. 3, p. 2), Ukraine (*ibid.*, SR. 5, pp. 5–6 and CDDH/SR. 11, p. 18–19), Cuba (CDDH/SR. 10, p. 5), Poland (CDDH/SR. 11, pp. 15–16), Czechoslovakia (CDDH/SR. 13, p. 17), Mongolia (CDDH/SR. 18, p. 13).

[7] See e.g. the statements by the representatives of Egypt (CDDH/I/SR. 2, pp. 3–4), Morocco (*ibid.*, p. 11 and CDDH/SR. 10, pp. 13–14), Nigeria (*ibid.*, p. 12); Syria (*ibid.*, SR., p. 7), Senegal (*ibid.*, S.R. 6, p. 6), Madagascar (CDDH/SR. 13, p. 14).

[8] See e.g. the statement made by the representatives of Mexico (CDDH/I/SR. 3, p. 7) and Venezuela (*ibid.*, pp. 8–9).

[9] See e.g. the statement by the delegate of Norway (CDDH/I/SR. 2, pp. 7–8).

[10] See the opening address by Lieutenant Colonel Hashim I. Mbita, Executive Secretary of the OAU Liberation Committee, at the OAU Seminar on Humanitarian Law (Dar Es Salam, 21 to 25 January, 1974): Permanent Delegation of the OAU in Geneva, *Summary Record of the OAU Seminar on Humanitarian Law*, Annex 4, pp. 2–5.

[11] See *Summary Record of the OAU Seminar* etc., cit., pp. 8–11.

[12] This was stressed, in particular, by the representatives of the German Democratic Republic (CDDH /I/SR. 2, p. 11) and USSR (*ibid.*, SR. 3, p. 2). See also Yugoslavia (*ibid.*, SR. 2, p. 5).

On this subject, see in general ABI-SAAB, *Wars of National Liberation and the Laws of War*, in *Annales d'Etudes Internationales*, 1972, vol. 3, pp. 93–117; Idem, *Legal Aspects of the Armed Struggles of the Liberation Movements*, in *International NGO Conference against Apartheid and Colonialism in Africa*, Geneva, September 1974, Conference Paper 4.

are two possible reasons for this. First, the other (extreme, ideologically-oriented) motivation has been advocated by very few States, though one of these is a country as important as the People's Republic of China. Secondly, only the proponents of the moderate motivation have put forward formal proposals embodying their own views and purposes. The opponents of the international character of wars of national liberation have therefore deemed it fit to concentrate their objections on the moderate approach. Yet, a few of them discerned an ideological overtone even in this approach, and consequently extended their criticism to the ideologically-oriented motivation. The spectrum of critical remarks levelled at the 'international-conflict-characterization' is therefore very wide and covers in substance all possible rationales of that characterization.

Let us now briefly mention the main objections raised by most Western countries against the majority view. First of all, it was observed that the legal assimilation of wars of national liberation to the status of international armed conflicts, and the consequent application of the 1949 Geneva Conventions and Additional Protocol I to such conflicts, would result in imposing heavy obligations on liberation movements, which they could not be in a position to fulfill. Consequently, such movements would be branded as being in violation of the Geneva Conventions.[13] For instance, movements fighting for self-determination would have to face serious problems in applying Article 23 of the Third Geneva Convention (the provision to shelter war prisoners against military operations), or Article 4 of the Fourth Convention (defining the persons protected by the Conventions as those who find themselves in the hands of a Party to the conflict or Occupying Power *of which they are not nationals*). It was further pointed out that the implementation of many provisions of the Geneva Conventions called for a complicated machinery which, generally speaking, is available only to Governments.[14]

A second major argument brought against the majority view consisted of the need to avoid placing undue emphasis on *subjective elements* for the purpose of distinguishing between the various forms of armed conflicts. As was stated by the United Kingdom representative, it is

a basic principle of the Geneva Conventions, the Hague Regulations and other instruments that legal and humanitarian protection should never vary according to the motives of those engaged in a particular armed struggle. Deviation from that principle would mean damaging the structure of the Hague and Geneva Conventions and would involve the need to reconstruct the whole of humanitarian law. Moreover, to discriminate between the motives of those engaged in the struggle, would violate essential principles of human rights.[15]

---

[13] Belgium (CDDH/I/SR. 2, p. 9); USA (*ibid.*, SR. 4, p. 2); United Kingdom (*ibid.*, SR. 4, p. 8); Brazil (*ibid.*, SR. 4, p. 12).

[14] Italy (CDDH/I/SR. 3, p. 11).

[15] CDDH/I/SR. 2, p. 13 and the final edition of the *Summary Records*, CDDH/I/SR. 2, p. 13. See also CDDH/I/SR. 4, p. 8, where the British delegate said that he strongly opposed 'the medieval concept of just warfare'.

These remarks were echoed by the representatives of other States.[16] Some States went so far as to suggest the possibility that the majority view would disrupt the principle of equality of treatment of the parties *durante bello*. They passionately argued that, since that view was based on the concept of the rightness or wrongness of a conflict, one might infer that the 'oppressor' alone should be bound to comply with the Geneva Conventions and Additional Protocol I. This would, of course, jeopardize the granting of an equal degree of protection to the parties to the conflict.[17] This argument was rebutted by several proponents of the majority view with the plain statement that they did not contemplate introducing any form of discrimination between the struggling parties. They added that, on the contrary, if wars for self-determination were regarded as internal armed conflicts, preferential treatment would be given to one of the parties, namely the colonial or racist country, for this country would enjoy great latitude in its repression of freedom fighters. If wars for self-determination were labelled international conflicts, a full equality was insured between the parties to the conflict since liberation movements are capable of and willing to abide by international rules governing armed conflicts; and in fact they are already applying, to a large extent, the 1949 Geneva Conventions.[18]

---

[16] France (CDDH/I/SR. 2, p. 14), Uruguay (*ibid.*, SR. 3, p. 2 and I/SR. 14, p. 9), Switzerland (*ibid.*, SR. 3, p. 5), Canada (*ibid.*, p. 6), Spain (*ibid.*, p. 6), Denmark (*ibid.*, SR. 5, p. 8 and SR. 14, p. 5), Belgium (*ibid.*, SR. 14, p. 2), Israel (*ibid.*, p. 3). See also the explanations of vote after the adoption of Art. 1 of Draft Protocol I: Belgium (CDDH/I/SR. 14, p. 2), Israel (*ibid.*, p. 3), Denmark (*ibid.*, p. 5), and Uruguay (*ibid.*, p. 9). Some States stressed that the majority view ultimately relied on the concept of 'just war'. Statements against introducing such a concept were made in Plenary by the Netherlands (CDDH/SR. 11, pp. 2–3), the United States (*ibid.*, SR. 11, p. 13–14), Belgium (*ibid.*, SR. 11, p. 20), the Holy See (*ibid.*, SR. 12, p. 11), the Federal Republic of Germany (*ibid.*, SR. 13, p. 9), the United Kingdom (*ibid.*, SR, 13, p. 11), Switzerland (*ibid.*, SR. 13, p. 15), New Zealand (*ibid.*, SR. 17, pp. 10–11), Iran (*ibid.*, SR., 18, p. 10). Cp. also Canada (*ibid.*, SR. 18, p. 2). See also the explanations of vote made in Committee I, after the adoption of Art. 1 of Draft Protocol I: Australia (CDDH/I/SR. 13) and the United States (*ibid.*, SR. 14, p. 9).

On this subject see in general Baxter, *The Geneva Conventions of 1949 and Wars of National Liberation,* in *Rivista di diritto internazionale,* 1974, pp. 196–197.

[17] USA (CDDH/I/SR. 2, p. 15; and cp. *ibid.*, SR. 14, p. 9), Netherlands (CDDH/I/SR. 4, p. 11).

[18] Norway (CDDH/I/SR. 4, p. 12; see also I/SR. 14, p. 5: 'Adoption of the amendment in doc. CDDH/I/71 did not amount to acceptance of the so-called "just war" concept. It was intended to ensure equal protection of all victims on both sides in wars of national liberation'); Egypt (*ibid.*, SR. 5, p. 4), Guinea-Bissau (*ibid.*, p. 12), Yugoslavia (*ibid.*, SR. 6, p. 10), India (*ibid.*, SR. 14, p. 6: 'The introduction into the discussion before and after the vote of the idea of just and unjust wars, and consequently that of discrimination, had only confused the issue. The question before the Committee had simply been to decide whether a specific type of conflict which was a major phenomenon of our time should be recognized as an international conflict. Different interpretations of the implications of that decision could only create difficulties in the work of the Conference'. See however CDDH/SR. 19, p. 6); Nigeria (*ibid.*, I/SR. 14, p. 11). See also Ukraine (CDDH/SR. 11, p. 19).

The same stand was taken by several liberation movements. See e.g. Frelimo, in CDDH/I/SR. 4, p. 13 and SR. 5, p. 6. Cp., however, the statement made in Plenary and quoted below, in this same note; PLO (Palestine Liberation Movement), *ibid.*, I/SR. 5, pp. 10–11.

The principle of inequality of treatment was on the contrary advocated by the representative of Romania in the general debate, in Plenary ('(H)umanitarian Law must distinguish between the aggressor and the victim of aggression and must guarantee greater protection for the victim in the

A third reason relied upon by Western countries was that the terminology used in the amendments aimed at characterizing wars of national liberation as international conflicts was vague, imprecise, and elastic. More specifically, the main target of Western criticism was the word 'peoples' which is found in the key-phrase 'self-determination of peoples'. It was contended that no exact and widely-accepted definition of 'peoples' has been given.[19] Consequently, in the view of the Belgian delegate 'it would be impossible to speak of an internal armed conflict every time an ethnic community wished to sever itself from a State'.[20]

exercise of his sacred right of self-defence': CDDH/SR: 11, p. 4). It is however significant that the Romanian delegate did not make a similar statement in Committee I, during the debate on Art. 1 of Draft Protocol I. Furthermore, Romania proposed an amendment (CDDH/I/13) in which wars of national liberation were labelled international 'with a view to ensuring more effective protection for the victims of aggression and oppression'. These words seem to convey the idea that Romania did not actually propose inequality of treatment, but rather that liberation movements be not treated less favourably than the parties against which they fight.

Other remarks which could be possibly interpreted, to some extent, as hints at the need for inequality of treatment can be found in statements made in the 1974 Diplomatic Conference and at the Dar Es Salam OAU Seminar on Humanitarian Law, as well as in comments of some States on one of the Reports of the United Nations Secretary-General. At the Geneva Conference the representatives of FRE LIMO and ZAPU (Zimbabwe African Peoples Union) stated *in Plenary* that a distinction must be made between the aggressor and the victim and between the oppressor and the oppressed (see respectively CDDH/SR. 19, p. 8 and *ibid.,* p. 12). They did not elaborate, however, on this point. The same view was taken by Byelorussia and Ukraine in their comments on a Report of the Secretary General of the United Nations (UN doc. A/8313, respectively p. 10 and 63).

More relevant appear to be some conclusions reached by the participants in the Dar Es Salaam OAU Seminar. Concerning Art. 35 sub-para. (c) of Draft Protocol I, whereby disguise of combatants in civilian clothes is prohibited, as perfidy, it was stated: '(In guerrilla warfare) the people engaged in the struggle do not always have or rarely have one single type of uniform. In most cases the freedom fighters do not have any other clothes apart from their own civilian clothes. In other cases the Liberation Movements have to use the uniforms captured from the enemy. This is why it would be desirable to work out a formula that will make this type of prohibition only applicable to those who in fact have the means to provide themselves with uniforms, I am referring here to the colonial powers. The demand for strictly identical requirements for the two parties in this field is tantamount to either penalizing the Liberation Movements or rendering the rules inapplicable. The proposal made by some Experts including the Norwegian [CE/COM. III/C. 55], to eliminate sub-para. (c), appeared to be much more realistic' (*Summary Record of the OAU Seminar,* quoted above, p. 17). This conclusion was possibly echoed—to some extent—at the Diplomatic Conference by the delegate of Ghana (CDDH/SR. 10, p. 9). Cp. also what was stated in the *OAU Seminar* on the protection of *civilian property* ('It was stressed that in any liberation war, to weaken or destroy the enemy's potentialities is one of the main aims of the struggle. This is particularly true in the case of projects and installation whether or not of an economic value, such as the projects of Cabora Bassa in Mozambique and Cunene in Angola, which the United Nations precisely considers as being instrumental in perpetuating and consolidating colonial domination') (*Summary Record of the OAU Seminar* etc., pp. 20–21).

It must not be overlooked, however, that at the OAU Seminar it was consistently emphasized, as a matter of principle, that liberation movements are ready and willing to apply humanitarian law, in particular the 1949 Geneva Conventions. See *ibid.,* p. 9, para. 5; see also the address by the Executive Secretary of the OAU Liberation Committee, *ibid.,* Annex 4, p. 4.

[19] Belgium (CDDH/I/SR. 2, p. 10), United Kingdom (*ibid.,* SR. 2, p. 13). The United States delegate furthermore observed that 'concepts such as "alien domination" and "racist regime" had yet to be defined' (*ibid.,* SR. 2, p. 15).

[20] CDDH/I/SR. 2, p. 10.

The Irish delegate pointed out that the expression 'armed struggles waged by peoples in the exercise of their right of self-determination' contained in one of the suggested amendments (CDDH/I/11) was

too vague and imprecise to serve as a justiciable standard in a legal document. It leaves scope for endless argument on when peoples may be said to exercise their right to self-determination. Any separatist movement would appear to come within this term, whether or not this was intended by all or any of its authors. Any band of armed criminals in a colonial territory could plausibly claim to be engaged in an armed struggle in furtherence of their peoples' right to self-determination. Equally disturbing is the failure of the proposal to distinguish and except the situation where peoples seek self-determination by constitutional non-violent means and a minority, with no popular mandate, resorts to violence in the same causes.[21]

He went on to say that:

the real difficulty with this proposal is not that it will impose an unacceptable burden on Governments but rather that it will ultimately injure the interests of those it seeks to protect. Its imprecision will allow Governments—especially insensitive and authoritarian Governments—endless scope to deny that a conflict comes within its terms.[22]

The representative of Uruguay observed for his part that the text of the provision which was, eventually adopted 'might open the door to any seditious movements which disturbed the internal life of States'.[23]

It is worth stressing that to these objections it was replied by supporters of the majority view that the right to self-determination was to be understood 'not as encouraging secessional and divisive subversion in multi-ethnic nations, but as applying to a struggle against colonial and alien domination, foreign occupation and racist regimes'.[24] It was also stated that 'any group of the people of a country which had succesfully overcome foreign domination and gained its national independence [could not] legitimately claim that a movement for secession from the national government was a struggle for self-determination'.[25]

Furthermore, it must be emphasized that a sufficiently precise delimitation of the concept of self-determination can be inferred both from the very text of the provision adopted at Geneva and from its 'legislative history'. The present wording of Article 1 embodies, by means of an express reference to the United

---

[21] See the full text of the statement, issued by the 'Mission permanente d'Irlande' at Geneva, p. 1. The statement is summarized in CDDH/I/SR. 4, p. 4.

[22] *Ibid.*

[23] CDDH/I/SR. 14, p. 9.

[24] Nigeria (CDDH/I/SR. 2, p. 12).

[25] Pakistan (CDDH/SR. 11, p. 11). The representative of Iran said that he 'agreed with the representative of Pakistan that the term "international armed conflict" could be applied to armed struggles for liberation from colonial domination and the acquisition of national independence, but that the term "non-international conflict" could not be applied to armed campaigns by a racial or ethnic group against the central government of its own country' (CDDH/SR. 18, p. 10. See the final edition of the *Summary Records*, CDDH/SR. 18, p. 189).

Nations Declaration on Friendly Relations, the notion of self-determination formulated in that Declaration. Therefore, it also takes up the qualification included
in the Declaration, whereby the principle of self-determination of peoples must
not be construed 'as authorizing or encouraging any action which dismembers
or impairs, totally or in part, the territorial integrity or political unity of sovereign and independent States conducting themselves in compliance with the
principle of equal rights and self-determination of peoples . . . and thus possessed
of a government representing the whole people belonging to the territory without distinction as to race, creed or colour'. As a consequence, Article 1 does not
consider as a war of national liberation any war fought by a secessionist or other
rebellious movement against an independent government that is representative of
the whole people and upholds the principle of equality. Any such secessionist or
rebellious movements in a sovereign and representative country cannot therefore
claim the right to be treated as a party to an international conflict. This conclusion is borne out by an examination of the process by which Article 1 was drafted.
While the amendment first proposed by Afro-Asian States only spoke in general
terms of wars for national self-determination, though it implicitly qualified this
concept by making reference to the Declaration on Friendly Relations,[26] the text
that was eventually adopted spelled out that reference and, above all, specified
in positive terms what should be meant by 'wars for self-determination'. For, as a
result of that amendment being amalgamated with amendments put forward by
some socialist countries,[27] the final text takes care to make it clear that the wars
it covers are only those of 'peoples fighting against colonial domination and alien
occupation and against racist régimes'.[28]

---

[26] See CDDH/I/11 and Add. 1 to 3. It must be pointed out that, in addition to several Afro-
Asian States, also Australia, Cuba, Norway and Yugoslavia co-sponsored the amendment. It
referred to 'armed struggles waged by peoples in the exercise of their right of self-determination,
as enshrined in the Charter of the United Nations and defined by the Declaration on Principles of
International Law concerning Friendly Relations and Co-operation among States in accordance
with the Charter of the United Nations'.

[27] See doc. CDDH/I/5 and Add. 1 and 2 (amendment proposed by Czechoslovakia, German
Democratic Republic, Hungary, Morocco, Poland, Tanzania, USSR), and doc. CDDH/I/13
(amendment proposed by Romania). The former amendment spoke of 'armed conflicts where
peoples fight against colonial and alien domination and against racist régimes'. The Romanian
amendment referred to 'armed conflicts in which the people of a colony, a non-self-governing
territory or a territory under foreign occupation are engaged, in the exercise of the right to self-
determination and the right to self-defence against aggression, with a view to ensuring more effective protection for the victims of aggression and oppression'.
The final vote was taken in Committee I on an amendment submitted by five Latin-American
delegations (doc. CDDH/I/71), which incorporated inter alia the substance of amendment
CDDH/I/5, and was orally amended by replacing the words 'colonial and alien occupation' with
the words 'colonial domination and alien occupation' and inserting the word 'against' before the
words 'racist régimes'. For more details on the various stages of the debates and the vote, see *Report
of Committee I*, CDDH/48, pp. 4–6, as well as the more exhaustive *Report of the Secretary-General
of the UN* on the Geneva Diplomatic Conference, A/9669, pp. 22–27.

[28] It is interesting to note that the delegate of Norway stated, after the vote on Art. 1, that,
although he had voted in favour of the provision, his delegation had, however, strong reservations

Going back to the objections which were raised by Western States to the majority view, it must be said finally that criticisms were levelled at the argument that the right to self-determination is firmly laid down in the United Nations Charter and has been subsequently developed and elaborated by innumerable resolutions of the United Nations General Assembly. It was held that the United Nations Charter only mentions the *principle* of self-determination: 'nowhere in the Charter [does] the right to engage in armed struggle appear'.[29] Furthermore, it was contended that General Assembly resolutions have no great relevance as to the possible trasformation of that principle into a legal right, for the very reason that they are not binding upon Member States nor can they amend the Charter, which remains 'inviolate until amended in the proper manner'.[30]

Before concluding our consideration of the legal classification of wars of national liberation, it may be useful to briefly stress that the adoption of Article 1 of Protocol I, if it is confirmed by the plenary of the Diplomatic Conference, will raise at least three major legal problems.

First of all, the very fact of deciding that the Protocol applies to wars of national liberation makes it logical and even imperative to allow liberation movements to accede to the Protocol. Should one of the parties to which the provisions of the Protocol address themselves not be permitted to somehow take part in the Protocol, the ensuing situation would greatly diminish the significance of the Protocol itself. It is plain that in the event of liberation movements not being bound by it, both such movements and States fighting against them would not feel obliged to comply with the Protocol in their reciprocal relationships.

The present Draft Protocol provides only for one way of 'accession': under Article 84, para. 2, liberation movements can make a declaration of acceptance of the Protocol. Their becoming parties to it is however made subject to reciprocity, in the sense that they will be regarded as parties so long as they comply with the Protocol. One may wonder whether the supporters of Article 1 will be content with this form of 'accession', or will instead ask for a modality of participation which delivers liberation movements from any condition of reciprocity.

---

against some of its wording, and regarded the phrase 'against colonial domination and alien occupation and racist régimes' as superfluous (CDDH/I/SR. 14, p. 4).

A quite different, but equally interesting declaration was made by the representative of Cuba. He stated that 'his delegation had voted in favour of the proposed amendment, on the understanding that the text was interpreted as referring not only to the national liberation movements present at the Conference and those recognized by the Organization of African Unity and the League of Arab States, but also others such as the Puerto Rico liberation group' (CDDH/I/SR. 14, p. 3). See the final edition of the *Summary Records*, CDDH/I/SR. 14, p. 105). The representative of the Federal Republic of Germany (a State that voted against Art. 1), observed in his explanation of vote that 'the definition of self-determination applicable to areas of fighting "against colonial domination and alien occupation and racist regimes", given in para. 2 of the amendment, was too limited: that principle should apply to all parts of the world' (*ibid.*, p. 4).

[29] United Kingdom (CDDH/I/SR. 2, p. 13).
[30] United Kingdom (CDDH/I/SR. 2, p. 13). See also Monaco (*ibid.*, SR. 4, p. 6); Turkey (*ibid.*, SR. 5, pp. 12–13).

The second problem raised by Article 1 is whether or not this provision can have the effect of making the 1949 Geneva Conventions applicable to wars of national liberation. The correct answer would seem to be in the negative, for two reasons. First, the 1949 Conventions on the one hand and the Additional Protocols on the other constitute two quite distinct and separate sets of rules, as is borne out by the provision whereby the Protocol does not revise, but only supplements the Conventions. Secondly, at least the II (on Prisoners of war) and the IV (on Civilians) Conventions rest on two main legal concepts, nationality and enemy-occupied territory, that can find no place in wars for self-determination, where the struggle is not carried out against enemy nationals, nor is the territory that can be militarily 'occupied' by one party to the conflict the territory of a foreign State. Those two Conventions could therefore not apply, as such, to the wars in question. Yet the nexus of Protocol I with the 1949 Conventions is much more complicated to define than would appear from the remarks I have just made. Many provisions of the Protocol presuppose that the Conventions are applicable, and indeed the basic assumption on which the Protocol rests is that the parties to it are also parties to the Convention. The conclusion can therefore be drawn that the framers of the Protocol should seek to clarify the legal relations between it and the Conventions, if they want the Protocol to be a viable and satisfactory instrument.

The adoption of Article 1 gives rise to a third problem. Many substantive provisions of Draft Protocol I, which were conceived and elaborated on the assumption that they would apply to inter-State conflicts only, will have to be adjusted to wars of national liberation.

3. Guerrilla Fighters

Let us turn now to our second question, namely, *who is to be regarded as a legitimate belligerent?*

The existing rules of international law are the result of a compromise between major Powers, possessing strong and well-equipped armies, and small or medium-sized countries, which have weak armies, are more likely to be occupied in case of war, and who rely strongly on popular resistance to combat a foreign invasion. The compromise was for the first time reached in 1874 at the Brussels Diplomatic Conference on the Laws of War. Its essence consists in the established principle that regular armies are entitled to be regarded as legitimate belligerents. Two categories of persons were assimilated to them: (1) militia and volunteer corps; (2) the inhabitants of a territory not under foreign occupation, who, upon the approach of the enemy, spontaneously take up arms to resist the invading troops ('levée en masse'). Militia and volunteer corps must, however, fulfil four strict conditions. They must (a) be commanded by a person responsible for his subordinates; (b) have a fixed distinctive sign recognizable at a distance; (c) carry arms openly; and (d) conduct their operations in accordance with the laws and customs of war. As for a people rising against invaders, in view of the rapidity with which they have to face the invasion, it is sufficient for them to fulfil two of those conditions: they must carry arms openly and respect the laws and customs of war.

It is apparent from a consideration of these provisions that big Powers, while they had eventually to satisfy the demands of small and medium-sized countries, nevertheless succeeded in requiring that all combatants other than members of regular armed forces should meet a series of stringent requirements. The purpose of these requirements is twofold: to allow the adversary to distinguish combatants from civilians, and to ensure that persons taking part in the hostilities shall comply with the laws of war. To achieve this compliance a system of internal discipline is required which should enable the enforcement of those laws in the case that an individual combatant behaves contrary to them. Also, the commander and, in the final analysis, the party to the conflict with which the militia or volunteer corps is linked, are made answerable for any breach of law by members of the group.

This regulation, which dates back to the Hague Conventions of 1899 and 1907, and which was updated in 1949 adding 'organized resistance movements' to militias and volunteer corps in the light of the experience of World War II, cannot cover a phenomenon which has become increasingly important—the emergence of guerrilla warfare. Guerrillas, as is well known, normally lack at least two of the four aforementioned conditions: they do not bear a distinctive sign, nor do they carry arms openly. Accordingly, under present international law they do not qualify for legitimate belligerent status and, if captured, are liable to be court-martialled.

The ICRC, for its part, proposed in 1974 to include in the Draft Protocol I a provision (Art. 42) wherein the two conditions under discussion are reduced to one, as follows: that combatants should distinguish themselves from the civilian population in military operations. This provision, which covers only guerrillas fighting within the framework of an international armed conflict and belonging to a party to the conflict, does not specify the manner in which the distinction between combatants and civilians should be made. It is sufficient for combatants to manifest their status in some way, either by carrying arms or by wearing a uniform, or by carrying a distinctive emblem, or in some other way. In addition to thus lowering the requisite conditions, the provision at issue favours guerrillas in the respect that they are required to distinguish themselves from civilians only during military operations, which are defined by the ICRC as 'offensive and defensive movements by armed forces in action'.[31] Consequently, a guerrilla who at the end of an operation resumes his civilian garb and is arrested by the opposing party, cannot be sentenced for having taken part in military operations if,

---

[31] ICRC, Draft Additional Protocols to the Geneva Conventions of August 12, 1949, *Commentary* (CDDH/3 October 1973), p. 51.

during those operations, he met the necessary requirements; he will be entitled to prisoner-of-war status.[32]

It was pointed out that these ICRC proposals may raise serious problems. As they do not specify the manner in which combatants should or can distinguish themselves from civilians, it will ultimately be for the captor State to establish in each case whether or not they meet the general requirement suggested by the ICRC. This wide discretionary power devolving upon the captor could give rise to grave abuses. Despite this undisputable drawback, the ICRC provision seems to a large extent to take into account the exigencies of modern warfare. At present, combats no longer take place between two armies facing each other at a short distance wherein the enemy is discernable at sight. The great mobility of armed forces, the use of long-distance weapons, the increasing resort to camouflage, have made nearly obsolete the requirements of visibility. It seems therefore appropriate to require only in a loose and general manner that combatants must be somehow distinguishable from civilians.

The position of the ICRC seems to be endorsed by Western countries. This applies, for instance, to the United States which during the Vietnam war was liberal in extending prisoner-of-war status to guerrillas captured.[33] In the opinion of the United States and other States the possibility of in some way distinguishing a combatant from a civilian during the hostilities is of paramount importance and cannot be abandoned. Alternatively one basic tenet of modern warfare, the immunity of civilians from hostilities, would be disrupted. Should such a possibility be lacking, civilians would be in constant danger. Indeed, if combatants were not certain about who constitutes the enemy, they would very easily attack civilians in fear that either they were guerrillas or that guerrillas had concealed themselves among them.

Some other States, such as Norway, Romania, Indonesia, Syria, and the Philippines[34] argue on the contrary that the condition under consideration should be dropped and that only two conditions should be required: namely (1) to be under a command responsible to a party to the conflict for its subordinates, and (2) to conduct military operations in accordance with international law. This is also the stance taken by the Organization of African Unity[35] and several

---

[32] ICRC, *Commentary*, etc., cit., p. 51.

[33] See the statements by Admiral Alan B. Shepard, US delegate, in the III Committee of the UN General Assembly, Nov. 29, 1971 (*Press Release* USUN-201 71, p. 3) and by G. Aldrich, US delegate, in the VI Committee of the UN General Assembly, 1973 (UN Doc. A/C.6/SR. 1450, p. 15), as well as the statement by Major General Prugh, US Judge Advocate General Department of the Army, before the House of Representatives, on Sept. 20, 1973, *Hearings Before the Sub-Committee on International Organizations and Movements of the Committee on Foreign Affairs, House of Representatives, Ninety-Third Congress, Ist Session,* Washington 1974, p. 104.

See also G. ALDRICH, *Human Rights and Armed Conflicts, Remarks,* in *Proceedings of the 67 Annual Meeting of the American Society of International Law,* 1973, pp. 145–146.

[34] See the proposals put forward by the experts of these Governments in the II Geneva Conference of Government experts, CE/Comm.III/15, 17, 41, 49, 54.

[35] See the opening address by the Executive Secretary of the OAU Liberation Committee, quoted above, note 10.

African liberation movements.[36] It is contended that the condition that combatants should distinguish themselves from civilians poses great practical difficulties to liberation movements, which would be unable to live up to it. Guerrilla warfare is based 'on mobility, surprise and camouflage. It does not involve a clearly defined front line and the distinction between combatants and civilian population is much more blurred and consequently much more difficult to operate than in conventional warfare'.[37] Usually freedom fighters and the civilian population fight side by side against colonialist troops, especially when such troops invade villages. By accepting this condition, freedom fighters would have to give up their principal method of combat. They are not prepared to do so, because colonial armies have superior technological development and thus superior military strength (mastery of the air, fire power, and so on). As a result, it is imperative for freedom fighters to resort to guerrilla warfare.

Whichever of the two aforementioned conflicting positions will prevail in the end, one important point can be stressed. The States, Organizations and liberation movements I have been referring to, admit that insurgents must abide by international law regarding prisoners of war and immunity of civilians. This is made clear by the general acceptance that guerrilla fighters must comply with the law of war in order to qualify for prisoner-of-war status. This implies inter alia that guerrilla fighters are willing to renounce such methods of combat as the terrorism and sabotage of exclusively civilian installations and are prepared to treat prisoners of war in conformity with the strict regulations of the III Geneva Convention of 1949.

4. Means of Combat

Let us now consider how the laws of war regulate the *means of combat* and whether the States' current law-making endeavours are improving the existing situation.

This is the area in which present international law is more favourable to great Powers than to small States. Indeed, the compromise solutions which have so far been reached between these two categories of States are not capable of actually imposing strict restraints on the use of those weapons which can have a decisive impact on the conduct of hostilities. International law has not been able to do away with or even to reduce the imbalance existing between the States which have technologically advanced weapons and equipment, or countries depending on such States, and the backward or small States.

So far States have adopted two different approaches to the banning of weapons. They have either laid down general principles concerning broad and unspecified

[36] *Summary Record of the OAU Seminar,* etc., cit., pp. 18–19.
[37] Opening address by the Executive Secretary of the OAU Liberation Committee, quoted above, note 10.

categories of weapons, or they have agreed upon restraints on the use of specific weapons.

The general-principle approach is the less satisfactory one. It has led to the formulation of the well-known rule embodied in Article 23(e) of the 1907 Hague Regulations whereby 'it is particularly forbidden to employ arms, projectiles or material apt to cause unnecessary suffering'. The wording of this rule is so vague that it has proved unworkable as a real standard of conduct. Each State has interpreted it in its own way. In addition, it has been invoked in very few instances; even when it was relied upon, no agreement was reached by the States concerned on whether the weapons at issue were actually prohibited by the principle.[38] No doubt, this state of affairs is eventually more profitable to great Powers than to small States.

Less unfruitful was the other approach, which led to the proscription of various agencies of destruction: explosive projectiles under 400 grammes weight (St. Petersburg Declaration of 1868), asphyxiating gases (Hague Declaration of 1899), expanding bullets (Hague Declaration of 1899), poison or poisoned weapons (Hague Conventions of 1899 and 1907), asphyxiating, poisonous or other gases and bacteriological methods of warfare (Geneva Protocol of 1925, and, as far as bacteriological warfare is concerned, the New York Convention of 1972). These specific bans, however important they may be, have two major deficiencies. First of all, they prohibit weapons which were not decisive in the battlefield at the time that they were proscribed. States, especially major Powers, agreed to outlaw those means of combat because they ultimately played, or could only play, a minor role. But whenever the banning of important weapons was envisaged, it was strongly opposed and subsequently never effected. This applies, e.g., to submarine torpedoes, whose prohibition was rejected in 1899 because of their military relevance, as well as to atomic and nuclear weapons after World War II. Furthermore, the use of flying objects for warfare purposes remained prohibited as long as they were scarcely developed. Thus, the Hague Declarations of 1899 and 1907 prohibiting the discharge of projectiles and explosives from balloons were qualified: the former was valid for five years only, the latter was to remain applicable for a period extending to the close of the Third Peace Conference, which had been scheduled for 1914, but could not be convened because of the outbreak of World War I. In any case, it had become obsolete as a consequence of the developments in air warfare beginning in 1911. The temporal qualification

---

[38] May I refer to my article *Weapons Causing Unnecessary Suffering: Are they Prohibited?*, in *Rivista di diritto internazionale*, 1974, no. 4 (also in this volume).

In general, on the international prohibitions of weapons, see the excellent remarks of SCHWARZENBERGER, *The Legality of Nuclear Weapons*, London, 1958, p. 13 ff.; Idem, *From the Laws of War to the Law of Armed Conflict*, in the *Journal of Public Law*, 1968, pp. 67–69. See also the exhaustive survey by BINDSCHEDLER ROBERT, *A Reconsideration of the Law of Armed Conflicts*, in *The Law of Armed Conflicts*, I, New York, 1971, pp. 28–37. Cp. ICRC, *Report on the Work of the Conference of Government Experts on the Use of Certain Conventional Weapons*, Lucerne, Sept. 24 Oct. 18, 1974.

of the two Hague Declarations is indicative of the awareness of States, primarily the great Powers, that air warfare could become a means of enormous military importance. Therefore, they did not intend to bind themselves in a manner that could prove in the future disadvantageous to military exigencies.

The second major deficiency of the specific-ban approach is that prohibitions of particular weapons can be easily by-passed by elaborating new and more sophisticated weapons which, though they are no less cruel than the proscribed ones, do not fall under the prohibition owing to their new features. It is apparent that the States more likely to dodge the ban (or at least capable of it) are the more industrialized ones, for they possess the technological resources which are needed to manufacture sophisticated weaponry. As a result, even as far as specific bans are concerned, great Powers can draw greater profit from existing law than can small countries.

This legal situation is very unsatisfactory, for since the last world war States have constantly been developing and occasionally using new and very cruel weapons: suffice it to mention incendiary weapons containing napalm and phosphorus, which produce dreadful burnings, and the so-called neo-conventional weapons, such as fragmentation and cluster bombs, as well as hypervelocity bullets, which become completely unstable on impact, tumbling in the wound and producing a large cavity. In addition, States have steadily been perfecting nuclear weapons of various sizes and have been manufacturing new chemical weapons of an increasing effectiveness. As the existing rules of international law are obviously inadequate to cope with these new agencies of destruction, what are the ICRC and the international community doing to outlaw or at least curb their use?

The ICRC suggested that Draft Protocol I should confine itself to including some general provisions, without mentioning specific weapons. Accordingly, that Draft Protocol contains only two rules: one (Art. 33) restates and reaffirms the customary international-law ban on weapons causing unnecessary suffering; the other provision (Art. 46, para. 3) is aimed at developing present international law in that it lays down a general principle on indiscriminate weapons or the indiscriminate use of weapons. It stipulates that 'the employment of means of combat, and any methods which strike or affect indiscriminately the civilian population and combatants or civilian objects and military objectives, are prohibited'. As to the possible banning of incendiary or neo-conventional weapons, the ICRC takes the stand that it should not be envisaged within the framework of the two Draft Protocols. It therefore convened a conference of government experts which could lay the basis for a future ad hoc diplomatic conference.

As regards States, most of them agree that there are two categories of weapons—nuclear and chemical—which call for a special solution. Owing to their strategic importance, their possible banning or restriction can only be discussed in a disarmament forum, where manufacturing and stockpiling are also considered as well as procedures for verifying whether possible prohibitions are complied with. The international forum which has so far been used to this effect is the Geneva Conference of the Committee for Disarmament (CCD) in which a limited number of States, including the Soviet Union, the United States and the United Kingdom, take part.

The opinions of States are divided about incendiary and neo-conventional weapons, as well as any future types of weapons. A group of States, made up of Afro-Asian countries, a few Latin American countries and some Western States (such as Sweden), strongly advocate that an ad hoc diplomatic conference should ban at least some incendiary and neo-conventional weapons. At the 1974 Session of the Geneva Diplomatic Conference six States, namely Egypt, Mexico, Norway, Sweden, Switzerland and Yugoslavia, submitted a working paper proposing that the use of some of these arms be restricted or prohibited, because they are either indiscriminate in their effects or cause unnecessary suffering, and also because they have no great military value.[39] The major Western countries have taken a rather cautious stand on the subject; they have pointed out that, should the possible banning of those weapons be discussed, the only appropriate forum would be the CCD.[40] The Soviet Union and other socialist countries have strongly supported the Third World requests that napalm and neo-conventional weapons be prohibited. They have however joined the major Western countries in maintaining that the examination of this matter should be taken up by an international forum directly concerned with disarmament, such as the CCD.[41]

The implications of the adoption of either solution are evident. In an ad hoc diplomatic conference those States which at present oppose the CCD solution would command a solid majority, and would fairly easily succeed in adopting sweeping bans on several weapons despite any possible resistance or opposition by the great Powers. The ensuing treaty or treaties could however run the risk of remaining a dead letter if they are not acceded to by the great Powers. The CCD, on the other hand, would be likely to take a more cautious and realistic stand. Nonetheless, the fact that it is composed of a limited number of States and that its wary attitude could cause great delays in reaching any agreement on the subject is looked upon adversely by Third World countries.

---

[39] See CDDH/DT/2, pp. 3–11.
Several other States have favoured the banning of cruel and inhuman weapons. See e.g. Ghana (CDDH/SR. 10, p. 10), Romania (*ibid.*, SR. 11, p. 4), Denmark (*ibid.*, SR. 12, p. 14), Uganda (*ibid.*, SR. 13, p. 3), Federal Republic of Germany (*ibid.*, p. 8), Bangladesh (*ibid.*, SR. 18, p. 5), Zaire (*ibid.*, SR. 19, pp. 2–3).
[40] See, e.g., the Comment by Canada and Denmark on the Reports of the UN Secretary-General on Respect for Human Rights in Armed Conflicts, UN Doc. A/8313 (15 June 1971), on pp. 13 and 22, 24–25 respectively.
The same stand was taken by some Latin American countries, such as Brazil (CDDH/SR. 10, p. 11).
[41] Ukraine (CDDH/SR. 11, p. 19), Hungary (*ibid.*, p. 22), USSR (*ibid.*, SR. 12, p. 8), Byelorussia (*ibid.*, SR. 14, p. 14).

5. The Protection of Civilians

It is common knowledge that *civilians* are among those who suffer the most from the scourge of war. The protection afforded by international law is indeed very unsatisfactory.

There exist at present a few general principles on the matter. One can mention, first, the principle whereby civilians must not be the object of deliberate attacks. Its weak point is that in the heat of a battle it is difficult to ascertain whether or not an attack on civilians is intentional. States that resort to such a course of action could claim that the attack was unleashed by mistake or by negligence. One could argue that in this case compensation must be paid. Yet, even assuming that this is correct, the authors of the attack would not be answerable as war criminals.

The second principle states that only military objectives can be hit, whether or not they are located in 'undefended places'. Accordingly, civilians and—subject to the considerations below—civilian objects must be spared. The big deficiency of this principle consists in the fact that no definition of 'military objective' has ever been agreed upon. As a result, States are free to regard as military targets—in addition to such military objectives as war depots, barracks, lines of communication and, generally speaking, those objectives that clearly have a military character—also industrial plants, dikes, and places where civilians work or receive social services.

The third principle provides that whenever military objectives are attacked, precautions must be taken for the protection of civilians. The rule is so vague that it can hardly amount to a safe standard of conduct.

The fourth principle states that any incidental damage caused to civilians by hitting a military objective must not be out of proportion to the military gain achieved by the attack. The rule of proportionality has a questionable value. Professor R. R. Baxter, a great authority on the laws of war, has said that: ' . . . proportionality to the military advantage to be gained. . .calls for comparing two things for which there is no standard of comparison. Is one, for example, compelled to think in terms of a certain number of casualties as justified in the gaining of a specified number of yards? Such precise relationships are so far removed from reality as to be unthinkable'.[42]

A further principle, open to the same criticisms because it relies also on proportionality, provides that civilian property, including means necessary for the survival of the population (such as crops and food supplies) can be legitimately

---

[42] BAXTER, *Criteria of the Prohibition of Weapons in International Law*, in *Festschrift für Ulrich Scheuner*, Berlin, 1973, p. 46. Although the above-quoted reference to proportionality is made by Baxter with respect to the principle prohibiting weapons which cause unnecessary suffering, his remarks, I submit, have a more general scope and hold true for any application of the concept of proportionality.

destroyed, if their destruction is required by military necessity and is not out of proportion to the military advantage gained.

One can add that international humanitarian law, as it stands at present, is inadequate in yet another respect: it allows the taking of reprisals against enemy civilians other than those interned on the territory of the adversary or living under occupation. As a result, civilians living in their own country or in combat areas are exposed not only to the daily risk of belligerent hostilities but also to legitimate reprisals.

Far from being improved by adequate changes in international law, in recent years the situation I have been describing has even worsened. As a consequence of fresh developments in military strategy and in war techniques new strains have been put on the relevant body of international law. What have been termed correctly the 'war of the poor' and the 'war of the rich' have both contributed to cause new tensions and difficulties, as well as unprecedented perils to civilians.

The 'war of the poor' assumes mainly the form of guerrilla warfare which is carried on by 'irregulars', namely by independent military groups often acting in connection with, or within the context of, an inter-state war, usually in the rear or on the flanks of the adversary. As a rule, guerrilla operations are characterized by three features which entail grave risks for the population. First, as I mentioned previously, guerrilla fighters normally do not fulfill all conditions required by the III Geneva Convention of 1949 for combatants in order to be considered legitimate belligerents: they usually have neither a fixed distinctive sign recognizable at a distance, nor do they carry arms openly. Consequently the adversary will find it difficult, if not impossible, to distinguish between civilians and irregular combatants; and the former will run the risk of being treated as guerrilla fighters and being subjected to the rigours of martial law. The second feature of guerrillas is that as a rule they rely heavily upon the support of the civilian population; at least a part of the population gives them shelter and provides them with essential material assistance. Since it is not easy to determine which sections of the population support guerrillas, the regular enemy combatants might be led to narrow down the protection to which the civilian population is entitled. Finally, a third feature of guerrilla warfare which is likely to cause, and has in fact frequently caused, grave perils to civilians is the practice of terrorism to which guerrilla forces often turn. The principal victims of this boundless violence are commonly the members of the civilian population.

The 'war of the rich' poses different, through equally serious dangers to civilians. This type of war takes the form of electronic warfare—war carried out by means of highly sophisticated devices such as guided missiles, bombs identifying their target through infra-red, radar or seismic instruments—or of ecological warfare, including the use of defoliants, herbicides etc.; or it can even entail resort to such destructive weapons as nuclear bombs, or chemical substances. There is no need to elaborate here upon the tremendous implications that such warfare as well as the resulting expansion of military objectives, can have for the civilian population. One needs no special knowledge or demonstration to realize that usually it is civilians who actually bear the brunt of these new methods of war; for the main feature of nuclear, electronic and ecological warfare consists in the far-reaching and indiscriminate devastation it brings about. This explains why, as it was recently pointed out, 'an increasing number of those killed in wars are civilians: some 5 per cent in the First World War, some 50 per cent in the Second World War, perhaps around 60 per cent in the Korean war. And for the Vietnam war some 70 per cent of the disabled have been stated to be civilians'.[43]

What are the efforts made by the ICRC and States to improve the present situation? The ICRC has taken a very progressive, though realistic and well-balanced stand. In Draft Protocol I, which it submitted to the Geneva Diplomatic Conference, it suggested a series of provisions which, if accepted, would greatly improve the plight of civilians. The ICRC has adopted a twofold course of action: it has strived to ameliorate the existing rules by greatly expanding the protection afforded to civilians; and also, it has endeavoured to fill the present gaps in international law by proposing regulations for cases and situations which so far have not been covered by any legal restraint.

Even a cursory examination of the ICRC proposals can show how progressive they are. First of all, the ICRC has restated the general principle concerning attacks against the civilian population as such, but by so doing, it has ruled out the notion of 'intention'.[44] Secondly, it has elaborated some provisions which aim at defining 'military objectives': any definition of such a difficult class of objects is open to criticism. Yet, the ICRC definition seems to be both sufficiently flexible and general, and capable of circumscribing to some extent the targets of military action.[45]

In addition, the ICRC has proposed that certain important objects should never be attacked. They are both 'objects indispensable to the survival of the civilian population' (such as foodstuffs and foodproducing areas, crops, livestock,

---

[43] Statement made by the representative of Sweden on March 7, 1974, in the general debate of the Diplomatic Conference (text provided by the Swedish Delegation to the Conference on Humanitarian Law), p. 7. The text is summarized in CDDH/SR. 14, pp. 2–8.

In general, on the protection of civilians in modern warfare, see the fundamental remarks of BINDSCHEDLER, *Die Unterscheidung zwischen Zivilbevölkerung und Bewaffneten Kräften—Ein Grundproblem des Kriegsrechts in der heutigen Zeit*, in *Festschrift für Verdross*, München, 1971, pp. 55–69.

[44] Art. 46, para. 1 provides: 'The civilian population as such, as well as individual civilians, shall not be made the object of attack. In particular, methods intended to spread terror among the civilian population are prohibited'. Thus, the notion of intention was retained only in connection with 'terror bombing'. The reasons for this stand are stated in ICRC, *Draft Additional Protocols etc., Commentary,* cit., p. 57.

[45] Art. 47, para. 1 provides: 'Attacks shall be strictly limited to military objectives, namely, to those objectives which are, by their nature, purpose or use, recognized to be of military interest or whose total or partial destruction, in the circumstances ruling at the time, offers a distinct and substantial military advantage'. See also para. 2, as well as Art. 43 ('In order to ensure respect for the civilian population, the Parties to the conflict shall confine their operations to the *destruction or weakening of the military resources* of the adversary and shall make a distinction between the civilian population and combatants, and between civilian objects and military objectives'; emphasis added).

drinking water supplies and irrigation works)[46] and 'works and installations containing dangerous forces' (such as dams, dykes and nuclear generating stations), whose damage or destruction could release natural or artificial elements that might gravely imperil the civilian population.[47]

The ICRC has then elaborated a rule prohibiting, in general terms, indiscriminate attacks and, in particular, the so-called carpet or target area bombings.[48] It has also greatly improved the traditional rules concerning proportionality[49] and the precautions which should be taken when attacking.[50] Furthermore, it has striven to develop the existing but so far unworkable rules on 'undefended places' and 'safety zones', so that they can offer belligerents a real possibility of agreeing on the setting up of 'sanctuaries' for civilians.[51] Lastly, the ICRC has filled a serious gap, by suggesting a provision whereby 'attacks against the civilian population or civilians by way of reprisals are prohibited' (Art. 46, para. 4).

What is the stand taken by States with regard to such ICRC proposals? The major Western military powers have adopted a somewhat negative attitude. They seem to consider that most of the ICRC draft rules cannot be reconciled with military demands. Thus, for instance, on several occasions the delegate of the United States pointed out that the provisions prohibiting indiscriminate attacks 'would fundamentally change the nature of conventional war and would preclude nuclear war almost completely'.[52] It seems that, in the view of the United States, this would have a negative impact on the present balance of power and global strategic situation. A United States delegate argued that his country favours the prohibition of any bombing of civilians which is intended to terrorize them; in addition the United States would prohibit 'a deliberate aerial bombardment of a city containing no military targets' and would equally oppose 'deliberate rocket attacks on urban population centers'.[53] And, at the same time, the United States is in favour of devising rules aimed at ensuring that armed forces avoid 'unnecessary injuries to civilians and damage to civilian property', and at making 'safety a workable concept'.[54] It would appear that the United States is not prepared to go beyond this limit; in particular, the United States is not disposed to accept any substantial restriction on those attacks on military objectives which can also involve civilians.

---

[46] Art. 48.

[47] Art. 49.

[48] Art. 46 para. 3 and lett. *a*.

[49] Art. 46 para. 3 lett. *b*.

[50] Arts 50 and 51.

[51] Arts 52 and 53.

[52] See e.g. the statement made by the US delegate (G. Aldrich) in the Sixth Committee of the General Assembly (1973), UN doc. A/C.6/SR. 1450, pp. 15–16 as well as before the US House of Representatives Sub-Committee on International Organizations and Movements, *Hearings* quoted above, at note 33, p. 98. See also BAXTER, *The Evolving Laws of Armed Conflicts,* in *Military Law Review*, vol. 99, 1973, p. 108.

[53] See the above-mentioned statement by Major General G.P. Prugh, pp. 104–105.

[54] See the statement made in 1973 by G. Aldrich, USA delegate to the Sixth Committee of the General Assembly, UN doc. A/C.6/SR. 1450, p. 16.

A similar stand has been taken by the United Kingdom, Canada, and France, who have argued that great restraint should be used in dealing with problems concerning aerial bombardment. To this effect Canada and France put forward some proposals which are aimed at narrowing the scope of the ICRC draft articles.[55]

By contrast most Afro-Asian countries seem to favour the ICRC suggestions and have even proposed some wordings which place greater restrictions on States, by better safeguarding the civilian population.[56] Some Western countries such as Australia, Austria, the Netherlands, Norway, the Federal Republic of Germany and Sweden have associated themselves with this attitude.[57]

As to the socialist countries, they have so far shown a great deal of caution. One could venture to say that generally speaking they have endeavoured to avoid taking any definite stand on the major problems involving methods of combat. It would seem, in particular, that the Soviet Union is somewhat divided between the need to safeguard its interests as a major military power and the desire to join the countries of the Third World.[58]

6. International Supervision

Next we come to the fifth area announced at the beginning of this paper—*the procedures for supervising the implementation of the laws of war*. It is well known that very often laws are not complied with by belligerents, and that there is no effective international mechanism responsible for verifying the existence of breaches and inducing belligerents to remedy them. Customary international law does not set up any such mechanism. States therefore can only rely on traditional means of supervision—such as Protecting Powers, which are third countries appointed by each belligerent to protect its interests, subject to the consent of the

[55] See e.g. the amendments proposed by Canada in doc. CDDH/III/79 and by France in doc. CDDH/III/41.

[56] See e.g. the amendments proposed by Ghana, Nigeria, Uganda and Tanzania in doc. CDDH/III/38 and by Algeria, Democratic Republic of Yemen, Egypt, Iraq, Libya, Morocco, Kuwait, Sudan, Syria, United Arab Emirates, in doc. CDDH/III/48/Rev. 1. See also the statements by the representatives of Egypt (CDDH/SR. 10, p. 3), Morocco (*ibid.*, SR. 13, p. 14) and Madagascar (*ibid.*, p. 14).

[57] See e.g. the amendments proposed by Australia in doc. CDDH/III/49 (definition of military objectives, and protection of foodstuffs and food producing areas), and in CDDH/III/55 and CDDH/III/60 (protection of the natural environment), as well as the statement by the Australian representative in CDDH/SR. 14, p. 13. See also the amendment co-sponsored inter alia by Austria, the Netherlands and Norway, in doc. CDDH/III/57 (on prohibition of reprisals against civilian objects), and the statements by the representatives of the Federal Republic of Germany (in CDDH/SR. 13, p. 7) and Sweden (*ibid.*, SR. 14, pp. 3–4; cp. also UN doc. A/8313, pp. 58–59).

[58] Some socialist countries have sponsored or co-sponsored amendments aiming at widening the protection of civilians. See e.g. doc CDDH/III/57, co-sponsored by USSR, prohibiting reprisals against civilian objects; doc. CDDH/III/58, submitted by Czechoslovakia and the German Democratic Republic, to the same effect; doc. CDDH/III/64 submitted by Czechoslovakia, the German Democratic Republic and Hungary, on the protection of natural environment.

See also the statements by the representatives of Romania /CDDH/SR. 11/p. 5), Hungary (*ibid.*, p. 21), Czechoslovakia (*ibid.*, SR. 13, p. 17).

other party to the conflict, and commissions of inquiry or other fact-finding bodies. The problem is, however, that all these bodies can only be set up if the States concerned agree to them, which normally is not the case. As to treaty law, the 1949 Geneva Conventions suggest two procedures: first of all, these Conventions take over from customary law the Protecting Powers system and improve it both by specifying the tasks of such Powers and by laying down that, in the event of their not functioning, the ICRC can step in as a substitute organization, provided that the belligerents so decide; secondly, the Conventions make provision for the possible establishment of commissions of enquiry. Yet, in the course of the various armed conflicts which have been occurring since World War II neither system has ever been resorted to. There is good reason for this attitude of States. The Protecting Power system envisaged in the 1949 Conventions is inadequate in that—in common with customary international law—it rests on the assumption that each belligerent is willing to appoint a Protecting Power and to accept the Protecting Power appointed by the adversary. If this will is lacking, no Protecting Power is designated, because the Conventions do not envisage any procedure for appointing them in the event that the belligerents do not come to an agreement. As to the possible stepping in of the ICRC as a substitute organization, it is made conditional on the express consent of all the parties to the conflict. Under the Conventions States are only bound to accept the offer by the ICRC to assume the 'humanitarian functions' performed by Protecting Powers. Such functions, however, do not include the task of supervising the application of the Conventions.[59]

The requirement that all belligerents concerned should be in agreement also underlies the enquiry procedure. This may well explain why no enquiry has ever been conducted concerning alleged violations of the 1949 Conventions, not even in the 1973 Middle East conflict, when the ICRC submitted some interesting suggestions to the parties concerned.[60]

This state of affairs has raised widespread anxiety and concern among States and stimulated international efforts aimed at improving the present systems of scrutiny. Two main questions have been raised and debated at great length. First,

[59] According to ABI-SAAB, *Le renforcement du système d'application des règles du droit humanitaire*, in *Séminaire sur l'enseignement du droit humanitaire dans les institutions militaires, Sanremo, 6–18 Novembre 1972,* Sanremo 1973, 'le contrôle de l'application des Conventions constitue également une tâche humanitaire, dans la mesure où il fournit une garantie aux stipulations substantielles dont le contenu est . . . humanitaire'. Yet, if supervision proper were also among the humanitarian functions mentioned in articles 10/10/10/11 para. 3 of the Conventions, why did the drafters of the Conventions specify that only 'the humanitarian functions performed by the Protecting Powers under the present Convention' could be assumed by the ICRC or another humanitarian organization? It is my submission that the framers of the Conventions decided to confer only 'humanitarian' functions on these organizations in order to counterbalance the fact that it was imposed upon States to accept the offer of the ICRC or another humanitarian organization to act in case of failure of the Protecting Powers system.

[60] The ICRC proposals are summarized in *The ICRC in Action: ICRC Information Notes,* Geneva, 20 Dec. 1973, No. 206 *b*, p. 6.

to what extent and by which means is it desirable to strengthen the Protecting Powers system? Secondly, with respect to which specific rules of warfare should this system work; that is to say, should Protecting Powers oversee the application of all rules of warfare or instead should they confine themselves to scrutinizing the implementation of rules other than those concerning combat operations?

Let us consider first the question of strengthening the Protecting Powers system. The proposals submitted by the ICRC in its Draft Protocol I are aimed at improving the present means of supervision. The ICRC elaborated a series of important devices designed to overcome various difficulties that so far have prevented the Protecting-Powers system from working.[61] These ingenious suggestions greatly increase the chances that this system actually will be set in motion in the future. Furthermore, the ICRC is willing to assume the role of substitute organization in the event of there being no Protecting Power. The ICRC has made clear, however, that it would be prepared to exercise this function only under several specific conditions. First, it has ruled out its serving as an automatic 'fall-back' institution. In other words, it considers that it should not be duty-bound to act, but should retain its liberty to offer its services to the parties to a conflict whenever it deems fit. Secondly, its intervention ought to be agreed to by the parties concerned; with the consequence that the opposition of one belligerent would prevent it from performing its functions. Thirdly, the ICRC would not have to function from the outset of a conflict, but only in case of failure of the Protecting Powers system to work. It is the opinion of the ICRC that its stepping in from the inception of the conflict might easily result in the parties to the conflict losing all interest in the designation of Protecting Powers. Fourthly, the ICRC has maintained that although its tasks would include consideration of alleged violations of the Conventions and the Protocol and reporting of the findings to the interested parties, it would not be appropriate for it to make enquiries as to the veracity of alleged violations, and publish the results thereof. In other words, it does not intend to exercise supervisory functions proper. Fifthly, the Committee has made known that in order to fulfil its functions it would need to be supplied with adequate funds and staff. Therefore, its functioning as a substitute organization would be greatly dependent on the possibility for it to secure appropriate financial support.[62]

---

[61] Thus, Art. 5, para. 4, of Draft Protocol I provides that 'The maintenance and acceptance of Protecting Powers for the sole purpose of applying the Conventions and the present Protocol *shall not affect the legal status of the Parties to the conflict or that of the territories over which they exercise authority*' (emphasis added). Para. 5 of the same Article states: '*The maintenance of diplomatic relations* between the Parties to the conflict does not constitute an obstacle to the appointment of Protecting Powers for the sole purpose of applying the Conventions or the present Protocol' (emphasis added).

[62] See the statements by ICRC representatives reported in: ICRC, Conference of Government Experts, IInd Session (3 May–3 June 1972), *Report on the Work of the Conference*, vol. I, 1972, pp. 180–181, paras 4.68–4.72; ICRC, Draft Additional Protocols etc., *Commentary*, cit., p. 13.

Let us now turn to the position taken by States on the Protecting Power question. The debates in the United Nations and at the Geneva Conference point to the conclusion that most Western and Afro-Asian States (the latter under the impulse of the Arab States) are keen on elaborating satisfactory procedures for the appointment of Protecting Powers and are ready to agree that, should this system fail to work, a humanitarian organization could step in and perform all functions of the Protecting Powers, even if one of the belligerents is not agreeable. In other words, the aforementioned groups of States pursue a twofold purpose. They endeavour to work out a procedure for facilitating an agreement between belligerents on the appointment of Protecting Powers. They also intend to take realistically into account the possibility that, despite the working of this procedure, no Protecting Powers may be appointed. It is for such a case that those States try to provide for the stepping in of a substitute organization capable of functioning without the ad hoc consent of belligerents.[63]

Against this common background, however, three main positions can be identified among the States just referred to. A solution which at present appears to command the greatest favour is supported by various States, among which are the United States,[64] Belgium and the United Kingdom,[65] Pakistan[66] and Greece.[67] It pivots on two elements. First, in the event of disagreement between the parties or unjustified delay in the designation and acceptance of the Protecting Powers, the ICRC will offer its good offices; some procedural devices are envisaged for the purpose of permitting the ICRC to attain the agreement of belligerents on the Protecting Powers. Secondly, if despite the action of the ICRC no Protecting Power is appointed, the parties to the conflict are duty-bound to accept a possible offer by the ICRC to act as a substitute. Clearly both elements constitute a great step forward. It is worth stressing that under this proposal the procedure for arriving at the creation of a supervisory machinery falls into three stages: in the first one contacts are envisaged between the belligerents with a view to reaching an agreed appointment of the Protecting Powers; if the contacts have not led to positive results, one moves to the second stage, which is dominated by the ICRC mediation aimed at promoting an agreement between the parties. If even this stage yields no results, the third one will start, in which the ICRC may decide to act as a substitute organization, regardless of the attitude or the reaction of the parties concerned.

---

[63] Among the States favouring the strengthening of the Protecting Power system were inter alia Egypt (CDDH/SR. 10, pp. 3–4), Pakistan (*ibid.*, SR. 11, pp. 8–9), Jordan (*ibid.*, SR. 12, p. 10), Holy See (*ibid.*, p. 12), Denmark (*ibid.*, p. 14), Venezuela (*ibid.*, SR. 13, p. 4), Republic of Korea (*ibid.*, p. 5), Federal Republic of Germany (*ibid.*, p. 8), United Kingdom (*ibid.*, p. 9), Switzerland (*ibid.*, p. 16), Austria (*ibid.*, SR. 14, pp. 14–15), Argentina (*ibid.*, SR. 17, p. 10), New Zealand (*ibid.*, pp. 11–12), Japan (*ibid.*, SR. 18, p. 7), Italy (*ibid.*, p. 8), Iran (*ibid.*, p. 9). As to the position of the United States, see *inter alia* A/C.6/SR. 1450, p. 14.

[64] Amendment contained in doc. CDDH/I/64.

[65] Amendment contained in doc. CDDH/I/67.

[66] Amendment contained in doc. CDDH/I/24.

[67] Amendment contained in doc. CDDH/I/31.

A second solution, which aims at strengthening the role of the ICRC, was suggested by Italy in an amendment submitted to the 1974 Session of the Diplomatic Conference.[68] Under it, the ICRC, instead of stepping in as the result of a failure to appoint the Protecting Powers, should start functioning as a substitute organization—provided of course it deems it expedient and advisable—from the outbreak of hostilities and until such time as the Protecting Powers begin to exercise their functions. The Italian amendment envisages also three stages in the procedure for appointing a body of scrutiny. But while in the view of the supporters of the first position considered above the initial stage would consist in contacts between the parties concerned, followed by the mediation of the ICRC and the possible functioning of the ICRC as a substitute; adding the provision of the Italian amendment, the ICRC would assume supervisory tasks at the first stage.

Finally, a third position was taken by a number of Arab States, who submitted an amendment, concerning the intervention of a substitute organization in the event of no Protecting Powers being appointed.[69] Under this amendment if no Protecting Power is appointed, 'the Parties to the conflict shall accept as a substitute for the Protecting Power an impartial humanitarian organization, such as the ICRC, appointed by one of the Parties and accepted by the other Party, or, in the last instance, appointed by the Conference of the High Contracting Parties, in conformity with article 7'. There are two major differences between the Arab proposal and that supported by the majority of States. First, while the latter proposal authorizes the ICRC to offer its services and obliges the States concerned to accept this offer, the former does not envisage solely the ICRC, but speaks of 'an impartial humanitarian organization, such as the ICRC'. Secondly, and more importantly, the Arab proposal does not oblige belligerents to accept the offer of the humanitarian organization. On the contrary, it requires their consent to the intervention of the substitute organization. It is apparent that under this amendment the role of the ICRC is eventually lessened. To be sure, the Arab proposal provides for a means to overcome a possible lack of consent by the concerned parties, by deferring the appointment of the substitute to a Conference of the Contracting Parties. The fact however remains that it ultimately attaches decisive importance to such a conference instead of to the ICRC. This tendency to downgrade the ICRC and to enhance instead the Contracting Parties is even more apparent in an amendment submitted by the Syrian Arab Republic, whereby, if the Protecting Powers system fails to work, the only way out appears to be the designation of a substitute by a conference of the Contracting Parties.[70]

Unlike the States so far discussed, socialist countries do not seem enthusiastic about the idea of actually improving international supervision. They insist on the need to avoid any kind of interference in the internal affairs of States and,

[68] CDDH/I/50.
[69] See doc. CDDH/I/75 (submitted by Algeria, Egypt, Iraq, Jordan, Kuwait, Lebanon, Libya, Morocco, Oman, Quatar, Sudan, United Arab Emirates, Democratic Yemen).
[70] See doc. CDDH/I/62.

generally speaking, reaffirm with respect to the laws of war their traditional mis-trust in international mechanisms of scrutiny. It may be useful to quote here what was stated in 1973 by the delegate of the Soviet Union, in the Sixth Committee of the General Assembly. He said:

> Although it was convinced of the need to put an end to the persistent violations of exist-ing rules, the USSR did not think that it would be useful to set up new machinery with supra-national functions. It was sufficient to use existing institutions and to punish those who were guilty of military crimes against humanity.[71]

In keeping with this general position, the Soviet Union, Byelorussia, and the Ukraine submitted to the 1974 session of the Geneva Diplomatic Conference an amendment which, though it includes some procedural devices suggested by the ICRC for the purpose of facilitating the appointment of Protecting Powers, ultimately does not represent any actual step forward with respect to the exist-ing system. Essentially, the amendment makes the creation and the functioning of any international system of scrutiny conditional on the consent of the parties concerned. It clearly provides that the ICRC may offer its services for the purpose of inducing the contending States to reach an agreement on the appointment of the Protecting Powers: yet, it is well stressed that such services may be offered 'subject to the consent of the Parties to the conflict concerned'. Furthermore, the assumption of the functions of substitute by any humanitarian organization in the event that no Protecting Powers are appointed, could take place only 'pro-vided the Parties to the conflict so agree'.[72] In that under this amendment the entire procedure in all its stages rests on the consent of the States concerned, one fails to see to what extent its adoption could improve on the provisions of the 1949 Geneva Conventions.

The second question framed at the beginning of this section was whether the Protecting Powers should perform their tasks solely with regard to international rules concerning victims of war, or should supervise also the application of rules concerning the actual conduct of hostilities as well as means and methods of com-bat. Thus far this question has not arisen, in practice, because the 1949 Geneva Conventions, which entrust Protecting Powers with supervisory functions, do not cover with their substantive provisions the area of the conduct of hostilities. As to customary international law, it is for belligerents to define in each case the competence of their Protecting Powers. It does not seem that so far belliger-ents have ever extended this competence so as to include the supervision of the conduct of military operations. The problem does arise now because the Draft Protocol on international conflicts, worked out by the ICRC, contains several provisions on means and methods of combat and the protection of civilians from the danger of hostilities.

---

[71] UN doc. A/C.6/SR. 1452, p. 19. See also the Soviet reply in UN doc. A/8313, p. 68.
[72] See doc. CDDH/I/70.

The ICRC has taken a rather cautious stand on the matter; yet it appears to disfavour the possibility for Protecting Powers to exercise their functions within the combat zone.[73] As to States, most of them have not yet said whether or not the supervisory system should work solely with respect to some parts of the Protocol. The inference could be that in the opinion of the majority of States the Protecting Powers or their substitute should perform their functions with regard to all sections of the Protocol, irrespective of their scope and contents. Yet, it would be more accurate to avoid any premature conclusion from the silence of those States.

For reasons of their own the United States and the United Kingdom have taken a stand essentially similar to that of the ICRC. A United States representative stated that 'outside supervision is neither traditional nor easy to visualize' with respect to the rules concerning the methods and means of war and the protection of civilians behind the enemy's line.[74] The British delegate endorsed this stand without however expanding on the reasons behind it.[75] Here again, it is not difficult to grasp why some States, especially major military powers, prefer such an approach to supervision. Military demands oppose the presence of any third party in the zone of actual combat. As was pointed out by a learned author, supervision of military operations would involve 'a direct inroad on the commander's power of decision'.[76] Furthermore, it would entail, for the supervising body, 'the awkward task of weighing immediate military interests against a set of insufficiently clarified, wide principles (such as protection of the civilian population, prohibition of unnecessary suffering, or prohibition of perfidy)'.[77]

One could object, however, that if the major military Powers deem it contrary to their interest to allow supervision of compliance with rules of combat, they should at least agree to the elaboration of somewhat more detailed provisions on the conduct of hostilities. This would compensate for the lack of supervision

---

[73] In this connection the following was pointed out by the ICRC: 'The First and Second Conventions, as well as Part II of the Fourth Convention, which apply mainly to the battlefield or its immediate surroundings, determine the role which the Protecting Powers are called upon to play in this field; that role will be similar with respect to the provisions in question in the present draft. The Conventions did not go further than to reaffirm tasks that were traditionally conferred upon the Protecting Powers by customary international law and did not provide for their presence in relation to the actual fighting . . . The mandate of a Protecting Power for the purposes of the application of the Conventions and the Protocol does not include enquiries into violations of those instruments, the findings of which would be made the subject of a public report which would be submitted to the attention of intergovernmental organizations. Besides, by laying down in a separate article (Art. 52/53/132/149) a special procedure for enquiries into violations, the Conventions clearly show that the supervision exercised by the Protecting Powers does not extend to such cases' (ICRC, *Commentary,* cit., p. 9).

[74] See the statement by Major General G.S. Prugh, quoted above (in note 33), p. 103.

[75] Statement of the UK delegate in the Sixth Committee of the UN General Assembly, 1973 (UN doc. A/C.6/SR. 1453, p. 17).

[76] KALSHOVEN, *The Law of Warfare, a Summary of its Recent History and Trends in Development,* 1973, Leiden, p. 115.

[77] *Op.loc.cit.*

on the matter, because the standards by which the conduct of States should be gauged would allow a more fair assessment of how belligerents behave.

7. Internal Armed Conflicts

The last topic to be considered in this paper is very tricky and complex: it refers to *the legal regulation of civil wars,* or—to use an up-to-date terminology—of armed conflicts not of an international character.

It is striking that despite the increasing frequency of such conflicts, the relevant international regulation is very poor and far from satisfactory. As stated above, only a few rules govern this sensitive area; for the main part, civil wars remain within the province of municipal criminal law, of course much to the benefit of the incumbent authorities. As to customary international law, very few rules concerning inter-state wars have evolved in such a way as to also cover internal conflicts. Mention can be made of some general rules concerning the protection of civilians: the rule prohibiting deliberate attacks upon civilian populations, the principle whereby military objectives only can be attacked, and the rule providing that reasonable care must be taken in attacking military objectives so that by carelessness a civilian population in the neighbourhood is not bombed.[78] Except for the rule forbidding deliberate attacks on civilians as such and for the general principle whereby 'distinction must be made at all times between persons taking part in the hostilities and members of the civilian population to the effect that the latter be spared as much as possible',[79] this small body of international laws also applies to high-level internal conflicts; that is to say, civil wars proper, in which the armed forces opposing the authorities in power are organized and occupy a part of the territory, and the hostilities are of considerable intensity and continue for a sufficiently long period of time.

Low-level internal conflicts are covered primarily by treaty law, namely by Article 3 common to the four Geneva Conventions of 1949, and by a few provisions of the United Nations Covenant on Civil and Political Rights of 1966.[80]

[78] See inter alia the statement on the Spanish civil war, made on June 21, 1938 in the House of Commons by the British Prime Minister. He listed the rules of international law that in the opinion of the British Government apply both to internal and international armed conflicts: *House of Commons, Debates,* vol. 337 (1938), cols. 937–939. See CASSESE, *The Spanish Civil War and the Development of Customary Law Concerning Internal Armed Conflicts,* in CASSESE (Editor), *Lectures in International Law,* Pisa 1975 (also in this volume).

[79] These rules were restated in operative para. 1 of the UN General Assembly resolution 2444 (XXIII), adopted unanimously in 1969. As this resolution refers to 'armed conflicts', hence both to international and internal armed conflicts, one could argue that, by adopting it, the General Assembly intended to confirm customary rules relating, *inter alia,* to all kinds of non-international armed conflicts (provided of course that they do not amount to mere riots or sporadic disturbances). Cp. KALSHOVEN, *Applicability of Customary International Law in Non International Armed Conflicts,* in CASSESE (Editor), *Lectures in International Law,* Pisa 1975.

[80] See Art. 4 of the Covenant.

Yet, the Covenant is not yet in force, and Article 3 has three major deficiencies. First, the minimum rules it contains do not cover the whole area of internal armed conflicts. They only protect certain fundamental human rights of two categories of persons: (a) non-participants in the armed conflict; and (b) persons who, having engaged in hostilities, have subsequently laid down their arms. Article 3 does not regulate actual combat, nor does it grant any specific protection to the civilian population against the effects of hostilities. Even from a strictly humanitarian point of view, the article has several serious gaps; thus, for instance, it does not provide for the passage of food and relief supplies for non-combatants.

The second shortcoming of Article 3 is that it leaves great latitude to Contracting States as to when its provisions begin to apply. It does not define the key term 'non-international armed conflicts'; consequently, it is not clear at what level of internal disturbance the provisions of Article 3 become applicable. Neither does Article 3 entrust any international authority with the task of verifying whether or not a domestic disorder is in progress which should be deemed to fall under the purview of its provisions.

The third deficiency of Article 3 is that it does not confer on any international body the power to supervise compliance with its provisions by the contending parties; it confines itself to providing that 'an impartial humanitarian body, such as the ICRC, may offer its services to the Parties to the conflict'. As a result, Contracting States, assuming that they decide to consider that an internal armed conflict falls under Article 3, retain a large margin of discretion as to the actual extent to which they apply Article 3. This explains why since 1949 that rule has been applied in so few instances, although domestic armed conflicts have been very numerous.[81]

This being so, in many international quarters, and above all in the International Conference of the Red Cross and the International Committee of the Red Cross, it was ardently urged that Article 3 be elaborated and supplemented by a new Protocol aimed at greatly expanding the protection it at present affords to victims of internal conflicts.[82] Any widening of the provisions of Article 3 amounts to

---

[81] On the practice concerning the application of Art. 3 see inter alia DRAPER, *The Geneva Conventions of 1949*, in *Recueil des Cours*, 1965-I, p. 91 ff.; FALK (Editor), *The International Law of Civil Law*, Baltimore and London 1971; MIGLIAZZA, *L'évolution de la réglementation de la guerre à la lumière de la sauvegarde des droits de l'homme*, in *Recueil des Cours*, 1972-III, pp. 212–220; BOND, *The Rules of Riot. Internal Conflict and the Law of War*, Princeton 1974; VEUTHEY, *Les conflits armés de caractère non international et le droit humanitaire*, in CASSESE (Editor), cit.

[82] On the endeavours to expand Art. 3 see WILHELM, *Problèmes relatifs à la protection de la personne humaine par le droit international dans les conflits armés ne présentant pas un caractère international*, in *Recueil des Cours*, 1972-III, pp. 340 ff., 385 ff., 410 ff.; KALSHOVEN, *Reaffirmation and Development of International Humanitarian Law Applicable in Armed Conflicts*, in *Netherlands Yearbook of International Law*, 1971, pp. 77–83, 1972, pp. 55–59; SIOTIS, *La protection de la personne humaine dans les conflits armés ne présentant pas un caractère international*, in *Séminaire sur l'enseignement du droit humanitaire dans les institutions militaires, Sanremo, 6–18 novembre 1972*, Sanremo 1973, pp. 281–287. See also CIOBANU, *The Concept and the Determination of the Existence of 'Armed Conflicts not of an International Character'*, in *Rivista di diritto internazionale*, 1975, no. 1, pp. 43–79.

placing greater restrictions on the freedom of sovereign States as to their internal affairs. That is why States belonging to all political groups and geographic areas have shown a marked reluctance to admit further inroads of international law, that is to say of the international society, in their own domestic jurisdiction. This reluctance has become strong opposition, among some developing countries. They fear any outside encroachments on their sovereignty to be a possible attempt on their territorial integrity and political independence.

What most States have particularly resisted is the idea of extending to rebels the status of legitimate combatants, thus treating them as prisoners of war once they fall into the hands of central authorities. This perspective aroused such widespread concern and opposition among States, that the ICRC eventually did not include any provision on the matter in the Draft Protocol it submitted to the 1974 Session of the Geneva Diplomatic Conference.

The Draft Protocol focuses on two basic ideas. First, it should be applicable to a wide range of non-international armed conflicts. Thus in Article 1 of Draft Protocol II it is proposed that the Protocol should apply to all armed conflicts other than inter-State conflicts, 'taking place between armed forces or other organized armed groups under responsible command'. By contrast, such situations as 'internal disturbances and tensions, inter alia riots, isolated and sporadic acts of violence and other acts of a similar nature' do not come within the purview of the Protocol. Even a cursory examination of the ICRC proposals indicates that the level of hostilities suggested by the ICRC for the applicability of the Protocol is rather low: it will suffice that the armed groups fighting against the authorities in power be 'organized' and carry out their military operations under a responsible command. The second basic idea underlying the ICRC Draft is that the Protocol should be exclusively humanitarian in character. In other words, rebels will enjoy no particular status, but will remain within the province of domestic criminal law; they will therefore be punishable for their insurrection. Yet they will benefit from a series of humanitarian safeguards, the most important of which are those concerning the guarantees for a fair trial, and the provision whereby 'the death penalty pronounced on any person found guilty of an offence in relation to the armed conflict shall not be carried out until the hostilities have ceased' (Art. 10, para. 3).

Another important point deserves special attention. The ICRC, though it has reduced its Draft Protocol essentially to a set of humanitarian rules, has not confined itself to submitting proposals for the protection of the victims of internal armed conflicts: wounded, sick, and shipwrecked persons; and persons in the power of the parties to the conflict. The Committee has also suggested rules concerning the conduct of hostilities; for instance, it proposed rules on means and methods of combat (Articles 20–23), and on the protection of civilian populations from belligerent activities (Articles 24–29).

How have States reacted to this Draft Protocol? So far many States have preferred not to take any definite stand; presumably they have deemed it advisable to keep open their options at the Second Session of the Diplomatic Conference (1975). As for those States that in some way have made their position known, two main trends have emerged.

Some States would like to narrow the field of application of Draft Protocol II, by making it applicable to high-level conflicts only. Thus a few States, among which are Pakistan,[83] Indonesia,[84] Brazil,[85] the United Kingdom,[86] France[87] and Australia[88] suggested, either in formal amendments or in official statements, that the Protocol should only apply when the insurrection has reached a certain intensity, and particularly when the following requirements are met: that rebels control a non-negligible part of the territory, and the hostilities continue for a considerable period of time. It is not clear whether, should the field of application of the Protocol be substantially reduced as a result of the adoption of this suggestion, its promoters would be prepared to accept the rest of the Protocol as it now stands, especially the provisions regulating the conduct of hostilities.

There is a second group of States including *inter alia* Canada[89] and the United States[90] which is willing to agree to the present low threshold of applicability of the Draft Protocol. They seem, however, inclined to counterbalance the breadth of the field of application of the Protocol by deleting all provisions concerning the conduct of hostilities, or at least most of them. They argue that the Protocol should have a primarily humanitarian content; as a result any provision other than those protecting victims of violence should be eliminated. Particularly unacceptable to these States seem to be the proposed rules regulating the use of weapons and methods of combat. In their view Protocol II should take a human rights approach to domestic disorders, thus becoming a sort of annex to the rules of the United Nations Covenant on Civil and Political Rights concerning public emergencies. In short, those States envisage the Protocol as a human-rights treaty rather than a laws-of-war convention.

[83] See the amendment by Pakistan in doc. CDDH/I/26.

[84] See the amendment by Indonesia in doc. CDDH/I/32. See also the statement by the representative of that country, in CDDH/SR. 11, p. 6.

[85] See the amendment by the representative of Brazil in doc. CDDH/I/79. Cp. also the statement by the representative of Brazil in CDDH/SR. 10, p. 12.

[86] See e.g. the proposals made by the United Kingdom experts in 1971 and 1972(CE/Com.II/8, in ICRC-1971 Conference of Government Experts, *Report on the Work of the Conference,* Geneva 1971, p. 62; CE/COM.II/14, in ICRC-1972 Conference of Government Experts, *Report on the Work of the Conference,* vol. II, Geneva 1972, pp. 35–36).

[87] See e.g. the proposals put forward by the French experts in 1971 and 1972 (CE/Com.II/5, in ICRC-1971 Conference of Government Experts, *Report,* cit., p. 62; CE/COM.II/3, in ICRC.1972 Conference of Government Experts, *Report,* cit., vol. II, p. 33).

[88] See the statement by the representative of Australia in CDDH/SR. 14, p. 13.

[89] See the amendment by Canada in doc. CDDH/I/37, and the statement made in Plenary by the representative of that State (CDDH/SR. 18, pp. 2–3).

[90] As to the United States position, see the statement made in 1971 by the US representative, Admiral Alan B. Shepard, in the III Committee of the General Assembly *(Press Release* USUN-201 (71), Nov. 29, 1971, p. 3), as well as the statements by G. Aldrich to the UN General Assembly's Sixth Committee, in 1973 (A/C.6/SR. 1450, p. 15), and by Major General G.S. Prugh before the House of Representatives, cit., p. 104.

It is difficult to predict which of the two tendencies referred to above will in the end prevail. One could however venture to conclude that the overwhelming majority of States appear to attach such a great importance to 'sovereignty' and 'domestic jurisdiction' that they will hardly be prepared to accept far-reaching restraints on their freedom of action.[91]

8. Concluding Remarks

The two branches into which the international law of war has traditionally been subdivided, the law concerning the conduct of hostilities and the law on the protection of war victims, are both being greatly eroded by various factors. In their present formulation the laws on the conduct of hostilities by far benefit the major military Powers. Therefore, it is not surprising that these laws are being assailed by the great majority of States, primarily small or medium-sized countries, who would like to reduce the imbalance between strong and weak countries codified, as it were, by international law.

By contrast, the law on war victims rests on reciprocity of interests between belligerents and, in theory at least, should take no account of the differences between powerful and small countries; because each belligerent, no matter how strong or weak he is, is interested in his wounded, sick, shipwrecked, civilians, as well as his soldiers who fall into the hands of the enemy, being treated in conformity with international law. In actual fact, however, small countries increasingly tend to counterbalance the military superiority of their adversaries by bargaining the treatment of the enemy citizens in their hands (especially prisoners of war) as a means of putting pressure on the adversary. In addition, medium-sized countries seem often inclined to disregard some sections of the law on war victims, as, for instance, the law of military occupation, presumably for the purpose of prolonging their military victory over militarily weaker countries.

---

[91] It may be interesting to quote a Soviet statement on the matter, which is contained in an official document sent in 1971 by the Soviet Union to the United Nations Secretary-General: 'One of the most important principles of contemporary international law is that of non-intervention in internal affairs . . . In elaborating additional rules for the protection of human rights in armed conflicts, any attempt to "internationalize" internal armed conflicts should be resisted. Such "internationalization" could be used to justify foreign intervention in the internal affairs of States, which might lead to flagrant violations of the generally recognized rules of international law' (UN doc. A/8313, p. 68).

See also the statements made at the 1974 Diplomatic Conference by the representatives of Romania (CDDH/SR. 11, p. 5), Yugoslavia (*ibid.*, p. 8), Ukraine (*ibid.*, p. 19), Mongolia (*ibid.*, SR. 18, p. 15), and Indonesia, *ibid.*, p. 5. Cp. also the statement of the representative of the People's Republic of China (*ibid.*, SR. 12, p. 7). The Chinese delegate said in Committee III that 'the concept of "non-international armed conflicts" was ambiguous and raised a problem of fundamental principle. The very need for a second protocol to deal with them required further study' (CDDH/III/SR. 10, p. 10).

Thus even this section of the laws of war is placed under great strain, prompting many States and, above all, the major military Powers, to complain that existing rules are not complied with.

The law-making efforts currently under way with a view to improving and updating the laws of armed conflict appear to be on the right track. Laudable efforts are being made to frame rules on the conduct of hostilities which place greater restraints on belligerents. Also, new means of ensuring strict compliance with international law are being devised. The new law cannot but result from a compromise between the major military powers, who ought to accept far greater restraints on their freedom to use force *durante bello,* and the great majority of States, who should agree to abide by the law concerning war victims, and accept to this end new means of ensuring compliance. If either category of States is not willing to relinquish a few advantages in return for some concessions by other States, the legislative endeavours now in progress are destined to achieve little change in the laws of war.

2. The Martens Clause: Half a Loaf or Simply Pie in the Sky?*

1. Introduction

The so-called 'Martens' Clause was first inserted, at the suggestion of the Russian publicist Fyodor Fyodorovich Martens (1845–1909), in the preamble of the 1899 Hague Convention II containing the Regulations on the Laws and Customs of War on Land, and then restated in the 1907 Hague Convention IV on the same matter. It is by now well known to any student of international relations and is couched as follows:

En attendant qu'un code plus complet des lois de la guerre puisse être édicté, les Hautes Parties Contractantes jugent opportun de constater que, dans les cas non compris dans les dispositions réglementaires adoptées par Elles, les populations et les belligérants restent sous la sauvegarde et sous l'empire des principes du droit des gens, tels qu'ils résultent des usages établis entre nations civilisées, des lois de l'humanité et des exigences de la conscience publique. Elles déclarent que c'est dans ce sens que doivent s'entendre notamment les articles 1 [on the requirements for lawful belligerents] *et 2* [on the so-called *levée en masse*] du Règlement adopté.[1]

Since 1907, the clause—at least in its mutilated form (i.e. without its last proviso) has been hailed as a significant turning point in the history of international humanitarian law. It has been argued, in this respect, that it represents the first time in which the notion that there exist international legal rules embodying humanitarian considerations and that these rules are no less binding than those motivated by other (e.g. military or political) concerns was set forth. Two features of the clause are striking. First, it is very loosely worded and has consequently given rise to a multiplicity of often conflicting interpretations. Secondly, perhaps precisely because of its evasive yet appealing contents, the clause has been very frequently relied upon in international dealings, restated by states in treaties, cited

* Originally published in 11 *European Journal of International Law* (2000) 187.
[1] According to the translation reported in J.B. Scott (ed.), *The Hague Conventions and Declarations of 1899 and 1907* (1915) 101–102, the English equivalent of this clause is as follows: 'Until a more complete code of the laws of war has been issued, the High Contracting parties deem it expedient to declare that, in cases not included in the Regulations adopted by them, the inhabitants and the belligerents remain under the protection and the rule of the principles of the law of nations, as they result from the usages established among civilized peoples, from the laws of humanity, and the dictates of the public conscience. They declare that it is in this sense especially that Articles 1 and 2 of the Regulations must be understood'. It should be emphasized that both commentators and states as well as courts tend to neglect the last proviso of this clause, which nevertheless proves to be of great help in understanding the historical origin of the clause, as will be shown *infra*.

by international and national courts, invoked by organizations and individuals. The combination of these two features warrants the conclusion that by now the clause has become one of the *legal myths* of the international community.

Be that as it may, undoubtedly the name of Martens is inextricably bound up with the clause, whilst all his other diplomatic achievements or scholarly works have fallen into obscurity. Whatever its inherent legal value, there is no gainsaying that the Martens Clause acquired a vast resonance and has had a significant impact on international law, in particular international humanitarian law. The principal—and general—merit of the clause—of which Martens may arguably have been unaware—is that it approached the question of the laws of humanity for the first time not as a *moral* issue but from a *positivist* (or, to put it more accurately, from an *apparently positivist*) perspective. Previously, international treaties and Declarations had simply proclaimed the importance of such laws or humanitarian considerations. As a consequence, states had not been enjoined to abide by any strict legal standard upholding the laws of humanity; they had merely been called upon to not disregard the principles of humanity, *qua moral principles,* while acting in the course of a war. Absent international courts with compulsory jurisdiction or even mandatory fact-finding bodies or commissions of enquiry, it was left to each belligerent to decide for itself whether or not it had behaved humanely while attacking the enemy or bombing its cities and villages. In short, these clauses had scant legal value. By contrast, the Martens Clause proclaimed for the first time that there may exist principles or rules of customary *international law* resulting not only from state practice, but also from the laws of humanity and the dictates of public conscience. Martens deserves credit for crafting such an ingenious blend of natural law and positivism. It was probably the combination of his diplomatic skill, his humanitarian leanings and his lack of legal rigour which brought about such a felicitous result.[2]

---

[2] On Martens, see in particular: Holland, 'F. De Martens', 10 *Journal of the Society of Comparative Legislation* (1909) 10–12; Kamarowsky, 'Frédéric de Martens', 23 *Annuaire de l'Institut de Droit International* (1910) 538–543; Wehberg, 'Friedrich v. Martens und die Haager Friedenskonferenzen', 20 *Zeitschrift für Internationales Recht* (1910) 343–357; V.E. Grabar, *The History of International Law in Russia, 1647–1917,* transl. W.E. Butler (1990) 381–388; Nussbaum, 'Frederic de Martens. Representative Tsarist Writer on International Law', 22 *Nordisk Tidsskrift for International Ret* (Acta Scandinavica juris gentium) (1952) 51–66; Miyazaki, 'The Martens Clause and International Humanitarian Law', in *Studies and Essays in Honour of J. Pictet,* (1984) 433–444; Pustogarov, Ф.Ф. МАРТЕНС: ЮРИСТ, ДИПЛОМАТ, ПУЪЛИЦИСТ (F.F. Martens: Jurist, Diplomat, Publicist), Советскнй журнал международного права (3–4 *Soviet Journal of International Law*) (1991) 76–94. V.V. Pustogarov, "…*Спальмовой ветвью МИРА*" *Ф.Ф. МАРТЕНС—рорист, дипломат, публииист* ("…with the palm branch of peace" *F.F. Martens, Jurist, Diplomat, Publicist* (1993)); Benvenuti,'La clausola Martens e la tradizione classica del diritto naturale nella codificazione del diritto internazionale umanitario', in *Studi in memoria di G. Barile* (1995), p. 173 ff.; Pustogarov, 'F.F. Martens (1845–1909), a Humanist of Modern Times', in *International Review of the Red Cross* (1996) 300–314. See also Lammasch. 'Friedrich von Martens und der Berliner Vertrag', 11 *Zeitschrift für das Privat und öffentliche Recht der Gegenwart* (1884) 405 ff. It is also worth mentioning the recent historical novel by the distinguished Estonian writer Jaan Kross, *Professor Martensi Äasöit,* 1984 (French transl.: *Le départ du professeur Martens,* 1990).

However, the clause is *ambiguous* and *evasive*—we do not know whether this was so intentionally or unwittingly. Indeed, as stated above, it lends itself to many and conflicting interpretations.

2. The Various Interpretations of the Clause Propounded in the Legal Literature

What is the proper legal significance to be attributed to the Martens Clause? A careful perusal of the legal literature shows that opinions are divided. Arguably, three different trends may be discerned.

A first trend includes authors who contend that the clause operates only at the level of *interpretation* of international principles and rules. Some of these commentators maintain that the clause serves to exclude the *a contrario* argument whereby the fact that certain matters are not regulated by the Hague Convention would render belligerents free to behave as they please and to disregard any possible limitations flowing from other international rules (whether they be customary or treaty rules). The clause would serve solely to avert this dangerous inference.[3] Other publicists argue instead that the clause serves as a general interpretative guideline whenever doubts concerning the construction of principles and rules of international humanitarian law arise; the clause would aim at enhancing the demands of humanity and public conscience, which should therefore be taken into account in the interpretation of these principles or rules.[4]

---

[3] See for instance G. Schwarzenberger, *The Legality of Nuclear Weapons* (1958) 10–11. For this distinguished scholar, the purpose of the clause was 'to forestall an unintended and cynical argument *a contrario*. Because the [Hague] Regulations on Land Warfare were not exhaustive, the Parties wished to avoid the interpretation that anything that was not expressly prohibited by these Regulations was allowed.... What, however, this clause was not meant to settle with binding force for the Parties was how rules of warfare came into existence. Its only function was to preserve intact any pre-existing rules of warfare, on whatever law-creating process they happened to rest'. A similar position would seem to have been taken by Abi-Saab, 'The Specificities of Humanitarian Law', in *Studies and Essays in Honour of J. Pictet* (1984) 274–275.

Another author that can be regarded as belonging to this category is N. Singh. In his view, 'the supreme intention of the Martens' clause is to negate any possibility of the omitted questions, not covered by written rules, being left to the 'arbitrary opinion of military commanders'. To ensure this. '...Martens rightly suggested that the appeal should be to "the best customs of the best peoples", and even to supplement or modify such customs by "moral considerations, in order to fill up the gaps in the laws of war on land as formulated by the quasi-legislative organ of the Society of Nations"' (N. Singh and E. McWhinney, *Nuclear Weapons and Customary International Law,* 2nd edn (1989) 47).

Cf. also Y. Sandoz, C. Swinarski, B. Zimmermann (eds), *Commentary on the Additional Protocols of 8 June 1977 to the Geneva Conventions of 12 August 1949* (1987) 39; Greenwood, 'Historical Development and Legal Basis', in D. Fleck (ed.), *The Handbook of Humanitarian Law in Armed Conflicts* (1995) 28.

[4] For some authors, the clause has primarily an interpretative value as well as the value of impelling states to take account of humanitarian considerations when drafting or agreeing upon new rules of international humanitarian law. See for example E. Spetzler, *Luftkrieg und Menschlichkeit—Die völkerrechtliche Stellung der Zivilpersonen im Luftkrieg* (1956) 129–131.

A second group of scholars as well as some judges instead maintain that the clause has had an important impact on the *sources of international law*. It has in fact, on this view, expanded such sources, at least in the area of international humanitarian law.[5] More specifically, some commentators contend that the

For G.L. Binz, 'Die Martens'sche Klausel'. *Wehrwissenshchaftliche Rundschau—Zeitschrift für die Europäische Sicherheit* (1960) 139–160, the clause 'hat ihren dreifachen Sinn keineswegs verloren: An die Einhaltung anerkannter Normen ernstlich zu mahnen, ihre Auslegung im Geiste der Zivilisation zu verlangen und schliessich dort Engpässe zu überwinden, wo das geltende Kriegsrecht überhaupt versagt. Vielleicht ist die Martens'sche Klausel heute das enzigeethische Korrektiv gegen den Kalten Utilitarismus der Politik und gegen den Formalismus der Diplomate' (at 160).

[5] For such commentators see in particular: B.V.A. Röling, *International Law in an Expanded World* (1960) 37–38. The distinguished Dutch scholar first of all harshly assails Schwarzenberger for his 'narrow historical interpretation of the clause', which 'is not borne out by later events', among which Röling includes the Nuremberg judgment, the ICJ's pronouncement in the *Corfu Channel* case, and the *Rauter* case. In his view, the clause, as laid down in the provisions on denunciation in the four 1949 Geneva Conventions, 'presupposes that the principles of the law of nations, as they result from the usages among civilized peoples, the laws of humanity and the dictates of the public conscience, contain specific rules of conduct in the event that the treaties are no longer binding' (at 38). Röling however does not specify how these principles have come into being. He adds only that 'the concept of civilisation, or the custom or general opinion of civilized peoples, was a source of standards, not merely in the laws of war, but also in the laws of peace…'

Mention should also be made of Strebel, 'Martenssche Klausel', in Strupp and Schlochauer (eds), *Wörterbuch des Völkerrechts,* vol. 2 (1961) 484–485. According to this author, the effect of the clause cannot be seen as immediately giving normative force (*normative Kraft*) to the usages of nations, the laws of humanity or the dictates of public conscience: rather, if there is a clear position of states on the matter, in case of doubt it is to be assumed that there exists in international law a principle based on one of these three categories (usages, laws of humanity and dictates of the public conscience), and this principle must be applied, unless there exists a conflicting principle of international law that ought to prevail because it enjoins states to make an exception. ('In der Klausel sind soziologisch und ethisch tragende Grundlagen von Völkerrechtsgrundsätzen derart aufgeführt, dass *bei klarer Stellungnahme* der unter gesitteten Völkern feststehenden Gebräuche oder der Gesetze der Menschlichkeit oder der Forderungen des öffentlichen Gewissens zu einem konkreten Phänomenon *im Zweifel anzunehmen ist, dass auch ein entsprechender Völkerrechtsgrundsatz besteht und verleizt ist,* es sei denn, dass überwiegende andere Völkerrechtsgrundsätze oder regeln eine Ausnahme gebieten', at 485, emphasis added.) Later this author slightly changed his position. He stated recently that the clause has three different legal meanings: first, 'it precludes conclusions to the effect that what is not forbidden by the [Hague] Regulations would be allowed'; secondly, it permits the application of established principles and rules 'to new technological developments and new situations in general': thirdly, it 'does not refer simply to three sources of law (established custom or usages, laws of humanity, and dictates of public conscience) but it refers also to principles of international law resulting from any of these three sources or from their combined significance,' Strebel. 'Martens' Clause', in R. Bernhardt (ed.), *Encyclopedia of Public International Law,* vol. 3 (1997) 327.

Another author also attributes normative value to the clause: Münch, 'Die Martens'sche Klausel und die Grundlagen des Völkerrechts', 36 *Zeitschrift für ausländisches öffentliches Recht und Völkerrecht* (1976) 347–371. According to him the three elements indicated in the clause do constitute sources of law: in his view 'die Gebräuche der gesitteten Staaten [werden] zur Norm, nicht nur die allgemein anerkannten und geübten Gebräuchen…die Menschlichkeit auch ohne Anerkennung und eingewurzelte Übung Normen hervorbringt und…das öffentliche Gewissen [kann] verbindliche Forderungen stelle…(at 365). This author concludes that the three elements of the clause must be seen as 'Leitideen der zwischenstaatlichen Lebensordnung' (at 368).

It would seem that, at least in some respects, a similar attitude was taken by a US Military Tribunal sitting at Nuremberg in the *Krupp* case. According to the Tribunal, the clause at issue was 'a general clause, making the usages established among civilized nations, the laws of humanity

clause has created two new sources of law; i.e. the laws of humanity and the dictates of public conscience. Others have adopted a more sophisticated approach.[6] In particular, in the view of one publicist, by virtue of the clause, the principles of humanity and the dictates of public conscience do become principles of international law *en bloc*; however, the precise content of these principles must be ascertained by courts of law in the light of changing conditions. This determination is made by establishing what standards states consider at a certain moment to be required by humanity or public conscience.[7] In other words, the clause does not immediately and directly transform the laws of humanity and the dictates of public conscience into international legal standards. Rather, it permits the crystallization into such legal standards of only those 'principles' that states consider, at a particular moment as consonant with humanity and the dictates of public conscience. Thus, the view of states acts as a sort of filter designed both to prevent

and the dictates of the public conscience into *the legal yardstick to be applied if and when the specific provisions* of the [Hague] Convention and the Regulations annexed to it do not cover specific cases occurring in warfare, or concomitant to warfare' (emphasis added), in *Trials of War Criminals before the Nuremberg Military Tribunals under Control Council Law no. 10*, vol. 9, Part II, 1341. See also this paper, *infra*.

[6] For instance, a rigorous and original view was set forth by G. Sperduti, *Lezioni di diritto internazionale* (1958) 68–74. According to this scholar, there exists in international law, next to the customary process, another norm-creating process which he calls 'legal recognition of demands of public conscience' ('riconoscimento giuridico di esigenze della coscienza pubblica'). Through this source, general rules come into being by a process that is different from that of custom because the norms produced through this other source (i) were originally *moral* norms (ii) before becoming international legal norms *were devoid of any legal or practical value in the international community,* a value that they acquire only once they come into existence as general norms through this norm-creating process, and (iii) their legal recognition in the international community often occurs through their *repetition in provisions of international treaties* or the *accumulation of state declarations.* Sperduti gives as examples of such norms those prohibiting the slave trade and the norm that prohibits wars of aggression and which in addition declares them to be international crimes. In his view, the Martens Clause envisages both customary law proper (in that it refers to the usages of civilized nations) and this norm-creating process (in that it adverts to the dictates of public conscience). See also the Dissenting Opinion of Judge Weeramantry to the Advisory Opinion of the International Court of Justice in the *Legality of the Threat or Use of Nuclear Weapons* case (ICJ Reports (1996) 260–269).

[7] A highly sophisticated and extremely well-argued construction of the clause was advanced by Judge Shahabuddeen in his Dissenting Opinion to the Advisory Opinion of the International Court of Justice on *Legality of the Threat or Use of Nuclear Weapons* (*ibid.* at 405–411). In his view, the clause 'provided authority for treating the principles of humanity and the dictates of public conscience as principles of international law, leaving the precise content of the standard implied by these principles of international law to be ascertained in the light of changing conditions' (*ibid.* 406). 'The basic function of the clause was to put beyond challenge the existence of principles of international law which residually served, with current effect, to govern military conduct by reference to the "principles of humanity and … the dictates of public conscience"' (408). He noted, further, that '[t]he word "remain" would be inappropriate in relation to the principles of humanity and … the dictates of public conscience' unless these were conceived of as presently capable of exerting normative force to control military conduct' (*ibid*). In short, according to Judge Shahabuddeen, the clause imported into international law principles of humanity and the dictates of public conscience. It would be primarily for courts to find whether there existed a general principle resulting from the laws of humanity or the diciates of public conscience. To make such a finding, courts must look to the views of states. However, in this respect, such views 'are relevant only for their value in indicating the state of the public conscience not for the purpose of determining whether an *opinio iuris* exists' (at 410), for instance as to the legality of the use of nuclear or other weapons.

arbitrariness (or at least subjective appraisals by courts and other interpreters), and to make the elevation of 'principles' to international legal standards contingent upon the approval of states. Clearly, under this construction, the opinion of states plays a different role from that required by the customary process; in addition, no practice is required, unlike the requirements of the customary law-making process.

Finally, according to a third group of commentators, the clause expresses notions that have *motivated and inspired* the development of international humanitarian law.[8]

3. Does the Clause Serve to Dismiss Possible *a contrario* Arguments?

Let us first of all deal with this construction of the clause, which is by far the most widespread. If this were to be the true meaning and purport of the clause, one could not escape the conclusion that the clause states the obvious and is therefore pointless. Indeed, it is self-evident that in international law, as in any other legal system, if a matter is not covered by a set of rules (say, treaty provisions), it can nevertheless be governed by another, distinct, body of law (for example, custom), if the requisite conditions are met. The warning issued by the clause would simply have a sort of moral or political value. From the viewpoint of law, it would be redundant. In addition, the authors advancing the view under discussion fail to explain why the clause, instead of simply limiting itself to referring to principles and rules 'outside' the treaty containing the clause, also mentioned—and this was indeed its novelty—the 'laws of humanity' and the 'dictates of public conscience'.

4. Does the Clause Create Two New Sources of International Law?

Of the three interpretative trends adumbrated above, the most radical is that which assigns to the clause a norm-creating character, whether directly (in that the clause is viewed as a norm establishing two new sources of law) or indirectly (in that the clause is regarded as a norm which raises to the rank of principles of international law standards of conduct perceived by states as required by, or at

---

[8] For some scholars, the Martens Clause 'states the whole animating and motivating principle of the law of war'. In their view, the three notions it sets out permeate, and constitute the driving force of, the whole of the body of international humanitarian law. See for instance the Foreword of Lord Wright to vol. XV of the *Law Reports of Trials of War Criminals,* at p. xiii (the words just cited are his), as well as Benvenuti, 'La clausola Martens e la tradizione classica del diritto naturale nella codificazione del diritto internazionale umanitario', *supra,* note 2, 173 *et seq.*

least consistent with, the laws of humanity or the dictates of public conscience). Let us therefore concentrate on this construction of the clause.

For this purpose, it may be worthwhile firstly to examine the preparatory work at the 1899 Hague Conference, the intention expressed in 1899 by Martens himself, and finally, the evolution of state practice. Indeed, to prove the validity of such a radically innovative proposition, one ought to show that this was in fact the intention of Martens when he proposed the clause and that the other delegates did not object to it. Still more importantly, one ought to demonstrate that, whatever the intention of Martens and the positions taken by states at The Hague, case law and state practice in fact consistently bear out this normative value of the clause. In other words, one should be able to show that, on the strength of and by virtue of the clause, courts and states have applied general principles resulting from the laws of humanity or the dictates of public conscience, or in other words that such principles have been acted upon in practice.

A. The Hague Negotiations in 1899

In reality, the famous clause was not proposed by Martens with a humanitarian goal in mind. It was viewed, instead, as an expedient way out of a diplomatic deadlock between the small powers, led by Belgium, and the major powers, consisting, amongst others, of Russia and Germany. It may be fitting briefly to recall how the deadlock emerged and what steps Martens took to end it.

In June 1899, the Hague Diplomatic Conference tackled the question of adopting the parts of the 1874 Brussels Declaration (which had not become a legally binding instrument) that dealt with belligerent occupation. The Belgian delegate immediately voiced strong objections in the Second Commission of the Conference, where the question was being discussed. In short, he took issue on two points with the major powers that were pushing for the adoption of the relevant provisions of the Declaration. First, he noted that some Articles of the Declaration granted extensive powers to occupying powers, particularly with respect to the possibility of changing the laws of the occupied state, of using its civil servants, of raising new levies and requisitioning goods. According to the Belgian delegate, although this was what actually occurred in the case of belligerent occupation, it was wrong, and contrary to the interests of small countries, to lay down in a treaty a legal right for occupying powers to do such things.[9] Secondly, the Brussels Declaration's provisions concerning lawful combatants did not provide for the right of all citizens of an occupied country to resist occupation, whereas in his view this was a fundamental right of all inhabitants of a

---

[9] The Belgian delegate Beernaert made his speech on 6 June 1899, in the Sixth Meeting of the Second Sub-Commission. His speech was reproduced in full (see *Conférence Internationale de la Paix*, La Haye 18 Mai–29 Juillet 1899, Troisième Partie (1899) 111–113).

country being invaded by the enemy.[10] In both these areas the Belgian delegate proposed generally to leave matters *unregulated by treaty*: in his view it was preferable to remit such matters to customary international law, however vague.[11] In addition, with regard to the first of the two areas, the Begian delegate also proposed the deletion of some provisions and the adoption of new ones.[12] In short, Belgium proposed on the one hand to limit the rights of occupying powers (both by adopting provisions that greatly restricted these rights and by leaving other matters unregulated by treaty) and, on the other hand, to suppress any provision on lawful combatants, so as again to remit the matter to general international law. These proposals were in part strongly supported by Great Britain, which put forward a proposal concerning lawful combatants in occupied territories that took up the main points made by Belgium,[13] and Switzerland.[14] They were, however, forcefully opposed by Russia[15] and Germany.[16]

Interestingly, in the case of Russia, a two-pronged strategy of attack was followed. Martens (regarded by other delegates as 'the real head of the Russian delegation'[17]) assailed the Belgian proposals with a conspicuous display of grandiloquent rhetoric. Another member of the Russian delegation, Gilinski (a colonel of the Russian General Staff) instead raised technical objections. In short, Martens advanced three arguments. First, he asserted that to leave matters unregulated by treaty, by remitting them to a vague body of law (principles and customary rules) was detrimental not only for the large powers (which would be uncertain about their rights), but also for smaller states (as they would not know which obligations bound the major powers). Secondly, to fail to agree upon

[10] *Ibid.* 112–113. Mr. Beernaert said the following: 'A vouloir restreindre la guerre aux Etats seulement, les citoyens n'étant plus en quelque sorte que de simples spectateurs, ne risque-t-on pas de réduire les éléments de la résistance, en énervant le ressort si puissant du patriotisme? Le premier devoir du citoyen n'est-il pas de défendre son pays, et n'est-ce-pas à l'accomplissement de ce devoir que tous, nous devons les plus belles pages de notre histoire nationale? D'aure part, dire aux citoyens de ne pas se mêler aux luttes où le sort de leur pays est engagé, n'est-ce pas encourager encore ce mal d'indifférence qui est peut-être l'un des plus graves dont souffre notre temps? Les petits pays sûrtout ont besoin de pouvoir compléter les éléments de leur défense, en disposant de toutes leurs ressources... Notre pays est de si peu d'étendue que, par surprise, il pourrait être occupé presque tout entier en deux jours, notre armée étant refoulée dans Anvers, réduit de la résistance. Pourrions-nous, en vue de cette situation si grave, dégager en quelque sorte nos concitoyens de leurs devoirs envers le pays, en semblant tout au moins leur déconseiller de contribuer à la résistance?' (at 112–113).

[11] *Ibid.* at 112 ('il y a là des situations qu'il vaut mieux abandonner au domaine du droit des gens, si vague qu'il soit'; see also 113). At the outset of his speech, the Belgian delegate had set forth the following general proposition: 'A mon avis, il y a certains point, qui ne peuvent faire l'objet d'une convention et qu'il vaudrait mieux laisser comme aujourd'hui, sous empire de cette loi tacite et commune qui résulte des principes du droit des gens' (*ibid.* at 111).

[12] *Ibid.* at 113.
[13] *Ibid.* at 154.
[14] *Ibid.* at 154–156.
[15] *Ibid.* at 113–116.
[16] *Ibid.* at 156–157.
[17] This was how he was described by the head of the United States delegation, White: see A.D. White, *Autobiography*, vol. II (1906) at 270.

specific treaty rules would have the consequence of showing to the military that for the second time (the first being the Brussels Conference of 1874) experts and diplomats could not fashion rules on the matter. Consequently, the military would feel free to interpret the laws of warfare as they pleased. Thirdly, and with specific reference to the question of lawful combatants, Martens emphasized that the Hague Conference in no way intended to remain blind to the heroism of the inhabitants of countries occupied by the enemy; the Conference, however, was not designed to codify all the cases that might arise, including cases of heroism and patriotism.[18]

It would seem that Martens himself was aware that his rhetorical fireworks were unable to change the mind of the Belgians.[19] In any case, the other Russian delegate preferred to be straightforward and even blunt. He took issue with a proposal made, after the speech of the Belgian delegate, by the British delegate which was *inter alia* designed to meet some of the concerns of Belgium by conferring the status of lawful combatant on the population of an occupied territory.[20] He simply stated that it was impossible to grant to the population of an occupied territory the right to attack lines of communication, for without such lines the foreign occupying army could not survive.[21] Similarly, the German delegate, also in criticizing the British proposal, noted that the interests of large armies imperatively required security for their lines of communication and their areas of occupation. In his view it consequently proved impossible to reconcile such interests with the concerns of occupied populations. The best way out was to pass over in silence matters upon which no agreement was possible.[22]

---

[18] *Ibid.* at 113–116 and 151–152. In the speech he made after tabling his proposal concerning the clause, on 20 June 1899 Martens stated the following: 'Il … faut se rappeler que ces dispositions [namely Articles 9 and 10, dealing with the classes of lawful combatants and *levée en masse*] n'ont pas pour objet de codifier tous les cas qui pourraient se présenter. Elles ont laissé la porte ouverte aux sacrifices héroïques que les nations seraient prêtes à faire pour se défendre: une nation héroïque est, comme tous les héros, au dessus des codes, des règles et des fails. Ce n'est pas à nous … de mettre des bornes au patriotisme: notre tâche est seulement d'établir par un commun accord entre les Etats, les droits des populations et les conditions à remplir pour ceux qui désirent légalement se battre pour leur patrie' (at 152).

[19] According to a Russian author who has recently studied Martens' diaries (V.V. Pustogarov), 'Martens objected [to the Belgian proposals] and objected brilliantly, evoking applause from those present. Yet he understood that rhetorical art alone was not enough to secure agreement'. In his diary he wrote: 'As if by eloquence one could make the representatives of the Powers break their obligations and not carry out their instructions! How stupid and naive!' [note 24: AVPR/Foreign Policy Archives of Russia. op.787,d.9,yed.khr.5.I.60]. Martens knew that the Belgian delegate in delivering his speech was acting not spontaneously but in accordance with instructions from Brussels (*supra* note 2, at 162, unofficial translation from the Russian original).

[20] *Ibid.* at 154. The British proposal was worded as follows: 'Rien dans ce chapitre ne doit être considéré comme tendant à amoindrir ou à supprimer le droit qui appartient à la population d'un pays envahi de remplir son devoir d'opposer aux envahisseurs, par tous les moyens licites, la résistance patriotique la plus énergique.'

[21] *Ibid.* at 157.

[22] *Ibid.* at 156–157.

Arguably the speech and the proposed amendments of the Belgian delegate had not been particularly disruptive. Generally speaking, the Belgian stance was rather weak and, in a way, legally and politically unfocused. As was admitted by the Belgian delegate himself, this position was essentially inspired by moral and patriotic sentiments as well as the fear that national parliaments of small countries would otherwise not authorize the ratification of the Convention.[23] The position of major powers was clear. Except for Great Britain, they were in favour of granting extensive rights to occupying powers. It was naive to hope that they would renounce their position by simply leaving the matter unregulated by treaty law, hence governed by the then vague customary principles. In addition, it was injudicious and indeed illusory to suggest that treaty law should refrain from defining the categories of lawful combatants in modern warfare and, once again, consign the matter to loose general principles of customary law. As for granting the status of lawful combatants to partisans and *franc-tireurs* in occupied territories, this proposal was totally unacceptable to the Great Powers; it was therefore unrealistic to think that it could have been adopted.

Strikingly, other major delegations perceived the difference between the competing positions as undramatic.[24] Nevertheless, the Belgian position frightened the President of the Sub-Commission, Martens. He felt that the Belgian attitude might have a snowball effect and lead to the Conference's failure. Such a failure would be a repeat of the 1874 Brussels Conference. More importantly, it would strike a serious blow to the prestige of the convenor of the Hague Conference, Tsar Nicholas II.[25] Accordingly, Martens proposed the adoption of the clause.[26]

---

[23] *Ibid.* at 111–112.

[24] Thus, for instance, within the United States delegation the disagreement was reported as follows: 'On one side are those who think it best to go at considerable length into more or less minute restrictions upon the conduct of invaders and invaded. On the other side, M. Beernaert of Belgium, one of the most eminent men from that country, and others, take the ground that it would be better to leave the whole matter to the general development of humanity in international law. M. de Martens insists that now is the time to settle the matter, rather than leave it to individuals who, in time of war, are likely to be more or less exasperated by accounts of atrocities and to have no adequate time for deciding upon a policy' (*supra* note 17, at 292).

[25] This was later emphasized by Martens in his book *La Paix et la Guerre* (1901). He pointed out the following: 'Cette manière de penser [of the Belgian delegate and the delegates of other small countries] mettait en péril toute l'oeuvre de la Conférence de Bruxelles en écartant la détermination des lois et coutumes de guerre qui sont d'une importance vitale pour les populations paisibles des territoires envahis. La suppression des articles les plus importants de la déclaration de Bruxelles aurait compromis toute cette oeuvre généreuse et désintéressée entreprise par la Russie' (at 122–123).

[26] *Ibid.* at 152 (Eleventh Meeting of the Second Sub-Commission, 20 June 1899). Already in its original version, as proposed that day by Martens, the clause had a final paragraph which stated as follows: 'C'est dans ce sens que doivent s'entendre notamment les articles 9 et 10 adoptés par la Conférence' (these two provisions, which correspond to the present Articles 1 and 2 of the Hague Convention, deal with the classes of lawful belligerents and *levée en masse*). The clear purpose of this paragraph was to specify that the clause primarily intended to cover the specific issue of who should be treated as a lawful combatant in occupied territories. According to what has recently been suggested by a Russian author who studied Martens' diaries, 'by agreement with the Belgian delegate, whom he had known long and well, [Martens] took the document sent from Brussels,

Plainly, the Martens Clause essentially referred to the question of lawful combatants in occupied territories. It totally ignored the other issue raised by Belgium, namely the rights and powers of occupying states concerning respect for, or modification of, local laws, the raising of levies, the requisitioning of goods, etc. In addition, no mention was made of the Belgian suggestions to delete certain provisions of the Brussels Draft on such rights and powers and to adopt instead new provisions. On all these matters Belgian demands were only minimally met in later negotiations at the Conference. Nevertheless the Belgian delegate— probably aware of the fragility of Belgium's position vis à vis the Great Powers— quickly declared that he was happy to accede to the proposal, although the clause did not entirely satisfy his concerns.[27] Indeed, he went so far as to call upon the British delegate to withdraw his specific proposal concerning lawful combatants in occupied territory, on account of Martens' statement and proposed clause.[28]

In the interpretation of Belgium, the clause proposed by Martens remitted to customary international law the major bone of contention, namely the question of which persons not belonging to the armed forces of the occupied country might be regarded as lawful combatants in occupied territory.[29] Seen within the context of its origin,[30] the celebrated clause appears to be a typical diplomatic ploy to paper over strong disagreement between states by skilfully deferring the problem for a future discussion. The clause met the concerns of the Great Powers,

---

edited it in his own way to include some positions of principle, and suggested its adoption' to the Conference. See Pustogarov, *supra* note 2, at 162.

[27] *Ibid.* at 153.

[28] *Ibid.* at 158. The British delegate, seeing that only his and the Swiss delegations were prepared to vote for his proposed article, withdrew his proposal (*ibid.* at 159).

[29] *Ibid.* at 153. The Belgian delegate noted the following: '*La Conférence laissait* non réglées *les* questions relatives aux *soulèvements en territoire occupé* et aux *faits de guerre individuels* . . . Il n'y a donc de réglé que ce point qu'il faut tenir comme belligérants les armées, les milices, les corps organisés et aussi la population, qui, même sans organisation, prend spontanément les armes dans le territoire non-occupé. Dans tous les autres cas, toutes les autres situations sont réglés par le droit des gens dans les termes de la déclaration que vient de lire le Président . . . Demain comme aujourd' hui les droits du vainqueur, loin d'être illimités, seront restreints par les lois de la conscience universelle et pas un pays, pas un général n'oserait les enfreindre, puisque ce serait se mettre au ban des nations civilisées' (emphasis added).

[30] In the event, the clause was adopted by the Sub-Commission, and subsequently by the Second Commission and the Plenary, as an integral part of the draft being discussed, and later became part of the preamble of the Convention. See the report presented, on behalf of the Second Sub-Commission, by the rapporteur Rolin, to the Second Commission (annex to the minutes of the Meeting of 5 July 1899, *ibid.* Troisième Partie, at 32–36). See also the report by Rolin, on behalf of the Second Commission, to the Plenary (annex to the minutes of the Fifth Meeting, of 5 July 1899, *ibid.* Première Partie, at 49–51). Furthermore see the minutes of the Eighth Meeting of the Plenary (27 July 1899), where the Martens Clause was adopted (*ibid.* Première Partie, at 195–197). It should be stressed that in his report to the Plenary, Rolin emphasized that the clause adopted by the Commission was primarily designed to answer the objections raised by Belgium to the two provisions (former Articles 9 and 10, new Articles 1 and 2) concerning lawful combatants (*ibid.* Première Partie, at 49–51). See the relevant part of the report made by Rolin to the Plenary (Annex to the Minutes of the Fifth Meeting of the Plenary, *ibid.* Première Partie, at 49–51) and the discussion in the Plenary (*ibid.* at 42–46).

for it obviated the need to tamper with the relevant provisions of the Brussels Declaration, which to a large extent upheld their demands. The clause, on the face of it, also satisfied the demands of smaller countries, because it left open the possibility of arguing that there existed principles or customary rules of international law granting the status of lawful combatants to nationals of an occupied country taking up arms against the occupying power.

Clearly, this possible argument was belied by international law and the practice of states. Both in 1899 and later, until at least 1949, civilians living in already occupied territories were *not allowed* by customary international law to take up arms against the occupying power. This notion was clearly spelled out by Martens himself in his writings of 1900–1901 on the application of the laws of warfare in the 1877–1878 war between Russia and the Ottoman Empire[31] (a circumstance that once again highlights how ingenious and indeed cunning Martens proved to be at the 1899 Hague Conference). Only at the 1949 Geneva Conference were partisans and members of organized resistance movements in occupied territory upgraded to the rank of lawful combatants, provided they met certain requisite conditions (see Article 4(A)(2) of the Third Geneva Convention).

Thus, in the event, the Martens Clause proved to be an adroit way for a number of Great Powers to outwit the smaller countries. Cleverly acting on behalf of those Great Powers, Martens, through his clause, ultimately promised to lesser countries pie in the sky. To put it better, he went through the pretence of giving them half a loaf, while in actual fact he handed to them merely a string of polished and high-minded words.

B. Martens' Intentions (and His 'Shaky' Positivism)

We could stop at this point and conclude that the preparatory work convincingly shows that the clause essentially served as a diplomatic ploy. Could one nevertheless argue that Martens *also intended* to introduce through it a novel and radical means of international lawmaking, by elevating humanity and the dictates of conscience to the rank of new sources of international law? In other words, can it be submitted that, beyond the diplomatic skirmishes at the Hague Conference, what in fact Martens sought to achieve was the introduction of a revolutionary idea in the international body of law concerning warfare?

To my mind, it is fitting to undertake this investigation, if only to leave no stone unturned and to clarify this point once and for all. However, one clearly enters uncharted waters, where great prudence is required, among other things because our scholarly search in this area can really only be based on circumstantial evidence.

---

[31] See *La Paix et la Guerre, supra* note 25, at 368–387. It appears from what is stated, for instance, at 380 (where the Hague Convention is mentioned) that at least this part of the book was written after the 1899 Hague Conference.

To argue for an affirmative answer to the question set out above, one could lay emphasis on the repeated reference by many delegates, in the debates preceding and following the adoption of the clause, to *'les principes du droit des gens'* as constituting customary law, and the widely accepted notion that the matter left unregulated at The Hague, but covered by the clause, fell within the ambit of such *principes*. This would seem to point to a positivist approach underlying the clause: matters left unregulated by the Hague Convention might have been governed by customary law resulting, amongst other things, from the laws of humanity or the dictates of public conscience. In addition, one could recall a general point rightly made by Wehberg with regard to Martens' attitude: Martens' humanitarianism was a blend of both idealism and a keen desire to advocate the official position of Russia.[32] True, other contemporaries of Martens such as the Austrian Lammasch[33] and the British Holland[34] instead emphasized Martens' general tendency to propound ideas and legal constructs which safeguarded the interests of Russia. Nevertheless, the general remark by Wehberg, which may appear to be more balanced than the other assessments, could lead one to support the following proposition: the famous clause, while admittedly designed to take account of Russia's interest in averting the Conference's failure, also intended to enhance the interests of humanity by using an innovative and forward-looking formula.

However, there are quite a few elements that would support the contrary interpretation. First of all, one thing should make us at least suspicious regarding both the true significance Martens intended to attribute to the clause and the motivations that led him to table it: Martens himself—a man ready to extol his own merits—never took pride in the clause. In his numerous books and writings he instead emphasized other contributions of his which he regarded as major accomplishments. Thus, it is striking that in the two writings he devoted to the 1899 Hague Conference, he totally ignored his own proposals concerning the clause. In a lengthy lecture he gave at St Petersburg in 1900, he mentioned only some insignificant trifles.[35] In a voluminous book of 1901 on peace and war, he gave an

---

[32] Wehberg, *supra* note 2, at 351 ('Man wird freilich in *v. Martens* keinen reinen Idealisten erblicken dürfen. Er war wohl gleichzeitig ein russischer Politiker').

[33] In a very critical survey of Martens' textbook on international law, Lammasch wrote, amongst other things, that one of the main features of Martens' writings lay in the fact that such writings tended 'to lay the scientific foundations of the Russian foreign policy in the East' (Lammasch, *supra* note 2, at 411).

[34] See the obituary published by T.E. Holland, *supra* note 2, at 11 ('He was essentially a patriot, and a faithful exponent of the humane theories of his Imperial masters: so much so that his arguments sometimes suggested rather the diplomatist, in constant touch with his Foreign Office, than the jurist who adorned the chair of International Law at St. Petersburg').

[35] See *La Conférence de la Paix à La Haye—Etude d'histoire contemporaine* (1900), especially at 23–27. After pointing out that the Hague Convention on the Laws of Land Warfare also contained provisions on military occupation, *levée en masse,* inviolability of private property, etc., Martens added: 'Il est certain que cette Convention contient encore quelques lacunes; il était impossible de tout prévoir. Ainsi, entre autres, on n'a pas visé le cas des prisonniers de guerre jouant au *foot ball* et au *cricket,* comme ont pu le faire dernièrement les prisonniers anglais à Prétoria' (at 27).

account of the Belgian opposition to the adoption at The Hague of some provisions of the Brussels Declaration, but then failed to mention the most significant fact: it was on account of his own counter-proposal aimed at inserting
the clause that the Belgian opposition was overcome.[36] Similarly, his contemporaries passed over the clause in silence and emphasized instead the importance of his fifteen-volume *Recueil des traités* (1874–1909) and his two-volume
Treatise of International Law (1882–3),[37] as well as—with specific regard to the
Hague codification of 1899 and 1907—his contribution to the establishment of
the institution of arbitration and the setting up of commissions of enquiry. The
fact that his fame should be linked to something which was during his lifetime
not regarded by him or others as significant is perhaps not so striking. After all,
Grotius—as was appositely stressed by Huizinga[38]—was chiefly renowned in his
century for his *De veritate religionis christianae,* whereas we now tend to believe
that he owes his lasting fame instead to *De iure belli ac pacis.* The fact remains,
however, that in Martens' lifetime, no one paid any attention whatsoever to the
clause and he himself—in spite of his evident and repeated boasting of other
diplomatic successes—did not look upon it as a major achievement nor even as a
notable contribution to the Peace Conference.

Furthermore, one should not overlook the fact that Martens' positivism was
not watertight. True, he insisted that modern international law theorists should
study only 'positive legal rules' as expressed in 'customs, treaties and reciprocal
relations of states', without indulging in political considerations.[39] However, he
also noted that the representatives of modern legal scholarship dealing with international law ought to have but one goal: 'to neatly establish the positive legal principles that must govern relations among states, by consulting not only history, the
material circumstances, the real conditions of life, but also the requirements of
scientific truth and the concept of law prevailing in the civilised world'.[40]

In addition, as was rightly underscored by Nussbaum,[41] Martens took into
account many factors that should have been extraneous to a rigorous legal analysis. This, for instance, holds true for Martens' conception of the degree of binding force of treaties, which he made contingent upon 'the extent to which they
conform to reasonable requirements of states and [on] their reciprocal relations'.

---

[36] See *La Paix et la Guerre, supra* note 25, at 119–127.
[37] It was translated into German, French, Spanish, Serbian, Persian and Japanese. I shall quote
here from the French translation in three volumes: *Traité de droit international* (1883–1887).
[38] Huizinga, 'Grotius' Plaats in de Geschiedenis van den Menschelijken Geest' (The Place of
Grotius in the History of the Human Mind) (1925), in *Verzamelde Werken,* vol. II (1948) 382–389,
at 382.
[39] *Traité,* vol. I, at 233 (para. 39).
[40] *Traité,* vol. I, at 201 (para. 34): 'établir nettement les principes juridiques positifs qui doivent
diriger les rapports entre les Etats, en consultant non seulement l'histoire, les circonstances matéri-
elles, les conditions réelles de la vie, mais encore les exigences de la vérité scientifique et le sentiment
du droit qui prévaut dans le monde civilisé'.
[41] Nussbaum, 'Frederic de Martens. Representative Tsarist Writer of International Law', *supra*
note 2, at 54.

(In contrast, one cannot share Nussbaum's criticism whereby another factor that should have remained foreign to legal analysis was Martens' concept of expediency, which, in his view should operate as the supreme principle of international administrative law.)[42]

The serious inconsistencies that marred most of Martens' writings should also be emphasized. Thus, for instance, Martens' insistence on human rights as a crucial element of the international community[43] was indisputably extremely modern and indeed forward-looking. However, it cannot be easily reconciled either with his view that in international relations, states' interest should be the overriding factor or his awe and admiration—at least around the period of the 1899 Conference— for the despotic Russian authorities, as aptly recalled by Pustogarov on the basis of the contents of Martens' diaries.[44] Furthermore, his emphasis on human rights (which, on close scrutiny, revealed a rather narrow view of such rights) under those circumstances and in that context may be taken to reveal a strong affinity for natural law doctrines.[45] At a higher level of abstraction, Martens' making the idea of 'international community' the lynchpin of his own conception of international law,[46] while again extremely modern and appealing, is at odds with his view of the scope of international law. According to Martens, this body of law only applied to so-called 'civilised countries' (which comprised the international community) whereas 'Muslim, pagan and savage' peoples, as well as such states as Turkey, Persia, China and Japan were outside that community. It followed that as between the former and the latter categories of states, only natural law might apply.[47]

---

[42] See Nussbaum *cit., supra* note 2, at 54. This criticism does not take into account that the criterion of expediency must be relied upon by administrative bodies in their day to day action.

It should be added that in quite a few writings Martens brilliantly combined legal analysis with historical and political investigation. See, in particular, *Par la justice vers la paix,* without date (but 1904).

[43] See in particular *Traité,* vol. I, at iii (preface), at 14–15, 427–431. See also vol. III, 186–187.

[44] Pustogarov, *supra* note 2, Ch. 8 ('F.F. Martens' Social and Political Views'), at 196–228.

[45] For Martens, the fundamental rights that civilized states recognized for any individual, regardless of his nationality, were: (1) the right to physical life; (2) the right to the development of one's intellectual faculties; and (3) to right to move freely within states united by international links, including the right to emigrate. From these fundamental rights others followed, including the right of all to respect for his person, honour and health, the right to property, the right to get married, etc. (*Traité,* vol. I. at 440–441). Martens clearly took a natural law approach to human rights ('Ces droits [de l'homme] découlent de la nature et des conditions de l'humanité et ne peuvent donc pas être créés par la législation. Ils existent par eux-mêmes', at 14; and see also at 441).

The natural law slant of Martens was also underscored by Pustogarov, *supra* note 2, at 82–83: 'Recalling Martens' constant references to the inalienable rights of the individual, or considering his theory of international intercourse, one cannot fail to find essential elements of an attachment to natural law. This is fully in line with his endeavour to synthesize the positive sides of both tendencies [i.e. positive law and natural law]. Considering what has been said [above], in my view Martens can be assigned to the positivist camp only very conditionally' (unofficial translation from the Russian original).

[46] See *Traité,* vol. I, 236, 265 *et seq.,* in particular 272–275.

[47] *Traité,* vol. I, at 238–241 (para. 41), 398, 240–241 and 398. It is notable that, as mentioned by Martens himself, one of his contemporaries, namely the Swiss Bluntschli (*Das moderne Völkerrecht der civilisirten Staaten als Rechtsbuch dargestellt,* 3rd edn (1878) paras 7–8) was of the view that the international community embraced all peoples, including those supposedly less advanced.

Another side of Martens' approach to international law deserves to be emphasized; namely, his conspicuous lack of legal exactitude, particularly as compared to those Swiss, German and Austrian contemporaries of his—Bluntschli, Jellinek, Bergbohm, Holtzendorf, Zorn, Lammasch—whom he nevertheless either knew and cited, or took issue with.

In short, all the aforementioned features of Martens' position make it possible to argue that in proposing his clause, the Russian publicist did not intend also to envisage the possibility of considering 'the laws of humanity' and 'the dictates of public conscience' as distinct sources of law. He used loose language for the purpose merely of solving a diplomatic problem.

C. The Evolution of International and National Case Law

Let us now consider whether, in spite of what can be concluded from the preparatory work and Martens' general outlook, judicial and legislative developments as well as state practice subsequent to the adoption of the clause in 1899 nevertheless render it possible to maintain that the laws of humanity and the dictates of public conscience have gradually taken the shape and significance of distinct sources of international law. An affirmative conclusion would by no means be surprising, for after all what counts in international dealings is actual practice, more than the intentions of diplomats or the contents of negotiations conducted in multilateral fora.

I shall start with case law. The Martens Clause has been cited in a number of cases, some national and others international. These cases may be grouped in three categories.[48] The first category, which is by far the most extensive, comprises cases where the clause was simply used to confirm or bolster the interpretation of other international rules of humanitarian law. The second category includes a case where the clause was resorted to in order to suggest an original construction of existing rules of humanitarian law, based on the demands of humanity as expressed in international standards on human rights. The third category embraces a case where the clause was used to exclude *a contrario* interpretations of humanitarian law treaties.

i. *Cases where the clause was substantially used* ad abundantiam

The first case is *Klinge,* decided in 1946 by the Supreme Court of Norway. The defendant, a member of the Gestapo, had been charged with 'maltreatment and torture of Norwegian patriots' under the Norwegian Criminal Code of 1902 jointly with a Royal Decree of 4 May 1945 that gave courts the power to impose death sentences instead of imprisonment for acts such as those perpetrated by Klinge. Having been sentenced to death by the Court of Appeal, the defendant

---

[48] To the cases examined in the text one should now add *Kupreškić,* decided by Trial Chamber II of the ICTY on 14 January 2000 (Case no. IT-95–16–T). See *infra,* in this paper.

appealed to the Supreme Court, claiming that the application of the Royal Decree to acts that he had committed before May 1945 was at variance with Article 97 of the Norwegian Constitution, whereby '[n]o law must be given retroactive effect'. The Supreme Court, by a majority, dismissed the appeal. Judge Skau, who delivered the judgment, held that the grave acts of torture, of which Klinge had been found guilty, were not only expressly prohibited by Norwegian law, but were also contrary to the 'laws of humanity' and the 'dictates of public conscience' mentioned in the Martens Clause. They were therefore war crimes and as such punishable 'by the most severe penalties, including the death penalty'.[49] The Court added the following:

> In other words, the criminal character of the acts dealt with in the present case as well as the degree of punishment are already laid down in International Law in the rules relating to the laws and customs of war. These rules are valid for Norway as a belligerent country.[50]

On the face of it, the Court's decision equated the 'laws of humanity' and the 'dictates of public conscience' with international legal standards. However, it is apparent that the Court's holding was based on a twofold misconstruction of international law. First, torture of enemy civilians, whether or not guilty of unlawful military operations against the occupying power, was implicitly prohibited by customary international rules resulting from the Hague Regulations of 1907—at least if these are liberally interpreted. Hence, it amounted to a war crime. This, in a sense, was acknowledged by the same Supreme Court, for after citing the Martens Clause as authority for its proposition, it referred also to Article 46 of the 'Rules of Land Warfare' (on the duty of occupants to respect 'family honour and rights, the lives of persons and private property' of the inhabitants of occupied territories) and 'Article 61' of the 'Geneva Convention'.[51] No resort to the Martens Clause would therefore have been necessary in this regard—except for supporting a liberal interpretation of Article 46 and the corresponding customary rule. Secondly, nowhere could one find in treaty or general international law, as it existed after World War II, any rules regarding penalties for war crimes. Clearly, this was a matter remitted to each state acting under its own legislation. The contention could, however, be made that, in spite of its manifestly fallacious interpretation of international law, the Norwegian ruling concerning the clause nevertheless carries some legal weight. It is doubtful whether the clause was referred to merely *ad adjuvandum* or was instead regarded as dispositive of

---

[49] See *Annual Digest and Reports of Public International Law Cases, Year 1946*, at 263.

[50] *Ibid.*

[51] It is not clear what Geneva Convention the Court intended to refer to. In 1946, when it delivered its decision, two Geneva Conventions were still applicable, that of 1929 on the Wounded and Sick and the other Convention, also of 1929, on Prisoners of War. The former contains only 39 articles; the latter, at Article 61, deals with the issue of sentencing of prisoners of war tried by the detaining power. It does not appear that other provisions of the Convention may be regarded as germane to the matter under discussion.

the matter. Probably the better interpretation is that the clause was relied upon by the Court primarily to bolster the construction of Article 46 of the Hague Regulations to the effect that torture is prohibited, with the consequence that, if acts of torture are committed, they amount to a war crime.

The fact that courts tend to use the clause primarily to strengthen propositions made on the basis of other arguments is even more evident in *Krupp,* a case decided in 1948 by a United States Military Tribunal sitting at Nuremberg. The defendants had been accused of 'having exploited. . .territories occupied by German armed forces in a ruthless manner, far beyond the needs of the army of occupation and in disregard of the needs of the local economy'.[52] The Tribunal mentioned the various provisions of the Hague Regulations on belligerent occupation, in particular Articles 46–56 and found that those provisions were binding upon Germany 'not only as a treaty but also as customary law'.[53] It then went on to quote (or rather to misquote) the Martens Clause and observed the following:

The preamble [to the 1899 and 1907 Hague Convention] is much more than a pious declaration. It is a general clause, making the usages established among civilized nations, the laws of humanity, and the dictates of public conscience into the legal yardstick to be applied if and when the specific provisions of the Convention and the Regulations annexed to it do not cover specific cases occurring in warfare, or concomitant to warfare.[54]

The Tribunal then stated: 'However, it will hardly be necessary to refer to these more general rules. The Articles of the Hague Regulations, quoted above, are clear and unequivocal.'[55] Indeed, the Tribunal applied those provisions, and not the Martens Clause, to the facts at issue. Thus, it is apparent that the *obiter dictum* in *Krupp* was merely an expression of the views of the judges concerning the legal value of the clause. In other words, the Tribunal did not use the clause to infer from it that, as a result of the clause, new sources of law had been instituted in the international community and that, *in casu,* rules deriving from such sources were applicable.

The same holds true for *Rauter,* decided in 1949 by the Dutch Special Court of Cassation. At issue was the question of whether the Germans occupying the Netherlands were entitled to take reprisals against the civilian population. The Court mentioned Article 50 of the Hague Regulations prohibiting 'collective penalties, pecuniary or otherwise' and rightly added that 'the basic idea (*grondgedachte*) of this Article is apparently that no Occupant of foreign territory may—any more than may the lawful sovereign of the Occupant in his own territory—take steps against those who are innocent [of] acts performed by others'.[56]

---

[52] See *Trials of War Criminals, supra* note 5, at 1338.
[53] *Ibid.* at 1340.
[54] *Ibid.* at 1341.
[55] *Ibid.*
[56] See text of the decision in *Nederlandse Jurisprudentie* 1949 no. 87. 155–156 (English translation in *Annual Digest and Reports of Public International Law Cases, Year 1949,* at 541).

The Court then noted that such behaviour was also contrary to the principles mentioned in the Martens Clause. Plainly, this reference to the clause was made *ad abundantiam* and without attributing to the clause any particular legal value.

The Court referred again to the clause when it examined another argument put forth by the appellant: the argument whereby he was being prosecuted for acts which were not unlawful at the time of their commission and that consequently, the Dutch Special Criminal Law applied by the Court of Appeal infringed the principle *nullum crimen, nulla poena sine praevia lege poenali.* The Court of Cassation dismissed the argument. It first noted that the Hague Regulations of 1907 forbade certain acts and at the same time included the Martens Clause in the preamble. Consequently 'every deliberate transgression of these international firmly established rules of warfare' constituted an international crime. The appellant's argument was flawed for it ignored the fact that for a long time these transgressions had been known as 'war crimes'.[57] Secondly, the Court held that the appellant's contention that the Dutch Special Criminal Law had introduced a new 'crime against humanity' was without merit; in this connection the Court pointed out that in fact 'the said Preamble prescribes in so many words submission to the "lois de l'humanité"'.[58] Thirdly, the Court emphasized that the principle of non-retroactivity of criminal legislation was not absolute 'in the sense that its application cannot thwart that of other principles whose recognition is of equally grave concern for the legal order'.[59] In this connection the Court averred that the interests of the legal order did not permit that extremely serious violations of generally accepted principles of international law should not be punishable solely on the basis that no threat of punishment had previously existed.

Clearly, the first two points were rather vague, shallow and misleading. In particular, it is not clear whether the Court intended to hold that, by virtue of the Martens Clause, any conduct contrary to the 'principles of humanity' and the 'dictates of public conscience' was to be regarded as amounting to a war crime or to a crime against humanity, even when such conduct was not prohibited by any international legal rule. Arguably the Court did not intend to go so far, and relied upon the clause essentially to bolster its third argument, to which it probably attached decisive importance (and indeed this argument seems by far to be the best articulated and decisive of the three).

A similar approach was taken by Trial Chamber I of the ICTY in the *Martić* decision, handed down in 1996 under Rule 61 of the ICTY's Rules of Procedure

---

[57] See *Nederlandse Jurisprudentie,* at 156 (the Court spoke of 'elke opzettelijke overtreding van deze internationaal vastgestelde regelen van oorlogvoering'); see also *Annual Digest,* at 542.

[58] See *Nederlandse Jurisprudentie, ibid.* (for a slightly different English translation see *Annual Digest, ibid:* 'In fact, this was covered by the said Preamble relating to the "laws of humanity"').

[59] See *Nederlandse Jurisprudentie,* at 157 ('Dit beginsel echter geen absoluut karakter draagt in dien zin dat de werking daarvan niet zou kunnen worden doorkruist door die van andere beginselen bij welker erkenning evenzeer gewichtige belangen der rechtsordre zijn betrokken'). For a slightly different English translation see *Annual Digest,* at 543 ('Its operation may be affected by other principles whose recognition concerns equally important interests of justice').

and Evidence. Martić, the former president of the self-proclaimed Republic of Serbian Krajina, had been accused of having ordered the shelling of Zagreb on 2 and 3 May 1995, which resulted in the killing of innocent civilians, in violation of the laws of warfare. The Trial Chamber found that the shelling was a war crime: it violated the rules of both customary and treaty law prohibiting attacks on civilians, in particular attacks on civilians by way of reprisals, as well as the principle whereby the right of the parties to an armed conflict to choose methods and means of warfare is not unlimited. The Trial Chamber then added that the prohibition against attacks on civilians and the general principle limiting the means and methods of warfare 'also derive from the Martens Clause'.[60]

Formally speaking, of greater weight is the Advisory Opinion delivered in 1996 by the International Court of Justice (ICJ) in the *Legality of the Threat or Use of Nuclear Weapons* case. In spite of what would seem at first glance, on close scrutiny it can be said that here as well the reference to the clause was substantially made *ad abundantiam,* for the sole purpose of strengthening a conclusion already reached on the basis of specific international rules and principles.

In surveying the law applicable to the threat or use of nuclear weapons, in particular international humanitarian law, the Court mentioned the clause three times. First, after considering the two cardinal principles of humanitarian law (concerning the protection of civilians and the prohibition of any means or method of warfare causing unnecessary suffering to combatants), the Court referred to the clause 'in relation to these principles', and stated that it 'has proved to be an effective means of addressing the rapid evolution of military technology' (para. 78). It may be noted, with respect, that the significance of this reference to the clause is obscure. Probably the Court intended to articulate the idea that the clause has served as the inspirational force prompting states to humanize war and ban weapons that cause excessive suffering. One fails to see what other meaning could be attributed to this rather terse statement of the Court.

The Court returned to the clause when dealing with the applicability of Additional Protocol I to states not parties to it. In this respect the Court recalled that 'all states are bound by those rules in Additional Protocol I which, when adopted, were merely the expression of the pre-existing customary law such as the Martens Clause, reaffirmed in the first Article of Additional Protocol I' (para. 84).

It may be noted that once again, the reference to the clause is far from illuminating. The Court neither explains how the clause has become part of customary international law, nor does it go into the implications of its customary nature. In particular, the Court does not tackle the crucial issue: if the clause is binding

---

[60] See the *Martić* case, ICTY, case no. IT-95–11–R61, para. 13. The Trial Chamber added the following: 'This clause has been incorporated into basic humanitarian instruments . . . Moreover, these norms also emanate from elementary considerations of humanity which constitute the foundations of the entire body of international humanitarian law applicable to all armed conflict' (*ibid.*).

upon all states, what are its legal effects? In other words, what are the obligations upon states that flow from the clause? Does the clause establish new sources of international law? Or does it instead bring into being humanitarian standards of conduct? If so, can these standards be identified by the addressees themselves, or may they only be elaborated by courts of law? None of these queries can be answered in the light of the Court's pronouncement.

The Court came back to the clause at the end of its perusal of existing legal principles on the threat or use of weapons, concluding as follows:[61]

Finally, the Court points to the Martens Clause, whose continuing existence and applicability is not to be doubted, as an affirmation that the principles and rules of humanitarian law apply to nuclear weapons.

It is difficult to grasp the purport of this proposition. One plausible meaning is that, for the Court, the clause elevates the principles of humanity and the dictates of public conscience to yardsticks by which to gauge the behaviour of states. It would follow that, judged on the strength of such yardsticks, the use of nuclear weapons might prove to be contrary to those principles and dictates. However, the Court does not go so far as to draw these implications. Instead, it states that 'the principles and rules of humanitarian law'—not the principles of humanity or the dictates of public conscience—apply to these weapons. The Court simply states that the clause is 'an affirmation' that the principles and rules of humanitarian law apply to nuclear weapons. On what basis the Court infers such in 'affirmation' is nevertheless arcane.

ii. *Cases where the clause served to advance an original interpretation of certain rules of international humanitarian law*

An innovative approach was taken by the Conseil de guerre de Bruxelles in the *K.W.* case (judgment of 8 February 1950). The Military Court, without being directly cognizant of *Klinge,* in fact took up one of the arguments made there by the Norwegian Supreme Court. However, it framed the legal issue at stake in a much more appropriate and correct manner.

The defendant, a police officer, had been accused of violations of the laws and customs of war, in that he had caused serious injury to a number of civilians detained after fighting against the German occupiers in occupied Belgium. The Court pointed out that Article 46 of the Regulations annexed to the IVth Hague Convention on the Laws and Customs of War on Land imposed upon the occupying power the duty to respect 'the lives of persons'. However, no provision of the Regulations expressly prohibited acts of violence and ill treatment (*violences et sévices*) against the inhabitants of occupied territories. The Court thus referred to the Martens Clause. It noted in this regard that in its search for the principles of international law resulting from the principles of humanity and the dictates

---

[61] *Legality of the Threat or Use of Nuclear Weapons, supra* note 6 at para. 87.

of the public conscience, it was to be guided by the Universal Declaration of Human Rights, Article 5 of which provides that '[n]o one shall be subjected to torture or to cruel, inhuman or degrading treatment or punishment'. The Court then found that the acts performed by the accused against his victims amounted to torture and cruel treatment and concluded that they constituted violations of the customs of war.[62]

This judgment is exceedingly interesting in at least two respects; first, because it demonstrates that the clause may be of invaluable importance at the interpretative level and secondly, because it points to the proper modalities of construction of customary principles or rules of humanitarian law. By virtue of the clause, reference should thus not be made to vague principles of humanity, but rather to those human rights standards that have been laid down in international instruments such as the Universal Declaration. They may, among other things, be used as guidelines for determining the proper interpretation to be placed upon vague or insufficiently comprehensive international principles or rules.

iii. *Cases where the Martens Clause was used to reject possible* a contrario *arguments*

Finally, one should mention a ruling made in 1995 by the Constitutional Court of Colombia on the constitutionality of the Colombian law implementing the 1977 Second Additional Protocol to the Geneva Conventions. After examining various provisions of the Protocol, the Court also considered the preambular paragraph of the Protocol which refers to the principles of humanity and the dictates of public conscience. The Court took it to be an illustration of the Martens Clause,[63] and stated that the purpose of this clause was to rule out the possibility of regarding as authorized any conduct not prohibited by the Protocol.[64]

iv. *Summing-up*

It is apparent from the above survey that mention of the clause has been made primarily to pay lip service to humanitarian demands, rather than for the purpose of supporting the notion that two new sources of international law had come into existence around 1899. Beyond mere general statements such as those

---

[62] See the text of the decision in 30 *Revue de droit pénal et de criminologie* (1949–1950) at 562–568.

[63] For the wording of that preambular paragraph, see *infra*, in the text of this paper, where it is also shown why this paragraph is substantially different from the Martens Clause.

[64] It stated the following: 'The clause indicates that Protocol II must not be interpreted in isolation but must be viewed at all times within the context of the entire body of humanitarian principles, as the treaty simply extends the application of these principles to non-international armed conflicts. Hence the Constitutional Court considers that the absence of specific rules in Protocol II relating to the protection of the civilian population and to the conduct of hostilities in no way signifies that the Protocol authorizes behaviour contrary to those rules by the parties to the conflict.' (Ruling no. *C-225/95*. English translation reported in M. Sassòli and A.A. Bouvier (eds), *How Does Law Protect in War?*, ICRC (1999) at 1363–1364).

in the *Krupp* case, no international or national court has ever found that a principle or rule had emerged in the international community as a result of 'the laws of humanity' or the 'dictates of the public conscience'. In other words, no international or national court has propounded and acted upon the notion that there existed in the international community two additional and distinct sources of law, in addition to the treaty and custom processes. Courts have referred to 'humanity', either explicitly citing the Martens Clause or implicitly adverting to it, only to spell out the notion that in interpreting international rules one should not be blind to the requirements of humanity,[65] or to find international standards serving the purpose of circumscribing the discretionary power of belligerents in the face of loose international rules, or to stress that the clause expresses the spirit behind the treaty or customary formation of most rules of international humanitarian law.[66] Thus, the clause has implicitly or explicitly been used as a sort of general instruction concerning the *interpretation* of certain international rules or as a means of better understanding the thrust of modern humanitarian law.

D. The Evolution of State Practice

i. Treaties

Our conclusion concerning the case law is confirmed by an appraisal of state practice. On some occasions when the clause has been restated in international treaties, no follow up has been given to such restatement at the practical level. This is the case with regard to the four Geneva Conventions of 1949, which contain the clause in their provisions on denunciation[67] (provisions that have never been applied in practice, possibly also because no state has ever denounced these Conventions) and of the 1981 'Convention on prohibitions or restrictions on the use of certain conventional weapons which may be deemed to be excessively injurious or to have indiscriminate effects' (this clause may be found in para. 5 of the preamble).

---

[65] See for example the *Corfu Channel* case, ICJ Reports (1949) at 22.

[66] See for example *Military and Paramilitary Activities in and against Nicaragua (Merits)*, ICJ Reports (1986) para. 218; *Legality of the Threat or Use of Nuclear Weapons, supra* note 6 at para. 78 (see also paras 84 and 86). In para. 87, the Court stated the following: 'Finally, the Court points to the Martens Clause, whose continuing existence and applicability is not to be doubted, as an affirmation that the principles and rules of humanitarian law apply to nuclear weapons.' However, to fully grasp the purport and meaning of this passage, one ought to take account of the fact that previously the Court had stated that 'in the view of the vast majority of states as well as writers there can be no doubt as to the applicability of humanitarian law to nuclear weapons' (para. 85) and had further noted that the same position had been taken by such states as the Russian Federation, the UK and the US (para. 86).

[67] Articles 63(4) of the First Convention, 62(4) of the Second, 142(4) of the Third and 158(4) of the Fourth. Article 63 of the First Convention stipulates that: 'The denunciation shall have effect only in respect of the denouncing Power. It shall in no way impair the obligations which the Parties to the conflict shall remain bound to fulfil by virtue of the principles of the law of nations, as they result from the usages established among civilized peoples, from the laws of humanity and the dictates of the public conscience.' The provisions of the other Conventions are identical.

On the other hand, on some occasions and with limited reference to certain segments of international humanitarian law, states have taken a position that might be interpreted as giving the clause a special legal dimension. This is confirmed by fairly recent legal developments. The states gathered at Geneva at the 1974–1977 Diplomatic Conference restated the clause in Article 1(2) of Protocol I (on international armed conflicts).[68] By contrast in the preamble of Protocol II (on internal armed conflicts) they took up the cause in a different manner, i.e. as a reference not to the *legal principles* deriving from the laws of humanity or the dictates of public conscience, but to the *principles of morals* ('*Recalling* that, in cases not covered by the law in force, the human person remains under the protection of the principles of humanity and the dictates of the public conscience'). The different wording of the two clauses clearly shows that, when states are wary of excessive intrusion into state sovereignty, they simply call upon states to act in keeping with moral standards. On the contrary, in cases where major interests are at stake but where it is simultaneously felt that states' conduct ought to be governed by law (this could be said of the area of international armed conflicts), states do not shy away from proclaiming the existence of principles and customary rules brought about by considerations of humanity or the dictates of public conscience.

Can one draw from these two different approaches the conclusion that the Martens Clause, while applicable to international armed conflict, may not be applied to internal conflicts? Such a conclusion would be contrary to the whole spirit of international humanitarian law: this body of law, in its contemporary state of development, does not make its applicability contingent on fine legal distinctions. Unnecessary suffering is prohibited whether it is caused by a belligerent within the framework of an international armed conflict or within a civil war. Indiscriminate attacks on civilians are banned, whatever the general context within which they occur. One therefore fails to see why the legal value of the clause should be confined to some classes of armed conflicts and not to others. The restrictive wording of the preamble of the Second Additional Protocol only reflects the recalcitrance of the states gathered at Geneva in 1974–1977 in extensively regulating internal armed conflicts. It would be fallacious and contrary to the object and purpose of international humanitarian principles to infer more from that preamble and its difference vis à vis Article 1(2) of the First Additional Protocol.

ii. Statements before the ICJ

Important indications as to the position of states and their *opinio iuris* concerning the clause may also be drawn from the statements made by many states in the

---

[68] This clause provides that '. . . in cases not covered by this Protocol or by other international agreements, civilians and combatants remain under the protection and authority of the principles of international law derived from established custom, from the principles of humanity and from the dictates of public conscience.'

written and oral proceedings before the ICJ in the *Legality of the Threat or Use of Nuclear Weapons* case.

A number of States, including Australia, Mexico, Iran, New Zealand, Zimbabwe, Nauru and Malaysia,[69] took the view that the threat or use of nuclear weapons was unlawful amongst other reasons because it would run counter to the clause. However, they did not specify in great detail what legal meaning could, in their opinion, be attributed to the clause. In substance, they stated that the clause refers to humanitarian principles and the dictates of public conscience and resort to nuclear weapons would be contrary to such principles or dictates. It would seem that they thus implicitly propounded the view that the clause has resulted in *importing* into international law, as legally binding standards, both the principles of humanity and the dictates of public conscience.

A contrary view was put forward by countries such as the United States and the United Kingdom. For these States, the clause merely encapsulates a ban on a possible *a contrario* argument: under the clause, if cases are not covered by the rules of the Hague or Geneva Conventions, it does not necessarily follow that they are unregulated, for they may be governed by customary rules—if such rules exist with regard to a particular matter—or other treaties.[70] A more radical view was

---

[69] As for Australia, see ICJ, CR, 30 October 1995, at 45 and 57; for Mexico, see CR, 3 November 1995, at 69 (for this state the purpose of the clause is 'to confirm the enforcement of international law even in cases where existing international conventions do not stipulate the rules to be applied in determined situations'; see also the Written Statement of Mexico, in *Compilation of Written Statements,* UNAW 95/3, 13); for Iran see CR, 6 September 1995, at 38 and 44, for New Zealand see CR, 9 September 1995, at 28 (for this state 'fundamental general principles of humanitarian law . . . continue to give life to the law, even although specific provisions regulating an area in a particular way have not yet been made'; see also the Written Statement of New Zealand, in *Compilation of Written Statements,* UNAW 95/3, at 19); for Samoa see CR, 13 November 1995, at 55–56; for Zimbabwe see CR 15 November 1995, at 37 (the clause states 'that in considering new weapons systems or methods of warfare, the principles of customary international law and the dictates of public conscience shall apply. The threat and use of nuclear weapons violate both customary international law and the dictates of public conscience'); for Nauru see the Response, in *Compilation of Written Comments,* AWW, 95/2, 13 July 1995, at 13 ('The Martens Clause seems to require the application of general principles of law. It speaks of the laws of humanity and the dictates of public conscience. General principles of law recognized by civilized nations would therefore seem to embody the principles of humanity and the public conscience. Inhumane weapons and weapons which offend the public conscience are therefore prohibited') and 32–34. As for Malaysia, see the Statement in *Compilation of Written Comments,* AWW 95/2, 13 July 1995, at 33–34 ('The Martens Clause makes it indisputably clear that the customary rules of armed conflict as well as the dictates of public conscience are relevant to the question before the Court', at 33; 'The United Kingdom's interpretation of the Martens Clause reduces it to a non-entity by requiring "a rule of customary international law" for its application. What if some horrible new weapon were invented, eagerly adopted by most of the world's generals and roundly condemned as inhumane by most of the world's peoples? The United Kingdom's position would, in effect, make the legal advisors to the world's Ministries of Defence and Foreign Affairs the guardians of the public conscience. That is not what Frederic [*sic*] de Martens had in mind', at 34).

[70] As the United States representative Matheson put it: 'The Martens Clause clarifies that the absence of a specific treaty provision prohibiting the use of nuclear weapons does not, standing alone, compel the conclusion that such use is or is not unlawful. At the same time, however, the clause does not independently establish the illegality of nuclear weapons, nor does it transform public opinion into rules of customary international law. Rather, it simply makes clear the important

advanced by Russia: 'today the "Martens Clause" may formally be considered inapplicable'.[71]

As noted above, the ICJ, faced with these conflicting views, did not take sides in its Advisory Opinion. It did not uphold the view of the majority of states appearing before it, and suggesting—either implicitly or in a convoluted way—the expansion of the scope of the clause so as to upgrade it to the rank of a norm establishing new sources of law. Nor did it confine itself to attaching an exclusively interpretative purport to the clause, as advocated by the United States and the United Kingdom. It can be respectfully submitted that the Court took a sort of middle-of-the-road attitude, by expounding rather loose and ambiguous propositions bound to raise more problems than they solved.

E. Concluding Remarks

The stark difference of opinion existing among states and the failure of the ICJ to articulate a clear-cut and specific view on the matter bears out the conclusion that can be reached on the basis of a detailed survey of case law. Surely the clause does not envisage—nor has it brought about the birth of—two autonomous sources of international law, distinct from the customary process.

It should be added that, were one to hold a contrary view, one would fail to discern the constituent elements of the new sources: would they consist, as custom, of *usus* and *opinio*? If so, in what respect would they differ from the normal customary norm-creating process? If not, what would be the specific structural elements of these new norm-creating processes? It is striking that, except for one or two publicists,[72] no court or state has ever tackled this crucial question. This, it is submitted, further bolsters the conclusion that these new sources have not in fact materialized.

protective role of the law of nations and clarifies that customary international law may independently govern cases not explicitly addressed by the Conventions. This is what gives content and meaning to the Martens Clause. Therefore, when as here, customary international law does not categorically prohibit the use of nuclear weapons, the Martens Clause does not independently give rise to such a prohibition' (ICJ, Verbatim Records, 15 November 1995, CR 95/34, at 98). See also the Written Statement of the UK, *Compilation of Written Statements*, UN AW 95/31, 47–48, para. 3.58, *ibid.*

[71] See *Compilation of Written Statements*, ANW, 13 July 1995, at 13. After noting that the clause began with the words '[u]ntil a more complete code of the laws of war has been issued' (*ibid.* at 11), the Russian Memorandum pointed out the following: 'As to nuclear weapons the "Martens Clause" is not working at all. A "more complete code of the laws of war" mentioned there as a temporary limit was "issued" in 1949–1977 in the form of Geneva Conventions and Protocols thereto, and today the "Martens Clause" may formally be considered inapplicable' (*ibid.* at 13).

[72] See the contributions of Sperduti, *supra* note 6, and Shahabuddeen, *supra* note 7.

5. The Legal Purport That Can Be Justifiably Attributed to the Clause: Or Is It Simply a Diplomatic Gimmick?

As a result of the above analysis, should we conclude that the clause is solely a manifestation of diplomatic skill, and is per se devoid of any legal impact on international humanitarian law? It cannot be gainsaid that over the years the clause has had a great resonance in international relations. Clearly, in spite of its ambiguous wording and its undefinable purport, it has responded to a deeply felt and widespread demand in the international community: that the requirements of humanity and the pressure of public opinion be duly taken into account when regulating armed conflict. If the clause had not struck a chord with the sentiments prevailing in the world community, one could not explain why it has been evoked or relied upon so often, both by international lawmakers, by national and international courts and by diplomats. There is a further reason for attaching some legal value to the clause: namely, the general principle of construction whereby international instruments should not be presumed to be devoid of any legal significance and practical scope.

In an attempt to ascribe plausible legal significance to the clause, three points can be made.

A. The Clause and the Interpretation of International Rules

First of all, the clause may serve as fundamental guidance in the interpretation of international customary or treaty rules. In case of doubt, international rules, in particular rules belonging to humanitarian law, must be construed so as to be consonant with general standards of humanity and the demands of public conscience. In order to avoid arbitrary constructions or abuse, the 'standards of humanity' should be deduced from international human rights standards and the 'demands of public conscience' ought to be ascertained by taking into account resolutions and other authoritative acts of representative international bodies.

However, the question arises as to how this interpretative principle should be coordinated with the view taken by the International Court of Justice in a string of cases (*Corfu Channel, Nicaragua* and *Legality of the Threat or Use of Nuclear Weapons*)[73] concerning 'elementary considerations of humanity'. It has been convincingly argued that, for the Court, those 'considerations' constitute a general principle of international law imposing direct obligations upon states.[74] However,

---

[73] See the *Corfu Channel* case, ICJ Reports (1949) 22; *Nicaragua* case (Merits), *ibid.* (1986) para. 218 and *Legality of the Threat of Use of Nuclear Weapons, supra* note 6, at para. 79. On these cases see the remarks of Dupuy, 'Les "considérations élémentaires d'humanité" dans la jurisprudence de la Cour Internationale de Justice', *Mélanges en l'honneur de N. Valticos* (1999) 117–130.

[74] See on this matter the important considerations of Dupuy, *ibid.* at 119–128.

it would seem that neither the Court nor scholars have clarified two important points. First, the question of the conditions under which the 'considerations of humanity' become applicable; in particular whether they come into play whenever the legal regulation provided by a treaty or customary rule is doubtful, uncertain or lacking in clarity, or whether instead they also become operational when treaty or customary rules exist that run contrary to them; in other words, whether these 'considerations' may be attributed the rank of *jus cogens*.[75] The second point that has not been clarified regards the content of the 'considerations of humanity': How does one establish their scope and purport or, in other words, by what yardstick can one determine whether or not certain obligations are imposed by them? In addition, may such a finding be made only by courts, or can states and other international subjects also determine what specific conduct is required by this general principle of international law in a particular case?

In any event, if the view is taken that there now exists a general principle of international law concerning considerations of humanity, it could be maintained that the relationship of this principle with the Martens Clause, as construed above, is twofold. First, the clause has been at the origin of the general principle. It can be reasonably argued that the principle has evolved after World War II chiefly as a result of its being spelled out and, in a way, 'codified' by the International Court of Justice in the *Corfu Channel* case. If this is so, it cannot be denied that one of the most prominent and forceful 'historical' sources of the principle was precisely the Martens Clause. Secondly, there is room for the view that the clause, in as much as it embodies the principle of interpretation advocated above, is a sort of *lex specialis* vis à vis the general principle of international law upheld by the ICJ, in that it only refers to humanitarian law, whereas the principle embraces the whole body of international law. In this respect, the clause would restate and strengthen the general principle in the specific area of international humanitarian law.[76]

B. The Clause and the Sources of International Law

A second legal effect of the clause can be seen in the area of sources of law. If one disregards the historical origin of the clause and the intentions of its proponent, and considers it in its present logical and legal dimension, the clause may be construed as having *some indirect impact* on traditional sources of international law, in particular the customary process. It is a fact that the clause puts the 'laws of humanity' and the 'dictates of public conscience' on the same footing as the 'usages of states' (i.e., state practice) as historical sources of 'principles of international law'. As we have seen, this fact does not entail that the three categories

[75] On this point see however the considerations of both the ICJ in *Legality of Use or Threat of Nuclear Weapons, supra* note 6, at para. 78 and of Dupuy, *ibid.* at 123–124.
[76] For an illustration of the role the clause may have for interpretative purposes, see the judgment of 14 January 2000 in *Kupreškić*, cited *supra* note 48, paras 535–536 (on the question of precautions to be taken for the protection of civilians in case of attacks on military objectives).

have the same importance for norm-creating purposes. However, equating the three 'sources' may at least entail that whenever a principle derives from the laws of humanity, it must not necessarily be based on either state practice or the dictates of public conscience (similarly, a principle resulting from state practice need not be grounded in the other two categories; by the same token, a principle stemming from the dictates of public conscience need not be supported by state practice or by considerations of humanity). It follows that it is logically admissible to infer from the clause that the requirement of state practice for the formation of a principle or a rule based on the laws of humanity or the dictates of public conscience may not be prescribed, or at least may not be so high as in the case of principles and rules having a different underpinning or rationale. In other words, when it comes to proof of the emergence of a principle or general rule reflecting the laws of humanity (or the dictates of public conscience), as a result of the clause the requirement of *usus* (*les usages établis entre nations civilisées*) may be less stringent than in other cases where the principle or rule may have emerged instead as a result of economic, political or military demands. Put differently, the requirement of *opinio iuris* or *opinio necessitatis* may take on a special prominence. As a result, the expression of legal views by a number of states and other international subjects concerning the binding value of a principle or a rule, or the social and moral need for its observance by states, may be held to be conducive to the formation of a principle or a customary rule, even when those legal views are not backed up by widespread and consistent state practice, or even by no practice at all. Thus, arguably the Martens Clause *operates within the existing system of international sources* but, in the limited area of humanitarian law, *loosens* the requirements prescribed for *usus,* while at the same time *elevating opinio* (*iuris* or *necessitatis*) to a rank higher than that normally admitted.[77]

---

[77] For original constructions of the role of *opinio iuris* in the case of humanitarian principles see Sperduti, *supra* note 5, 68–74; Shahabuddeen, Dissenting Opinion in the case of *Legality of the Threat or Use of Nuclear Weapons, supra* note 6, 409–411 (the issue is also briefly discussed by Dupuy, 'Les "considérations élémentaires d'humanité" dans la jurisprudence de la Cour Internationale de Justice', *supra* note 73, at 127).

The legal construct suggested in the text is however different from that proposed by the two eminent international lawyers. First, as for Sperduti, he conceives the new norm-creating process as applicable to the whole body of international law, while the view propounded here only applies—more realistically, it would seem—to humanitarian law. Secondly, Sperduti tends to play down the 'laws of humanity' while by the same token overemphasizing the 'dictates of public conscience'; this would seem contrary to the spirit of the Martens Clause. Thirdly, his examples of norms produced through the norm-creating process at issue are questionable, for both in the case of slave trade and in that of aggression some state practice evolved before it was widely admitted that a general norm had emerged on the matter.

As for the view of Judge Shahabuddeen, it is different from that propounded here. The distinguished judge argues that the clause imports into international law all the laws of humanity and dictates of public conscience, thus transforming them into legal standards; it would then be for courts of law to ascertain the content of these standards, by reference to states' views. Whatever the role of courts in this process, the fact however remains that the clause would turn out to be a principle which brought into being *two new norm-creating processes.* This, however, has not been accepted by case law and state practice, as we have seen above. What would then legally justify this

What would justify this conclusion? From the viewpoint of substance, one could mention the need—in the area of the law of warfare—for humanitarian demands to efficaciously counterpoise compelling military requirements and their devastating impact on human beings, even before such humanitarian demands have been translated into actual practice. What would be the purpose of requiring prior state practice for the formation of a general legal prohibition, when what is at stake is, for instance, the use of extremely deadly means or methods of warfare seriously imperilling civilians? To wait for the development of practice would mean, in substance, legally to step in only after thousands of civilians have been killed contrary to imperative humanitarian demands. The original and unique 'restructuring' of the norm-creating process in the area of humanitarian law, as suggested here, would thus serve as a sort of *antidote* to the destructiveness of war: restraints on the most pernicious forms of belligerence must be complied with by combatants whenever authoritatively required by states and other international subjects, even if such restraints have not been previously put into practice.

From the angle of legal interpretation, the above conclusion would seem to rest on two arguably solid grounds. First and more generally, it rests upon the need to take account of the aforementioned fundamental principle whereby legal clauses must be so construed as to prove meaningful, with the consequence that any interpretation making them pointless must be dismissed whenever possible. Secondly, it rests upon the necessity to draw some legal sense from the widespread acclaim which the clause has attracted over the years in international relations, as a means of at least attenuating the most pernicious effects of modern warfare.[78]

C. The Future of the Clause

Thirdly, it seems appropriate to suggest *de lege ferenda* that states should cease restating the clause in treaties or other international instruments. Given the ambiguity marring the clause, what is the purpose of continuing with the ritualistic and rather hollow habit of proclaiming it again and again? To be sure, states should be commended for feeling the need to uphold the clause. They proclaim

---

theoretical construct? In addition, what would justify the proposition that, although the laws of humanity and the dictates of public conscience are transformed by the clause into legally binding standards they cannot however be applied before a court of law makes a finding about their exact contents? Given the present conditions of adjudication in the international community, this proposition would entail that states and other international subjects would not be in a position to act upon one of the standards produced through these new sources until a court has pronounced on the matter. Thus the laws of humanity and the dictates of public conscience would be very slow in coming into effect as standards of behaviour. What is even more serious, they would only operate subject to the condition that a court of law has made a finding on the matter. What would warrant such a unique and indeed odd legal condition?

[78] For a very recent case where a court has played down the role of *usus*, on account of the entry into force of the Martens Clause, see *Kupreškić, supra* at note 48, paras 537–544 (on the question of reprisals against civilians).

it because they admit that humanitarian demands should not go unheeded in international dealings. However, if this is so, states should endeavour to act in a more meaningful manner and attach some significance to the restatement of the clause. For instance, they could reword it as a general principle for the interpretation of international humanitarian law.[79] Or, in addition to this step, states could couch the clause as a norm concerning the formation of this body of law: the clause would aim at taking into account the demands of humanity as they are articulated by the public conscience emerging in the world community, regardless of any attendant practice.[80]

6. Conclusion

The introduction into international law, through the Martens Clause, of a means of taking into account humanity was not achieved out of humanitarian motivations. Rather, it formed part of diplomatic manoeuvring designed to overcome political difficulties in the international arena. The clause, so appealing both because, and in spite of, its ambiguity, brought about considerable confusion in international relations and has been at the source of many illusions and demands which were not matched by the harsh realities of international dealings.

However, the initial rationale behind this undertaking and the uncertainties to which it gave rise should not lead us to underestimate its importance for international relations. Here, as in any other path of life, what ultimately matters is the overall effect that a legal construct may produce, regardless of the intentions of its author or proponent. One could go so far as to argue in Hegelian terms that what matters is the action of the 'Wiles of Reason' (*List der Vernurft*), which may use individuals as mere tools to build the most significant edifices of history.[81] Be that as it may, it cannot be denied that advances in the world community may sometimes take strange and often mysterious paths. What counts is of course not so much *how* these advances are made, but rather that they *be made*, lest this body of law remain encumbered by the numerous fetters imposed by the traditional respect for state sovereignty.

---

[79] For instance, states could lay down that, in case of doubt, rules of international humanitarian law should always be construed so as to take account of the laws of humanity and the dictates of public conscience.

[80] For instance, states could proclaim that in cases not specifically regulated by treaty law or by customary rules, states and other parties to an armed conflict should comply with general principles emerging in international dealings and recognized by states, intergovernmental and non-governmental organizations as imposed by the demands of humanity and the dictates of public conscience.

[81] See the splendid pages of G.W.F. Hegel, *Vorlesungen über die Philosophie der Geschichte* (1840) in *Werke*, vol. IX (1927–1930) 83–84.

3. The Diffusion of Revolutionary Ideas and the Evolution of International Law*

1. Preliminary Observations on the Main Factors Behind the Evolution of the International Community

Until now, critical changes in both the organization and the functional rules of the international community have occurred mainly as the result of three types of phenomena: widespread wars; drastic changes in the social composition of the international community; and revolutions within States.

Even the uninitiated are not ignorant of the fact that it was the end of the Thirty Years War (1618–1648) that laid the foundations of the contemporary international community. This conflict shook the heart of the world—at that time Europe. Fundamental rules that were to govern the coexistence of sovereign and independent States were established at the end of these bloody confrontations. These confrontations, marked at the outset by religious wars (between Catholic and Protestant States), were actually an expression of conflicts for the domination of Europe. The first attempt to create an entente among great powers took place in the aftermath of the revolutionary and Napoleonic wars (1792–1815) when specific rules for the preservation of the status quo were established. These rules created a system of collective (or individual, upon collective authorization) intervention in States in which revolutionary uprisings could create dangerous situations for the conservative monarchies which had attempted to share control over Europe. The end of World War I prompted a second attempt at institutionalization of the international community through the League of Nations and especially the will to impose, at least procedural, restrictions on the unrestrained resort to war. Finally, after the Second World War, a first step towards the reorganization of the international community was achieved by imposing upon States a definite goal (peace, defined as the absence of armed conflict) and by establishing a new 'directory' of great powers who had the monopoly—at least on paper—of collective force.

Institutional and normative changes occurring in the international community are quite clearly linked to critical world conflicts ('world' conflicts in the sense that they shake the world 'that counts', for example Europe in earlier eras, or because they directly or indirectly involve most States in the world). This is mainly due to the fact that, after upheavals and conflicts that provoke a crisis

* Originally published in French, 'La diffusion des idées revolutionnaires et l'évolution du droit international', in *Révolution et droit international* (Paris: Pedone, 1990) 295.

within traditional norms and values, States feel the need to create new values and new norms. However, the diverse attempts at radical reform that I have just mentioned have clearly not succeeded in profoundly undermining the fundamental structure of the international community. It remains a set of sovereign and independent entities, all equal in legal terms, but substantially different in reality, mainly because of the military, economic and political domination of a group of Great Powers. The wars I have referred to (Napoleonic wars and the two World Wars) have only introduced new rules of the game and have created structures and institutions to coordinate the action of States. Indeed, the most important rules of conduct remain those that derive from the equal and individualistic structure of the traditional international community.

A second critical phenomenon has profoundly modified the operation and some of the rules of conduct of the international community. It is the result of a social revolution that took place inside the community: decolonization. In the 1950–60s, the community of States evolved: from an exclusive club of European countries (or of countries of European origin or linked to European countries), it became a set of States of profound cultural, political and ideological diversity. It follows that today, as everyone knows, the *majority* of the international community is no longer composed of rich and Christian-rooted States but of States with a different common denominator: economic under-development.

This revolutionary event has not provoked a radical change in the organization of the international community. Numerous traditional rules have nevertheless been abolished or adapted during that period; new germs of ideas have been introduced into existing international institutions and norms, and gradually the United Nations itself has adapted to the active presence of a majority of States that simply did not exist within the international community in 1945.

Finally, *two great national revolutions* (the 1789 French Revolution and the 1917 Soviet Revolution) represent the third type of event that has been able to provoke radical change in the community of States. The radical and extreme nature of these revolutions make them stand apart from the numerous upheavals that took place in other States. In contrast to other civil wars, these revolutions not only ruptured the internal organization of the State by replacing the holders of state power with a rebel group, but also went much further in that they violently announced and imposed a *new vision* of relationships among individuals, and among individuals, the State and society. The new vision and the new ethos created by both of these two revolutions were more likely to affect the international community.

It was this very absence of repercussions on the rules of the international community that prompted me to put aside other national revolutions, such as the fascist 'revolution' in Italy, the Nazi revolution in Germany, or the more recent Islamic revolution in Iran. If taking up and reversing what Hegel wrote on the French revolution in his great *Lessons on Philosophy of History*,[1] one could say that

---

[1] W.F. Hegel, *Vorlesungen uber die Philosophie der Geschichte,* mit einer Einleitung herausgegeben von F Brunstad (Verlag P. Reclam, Leipzig, sd, May 1925) 547–558.

the *Weltgeist,* the spirit of the world, was not present or did not operate in those latter revolutions.

Before beginning the discussion of the two revolutions mentioned earlier, I must set out my reasons for focusing my analysis more on the French revolution than the Soviet revolution. The first reason is the celebration of the bicentenary of the French revolution at the time of this colloquium. It therefore seems more germane to linger over the French revolution. More substantially, it is my opinion that the Soviet revolution, as original as it may have been, took up and deepened, or developed in a novel manner, some great themes of the 1789 revolution.

2. The French Revolution

A. General Observations

In 1789, the international community was almost exclusively composed of monarchies formed or consolidated as a result of hereditary succession or wars of conquest. The United States of America formed, of course, the most remarkable exception, a very young republic (1787), based on a particular mixture of ideals drawn from Enlightenment philosophy and from the principles of Protestant ethics (other exceptions were the Swiss Confederation and the Confederation of the United Provinces, which included among others the Netherlands). Save some specific cases, the world was thus mainly constituted of European, Christian and monarchic countries. A patrimonial conception of the State prevailed. According to this view, the State, as the property of the monarch, could be used by the monarch according to his personal or dynastical interests. International relations amounted to relationships between Princes and reigning Houses: territory, peoples and individuals were nothing but pawns in Princes' hands. The French Revolution represented a violent rebellion against the aristocracy's privileges; it dethroned monarchs and raised individuals, nations and peoples to the rank of the main protagonists and wellsprings of history. All human beings are born free and equal; only the people are sovereign; only Nations—all equal among themselves—can intervene within the international community. Negotiations and conflicts between Princes found themselves replaced by negotiations and conflicts between sovereign Nations.

The French Revolution thus projected some of the great principles and values, once tested within French society, onto the relations between States. Let us see how this change occurred and what marks it has left in the contemporary international community.

In this regard, and for the sake of clarity, two distinctions should be made.

First of all, one should distinguish between the principles proclaimed and implemented by French revolutionaries *in the field of international relations,* from those proclaimed and implemented *at the national level but in the field of foreign policy.* We will see that the French Revolution made an important contribution to each of these fields.

Then, one should distinguish the *immediate and direct effects* of revolutionary ideals and principles upon the rules of the international community on the one hand and their *long term effects* on the other hand. The latter comes to light so to speak 'after the event', only after many years—that is to say, once new historical circumstances inherent to the international community have emerged to nurture the seeds previously sowed in the revolutionary age, but which have remained dormant in the immediate aftermath of the revolution.[2]

B. Direct Effects on the Rules of the International Community

i. *Principles and norms in inter-State relationships*

Sovereign equality among States

Even before the French Revolution exploded, statesmen and diplomats had already proclaimed on numerous occasions the equality between States. However, the new ideas of the Enlightenment and natural law provided a new foundation and a new justification for the principle of sovereign equality. The premises of the revolutionary conception were set by Vattel in 1774. He observed that 'Nations... are naturally equal, and inherit from nature the same obligations and rights', and added the famous sentence: 'Power or weakness does not in this respect produce any difference. A dwarf is as much a man as a giant; a small republic is no less a sovereign state than the most powerful kingdom'.[3] In substance, the meaning of this principle was that no monarch had more rights than others—even if this principle was largely weakened as soon as the right freely to use force featured amongst these rights, whatever the purposes of that use of force might be.

---

[2] On the French Revolution and International Law, see generally: F. Laurent, *Histoire du droit des gens et des relations internationales* vol.15 (Paris, 1969) 55ff.; R. Redslob, *Die Staatstheorien des Französischen Nationalversammlung von 1789* (Leipzig, 1912) 75–104; R. Redslob, *Histoire des grands principes du droit des gens* (Paris, 1923); G. Scelle, *Précis de droit des Gens* (IIème partie, Paris, 1934) 263–264 and 279ff.; A. Wegner, *Geschichte des Völkerrechts* (1936) 218ff.; R. Reslob, *Traité de droit des gens* (Paris, 1950) 35–40; G. Stadtmüller, *Geschichte des Völkerrechts,* I (1951) 170ff.; A. Nussbaum, *A Concise History of the Law of Nations* (2nd edn, 1954); W.C. Gewe, *Epochen des Völkerrechtsgeschichte* (Baden-Baden, 1984) 485–498.

See also the specific following books: E. Nys, 'La Révolution française et le droit international', in *Etudes de droit international et de droit politique* (Bruxelles, 1896) I 318ff; J. Basdevant, *La Révolution Française et le droit de la guerre continentale* (Paris, 1901); R. Reslob, 'Völkerrechtliche Ideen des französischen Revolution', in *Festgabe für Otto Mayer* (Tübingen, 1916) 273ff; A. Aulard, 'La Société de Nations et la Révolution française', in *Etudes et Leçons sur la Révolution française* (vol. 8 Paris, 1921) 135ff; B. Mirkine-Guetzévitch, '*L'influence de la révolution française sur le développement du droit international dans l'Europe Orientale*', in *RCADI* (1928-II) vol. 22, 305–333; R. Schnurr, 'Weltfriedensidee und Weltbürgerkrieg 1791–92', in *Der Staat* (1964) 3, 295ff.

[3] E. de Vattel, *Le droit des gens ou principes de la loi naturelle appliquée à la conduite et aux affaires des nations et des souverains* (Paris, 1830) 47.

Vattel's ideas were taken up by many revolutionaries. It is sufficient to quote the draft declaration presented by Volney on 18 May 1790 (but not adopted by the French National Assembly): *'Dans cette grande Société générale, les peuples et les Etats considérés comme individus jouissent des même droits naturels et sont soumis aux même règles de justice que les individus des sociétés partielles et secondaires'.*[4] One should also recall that the Abbé Grégoire, in his presentation of the *'Déclaration du droit des gens'* to the Convention underlined that *'la souveraineté n'est pas susceptible de plus ni de moins; elle ne résulte ni de la force, ni de la richesse; elle appartient à Saint-Marin dans un degré aussi éminent qu'à la France'.*[5]

Equality is thus founded on a new basis: all inter-State relations are or must be equal and sovereign, as every individual shall be; all these nations express a sovereign will, one by which none can be superior to any other. Therefore, what previously only amounted to a legal condition ensuing from the normative system became a theoretical proposition based upon premises laid down as undisputable. As rightly identified by the German lawyer Grewe, this view implied that international law as a whole is based on the free agreement of States' will (*communis consensus gentium*). This conception thus constitutes the necessary premise of legal positivism that developed during the nineteenth century, that is, at least in its initial version of voluntarist positivism.[6]

The principle of equality conceived and theorized in this way constitutes one of the cornerstones of the international community, until this time. Of course, it has been affirmed in the United Nations Charter (Article 2§1 provides that 'The Organization is based on the principle of the sovereign equality of all its Members'), despite the deviations provided for in Article 27§1 (on the veto power of the five permanent members of the Security Council). Later, the same principle was vigorously proclaimed by 'emerging' countries in the Final Communiqué of the Bandung Conference (24 April 1955), where equality of race was added to the equality of States. While the second of the ten principles proclaimed in Bandung lays down 'respect for the sovereignty and territorial integrity of all nations', the third principle proclaims the 'recognition of the equality of all races and of the equality of all nations large and small'. However, in 1970, the traditional wording concerning the relations between States was reactivated, with the General Assembly Declaration on Friendly Relations and co-operation among States ('All States enjoy sovereign equality. They have equal rights and duties and are equal members of the international community, notwithstanding differences of an economic, social, political or other nature').

---

[4] 'In this general Society, peoples and States are to be treated like individuals. They enjoy the same natural rights and are subjected to the same rules of justice which are applicable to individuals in the secondary and partial societies to which they belong.' Quoted in Mirkine-Guetzévitch, *'L'influence de la Révolution française...'*, 309.

[5] 'Sovereignty cannot vary in degree; it is not the result of force, nor of wealth; it belongs to San Marino to the same degree as France'. *Moniteur Universel* (1795), An III (Séance du 4 Floréal) 334.

[6] W.G. Gewe, *Epochen des Völkerrechtsgeschichte,* op cit, 489.

Two of the features currently emphasized within the concept of equal sovereignty are: the right to respect for territorial integrity and political independence on the one hand; and the right for each State to choose freely, without interference, its own political, social, economic and cultural system on the other hand.

Self-determination

The concept that individuals, peoples and nations are the only social categories that count and that must count, has had another consequence in the field of international relations: that these relations must not be conducted by monarchs in a fashion that treats their subjects as objects capable of being transferred, alienated, handed over or protected according to the monarch's own interests. The rulers of each nation must be accountable to the sovereign people—while taking into account the wishes of the sovereign people of every other nation. It follows that one cannot annex other territories and other peoples without consulting these peoples beforehand through plebiscites. Article 2 of Title XIII of the draft Constitution presented on 15 February 1793 by Condorcet on behalf of the Constitution Comittee provided that *'[La République française] renonce solennellement à réunir à son territoire des contrées étrangères, sinon d'après le voeu librement émis de la majorité des habitants, et dans le cas seulement où les contrées qui solliciteront cette réunion ne seront pas incorporées et unies à une autre nation, en vertu d'un pacte social exprimé dans une constitution antérieure et librement consentie'.*[7]

This concept inspired the French authorities on several occasions. Thus, on 28 October 1790, Merlin de Douai supported the idea that Alsace was French; that it should no longer be subjected to the rule of German Princes claiming sovereignty over it on the basis of the Treaty of Westphalia, because the Alsatian population had expressed its opinion in favour of France. Commenting upon this statement, the historian Droz rightly observed that *'aux engagements de souverain à souverain l'Assemblée substituait ainsi un nouveau droit international public en vertu duquel il était possible d'annexer pacifiquement les pays révoltés contre leur souverain légitime'.*[8] We also know that in 1791 the territory of Avignon was united with France in accordance with this criterion; the same applied to Belgium and the Palatinat in 1793, after referendums were hastily organized.

One can easily infer from these few observations that the principle of self-determination of peoples was conceived and affirmed only in relation to a possible annexation of territories, that is to say as a criterion to *legitimize—or not—the attribution of some territories* to a State rather than to another. As such, it is to be

---

[7] '[The French Republic] solemnly renounces the annexation of foreign territories, unless the majority of the people of those territories so wishes, and only where these territories would not be joining another nation on the basis of a social pact enshrined in a previous constitution freely proclaimed'. Quoted in Redslob *Völkerrechtliche Ideen*, 293.

[8] '[T]he Assembly replaced the traditional agreements between sovereigns with a new notion of public international law according to which it would have been possible to peacefully annex countries which had revolted against their sovereign'. J. Droz, *Histoire diplomatique de 1648 à 1919* (2nd edn, Paris, 1972) 178–179.

found today in the 1958 French Constitution, in which Article 53§3 states that 'No cession, exchange or addition of territory shall be valid without the consent of the population concerned'.

However, the principle of self-determination was applied neither to *colonies* (we know that the majority of the Assembly members and then of the Convention were in favour of the upholding of colonies), nor to *minorities* or *ethnic, religious or cultural groups*. Nor did the principle *explicitly* refer to the free choice by the people of its own rulers: what we call today the right to *internal* self-determination (self-determination as a criterion of democratic legitimization of a State). Regarding this last case however, although not explicitly expressed in terms of self-determination, the right to choose freely one's own rulers flowed logically from the deeply anti-despotic and democratic spirit which was the revolutionaries' driving force (at least between 1789 and 1792).

Although the self-determination proclaimed by the French Revolution referred explicitly to only one aspect of the wide range of situations comprehended by the contemporary concept of self-determination, the principle has remained, in this sense, a sustaining factor in the evolution of the international community. Indeed, it was repeated during the nineteenth century in the form of the principle of nationalities, among others by the Italian politician and lawyer P.S. Mancini; in 1916–17, after having been revived in W. Wilson and V.I. Lenin's political programmes; and in the aftermath of the First World War. Nowadays, the principle of self-determination does not play a significant role as a defining criterion for the modifications of States' borders. [Note that this article was written prior to the Yugoslav conflict, the secession of East Timor, and the ongoing dispute over the status of Kosovo and of Russian minorities in the Republic of Moldova and elsewhere.] This is all the more so since such a principle was largely 'twisted' when it clashed with its 'anti-colonialist version'. As is well known, too often independence was granted to the ex-colonies without taking into account the wishes of the various minorities and ethnic groups, in accordance with the criterion of respect of 'colonial borders'.

The internal aspect of the self-determination principle proclaimed by the French Revolution, regarding the free choice of the rulers, has been less productive in practice (although it has been extremely fruitful in the field of ideals). It is mainly the western States that have insisted on this aspect, be it during the drafting of the United Nations Covenants on Human Rights (1966)[9] or during the negotiations re the Helsinki Declaration (1975).[10] The resistance by other groups of States and the persistence of so many authoritarian or despotic regimes in the

---

[9] See Cassese, 'The Self-determination of Peoples', in L. Henkin (ed.), *The International Bill of Rights* (New York, 1981) 92ff.
[10] See Cassese, 'The Helsinki Declaration and Self-determination' in T. Buergenthal (ed.), *Human Rights, International Law and the Helsinki Accord* (Montclair, New York, 1977) 93ff.

world has meant that until now, at least in practice, this idea of self-determination has been relegated to the background.

The prohibition of interference in internal affairs of States

One of the logical consequences of the sovereign equality between all nations is that each of them should not interfere in the internal affairs of others. If, in every nation, the people alone are sovereign, and if the people are the only ones who, through the intermediary of its representatives in the government, can decide on the orientation of internal and external policies, then it is obvious that no other person, and all the more so, no other monarch, has the right to interfere in these freely decided choices. The principle is explicitly presented in Article 119 of the Constitution of 24 June 1793, in the following wording: *'[Le Peuple français] ne s'immisce point dans le gouvernement des autres nations; il ne souffre pas que les autres nations s'immiscent dans le sien'.*[11]

In this case, contrary to what had occurred regarding the principle of self-determination, the French Revolution clearly affirmed a principle already asserted by other States. One can simply mention Article VIII of the Treaty of Nystadt, concluded on 30 August 1721 by Russia and Sweden, which laid down that *'Sa majesté Czarienne promet (…) de la manière la plus solennelle qu'Elle ne se mêlera point des affaires domestiques du Royaume de Suède'.*[12] Vattel also insisted on the duty not to interfere.[13] Nevertheless, the contribution of the Revolution lies in the fact that it gives a rational foundation and a new logic to this old principle. Non-interference not only ensues from mutual independence of States, but also, and above all, from the fact that—as I said earlier—the people makes its choices with sovereign power and no other people can restrict its sovereignty.

Even if events later led the revolutionaries to deny this principle on many occasions, it has remained one of the fundamental postulates of international relations. Indeed, it has been taken up and repeated several times, for example in 1970, in the United Nations Declaration on Friendly Relations, as well as in other international texts specifically dedicated to this question (I am referring especially to the General Assembly resolution No 2131–XX of 20 December 1965, and to

---

[11] '[The French People] does not interfere with the government of other Nations, and it cannot accept that other Nations interfere with its affairs'.

[12] 'The Czar [...] solemnly promises that he will not interfere with the domestic affairs of the Kingdom of Sweden' See the text in C. Parry (ed.), *The Consolidated Treaty Series* (vol. 31) 345.

[13] Indeed, regarding *internal issues*, he observes that *'toutes ces choses n'intéressant que la Nation, aucune puissance étrangère n'est en droit de s'en mêler, ni ne doit y intervenir autrement que pas ses bons offices, à moins qu'elle n'en soit requise, ou que des raisons particulières ne l'y appellent'.* Indeed, if *'quelqu'une s'ingère dans les affaires domestiques d'une autre, si elle entreprend de la contraindre dans ses délibération, elle lui fait injure'.* Here is the foundation of these propositions: 'It is an evident consequence of the liberty and independence of nations, that all have a right to be governed as they think proper, and that no State has the smallest right to interfere in the government of another', (online translation) E. Vattel, *Le droit des gens ou principes de la loi naturelle appliquée à la conduite et aux affaires des nations et des souverains,* op cit, vol. I, para. 57; vol. II para. 54.

the resolution No 36/103 of 9 December 1981). This same principle was also vigorously affirmed by the International Court of Justice in the case *Nicaragua v
United States of America* (judgment of 27 June 1986), where the Court referred
more specifically to interference through the use of force (which consisted more
precisely of an *intervention*).

However, I would like to point out that, when the principle was set out, it
clearly contrasted with all the other fundamental postulates of the international
community: at this time, not only the use of force, but also every other form of
interference (political, diplomatic, military or economic) into internal or external
affairs of other States ended up, in practice, being legitimized by the legal system.
Indeed, according to *general* international law, every State used to have the right
to cut into the sovereignty of other States in order to pursue the implementation
of a right (in this case, one could speak of the implementation of the law by the
use of force or, more generally, of sanctions against the other State) or simply
in order to pursue its own interests. As a consequence, both between 1789 and
1793 and afterwards, the proclamation of the principle of non-interference had
above all a political and ideological impact. It was only after the introduction in
the international community of the prohibition on the threat or use of force to
defend a State's rights or interests, that the principle of non-interference has gradually acquired quite precise legal parameters—even though it is still surrounded
by an halo of uncertainty and a grey zone which does not yet allow us to say with
certainty what exactly the international law establishes.

The prohibition of wars of aggression or conquest

The sovereign equality of peoples and nations as well as the general proclamation of the principle of liberty necessarily entailed, in the sphere of international
relations, the prohibition of wars intended to conquer other peoples or nations,
or the whole or parts of their territory.[14] This principle is proclaimed in an especially incisive way in the first proposition of Title VI of the Constitution of
3 September 1791: 'The French nation renounces the undertaking of any war with
a view to making conquests, and it will never use its forces against the liberty of
any people'.[15]

---

[14] In 1795 Kant would write that 'in a constitution which is not republican, and under which
the subjects are not citizens, a declaration of war is the easiest thing in the world to decide upon,
because war does not require of the ruler, who is the proprietor and not a member of the state,
the least sacrifice of the pleasures of his table, the hunt, his country houses, his court functions
etc... He may, therefore, resolve on war as on a pleasure party for the most trivial reasons, and with
perfect indifference leave the justification which decency requires to the diplomatic corps who are
ever ready to provide it', Kant, *Projet de Paix Perpétuelle,* translation J. Gibelin, J. Vrin (Paris, 1982)
17–18 available online at: <http://www.mtholyoke.edu/acad/intrel/kant/kantl.htm>.

[15] However already in his project of declaration of 18 May 1790, Volney had suggested noting
that *'nul peuple n'a le droit d'envahir la propriété d'un autre peuple ni de le priver de sa liberté et de ses
avantages naturels'* ('no people have the right to invade the property of another people nor to deprive
them of their natural freedom and advantages'). Then, it was established that *'toute guerre entreprise
pour un autre motif et pour un autre objet que la défense d'un droit juste est un acte d'oppression qu'il*

Moreover, besides wars of conquest, the revolutionary principles also prohibit in a more general way wars of *aggression*—this point being correctly underlined by W. Martens.[16] Several members of the National Assembly proclaimed very clearly that every 'offensive' war was unjust;[17] the Abbé Maury ended up giving a very wide definition of what constitutes aggression, stating that *'On est agresseur quand on forme des parties, quand on entre dans une ligue, quand on nuit au commerce, quand on refuse d'exécuter un traité, enfin quand on attaque directement ou indirectement l'intérêt de ses voisins'.*[18] The revolutionaries drew logical conclusions from these concepts: preventive war is illegal,[19] only war in self-defence is just,[20] and it is the same for collective self-defence;[21] it is not the case for 'offensive alliance',[22] as laid down in Article 16 of the Abbé Grégoire's 'Déclaration du droit des gens': *'Les ligues qui ont pour objet une guerre offensive, les traités ou les alliances qui peuvent nuire à l'intérêt d'un Peuple, sont un attentat contre la famille humaine'.*[23]

With these principles in mind, the revolutionaries intended that relations between monarchs based on conquest should be substituted with relations between free nations, each of them respecting the other's freedom. It is clearly a self-limitation which, at the time of its proclamation, is restrained to the field of external policy orientation and which is only valid for the State who makes it a rule. However, these principles, later trampled underfoot by the revolutionaries themselves, have become fundamental rules of the international community—still under uncertain terms—in 1928—with the Pact of Paris (prohibiting the use of war as a tool of national policy), and then, in 1945, with Article 2§4 and Article 51 of the United Nations Charter. It can be seen that some principles set forth in 1790 and 1791 as foreign policy postulates naturally emerging from the new ideals of the French Revolution, would have to wait for two great social

---

importe à toute la grande société de réprimer, parce que l'invasion d'un Etat par un autre Etat tend à menacer la liberté et la sûreté de tous' ('all enterprise of war for any reason or object other than the defence of a just right is an act of oppression which oppresses society as a whole, because the invasion of a State by another State threatens the freedom and safety of all').

[16] W. Martens, *Völkerrechtsvorstellungen der französischen Revolution...*, op cit, 297.

[17] Le Duc de Lévis, Dupont and Mirabeau at the National Assembly, on 16, 17 and 20 May 1790, in *Archives Parlementaires,* XV, 256, 586 and 619.

[18] 'One is to be considered an aggressor when one constitutes parties; when one creates a league; when one damages trade relationships; when one refuses to respect a treaty; when one directly or indirectly attacks the interests of one's neighbours', The Abbé Maury, National Assembly, 18 May 1790, *ibid,* XV, 567.

[19] Le Duc de Lévis, National Assembly, 16 May 1790, *ibid,* XV, 526.

[20] Le Duc de Lévis, National Assembly, 16 May 1790, *ibid,* XV, 526; le Comte de Clermont-Tonnerre, 18 May 1790, *ibid,* 560; Dupont, 19 May 1790, *ibid,* 586; Art. 17 of the 'Déclaration du droit des gens' of the Abbé Grégoire, in *Moniteur Universel,* An III (Séance du 4 floréal), 333.

[21] Dupont, 19 May 1790, *ibid,* 587 (*'il est permis de s'associer à la légitime défense d'autrui'*).

[22] Pétition de Villeneuve, 17 May 1790, *ibid,* 542; Clermont-Tonnerre, 18 May 1790, *ibid;* Dupont, 19 May 1790, *ibid,* 588.

[23] 'Leagues with the purpose of fighting aggressive wars, agreements and alliances that can damage the interests of a People are a threat to mankind', *Moniteur Universel,* An III (Séance du 4 floréal), 333.

upheavals of another kind (the two World Wars) to emerge as universally valid (with peremptory force) legal norms for all the members of the international community.

I would like to add that the international norms that I have just touched upon not only repeat the content, but also often the wording of the revolutionary principles. In addition, many modern *constitutions* have repeated the concepts as well as the wording of the revolutionary principles: for example, it is possible to quote Article 6 of the 1931 Spanish Republican Constitution, Article 9 of the 1946 Japanese Constitution, and above all Article 11 of the 1947 Italian Constitution which was written with words no less incisive than those of the French revolutionaries.[24]

The principle of armed intervention in favour of oppressed people

It was inherent to the concept of liberty defended by the revolutionaries that freedom could not be stopped at the French borders, but that it should be extended to all people (or 'all persons', or 'every people'). Besides, it derived logically from the concept of fraternity that French people should not be inactive in the face of the oppression of other peoples by tyrants and despots. It is thus not surprising that the revolutionaries declared themselves ready to help any oppressed people. The 19 November 1792 decree stated that: '*la Convention nationale déclare, au nom de la nation française, qu'elle accordera fraternité et secours à tous les peuples qui voudront recouvrer leur liberte*'.[25] Article 118 of the 1793 Constitution lays down that 'The French people are the friend and natural ally of free peoples'. These concepts were taken to their extreme by Robespierre in 1793 in his draft of the Declaration of the rights of man and of the citizen. Towards the end of this draft, he not only suggested fighting against tyrants who oppress foreign peoples, but also prosecuting them criminally as murderers: '*Celui qui opprime une seule nation, se déclare l'ennemi de toutes. Ceux qui font la guerre à un peuple, pour arrêter les progrès de la liberté, et anéantir les droits de l'homme, doivent être poursuivis partout, non comme des ennemis ordinaires, mais comme des assassins et des brigands rebelles*'.[26]

The principle of armed intervention in favour of oppressed peoples is closely tied to the concept of self-determination of peoples, and can even be considered as one of its direct consequences. However, it constitutes an exception to the general prohibition on interference in the internal affairs of other nations. This exception is justified by the pre-eminence given to 'liberty' and 'fraternity' over a

---

[24] The first proposition of Art. 11 of the Italian Constitution lays down that 'Italy rejects war as an instrument of aggression against the freedoms of others peoples and as a means for settling international controversies'. On this provision, see A. Cassese, 'Wars Forbidden and Wars allowed by the Italian Constitution' in *Studi in onore de G. Balladore Pallieri*, vol. II, (Milano, 1978) 131ff.

[25] 'The National Convention declares, in the name of the French Nation, that it will provide brotherhood and assistance to all people who will want to restore their freedom'.

[26] 'Those who oppress one nation, they are the enemies of all nations. All those who fight war against a people to stop the progress of freedom, and to annihilate human rights, must be prosecuted everywhere, not just as ordinary enemies, but as murderers and criminals'. In 'Lettres a ses commettants', *Œuvres complètes de Robespierre*, vol. V (Paris, 1961) 363.

formalist idea of 'equality' (nevertheless, the principle of 'equality' could also justify an armed intervention as it intends to put all nations on an equal footing as far as the respect of liberty is concerned).

Two points must be underlined. First of all, more than all the other principles proclaimed by the French Revolution, the principle of armed intervention in favour of oppressed peoples is ambiguous and entails numerous abuses because of its broad wording. Moreover, because of its ambiguity it has been violated on many occasions since 1792, even more than the other principles proclaimed by France.[27]

What was the influence of this principle on the normative foundation of the international community? For several years, it was used only on a political level to more or less justify concealed right-wing or left-wing imperialistic interventions. On the normative level, it left no mark, at least until 1945 and the reason for this was simple: until World War I, the use of force was allowed in every situation (except obviously when contrary to specific agreements). Subsequently, during the League of Nations era, States' efforts were focused on limiting the resort to war and as a consequence, no one was willing to give a free hand or any formal recognition to armed interventions intended to defend the liberty of other peoples.

A first turning point occurred in 1945 when the United Nations Charter established the right for every Member State to come to another State's assistance, if it is subject to an armed attack (Article 51). It thus proclaimed the right of armed intervention to defend the victim of an act of aggression. However, it is necessary to underline two basic differences *vis-à-vis* the principle established by the French Revolution. On one hand, the emphasis in this case is not on the fact that the intervening State is assisting another to get rid of the *oppression,* but rather on the fact that the latter is subjected to an *armed aggression.* On the other hand, no latitude is given with respect to cases of *internal oppression:* the fact that a people are victim of a dictatorship does not allow another State to rescue them by virtue of the right to 'collective self-defence'.

There was however an attempt to 'go back' to the revolutionary principle at the beginning of the 1960s, when the United Nations General Assembly began to proclaim the principle that wars of national liberation are legitimate forms of implementation of the people's right of self-determination and that assistance given to national liberation movements is fully legitimate. We know that socialist countries and especially several Third World States at first supported 'assistance' to oppressed peoples as a means to provide military aid, among other things by supplying troops. However, the opposition of western States, subsequently followed by many developing countries, did not allow for these claims to be

---

[27] Amongst others, Jacques Droz has demonstrated very well the fluctuations of the revolutionaires regarding the implementation of this principle, and above all the change from the 'revolutionary war' to the 'fruitful war', in which the aim of the war is no longer to export the revolution and freedom, but rather to widen the sphere of influence of France, and even to seize the goods of the conquered countries: Droz, op cit, 189–191.

translated into positive law. Thus, if there is today an agreement on the legitimacy of economic and humanitarian assistance, and maybe also on the supplying of weapons to national liberation movements, there is no agreement on the legitimacy of logistical assistance, the sending of troops or on the granting of 'sanctuaries' to these groups. No legal norm has thus crystallized on this point.

The prohibition of slavery

After many vicissitudes, the Convention abolished slavery on 4 February 1794 (16 pluviôse year II) with a brief but very incisive decree: 'The Convention declares the abolition of Negro slavery in all colonies; in consequence it decrees that all men, without distinction of colour, dwelling in the colonies, are French citizens and will enjoy all the rights guaranteed by the Constitution'. This decree was notably motivated by the necessity to gain the support of the slaves of Saint-Domingue to fight against the English.[28] We also know that slavery was reintroduced by Napoleon in 1802. Despite this, the words pronounced by Danton at the Convention on 4 February 1794 remain valid: *'Nous travaillons pour les générations futures, lançons la liberté dans les colonies: c'est aujourd'hui que l'Anglais est mort!'*.[29] The revolutionary ideal of equality, implemented in 1794 for a few years, would have important consequences for the international community during the nineteenth and then the twentieth centuries. During the nineteenth century, the European powers concluded several treaties to abolish the trade of slaves,[30] but it was only in 1926 that a multilateral convention was concluded to abolish, in addition to the trade in slaves, slavery itself. This convention was followed in 1956 by a more elaborate and comprehensive one.

The issue of the principles related to the conduct of wars

The smallest contribution of the French Revolution in the development of international law was the one related to the laws of war. Before the wars that took place between 1792 and 1815, the conduct of war was codified in a few main rules on the treatment of prisoners of war and the protection of the wounded, the sick and civilians. The major humanitarian principles of the laws of war had already been expressed to a great extent by Vattel, and they were widely observed in practice. However, their respect was eased by the kind of war prevailing at this time. Until the Revolutionary era, war consisted primarily of confrontations between professionals and elites who were not only well trained but also were aware of the existence of a range of behavioural rules. During the wars occurring between 1648

---

[28] See D. Brion Davis, *The Problem of Slavery in the Age of Revolution 1770–1823* (Ithaca and London, 1977) 137–148.

[29] 'We are working for future generations, let us pursue freedom for the Colonies: it is today that the English are dead'. Quoted by J. Tulard, J.F. Fayard, and A. Fierro, *Histoire et Dictionnaire de la Révolution française* (Paris, 1987) 802.

[30] See for all of these Oppenheim-Lauterpacht, *International Law*, I, 8 edn (London, 1955) 733–734.

and 1792, the civilian populations were seriously involved only in a few cases. Everything changed with the French Revolution, as underlined vigorously by von Clausewitz in his bulky book, *Vom Kriege* (1832–1834). Wars were no longer conducted by limited professional elites but by whole nations under arms. He observed that *'la guerre était soudain redevenue l'affaire du peuple et d'un peuple de 30 millions d'habitants qui se considéraient tous comme citoyens de l'Etat… La participation du peuple à la guerre, à la place d'un Cabinet ou d'une armée, faisait entrer une nation entière dans le jeu avec son poids naturel'.*[31] If war turns into a confrontation of entire peoples under arms, it is then difficult to ensure that the existing rules to protect the wounded, the sick, civilians and prisoners of war will be respected. The revolutionaries tried to ensure human treatment to enemies *'hors de combat'.*[32] However, according to several sources, during the 23 years of war, it was not only civilians who were subjected to abuses and suffering that would have been unthinkable until then—such was also the case for the wounded and for prisoners of war.[33]

From this point of view, the French Revolution contributed more by *introducing a new kind of war*—with all the ill-fated consequences which resulted from it and which led to the 'absolute' (as it was called by Clausewitz) or 'total' (as we call it today)[34] war—rather than by pushing towards new norms of international law.[35]

ii. Principles related to the internal organization of international relations

The expanding force of the great ideas of the Revolution was extremely likely also to influence the organization of the conduct of the foreign policy within the French State.

[31] 'War suddenly became something concerning the people as a whole, and a people of 30 million individuals who considered themselves as citizens of the State. The participation of the people in the war, instead of a Cabinet or an army, made an entire nation take part in the game with all its natural weight'. C. von Clausewitz, *De la guerre*, translation by D. Naville, (Paris, 1955) 687.

[32] Concerning this, it is possible to quote the decree of the legislative assembly of 4–5 May 1792, according to which *'les prisonniers de guerre sont sous la sauvegarde de la nation et la protection spéciale de la loi'* ('prisoners of war are under the safeguard of the nation and the special protection of the law'), as well as the decree of 25 May 1793, which ensured to wounded enemies the same medical and hospital treatment as that granted to the French, under the condition that reciprocity was ensured.

[33] For the best analysis of the practice of the revolutionaries regarding the law of war, see J. Basdevant, *La Révolution française et le droit de la guerre continentale*, op cit (especially on prisoners of war, 88–105, 109–110; on the wounded, 106–109). Also see P. Boissier, *Histoire du Comité international de la Croix-Rouge: de Solférino à Tsoushima* (Paris: Plon, 1963) 176–177, 205–212; J. Best, *Humanity in Warfare* (London, 1980) 75–127.

[34] The trend of total war and against 'everybody else', inherent to the revolutionary ideology, is rightly underlined by R. Schnur, *Weltfriedensidee und Weltbürgerkrieg…* op cit, 310–317.

[35] Concerning this, the conclusions of J. Basdevant op cit, 109–110, on prisoners of war, and 211–214, on the general impact of the French Revolution on the law of war, seem optimistic and hardly consonant with the practice that he himself identified and illustrated.

According to one of the great postulates of pacifism stemming from Enlightenment philosophy, and notably supported by the Abbé de Saint-Pierre, war results from a despot's whims. In other words, war is the natural outcome of a certain kind of political regime (the authoritarian regime of monarchs who are unconcerned about the wishes of the people). To implement the pacifist ideals, it was thus necessary—and sufficient—to leave decisions related to war in the hands of the people, *a priori* considered to be wise and sensible, as well as in the hands of the institutions they have freely chosen. The notion of popular sovereignty according to which all power lies in the hands of the people and must come from these same hands led to the same conclusion.

The norms in the different constitutions of revolutionary France were directly inspired by these notions: the power to *determine* the state of war was given to the national assembly, whereas the power to *declare* war was granted to the monarch (and afterwards, in the 1799 Constitution, to the first Consul).[36]

According to another fundamental principle, also corollary to the principle of popular sovereignty, the main treaties of political importance—peace treaties but also alliances and trade treaties—should no longer be concluded by the monarch, but should be authorized, that is to say concluded, by the legislative assembly.[37] The monarch (and afterwards the Directory and the first Consul) could only sign them.

One only needs to underline the following point to realize the huge innovative weight of these constitutional provisions on the democratic conduct of foreign policy. Before the French constitutions, the only constitution which was already providing for the participation of a legislative organ in the conclusion of treaties, that is to say the Constitution of the United States of America of 1787, required the Senate to participate in the conclusion of international treaties, not out of respect for democratic principles (meaning by virtue of popular sovereignty), but to ensure that the representatives of the federal states would not be deprived of their authority by the central power, embodied by the President. In other words, the American provision was more intended to protect the States against the centralization of power than to ensure the participation of the people—through the intermediary of its representatives—in the conclusion of international treaties. Indeed, the 'House of Representatives' was not entrusted with the power to conclude treaties.

According to another important principle proclaimed by the French Revolution, political asylum must be granted to every person persecuted abroad for his political beliefs. As it was laid down in Article 120 of the 1793 Constitution, '[the French people] gives asylum to foreigners who, in the name of liberty, are banished from their homelands, and refuses it to tyrants'. It is obvious that this provision is meant to proclaim the universal nature of liberty, and thus ensure a

---

[36] See Art. 2 of Ch. 3 and Arts 1–3 of section II of Ch. IV; Arts 326–334 of the 1795 Constitution and Art. 50 of the 1799 Constitution.

[37] See Art. 3 of Ch. III and Arts 1 and 3 of section III of Ch. IV of the 1791 Constitution; Arts 329–333 of the 1795 Constitution and Art. 50 of the 1799. Constitution.

safe shelter to every person who can not enjoy freedom in his or her own country. The profound innovative scope of this principle can be better seen if one looks at Vattel's observations in 1774. In establishing and theorizing the practice of States, Vattel observed that sovereign States could not refuse entrance to foreigners who had come to the border 'driven by a storm or another necessity'.[38] The French Revolution specifically sets up political persecution resulting from the fight for liberty as a fundamental ground for an automatic right to political asylum.

I must add that the three sets of constitutional provisions that I have just touched upon have not led to the creation of inter-States norms—even if in some cases, they have had a certain influence on their content.[39] Their transformation into international norms was among other things made difficult by the 'organizational' nature of the constitutional norms in question. These revolutionary provisions have had a considerable impact on the constitutions of several States, to the point of being taken up and imitated by European, Latin-American countries and even nowadays, by many socialist or developing countries.[40] As for developments in the democratic control of foreign policy, they have also been largely encouraged by the decline of the power of monarchs, the development of parliamentary regimes and the generalization of the principle of separation of powers.

C. Long Term Effects

Unlike the principles that I have examined earlier, what I am about to discuss below is a myriad of ideas, sketches, statements and proclamations that were formulated by the *men of the Revolution* but that were not adopted by the majority of the collegial organs of the Revolution (and thus were not established by formal acts). I may also touch upon principles and postulates that have received a formal consecration but that have been above all considered suitable for the national level—in other words, that have not been explicitly projected by the revolutionaries onto the international level, *that is to say the level of the relations between States, Peoples and Nations.* This partially explains the second, rather essential, characteristic of the principles, ideas and sketches in question. These principles have produced effects *only in the long term,* being transformed only much later, when favourable historic circumstances arose. From the rank of vague declarations and principles or from the status of norms only ruling over internal relations, they

---

[38] *Le Droit des gens . . .* , II, Ch. VII, para. 95; Ch. VIII, para. 100; Ch. IX, para. 123.

[39] J. Basdevant, *La Révolution française et de droit de la guerre continentale*, op cit, underlines (at 32–33, 41) that conferring upon the legislative assemblies the power to determine the state of war contributed to the formation of an international norm by virtue of which 'the state of war' between two or several States can result from a public act (notification, declaration of war) and not only from the opening of hostilities.

[40] See A. Cassese (ed.), *Parliamentary Control over Foreign Policy* (Alphen aan den Rijn, 1980); A. Cassese, *Modern Constitution and International Law* in *RCADI* 1985-III, vol. 192, 341ff.

have reached the rank of international norms or guidelines for the conduct of
States.

i. *The notion of international community*

Among the ideas suggested by some revolutionaries and left inert for many years
to be later, indeed rather recently, revived, the concept of international community must be highlighted.

The idea that 'mankind' constitutes a whole to which each individual and
each human group indissolubly belongs, is clearly not new. Diogenes of Sinope
used to define himself as a 'world citizen', and many catholic thinkers—especially F. Vitoria—underlined the unity of mankind and the universal nature of
the *'republica Christiana'*. States had already mentioned 'humanity' before the
French Revolution; in a peace treaty concluded in 1783 between England and
France, there is a reference to the 'good of humanity in general'.[41]

What is new with the French revolutionaries taking up the notion is the particular accent that they give to the concept of world community. In Volney's draft
of the decree presented to—but not adopted by—the Assembly on 18 May 1790,
Volney suggested in Article 1 the following wording: *'L'Assemblée déclare solennellement qu'elle regards l'universalité du genre humain comme ne formant qu'une
seule et même société dont l'objet est la paix et le bonheur de tous et chacun de ses mem-
bres'.*[42] The draft of Abbé Grégoire's *'Déclaration du droit des gens'*, also submitted
to the Convention (23 April 1795) and then rejected, established that *'l'intérêt
particulier d'un peuple est subordonné à l'intérêt général de la famille humaine'*[43]
(Article 4). The assertions of Jean-Baptiste Cloots (stated within the Constituent
Assembly, the Convention, or in one of his numerous writings) are also noteworthy. His constant and hyperbolic references to 'mankind' have led many people to think of him as a fool or a fanatic.[44]

In these statements of a few revolutionaries, a critical element lies in the fact
that the emphasis is placed on the *unity of mankind,* conceived as a myth above
the barriers of race, religion, language and customs, despite borders and the diversity of political regimes. The international community is no longer considered as
a mishmash of potentates, each one being independent, self-sufficient and pursuing its particular interests. On the contrary, the international community is envisaged as a true 'community', that is to say as a whole within which every individual

---

[41] In C. Parry, *The Consolidated Treaty Series*, op cit.

[42] 'The Assembly solemnly declares that given the universal character of mankind, it considers
humanity as a single society whose purpose is peace and the wellbeing of each and all of its members'. Quoted by Redslob, *Histoire des grands principes*, op cit, 280ff.

[43] 'The specific interests of one people are conditioned by the general interests of the human
family'. In *Moniteur Universel*, An III (Séance du 4 floréal) 333.

[44] See S. Stern, *Anarcharsis Cloots. Der Redner des Menschengeschlechts* (Berlin, 1914); A. Mathiez,
Anarcharsis Cloots, 'l'Universel', in *La Révolution et les étrangers* (Paris, 1918) 48ff; R. Schnurr,
Weltfriedensidee und Weltburgerkrieg, 1791–92, op cit, 300–306.

has to try to harmonize his or her own goals and interests, and must above all endeavour to act as though in a 'family'.

It is clear that this view mainly feeds on utopian ideas. What counts is that it was to be restated in the society of States, after decolonization and above all in the 1960s, when the necessity of a true 'community' in charge of all humanity and protecting the interests of everybody, especially the underprivileged, would be proclaimed. This has been very well demonstrated by R.J. Dupuy.[45] For the time being, we are still at the 'prospective' stage, or to repeat a term used by R.J. Dupuy, at the stage of a 'myth' or a 'utopia'; but little by little, this ideal works its way up to the world level and starts to be embodied into concrete institutions.

ii. International 'solidarity'

Another concept—closely linked to the one I have just illustrated—has emerged in the declarations of many revolutionaries without reaching the gestation stage; that is to say without becoming a fundamental postulate of revolutionary France. It is the principle according to which people ought to pursue *ideals of human solidarity*. It has been proclaimed by Robespierre,[46] Pétion de Villeneuve,[47] Clermont-Tonnerre,[48] Mirabeau l'aîné[49] and has found a particularly incisive resonance in the Abbé Grégoire's *'Déclaration du droit des gens'*.[50]

These ideals remained dormant for years, but they were revived within the international community after decolonization, when the 'emerging' countries started to insist on the necessity for the industrialized countries to repair so many past injustices, through some form of international solidarity. This postulate has been gradually translated into a general legal principle. We will find it again in one of the seven principles of the 1970 Declaration on Friendly Relations, where a 'duty of States to co-operate with one another in accordance with the Charter' is mentioned. As I have tried to show on another occasion,[51] this principle remained general and only imposed a duty to co-operate, without acquiring more incisive connotations. Nevertheless, the duty of solidarity is taking on a more concrete form in some other institutions; the seabed is, for instance, considered as a common heritage of mankind.

---

[45] R.J. Dupuy, *Communauté internationale et disparités de développement,* in *RCADI,* vol. 165, 21ff.

[46] National Assembly, 15 May 1790, in *Archives Parlementaires,* XV, 517.

[47] National Assembly, 17 May 1790, *ibid,* 542.

[48] National Assembly, 18 May 1790, *ibid,* 561.

[49] National Assembly, 25 August 1790, *Archives parlementaires,* XVIII, *ibid,* 263.

[50] Art. 3 laid down the following: *'Un peuple doit agir à l'égard des autres comme il désire qu'on agisse à son égard; ce qu'un homme doit à un homme, un Peuple le doit aux autres'.* Art. 4 established that *'L'intérêt particulier d'un Peuple est subordonné à l'intérêt général de la famille humaine',* *Moniteur Universel,* An III (Séance du 4 floréal) 333.

[51] A. Cassese, *International Law in a Divided World* (Oxford, 1986) 15–152.

iii. Respect for human rights

The French Revolution also enunciated a rather innovative view on the relationship between the individual and the State, as established in the 1789 Declaration of the rights of man and of the citizen (and in subsequent Declarations). Although the list of fundamental rights elaborated by the National Assembly was not new (some rather important texts had already been adopted in Great Britain and in the United States of America) and although it was primarily conceived to fit French society, no one can deny that the wording of the declaration had a scope and an expanding force of a *universal* nature.[52] In other words, this document had been conceived as applicable *to all men and all societies*. This was clearly stated by different members of the National Assembly, notably by Duport[53] (who talked about a declaration suitable for all men at all times and in all nations) and by the Count Mathieu de Montmorency.[54]

As everyone knows, the Declaration was trampled underfoot, even before the Terror, by the revolutionaries themselves.[55] Although it has been taken up by many modern States in their constitutional Charter, it has been violated several times by the authorities of these States. This has not prevented the Declaration itself (and even the preceding important texts) from gradually slipping into the field of international relations, where it made timid appearances before 1948. I should recall, by way of example, that the judgment of the Central American Court of Justice of 6 March 1906 in the case *Dr Pedro Andrez Fornos Diaz v The Government of the Republic of Guatemala*, defines the rights that a foreigner should enjoy and not be deprived of as 'international rights of man'.[56] As we

---

[52] See L. Olivi, 'De quelques conséquences de la Déclaration des Droits de l'Homme dans le domaine du droit des gens' in *Revue catholique des Institutions et du Droit*, (1889) vol. 17 97–108.

[53] For the text of M. Duport's statement, see *L'An I des Droits de l'Homme*, textes réunis par A de Baecke (Paris: Presses du CNRS, 1988) 131–132 (the quoted sentence is at 132).

[54] For the text of his statement see *L'An I des Droits de l'Homme*, op cit, 99–100. The universal scope of the Declaration of 1789 has been underlined by J. Rivero, *Les Libertés publiques*, I, (4th edn, Paris: PUF) 63. But already in 1901 J. Basdevant (op cit, 1) had described that *'Ils [les hommes de la révolution] entendent fonder les institutions françaises sur la raison et la raison étant universelle les principes qu'ils posent ont une portée absolue. Ils ne font pas une déclaration des droits du Français mais une Déclaration des droits de homme. Par suite les règles ainsi obtenues auront une portée non pas seulement nationale mais internationale'*. ('They (the men of the revolution) intend to base the French institutions on reason and reason being universal the principles which they pose have an absolute range. They do not make a statement of the rights of the French but a Statement of the rights of man. Consequently the rules thus obtained will have a significance not only national but international').

[55] The violation of some fundamental rights established in the Declaration had already started in 1789. It is sufficient to recall the decision taken on 29 October by the Constituent Assembly, which set the payment of a contribution of at least one Mark of silver (meaning 54 pounds) on top of the condition of possession of a 'land property', as a condition of eligibility for the legislative Assembly. As we know, this discrimination was strongly criticized by Robespierre (H. Guillemin, *Robespierre politique et mystique* (Paris: Ed. Du Seuil, 1987) 48, 57–58, 78 and 90) and was rightly underlined by Michelet (*Histoire de la Révolution française* (Paris: Pléiade, 1980) I, 185).

[56] In *American Journal of International Law*, vol. 3 (1909) 743 ('the fundamental rights and power of the human individual in civil life are placed under the protection of the principles governing the commonwealth of nations, as international rights of man').

can see, at this stage the individual still appeared in the international community only as a 'foreigner', that is to say a citizen from another State. However, an improvement can already be noticed as it was stated that some of these rights were 'international rights of man'. The decisive step would be taken when the individual is to be taken into consideration, no longer as a foreigner, or (after 1919) as a member of a minority group or a worker, but as a *human being*. This turning point—and this is not a coincidence—occurred after the Second World War, that is to say after a profound upheaval of the international community resulting from *racist dictatorships*. Following this cataclysm, there was a recognition of the need to establish *also* at the inter-State level these values that the French Revolution, and before it Great Britain and the United States of America, had proclaimed, thinking above all of their own societies.

Once again, a radical event occurring within the international community led to these principles, proclaimed almost two centuries earlier, being taken up at the world level. The seed previously sown finally had a chance to germinate and to blossom under the rise of a new traumatic event, no longer 'internal' or 'national', but precisely occurring within the international community.

iv. *The principle of democratic legitimization of states*

Among the principles that were supported by various revolutionaries without being repeated in general declarations adopted by legislative organs, one can find a principle according to which *only those States founded on people's sovereignty are internationally legitimized*. This concept has never been explicitly stated but one can deduce it from the declarations of many revolutionaries.[57] It actually constitutes a vital thread linking the thoughts of many of them. One can find an account of this in Article 4 of the draft Constitution presented by the Girondists to the Convention, on 15 and 16 of February 1793, according to which *'Dans ses relations avec les nations étrangères, la République française respectera les institutions garanties par le consentement de la généralité du peuple'.*[58]

This principle was only a logical implication of the thoughts of many revolutionaries, and was not raised to the rank of postulate in the foreign policy of the Revolution. For several years, it remained within the international community as if hidden or asleep; it has only regained force during the last decades. Indeed, nowadays, following the acceptance of many fundamental texts on human rights by States (especially the 1948 Universal Declaration and the 1966 Covenants), respect for human rights and for the political choices freely decided by the people have become criteria of *political legitimization of States*. This means that States that are not complying with these values, even if they fully enjoy the right

---

[57] W. Martens, *'Völkerrechtsvorstellungen des französischen Revolution...'* op cit, 305–306.

[58] 'In its relationships with foreign nations the French Republic will respect their institutions based on the general agreement of the people.' Text in Dugit, Monnier, Bonnard, Berlia, *Les Constitutions et les principales lois politiques de la France depuis 1789* (Paris, 1952) 33ff.

to be considered as legal subjects of the international community, still do not enjoy the political *legitimacy* that one can obtain only by respecting the values in question.

D. Conclusion

To conclude, I would like briefly to discuss the impact of the French Revolution upon the law of the international community; for that purpose, I will lay down three observations.

First of all, the Revolution did not alter the fundamental rules of the international community, and it did not affect the basic organization of this community (and in any event it would not have been able to do so). It has *hugely influenced the content* of some international principles, in several respects and in several directions. In some cases, States have gradually restructured some traditional norms, by giving them the foundation and the content defended by the Revolution. Such was the case for the principle of equal sovereignty of States, and for the prohibition of any interference in internal affairs. In other cases, subsequent traumatic events that occurred within the international community have led States to take up some concepts and ideas of the Revolution, upgrading them to the level of international norms. This was the case for the right to self-determination of peoples and for the prohibition of wars of aggression (and also to a lesser extent for the principle which legitimizes armed intervention in favour of oppressed peoples). Finally, in other cases, the Revolution planted a seed which bore fruit much later. 'Internal' revolutionary events arising within the international community recalled a number of subjects that initially arose in 1789. For instance, the concepts of universal community and of international solidarity, as well as the concept of respect for human rights, have become considered as necessary criteria for the political legitimization of States. In this case, the ideas of the Revolution have behaved like the waters of rivers in certain mountainous regions, which suddenly disappear underground and seem to vanish, only to later reappear much further downstream after a long subterranean journey, without having lost their force or their coolness, to produce once again their beneficial effects far away from their source.

My second observation seeks to emphasize that, besides the particular effect that I have just mentioned, the French Revolution has played another very important role. In the international community, one used to talk only about sovereigns, princes, monarchs, ruling dynasties, wars of conquest and transfers of territories. As Montesquieu wrote in the *Esprit des lois* (1748), 'The object of war is victory; that of victory is conquest; and that of conquest preservation. From this and the preceding principles all those rules are derived which constitute the law of nations'.[59] After the Revolution, the concepts of *individual, nation, people* and

---

[59] Montesquieu, *De l'Esprit des lois,* vol. I (Paris: Flammarion, 1979) 127.

equal sovereignty started to circulate among States. A new perspective then began to emerge: States did not consider themselves in their mutual relations as absolute potentates, but as simple managers of human communities (of individuals, of nations and of peoples).[60]

My third observation is intended to dismiss a possible objection to what I have argued so far. One may argue that, after a few years, the French Revolution had hastened to 'violate and trample underfoot' all the principles it advanced, sometimes in a spectacular way. The French Revolution violated the right to self-determination of peoples, it infringed the most basic human rights, it supported slavery in the colonies, it undertook wars of conquest, and it interfered in the internal affairs of other States, clearly trying to export the Revolution. Such behaviour would deeply undermine these principles, reducing them to mere utopias. To this possible objection, the following answer can easily be given. It is precisely because the influence of the French Revolution has been manifest, as I said earlier, by an impact, in the end, on the *content* of international law, or by a *dissemination of ideas and concepts* previously ignored or neglected by the sovereigns, that the denial of these principles and ideas in fact has not diminished their spreading force. In essence, Georges Sorel answered this objection long ago, even though in very general terms. Speaking about the force of myths in history, he observed in his reflections on violence that myths—the 'framing of a future indeterminate in time'—help societies to progress (or regress), even if these myths are only partially implemented, or even if not at all implemented. Writing specifically of the French Revolution, he writes: *'On peut reconnaître facilement que les vrais développements de la Révolution ne ressemblent nullement aux tableaux enchanteurs qui avaient enthousiasmé ses premiers adeptes; mais sans ces tableaux la Révolution aurait-elle pu vaincre? Le mythe était fort mêlé d'utopie... Ces utopies ont été vaines: mais on peut se demander si la Révolution n'a pas été une transformation beaucoup plus profonde que celles qu'avaient rêvées les gens qui, au XVIIIème siècle, fabriquaient des utopies sociales'.*[61] Nobody can deny the value, probably mythological and certainly utopian, of the concepts of the self-determination of peoples, human rights, respect for the sovereign equality of States and prohibition of wars of conquest. But it is precisely thanks to these huge myths that, gradually, the normative fabric of the international community and the effective behaviours of States have transformed until adopting the appearance and the contents that we find today in the world community—a community where today, without any

---

[60] Kant would write in 1795 that 'A state is not, like the ground which it occupies, a piece of property (*patrimonium*). It is a society of men' (I. Kant, *Projet de Paix Perpétuelle,* translation J. Gibelin, J. Vrin (eds) (Paris, 1982) 127).

[61] 'It is hard to deny that the true developments of the Revolution did not reflect the fascinating pictures which had created a great deal of enthusiasm in its first adepts. Would the Revolution ever have been successful without such grandiose pictures? The myth was very strongly influenced by utopias. These utopias have been nullified: however, one can certainly wonder whether the Revolution has not led to much more profound transformation than the changes dreamt by those who imagined the social utopias in the 18th Century', *Réflexions sur la violence* (Paris-Genève, 1981) 150–151.

doubt, 'the myth' in general, and above all the myths coming from the French Revolution, still play an enormous role.

3. The Soviet Revolution

A. General Observations

The French Revolution served as a breaking-off point in the international community, to the extent that, as I have already mentioned above, it introduced—nationally and internationally—concepts and ideas meant to gradually erode the conceptions prevailing among States.

The 1917 Revolution had the same effect.[62] Its main impact on the community of States lies in the fact that it was, for the first time, a breaking off of the ideological and political front that used to unify the members of the international community (including the non-Christian States such as the Ottoman Empire, Siam, China and Japan). For the first time a State asserted an ideology (the concept of the superiority of socialism over capitalism as well as the concept of proletarian internationalism closely linked to the preceding concept) which was radically contrary to the dominant ideologies. The international community thus became *un-homogeneous;* from 1917, two sides sprang up: the capitalist Western camp and the socialist camp. Later on, another traumatic event (the Second Word War) deepened the crisis by enlarging the socialist camp, and by creating a third camp, consisting of developing countries.

B. What the October Revolution Brought to International Law

i. *The principle of self-determination of peoples*

This principle, already vigorously proclaimed by Lenin in the 'January–February 1916 Theses' and then in the well-known 26 October 1917 Decree on Peace, was then officially taken up by Lenin himself and other Soviet political leaders in subsequent documents.[63]

When looking at the various declarations made at the time, it is clear that Soviet leaders have given three different meanings to the principle of self-determination.

---

[62] On the impact of the 1917 revolution on international law, see above all P.A. Steiniger, *Oktoberrevolution und Volkerrecht, eine popularwissenschaftliche Studie* (Berlin, 1967); W.A. Uschakow 'Volkerrechtliche Aspekte der grundung der USSR', in *Soviet Yearbook of International Law* (1972) 11–24; G.I. Tunkin, *Theory of International Law,* translation by W.E. Butler (London, 1974) 3–20; H. Kröger (ed.), *Volkerrecht, Lehrbuch,* I (Berlin, 1981) 86–93.

[63] On this principle and for reference to the different sources, see R. Arzinger, *Das Selbstbestimmungsrecht im allgemeinen Volkerrecht der Gegenwart* (Berlin, 1966) 44–78. See also 161–239 on the impact of the principle on modern international relations, P.A. Steiniger, *Oktoberrevolution und Volkerrecht,* op cit, 42–78; G.I. Tunkin, *Theory of International Law,* op cit, 7ff.

First of all, it is a principle that *deals with territories of sovereign States in instances of political or military conflicts:* from this point of view, the principle entails the prohibition of territorial annexations contrary to the will of the peoples in question.[64] In a way, it amounts to taking up the principle of self-determination proclaimed during the French revolution, already discussed above.

The principle is then proclaimed as an *anti-colonialist postulate:* in that sense, self-determination is to be understood as the right for peoples subjected to colonial rule to gain independence.[65] As laid down in 1922 by the Minister of Foreign Affairs, Chicherin: '. . .The World War has resulted in the intensification of the liberation movement of all oppressed and colonial peoples. World states are coming undone at the seams. Our international programme must bring all oppressed colonial peoples into the international scheme. The right of all peoples to secession or to home rule must be recognized. . .The novelty of our international scheme must be that the Negro and other colonial peoples participate on an equal footing [with Lenin's comment 'True!' in the margin (underlined)] with the European peoples in conferences, commissions and have the right to prevent [again, double underline] interference in their internal affairs. . .'[66]

The principle of self-determination was also conceived in a third manner: as *a principle according to which ethnic or national groups can legitimately and freely determine their destiny* by choosing to secede or to acquire a new and fully autonomous identity and structure. This principle was developed in several documents.[67] It was later confirmed and taken up in the different Soviet constitutions, from 1918 onwards. In the 1918 Constitution, the right to self-determination, including the right to secede for the different republics of the Union, was explicitly expressed.

The right to self-determination was nevertheless not accepted in other formulations, for instance as a principle of governmental democratic legitimization, i.e. a principle according to which people can freely decide upon and choose their public authorities. One could argue that this last meaning of the principle, although not explicitly formulated, could still be inferred from the general wording of this same principle.[68] If that is the case—which I very much doubt—it would

---

[64] See the Decree on Peace, in V.I. Lenin, *On the Foreign Policy of the Soviet State* (Moscow: Progress Publishers, 1968) 12.

[65] See Lenin, 1916 Theses, in *Selected Works* (London, 1969) 159–167; Report on the programme of the Party, March-April 1919, in Lenin *On the Foreign Policy...*, op cit, 141–142; V.I. Lenin ('Letter to G.V. Chicherin, March 14') [with notes on the margins of Chicherin's letter of 10 March 1922], *Collected Works*, vol. 45 (translation by Y. Sdobnikov (Moscow: Progress Publishers, 1970); this reprint, Lawrence and Wishart, London, n.d.) 506–511.

[66] V.I. Lenin ('Letter to G.V. Chicherin, March 14') [with notes on the margins of Chicherin's letter of 10 March 1922], *Collected Works*, vol. 45 (translation by Y Sdobnikov (Moscow: Progress Publishers, 1970); this reprint, Lawrence and Wishart, London, n.d.) 506–511.

[67] See for example the 1918 Declaration of the Rights of the Working and Exploited People, in which the right to self-determination of the Armenian people is explicitly stated: in Lenin, *On the Foreign Policy...*, op cit, 26; see also the report on the programme of the Party (March–April 1919), ibid 141–142.

[68] See Lenin, 1916 Thesis, in *Selected Works,* op cit, 141–142; 1922 Chicherin's letter, op cit, 506–511.

nevertheless be necessary to add that this fourth version of the principle is vague and uncertain in the ideological declarations of the socialist leaders. This is mainly because they gave more importance to the other meanings of the self-determination principle, in particular to the anti-colonialist one. Indeed, Lenin and the other revolutionary leaders were more interested in the 'self-determination of the working class' of all countries than in the self-determination of one people (and thus of other social classes as well).[69]

This said, it is important to underline that, as for the French Revolution, ideological declarations have not been followed by actual facts, at least the first and third meanings of the self-determination principle. Regarding anti-colonialism, one can note the remarkable coherence of the USSR and then the socialist states, mainly because this principle was objectively consonant with their political and ideological interests. During the October Revolution, the facts clearly challenged the principle of self-determination, both regarding the annexation of foreign territories (Latvia, Estonia and Lithuania for instance) and the national groups composing the USSR (the right to secession proclaimed by the different Soviet constitutions remained purely theoretical).

The effective denial of the principle should not only be attributed to political, economic and military considerations, even if those got the upper hand over ideology and self-determination. The possibility of a rejection of the self-determination principle is inherent in the socialist conceptions. It is notably clear in Lenin's article published in the *Pravda* on 21 February 1918. This article was written to challenge a peace treaty with Germany. The Germans notably suggested that several territories (Poland, Lithuania, a part of Latvia, Estonia and Byelorussia) be placed under their authority; Lenin thus dealt, in his article, with the issue of whether or not the cession of these territories would amount to treason towards the people living in these territories: 'Let us examine the argument from the standpoint of theory; which should be put first, the right of nations to self-determination, or socialism?' His answer was clear: 'Socialism should.' He then added: 'Is it permissible, because of a contravention of the right of nations to self-determination, to allow the Soviet Socialist Republic to be devoured, to expose it to the blows of imperialism at a time when imperialism is obviously strong and the Soviet Republic obviously weaker? No, it is not permissible—that is bourgeois and not socialist politics.'[70]

Leaving aside the effective rejection of these principles, what matters here is that the proclamation of the principle of self-determination—above all as an anti-colonialist principle—has had a critical influence on the foreign policy of States, on the mindset of political leaders in colonialist countries but also on

[69] This can be easily inferred from Lenin's Report on the programme of the Party (1919) already mentioned above, *On the Foreign Policy*, op cit, n 64.
[70] V.I. Lenin, 'The Revolutionary Phrase' [Pravda No. 31, 21 Feb 1918], *Collected Works*, vol. 27 (Feb–July 1918) (translation by C. Dutt; Moscow: Progress Publishers and Lawrence and Wishart, London, 1965; 1974).

international law. It is mainly thanks to the USSR that this principle was first accepted by the United Nations (even if it appeared in a toned-down version after the resistance of several Western countries)[71] and then gradually turned into a general principle of international law. It is important to underline that this principle only covers a limited part of the concept of democratic legitimization of governments, a concept that was absent from Soviet conceptions.[72]

ii. The principle of substantial equality among States

The Bolshevik revolution, in total harmony with the postulate of self-determination of peoples, asserted that not only all peoples, but also all States, should not be treated in a discriminatory manner, and that more generally, they were to be guaranteed more than mere legal equality. The sixth point of the propositions made by Adolf Joffe, leader of the Soviet delegation to the Brest–Litvosk Peace Conference (opened on 22 December 1917 and ended on 3 March 1918 with the conclusion of a peace treaty) laid out that '... The Russian delegation proposes that the contracting parties should condemn the attempts of stronger nations to restrict the freedom of weaker nations by such indirect methods as economic boycotts, economic subjection of one country by another, by means of compulsory agreements, restricting the freedom to trade with third countries, naval blockade without direct military purpose, etc. . . .'.[73]

Following this line, the USSR abolished in 1921, through a series of international agreements, the system of capitulations laid out in the previous treaties with Turkey and Persia; and in 1924 it did the same with China. The three agreements concluded by the Soviet State with the States mentioned above included the renouncement by the Soviet Union of all privileges inherent to the system of capitulations (consular jurisdiction, extra-territoriality, and so on).

These declarations have not substantially influenced the content of international law, for obvious political and military reasons. For instance, they have not prevented the USSR from accepting the UN Charter provision that gives a privileged position to the five permanent Members of the Security Council (Article 7§3). These declarations have nevertheless had an indirect influence: they have deeply inspired developing countries when reaching independence in the 1950–60s and they have strengthened these countries' aspirations. Of course, we have not yet reached the explicit and detailed legal prohibition of economic coercion or even the most subtle and ambiguous forms by which powerful countries can shape and influence weak countries' wills through economic mechanisms. But the arguments advanced by the Bolshevik revolution are the basis of

---

[71] See A. Cassese, in J.P. Cot and A. Pellet, *Commentaire de la Charte des Nations Unies* (Paris: Economica, 1985) 39–55.

[72] See A. Cassese, *The Right of Self-determination and Non-State Peoples.*

[73] *Soviet Documents on Foreign Policy,* ed Jane Degras, vol. I (1917–1924) (London: Royal Institute of International Affairs and OUP, 1951) 22.

the requests made by the least developed countries for the establishment of international economic conditions that are effectively fairer (the New International Economic Order in 1974) and for the creation of forms of international solidarity meant to rectify the current imbalance between powerful and weak countries. These forms of international solidarity are, for example, provided by international norms on the ocean floor as the common heritage of mankind.

In this field more than in any other, the October Revolution has sowed seeds that were not reaped by the USSR but whose fruits have been reaped by other States, in this case the underprivileged ones.

iii. Questioning the traditional content of international law

The October Revolution has had a much more significant effect in another— more general—field. For the first time in history, a member state of the international community explicitly rose up against numerous rules of this community for ideological reasons. The Soviet Union did not reject all international norms: it could not have done so without being viewed as an 'outlaw' or a 'pariah' in this community. It is obvious that every member of a social group has to accept at least some basic rules of communal life, if it does not want to be put in the position of an alien and hostile element of the group. In addition, numerous norms of the international community were to be useful for the USSR, for example the norms on respect for sovereign equality, on the immunity of State entities, on the immunities and privileges of diplomatic and consular agents and on the conclusion of treaties.

The USSR chose to adopt a two-faceted attitude towards the international rules it did not want to 'accept'. It first jettisoned a series of specific treaties concluded by the Tsarist government on the basis that the latter were only meant to protect the interest of landowners and Russian capitalists.[74] The USSR then—politically and ideologically—contested a series of general international norms that were— according to it—founded on 'capitalist interests'. An illustration can be found in the rules related to the expropriation or the nationalization of property and investments abroad or the norms re 'unequal treaties', where a weak contracting party is forced by a more powerful state to accept a treaty.

The October Revolution launched a general process of review and update of international law through this partisan challenge to traditional international law. The process was then critically boosted by the reorganization of the community after World War II and—above all—by the emergence of new States from 1950 onwards.

---

[74] See for instance, Lenin's 'Fourth Letter from Afar', 25 March 1917, in Lenin, *Collected Works,* XVIII (New York, 1929) 54–55; and the peace decree already referred to earlier, in Lenin, *On the Foreign Policy of the Soviet State,* op cit, 13.

4. Concluding Remarks

To summarize and conclude the considerations set forth above, four general comments can be made.

First of all, if the international community today recognizes some fundamental values, this is *notably*—and to a large extent—thanks to the two major revolutions that I have discussed here. These values are: respect for human beings; the concepts of nation and people; self-determination of peoples; solidarity between nations and people; real and non-fictive equality between individuals, groups and State entities.

The two revolutions have contributed to the profound *democratization* of the international community; in other words, to the transformation of this cluster of potentates and monarchs only attentive to dynastic battles, territorial conflicts, and attempting economic, political and territorial expansion, into a *genuine community*. The latter has two critical features. First, it is composed of governmental entities that handle human groups on the basis of a territory and strive to respect certain fundamental rights of the individuals, nations and people living on these territories. Secondly, representatives of human groups now also have a say in international dealings, at least to a certain extent: these are the movements of national liberation and individuals (no matter whether as persons or as representatives of ethnic, religious, cultural or racial minorities).

My second comment is that the values advanced by both revolutions are not antithetical; on the contrary, they complement and reinforce each other. The October Revolution took up and enriched the two main concepts launched during the French Revolution: the self-determination of peoples and the sovereign equality of States. In addition, even if it ignored to a certain extent the concept of human rights developed during the French Revolution, the October Revolution stood up towards a radical contestation of numerous traditional norms of the international community, following in that matter the guiding lines already opened up by France of greater respect for people and nations, and greater respect for the equality of States. My third point is that the impact of the two revolutions on international law has mainly been achieved by contributing to the dissemination of *ideas and conceptions* that have later influenced the content of numerous fundamental international rules.

Finally, their influence on the content and substance of the norms has been apparent *in concomitance* with or on *traumatic events* inherent to the international community: the two great world wars and the fundamental revolution in the composition of the international community prompted by the independence of people and countries which had until then been under colonial rule. These purely inter-State traumatic events have served as catalysts, provoking the crystallization of rules whose content had been defended by either revolution (or by both). These events have thus created the real historical conditions by which revolutionary ideas have been able to coagulate and take the form of international legal norms.

However, the opposite is also true, to the extent that these great world events peculiar to the international community were largely conditioned and encouraged by the two national revolutions. There is no doubt about this point as far as World War I is concerned. World War I broke out, among other things, because of the desire of various nations to rebel against the oppression of centralized States, who were not taking into account these nations; it ended up creating a new organization of Europe and of part of Asia. This organization was precisely based on the principle of self-determination launched by the French Revolution and taken up by the Soviet Revolution (self-determination as a criterion of legitimacy of territorial merger or dismemberment). To some extent, a similar phenomenon occurred during World War II. One can recognize the basic reasons for this war in the ideological and political conflicts that were also present during the October Revolution, as well as in the creation of opposing camps based on totalitarian ideologies. The conflict turned into a direct clash between States supporting ideals inherent to the French Revolution (liberty, equality) and authoritarian and racist States who would violate these ideals on a large scale. But the first merit of the suggestion laid out above is to be seen in relation to the social revolution that took place in the international community between 1950 and 1960. There is no doubt that the principle of self-determination of peoples, in the anti-colonialist meaning proclaimed by the October Revolution, served as a powerful weapon against colonial empires. From this point of view, this principle has thus served as 'the midwife of history', being a deciding factor to the birth of new international subjects.

As we can see, the three categories of events at the foundation of the changes and evolution of international law (world conflicts, international social revolutions and some national radical revolutions) that I mentioned in the introduction have interacted, causing modifications to international norms destined to leave definite marks on the life of the international community.

B. Classes of Wars and Belligerents

4. Wars of National Liberation and Humanitarian Law*

1. The Drive Towards the Assimilation of Wars of National Liberation to International Conflicts

It is common knowledge that as soon as the upsurge of national independence started in colonial territories in the early 1950s, liberation movements attempted to blow up the traditional distinction between 'international wars' and 'internal armed conflicts'. To this dichotomy they added a new category: 'wars of national liberation'. Admittedly the latter conflicts were not 'inter-state' clashes, yet in the opinion of liberation movements they did not fall within the class of civil strife either, for they actually amounted to international conflicts, with the consequence that all the rules of *jus in bello* ought to be applied to them.

The attempt to introduce this new category is one of the major novelties of the aftermath of World War II. To be sure, armed struggles of peoples under colonial domination are not a hallmark of this century. Suffice it to recall the fight of the American settlers against the British rule in the late 18th century, or the fight of Latin American countries against Spanish or Portuguese domination in the early 19th century. Furthermore, it is possible that the expression 'wars of national liberation' was used as early as the 19th century. However, the new struggles that started after World War II are remarkable, first, because they proliferated so rapidly and came to constitute a phenomenon of great magnitude and intensity, and, second, because 'national liberation' was now no longer merely a political concept, but was given a legal turn: indeed it was now claimed that these wars called for the application of rules commensurate with their importance and international dimension.

What political and ideological factors impelled liberation movements to demand the applicability of the whole of *jus in bello*? Arguably, there were three main motivations. First, if the State against which they were fighting was forced to concede that the rules of warfare applied to the conflict, this admission automatically entailed a conspicuous meta-legal consequence: the liberation

* Originally published in C. Swimarski (ed.), *Studies and Essays on International Humanitarian Law and Red Cross Principles in Honour of Jean Pictet* (Geneva, The Hague: M. Nijhoff, 1984) 313.

movement acquired international standing and a sort of legitimation, for it was no longer treated as a bunch of rebels fighting against the established authority; it could claim to be an international subject entitled to exercise rights and duties on the international level. The second possible motivation was legal in character but had important political implications. By acquiring the status of a party to an international armed conflict, the liberation movement was able to claim that its combatants should not be treated as bandits, liable to criminal punishment by the incumbent Government for the mere fact of having taken up arms in an armed insurrection; they were to be regarded as lawful belligerents (if of course they met the various requirements laid down in customary international law). Naturally, this consequence made a lot of difference to liberation movements. The third motivation was probably that liberation movements, being the weaker side in the armed struggle, had much to gain from the introduction of a modicum of humanity and legal restraint in the conduct of hostilities. In civil wars the actual conduct of hostilities is substantially left to the discretion of the contending parties, with the consequence that both insurgents and the civilian populations are likely to suffer most from the lack of legal control. By contrast, the rules governing international armed conflicts set a range of restrictions on the conduct of belligerents; this, no doubt, could prove beneficial both to the liberation movements and to the civilian population (it should not be forgotten that the former are usually keen to protect the latter from the adverse consequences of fighting and all the attendant hardships, if only because they have to rely on the population when conducting guerrilla warfare).

At the instigation of socialist and developing countries, in the 1960s and the early 1970s the UN General Assembly adopted a string of resolutions (ranging from res. 2383-XXIII of November 1968 to res. 3103-XXVIII, of December 12, 1973, no doubt the clearest and most noteworthy), proclaiming that wars of national liberation were to be treated as international conflicts proper. A number of *legal justifications* were propounded to bolster this political move. Among other things, it was claimed that the territories where liberation movements conducted their fight were not under the sovereignty of their opponents but constituted distinct and separate territories. It was also contended that liberation movements, being the holders of an international right to self-determination, possessed international status; hence they could not be equated with private individuals but were to be treated as international subjects proper. It was also suggested on many occasions (although the claim was subsequently toned down or dropped altogether) that liberation movements and the peoples for which they were fighting exercised an international right of self-defence against the aggression constituted by colonialism, racism or foreign occupation.

These claims were however rejected by Western countries which consistently held that wars of national liberation were not dissimilar from civil strife: if one looked at them dispassionately one could not help concluding that they possessed the same objective features as internal armed conflict (a group of persons take up arms against the central authorities and seek by dint of armed violence to wipe them out and gain control over the territory previously under the sway of those authorities). In the view of Western countries, upgrading one particular class of civil strife to the category of international conflict on account of the political motivations of liberation movements would mean the introduction of the 'just war' concept into international relations—a dangerous concept that was all the rage in the Middle Ages but was subsequently set aside with beneficial consequences for the humanitarian law of armed conflict. These and similar considerations led most Western States to vote against the General Assembly resolutions referred to above, although their opposition to some extent gradually dwindled with the decline of colonial domination.

2. The Application of Humanitarian Law

A. The 1949 Geneva Conventions

To what extent has the political drive referred to above led to a change in international legislation? In other words, what provisions of international humanitarian law can be regarded as applicable to wars of national liberation as a result of the pressure put by socialist and developing countries on the international community as a whole? Let us first consider the four Geneva Conventions of 1949 and then the Protocol I of 1977.

The contention has been made that under certain conditions wars of national liberation are governed by the four Geneva Conventions.[1] The Conventions, which are in principle open to States only, include two provisions regulating the possible accession to them, or their acceptance. The first is common Article 60/59/139/155, which provides for *accession* ('From the date of its coming in force, it shall be open to any Power in whose name the present Convention has not been signed, to accede to this Convention'). The other provision is common Art. 2, para. 3, which regulates the participation in the Conventions through *acceptance and actual application* ('Although one of the Powers in conflict may not be a party to the present Convention, the Powers who are parties thereto shall remain bound by it in their mutual relations. They shall furthermore be bound by the Convention in relation to the said Power, if the latter accepts and applies the provisions thereof'). It has been argued that the term 'Power' can also refer to liberation movements and that therefore the latter are entitled to become bound by the Conventions under one of the two aforementioned provisions.[2]

---

[1] G. Abi-Saab, Wars of National Liberation and the Laws of War, *Annales d'Etudes Internationales*, 1972, p. 104; J. Salmon, Les guerres de libération nationale, in A. Cassese (ed.), *The New Humanitarian Law of Armed Conflict*, Napoli, 1979, pp. 72–73; G. Abi-Saab, Wars of National Liberation in the Geneva Conventions and Protocols, RCADI, vol. 165, 1979-IV, pp. 400 ff.

[2] G. Abi-Saab, Wars of National Liberation in the Geneva Conventions and Protocols, op cit, pp. 400–401.

This view is open to criticism.[3] The whole context and the wording of the various provisions of the Geneva Conventions make it clear that when they mention 'Powers' they intend it to apply to States only. This is particularly evident in the case of the first of the two provisions mentioned above (in 1949, when the States framing the Conventions spoke of the possibility of a 'Power' signing them, they clearly had in mind States, and States only). This interpretation is borne out by subsequent practice. As stated in the ICRC Commentary to the First Geneva Convention, 'the invitation [to accede to the Conventions] is addressed [by the Swiss Government] to *all States* whether they are or are not parties to one of the earlier Conventions'.[4] The same interpretation is corroborated by the preparatory work. When the present text of common Art. 2, para. 3 was adopted by the 'Special Committee of the Joint Committee', the Rapporteur explained its rationale by observing among other things the following: 'The text adopted by the Special Committee . . . laid upon the Contracting State . . . the obligation to recognize that the Convention be applied to the non-Contracting adverse *State*, in so far as the latter accepted and applied the provisions thereof'.[5]

It therefore seems plausible to argue that in 1949 the States gathered at Geneva neither took wars of national liberation into account nor envisaged the possibility for liberation movements to become a contracting party to the Conventions or at any rate to be bound by them. Under the 1949 Geneva Conventions the only way a liberation movement might join the Conventions is by means of the 'special agreements' contemplated in common Art. 3, para. 3 ('The Parties to the [non-international armed] conflict should further endeavour to bring into force by means of special agreements, all or part of the other provisions of the present Convention'). In short, when the four Geneva Conventions were drafted the traditional dichotomy international/internal armed conflicts was still considered valid.

B. The Protocol I of 1977

In 1974, Third World and socialist countries managed to have the first session of the 1974–1977 Geneva Diplomatic Conference adopt a provision equating wars of national liberation with international conflicts. Once again, almost all Western countries cast a negative vote (the provision was adopted by 70 votes to 21 with 13 abstentions).

Interestingly, Western opposition to the provision gradually diminished during the Conference, so much so that when it was finally voted upon in 1977 in the plenary session, a general agreement emerged. This accounts for the proposal by

---

[3] For a detailed criticism of the main arguments put forward by G. Abi-Saab and taken up by J. Salmon, may I refer to a statement I made in 1976 (A. Cassese (ed.), *The New Humanitarian Law of Armed Conflict*, Proceedings of the 1976 and 1977 Conference, Napoli, 1980, pp. 26–27).

[4] J. Pictet, Commentary I, p. 408.

[5] Final Record of the Diplomatic Conference of Geneva, 1949, vol. II-B, p. 108 (emphasis added).

the US delegate that the relevant provision be adopted by consensus,[6] a proposal not upheld because of the Israeli request that a vote be taken.[7] The result of the vote was 87 in favour, one against (Israel) and 11 abstentions (Western countries such as the UK, the USA, the FRG, Canada, Italy, France, Spain, Ireland, Monaco, Japan, as well as Guatemala). The provision adopted became Art. 1, para. 4, which lays down as follows:

> The situations referred to in the preceding paragraph [i.e. international armed conflicts] include armed conflicts in which peoples are fighting against colonial domination and alien occupation and against racist régimes in the exercise of their right of self-determination, as enshrined in the Charter of the United Nations and the Declaration on Principles of International Law concerning Friendly Relations and Co-operation among States in accordance with the Charter of the United Nations.

The drafting history of this rule makes it clear that most of its framers intended to word it in such a way as to make it exclusively applicable to the three classes of situations it explicitly provides for. This, in particular, is patently demonstrated by the fact that the proposal made by a group of developing countries (plus Australia and Norway), which merely referred to the UN Declaration on Friendly Relations and therefore left much leeway for an extensive interpretation of the category of wars of national liberation,[8] was subsequently merged with the proposal of some socialist States (plus Algeria, Morocco and Tanzania), which instead propounded the three clear-cut situations.[9] Furthermore, it is apparent from the legislative history of the provision that even the three categories were intended as unsusceptible of a liberal interpretation (it is well known that while a previous proposal spoke of peoples fighting against 'alien domination', at the behest of five Latin American countries this expression was changed into 'alien occupation',[10] which no doubt has a much narrower scope and substantially refers to belligerent occupation or at any rate military occupation by a foreign State). In short, at least the majority of the framers of Art. 1, para. 4, manifestly intended to 'issue a legal command' having a well-defined and very narrow field of application.

It should however be pointed out that after the rule was adopted in plenary, the delegate of Australia made an important declaration: he stated that Australia had decided to support the provision, for it considered that the enumeration of the three categories was not exhaustive, but merely exemplary, with the consequence that in his view Art. 1, para. 4, could also cover other classes of wars of national liberation contemplated by the principle of self-determination of peoples as set forth in the

---

[6] Official Records of the Diplomatic Conference on the Reaffirmation and Development of International Humanitarian Law Applicable in Armed Conflicts: Geneva 1974–77 (henceforth: CDDH etc.), CDDH/SR. 36, para. 52.

[7] CDDH/SR. 36, para. 53.

[8] CDDH/I/11.

[9] CDDH/I/5.

[10] CDDH/I/71 (Argentina, Honduras, Mexico, Panama, Peru).

various UN instruments.[11] This declaration, which set the stage for a less restrictive construction, has been taken up in the legal literature[12] and might gradually lead to the acceptance of a liberal interpretation of the provision under discussion.

We should now ask ourselves whether the adoption of Art. 1, para. 4, was a positive step from the viewpoint of the development of humanitarian law, or whether it was instead merely a political victory for the Afro-Asian and socialist majority, with adverse consequences for humanitarian law (as was indeed claimed by some Western States).

I shall confine myself to two remarks. First, it is not true that the rule adopted at Geneva introduced much subjectivity, uncertainty and ambiguity in the laws of war. Indeed, as has been pointed out,[13] one of the two basic elements of that rule—namely the Governments against which a war of national liberation is fought—is objectively defined: colonial regimes, racist Governments or Governments occupying the territory of another country. Admittedly, the other basic element of the definition, i.e. the liberation movements fighting against one of those regimes, is not clearly identified. Consequently, under that rule any movement or rebellious group struggling against one of the three aforementioned classes of Governments may claim that it is engaged in an international armed conflict. Yet, the extreme narrowness of the three categories (defined by the reference to the class of regime) should dispel any fear that the broad category of 'national liberation movements' might lead to Art. 1, para. 4, having an excessively wide field of application.

Arguably, the major flaw of the rule is not its alleged looseness. Its basic deficiency is, instead, that it is 'dated', in that it only refers to three situations that are bound to disappear in the near future. This deficiency might *to some extent* also be attributed to the Western delegations, not because they originated the present formula (which, as stated above, was mainly authored by the socialist countries), but because they failed to negotiate with the majority (which had also hardened into a highly inflexible attitude), in order to improve the wording eventually adopted. The improvement could have resulted in slackening the formula so that it could be applied less tightly to those three categories of situation. The efforts of the more progressive Western countries could have helped to give wider scope to the rule, so as to include wars for self-determination conducted by peoples or minorities who are gravely and systematically oppressed by authoritarian regimes—even if these regimes are not racist like that of South Africa, are not colonialist like that of Portugal (when the African territories under Portuguese

---

[11] CDDH/SR. 22, para. 14.

[12] See the statement by J. Salmon in A. Cassese (ed.), *The New Humanitarian Law of Armed Conflict*, Proceedings, op cit, pp. 34–35. May I also refer to the views I expressed in 1977 (A. Cassese (ed.), *The New Humanitarian Law of Armed Conflict*, Proceedings; op cit, p. 245, where I referred *inter alia* to statements made by the representatives of the PLO and of the Socialist Republic of Vietnam in the Geneva Conference). For a similar and authoritative view, which strongly relies on the Australian statement, see G. Abi-Saab, in RCADI, op cit, pp. 398 and 432–433.

[13] C. Lysaght, The Attitude of Western Countries, in A. Cassese (ed.), *The New Humanitarian Law of Armed Conflict*, Napoli, 1979, p. 351.

dominion had not yet gained independence) and do not carry out a military occupation like that of Israel in Arab territories.

To be sure, this widening of the scope of Art. 1, para. 4, would have had a drawback: the rule would have been rendered more open to subjective interpretation.
Indeed, the class of regimes against which a liberation movement must fight in order
to be regarded as engaged in an international conflict would have become less clear-
cut than it is now. On this score however, two arguments may be put forward.

First, one could have set certain basic requirements which a liberation movement must fulfill in order to claim the applicability of Protocol I. Thus, for
instance, one could have required a certain control over the territory, some degree
of organization and above all the ability to comply with the provisions of the
Protocol (e.g., in matters relating to the protection of civilians or the treatment
of war prisoners). Furthermore, one could have specified the (fourth) category
of wars of national liberation falling under the rule by pointing to the features a
central Government should display in order for a rebellious group to claim that
it is exercising its right to self-determination (thus, one might have pointed to the
existence of a consistent pattern of gross and reliably attested violations of human
rights, amounting to a denial of the people's right to freely determine its—internal
or external—political and economic status).

Secondly, from a *strictly humanitarian* standpoint, extending the applicability
of Protocol I to a larger category of armed conflicts could not but appear positive.
Such an extension would involve the application of a greater number of humanitarian rules to these conflicts, and hence would mean greater safeguard of human
life. Of course, this also means that combatants are not longer considered common law criminals but lawful combatants, and are exempt from punishment
for the mere fact of fighting against the central government. But is this really so
bad? Is not what counts the fact that all those who participate in armed conflicts
behave in conformity with international law, without committing war crimes or
crimes against humanity? By considering wars of national liberation, other than
those falling under Art. 1, para. 4, as simple internal conflicts one neither exorcises
such wars nor brings them to a more rapid end. One merely places fewer restrictions on violence and thus attenuates to a much lesser extent the bitterness and
cruelty of armed conflict. It may seem difficult for a State to treat insurgents fighting for self-determination as lawful combatants rather than as criminals; but it
must be borne in mind that the counterpart to such treatment is greater protection for the civilian population, a much more extensive restriction on the methods
and means of warfare and thus much greater humanitarian protection for all those
embroiled in the armed conflict. Hence it seems to me that several humanitarian considerations should have made the solution advocated here acceptable, even
though the classification of an internal conflict as a war of national liberation is not
rigidly and surely predetermined by the rules, but is achieved mainly on the basis of
various elements, including the goals of the rebels. Of course, this solution implies
that only a few of the numerous internal armed conflicts could be elevated to the

rank of international wars; but this is already a substantial step towards broadening humanitarian protection. Although the choice is based on political criteria, they express the present trends and political orientations of the majority of States. Why must international rules not make choices on the basis of political criteria? Why must they claim instead to be inspired by allegedly 'neutral' considerations?

3. Art. 1, Para. 4, of the 1977 Protocol and Customary International Law

Let us now look into a very important issue, namely the question whether Art. 1, para. 4, has merely a contractual value, with the consequence that it only binds the States which ratify the Protocol, or whether instead its adoption has generated a *general rule* going beyond the conventional bonds instituted by the Protocol.

Despite the result of the vote taken when the provision was adopted in 1977, it is apparent from the declarations made by various countries that in actual fact only one State, namely Israel, totally rejected the rule. Those which abstained voiced misgivings about the possibility of applying the provision without difficulties and differences of opinion; they challenged the political and practical wisdom of the rule; however, they did not dismiss it out of hand as inapplicable in the future. Italy, for instance, stated that wars of national liberation were 'indefinable from an objective point of view'. The inclusion of a conflict in the category depended on a 'largely subjective element: the aim of the struggle. That factor seriously prejudiced the uncontroversial application of the rules of international law, since it completely blurred the borderline between international and non-international armed conflicts';[14] in the view of Italy the rule 'could not serve the legitimate interests of peoples, since it rendered uncertain both the legal system applicable to their struggle and the guarantees to which those peoples were entitled'.[15]

The UK delegation was less critical. It stated that it still had 'certain doubts' about the rule,[16] primarily for reasons of law, that is because the rule 'introduced the regrettable innovation of making the motives behind a conflict a criterion for the application of humanitarian law'.[17] These considerations were substantially echoed by Spain.[18] France stressed that 'the lack of criteria for a precise distinction' between the various classes of armed conflict 'was bound to be a constant source of trouble and confusion both legally and politically'.[19] Ireland pointed out that although it fully sympathized with the aims behind the rule, it nevertheless regretted that 'a clearer and more precise definition' of the conflicts had not been produced.[20] Finally, the FRG put forward two criticisms: first, the criteria

[14] CDDH/SR. 36, para. 77.
[15] CDDH/SR. 36, para. 78.
[16] CDDH/SR. 36, para. 86.
[17] CDDH/SR. 36, para. 83.
[18] CDDH/SR. 36, pp. 63–64.
[19] CDDH/SR. 36, para. 91.
[20] CDDH/SR. 36, para. 112.

laid down in the rule lent themselves 'to arbitrary, subjective and politically motivated interpretation'; secondly, they were chosen 'rather with a view to short-term political problems and objectives' and consequently did not fit well into a legal instrument 'intended to be of long-term value'.[21]

It is apparent from these statements that the few States which voiced misgivings about the rule were not motivated by strong opposition to it, but rather considered that the rule was *bad law*. Arguably, the result of the vote and the tenor of the 'reservations' entered by some States make it clear that even the latter States had eventually come to accept that the rule represented *a new law of the international community*—although, as I have just emphasized, in their view it was not good law.

Another important factor supporting the *general* character of the rule is that at least three delegations (two of them from the Western area) underscored that the provision actually embodied a general norm binding on all States, in that it codified a previous practice. Thus, the delegate of Egypt stated that:

International practice on the universal, regional and bilateral levels had established beyond doubt the international character of wars of national liberation. The purpose of the amendment which had been adopted as para. 4 of Art. 1 had not been to introduce a new and revolutionary provision, but to bring written humanitarian law into step with what was already established in general international law, of which humanitarian law was an integral part. His delegation therefore considered that the importance of the article lay in narrowing future divergencies in interpretation rather than in introducing new solutions.[22]

The delegate of Greece pointed out that:

Para. 4 was fully in accordance with modern international law as expressed in the United Nations Charter and as it had been applied during recent years.[23]

Commenting on the rule, the delegation of Australia declared that:

This development of humanitarian law is the result of various resolutions of the United Nations, particularly resolution 3103 (XXVIII), and echoes the deeply felt wish of the international community that international law must take into account political realities which have developed since 1949. It is not the first time that the international community has decided to place in a special legal category matters which have a special significance.[24]

These declarations are important both *per se* and also because no other delegation felt it necessary to challenge them. The conclusion is therefore warranted that in 1977 there emerged at the Conference general consensus to the effect that wars of national liberation falling within the three classes mentioned in Art. 1, para. 4, were to be regarded as international armed conflicts. It seems however that the consensus solidified around the *literal and strict interpretation* referred to above, not around the

---

[21] CDDH/SR. 36, p. 61.
[22] CDDH/SR. 36, paras 70–71.
[23] CDDH/SR. 36, para. 122.
[24] CDDH/SR. 36, p. 62.

liberal construction propounded by Australia (see para. 2 above). The general consent consolidated and gave shape to an emergent customary rule, evolved in the UN, that could not crystallize as a fully-fledged international norm until the Western countries (one of the three major segments of the international community) came to adhere to it. The adoption of Art. 1, para. 4, testified to the formation of a rule binding on all the States participating in the Conference (irrespective of whether or not they ratify the Protocol), save for Israel, which consistently rejected the provision.

Against the foregoing considerations one might object that in point of fact Western States refrained from opposing the provision in 1977 not because they intended to abide by it but only because they planned either to refrain from ratifying the Protocol or, in case of ratification, to enter a reservation on the provision. To this possible objection it is easy to rebut that if this were so, one fails to understand why Western States that voted against the rule in 1974 abstained or even voted for it in 1977; if they were opposed to it, they ought to have voted against it again in 1977. In fact the change in attitude of the Western countries had been brought about by two factors: first, the gradual disappearance of colonial empires, and the consequent removal of a major bone of contention; secondly, their becoming convinced that after all the rule in question was not dangerous for humanitarian law since it safeguarded all the basic principles of this law. This motivation came out with great clarity in the statements of the British and Japanese delegations.[25]

4. *Jus in bello* in Wars of National Liberation

The fact that Art. 1, para. 4, embodies a rule of customary law is not devoid of practical consequences on the legal plane. It follows from this rule that States are enjoined to apply to the categories of wars of national liberation it contemplates at least the fundamental principles of *customary law* on the conduct of hostilities and protection of war victims governing inter-State conflicts. Consequently, States are duty-bound to apply to wars of national liberation both the most basic customary rules existing before 1977 and those evolved as a result of the Geneva Diplomatic Conference.

One might object that this conclusion has only theoretical value, for in fact the two major countries against which Art. 1, para. 4, was actually aimed, to wit Israel and the Republic of South Africa, did not become bound by it, the former on account of its explicit 'opting out', the latter primarily because it did not participate in the final session of the Geneva Conference (it took part in the 1974 session solely, and of course cast a negative vote when the rule was adopted). Consequently even the substantive rules of customary law on warfare would not apply to the struggles opposing the PLO to Israel, SWAPO to Namibia and the various South African liberation movements to South Africa. However, international rules often have a significance transcending their legal

---

[25] As regards the British 'reservations', see CDDH/SR. 36, paras 84–86; as far as the Japanese objections are concerned, see CDDH/SR. 36, para. 105.

force; they possess an 'agitational' or 'rhetorical' value that explains why States are so eager to enact them despite the fact that the rules may have scant effectiveness as legal standards of behaviour. *Qua* 'rhetorical' values they can serve the useful purpose of making it possible to expose the conduct of States that do not live up to them. Art. 1, para. 4, however, has a legal scope too. It is not confined to the occurrences in which the two aforementioned States are involved; it can apply to other, fresh situations as well, witness the Soviet occupation of Afghanistan, which no doubt comes within the purview of the rule although the USSR has not ratified the Protocol and will probably refrain from doing so in the near future, as well as the Indonesian occupation of East Timor or the Vietnamese occupation of Kampuchea. To all these situations both Art. 1, para. 4, and the general principles on warfare that it renders operative, should be deemed applicable. If in point of fact it has not been applied, this cannot be taken to mean that States do not feel bound by it. For, in the aforementioned instances the States concerned, firstly, claimed that they were not faced with a war of national liberation and, secondly, found various legal justifications for their using military force. In the cases of Afghanistan and Kampuchea, the intervening States have claimed that they had been requested by the lawful authorities to enter the country to put down insurgency or foreign interference; in the case of East Timor, Indonesia has claimed that the island is in fact under its sovereignty and that therefore the fighting there is merely a case of civil strife. Thus, the general rule of wars of national liberation has not been deemed applicable for the simple reason that in the opinion of the States concerned the requisite circumstances were not present. This only proves that although the general rule has undisputedly evolved, the lack of any central agency capable of pronouncing on its concrete application greatly weakens its purport.

It should be added that those provisions of Protocol I which do not crystallize or reflect general rules but have merely contractual force (in particular the second sentence of Art. 44, para. 3 of Protocol I),[26] apply to wars of national liberation only if two conditions are met: (i) the (colonial, racist or occupying) Power against which the war is conducted is a party to the Protocol; and (ii) the national liberation movement fighting for self-determination makes the declaration provided for in Art. 96, para. 3, by which it undertakes to apply the four Geneva Conventions of 1949 and the Protocol.[27] Plainly, the first requirement is most unlikely to be met. It follows that only general rules on warfare will apply. In particular, as the whole of Art. 44, para. 3, of the Protocol I has not yet turned into a customary norm, irregular combatants fighting in wars of national liberation are to meet the requirements laid down in the first sentence of Art. 44, para. 3.[28]

[26] On this point may I refer to my paper Regular and Irregular Combatants (unpublished).
[27] On the requirements that national liberation movements should meet in order to be entitled to make the declaration provided for in Art. 96, para. 3, see the penetrating remarks of G. Abi-Saab, Wars of National Liberation in the Geneva Conventions and Protocols, op cit, pp. 407 ff.
[28] Under Art. 44, para. 3 (first sentence), 'freedom fighters' must 'distinguish themselves from the civilian population while they are engaged in an attack or in a military operation preparatory to an attack'.

5. Civil War and International Law*

1. Spreading of Civil Wars

In his 'Philosophical Dictionary', Voltaire wrote that together with 'starvation and plague', war constitutes one of the 'three most famous ingredients of this lowly world'. This 'ingredient' knows various forms, but one of its cruellest and most common expressions comes in the form of civil war. Civil wars have always existed. One can mention the war that opposed American colonists to the British colonial power between 1774 and 1783 as one of the bloodiest internal conflicts of the eighteenth century, and also the conflicts that sprung up against Spanish and Portuguese rule for the same reasons between 1810 and 1824, the American civil war of 1861–1865, and the numerous insurrections that took place on the European continent in the nineteenth century. More recently, after the Russian Revolution of 1917 and the Spanish civil war of 1936–39, serious internal armed conflicts have devastated the Congo (1960–61), Indonesia (1961–68), Yemen (1962–69), South Vietnam (1964–74), Western Pakistan (1972–73), Nigeria (1967–70), Northern Ireland (since 1969), as well as Nicaragua, El Salvador and Lebanon, where conflicts are still ongoing. Likewise, internal disturbances of significant scope have occurred in several countries, including Hungary (1956) and Czechoslovakia (1968).

It is clear from the historical landmarks mentioned above that no continent has been spared from internal armed conflicts and serious internal disturbances. What is more worrying though is that, for various historical and political reasons which I shall discuss later, internal conflicts have now become more numerous than international conflicts and they tend to be more prevalent in Third World countries.

2. Rarity of International Norms on Civil Wars

The most striking aspect of the international law on civil wars is the rudimentary nature of the existing rules on the issue. Whilst *armed conflicts between States* are regulated by many customary norms and treaties, *internal conflicts* have mostly remained under-considered. The main reasons for such a blatant divide require some reflection.

One particular reason for this state of affairs deals with the manner by which international law is made. International law remains the creation of States, and

* Originally published in French, 'La guerre civile et le droit international', in *Revue générale de droit international public* (1986) 553.

States act internationally through their own institutional organs, that is to say, mostly through their governments. Entities other than States (in particular peoples, individuals and international organizations) contribute only marginally to the making of international law. States remain the main actors on the international scene. The twilight of the Gods has not yet arrived! Because international law has mostly been made by States, the incentive to develop a body of law limiting States' discretion is limited, especially with respect to the most constitutionally traumatic of events: civil war. A civil war is like an injury that can lead the State either to its death, to a complete regeneration (for instance, where rebels win the war or form a revolutionary government), or to its fragmentation into several new States. So why should States be expected to set international limits to their ability to defend themselves against an internal enemy, against the sudden eruption of a cancer that could destroy them at any time? Where a civil war has erupted, the utmost concern of the State is to subdue the rebellion at its earliest stage or, where this fails, to prevent it from spreading and leading to the death of that State.

In addition, there are intrinsic reasons, that is, reasons that are inherent in the very nature of civil wars. Civil wars are *asymmetrical* conflicts.

Asymmetrical: first, in the most obvious sense—that is to say, opposing parties (the legitimate government and the insurgents), as a general rule, are not on an equal footing: on the one side is the State with all its might, its armed forces and its traditional apparatus, whilst on the other side are rebels with the most rudimentary organization and often very limited control over their territory.

Asymmetrical: secondly, in a more profound way. War legitimizes certain types of conduct which would otherwise be regarded as unacceptable. As H. Bergson once noted, in times of war 'murder and plunder as well as treacherousness, fraud, and lies not only become permissible; they become meritorious actions.'[1] The use of force to physically remove the Other—which connotes the earliest stages of civilization and is thus normally banned from civil society in times of peace—becomes once again an acceptable way *to relate to one another*. The natural consequence of this situation is that—in wars between States—belligerents realistically accept that the opposing soldiers are licensed to fight and kill, which is why they regard enemy soldiers not as criminals but as legitimate combatants. If they are captured by their adversaries, they will not be punished for taking up arms against the State against which they fought or for killing its soldiers, but will be entitled to the status of prisoners of war. This applies in the context of international armed conflict.

Conversely, in time of civil wars, the legitimate government considers armed rebellion to be a serious offence and treats insurgents as common criminals who have violated the core principles of the constitution. The legal government permits its own armed forces to kill rebels but does not consider the latter authorized

---

[1] H. Bergson, *Les deux sources de la morale et de la religion* (Paris: PUF, 1932) 26.

to kill regular forces. There is thus a colossal imbalance. On one side there is a belligerent who sees himself as the unique legitimate force authorized to kill and who regards any murder committed by him as a just and licit act; and on the other side there is a belligerent (the rebel) who is aware that he is perceived by the opposite party as a common criminal.

The consequence of this double asymmetry is that civil wars are *more barbaric and cruel* than wars between States, mainly because the two parties are not on an equal footing. States have thus not seen fit to create international restraints, so as to have free rein to fight potential rebels.

The third reason for the rarity of international norms applicable to civil wars is one of a historical and political nature. As I have already mentioned, civil wars usually spread further than international conflicts, in particular in Third World countries.

There are two reasons for this. On one hand, numerous African, South American or Asian countries are composed of ethnic groups in conflict, and the structures of the respective States are both weak and rigid. They do not rely on a traditional and deep-rooted civil foundation, unlike Western countries. Even if, in Western countries, civil societies are often composed of many ethnic groups and minorities who coexist either with difficulty or without peace, there are nevertheless many channels of mediation between the community and the state apparatus. This allows the State smoothly to adapt to the endeavours of the many human communities.

The second reason is that the danger of a nuclear catastrophe has pushed the two superpowers to freeze their nuclear weaponry and to conduct ideological wars either through political channels or third parties. Wars are thus either conventional wars stirred up or supported by one or the other superpower, or civil wars masterminded by great powers to the point where they are defined as 'wars by proxy'. Great powers supply arms and ammunitions, logistical support and often even 'military advisers'.

It might be expected that the increasing number of civil wars would bring States to adapt law to reality and to enact international norms that would curb a frequent and dangerous phenomenon.

Once again, the reaction of the States has been contrary to what any sensible person would expect. The majority of States, indeed Third World countries, i.e. the States suffering the most from civil wars and from enormous international military and political conditioning, are those who are reluctant to accept any international norm on the issue. According to them, the creation of new international norms would automatically legitimize the intervention of the international community in their sovereign domains and would make internal unrest worse.

I will return to this point. For now, I simply wish to highlight the fundamental reasons for international law's lack of interest in this critical issue.

3. How International Law Takes into Account Civil Wars

These wars have gained importance on the international plane in three respects.

One: from the perspective of the international rights and obligations of Third States to the State where the armed conflict breaks out. From this perspective, international law is very simple: it prohibits third parties from providing assistance to rebels whereas it allows them to assist legitimate governments. Here again we have an eloquent illustration of the fact that international norms are created by States to accommodate their own interests.

Two: the international personality of rebels. When and under what circumstances can rebels claim to be acting as subjects of the international community? In other words, when can rebels put forward rights and international claims and be bound to respect the obligations deriving from international rules?

International norms on this subject are extremely uncertain and vague. They do not establish with certainty the reasons and the circumstances in which rebels, once a group of bandits, become subjects of international law; nor do they ascertain the effect of potential international recognition from States.

The only thing to say is that if the civil war continues, if the insurgents steadily control a major part of the national territory and some States recognize this control, then the rebels acquire some international rights, for instance the right to make treaties; they also assume some obligations, for instance the obligation to protect Third States' citizens on the territory they control.

As we can see, the uncertainty on the issue—which is probably deliberate—is such that one is led to think that in practice States have the last word.

Finally, the third aspect concerns the conduct of hostilities, i.e. the course of civil wars: it is in this feature that international norms have developed in a less random way, because, in spite of States' reticence, it is above all in this sector that there is the greatest need to intervene, in order to stop the most barbarous acts. It is on this point that I will fix my attention.

4. *Jus in Bello Interno*: The Traditional Law

The distinction between traditional international law and modern international law must be highlighted. In this context, traditional law dates from the birth of the international community (around the conclusion of the Treaty of Westphalia 1648) to the Spanish civil war (1936–1939). The modern law begins at that point and continues until now.

Traditional law was at least relatively clear and simple. Civil wars were a matter of internal affairs, as would be, for example, the careers of university professors or the organization of popular fairs in villages. No other State could look into the internal issues of a State where serious and tragic events such as a civil war were taking place. The only international norm which deviated from this state of affairs was that imposing the obligation on Third States not to provide assistance to rebels, as mentioned earlier.

However, the international community's wilful ignorance of a phenomenon that had serious repercussions, at least on some States, was not total.

States gradually admitted (in particular around the middle of the nineteenth century) that in extreme circumstances, it was possible to bring an internal armed conflict to the level of an international conflict, with the consequence of enforcing the customary norms applicable to wars between States. This result was reached through the 'recognition of belligerency' that could be granted either by Third States or by the legitimate government. It is clear that the government's stance on the issue was decisive; it is only when the government decided to enforce the norms on international conflicts that the insurgents could be considered as legitimate belligerents.

The reasons for recourse to the 'recognition of belligerency' are manifest. When a civil war has grown too large or has become too serious to remain as an internal rebellion, it is in the very interest of the legitimate government to internationalize the conflict. Yet, it would be erroneous to think that this internationalization often took place. In fact, there are very few occasions of recognition of belligerency, the most notorious being the American Civil War (1861–1865). According to some authors, the last case is the Boer War (1899–1902) in which the rebellion rose up against the British dominion. However, this conflict should be considered as an international conflict from its outset and thus should not be mentioned as an example of 'recognition of belligerency'.

5. The Evolution of Contemporary Law

A. The First Phase (1936–1939)

Modern international law on this topic was born, as I have already mentioned, during the Spanish civil war, and proceeded to go through three main stages. The first was the Spanish civil war, the second was the 1949 normative revision, and the third corresponds to the reaffirmation and the development of humanitarian law in 1977. I will examine each of these phases in turn to highlight what progress was accomplished.

During the Spanish civil war, a new means of warfare, aerial warfare, already successfully employed during the war between Italy and Turkey (1911–1912) and World War I, gained momentum. The German air force first, but also the Italian air force, brought death and destruction especially among the civilian population. The importance and the scope of the massacres pushed the international community to go beyond the Pontius Pilate attitude of indifference and to adopt a clear position. The traditional process by which an internal armed conflict was transformed into an international one was, as discussed earlier, the 'recognition of belligerency'. The Republican Spanish government refused to undertake this process because, in its opinion, this would have brought international legitimacy to the pro-Franco insurgents. As for other States, it is to be remembered that France, Great Britain and the United States supported the principle of non-intervention of European powers. Great Britain asserted, notably through its Secretary of State to the House of Commons in 1937, that the 'recognition of belligerency' could not be granted because this concept—in its traditional form—could not be applied in a situation where hostilities had lost their 'civil war' nature because of the illegitimate intervention of foreign States. The Soviet Union was also opposed to this recognition, stating that it would be equivalent to taking a positive stand in favour of the insurgents.

In 1937, the Nyon Agreement on non-intervention (an agreement that patently favoured the rebels by engaging the contracting parties, among other things, not to use the right to assist the legitimate government) was signed. In the preamble, the contracting parties specifically stated that they were unwilling to admit the right of either party to the conflict in Spain to exercise belligerent rights.

Faced with the necessity of setting up legal limitations to a war which was becoming increasingly inhumane and gradually closer to an international war, but unwilling to choose between leaving the conflict in the ambit of Spanish national law or legally assimilating the conflict, *in all respects*, to a real international conflict, the parties to the conflict and third-party States progressively adopted a *third solution*. They ended up enforcing a series of *specific* international norms applicable to armed conflicts between States. As a consequence, the pro-Franco insurgents remained, in the eyes of the Republican government, a group of rebels who could be held responsible under the Spanish criminal code and who did not enjoy the status of legitimate belligerents. Nevertheless, in certain fields, they were considered capable of taking on international obligations. This may seem contrary to the logic and strictness of the law, but this situation was the result of both political and humanitarian considerations.[2]

States, in deciding to apply some international norms to the Spanish civil war, expressed the legal conviction that these rules should be applied to all internal armed conflicts with the same characteristics of intensity and length as the Spanish war. We can conclude that by the end of the 1930s far-reaching international norms on internal armed conflicts were created and these norms were substantially modelled on the ones applicable to inter-State conflicts.

The Spanish civil war thus represented a watershed in the legal conceptions of the international community. From then on, we were engaged in a new path, one departing from the traditional way which was characterized by an unavoidable dilemma: the armed conflict was either completely ignored or was upgraded to be

[2] On the customary rules emerging during the Spanish civil war, see my article 'The Spanish Civil War and the Development of Customary Law Concerning Internal Armed Conflicts' in A. Cassese (ed.), *Current Problems of International Law* (Milano: Giuffrè, 1975) 287 et seq. (also in this volume). These rules were mainly meant to protect the civilian population.

ranked as a conflict between States. In 1937–39, a new path, more realistic and more flexible, opened. The foundations to make internal conflicts—at least the most serious ones—to a certain extent less inhumane were laid.

B. The Second Phase (1949)

The second phase began in 1949 when, on the initiative of the ICRC, it was decided to revise a significant part of the humanitarian law on armed conflicts, in particular the sections related to victims of war: the wounded, the sick, the ship-wrecked, prisoners of war and civilians.

On this occasion, the idea of extending these new conventions to civil wars was launched. The reason was simple: the two conflicts that occurred between the two World Wars in which the ICRC intervened on a humanitarian level (that is the civil war in the territory of Upper Silesia in 1921 and the Spanish civil war, in particular the latter) clearly illustrated that internal conflicts are not less serious and less cruel than those between States.

However, in Geneva when the ICRC presented its proposal to extend the new Conventions *in toto* to internal conflicts, at least three main orientations emerged in the conference.

On one side there were the States completely in favour of the ICRC proposal: Western States such as Norway and Denmark, Third World countries such as Mexico and some socialist States present in Geneva, that is, the Soviet Union, Hungary, Romania, Byelorussia and Bulgaria. At the opposite extreme, there were States fundamentally opposed to the proposal because the proposal would, according to them, undermine State sovereignty and national security. Some of them, however, were prepared to accept it conditionally, i.e. the Conventions could only be applied to civil wars once the legitimate government granted the recognition of belligerency to insurgents. This amounted to giving to the State in question the absolute power to decide whether and when to extend the con-ventions to the civil war; in other words, this, in fact, came down to imposing a legal obligation dependent on the will of one of the parties to the obligation. This second group of States notably included Burma, the United Kingdom (which nonetheless had a balanced position), Greece and Australia. There was finally an intermediate group, mainly composed of Western States including France, Spain, the United States, Italy and the Principality of Monaco, as well as nation-alist China, who were willing to accept the ICRC proposal while at the same time defending 'States' rights'. These States specifically asked that the Conventions be restricted so as to only apply to situations where the insurgents constitute an organized group in control of a part of the territory and prepared to respect inter-national norms.

While the motivation of the last two groups of States is relatively self-evident, the impetus of the first group requires further investigation. In all States that took this position, there certainly were some purely humanitarian motivations;

however, in the case of the socialist States, political and ideological motivations also emerged. It is not a coincidence that the representative of the Soviet Union kept referring to 'civil wars and colonial wars', clearly implying that the latter were a category of civil wars. If we consider the political stance of the Soviet Union at the end of the 1940s (when the Cold War was at its zenith), it is clear that the extensive protection, and thus the international legitimization, of those who fight in civil or colonial wars was in line with the political programmes and interests of the Soviet Union. The aim of this was to encourage as much as possible the disintegration of the colonial empires as well as the destabilization of Western countries. The hostile reactions of the Western countries to the ICRC proposals can be explained through the interpretation and the use that the Soviet Union made of these proposals.

The clash was mainly between the first group (the one in favour of a large extension of international law to civil wars and which was powerfully led by the Soviet delegates) and the intermediate group which was essentially led by France—that presented some constructive proposals. The natural outcome was a compromise that brought together all the arguments. Internal armed conflicts were not ignored: a common article to the Conventions was dedicated to them (Article 3). On the other hand, internal armed conflicts were not brought under the scope of all norms of the Conventions but only of a few general humanitarian principles that were expressly formulated. Article 3 is in the end a short catalogue of *humanitarian principles* applicable to situations of civil wars. It was with a hint of criticism that the Soviet delegate Morozov defined it as a 'convention in miniature'.

Let us now look, just briefly, at the content of this famous Article 3. In substance, it does not contain rules applicable to combat, and all the more so, does not provide the status of legitimate combatants to rebels. It only lays down the principles of humanity to be applied by parties to a conflict to non-combatants, i.e. those who do not take part in the hostilities (civilians, women, children...) or those who are no longer active combatants because they have been wounded or captured.

Yet Article 3 does not lay down specific objective conditions determining its application to internal armed conflicts. The proposal of listing a series of objective conditions for the application of Article 3 with the idea of limiting the scope of this provision was not welcomed. The rejection of that proposal was certainly the price to pay for the removal of the clause advocated by the Soviets regarding the extension of all Conventions to civil wars.

All things considered, and even in light of the *travaux préparatoires,* it is quite certain that Article 3 does not apply to acts of a criminal nature, to isolated and sporadic acts of violence, and to riots, but does apply to conflicts between organized dissident forces and governmental armed forces. This article thus covers situations *broader* in scope than the Spanish civil war and other wars mentioned earlier, for which some customary principles had emerged.

There is another difference between Article 3 and these customary principles: Article 3 enjoys at least two guarantee mechanisms. One is contained in the article and allows the ICRC to intervene; as a result of this norm—and of its practice—it is clear that if the ICRC decides to 'offer its services', the parties to the conflict cannot refuse, nor hamper its humanitarian action and control.

The other guarantee mechanism laid down in common Article 1 to the four 1949 Geneva Conventions reads as follows: 'The High Contracting Parties undertake to respect and to ensure respect for the Present Convention in all circumstances'. This critical norm stipulates that in practice every Contracting Party has the right and the duty to ensure respect for the Conventions by other States. As a consequence, in cases of civil war on the territory of a Contracting Party, another Contracting Party can require compliance with Article 3 by the former.[3] In concrete terms, what can be done? First, diplomatic steps can be taken towards the State in which the conflict broke out; then, the intervention of the ICRC can be requested; finally, if absolutely necessary it is possible to put forward the case that the liable State violates the obligations it has towards all Contracting Parties to the Conventions and that in that sense it has committed an international wrongful act of *erga omnes* nature; as a consequence peaceful sanctions can be taken by third states, for instance the suspension of a treaty or the expulsion of citizens from the responsible State.

Perhaps one could even envisage a third type of guarantee. It is well known that all four 1949 Geneva Conventions require the Contracting Parties to look for and bring to court (or extradite) the perpetrators of ('grave breaches'), i.e. the most serious offences committed against persons or property protected by the Conventions. It could therefore be argued that nothing formally excludes that the violations of the main rules of Article 3 could fall within the 'serious offences' in question. If that was accepted, we would reach the conclusion that even Article 3 enjoys the momentous system of internal criminal guarantees generally established by the four Conventions. On a practical point of view, the most realistic hypothesis for the implementation of this system would be the following: a Third State refers to its own courts a perpetrator (from the legitimate government or the rebels) who allegedly violated Article 3 and who then entered the territory of the Third State.[4]

---

[3] According to the ICRC Commentary (*Commentary of Geneva Convention I* under the direction of J. Pictet (Geneva, 1952) 27), Article 1 of the Convention does not address civil wars; 'the reason is that since [the 1929 convention], the States have bound themselves explicitly in the case of non-international conflicts—a development which is tantamount to a revolution in international law'. One can argue that, since Article 1 states that 'The High Contracting Parties undertake to respect and to ensure respect for the Present Convention in all circumstances' and since Article 3 is part of the Convention, there is no basis for excluding Article 3 from the scope of Article 1. This exclusion, to be acceptable, should be the result of either Article 1 itself or of the *travaux préparatoires*, which does not seem to be the case. On the other hand, not only the letter of Article 1 but also the spirit and the purpose of the Conventions aim at protecting human beings; this supports the position of which I am in favour.

[4] Against the interpretation outlined in the text, one can point out the next to last paragraph of Article 3 that reads: 'The Parties to the conflict should further endeavour to bring into force, by

I have to add that Article 3 contains a real legal enigma over which many distinguished scholars have racked their brains. The enigma lies in the last paragraph of the article that reads: 'The application of the preceding provisions shall not affect the legal status of the Parties to the conflict'.

What does this paragraph mean? It clearly implies that Article 3 does not grant rebels an international legal status. Article 3 neither adds nor removes anything to their legal status. Laid down in these terms, the question seems relatively simple, and the political impetus relatively clear: international law-makers wanted to dispel the fear expressed by States that such a norm on civil wars would give more power, and to some extent a promotion, to the rebels by having them gain international legitimacy. The issue arises when one reads the other provisions of Article 3 which clearly address both the legitimate government and the rebels, and that tend to impose the same obligations on both sides. We thus have—and it cannot be denied—an international norm imposing obligations (and granting correlative rights) on to the rebels. It naturally follows that those rebels are entitled to claim rights and obligations, and are subjects (even if very limited ones) of international law. But we then lose the value and the meaning of the last paragraph of Article 3. In fact, we are faced with a serious contradiction dictated by opposing political motivations. *Article 3 has two souls*: one is humanitarian and open to insurgents; the other favours respect for State sovereignty and is thus opposed to the rebels.

The task for lawyers is to harmonize the contradictions left by diplomats. In my opinion, this contradiction can be overcome through interpretation, if we first accept that Article 3 is meant to impose obligations on both the State and the rebels. This premise is unquestionable to me. It can be inferred from the letter of the provision ('each Party to the conflict shall be bound to apply, as a minimum, the following provisions'; 'the Parties to the conflict should further endeavour...by means of special agreements, all or part of the other provisions of the present Convention'); it is also in accordance with *logic*. What sense would it make to impose obligations solely on the State whilst leaving the rebels free to do what they want? In fact, Article 3 gives obligations and correlative rights to both parties.

---

means of special agreements, all or part of the other provisions of the present Convention'. We can infer that civil wars are only regulated by Article 3. In fact, this conclusion is the one reached in the ICRC Commentary (*Commentary of Geneva Convention I*, 59: 'the Parties to the conflict are only bound to observe Article 3 and may ignore all other Articles [...]. [T]he only provisions which individual Parties are bound to apply unilaterally are those contained in Article 3'.

We could nevertheless consider that this paragraph essentially refers to the *substantial rules* of the Conventions, and not to the rules of implementation. For sure, this paragraph does not refer to Article 1 for the reasons I have mentioned above in the text and in footnote 3. The extension of the rules on criminal enforcement of the Convention to civil wars is however justified by the humanitarian purpose of the Conventions and thus by the requirement to broaden the protection of victims in times of armed conflicts.

The main impediment, of a literal nature, to the extension is to be found in the provisions of the Conventions that limit the scope of 'grave breaches', specifying that they should be acts 'committed against persons and property protected' by the Conventions. The question is thus whether or not victims of internal armed conflicts fall within the category of 'protected persons'. The answer to this question is not always easy.

The last paragraph should thus be read in a restrictive way. According to this interpretation, through ambiguous, even contradictory wording, Contracting States wanted to express the idea that rebels have obligations and rights derived *only* from Article 3. The rebels cannot claim other international rights regarding the conduct of hostilities (in particular, they cannot claim to be legitimate combatants and thus prisoners of war in case of capture), nor can they claim rights that could be inferred from other international rules by the mere fact that Article 3 addresses rebels.

What has been the implementation of Article 3 in international practice?

Unfortunately the results are modest because this article, whilst extensively mentioned, has rarely been observed in its entirety.

The reasons are self-evident. States in which civil wars break out prefer to deny the application of Article 3, stating that the disturbances are sporadic, thus remaining free to quell the rebellion. The rebels, on the other hand, as I have already mentioned, have little interest in applying the humanitarian provisions of Article 3 because they know that they will be punished for their rebellion anyway. Even when States have to admit, in view of the length of the civil war, that this is an internal armed conflict under Article 3, they carefully avoid respecting all provisions of the article.

In addition, while the ICRC has always been vigilant and has always rapidly intervened at least to fulfil its humanitarian tasks, if not its supervisory powers, Third States in practice have never relied upon their rights provided by Article 1 of the four Geneva Conventions, nor have they held criminally responsible perpetrators of serious violations of Article 3 who have fallen into their hands. Unfortunately, individualism remains an important characteristic of the international community, and not all opportunities offered by the law—often in advance of historical and political reality—are exploited.

Shall we then express an overwhelmingly negative view? Article 3 certainly does not regulate the main problems of civil wars, i.e. the hostilities and the way they should be conducted. In addition, despite its purely humanitarian content, it has largely remained a dead letter. It would nevertheless be a mistake to underestimate its importance. This can only be understood if we take history into account, in particular the fact that internal armed conflicts were previously the exclusive 'hunting ground' of individual States (except for the norms on civilian population implemented during the Spanish civil war). The international community could not intervene unless the individual State in question expressed interest in such an involvement. G.I.A.D. Draper, a distinguished British lawyer, rightly said in 1965, regarding Article 3: 'The establishment of a legal norm may precede its regular enforcement, but the existence of such a norm is a value in itself'.[5]

[5] G.I.A.D. Draper, 'The Geneva Conventions of 1949', *Recueil des Cours de l'Académie de Droit International*, vol. 114 (1965–1) 100.

C. The Third Phase (1977)

The third phase opens with the Diplomatic Conference of Geneva in 1974–77 on the revision and modernization of humanitarian law on armed conflicts. This Conference notably led to the adoption of Protocol II on non-international armed conflicts.

Before discussing the Protocol, I would like to highlight the evolution of civil war since 1949. I have already said that internal armed conflicts have increased these last years, for the reasons previously discussed. In addition, these conflicts have been more and more internationalized, in two ways. On one hand, Third States have increasingly been involved in the conflicts by providing arms, material supplies, political support and so on to one party to the conflict; but they have not taken official legal positions—that is to say they have not granted recognition to rebels and they have not explicitly affirmed that there is an internal armed conflict. On the other hand, the second type of internationalization refers to the birth of 'hybrid' armed conflicts, i.e. conflicts both national and international in nature (for instance Vietnam, Bangladesh, Cyprus, and Lebanon).

That is why the development of civil wars, their increasing barbarity as well as the increased involvement of Third States have taken place, and this within a quasi-absolute legal void, namely; without creating norms regulating such issues.

We thus understand why in the early 1970s the ICRC took the initiative to elaborate a Protocol regulating, if not the relationship between Third States and the parties to conflict, at least the behaviours of these parties. In Geneva, during the Diplomatic Conference, three trends emerged. On one side, some Western countries, including Austria, Italy, Belgium and Switzerland were very much in favour of a radical broadening of Article 3. This group shared its vision with Third World countries such as Egypt and, to a certain extent, Syria.

Another group of Western countries (including France, the United States and the Federal Republic of Germany) was also in favour of such a broadening but required some precautions and above all more precision regarding the objective conditions under which an internal armed conflict would exist. They suggested conditions at the level of the Spanish civil war or the conflict in Nigeria. Very close to this position were socialist States (not including Romania): they did not take the leading role they took in 1949, nor did they show particular support for the widening of humanitarian law. They were more cautious and moderate and, like the majority of Western States, they asked that the threshold required to be reached by non-international armed conflicts in order to fall under Protocol II be higher.

The last group of States, composed of many Third World countries led by Nigeria, India, Pakistan and Indonesia, was decisively hostile to the widening of humanitarian norms to include civil wars. They feared that such an opening out would encourage the intervention of superpowers in their internal affairs. These countries, along with other Third World States and the socialist bloc, argued at the Diplomatic Conference that some categories of civil wars should be upgraded to the level of international armed conflicts: the armed struggle of peoples under colonial dominion; the rebellion against racist governments, as in South Africa; and uprisings by the people in occupied territories: in a word, 'wars of national liberation'. Once this point was achieved, some Third World countries sought the widest restriction possible of international norms applicable to other civil wars; they were scared of secessions or the division of their territories. They had the upper hand and succeeded in 'disfiguring' and toningdown numerous provisions of the Protocol.

Let us now take a look at the content of the Protocol. Three main elements are to be considered.

First, accepting the entreaties of a majority of Western States and some socialist countries, the Protocol holds a very high threshold of application; in other words, it does not regulate any civil war but only those which are long-lasting and of great intensity.[6] The Protocol thus has the same scope of application as the customary rules that emerged during the Spanish civil war.

The second element to consider is that, even if the material norms of the Protocol were partly elaborated in the same perspective as Article 3 (they are purely humanitarian and their main purpose is the protection of non-combatants), they also deal with the hostilities themselves to a certain extent. Let us first look at the latter. A provision sets out limits to the actions of combatants: for example the last sentence of Article 4, paragraph 1 reads: 'It is prohibited to order that there shall be no survivors'. There is then a set of norms that aim at protecting civilian populations from hostilities, by narrowing the means of warfare of either the legitimate government or the insurgents. Article 13 sets out the general principle according to which 'the civilian population as such, as well as individual civilians, shall not be the object of attack' but also includes other provisions specifically prohibiting attacks against civilian persons.

Despite these highly significant norms, *the core of the Protocol remains the protection of non-combatants.* Parties to the conflict are thus free to use the arms they desire, even those whose use is prohibited in international armed conflicts (for example, toxic and poison gas, defoliant and napalm under certain circumstances, explosive bullets, expansive or 'dumdum' bullets, and so on). Here again lies a paradox: a State can use against its own citizens arms that it cannot use against nationals of other States. Likewise, some methods of violence forbidden in wars between States are not illegal during civil wars: for example perfidy or disloyal

---

[6] According to Article 1, the Protocol applies to conflicts 'which take place in the territory of a High Contracting Party between its armed forces and dissident armed forces or other organized armed groups which, under responsible command, exercise such control over a part of its territory as to enable them to carry out sustained and concerted military operations and to implement this Protocol'. In order to dispel any remaining doubt, para. 2 adds that the Protocol 'shall not apply to situations of internal disturbances and tensions, such as riots, isolated and sporadic acts of violence and other acts of a similar nature, as not being armed conflicts'.

means (as for instance 'the feigning of an intent to negotiate under the flag of truce or of a surrender' or 'the feigning of an incapacitation by wounds or sickness').

Let me add that even in its purely humanitarian parts, the Protocol has serious shortcomings.

For example, it does not suspend the enforcement of the death penalty during hostilities, as suggested the escalation of violence to avoid to ever-growing atrocities.

Another crucial point was dealt with in a very unsatisfactory manner. We know that legitimate governments often prevent relief charities or international organizations from helping (in humanitarian terms) the population under the control of rebels (so that they can be provided with necessary supplies and medicines). Article 18, para. 2 of the Protocol contemplates such relief actions 'if the civilian population is suffering undue hardship owing to a lack of the supplies essential for its survival' but adds that such relief actions 'shall be undertaken subject to the consent of the High Contracting Party concerned'. This means that the latter can forbid these actions as it pleases. Likewise, another provision (Article 18, para. 1) dealing with a critical issue is very weak and somehow ambiguous. It concerns the possibility of Red Cross societies being able to operate in rebels' territories and to fulfil their tasks without any ban or sanctions from the government or the 'mother organization' present in the territory controlled by the legitimate government.

The third element is, in my view, the most worrying; it relates to the implementation of the Protocol. Not only does the Protocol fail to establish any international mechanism monitoring its implementation, but it also takes a step back from Article 3 of the 1949 Convention, and does this in two ways.

On the one hand, while this article, granted the ICRC the power to intervene, the Protocol fails to mention anything on the matter.

On the other hand, as I have already mentioned, Article 1 common to the four Geneva Conventions gave all Contracting Parties the right to require the respect of Article 3 by other Contracting Parties. Not only does the Protocol not take up this norm, but it actually includes a provision that seems to go the opposite way. Article 3, para. 2, indeed states that 'nothing in this Protocol shall be invoked as a justification for intervening, directly or indirectly, for any reason whatever, in the armed conflict or in the internal or external affairs of the High Contracting Party in the territory of which that conflict occurs'. This may imply that no other Contracting Party can demand compliance with the Protocol from a State where a civil war is ongoing, because the State could see such a step as a serious interference in its internal affairs.

The only consolation that remains is that Article 3 is encompassed by the Protocol. What I mean is that every time we apply the Protocol, Article 3 will automatically be applied, and the internal armed conflict will enjoy the guarantees laid out in Article 3. The ICRC and other Contracting Parties to the four Geneva Conventions will not be able to demand the strict implementation of the Protocol; they will only be able to require Article 3's implementation. That is why the Protocol can be seen as a warrior without arms: it enacts orders but does not have powerful mechanisms available to have them executed.

The overall conclusion is, in some respects, rather disappointing. Even the authors of the Protocol became conscious of the shortcomings of the Protocol; they turned to natural law, or to a new form of natural law, as is the case every time positive law is inadequate. The preamble of the Protocol notably states that 'in cases not covered by the law in force, the human person remains under the protection of the principle of humanity and the dictates of the public conscience'. It is interesting to underline that this formula in some respect repeats the celebrated Martens clause propounded in 1899 by the Russian delegate F.F. Martens at the First Hague Conference and then incorporated in the preamble to the 1907 Hague Convention IV. The Martens clause was inspired by positivism: to fill possible gaps it did not advert to the notion of *'non-droit'* or moral principles but to other legal rules capable of palliating the shortcomings of Convention IV. Indeed, it provided that, in cases not covered by Convention IV, 'the inhabitants and the belligerents remain under the protection and the rule of the principles of the laws of nations, as they result from the usages established among civilized peoples, from the laws of humanity, and the dictates of the public conscience.' It is not a coincidence that this clause marked by positivism was taken up by the 1977 Protocol I (Article 1, para. 2), whereas it was transformed in a clause seeking support from ethics as far as Protocol II is concerned.

Beyond the complexities lying in the content of Protocol II, there is a worrying element that should be highlighted: many Third World States expressed scepticism regarding the importance of the Protocol and did this after its approval. For example, the Indonesian delegate underlined that the rules of Protocol II 'were not adequate for safeguarding the principles of sovereignty and integrity of States' because according to him, these rules deal with issues 'coming within the domain of internal affairs of a sovereign State'.[7] India adhered to this view: its delegate notably stated that '[i]t would be dangerous for the [Geneva Diplomatic] Conference to encourage the dissident and secessionist elements and thus weaken national sovereignty and unity'.[8] According to the representative of Mexico, 'in internal armed conflicts, national law [holds] the rein'; as a result, Protocol II is 'a superfluous instrument'.[9] Uganda took the same path stating that the Protocol was 'quite unnecessary'.[10] As for the Sudanese delegate, he pointed out that the Protocol 'did not involve any international agreements but simply a concession on the part of States which agreed to apply it to their own nationals'.[11]

---

[7] CDDH/SR. 56, para. 21.
[8] CDDH/SR. 56, para. 51.
[9] CDDH/SR. 56, para. 28.
[10] CDDH/SR. 56, p. 251 (no para. number is available).
[11] CDDH/SR. 56, para. 37.

6. Conclusion

It is now time to draw the main threads out of this discussion. I would like to make three general remarks.

First, the inadequacy and the traditional shortcomings of the norms applicable to civil wars particularly stand out in the current organization of the international community, because the international community as it works today tends to intervene to a greater extent and to regulate more matters belonging to the internal affairs of States. There is a similar phenomenon in State-led societies where enormous public and private industrial machinery and state organisms have increasingly swept up our private lives, to the point where they try to manipulate our thinking. While this phenomenon is certainly negative, the incursion of international law into internal affairs is on the contrary beneficial. Indeed it holds back nationalisms and individualisms to introduce solidarity— indeed pacifism—into national legal systems.

But civil wars brutally elude this tendency, or at least this tendency stagnates and sinks in face of civil war. Why? There is little doubt that this issue actually touches the most intimate and delicate nerves of the sovereign State. Civil wars involve a questioning of state authority and represent an attempt to deny legitimacy and power to persons of authority. As a consequence, it is generally argued that even if a sovereign State can at a pinch accept international limitations with regard to its economy or the fundamental rights of its citizens, for instance, it will be reluctant to remain inactive when it is threatened by a group of citizens.

I think that this is an inadequate explanation. Indeed it has rarely been suggested in international practice that rebels should be treated as legitimate combatants. What is commonly asked is that some humanitarian principles should apply to insurgents, even if they remain common criminals in the eyes of the legitimate government and Third States. It is also asked that civilians should not suffer, that no massacre should take place, that indiscriminate and inhuman methods of warfare are not used, that no hostages are taken, that acts of terrorism should not occur, and so on. All of this should be in the interests of the legitimate government, because after all rebels belong to the national population, and civilian populations are composed of States' citizens. States, especially Third World countries, opposed to new international rules or to Protocol II *make a terrible mistake and are short-sighted*. They believe that international norms applicable to civil wars can provide big powers and superpowers an opportunity to intervene in their internal affairs. They do not realize that this intrusion takes place anyhow, regardless of the presence of international rules. International rules are intended to make internal conflicts less inhuman by protecting victims or potential victims.

My second comment deals with the status of insurgents. As I have already mentioned, no one dares to suggest that rebels should be considered as legitimate combatants. I have also said that this lack of status has resulted in civil wars becoming more savage. Rebels know that they have nothing to lose and thus feel free to commit atrocities against regular forces and against the civilian population. Governments may want to be more courageous and grant insurgents fulfilling some predefined criteria the status of legitimate combatants, in order to *humanize* civil wars.

This would of course bring some legitimacy to the insurgents. However, we could apply here what Third World countries have rightly argued for years against the Western States' position on 'guerrillas'. Some western States claimed that guerrillas taking part in conflicts of national liberation and in occupied territories could only be considered as legitimate combatants if they were to fulfil very strict conditions (such as carrying arms openly and having a fixed and distinctive sign recognisable at a distance). It is impossible for guerrillas to fulfil these conditions since guerrilla war is a technique of warfare based on surprise attacks, ambushes, the utmost mobility and above all on the fact that the guerrillas are mixed with the civilian population. Some Western States, Norway, the United States, and France for instance, have realized that, by welcoming the suggestions of the Third World countries, one could generate situations where guerrillas would be inclined to respect rules of warfare because of their status as legitimate combatants. These Western countries were well-advised and sagacious enough to understand that if we want guerrillas to observe humanitarian rules, special treatment will have to be given to them.

I would argue that this open attitude towards irregular combatants in conflicts of national liberation could be progressively taken with regard to civil war situations. After all, the objective is the same in both cases: to push the combatants to act as humanely as possible towards the enemy and above all towards the civilian population. The least we can say is thus that those States in favour of a privileged status for guerrillas have been clearly incoherent when they excluded the same status for other rebels.

Finally, my last comment is that, if international law in this area seems very fragile and shaky and if its normative value is limited, it is because the 'model' of traditional international law (the one formed at the time of the Treaty of Westphalia and which lasted until the 1940s) has not been replaced by modern international law. This is particularly true for this domain. Traditional law was based on the sovereignty of States and on their formal equality; it was deeply imbued with individualism, it did not place any limit on the use of force and it was mainly meant to regulate the coexistence between States. Modern law on the other hand is inspired by values such as solidarity; it poses some shrewd limitations on the use of force and recognizes the international role of entities other than States; it also establishes international cooperation, it seeks to fill in substantial inequalities, and above all it is meant to protect human beings as such, wherever and whoever they are. In the area of internal armed conflicts, the model of modern international law has only scraped the surface of the old model. As I have already argued, even if new rules have been created since 1949, they have come up against the bedrock of traditional international law: the sovereignty of States. Civil war affects the core of the State; it shakes the existence of the State. It is thus obvious that sovereign States—still ruling the international community—have seen innovations in this area as unnecessary. The *progress* in this domain, relatively *limited* in scope, has mainly focused on normative evolution. Indeed, the sovereignty of States—'the mortal gods', according to Hobbes—has impeded the effective implementation of new norms.

In cases like this when law is inefficient, extrajudicial forces such as public opinion, lobbies and non-governmental organizations are powerful channels. They have the moral obligation to substitute for the law, to give life and blood to the few existing legal rules, and to put forward moral authority where the law is silent.

6. The Spanish Civil War and the Development of Customary Law Concerning Internal Armed Conflicts*

1. Introductory Remarks

It is usually held that when civil strife or armed rebellion break out in the territory of a sovereign State, the whole legal regulation of hostilities falls within the competence of that State, more exactly, of the incumbent Government, even though rebels have been granted recognition as insurgents. As a result, all acts of violence committed by rebels come within the competence of domestic criminal law, and are accordingly subject to the prescribed penalties. Only in the event that the insurgents are recognized as a belligerent Power either by the lawful Government or by third States, does the internal conflict turn into an international war and the rules regulating warfare become applicable. This opinion, expressed by most authorities, is also upheld in official texts; for instance, the 1956 United States Army Field Manual specifies that 'the customary law of war becomes applicable to civil war upon recognition of the rebels as belligerents' (para. 11 *a*).

I suggest that this view, while it was correct in the past, has become *at present* inaccurate, inasmuch as it does not take into account developments in international law of the 1930s. During the Spanish Civil War (1936–1939) a general conviction took shape among States that some fundamental principles and rules of the laws of war would have to be extended to cover civil strifes as well, regardless of any recognition of belligerency. It must be pointed out, however, that, according to the practice of States, the extension of some basic rules of warfare does not benefit all kinds of internal armed conflicts, but only instances of large-scale civil wars—cases where rebels form an organized entity effectively controlling a portion of the territory by means of an administration and organized armed forces; and furthermore, the hostilities between the lawful Government and rebels reach a considerable degree of intensity and duration. By contrast, internal armed struggles or disturbances falling below this standard remain outside the scope of such an extension.

In order to substantiate this view, I shall quote some statements made during the Spanish Civil War both by the parties to the conflict and by third Governments. Before doing so, it is useful to emphasize that in that civil war the insurgents were

* Originally published in A. Cassese (ed.), *Current Problems of International Law* (Milano: Giuffrè, 1975) 287.

never recognized as belligerents, although General Franco asked Third States to accord him belligerent rights and expressly stressed that his forces fulfilled all conditions required for that status.[1] States refused to accede to his request. There were three main reasons for this. First, some States thought that such a recognition would have been inconsistent with the non-intervention policy agreed upon by many States; in fact, since the insurgents were much stronger on the sea, the

---

[1] See the declaration by General Franco of July 17, 1937 ('According to international laws and customs, we have the right to be granted recognition as belligerents. This right is implicit when a party to the conflict occupies and controls a vast territory, and has a government organization and a regular army abiding by the laws and customs of war. As far as Nationalist Spain is concerned, these conditions exist, even to a greater extent than in other cases where belligerent rights were granted'). See the Italian text of this declaration in *Diritto internazionale* 1937, ISPI, p. 117. See the more detailed diplomatic notes of the Nationalist authorities, of November 18, 1937 (in *New York Times*, November 24, 1937) and August 21, 1938 (in PADELFORD, *International Law and Diplomacy in the Spanish Civil Strife*, New York 1939, pp. 597–598).

A request for granting belligerent rights to the contending parties in Spain was made on July 2, 1937 by Italy and Germany in the Non-Intervention Committee. See the text of the Italian-German proposal (in French) in *La Documentation Internationale, Politique, Juridique et Economique*, vol. 5, nos. 47–48, Mai-Juin 1938, p. 75. (English text in *Keesing's Contemporary Archives, 1937–1940*, p. 2643). On July 9, 1937 the Italian delegate to the Committee justified the proposal with the following words: 'Certains pouvoirs ont soulevé des objections au principe de la neutralité juridique comprise dans nos propositions, parce qu'une telle neutralité représente de trop grandes concessions en faveur du Gouvernement de Salamanque. On oublie un fait indiscutable, à savoir que le Gouvernement de Salamanque contrôle deux tiers du territoire espagnol et le total du territoire espagnol colonial. Le Gouvernement de Salamanque représente 14 millions des 22 millions de l'Espagne. C'est un Gouvernement possédant une armée, une flotte, une aviation bien organisée et entraînée. Il dispose d'une administration bien organisée. Il remplit, en effet, toutes les conditions nécessaires pour un Etat souverain. Le Gouvernement de Salamanque est donc d'autant plus en état de revendiquer justement la reconnaissance du droit de belligérant dont les conditions, selon le droit et la pratique internationale, dans le cas des "insurrections contre les Gouvernements reconnus" sont comme suit: 1° d'avoir conquis une certaine partie du territoire national; 2° de posséder tous les éléments d'un gouvernement régulier; 3° de se battre avec des troupes organisées avec la discipline militaire et en conformité avee la loi et les coutumes de la guerre' (*La Documentation Internationale* cit., nos. 49–50, Juillet–Août, 1938, p. 93). Cp. the statement by the representative of Germany (*ibid.*, nos, 51–52, Septembre–Octobre 1938, p. 118). The same position was taken by Mussolini in an article in the Italian newspaper 'Popolo d'Italia' of July 24, 1937, where he wrote: 'Mr. Eden himself in the House of Commons has recognised the absurdity of denying belligerent rights to a General whose army has fought for a year, who governs and controls two-thirds of Spain and all its colonies, and who has 14 out of 22 million Spaniards behind him' (in *Keesing's Contemporary Archives, 1937–1940*, p. 2676A).

On July 16, 1937, the British representative declared in the Non-Intervention Committee that Great Britain could grant the recognition of belligerency, on condition, however, that foreign armed forces would be withdrawn from Spain (*La Documentation Internationale* cit., nos. 53–54, Novembre–Décembre 1938, pp. 134–135). As the condition was not fulfilled, the recognition was not granted.

The Nationalist authorities' request to be accorded belligerent rights was strongly denied, on several occasions, by the Spanish Republican Government, which forcefully contended that the contest was merely a civil war. See the notes of the Madrid Government of August 10, 1936 (text in *La Documentation Internationale* cit., vol. 4, nos. 32–33, Février–Mars 1937, p. 21) of December 16, 1936 (*ibid.*, vol. 4, nos 37–38, Juillet-Août 1937, pp. 102–103), and of August 2, 1938 (in PADELFORD, op cit, p. 595).

On the recognition of belligerency see above all the excellent survey of Ch. ROUSSEAU, 'La Non-Intervention en Espagne', *Revue de droit international et de législation comparée*, vol. 18, 1938,

exercise of belligerent rights would have allowed them to intercept and seize, as contraband goods, most supplies of arms going to the Republican Government. An imbalance between the two conflicting parties would thus ensue.[2] The second reason was that the exercise of belligerent rights on the sea by both the incumbent Government and insurgents would have easily caused incidents with third States. For, the contending parties would have been granted the belligerent right to submit neutral ships to search, in order to discover whether they were breaking a blockade, carrying contraband goods, or rendering unneutral service. This might have given rise to the dangerous possibility for the civil war to widen into a European conflict.[3] The third reason was that the illegal 'intervention' of foreign States in the conflict had altered the civil war character, which the Spanish contest had had at the outset. In the opinion of third States, the accepted rules on recognition of belligerency could therefore not apply to such a situation.[4]

Although, however, the Spanish strife was never elevated to a war proper, it did not remain within the traditional bounds of a 'civil war'. It was, rather, regarded as a conflict belonging to a *tertium genus,* intermediate between mere 'civil wars' and those civil wars where the contending parties are recognized as belligerents. For, in civil wars third States are duty bound not to help insurgents, while they can give any assistance to the rightful Government. It is common knowledge that international law benefits the incumbent Government, much to the detriment of rebels. By contrast, in the case of the Spanish contest many States, through the non-intervention agreements, decided to treat both the lawful Government and insurgents in the same way, by refraining from giving military assistance to either. This gave rise to many criticisms on the part of the lawful Government. Thus, its representative pointed out in 1936 in the Assembly of the League of Nations that

The legal monstrosity of the formula of non-intervention is manifest. That formula . . . places on the same footing the lawful Government of my country and the rebels, whom

---

pp. 510–520. See also as McNair, 'The Law Relating to the Civil War in Spain', *Law Quarterly Review,* vol. 53, Oct. 1937, pp. 491–492; O'Rourke, 'Recognition of Belligerency and the Spanish War', *American Journal of International Law,* vol. 31, 1937, p. 408 ff.; Le Fur, *La guerre d'Espagne et le droit,* Paris, 1938, p. 47 ff.; Garner. 'Recognition of Belligerency', *American Journal of International Law,* vol. 32, 1938, p. 106 ff.; van der Esch, *Prelude to War, the International Repercussions of the Spanish Civil War,* The Hague 1951, pp. 83–85, 121 f.

[2] See e.g. the statements made in the Non-Intervention Committee by the representatives of France and USSR on July 2, 1937 (text in *La Documentation Internationale,* vol. 5, nos. 47–48, Mai-Juin 1938, respectively at p. 76 and 77) and on July 9, 1937 (respectively at p. 111 and 113). See also the statement made on November 1, 1937 by the British Foreign Minister, A. Eden, in the House of Commons, *House of Commons Debates,* vol. 328 (1937–1938), cols. 589–590.

[3] See the statements made in the House of Commons on June 25, 1937 by British Prime Minister N. Chamberlain, *House of Commons Debates,* vol. 325 (1936–1937), cols. 1546–1547. See also the statement made on July 9, 1937 in the Non-Intervention Committee by the representative of France (text in *La Documentation Internationale,* cit., nos. 51–52, Septembre–Octobre 1938, p. 110).

[4] See the statement made on June 25, 1937 by the British Secretary of State in the House of Commons, *House of Commons Debates,* vol. 325 (1936–1937) col. 1608. See also the statement by the representative of USSR in the Non-Intervention Committee, on July 2, 1937 (in *La Documentation Internationale* cit., nos. 47–48, Mai-Juin 1938, p. 77) and on July 9, 1937 (*ibid.,* nos. 51–52, Septembre–Octobre 1938, pp. 118–115).

any Government worthy of the name is not only entitled but bound to suppress and punish. From the juridical point of view, non-intervention, as applied to Spain, represents an innovation in the traditional rules of international law, for it means withholding means of action from a lawful Government.[5]

Yet, the behaviour of the States parties to the non-intervention agreements was impeccable from a legal point of view. Customary international law merely confers a right on States to help the lawful Government. States are therefore at liberty to waive this right by mutual agreement. Moreover, by agreeing not to help the rebels, they merely confirmed an obligation deriving from customary law. Apart from this, it can be noted that third States decided to act in a way that to some extent may resemble the position of neutral States vis-à-vis belligerents (impartiality is typical of the attitude of neutral States).[6] Despite this attitude, the behaviour of third States towards the contending parties in Spain never amounted to a recognition of belligerency. Although the insurgents undoubtedly met all the requisite conditions for the application of belligerent recognition, many States took care on several occasions to stress that they regarded the Spanish conflict as an internal strife, and expressly refused to grant recognition.[7] It is

---

[5] League of Nations, *Official Journal,* Special Supplement no. 155, Records of the XVIIth Ordinary Session of the Assembly, Plenary Meetings, 1936, p. 49.

[6] On November 1, 1937 in the House of Commons the British Foreign Minister, A. Eden, made the following remark: 'What happened was that non-intervention sought to create a new form of neutrality. Say if you will, that it has succeeded or failed, but a result of that new form of neutrality has been that belligerent rights have not been granted' (*House of Commons Debates,* vol. 328 (1937–1938), col. 589).

[7] See e.g. the statements made by several States in the Non-Intervention Committee, quoted *supra,* at note 1 and the British statements quoted at notes 2, 3 and 4, as well as the statement made on December 8, 1937, by the British Foreign Minister, A. Eden, in the House of Commons (*House of Commons Debates,* vol. 330 (1937–1938), col. 357). See also the declarations of several Governments quoted by ROUSSEAU, op cit, pp. 510–520, 525–526.

The Preamble of the Nyon Arrangement of September 14, 1937 must also be quoted. After noting in the first paragraph that 'Arising out of the Spanish conflict attacks have been repeatedly committed in the Mediterranean by submarines against merchant ships not belonging to either of the conflicting Spanish parties', it was stated in the second paragraph that 'these attacks are violations of the rules of international law referred to in Part IV of the Treaty of London of April 22, 1930, with regard to the sinking of merchant ship and constitute acts contrary to the most elementary dictates of humanity, *which should be justly treated as acts of piracy*' (italics added). The third paragraph read as follows: '*Without in any way admitting the right of either party to the conflict in Spain to exercise belligerent rights* or to interfere with merchant ships on the high seas even if the laws of warfare at sea are observed . . . it is necessary in the first place to agree upon certain special collective measures against *piratical acts by submarine*'. It is clear that the framers of the Arrangement intended to withhold belligerent status to the Spanish contending parties, both by laying down the express proviso in preambular para. 3, and by branding the acts of those (and any third) parties as 'piratical' in preambular paras 2 and 3 (on this last point see GENET, "The Charge of Piracy in the Spanish Civil War", *American Journal of International Law,* vol. 32, 1938, p. 253 ff.; PADELFORD, *International Law and Diplomacy* cit., pp. 43–49).

It can be added, though it may appear to be less significant, that many States referred in the Assembly on the Council of the League of Nations to the Spanish conflict as a 'civil war'. See, for example, the statements by the representative of Bolivia and Peru in the Council: League of Nations, *Official Journal,* Minutes of the 103rd Session of the Council (September 1938), November 1938, p. 884.

therefore appropriate to maintain that the conflict at issue must be brought under a *tertium genus*.

2. The International Rules Applied in the Spanish Civil War: General

Although, as we have seen above, the Spanish Civil War was regarded as an internal armed conflict, many third States felt that some international rules concerning inter-State warfare should be extended to govern certain aspects of that conflict. The most strenuous advocates of this stand were precisely those States (the United Kingdom, France and the United States) which had more consistently stressed that they did not intend to grant belligerent rights. There is no contradiction in this behaviour. The States at issue, on the one hand did not want the contending parties to be recognized as belligerents, for they wished the conflict to remain in principle within the bounds of a domestic strife. On the other hand, they realized that compelling humanitarian demands required that the most strikingly inhumane aspects of the conduct of hostilities should be taken out of the domestic sphere and be governed by international rules. They, therefore, consistently tried to impose the application of some international rules on the contending parties. This behaviour cannot be construed as a kind of 'partial' recognition of belligerency—the States concerned, all too clearly, emphasized that they withheld any such recognition—but rather as indicative of the gradual development of international customary rules governing civil war.

Among the aspects of armed violence which were considered by the parties involved to be covered by rules of international law, mention must first of all be made of the protection of war victims. In 1936, on the initiative of the International Committee of the Red Cross (ICRC), both the Republican Government and the insurgents (the Burgos authorities) agreed in formal declarations to the ICRC to apply the 1929 Geneva Convention concerning the Wounded and Sick. They also undertook to have the Red Cross emblem respected, to facilitate the humanitarian tasks of the Red Cross institutions and to co-operate in the setting up of

---

The view of BALLADORE PALLIERI, 'Quelques aspects juridiques de la non-intervention en Espagne', *Revue de droit internationale et de législation comparée*, vol. 18, 1937, pp. 285–309; WALKER, 'Recognition of Belligerency and Grant of Belligerent Rights', *Transactions of the Grotius Society*, vol. 23, 1937, p. 179; SMITH, 'Some Problems of the Spanish Civil War', *British Yearbook of International Law*, vol. 18, 1937, p. 26 ff., and Bosco, 'La guerra civile in Spagna e il diritto internazionale', *Civiltà Fascista*, vol. 5, 1938, p. 507 ff., that belligerent rights were tacitly granted to the contending parties, is therefore ill-founded. The contrary view was expressed by many other learned authors, among whom I shall mention here the following ones: PADELFORD, op cit, pp. 14–18; SANDIFORD, 'Le guerre civili e il diritto internazionale marittimo', *Rivista marittima*, 1937, pp. 18–19; SCELLE, 'La reconnaissance des insurgés et la guerre espagnole', *Die Friedenswarte*, 1937, pp. 67–70; LAUTERPACHT, *Recognition in International Law*, Cambridge, 1947, pp. 250–253.

a Prisoners of War Information Agency. The rebels, in addition, declared to be ready to comply with the 1929 Geneva Convention on Prisoners of War.[8] In a circular letter sent, in 1937, to all national Societies of the Red Cross, the ICRC pointed out that 'the application by analogy' of the 1929 Geneva Convention on the Wounded and Sick was in a general way admitted in fact by both contending parties.[9]

Other international rules were also made applicable to the Spanish conflict.[10] Thus, for instance, many States agreed *inter se* to apply to some extent the substance of the rules of customary law codified in Article 22 of the London Treaty of April 22, 1930 for the Limitation and Reduction of Naval Armament, concerning the conditions on which warships can sink or destroy merchant vessels in time of war.[11] They agreed in the Nyon Arrangements and Supplementary Agreement, of September 14, and 17, 1937, respectively, that they would counterattack and, if possible, destroy, submarines, surface vessels, or aircraft which would attack in the Mediterranean—without complying with the principles of the London Treaty—any merchant vessel not belonging to either of the conflicting Spanish parties.[12] These agreements were subsequently endorsed by the Council of the League of Nations.[13] By these agreements the contracting States

---

[8] See the text of the official letters of the Spanish Government and the Burgos authorities in *Rapport général du Comité international de la Croix Rouge sur son activité d'août 1934 à mars 1938,* p. 132 and 133–134.
   See on these letters the remarks by SIORDET, 'Les Conventions de Genève et la guerre civile', *Revue internationale de la Croix-Rouge,* février 1950, vol. 32, pp. 112–114.
[9] *L'action de la Croix-Rouge en Espagne, 335me Circulaire du Comité international de la Croix-Rouge,* Geneva, March 31, 1937, p. 4.
[10] See on this matter the extensive survey by ROUSSEAU, op cit, pp. 474–510; PADELFORD, *International Law and Diplomacy* cit., pp. 25–52, 196–202.
[11] Part IV of the London Treaty consists of Art. 22, which reads as follows: 'The following are accepted as established rules of International Law: (1) In their action with regard to merchant ships, submarines must conform to the rules of International Law to which surface vessels are subject. (2) In particular, except in the case of persistent refusal to stop on being duly summoned, or of active resistance to visit or search, a warship, whether surface vessel or submarine, may not sink or render incapable of navigation a merchant vessel without having first placed passengers, crew and ship's papers in a place of safety. For this purpose the ship's boats are not regarded as a place of safety unless the safety of the passengers and crew is assured, in the existing sea and weather conditions, by the proximity of land, or the presence of another vessel which is in a position to take them on board. The High Contracting Parties invite all other Powers to express their assent to the above rules'.
[12] For the Preamble of the Nyon Arrangement, *see supra,* note 7.
   Art. 2 of the Arrangement stipulated that 'any submarine which attacks such a ship (a merchant ship) in a manner contrary to the rules of international law referred to' in the London Treaty and confirmed in the London Protocol of November 6, 1936, must be 'counter-attacked and, if possible, destroyed'. Art. 2 of the Agreement applied to 'any attack by a surface vessel or an aircraft . . . when such attack is accompanied by a violation of the humanitarian principles embodied in the rules of international law with regard to warfare at sea', which were referred to in the London Treaty and Protocol.
[13] In a resolution adopted on October 5, 1937, the Council stated in paras 7 and 8:
   '[It] Notes that attacks have taken place in violation of the most elementary dictates of humanity underlying the established rules of international law which are affirmed, so far as war time is concerned, in Part IV, of the Treaty of London of April 22nd, 1930, rules which have been formally accepted by the great majority of Governments.

de facto imposed on either Spanish contending party the duty of complying with the requirements of the London Treaty. In other words, these States held that some rules of customary international law concerning sea warfare applied to the Spanish civil strife. They, however, stressed quite clearly that this application did not entail a recognition of belligerency.[14] It was their intention that only some specific customary rules of warfare should be extended to the Spanish conflict, without however the contending parties being granted *the full status of belligerents*. As stated before, there is no contradiction in this behaviour of the States parties to the Nyon Accords. They held that compelling reasons—the ones referred to in para. 1—made it necessary for them to withhold the recognition of belligerency. Yet, they found it expedient and useful that some international rules of warfare concerning the conduct of hostilities, should become applicable to the conflict, because these rules could better protect the life and the assets of persons not taking part in the hostilities.

The greatest body of law which was relied upon related to the protection of civilians on land. The reason is simple: civilians on land suffered most from civil strife and new methods of warfare, especially aerial bombardment. It was only natural that third States, international Organizations, as well as the contending parties, primarily concerned themselves with the protection of civilians. Some of these rules are also very interesting from a legal point of view for the following reason. Most of the rules of warfare applied in the Spanish civil strife did not give rise to a general legal conviction concerning the need for their application to any internal armed conflict. The contending parties applied the rules on wounded and sick by themselves making an agreement which, except of course for the ICRC, remained for third States or Organizations a *res inter alios acta*. The same holds true for the agreement concluded between the parties to the conflict, through the ICRC, with regard to the creation of a 'neutralized zone' in Madrid[15] and for the rules concerning attacks by submarines, surface vessels, or

[It] Declares that all attacks of this kind against any merchant vessels are repugnant to the conscience of the civilised nations which now finds expression through the Council' (League of Nations, *Official Journal*, December 1937, p. 945).

It must not be overlooked that the Council avoided stating that the attacks concurring during the Spanish Civil War were in violation of the rules embodied in the London Treaty. Had it said so, this would have meant that in the view of the Council the rules in question were, as such, applicable to the Spanish strife. As a consequence, belligerent rights would have been extended to the conflicting parties. The Council, instead, advisedly confined itself to declaring that those attacks were contrary to the 'most elementary dictates of humanity underlying' those rules.

[14] See the Preamble of the Nyon Accords quoted *supra*, note 7.

[15] 'A la demande du Gouvernement suisse il (le CICR) a fait des démarches pour obtenir la délimitation d'un quartier de Madrid où la population non combattante pourrait se trouver en sûreté. Le Gouvernement de la République espagnole répondit que selon lui, toute la population civile de Madrid devrait être considérée comme non combattante. Le chef de cabinet diplomatique du Gouvernement de Salamanque affirma par télégrammes les 17 et 28 novembre 1936 l'intention du général Franco de respecter néanmoins la zone neutre de Madrid et cela avec le souci d'éviter dans la mesure du possible de porter préjudice à la population non combattante. Cette zone a été respectée par les assiégeants. Une zone neutre analogue établie par les consuls à Las Arenas près de

aircraft, on merchant vessels of third States, which were extended to the Spanish Civil War as a result of the Nyon Accords. It can be added that Great Britain and the Spanish lawful Government made reference to the prohibition to use toxic gases during the civil war.[16] This prohibition, however, was not invoked so consistently as to give rise to the view that it was incumbent upon the parties to the conflict to refrain from using that means of combat.

By contrast, several rules on the protection of civilians in land or air warfare were invoked so many times and by so many parties (the contending parties, third States and intergovernmental Organizations) that—as I shall demonstrate—a *general* legal conviction evolved as to their applicability to all large-scale civil wars. In other words, reliance on those rules transcended the Spanish conflict and gave a decisive impulse to the formation of rules of customary international law on civil wars at large. Therefore, the focus in this paper is on the protection of civilians.

3. The Rules Concerning the Protection of Civilians which Were Considered Applicable

A. The Prohibition of the Intentional Bombing of Civilians

The most important rule invoked during the period 1936–1939, is the rule forbidding the bombardment of civilian populations as such, and, more specifically, the bombing of civilians for the purpose of terrorising or demoralising them. This rule was expressly mentioned in 1937, with reference to Spain, by Prime Minister N. Chamberlain, in the British House of Commons. He pointed out that this rule surely applied to the war raging in Spain, although in the opinion of the British Government far too many instances had occurred where the rule had been plainly disregarded.[17] The same rule was reaffirmed by the Assembly of

---

Bilbao a été respectée pareillement' (XVIe Conférence internationale de la Croix-Rouge, Londres 20–24 Juin 1938. *Rapport Général du Comité International de la Croix-Rouge sur son activité d'août 1934 à mars 1938,* p. 130). The text of one of the abovementioned cables is quoted by Le Goff, 'Les bombardements aériens dans la guerre civile espagnole', *Revue générale de droit international public,* vol. 45, 1938, p. 604.

Reference to the 'neutralized zone' in Madrid is made in a letter of June 18, 1938 sent by the Under-Secretary for Foreign Affairs of the Burgos Government to the ICRC. It is stated in this letter: 'No ha sido nunca propósito del Gobierno Nacional el provocar, en la dolorosa guerra civil en que participa, daños innecesarios antes bien se ha inspirado siempre en principios de humanidad. Buena prueba de ello la ofrece tanto la invitación a evacuar la población civil de las ciudades del Norte a lugares en que no corriese peligro, como el haber fijado en Madrid una zona neutral respetada por nuestra artilleria y nuestra aviación' (the original text of this letter can be found in the files of the ICRC, at Geneva. The author is indebted to the officials of the ICRC for allowing him to consult this and other relevant documents).

[16] See the declarations quoted by Rousseau, op cit, pp. 484–485.

[17] *House of Commons Debates,* vol. 337, 21 June 1938, col. 937. The Prime Minister went on to say: 'Let me say at once that we cannot too strongly condemn any declaration on the part of anybody, wherever it may be made and on whatever side it may be made, that it should be part of

the League of Nations in 1938. On the initiative of the delegate from the Spanish lawful Government, the Assembly discussed at length the question of protection of civilian population against bombing from the air. During the debates reference was made both to civil wars, in particular to the one then in progress in Spain, and to inter-State conflicts, such as the Sino-Japanese war also raging at that time. At the conclusion of the debate the Assembly adopted, on September 30, 1938, a resolution stating in general terms that 'the intentional bombing of civilian population is illegal'.[18] No less important than the resolution itself, many

a deliberate policy to try and win a war by demoralising the civilian population through a process of bombing from the air. That is absolutely contrary to international law . . .' (*ibid.*, col. 938). He added, however, the following: 'The difficulty arises when one of the forces engaged in aerial warfare, being accused of deliberate bombing of civilians, deny that they were bombing civilians or that it was deliberate, and allege that they were in pursuit of military objectives' (*ibid.*).

[18] See the records of the debates in League of Nations, *Official Journal*, Special Supplement no. 186, Records of the XIXth Ordinary Session of the Assembly, *Minutes of the IIIrd Committee*, pp. 9–36. See at p. 37 the text of the Spanish request to place on the agenda of the Assembly the item 'Protection of the civilian non-combatant populations against bombing from the air in case of War'.

Many delegates referred to the situation in Spain, or to that situation and the Sino-Japanese conflict. See, for example, the statements by the representatives of Spain (*Minutes of the IIIrd Committee* etc. cit., pp. 18–19) of China (*ibid.*, pp. 20–22 and p. 31), of France (*ibid.*, pp. 22–23), of Mexico (*ibid.*, pp. 23–24), of Cuba (*ibid.*, p. 26) and of Haiti (*ibid.*, p. 31). All these delegates substantially put the Spanish Civil War and the Sino–Japanese War on the same footing (the Cuban representative stated *inter alia* that 'civil wars and international wars were taking on a new shape' *ibid.*, p. 26).

For the text of the 'resolution' and the 'recommendation' annexed to it, see *ibid.*, pp. 48–49, or League of Nations, *Official Journal*, Special Supplement no. 183, Records of the XIX Ordinary Session of the Assembly, Plenary Meetings, Text of the debates, pp. 135–136 (the resolution and the recommendation were adopted by the IIIrd Committee of the Assembly 'unanimously... the delegates of Hungary and Poland abstaining': *Minutes of the IIIrd Committee*, cit., p. 36. In Plenary, it would seem that the Assembly adopted the texts unanimously: *Plenary Meetings. Text of the Debates*, cit., p. 96).

The resolution reads as follows:

'The Assembly,

Considering that on numerous occasions public opinion has expressed through the most authoritative channels its horror of the bombing of civilian populations;

Considering that this practice, for which there is no military necessity and which, as experience shows, only causes needless suffering, is condemned under the recognised principles of international law;

Considering, further, that though this principle ought to be respected by all States and does not require further reaffirmation, it urgently needs to be made the subject of regulations specially adapted to air warfare and taking account of the lessons of experience;

Considering that the solution of this problem, which is of concern to all States, whether Members of the League of Nations or not, calls for technical investigation and thorough consideration;

Considering that the Bureau of the Conference for the Reduction and Limitation of Armaments is to meet in the near future and that it is for the Bureau to consider practical means of undertaking the necessary work under conditions most likely to lead to as general an agreement as possible:

I. Recognises the following principles as a necessary basis for any subsequent regulations:

(1) The intentional bombing of civilian population is illegal...'

As is quite apparent from this text, as well as from the debates that preceded its adoption, the Assembly considered that the intentional bombing of civilians is prohibited by international law in any case, regardless of whether it is carried out in inter-State armed conflicts or in civil wars. This is also borne out by the preamble of the 'recommendation' adopted by the Assembly at the same time as the 'resolution', which stated 'The Assembly, Referring to its resolution of this day's date on the general question of the bombing of civilian populations from the air; Bearing in mind the present situation, notably in Spain and in the Far East . . .'.

delegates stated in the most explicit terms, before the passing of the resolution, that that type of attack on civilians was in breach of an existing rule of international law—a rule that, in the view of those delegates, clearly applied to the Spanish civil strife as well.[19] That very year, after insurgents intensified aerial bombardment of Barcelona, thus causing heavy loss of life among the civilian population, the British and French Governments sent representations to General Franco's administration, drawing its attention to the fact:

that direct and deliberate attacks on civilian population are contrary to the principles of international law as based on the established practices of civilised nations, to the laws of humanity and to the dictates of public opinion.[20]

The same view was expressed by the representative of the Spanish lawful Government in 1939, before the Council of the League of Nations.[21] And the Council adopted a resolution in which, after noting that several air attacks which had been directed 'intentionally against civilian populations' had taken place in Spain, it condemned 'recourse to methods which are contrary to the conscience of mankind and to principles of international law'.[22]

B. The Rule Forbidding Attacks on Non-Military Objectives

A second rule concerning civilians generally deemed applicable is the one stipulating that only military objectives may be attacked. This rule, however, was not always invoked in the same manner. Sometimes reference was made to the notion of 'open towns' by stating that such towns must be spared by the contending parties. On other occasions only the notion of 'military objectives' was relied upon. In other cases both notions were applied, either supplementing each other, or as interchangeable concepts.

The greatest body of pronouncements—only some of which I will mention here—make reference, however, to the notion of 'military objectives'.

In June 1938, British Prime Minister N. Chamberlain, stated in the House of Commons that a rule which undoubtedly applied to the Spanish Civil War was that whereby:

---

[19] See the statement by the representatives of Great Britain (*Minutes of the IIIrd Committee* etc. cit., p. 20), of Greece (*ibid.*, p. 24) of Irelend (*ibid.*, p. 30), of Haiti (*ibid.*, p. 35); cp. also the statement by the French delegate (*ibid.*, p. 22). Some other delegates spoke of the need to draw up new rules 'to serve as a guide for the future' (Poland, *ibid.*, p. 31; China, *ibid.*, p. 31). But, as was pointed out by the representatives of Haiti (*ibid.*, p. 35; cp. also the statement of the Chairman of the Committee, *ibid.*, p. 34), and was apparent from the text of the resolution that was eventually adopted, the three principles enunciated by Mr. Chamberlain in the House of Commons and taken up in the resolution of the Assembly were regarded as *already in force,* although they needed to be developed and specified.

[20] League of Nations, *Official Journal,* 104th Session of the Council, Fourth Meeting (18-I-1939), February 1939, p. 86.

[21] Resolution of January 20, 1939, in League of Nations, *Official Journal,* 104th Session of the Council, Fifth Meeting (20-I-1939), pp. 97 and 99.

[22] *House of Commons Debates,* vol. 333, 21 March 1938, col. 825.

targets which are aimed at from the air must be legitimate military objectives and must be capable of identification.[23]

In July the same position was again taken up in the House of Commons by Mr. Butler, the British Under-Secretary of State for Foreign Affairs.[24] And in September of the same year the Assembly of the League, after a debate on protection of civilian populations against bombing from the air, adopted the British view, by proclaiming in a resolution that 'objectives aimed at from the air must be legitimate military objectives and must be identifiable'.[25] Before the passing of the resolution, several delegates had proclaimed the same principle.[26] Not less significantly, in 1939, in the course of a debate on the Spanish question in the Council of the League of Nations, the representatives of the Soviet Union,[27] of China,[28] and of France[29] referred to 'military objectives' as the only targets that the contending parties were entitled to attack. Furthermore, it may be mentioned that, in a message of condolence to the civil Governor of Alicante, following an air raid on the town in which hundreds of civilians were killed, the Consular representatives of 28 nations stated:

The fact that, unfortunately, the attack was in the centre of the city, far from military objectives, and that the victims were principally civilians, only increases our sorrow over the great tragedy.[30]

The International Committee of the Red Cross adopted the same terminology when it addressed an appeal to both parties on February 15, 1938, stating *inter alia* that:

it [the Committee] beseeches them to make every possible endeavour to do away with . . . any bombardment striking the civilian population of localities in the rear, as well as any bombardment of localities which do not constitute strictly military objectives.[31]

[23] *House of Commons Debates,* vol. 337, 21 June 1938, col. 937.
[24] *House of Commons Debates,* vol. 338, 4 July 1938, col. 6. On March 18, 1939, the Prime Minister informed the House of Commons about bombing of Barcelona by the Franco's air forces. After a Member of Parliament asked whether the bombing 'was directed with a view to terrorism on the civilian population and not at military objectives', the Prime Minister answered: '. . .The statement which I have just read out . . . does not contain anything to that effect, but the reports which I have seen in the Press do appear to describe the damage as being done largely to living quarters and not to military objectives' (*ibid.,* vol. III, 18 march 1938, col. 747).
[25] League of Nations, *Official Journal,* Special Supplement no. 183, cit., p. 136. See *supra,* notes 17 and 18.
[26] Spain (League of Nations, *Official Journal,* Special Supplement no. 186, Records of the XIX Ordinary Session of the Assembly, *Minutes of the IIIrd Committee,* p. 18), Great Britain (*ibid.,* p. 20), France (*ibid.,* p. 23).
[27] League of Nations, *Official Journal,* February 1939, p. 89.
[28] *Ibid.,* p. 89.
[29] *Ibid.,* p. 90.
[30] *New York Times,* May 27, 1938, quoted in the *Information Bulletin* issued by the 'The New Commonwealth Institute', vol. III, July 7, 1948, p. 4.
[31] French text in *Revue Internationale de la Croix-Rouge,* Juin 1938, vol. 69, n. 430, p. 556.

It is quite significant that the insurgents themselves, when accused of bombing civilians, admitted by implication that they were not allowed to attack non-military objectives: this is clearly proved by their claiming that the targets of their bombing were only military objectives. Thus, in March 1938 the nationalist authorities sent a note to the British agent at Burgos repudiating the British contention that the civilian population had been the object of deliberate attack either in Barcelona or elsewhere. The note alleged that Barcelona constituted a military objective of great importance with 200 factories and industrial undertakings for the production of war material. General Franco's authorities expressed at the same time their sorrow at the loss of innocent lives and stated that they desired, so far as they could, to minimize the effects of aerial activity on the populations of towns and to employ only such means when imperative military necessity left them no alternative.[32]

In June 1938 Mr. Butler, British Under-Secretary of State for Foreign Affairs, stated in the House of Commons that:

The Burgos authorities, in reply to His Majesty's Government's protests regarding the indiscriminate aerial bombardment of towns and villages, in particular of Alicante and Granollers, contend that these towns contain military objectives placed in or close to inhabited districts, and that their bombardment is unavoidable.[33]

---

[32] The note was quoted to the House of Commons by the Prime Minister, N. Chamberlain; see *House of Commons Debates,* vol. 333, 29 March 1938, cols. 1828–1829. After relating the note, Mr. Chamberlain pointed out the following: 'His Majesty's Government cannot regard this reply as an adequate justification in view of the exceptional loss of life and injury to the civilian population of Barcelona, but they have been glad to note that no further bombardments of Barcelona itself have taken place since their recent communication on this subject was addressed to General Franco's administration' (*ibid.,* col. 1829).

See also the declaration made in June 1938 by the Minister for Interior of the Nationalist Government, Mr. Serrano Suner, published in *Temps,* 21 juin 1938, and quoted in LE GOFF, 'Les bombardments aériens' etc. cit., pp. 592–593. Cp. also the declaration by the same Minister, made on July 21, 1938, *ibid.,* p. 593.

A Spanish newspaper, *Heraldo de Aragon,* published on February 1938 a declaration of General Franco's Government whereby 'La glorieuse aviation nationale a opéré toujours, sur des objectifs militaires. Les stations frontières, les ports par où entre la contrebande française d'armes, de munition, d'éléments de trasports, etc... les concentrations de miliciens rouges, les usines où l'on travaille pour la guerre . . .' (the French translation here quoted, can be found in *Revue générale de droit aérien,* 1938, vol. 7, p. 45).

[33] *House of Commons Debates,* vol. 337, 20 June 1938, col. 680. It is useful to quote *in extenso* a further statement by Mr. Butler, which casts light both on the view of the British Government about what objectives are 'military' and on how bombings were actually carried out by the Nationalist authorities. Replying to a Member of Parliament who had asked what report had been received from the British Minister in Barcelona with regard to the presence of military objectives in Granollers, Mr. Butler said: 'His Majesty's Minister at Barcelona has reported that the town of Granollers contains a small barrack lived in by some 300 troops, a garage used to erect aeroplane engines, a small generating station for the supply of the town, a railway bridge and a railway station. These points were, however, well outside the area which suffered the full force of the bombardment. With the exception of a group of six or seven bombs, which fell in a field outside the town and far away from any target, and of three which burst at the railway station, all fell in the centre of the town' (*ibid.,* col. 681).

Unlike the statements we have seen thus far, other pronouncements condemning the methods of warfare of the Spanish Civil War, only made reference to the notion of 'open town'. Thus the Spanish Republican Government, when accusing the nationalist insurgents of behaving inhumanely in bombing defenceless civilians, nearly always stressed that the unlawful attacks had been made against 'open towns'.[34] On May 29, 1937, after a debate in the course of which reference was made to the bombing of Guernica and to other instances of attacks designed to spread terror among the civilian population, the Council of the League of Nations adopted a resolution stating, among other things, that:

profoundly moved by the horrors resulting from the use of certain methods of warfare, (the Council) condemns the employment, in the Spanish struggle, of methods contrary to international law and bombing of open towns.[35]

A similar resolution was adopted by the Assembly of the League of Nations on September 28, 1937.[36] The notion of 'open towns' was further invoked by several States, in the Assembly, in 1938[37] and, in 1939, in the Council of the same Organization[38] during the debate on the Spanish Civil War.

It follows from the statements we have seen that during the Spanish Civil War many States, international bodies as well as the parties to the Spanish conflict, developed a strong legal conviction that bombing civilian objectives was illegal. This amounts to saying that a legal conviction had emerged which specified that the rules of warfare protecting civilians in time of international conflicts were

[34] See the Spanish note to Great Britain and France of May 28, 1938, (in French), in *Revue générale de droit aérien*, 1938, p. 207 and 208. See also the communiqué of the Spanish Embassy in Paris of May 25, 1938, *ibid.*, p. 210, as well as the note of the Spanish Republican Government to Great Britain, of June 27, 1938, *ibid.*, p. 212.
It must be stressed that in a note of January 29, 1938 to the British Government, the Spanish Government spoke of 'civilian populations in the rear' ('L'aviation républicaine s'abstiendrait résolument de bombarder les populations de l'arrière si l'ennemi y consentatit également', *ibid.*, p. 207); in a further note of February 3, 1938 to the British Government, the Spanish Government referred to 'towns far away from the combat zone' ('éviter le bombardment de cités distantes du théatre des opérations', *ibid.*). It seems that this terminology was regarded by the Spanish authorities as equivalent to the more common expression 'open towns'.
However, it must not be overlooked that on some occasions the Spanish Government made reference to 'military objectives' instead of 'open towns'. See, for example, the statements made by the Spanish delegate on September 17, 1938, in the Assembly of the League of Nations (League of Nations, *Official Journal*, Special Supplement no. 186, Records of the XIXth Ordinary Session of the Assembly, Minutes of the Third Committee, p. 18) and on January 18, 1939, before the Council of the League (League of Nations, *Official Journal*, February 1939, p. 86).
[35] League of Nations, *Official Journal*, May–June 1937, p. 334.
[36] League of Nations, *Official Journal*, Special Supplement no. 168, p. 34.
[37] Mexico (League of Nations, *Official Journal*, Special Supplement no. 186, Records of the XIX the Ordinary Session of the Assembly *Minutes of the IIIrd Committee*, p. 23), Haiti (*ibid.*, pp. 30–31; see, however, p. 27).
[38] Great Britain (League of Nations, *Official Journal*, February 1939, p. 88. Cp. also the statement made on February 7, 1938 by the British Foreign Minister, Mr. A. Eden, in the House of Commons, in *House of Commons*, vol. 331, 7 February 1938, col. 652) and Bolivia (League of Nations, *Official Journal*, February 1939, p. 98).

also applicable to civil war. However, there were some variations and a certain amount of confusion concerning the exact determination of which objects must not be bombed, some parties stating that only 'open' or 'undefended' towns were not to be made targets of bombings, with others referring instead to 'non-military objectives'. Which of the two notions was really relied upon? This question is important for two reasons. First, the two notions at issue may to some extent be incompatible; in fact a town may be regarded as 'open' or 'undefended', and hence immune from attack, even though it contains military objectives provided, however, that it does not offer any active resistance to the enemy.[39] On the contrary, according to the doctrine of military objectives, combatants may strike every such objective, even if it is located in a town which the enemy can enter without opposition. Secondly, it is important to try to give an answer to the above question because in the 1930s the very same question arose with regard to inter-State armed conflicts as well. Also in this area States started invoking the notion of 'military objectives', without clarifying, however, whether or not it completely replaced the older concept of 'undefended towns'. Therefore, were it possible to reach a conclusive solution with regard to the Spanish civil strife, some light could be shed on a significant aspect of the evolution of international law concerning inter-State armed conflicts.

It would seem that in the final analysis most, if not all, parties who took a stand on this matter actually intended to exclude from legitimate war targets 'non-military objectives', even when referring to 'open towns'. In other words, it can be submitted that the notion of non-military objectives in fact replaced the older concept of 'open (or "undefended") town', in that towns were considered 'open' or 'undefended' only when devoid of military objectives. This seems to be borne out by some authoritative statements, which it will be useful to quote.

On June 18, 1937 the International Committee for the Application of the Agreement regarding Non-Intervention in Spain, on behalf of the 27 Governments which were parties to such Agreement, dispatched an appeal to both contending sides, stating *inter alia:*

The International Committee urge that both sides should abstain from the destruction of all open towns and villages and other objectives of a non-military character, whether by bombardment from the air, or by land or sea, or by fire, mining, or any other means.[40]

This statement clearly places open towns on the same footing as non-military objectives, thereby implying that towns are entitled to protection only in so far as they do not contain military objectives.

[39] See SCHMITZ, 'Die "offene Stadt" im geltenden Kriegsrecht', *Zeitschrift für ausländisches öffentliches Recht und Völkerrecht,* vol. 10, 1941–42, pp. 618–622; JENNINGS, 'Open Towns', *British Yearbook of International Law,* vol. 22, 1945, pp. 258–262.

[40] See the full text of the appeal in (London) *Times,* June 19, 1937, quoted in PADELFORD, *International Law and Diplomacy,* cit., p. 95, note 109. The French text can be found in *La Documentation internationale,* cit., vol. 5, nos. 45–46, Mars–Avril 1938, p. 54.

This is further confirmed by a discussion on the matter which took place in the British House of Commons. On March 1938 a member of the House, in view of the British protest to General Franco over the bombing of Barcelona, asked the Prime Minister to give a definition of 'open town' and to explain why Barcelona was classed as an open town and therefore immune to attack, although it contained the seat of government, offices of government departments, military bases, munition factories, docks, and railways available for the transport of troops and munitions. The Prime Minister N. Chamberlain replied *inter alia* as follows:

> ... The rules of international law as to what constitutes a military objective are undefined and pending the conclusion of the examination of this question ... I am not in a position to make any statement on the subject. The one definite rule of international law, however, is that the direct and deliberate bombing of non-combatants is in all circumstances illegal, and His Majesty's Government's protest was based on information which led them to the conclusion that the bombardment of Barcelona, carried on apparently at random and without special aim at military objectives, was in fact of this nature.[41]

Although the Prime Minister avoided giving any definition, he referred not to 'open towns' but only to 'military objectives', thereby showing that in his Government's view the latter notion had superseded the former.

Another authoritative statement which can be quoted in support of my thesis was made on June 3, 1938, by the Acting Secretary of State of the United States, Summer Welles. He declared:

> When the methods used in the conduct of ... hostilities take the form of ruthless bombing of unfortified localities with the resultant slaughter of civilian populations and in particular of women and children, public opinion in the United States regards such methods as barbarous. Several times during the past year, especially on September 28, 1937, and on March 21, 1938, the Secretary of State has expressed the views of this country to the effect that any general bombing of an extensive area wherein there resided a large population engaged in peaceful pursuits is contrary to every principle of law and of humanity. During the past few days there have taken place in China and in Spain aerial bombings which have resulted in the death of many hundreds of the civilian population. This Government, while scrupulously adhering to the policy of nonintervention, reiterates this nation's emphatic reprobation of such methods and of such acts, which are in violation of the most elementary principles of those standards of humane conduct which have been developed as an essential part of modern civilization.[42]

It is apparent from the wording of this declaration that in the view of the United States Government 'fortified localities' can be legitimately bombed whereas strictly civilian areas must be spared. This is tantamount to maintaining the distinction between 'military' and 'non-military' objectives. In this connection it is interesting to note that, under Article 25 of the 1907 Hague Regulations, a

---

[41] *House of Commons Debates*, vol. 333, 23 March 1938, col. 1177.

[42] *Documents on American Foreign Relations, January 1938–June 1939*, Boston 1939, pp. 208–209. See *ibid.*, at p. 209, note 1, the text of the Secretary of State's statement of March 21, 1938.

locality is 'undefended' even if it is fortified, provided it is open to entry by the enemy. Now, in the American declaration the existence of fortifications is sufficient for giving a locality the character of a legitimate target. The replacement of the 'open' or 'undefended' locality concept by the 'military objective' concept is once again confirmed.[43]

Lastly, a declaration which, to my mind, substantiates the view I have expressed, was made by the insurgents. In March 1938 the Salamanca authorities received an offer of good offices, made by the British Government with a view to inducing both sides to discontinue bombing of open towns. In their reply the Salamanca authorities pointed out that, while they deeply regretted the bombardment of open towns, and had avoided on every occasion causing useless ravages, they must nevertheless reserve to themselves freedom of action as far as the free development of the campaign was concerned, which necessitated striking at military objectives wherever they might be found.[44]

C. The Rule Concerning the Precautions that Must Be Taken when Attacking Military Objectives

Let me now turn to consider a third rule protecting civilians, which was clearly affirmed by several parties. It was first spelled out by the British Prime Minister in the House of Commons, in 1938. He stated that one of the three rules or principles of international law equally applicable to air, land, or sea warfare in any armed conflicts (hence both international and internal), was the rule whereby:

Reasonable care must be taken in attacking . . . military objectives so that by carelessness a civilian population in the neighbourhood is not bombed.[45]

As in the case of the other rules previously mentioned, this formulation by the British Prime Minister was substantially taken up by the Assembly of the

---

[43] Furthermore, it may be recalled that in 1938, in the Assembly of the League of Nations the delegate of Greece stated that regulations had to be adopted with a view to allowing to draw 'a pratical distinction' 'between open and other towns, between towns with military defences and those without' (League of Nations, *Official Journal,* Special Supplement no. 186, Records of the XIX Ordinary Session of the Assembly, *Minutes of the IIIrd Committee,* p. 25). The delegate from Haiti stated that 'undefended open towns without any military objective might be specified in peacetime by means of a preliminary agreement . . .' (*ibid.,* p. 27).

[44] The Spanish reply was related to the House of Commons by the British Under-Secretary of State for Foreign Affairs, Mr. Butler: see *House of Commons Debates,* vol. 333, 14 March 1938, col. 5.

[45] *House of Commons Debates,* vol. 337, 21 June 1938, cols. 937–938. The Prime Minister added however: 'We must try to lay down rules which will be accepted by all sides and will be carried out in practice. I say that reasonable care must be taken, in attacking military objectives, not to go outside those objectives, but it is extremely difficult in practice to determine whether in fact the dropping of bombs which have killed civilians in the neighbourhood of military objectives is the result of want of care or not. Suppose a man makes a bad shot, which is not at all unlikely when machines are going at over 300 miles an hour and when, as I am informed, in taking aim you have to release the bomb miles away from its objective—it seems to me that it is extremely difficult to lay down exactly the point at which reasonable care turns into unreasonable want of care' (*ibid.,* cols. 938–939).

League of Nations in 1938. The Assembly adopted a resolution stating *inter alia* that 'any attack on legitimate military objectives must be carried out in such a way that civilian populations in the neighbourhood are not bombed through negligence'.[46] The same rules were invoked by the representative of the Spanish lawful Government in the Council of the League of Nations, in 1939.[47] The Council itself adopted a resolution condemning *inter alia* as 'contrary to the conscience of mankind and to the principles of international law', air attacks by the insurgents directed 'by negligence' against civilian populations.[48]

It would seem that even the insurgents relied upon the same rule. For, on December 1, 1938, on the eve of the offensive against Catalonia, the nationalist authorities announced on the radio all places in the areas controlled by Republicans containing military objectives that would be bombed by nationalist armed forces. This announcement, according to General Franco's administration, was made in order to enable Republican authorities to take all measures necessary for protecting or evacuating civilians.[49]

D. The Rule Authorizing Reprisals against Enemy Civilians

A fourth rule whose application to the Spanish Civil War was clearly affirmed by some States was the rule whereby reprisals are legitimate against enemy civilians, in the event that the adversary should breach international law by bombing the civilian population. In a note addressed to the French Foreign Minister, the Minister for Foreign Affairs of the Spanish Republican Government stated, in 1938, that the Republican Government was fully entitled to resort to reprisals, though this did not correspond to its humanitarian attitude.[50] The same stand was taken by the Spanish representative in the League of Nations.[51] No member of the Organisation challenged the right of the Spanish Government to resort to

---

[46] League of Nations, *Official Journal,* Special Supplement no. 183, cit., p. 136. See *supra,* para. 3 (A) and notes 17 and 18.

[47] League of Nations, *Official Journal,* February 1939, p. 86.

[48] League of Nations, *Official Journal,* February 1939, p. 97.

[49] See XVIIe Conférence internationale de la Croix-Rouge, Stockholm, août 1948, *Rapport complémentaire sur l'activité du Comité international de la Croix-Rouge relative à la guerre civile en Espagne* (du 1er juin 1938 au 31 août 1939) *et à ses suites,* Genève, mai 1948, p. 12. The reaction of the Republican Government was as follows 'Les Autorités républicaines firent valoir que cette publication (viz. the Burgos authorities' announcement) n'avait nullement un caractère humanitaire, mais celui de tromper l'adversaire sur les directions de la prochaine offensive' (*ibid.*).

[50] For the French text of the Spanish note, see the French Journal *La protection de la population civile,* 1938, vol. 1, pp. 172–173.

[51] See the statement made by the Spanish representative on September 17, 1938 in the Assembly of the League (League of Nations, *Official Journal,* Special Supplement no. 186, Records of the XIXth Ordinary Session of the Assembly, Minutes of the IIIrd Committee, p. 19) and on February 1939 in the Council of the League (League of Nations, *Official Journal,* February 1939, p. 87).

reprisals.[52] The resolution adopted by the Council contained a preambular paragraph in which the Council noted:

. . . with satisfaction the declaration made by the representative of Spain before the Council according to which the Spanish Government maintains the decision mentioned in that declaration not to take reprisals in consequence of the aerial bombardments of which the civilian population in its territory is the victim.[53]

This statement, by not questioning the right of the Spanish Government to visit reprisals on the insurgents, clearly implies that in the opinion of the Council the Government was fully entitled to do so, although such a course of action would have displeased the Council.

4. Legal Problems Raised by Reliance Upon the Above Rules in the Spanish Civil War

The four rules I have been discussing were surely recognized as binding by both contending parties: even when either of these did not actually comply with them, it did uphold them formally, and only denied the facts of which it was accused. Moreover, as we have seen, the same rules were proclaimed time and again by several third States, either separately or jointly, through the organs of the League of Nations. They expressly emphasized that those rules must regulate the behaviour of the lawful government and the insurgents alike. Hence, no doubt a strong and general legal conviction emerged as to the full applicability of those rules to the war raging in Spain.

We must now ask ourselves three questions: first, how did it happen that international rules were regarded as applicable to a civil war even though a recognition of belligerency was lacking; second, by which formal process did this legal development take place; and finally, did these international rules emerge with specific reference to the Spanish Civil War alone, or is their scope much wider, so as to cover any large-scale civil war?

The reason why both contending parties and third States considered the four abovementioned rules applicable to the Spanish Civil War, may be found in the magnitude assumed by this war, and in its duration and scope. This internal strife was so long and complex and had such wide international repercussions that it greatly resembled an inter-State war. These features explain *inter alia* why, as was pointed out above (para. 1), third parties, although they did not assimilate it to a war proper, did not regard it as a mere internal conflict either, and mutually undertook non-intervention obligations that are at variance with traditional practice in case of civil wars proper. The main reason for the application of the rules

---

[52] See League of Nations, *Official Journal,* February 1939, pp. 88–98.
[53] *Ibid.,* p. 97.

on civilians to the Spanish conflict lies, however, in the fact that the massive use of weapons and new methods of warfare, especially of aerial bombardment, caused so much loss to civilians that it aroused the greatest indignation among the civilized world. Many States, first among them Great Britain and France, exerted strong pressure, both outside and inside the League of Nations, for the adoption by the contending parties of standards of conduct capable of protecting civilians from the horrors of warfare to the maximum possible extent. The havoc wrought by the new methods of warfare was so great that the parties concerned, and third States, fully realized that certain human values must be proclaimed and protected at all times, regardless of whether the conflict is internal or international. It was not accidental that those values were forcefully enunciated by the members of the League of Nations in 1938, while discussing two different situations, that of Spain and the conflict between China and Japan. Although the Spanish struggle was internal and the Sino-Japanese international, the very same principles concerning the protection of civilians were upheld with regard to both of them.

By which formal process did these rules apply to the Spanish war?—this is our second question.

The International Committee of the Red Cross made reference to 'application by analogy' when it stated that the contending parties applied the 1929 Geneva Convention on Wounded and Sick. It is self-evident that in that case there was no analogy proper. In fact, the parties to the conflict concluded through the ICRC an agreement that took over its basic contents from the Geneva Convention. The Convention served as a model from which provisions were drawn and adjusted to the exigencies of a civil war. Is it appropriate to refer to analogy in those other cases where customary international rules evolved concerning civil wars? It is common knowledge that the basic condition underlying resort to analogy is the lack of any international rule, or any *practice of States* pointing to a legal regulation of a certain matter. However, in the case at issue we have noted that States repeatedly affirmed that certain rules were to be applied to the Spanish conflict. It would therefore seem that the basic condition for recourse to analogy did not exist. The reason why reference was made to 'analogy' lies in a confusion between analogy proper, which is a supplementary means of finding law when customary or treaty rules are lacking or defective, and 'analogy' as a practical and psychological process whereby some rules of law are shaped by States themselves on the model of (or by 'analogy' with) other pre-existing rules. In the case under consideration some of the rules on civil war evolved on the pattern of those governing inter-State conflicts.

Hence, the best way for legally explaining how the international rules in question grew up is to go back to the traditional law-creating process of customary law. In the case in point there were both the constitutive elements of customary law, namely the *usus* and the *opinio juris*. For, as I have been showing, there evolved a general practice among third States and concerned parties, and evidence exists that this practice was recognized as flowing from a legal obligation.

What pointedly characterized the creation of the rules under consideration is the particular way their content took shape. In part their content was *materially borrowed from existing rules on international war* (this is the case for the prohibition against attacking civilian population as such); in part they *emerged at the same time as the new rules regulating inter-State wars* (this applies to the rule on military objectives and on precautionary measures to be taken when attacking these objectives).

Turning to the third question (that of whether the four above-mentioned rules were regarded as applicable to the Spanish war only, or whether they have a wider scope), I am firmly convinced that the latter solution is correct. This, I submit, is amply proved by a number of statements and declarations of third States, in which, though generally referring to Spain, they took the view that the applicability of those rules was called for by the very nature of the civil war, not by the mere fact of that war taking place in that specific area and between those specific parties. Those States, and even, occasionally, the contending parties, insisted on the humanitarian basis of the rules protecting civilians, and expressly stressed that they had been induced to uphold them by humanitarian feelings. How could it then be argued that these States meant to apply the rules to the Spanish war only, and disregard of the victims of *any* internal armed conflict? Secondly, in recent years the Afro-Asian majority, in concert with the socialist countries, have promoted the passing by the United Nations General Assembly of a number of resolutions which are designed to legitimize some categories of internal rebellions, i.e. wars of national liberation. These resolutions, in particular, urge that members of liberation movements, or, more generally, 'freedom fighters', should be treated as legitimate belligerents, and should be assisted by member States. To be sure, these resolutions cannot amount to an implicit recognition of belligerency, for there is no evidence that their sponsors or the States voting in favour of them have ever meant to draw from them all the consequences following from the granting of belligerent rights. Yet, the resolutions are significant inasmuch as they show that, in the opinion of vast segments of international society, some categories of internal armed conflicts *should* be governed by rules which traditionally apply to inter-State armed conflicts only.

Of course, the best way of completely and satisfactorily filling the gap resulting from the obsolescence of the recognition of belligerency, would be to pass a set of international rules regulating those aspects of internal armed conflicts which are most in need of being governed by international legislation. This is precisely the path taken by the International Committee of the Red Cross, which has proposed that a Diplomatic Conference should adopt a Protocol Additional to Article 3 Common to the 1949 Geneva Conventions. It is strongly to be hoped that the efforts of the ICRC will find a positive response among States.

7. The Status of Rebels under the 1977 Geneva Protocol on Non-International Armed Conflicts*

1. Introduction

The question to which I wish to address myself in this paper relates to the possible legal standing of rebels in the case of civil war under the II Additional Protocol to the four 1949 Geneva Conventions, which was adopted by a Diplomatic Conference in 1977. I shall examine the question whether insurgents have rights and duties under the Protocol and in particular, whether they can claim respect for the Protocol by the incumbent Government and, if so, at what stage of civil war they become bound by the obligations of and benefit from the Protocol.

It should be pointed out at once, for the sake of clarity, that the above issues are not merely theoretical. Indeed, they are of great practical significance, for two reasons. First, internal wars are increasingly common all over the world, in particular in Third World countries. Fully-fledged international wars are more and more risky because they may grow into nuclear wars or because many States may become entangled in the conflict. Therefore, large and medium-sized powers either refrain from settling disputes by armed force or fight their wars by proxy, in the territory of other States. The latter are usually developing countries, whose political structures are fragile and often beset with tribal or other conflicts.[1]

The second reason why the legal status of rebels under Protocol II is of practical consequence is more specific. To grant rebels international rights and duties means that the divide between insurgents and the legal government has reached such a point that the former have a standing, albeit limited, in the international community. To acknowledge that rebels are entitled to invoke international rules implies that they are outside both the physical and legal control of the national authorities. By contrast, to suggest that insurgents cannot rely on international law means that the only body of law applicable to them is domestic criminal law and consequently that the government in power is free from international constraint and can treat them as it thinks best.[2]

---

* Originally published in 30 *International and Comparative Law Quarterly* (1981) 416.

[1] See in particular Falk, *Janus Tormented: the International Law of Internal War*, in International Aspects of Civil Strife 185 ff. (Rosenau ed. 1964); Roting, *The Legal Status of Rebels and Rebellion*, 13 Journal of Peace Research 149–151 (1976).

[2] It should be pointed out that under the Protocol the lawful Government is authorized to consider insurgents as criminals to be prosecuted under its own criminal legislation, despite the fact

It should be added that the importance of the question raised above is in no way belittled by the fact that an admittedly important category of internal armed conflict, namely wars of national liberation, has been 'upgraded' by the 1977 Geneva Protocol I to the class of international conflicts, and therefore those engaged in such wars enjoy the full status of lawful combatants and are even entitled formally to derive rights and duties from Protocol I. This diminishes the importance of civil wars to a limited extent because—at least on the face of it—Article 1, para. 4 of Protocol I takes a rather restricted view of wars of national liberation, and actually only includes three categories, namely wars against colonial domination, against alien occupation or against racist regimes.[3] It follows that most of the civil wars which have lately broken out in Third World countries, or are at present being fought there, do not fall under this heading. Suffice it to mention here the recent war in Nicaragua, or the disturbances and clashes currently taking place in Chad or El Salvador.

2. General Features of the 1977 Geneva Protocol

Before considering whether the 1977 Geneva Protocol confers rights and imposes obligations on insurgents it may be appropriate briefly to look at a few of its general features germane to the specific issue to be considered in this paper.

The Protocol was given its title ('Protocol Additional to the 1949 Geneva Conventions') because it was conceived as an international treaty to supplement and develop Common Article 3 of the Geneva Conventions. It is therefore closely linked to those Conventions, and indeed only States party to them are allowed to sign and ratify, or to accede to the Protocol.[4]

---

that they may belong to an international body (the central authorities controlling the rebels) which derives rights and duties from the Protocol (see *infra*). It could be suggested that this is a striking contradiction. Admittedly, it is somewhat inconsistent to consider insurgents as persons fighting on behalf of an international entity and yet subject them to criminal legislation for the very fact of fighting. This contradiction was motivated by the fact that the States participating in the Geneva Diplomatic Conference did not intend to go so far as to upgrade rebels to the status of *lawful combatants*. This, in their view, would have entailed legitimizing the rebels' struggle; they would thus have abdicated their role of sovereign Governments exercising *exclusive* control over the territory belonging to them.

[3] See Abi-Saab, *Wars of National Liberation and the Laws of War*, Annales d'Etudes Internationales, 93 ff. (1972); Salmon, *Les guerres de libération nationale,* in The New Humanitarian Law of Armed Conflict 55 ff. (Cassese ed. 1979). See, however, Cassese, *A Tentative Appraisal of the Old and New Humanitarian Law of Armed Conflict,* in The New Humanitarian Law of Armed Conflict, at pp. 466–470.

[4] So far (June 1980) 10 States have ratified, or acceded to the Protocol: Botswana, Ecuador, El Salvador, Ghana, Jordon, Libya, Niger, Sweden, Tunisia and Jugoslavia (see ICRC, *Signatures, Ratifications and Accessions to the Geneva Conventions of August 12, 1949 and to the two Additional Protocols of June 8, 1975,* DD/JUR—No 9/3, 5.7.1977).

On the Protocol, see Kalshoven, *Reaffirmation and Development of International Humanitarian Law I, 8* Netherlands Yearbook of International Law, 107 ff. (1977); Bothe, *Conflits armés internes*

In order to grasp the full importance and the limitations of the Protocol, one should bear in mind that most Third World countries opposed it at Geneva and consistently endeavoured to hamstring, or at least water it down. A vocal alignment consisting of western and socialist States tried to convince the recalcitrant majority to hammer out an international instrument strongly geared to humanitarian demands. It is a matter for some regret that the nations hostile or lukewarm towards the Protocol eventually won the upper hand.[5] This accounts for the modest character of the final outcome—a Protocol which is indeed an emasulated version of what might have been desired. In addition, it is replete with general or ambiguous clauses designed to please both the States hostile to the development of international legislation on the matter and those which desired to create an international instrument of considerable substance. A few observations may be enough to give an idea of the scope and significance of the Protocol.

First, it does not apply to all internal conflicts, but only to those which are prolonged and of great intensity. Article 1 states that the insurgents must be 'organised armed groups' which 'under responsible command, exercise such control over a part of the territory of the State as to enable them to carry out sustained and concerted military operations and to implement the Protocol'. Paragraph 2 of the same article spells out this notion by specifying that the Protocol does not apply 'to situations of internal disturbances and tensions, such as riots, isolated and sporadic acts of violence and other acts of a similar nature'. It is therefore apparent that the Protocol has a high 'threshold of application', and in substance only covers those civil wars which by their scale reach a level comparable to that of the Spanish war or the Nigerian conflict. All conflicts which fall short of the strict conditions required by Article 1 without, however, being minor domestic incidents, are covered only by Common Article 3, which no doubt retains a much broader field of application than Protocol II.

A second feature of the Protocol is that it has an almost exclusively *humanitarian* content; in other words, it is primarily designed to protect *'victims'* of the armed conflict, i.e. those who do not take a direct part in the hostilities, as well as those who have ceased to take part in the armed conflict because they have been taken prisoner, have been wounded, shipwrecked or are ill. However, the Protocol

et droit international humanitaire, 82 Revue Générale de Droit International Public, 82 ff. (1978); Forsythe, *Legal Management of Internal War: The 1977 Protocol on Non-International Armed Conflicts*, 72 AJIL 272 ff. (1978); Dupuy and Leonetti, *La notion de conflit armé à caractère non international*, in The New Humanitarian Law of Armed Conflict, at p. 258 ff., Eide, *The New Humanitarian Law in Non-International Armed Conflict*, *ibid*. p. 277 ff.

[5] On the attitude taken by the various States gathered at Geneva see Lysaght, *The Attitude of Western Countries*, in The New Humanitarian Law of Armed Conflict, at pp. 382–385; Condorelli, *Les Pays Afro-asiatiques*, *ibid*. at pp. 387–391; Forsythe, op cit *supra* n. 4, pp. 280–281; Bothe, op cit *supra*, n. 4 at pp. 86–87; Cassese, *A Tentative Appraisal of the Old and the New Humanitarian Law of Armed Conflict*, op cit *supra*, pp. 494–497.

includes a few rules impinging upon the conduct of the hostilities themselves.[6] Even these provisions, although they put restraints on the methods used in combat, mostly favour those who do not take part in the hostilities or have ceased to participate in them, as well as medical personnel. Nevertheless, at least one provision protects those who actually carry out military operations: namely the rule forbidding the denial of quarter (Article 4, para. 1).[7] All in all, however, the greater number of the restraints set by the Protocol benefit persons who are not, or who are no longer, engaged in combat.

A third feature of the Protocol is that it does not provide any machinery for its supervision or enforcement. The Protocol has not bestowed on any international body the right to determine whether in a given case the circumstances have arisen conditional upon which the Protocol becomes operative. Furthermore, no international body is called upon to pass judgment on whether or not the parties to the conflict have kept to the standards imposed by the Protocol. This lack of any international scrutiny, which clearly resulted from the joint view of Third World and socialist countries is no doubt most unfortunate, for it may result in stultifying the effect of the Protocol. However, this situation is somewhat remedied by the fact that, as has been pointed out, the Protocol is closely linked and even enmeshed with Common Article 3. Indeed, Article 1, para. 1 of the Protocol starts by stating that the Protocol 'develops and supplements Article 3 common to the Geneva Conventions of August 12, 1949.' A few States at Geneva,[8] and subsequently some commentators[9] have inferred from that provision that the Protocol remains under the aegis of Common Article 3 and consequently benefits from its major advantages. As Common Article 3 provides among other things that 'an impartial humanitarian body, such as the International Committee of the Red Cross, may offer its services to the Parties to the conflict', the conclusion is surely justified that the ICRC is authorized to offer its services to the parties at war for the purpose of enabling them to comply more completely with the Protocol. It would of course be unsound to contend that, in the case of an internal armed conflict covered by both Article 3 and the Protocol, the ICRC (or for that matter, any other impartial humanitarian body) could propose to help only in operating the provisions of Article 3, being therefore barred from offering to scrutinize the application of the Protocol. Indeed, the terms of reference set out in Article 3 are

---

[6] For example, the rule against giving no quarter (Art. 4, para. 10), the prohibitions on taking hostages, on terrorism and pillage (Art. 4, para. *2c, d* and *g*), the prohibition on attacking medical units and transport (Art. 11), the rule protecting the civilian population against the dangers arising from military operations (Art. 13), the provision protecting objects indispensable to the survival of the civilian population (Art. 14), the rule protecting works and installations containing dangerous forces (Art. 15), and the rule protecting cultural objects and places of worship (Art. 16).

[7] Indeed, to prohibit belligerents ordering that there shall be no survivors amounts to protecting their enemy from being killed out of hand instead of being taken prisoner.

[8] See *e.g.* the declaration by Belgium (CDDH/SR. 49, Annex, p. 76) as well as that made by Italy (CDDH/SR. 50, Annex, pp. 100–101).

[9] See, for instance, Bothe, op cit, p. 100; Forsythe, op cit, p. 288.

very broad ('may offer its services to the Parties to the conflict'): they can therefore legitimately cover monitoring the implementation of the Protocol as well.

A fourth feature of the Protocol is that it is only open for signature and ratification, or accession by *States,* more specifically, by those States which are parties to the 1949 Geneva Conventions (Articles 20–22). No provision is made for the 'participation' in the Protocol by rebels, when civil war breaks out on the territory of a contracting party. This is all the more striking as Protocol I, relating to international armed conflicts, includes a clause (Article 96, para. 3), which allows 'liberation movements' to 'participate' in the Protocol, by means of a unilateral declaration addressed to the Swiss Federal Council, the depositary of the Conventions and the Protocol. This difference can of course be explained to some extent by the fact, as has been pointed out before, that Protocol I has 'upgraded' wars of national liberation to the rank of international armed conflicts. The fact remains, however, that the States gathered at Geneva preferred to omit any clause that might grant insurgents a right to accede formally to Protocol II. Does this mean that those States intended to rule out any legal standing for the rebels, in the case of civil war?

3. The Status of Rebels Under the Geneva Protocol

I shall now endeavour to grapple with the problem raised at the outset of this paper, namely whether insurgents derive rights and duties from the Protocol, or whether it is binding merely on the contracting States.

As I have pointed out above, the Protocol, at least taken at face value, does not confer rights or impose obligations on rebels, in that it does not permit them formally to become a party to it. It would therefore seem that States are the only international entities to which the Protocol applies. This would by no means amount to a legal aberration. Each contracting State would undertake (*vis-à-vis* all the other contracting parties) to respect the provisions of the Protocol in the case of a civil war breaking out within its territory. The right to demand that a Government fighting insurgents should comply with the Protocol would thus only belong to all the other ratifying States, not the insurgents themselves.

This view was put forward by Italy at the Geneva Conference. When Article 10 *bis* (which required unconditional respect for the Protocol) was deleted,[10] Italy put on record a full statement enunciating its view that, despite the rejection of that article, the Protocol's provisions demanded unconditional respect and, therefore, had to be met even when one of the parties to the conflict ignored them. The Italian declaration pointed out that this thesis was 'fully in keeping with the essential legal significance' of the Protocol, and then went on to state:

In ratifying this instrument, the High Contracting Parties will assume obligations, not towards rebel forces (which are neither subjects of international law nor Parties to Protocol

---

[10] For the text of this Article, see *infra,* n. 42. Art. 10 *bis* was rejected by 41 votes to 20, with 22 abstentions (CDDH/SR. 51, para. 16).

II), but towards the other Contracting Parties, the international community and world opinion. Clearly, therefore, each Contracting Party's obligation to respect Protocol II cannot be conditioned or modified by the conduct of rebel forces.[11]

Italy was not without support in this view—indeed several other States took a very similar stand on the issue. For example, various Third World countries suggested that the expression 'the parties to the conflict', found in various provisions of the draft Protocol, should be deleted, lest the Protocol seem to endorse the view that insurgents were on the same footing as Government forces. The phrase was consequently removed from the Protocol. In addition, and for the same reasons, draft Article 3 on the 'legal status of the parties to the conflict' and Article 5, on the equality of the parties to the conflict,[12] were dropped in the final stage of the adoption of the Protocol.[13] The States that pushed for these changes, and which eventually succeeded in imposing their views, were clearly motivated by the desire to reduce rebels to the level of criminals devoid of any international status. This attitude was made completely clear by some of these States, in the final declarations which they made after the adoption of the Protocol as a whole. Thus, for instance, the representative of Sudan stated that:

The Protocol did not involve any international agreements but simply a concession on the part of States which agreed to apply it to their own nationals.[14]

The representative of Zaire, for his part, stressed that the original draft Protocol had suffered from the major drawback that at least some of its provisions treated 'a sovereign State and a group of insurgent nationals, a legal Government and a group of outlaws, a subject of international law and a subject of domestic law, on an equal footing'. The final draft had instead the 'great virtue' that it 'toned down the legal character which draft Protocol II, as adopted in Committee, had conferred on rebellious elements'. Under the final version of the Protocol:

[Rebels] had not the same rights as the national Government, which was the embodiment of State sovereignty and which held general responsibilities. Indeed, they did not possess any rights at all, but simply had an obligation to deal humanely with all those who did not take part in hostilities or with other prisoners of war who might fall into their hands.[15]

---

[11] CDDH/SR. 51, Annex, p. 122.

[12] Art. 3, as adopted in 1975 (see CDDH/2 9/Rev. 1, para. 103), provided as follows: 'The application of the provisions of the present Protocol, or of all or part of the provisions of the Geneva Conventions of August 12, 1949, and of the Additional Protocol relating to the protection of victims of international armed conflicts brought into force in accordance with Art. 38 or by the conclusion of any agreement provided for in the Geneva Conventions and the Additional Protocols shall not affect the legal status of the parties to the conflict.' Art. 5, as adopted in 1975 (CDDH/219/Rev. 1, para. 116), stipulated as follows: 'The rights and duties which derive from the present Protocol apply equally to all the parties to the conflict.'

[13] CDDH/SR. 50, paras 2–9.

[14] CDDH/SR. 56, para. 37.

[15] CDDH/SR. 56, para. 126.

The attitude of Zaire was made even more explicit in another statement:

Only a sovereign State can claim to have international legal personality and, as such, it enjoys all the prerogatives of sovereignty, including that of entering into international agreements and conventions, that is to say, of becoming a party to them. Accordingly, dissident armed forces are primarily a group of rebels with no international legal personality. Their only legal status is that granted them under the domestic laws of their national State. To claim otherwise is to place a sovereign State on the same footing as a rebel movement, and that would imply *de facto* recognition of the movement.[16]

However, it should be noted that other countries disagreed with this view. Thus for instance, as early as 1975, the representative of the Soviet Union emphasized that in his opinion the Protocol would be binding on both the contracting States and insurgents. The occasion for this statement was the discussion of draft Article 22 concerning the prohibition of the refusal of quarter (a rule that fortunately did not undergo the mutilation that eventually maimed so many parts of the original draf and is at present incorporated in Article 4, para. 1). Commenting on Article 22, the Soviet delegate said:

If it was accepted, it [Article 22] would impose an obligation not only on Governments but on those who, for various reasons, were engaged in movements against Governments. Once adopted, the text would become a national law imposing an obligation on all persons within the territory of the State in question. Any international instrument signed by a Government was binding on all those within its territory. . . . Some delegations had thought that the text in question would impose an obligation on Governments only. That would be a serious mistake. The obligation was in fact valid for all citizens. . . .[17]

The same conclusion was reached by Belgium, which however gave different reasons for its view. The starting point for Belgium was not the necessary transformation of the Protocol into the domestic law of all the contracting States, but rather the link between Common Article 3 and the Protocol. Belgium propounded the following syllogism: as Common Article 3 is binding on both States and rebels and as the Protocol takes up and embodies all the basic principles of Article 3, hence the Protocol too is addressed to both States and insurgents. The Belgian 'doctrine' was set out in a declaration made in plenary session after the adoption of Article I of the Protocol. It was stated there that:

. . . The entire philosophy of the provisions of Common Article 3, whether explicitly reaffirmed or not, is included in the Protocol. It is implicit that the same applies to the basic sovereign principle that the obligations of the Protocol are equally binding on both Parties to the conflict. . . .[18]

Faced with this sharp divergence of view on the status of rebels, I believe that a solution can be found only if the question is put in the right legal perspective.

[16] CDDH/SR. 50, Annex, p. 104.
[17] CDDH/III/SR. 32, paras 21–28.
[18] CDDH/SR. 49, Annex, p. 76.

Upon analysis, the problem revolves around whether the Protocol can produce legal effects for 'third parties'. To solve this, one should of course start from the customary rules on the effects of treaties on third parties, as they have been codified in the Vienna Convention on the Law of Treaties. To be sure, this Convention only relates to States, while the customary rules on the matter have a broader scope, in that they govern the effects of treaties on *any international subject* taking the position of a third party *vis-à-vis* a treaty. However, it is appropriate to rely on the Convention, for two reasons. First, general international law does not differentiate in this matter between States and other international legal persons, as far as the effects of treaties between States are concerned. Secondly, the Vienna Convention does not deviate from that law; rather it codifies it and spells it out. Although it explicitly refers to treaties between States only (see Article I), it does not rule out the applicability of its provisions to other international entities. One can therefore legitimately draw on the Convention in order to ascertain the contents of general principles, to the extent that the Convention does not depart from them.

Articles 34–36 of the Convention[19] lay down correctly the principle that a treaty can create either obligations or rights for a third party only if two conditions are met: first, the contracting parties must have intended the treaty to grant such rights or impose such obligations on third parties; and secondly, a third party must accept the rights or obligations. The test is, therefore, twofold; combining the intention of the draftsmen and the attitude of third parties.

The first requirement, regarding the intention of the States which worked out the treaty, is in our case rather difficult to apply. Indeed, as is abundantly proven by the conflicting statements which I mentioned above, the framers of the Protocol did not express a common view on whether they intended to 'open up' the Protocol to insurgents. Two sharply opposing views were propounded on this issue, neither of which can be said to have won the upper hand. It is probably fair to contend that the view opposed to any extension of legal rights or duties to rebels was far more widespread. However, the contrary stance, although it was only taken by a minority, was clearly regarded by them as a basic condition for their acceptance of the Protocol. We are consequently at a loss to pinpoint any single intention of the draftsmen. I suggest, however, that one should not confine oneself to the intention of the parties as it appears from their statements or declarations. More important than these is the 'intention' which emerges from the text of the Protocol itself: in other words, the intention that was incorporated into the Protocol's provisions; this, unlike that sketched in the various and contradictory statements, was 'crystallised' and objective. It is this intention that should play a decisive role in assessing whether the authors of the Protocol really meant it to be binding on insurgents as well.

[19] See thereon Sinclair, *The Vienna Convention on the Law of Treaties,* at pp. 76–79 (1973); Elias, *The Modern Law of Treaties,* at pp. 59–70 (1974).

I shall identify this 'objective' intention of the draftsmen under three heads.

First, attention should be drawn to the relationship between Common Article 3 and the Protocol (the argument put forward by Belgium, as mentioned above). Article 1, para. 1 of the Protocol states that the Protocol 'develops and supplements Article 3.' This, among other things, means that whenever an internal armed conflict arising in the territory of a State that is party both to the Geneva Conventions and Protocol II comes within the purview of both Article 3 and Protocol II, the effects of the two instruments are inseparably connected. The one cannot be applied without the other. But if the Protocol 'develops and supplements' Article 3, this of necessity means that it follows the same lines as that article and only expands and broadens the protection granted by it. Since it is undisputed that Article 3 is binding on and grants rights to insurgents,[20] the conclusion is inescapable that Protocol II was destined by its authors to operate for rebels. It would indeed be absurd to contend that Article 3 gives rights and imposes obligations on rebels, while Protocol II—which is but an elaboration of that article—refuses to make itself available to them. It can therefore be maintained that, on the wording of Article 1, para. 1, the States gathered at Geneva did not mean to deviate from the approach of Article 3 and therefore intended to put the Protocol at the disposal of rebels.

A second argument based on the wording of the Protocol can be advanced. Article 1, para. 1, stipulates that the Protocol can only apply when rebels fulfil certain conditions. These conditions include the existence of a 'responsible command' controlling the 'organised armed group' which fights against the Government in power. The 'responsible command' and the 'organised' character of the rebels are considered as prerequisites for permitting insurgents to implement the Protocol. In short, the Protocol only begins to apply when rebels prove to be able to, and do in fact, implement it. This being so, it would plainly be absurd to contend that the rebels must comply with the Protocol, in order for it to become applicable, yet do not acquire any rights or duties. There would be no reason for insurgents to fulfil the obligations deriving from the Protocol if they could not benefit from the rights it confers, once the Protocol becomes applicable as a result of their compliance. If that were so the insurgents would clearly never begin to keep the rules of the Protocol, aware that in any case they would not gain in the least from such behaviour. If the activation of the Protocol is made conditional on their respecting it, this of necessity must entail that once they prove to be able to implement the Protocol, its provisions become legally binding on them. A contrary interpretation would render the whole Protocol nugatory; it should

---

[20] See e.g. Pictet (ed.), *Commentary, I Geneva Conventions,* at 51 (1952); Guggenheim, *Traité de Droit International Public, II,* pp. 313–314 (1954); Draper, *The Red Cross Conventions,* at p. 17 (1958); Siotis, *Le Droit de la Guerre et les Conflits Armés d'an Caractère Non International,* at pp. 217–218 (1958); Draper, *The Geneva Conventions of 1949,* Hague Recueil 1965–1, at 96; Zorgbibe, *La guerre civile* Annales de la Faculté de Droit et des Sciences Economiques (Université de Clermont), 163 ff. (1969). Cf. also Barsotti, *Insorti,* 21 Enciclopedia del Diritto, 807–810 (1971).

therefore be discarded as contrary to the principle of 'effective interpretation' (*ut res magis valeat quam pereat*).[21]

An objection to this could be raised using the lines of the 'doctrine' propounded at Geneva by Italy and referred to above. It would be as follows: the Protocol waits for the rebels be 'responsible' and well-organized so as to live up to its standards; then it applies. Since it is in the interest of insurgents to make the Protocol operational (they cannot but take advantage of all its humanitarian safeguards in favour both of the victims of the conflict and those who are or have been engaged in the war itself), they may consider it advantageous to show their willingness to respect its provisions. Once this condition is present, along with all the others set forth in Article 1, the Protocol becomes immediately and automatically applicable. From that moment on, the State fighting the rebels has a duty to the other contracting parties to comply with the Protocol, irrespective of whether or not the rebels continue to respect it. Any other contracting State has the right to demand the full application of the Protocol by the State within whose boundaries the civil war has broken out. Any breach of the Protocol by insurgents, while it does not authorize the established Government to disregard it, would legitimize any harsher criminal measures taken against them. On the other hand, any violation of the Protocol by the Government would make it answerable before the whole community of contracting States, and any one of them might bring it to book.

The above legal configuration of the Protocol's working seems logically flawless, and no doubt manages to explain the possible role of rebels under the Protocol without according them any legal standing. It has, however, one major deficiency: it completely disregards the real state of affairs—placing the Protocol in a utopian world. It sees the Protocol against a distorted background of States only motivated by humanitarian considerations, ready unreservedly to live up to their international obligations, and firmly committed to putting pressure on other States which might neglect their international duties. However, the international community by no means reflects this model. In practice, insurgents are not willing to live up to international standards they have not accepted.[22] What

---

[21] It may be noted that in some respects Art I is reminiscent of Art. 35, para. 2 of the U.N. Charter (whereby 'a State which is not a member of the United Nations may bring to the attention of the Security Council or of the General Assembly any dispute to which it is a party *if it accepts in advance, for the purposes of the dispute, the obligation of pacific settlement provided in the present Charter*'). This provision clearly makes the conferment of a right conditional on the fulfilment by the third party of the obligations laid down in the treaty; similarly, under Art. I of the Protocol insurgents must prove to fulfil the obligations deriving from the Protocol, before they can be entitled to claim respect for it by the established Government, that is to say before they can invoke the rights deriving from the Protocol.

On the aforementioned provision of the U.N. Charter, see Jimenez de Arechaga, *Treaty Stipulations in Favor of Third States*, 50 AJIL, at 356 (1956).

[22] What R. Baxter said in 1974 with respect to Art. 3 common to the 1949 Geneva Conventions fully applies to the Protocol ('. . . whether a group of any sort has or has not expressly accepted the obligations of an agreement does have a great deal to do psychologically with the willingness of

is even more important, States engaged in an internal armed conflict do not read-ily concede that civil strife calls for the application of international regulations. They try to postpone as much as possible the application of international rules, in the hope of quashing the domestic trouble before the matter becomes of inter-national concern. Therefore States are likely to refuse to admit that rebels really do live up to international standards so that the Protocol should apply. Or, it is most probable that States will minimize, or deny the existence of, the other factual circumstances (*e.g.* control by the insurgents over a part of the territory, the carrying out of sustained and concerted military operations, or the existence of a responsible command) that would render the Protocol applicable.[23] On the other hand experience has abundantly proved that other States only reluctantly demand the application of international rules governing civil strife, preferring to keep aloof. Even the ICRC has desired to avoid putting pressure on Governments; only in exceptional cases has the ICRC broken its usual attitude of a studied dis-cretion and publicly requested a State to apply the humanitarian law of armed conflict. It is no coincidence that in these cases the civil war strongly resembled an international conflict proper.[24]

This being so, to advocate the interpretation of the Protocol referred to above may amount to thwarting its purpose. If it were to prevail, the Protocol might become a dead letter. This, it is submitted, can only be considered contrary to the principle of interpretation whereby States are presumed not to enact international legislation that proves pointless. States are presumed not to undertake exercises in futility. Whenever possible, their action must be so interpreted as to be given prac-tical significance. If insurgents are regarded as beneficiaries and addressees of the Protocol, this means that they are *authorized to demand from the Government in power the full application of the Protocol*, once its activating conditions are present. *The very men for whose sake the Protocol has been elaborated are the best equipped to*

that group to carry out its purported obligations. The climate for compliance is even less propitious when the insurgents are rebelling against the authority of the very government that has assumed the obligations of the Conventions. And even if the obligations of Art. 3 are not particularly oner-ous for the rebels, they will still see a certain lack of reciprocity in the government's having been afforded the opportunity to determine whether to assume the obligations of the Conventions while they, the rebels, have not been given the occasions for a like decision' (Baxter, *Jus in Bello Interno: the Present and the Future Law* in *Law and Civil War in the Modern World* 528, Moore (ed.) 1974).

[23] For the various cases where Governments have refused to acknowledge the existence of an internal armed conflict, see Baxter, *ibid*, pp. 528–529.

[24] A case in point is the appeal made on March 20, 1979 by the President of the ICRC to all the parties to the conflict in Rhodesia/Zimbabwe, calling upon them 'to respect and to observe most scrupulously the fundamental humanitarian principles and to allow the ICRC to carry out fully its tasks for the protection and assistance of war victims' (ICRC *Bulletin*, No 39, April 4, 1979, p. 1). The ICRC itself called its step 'unprecedented'. The ICRC's President said: 'This departure from our habitual policy of diplomatic circumspection is deliberate. . . . For too long we have witnessed, on the part of both sides to the conflict, the systematic violation of the code of human conduct. The degree of misbehaviour has risen to such levels that the ICRC feels it can no longer remain silent' (*ibid*). The contention can be made that the situation in Rhodesia/Zimbabwe was a 'war of national liberation' fought against a racist regime, and not at all an internal armed conflict.

prompt the Government concerned to respect it. We shall see shortly what means are available to insurgents to this effect.

A third textual argument can be put forward to support the thesis I am advocating. Article 6, para. 5 of the Protocol provides that 'at the end of the hostilities the authorities in power shall endeavour to grant the broadest possible amnesty to persons who have participated in the armed conflict, or those deprived of their liberty for reasons related to the armed conflict, whether they are interned or detained'. This provision imposes a duty on the 'authorities in power at the end of the hostilities'. Hence, it refers both to the State (in the event of its being successful in quelling the insurrection) and to rebels (in the event of their defeating the central Government and installing themselves in power, or else managing to secede from the State and to create a new entity). If this duty is made incumbent on the rebels once they seize power in the territory or in part of the territory, it is logical to maintain that the other rules of the Protocol also bind the rebels before that final moment. Otherwise one could reach the strange conclusion that the Protocol, while it does not grant any legal status to rebels, nevertheless takes them into account once they have attained power. This absurdity becomes even more apparent when one considers the content of the provision under consideration. Article 6 provides for a series of guarantees in the case where a person engaged in the armed conflict, upon capture by the adversary, is punished for participating in the conflict or for other offences related to the conflict. The article lists all the safeguards of a proper trial that opposing forces must accord the offenders.[25]

It would be absurd to argue that these guarantees must be respected by the Government only, and are not duties binding the rebels. Otherwise one should conclude that the article does not impose duties on rebels relating to the punishment of offenders belonging to the Government's armed forces, while it

---

[25] Art. 6 provides as follows: '(1) This Article applies to the prosecution and punishment of criminal offences related to the armed conflict. (2) No sentence shall be passed and no penalty shall be executed on a person found guilty of an offence except pursuant to a conviction pronounced by a court offering the essential guarantees of independence and impartiality. In particular: (*a*) the procedure shall provide for an accused to be informed without delay of the particulars of the offence alleged against him and shall afford the accused before and during his trial all necessary rights and means of defence; (*b*) no one shall be convicted of an offence except on the basis of individual penal responsibility; (*c*) no one shall be held guilty of any criminal offence on account of any act or omission which did not constitute a criminal offence, under the law, at the time when it was committed; nor shall a heavier penalty be imposed than that which was applicable at the time when the criminal offence was committed; if, after the commission of the offence, provision is made by law for the imposition of a lighter penalty, the offender shall benefit thereby; (*d*) anyone charged with an offence is presumed innocent until proved guilty according to law; (*e*) anyone charged with an offence shall have the right to be tried in his presence; (*f*) no one shall be compelled to testify against himself or to confess guilt. (3) A convicted person shall be advised on conviction of his judicial and other remedies and of the time-limits within which they may be exercised. (4) The death penalty shall not be pronounced on persons who were under the age of eighteen years at the time of the offence and shall not be carried out on pregnant women or mothers of young children. (5) At the end of hostilities, the authorities in power shall endeavour to grant the broadest possible amnesty to persons who have participated in the armed conflict, or those deprived of their liberty for reasons related to the armed conflict, whether they are interned or detained'.

would impose on those rebels—once they have seized power—the duty to grant amnesty.

It is apparent from the above discussion that the intention of the parties, inasmuch as it was embodied in the text of the Protocol, is to the effect that insurgents may derive rights and duties from that international instrument. To put it differently, the draftsmen conceived of the Protocol as a treaty destined to bind not only the contracting States but also those rebels who show their willingness to abide by its provisions. Hence, one may conclude that, under the first of the two tests required by the Vienna Convention for an international treaty to produce legal effects on third parties, the Protocol can be regarded as able to produce those effects on insurgents.

As for the second test, i.e. the assent by the third party to the rights or duties deriving from the treaty, it will of course be necessary to determine in each civil war whether rebels are ready and willing to accept the Protocol. This willingness may be shown in various ways: by a unilateral declaration addressed to the Government, by tacit compliance with the Protocol, by a request to the ICRC to intervene and guarantee respect for the Protocol, or by any other similar means. The war in Chad is a recent illustration of an offer by rebels to apply humanitarian standards (in this case, Article 3 and possibly some provisions of the III Geneva Convention of 1949, on prisoners of war). In the strife, categorized by the ICRC as a typical armed conflict falling within Common Article 3,[26] both the Frolinat forces and the Government of Chad expressed their determination to observe humanitarian principles for the benefit of the 'victims', and in addition called upon the ICRC to intervene to ensure that protection.[27] In this, as in similar cases, the attitude of the rebels or their declarations give rise to a *tacit agreement* between them and the lawful Government. The effect of this agreement—which could be defined as 'collateral'[28]—is to extend the application of the Protocol (or, in the case of Chad, of the rules referred to above) to the insurgents. It results in the bulk of the provisions of the Protocol becoming applicable to the dealings between the Government and the rebels. It should be pointed out that rebels *do not become formal parties to the Protocol*. Only States are entitled to do that, as is explicitly provided for by Articles 20–22. Only States, therefore, may propose amendments, in accordance with Article 24, and have the right to receive the notifications provided for under Articles 26 and 27, para. 2. Rebels, while not parties to the Protocol, can derive rights and duties from its substantive provisions. This distinction between two categories of international subjects is easy to

---

[26] See the declaration made by L. Marti, head of the ICRC delegation to Chad, in ICRC *Bulletin* No. 27, April 5, 1978. p. 6.

[27] See ICRC *Bulletin,* No. 27, April 5, 1978, p. 2.

[28] The agreement by which a third party assents to accepting the rights and obligations derived from a treaty is termed 'collateral' by some authors: Sinclair, *The Vienna Convention on the Law of Treaties* at pp. 77–78. See *e.g.,* however, Jimenez de Arechaga, *International Law in the Past Third of a Century,* Hague Recueil, 1978-I at pp. 54–57.

explain. States tend to be stable and permanent. Rebels, by contrast, are by definition transient creatures. Their temporary character fully justifies their participating in the Protocol solely as long as the civil war is in progress. As the Protocol is designed to regulate this strife, it is quite right that rebels be bound by it only for the duration of such a conflict.[29]

I submit that the above explanation of how insurgents become bound by the Protocol is more satisfactory than the views hitherto advanced to justify the binding nature of Article 3, or the Protocol, on rebels. The more widespread opinion is that Article 3 (or, for that matter, the Protocol) is able to confer rights and impose obligations on insurgents because, as a consequence of the State's ratification, the treaty becomes part of domestic law and therefore obliges all citizens, including rebels. This view, put forward by some prominent scholars,[30] has also been accepted by the ICRC[31] and a few States,[32] but is plainly based on a misconception of the relationship between international and domestic law. Indisputedly, in most States international treaties become part of domestic law upon ratification, but they then bind individuals and State authorities *qua* domestic law, and indeed benefit from all the judicial guarantees provided for by that legal system. However, what is at stake in the present case is not whether rebels are subjects of domestic law, but their legal standing in *international* law—their status vis-à-vis both the lawful Government and third States and the international community at large. It should be added that the view referred to above would not explain the legal impact of the Protocol on rebels, were they to declare null and void in a territory under their control its domestic legislation, and hence the domestic rules incorporating the Protocol.

No more satisfactory is another view,[33] whereby the Protocol may become binding on insurgents on the strength of a rule of customary international law which extends the effects of the ratification made by a State to any new international entity establishing itself, albeit provisionally, in the territory of that

---

[29] A serious problem might arise if the States parties to the Protocol decided to revise it while a civil war is raging in the territory of one of them. It is submitted that in this case the insurgent faction would not be bound automatically by the revised rules of the Protocol. For it to acquire the rights and duties following from the new rules a (tacit or explicit) assent to those rules would be necessary.

[30] See *e.g.* Draper, *The Geneva Conventions of 1949*, Hague Receuil 1965–I at p. 96. Previously, this author had expressed a slightly different view: Draper, *The Red Cross Conventions,* at p. 17 (1958).

[31] Pictet (ed.), *Commentary, II Geneva Convention of 1949,* at p. 34 (1960). A slightly different view had been expressed in the Commentary to the Ist. Geneva Convention: Pictet (ed.), *Commentary, I Geneva Convention of 1949,* at p. 51 (1952). In the latter work it had been maintained that 'if the responsible authority at their [the rebels] head exercises effective authority, it is bound by the very fact that it claims to represent the country, or part of the country'. In the Commentary to the 2nd Convention, this justification is given in addition to the more general one based on the incorporation of the Conventions into domestic law.

[32] See *e.g.* the statement made in 1975 by the Soviet delegate to the Geneva Diplomatic Conference and quoted above, at n. 16.

[33] Bothe, op cit, *supra* n. 4, at p. 92.

State. Apart from the fact that participation of rebels in the Protocol should not be equated with ratification by a State, because ratifying or acceding parties retain a status different from that acquired by rebels, it should be stressed that the view under consideration is based on an artificial legal construction. Indeed, it would be difficult to produce evidence to support the assertion that there exists such a rule of customary international law, and there is room for believing that it ultimately rests on a legal fiction.[34]

4. Legal Consequences of the Participation of Rebels in the Protocol

If the above view of the manner by which the Protocol becomes binding on insurgents is correct, some consequences necessarily follow.

First, once rebels have shown their willingness and ability to apply the Protocol and demonstrated that they indeed do abide by its provisions, the Protocol becomes automatically binding on both parties. The authorities in power cannot claim that rebels are not entitled to invoke the Protocol. Whenever it is beyond dispute that the rebels meet the objective requirements laid down in Article 1 (i.e. that they exercise control by means of a responsible command and organized armed groups, wield power over a part of the territory and are able to carry out sustained and concerted military operations in compliance with the Protocol) the Government cannot refuse to apply the Protocol. In the event of such a refusal, and of other contracting States not intervening to induce that Government to apply the Protocol, rebels can call upon the ICRC to approach the Government and request it to behave in accord with the Protocol. If all these steps are of no avail, rebels are entitled to disregard some provisions of the Protocol. In other words, they are entitled to resort to action that would be contrary to the Protocol, yet not unlawful because it constitutes a reaction to the unlawful behaviour of the Government in power. Resort to these 'reprisals' may however be admitted only under certain well defined conditions, as will be specified shortly. However, one point should be made clear immediately. Disregard of the Protocol can only be justified as a means of putting pressure on the Government to implement

---

[34] However, Bothe's theory could be regarded as valid with respect to Art. 3 common to the 1949 Conventions. One might agree that 'there is strong indication that State practice assumes that these provisions [i.e. Art. 3 referred to above and Art. 19 of the Hague Convention on the Protection of Cultural Property] are binding also for the rebels . . . ' and therefore one can point both to 'State practice and *opinio juris*' to the effect that the 'ratification of Art. 3 of the Geneva Conventions and Art. 19 of the Hague Convention has the effect that also rebels are bound' (from a letter Professor Bothe sent to the author). Yet, even assuming that this view is correct, it would not be applicable to Protocol II, for there seems to be no indication in practice that a customary rule of international law relating to the effects of ratification of the Protocol was evolved at Geneva in 1974–1977, or afterwards.

it. Furthermore, resort to such measures can only be lawful after certain international steps have been taken (see *infra*).

A logical corollary of the above proposition is that if rebels do not observe its provisions once there has been a tacit agreement of a kind referred to already, the lawful authorities are entitled to suspend application of specific provisions of the Protocol, as a means of inducing the rebels to abide by it. Again, in this case, the same safeguards are to be observed as are called for in the event of rebels resorting to this means of enforcing the Protocol.

A second consequence following from the above legal analysis of rebels' standing under the Protocol is that, once the tacit agreement has been made, rebels become bound to observe the Protocol not only towards the authorities they are fighting, but also *vis-à-vis* all the other States that are parties to the Protocol. There would indeed exist too blatant an imbalance if the government in power only were to have a duty towards all the other contracting States. It seems logical and consonant with the humanitarian spirit of the Protocol to assume that rebels have a similar duty towards third States. So, any other contracting party can demand from rebels compliance with the humanitarian standards laid down in the Protocol. This, it is submitted, should greatly enhance the practical importance of the treaty and contribute to making it a workable instrument. If the above is correct, one should of course assume that the tacit agreement concluded by the rebels with the authorities in power extends its legal effects to all the other contracting States. It is not necessary for third States to make an explicit declaration for the purpose of acquiring the right to claim compliance with the Protocol by insurgents. This right logically follows from the whole system envisaged in the Protocol, particularly from the principle of symmetry underlying it.

A third legal consequence following from the above construction relates to the denunciation of the Protocol. This matter is governed by Article 25, whereby contracting parties can denounce the Protocol, but their denunciation takes effect six months after its receipt by the depositary, and in any case, if on the expiry of six months the denouncing party is engaged in an internal armed conflict, the denunciation does not take effect before the conflict ends.[35] The question arises whether rebels can denounce the Protocol while the civil war is in progress. The answer has to be in the negative, otherwise insurgents would find themselves in a better position than the lawful authorities. As long as the civil strife continues, neither party can free itself from the obligations deriving from the Protocol. This,

---

[35] Art. 25, para. 1 provides as follows: 'In case a High Contracting Party should denounce this Protocol, the denunciation shall only take effect six months after receipt of the instrument of denunciation. If, however, on the expiry of six months, the denouncing Party is engaged in the situation referred to in Art. 1, the denunciation shall not take effect before the end of the armed conflict. Persons who have been deprived of liberty, or whose liberty has been restricted, for reasons related to the conflict shall nevertheless continue to benefit from the provisions of this Protocol until their final release'.

Para. 2 stipulates that 'the denunciation shall be notified in writing to the depositary, which shall transmit it to all the High Contracting Parties'.

it is submitted, is in keeping with the humanitarian purpose of the Protocol and is a means of ensuring that its basic provisions are respected, once the parties to the conflict have agreed to abide by them.

5. Does the Protocol Impose Absolute Obligations?

What has been set forth in the preceding paragraph is based on an assumption that should now be examined, namely that the Protocol does not rule out 'reciprocity of obligations', but is founded, to a large extent, on a symmetry of obligations between the parties. It can thus allow for some provisions to be disregarded in reaction to non-compliance with the Protocol by the other party. This is a very sensitive and tricky issue that deserves to be looked into at some length.

At the close of the Geneva Diplomatic Conference, it was suggested that the observance of the Protocol by a contracting party is not made conditional on compliance by the opposing party.[36] In other words, no provision of the Protocol may, in any circumstances or for any reason whatsoever, be violated, even in response to a violation by the other party. Under this interpretation any form of 'reciprocity' is excluded from the Protocol. Reflecting on what the ICRC stated in 1973 with respect to the 1949 Geneva Conventions and applying it to the present issue, one might say of the Protocol that 'the commitments arising out of it are of a binding and absolute nature. Under those circumstances each State [as well as rebels, we may add] unilaterally undertakes, *vis-à-vis* all other States, without any reciprocal return, to respect in all circumstances the rules and principles they have recognized as vital. These do not involve an interchange of benefits but constitute a fundamental charter that proclaims to the world the essential guarantees to which every human being is entitled'.[37]

Several objections can be raised against this view. Before expounding them the issue must be clarified, because two different phrases were used in the discussion at Geneva. Some delegates spoke of 'reciprocity of obligations', while others referred to 'reprisals'. There is, however, a notable difference between the two notions. 'Reciprocity of obligations' means that a party to the Protocol is bound by one of its provisions subject to the other's respect for that provision (*'inadimplenti non est adimplendum'*). By contrast, the right to resort to reprisals under the Protocol entails that a party is authorized to ignore an obligation deriving from the Protocol, if the adversary has violated that obligation *or any other obligation* imposed by it. I submit that the problem arising under the Protocol is not so much that of 'reciprocity of obligations'; it is rather the question whether obligations are absolute or may be disregarded in reaction to a violation by the adversary.

[36] See the declaration made by Italy, CCDH/SR. 51, pp. 120–122.
[37] This declaration was made by the ICRC in relation to the Arab-Israeli conflict; see *The ICRC in Action—Information Notes*, December 5, 1973, no. 205b, at p. 9.

Indeed, the crucial question for the Protocol is whether a party to the civil conflict has a *means of enforcing* the Protocol directly, by inducing the adversary to cease its violations. Furthermore, to view the issue as a question of 'reciprocity of obligations' might lead to the disruption of the whole Protocol, or at least render its application highly problematic. This is because for each of its provisions, a party would always have to determine—before applying it—whether or not the adversary complies with it.

It has been suggested that the term 'reprisals' should not be used here because it is inappropriate in the context of civil strife.[38] Admittedly, the notions has negative overtones. Also, it is generally applied to inter-State conflicts. Nevertheless, no logical obstacle seems to prevent its use in reference to the Protocol. Once it is accepted that this instrument grants international rights and obligations both to Governments and rebels, the appropriateness of using the concept of reprisals only depends on whether the Protocol makes allowance for it. If it does, the utmost care should of course be taken to define the proper scope of reprisals. Furthermore, it should be made clear that resort to reprisals under the Protocol only results in *authorized non-compliance* with it in the event of the enemy violating its provisions.

After this digression, we return to our main problem, namely the objections which can be raised against the view that the Protocol imposes absolute obligations. My first objection is that if the Protocol in its entirety is conceived of as a set of obligations to be fulfilled even in the case of non-fulfilment by the other party, either the authorities in power or the rebels may consider it more convenient to avoid applying the Protocol altogether. Governments, knowing that they would have to apply the Protocol even if confronted with violations by the insurgents on a large scale (after their initial compliance), would naturally tend to refuse either to acknowledge the existence of an internal armed conflict or to apply the Protocol, on the pretext that the civil strife is not of the intensity required by it. Rebels may easily take a similar attitude. In the event of the established regime deciding to apply the Protocol, rebels may take advantage of the fact that the Government is bound to respect it in any event. Therefore, after an initial compliance with the Protocol, they would easily be led largely to ignore it. They would do so not only because they would feel safe from any counter-violation by the Government, but also because they would be aware that, if captured, they would be severely punished by the lawful authorities merely for having taken up arms. Committing the atrocities prohibited by the Protocol would hardly aggravate their treason and rebellion, which are normally among the most serious offences in any national legal system. In short, the 'unilateralist' or 'absolute obligations'

---

[38] This view was put forward by various States, which however gave varying justifications in its support. See *e.g.* the statements by the delegates of the Federal Republic of Germany (CDDH/I/ SR. 32, para. 11), of Iraq (*ibid.,* para. 16), of Nigeria (*ibid.,* para. 21), of India (*ibid.,* para. 22) and of Iran (*ibid.,* para. 37). See also the statement made by the representatives of the United States in plenary: CDDH/SR. 51, para. 7.

theory referred to above may act as a powerful *disincentive* for Governments and insurgents to apply the Protocol. Thus, the very purpose of the Protocol, i.e. to broaden and strengthen the protection given to persons engaged in, or victims of, armed conflicts, would be thwarted. This would be at sharp variance with the basic legal principle alluded to whereby international treaties are always to be interpreted in such a way as to render their provisions effective.[39]

A second objection hinges on the wording of the Protocol's provisions. On closer inspection it is possible to identify some provisions which demand obedience 'in all circumstances' or 'at any time and in any place whatsoever', while others do not include any such clause. The former category comprises Article 4, paras 1 and 2 (fundamental guarantees); Article 7 (the protection and care of the wounded, sick and shipwrecked); Article 10, para. 1 (general protection of medical duties); Article 11 (protection of medical units and transport); Article 12 (protection of the distinctive emblem); Article 13 (protection of the civilian population); Article 14 (protection of objects indispensable to the survival of the civilian population); Article 15 (protection of works and installations containing dangerous forces); Article 16 (protection of cultural objects and places of worship).[40]

---

[39] It is fitting to recall that as early as 1971 a great authority, R. Baxter pointed out as follows: 'The greatest care must be taken to ensure that both the lawful government and the insurgents will be in a position to carry out the provisions of any new protocol. Not only must there be reciprocity of obligation, but the rules must be framed with a realistic understanding of what the capacities and purposes of insurgents are' (op cit, *supra*, n. 22, at p. 536).

[40] It should be mentioned that a provision of the Protocol, Art. 5 (relating to persons whose liberty has been restricted), contains a clause which could be regarded as equivalent to the 'in all circumstances' clause. It stipulates in para. 1: 'In addition to the provisions of Art. 4, the following provisions *shall be respected as a minimum* with regard to persons deprived of their liberty for reasons related to the armed conflict, whether they are interned or detained'. It was contended by Italy (see the declaration made in the plenary meeting, after the deletion by the Conference of Art. 10 *bis*: CCDH/SR. 51, Annex, at p. 121) that the above expression implies that the Article containing it requires unconditional respect. It is submitted, however, that the contrary view is sounder, namely that the phrase 'shall be respected as a minimum' has a meaning different from that of the 'in all circumstances' clause. Two reasons seem to support this view. First, a logical interpretation leads to believing that, had the drafters intended to require unconditional respect for Art. 5 as well, they would have used the 'in all circumstances' clause. The choice of a different expression, which is also different from other expressions used in the Protocol (*'e.g.:* it shall remain prohibited *at any time and in any place whatsoever'*, Art. 4, para. 2) implies that the framers of the Protocol intended to give Art. 5 a different purport and meaning.

Second, resort to preparatory work seems to corroborate the above view. The draft proposed by the ICRC included the words 'the parties to the conflict shall respect *at least* the following provisions'. When the Article was presented to Committee 1, the ICRC delegate suggested that the words 'in all circumstances' should be used (CDDH/I/SR. 32, para. 66). This suggestion was not taken up, however. The ICRC draft gave rise to a lot of objections. In particular, it was felt that the obligations proposed by the ICRC were too onerous, especially for developing countries; it was therefore suggested that they should be made 'less mandatory' and be placed 'within the capabilities of both parties' (see that statements made by the delegates of Canada, CDDH/I/SR. 32, para. 71; Mexico, *ibid.,* para. 76, Iran, *ibid.,* paras 82–83; Nigeria, *ibid.,* para. 84; India, *ibid.,* para. 87; Iraq, *ibid.,* para. 89). Only the representative of Italy insisted on the 'absolute nature' of the obligations of the Article (*ibid.,* p. SR. 33, paras 18–19). Nevertheless, the text adopted in Committee I stated in para. 1 that 'The parties to the conflict shall respect *at least* etc' while para. 2 included the

If the Protocol makes this distinction, it is to be assumed that it wants to differentiate between two categories, one consisting of provisions that permit no derogation, the other made up of rules that may be exceptionally disregarded when the other party to the conflict grossly and systematically violates the Protocol. It is evident that the two categories have not been set up in a capricious or haphazard way. Indeed, the rules belonging to the first category, i.e. those which lay down absolute obligations, are designed to protect the most basic human values: they constitute what can be called the 'hard core' of humanitarian safeguards which should not be disregarded if civil war is not to degenerate into barbarity. They safeguard the most precious aspects of human dignity (by prohibiting torture, rape, the taking of hostages, acts of terrorism and slavery), or they protect those persons whose action is indispensable for the care of the wounded and sick (hence the duty to respect and protect medical units and transport); furthermore, they guard the civilian population and the most important civilian objects against the dangers arising from military operations. All the other provisions, although they set important safeguards for the victims of internal conflicts, have been regarded as less crucial, and their observance may therefore be dispensed with under exceptional circumstances.

A third objection against the 'absolute obligations' theory is based on the preparatory work. The plenary session of the Diplomatic Conference rejected by a vote of 41 to 28, with 21 abstentions,[41] a provision adopted in Committee (Article 10 *bis*),[42] which laid down that certain provisions of the Protocol should not, 'in

---

phrase 'within the limits of their capabilities' (CDDH/219 Rev. 1, para. 175 and CDDH/I/SR. 39, paras 19–64). The replacement of 'at least' by the words 'as a minimum' occurred in plenary. In 1977, when the Pakistani draft (CDDH/427) was adopted, the Pakistani delegate pointed out that in his proposed amendment 'he had merely deleted the words "Parties to the conflict"' (CDDH/SR. 50, para. 49). It seems to me that both the failure to accept the suggestion made in 1975 by the ICRC delegate and various objections against the 'too mandatory' character of the Article lead one to maintain that the draftsmen did not intend to require absolute compliance with Art. 5. The phrase 'as a minimum' conveys the idea that the parties to a conflict should normally apply its provisions, and should also endeavour to grant greater and better protection to persons deprived of their liberty for reasons related to the armed conflict. In other words, that expression contains an invitation to the parties to go beyond the level of protection provided for in Art. 5. The Article however, can be disregarded by way of reprisal. This should not be surprising, if one thinks of the very content of some of the provisions included in the Article (mention can be made, for instance, of para. 1*c*: 'they shall be allowed to receive individual or collective relief'; para. 1*d*: 'they shall be allowed to practice their religion and, if requested and appropriate, to receive spiritual assistance from persons, such as chaplains, performing religious functions'; para. 1*e*: 'they shall, if made to work, have the benefit of working conditions and safeguards similar to those enjoyed by the local civilian population'). It does not seem that the *exceptional suspension* of these guarantees could give rise to major objections, especially if one compares these provisions with those embodying the basic values that no party to the conflict is allowed to disregard (one may think, for instance, of the prohibition on terrorism, the taking of hostages, slavery, pillage, etc.: Art. 4, para. 2).

[41] CDDH/SR. 51, para. 16.

[42] This Article, adopted by Committee I on May 16, 1977 by 33 votes to 15, with 28 abstentions, reads as follows: 'The provisions of Parts II [on Humane Treatment of Persons in the Power of the Parties to the Conflict] and III [on Wounded, Sick and Shipwrecked] and of Articles 26 [on the Protection of the Civilian Population], 26 *bis* [on the General Protection of Civilian Objects], 27 [on the Protection of Objects Indispensable to the Survival of the Civilian Population] and 28 [on

any circumstance or for any reason whatsoever, be violated, even in response to a violation of the provisions of the Protocol'. The opponents of this Article included most Third World countries, plus a few Western States (*e.g.* the United States, New Zealand, France and the United Kingdom). Although the reasons for the rejection of the Article turned out to be contradictory,[43] it would seem that two representations of the Third World best expressed the basic reason why the Article was deleted. The delegate of India, appealing to all developing countries to vote against the Article, pointed out that it 'tended to jeopardise the national sovereignty of States.'[44] After the vote, the delegation of Nigeria put on record a declaration which stated *inter alia:*

... The inclusion of an article on reprisals in this Protocol could lead Governments and States into embarrassing situations. This is because it is not inconceivable that in the course of an internal conflict rebels may deliberately commit acts to which the normal reaction would be in the nature of reprisals but because of a prohibitory article such as this, Governments would feel bound to fold their arms while dissident groups go on the rampage killing and maiming innocent civilians and burning dwellings and food crops. No responsible Government can allow such a situation to develop, but if this article had been adopted this is the kind of scenario that would repeat itself time and again.[45]

Although great caution should be displayed in assessing the significance of the rejection of Article 10 *bis,* it seems to me that at least the following contention can be made: the great majority of States did not wish the Protocol to include a clause which provided, in sweeping terms, for entire Sections of the Protocol, plus a cluster of other provisions, to be observed in every circumstance. In other words, the conclusion to be drawn from the rejection of that Article is that the States gathered at Geneva ruled out a general 'unilateralist' solution for the bulk of the Protocol in the belief that, apart from a number of provisions to be identified by their own terms and not in a general way, Governments should be left free to disregard the Protocol in response to gross violations by the rebels.

The three arguments set out above lead to the conclusion that the Protocol includes a category of obligations which may be ignored for a time by one of the parties to the conflict, in retaliation to serious violations by the opposing party. But under what circumstances are parties to an internal armed conflict free not to fulfil these obligations? This is a very sensitive point, the answer to which may lead either to ensuring better compliance with the Protocol, or to disrupting completely the system of rules established by it. One should therefore proceed with the utmost caution.

the Protection of Works and Installations Containing Dangerous Forces] shall not, in any circumstances or for any reason whatsoever, be violated, even in response to a violation of the provisions of the Protocol'.

[43] Thus, for instance, the delegate of the United States declared that he opposed the Article 'since the whole concept of reprisals had no place in Protocol II' (CDDH/SR. 51, para. 7).

[44] CDDH/SR. 51, para. 8.

[45] CDDH/SR. 51, Annex, p. 22.

In trying to find a solution to this problem, attention should first be drawn to the contents of the provisions which lend themselves to being broken by way of reprisals.[46] One could mention by way of illustration Article 6, which sets out a list of basic safeguards that each party to the conflict should respect in the prosecution and punishment of criminal offences related to the armed conflict.[47] This rule does not include the qualification 'in any circumstance' and consequently one could contend that its application by one party may be suspended in retaliation to grave violations of the Protocol committed by the other party. However, given the subject-matter of the provision, not applying it may easily lead to a more savage and cruel manner of conducting the war. Thus, for instance, in response to atrocities committed by rebels against captive civilians the authorities might decide to suspend the application of Article 6. Consequently, they would proceed summarily to put on trial their captured rebels without affording them all the reasonable means of defence or without granting them the proper judicial remedies after their conviction. Plainly, these Government measures may prompt the insurgents to increase violence and the number of atrocities, instead of inducing them to discontinue the violations of the Protocol. This outcome would of course be absolutely contrary to the Protocol's purpose. One should therefore endeavour to place an interpretation on the Protocol which restricts the potentially dangerous consequences of reprisals.

I submit that, in order to take account of the humanitarian purpose of the Protocol and ensure that breaches of it should be kept to a minimum, reprisals should only be resorted to subject to the following strict conditions. First, a party to the conflict may suspend the application of one of the provisions mentioned above only if the opposing party has committed *systematic violations* of the Protocol on a large scale. One or two isolated incidents surely cannot authorize resort to reprisals. The violations must be serious and repeated. To use a well-known United Nations phrase one might say that it is necessary for a party to commit 'a consistent pattern of gross violations'.[48] A second condition relates to the determination of violations. It is apparent that the task of ascertaining whether infringements are committed by one party cannot be left to the other party allegedly suffering from them. If each party were free to disregard the Protocol simply by establishing that the other has violated it, the risk of abuse would be enormous. It is in keeping with the humanitarian object of the Protocol to maintain that, if one of the parties to the conflict wishes to avail itself of the 'reprisals system', it may do so only on condition that gross and repeated violations

---

[46] They are the obligations provided for in Art. 4, para. 3 (protection of children); Art. 5 (persons whose liberty has been restricted); Art. 6 (penal prosecutions); Art. 8 (search for the wounded, sick and shipwrecked); Art. 9 (protection of medical and religious personnel); Art. 10, paras 2–4 (protection of medical duties).

[47] For the text of this Article, see *supra*, n. 25.

[48] See *e.g.* ECOSOC resolutions 1235 (XLII) and 1503 (XLVIII). It should be stressed that the above requirement greatly narrows the range of possible reprisals.

by the other party have been authoritatively established by *an independent body,* such as the ICRC or any other humanitarian institution which affords guarantees of impartiality and independence. As long as a party is unwilling to request such a body officially to verify the existence of the alleged violations, that party should be barred from invoking the right to be excused from an obligation under the Protocol.

A third condition dictated by the purpose of the Protocol is that a party to the conflict, once it is established that violations have been committed by the opposing party, should give a *warning* to that party, before actually beginning reprisals contrary to its provisions. The purpose of the warning is clearly to allow the offending party to discontinue its action before the appropriate counter-measures are taken.

A fourth condition is that, in the case where one or more provisions are disregarded by way of retaliation, *this non-compliance should stop as soon as the delinquent party discontinues its violations* of the Protocol. Since the purpose of 'reprisals' is not so much a penalty on the enemy as to induce him to abide by the Protocol, once the violations cease, the suspension of the Protocol's provisions should also come to an end.[49]

It is submitted that the four above-mentioned conditions are indispensable. Their fulfilment is called for by the nature of the Protocol and the contents of its provisions. To affirm that certain obligations of the Protocol can be suspended in retaliation to serious violations by the enemy ultimately allows a party to the conflict to behave towards prisoners, children, women and other innocent members of the civilian population, in a manner that the international community has come to consider as contrary to the basic demands of humanity. Those who suffer from the application of 'reprisals' are likely to be innocent people, who have nothing to do with the conflict. Even if the provisions disregarded relate to combatants who have fallen into enemy hands, nevertheless, 'lawful non-compliance' means not to apply basic humanitarian safeguards (such as those concerning a proper and fair trial) that have become essential for any form of respect for human dignity. Therefore, *a strict interpretation* of the 'doctrine of reprisals' is called for—a doctrine which is countenanced by the Protocol, on the realistic assumption that without it the parties to the conflict might easily evade all their obligations. On the other hand, acknowledging a place for reprisals should not entail offering an opportunity for the increase of inhumane violence. That would lead to the very result which the 'reprisals system' was intended to avoid.

[49] It follows from this requirement (coupled with that relating to the gross and systematic character of the violations by the adversary) that the reprisals are not allowed to be *disproportionate* to the violations to which they react. If the party violating the Protocol systematically goes on with its consistent pattern of gross infringements after the reprisals by the adversary, that of course means that the former party has decided to ignore the Protocol altogether. As this situation is however unlikely to occur, it must be presumed that it is sufficient for the reprisals to reach the same level of intensity of the violations by the adversary, for the latter to discontinue its misbehaviour.

Before concluding, it is appropriate to point out that although the aforementioned conditions for resorting to reprisals follow from the very object and nature of the Protocol, to a large extent they conform to the general requirements for reprisals set by customary law. In particular, the first of the four above conditions, i.e. the need for the violations to which a party reacts by way of reprisal to be gross and systematic, actually corresponds to the principle of proportionality governing the reprisals system under general international law. One might submit that what is actually suggested in this paper is that the general rules on reprisals should be read into the application of the Protocol. More correctly, the system of reprisals envisaged in the Protocol should be viewed against the background of general international law. Similarly, as has been emphasized at the outset, in order to understand how the Protocol produces legal effects for insurgents, one should place it against the background of customary principles governing the binding force of treaties for third parties. *It is the main thesis of this paper that one cannot really grasp the meaning of this new treaty if one does not place it in the right context,* i.e. *that of general international law.* Indeed, Protocol II is not a flower in the desert. It is the offshoot of a long legislative process that reflects the efforts made by the international community over a long period of time to control and humanize civil strife. It does not mark an abrubt departure from traditional law; nor does it reflect a radically new approach to the thorny problems of internal wars. Rather, it develops and enhances a host of elements that were already to be found in international legislation. It substantially builds upon the foundations of international institutions and brings to the fore or spells out traditional concepts and ideas. It is therefore necessary to look at the Protocol not in isolation, but as part and parcel of the whole international law-making process. This attitude does not necessarily mean taking a traditional, conservative view of the Protocol. On the contrary, it is submitted that the interpretation proposed in this paper is forward looking. It gives to insurgents the proper role they deserve in the present situation of conflict within the international community, and it emphasizes the humanitarian demands of all who are caught up in civil strife or deliberately participate in it without wishing to renounce the imprescriptible exigencies of human dignity.

C. Means of Warfare

8. The Prohibition of Indiscriminate Means of Warfare*

1. Introduction

It is common knowledge that all weapons can be used indiscriminately, i.e. in such a way as to strike combatants and civilians alike. There are, however, some weapons that are by their nature incapable of being directed with any certainty at specific military objectives, or which in their typical or normal use are not delivered with any certainty to such targets. Although as a result of technological advances there is now a tendency to manufacture more and more accurate and 'discriminate' weapons (such as the so-called 'smart' bombs, 'tactical' nuclear bombs, etc.), most States still have in their arsenals, and often use, means of destruction that are 'blind', in that they do not differentiate between military and civilian objectives. Mention can be made, for example, of delayed-action weapons which, by the very fact that they do not release their lethal effects as soon as they hit their objectives, are likely to kill or wound civilians who subsequently happen to be in that locality. Booby-traps, mines, some electronic devices and other new weapons can also kill indiscriminately.[1]

In this paper I propose to consider to what extent current international law protects civilians against the use of these weapons, and the trends which are discernible in the new law that States are now endeavoring to draft at the Geneva Diplomatic Conference on the Humanitarian Law of Armed Conflicts, [at the time of writing, the Geneva Conference that led to the adoption of the two Additional Protocols to the Geneva Conventions was still under way]. (The works on chemical and nuclear weapons of the Conference of the Committee on Disarmament will not be dealt with here).

---

* Originally published in R.J. Akkermann et al. (eds), *Declaration of Principles: A Quest for Universal Peace* (Leyden: Sijthoff, 1977) 171.

[1] For a description of some of these weapons see ICRC, *Weapons that May Cause Unnecessary Suffering or Have Indiscriminate Effects,* Geneva, 1973; *Conventional Weapons. Their Deployment and Effects from Humanitarian Aspect—Recommendations for the Modernization of International Law,* by a Swedish Working Group Study, Stockholm, 1973.

2. The General Prohibition Following from Customary International Law

There is widespread agreement that the use of indiscriminate weapons is prohibited by customary international law. This prohibition is a natural corollary of the general principle whereby 'distinction must be made at all times between persons taking part in the hostilities and members of the civilian population to the effect that the latter be spared as much as possible' from the horrors of war.[2]

The argument can be made that a belligerent who knowingly makes use of a weapon which by its very nature cannot but cause injuries both to combatants and civilians, intended to hit civilians or at any rate consciously brought them under his attack. This belligerent would thus be violating the rule forbidding deliberate attack on civilians—a rule that significantly specifies the aforementioned general principle. This argument, however, can hold true only for some extreme cases. We should consider, for example, that there are certain categories of 'blind' weapons, such as the V.1 and V.2 used by Germans in World War II, which lack precision to such an extent that they cannot be aimed at any specific target. Such weapons are therefore very likely to strike civilians or civilian objects only. For this reason their use can be equated to the deliberate use of weapons against civilians, and is as such unlawful. This contention is borne out by State practice: suffice it to recall that resort to the V.1 and V.2 by Germany was considered illegal in substance, by the British Prime Minister, W. Churchill, in 1944;[3] the same stand is ultimately taken by the Military Manual of the Federal Republic of Germany which considers, however, that those weapons, although inherently illegal, were not illegal when they were actually used, since they were employed by way of reprisal for Allied delinquencies.[4]

Far more relevant and frequent is the case of weapons that are not so 'blind' and, while they also hit civilians, are primarily aimed at military objectives. The use of these means of warfare necessarily falls under the rule whereby if belligerents

---

[2] The words quoted above were used by the UN General Assembly in its resolution 2444 (XXIII), adopted unanimously on December 18, 1968. In 1972 the General Counsel of the US Department of Defense stated that the US regards this principle 'as declaratory of existing customary international law' (67 *American Journal of International Law* (1973) p. 122); see also the G.A. resolution 2675 (XXV), adopted on December 9, 1970 ('Basic Principles for the Protection of Civilian Population in Armed Conflicts').

[3] In a statement made in the House of Commons on July 6, 1944, Churchill said *inter alia:* 'A very high proportion of these casualties I have mentioned . . . have fallen upon London, which presents to the enemy . . . a target 18 miles wide by over 20 miles deep. It is, therefore, the unique target of the world for the use of a weapon of such proved inaccuracy. The flying bomb is a weapon literally and essentially indiscriminate in its nature, purpose and effect. The introduction by the Germans of such a weapon obviously raises some grave questions upon which I do not propose to trench today' (*Keesing's Contemporary Archives*, 1943–1956, pp. 6536–6537).

[4] *Kriegsvölkerrecht, Allgemeine Bestimmungen des Kriegsführungsrechts und Landkriegsrecht*, ZDv 15/10, März 1961, para. 90.

resort to methods or means of warfare which result in incidental civilian losses, such losses must not be out of proportion to the military advantage gained. This rule of proportionality represents an important development and specification of the general principle on the distinction to be made between combatants and civilians. It has, however, been widely criticized. Thus, it was contended that this standard 'calls for comparing two things for which there is no standard of comparison. Is one, for example, compelled to think in terms of a certain number of casualties as justified in the gaining of a specified number of yards? Such precise relationships are so far removed from reality as to be unthinkable . . . One rebels at the thought that hundreds of thousands of civilians should be killed in order to destroy one enemy soldier who may be in their midst. But under more reasonable circumstances, how can a proper ratio be established between loss of civilian life and the destruction of railway carriages?'[5] Admittedly, the proportionality rule is vague and contains loopholes. Still, it provides a standard for at least the most glaring cases. Moreover, criticisms of this rule are warranted provided they are aimed at suggesting more workable and safer standards, that better meet humanitarian demands. Otherwise attacks on that rule could paradoxically even result in belittling the protection of civilians it currently provides.

3. Conventional Bans or Restrictions on the Use of Indiscriminate Weapons

Treaty restraints on the use of specific indiscriminate weapons are not numerous. They were mostly enacted in the 'golden age' of the codification of the laws of war, namely between the first Hague Peace Conference (1899) and 1925. The only treaty adopted in recent times, the Convention on bacteriological weapons, does not provide for new bans on the use of weapons, as it reaffirms a prohibition made as early as 1925 and primarily aims at supplementing that prohibition with bans on the manufacturing, stockpiling, etc. of weapons. If so far States have conspicuously shied away from outlawing the use of such new weapons as atomic and nuclear bombs, so called neo-conventional weapons, etc., this is probably due to their great military effectiveness.

Means of combat which were prohibited because of their indiscriminate effects are the projectiles which spread asphyxiating and deleterious gases. In the 1899 Hague Conference, which produced the Declaration concerning those weapons, the supporters of the prohibition pointed to two grounds for banning asphyxiating gases. First of all, they are 'barbarous in character'[6] for they render

---

[5] R.R. Baxter, 'Criteria of the Prohibition of Weapons in International Law', *Festschrift für Scheuner,* Berlin, 1973, 46, pp. 48–49.

[6] Delegate of Russia (*Proceedings of the Hague Peace Conferences,* edited by J.B. Scott, The Conference of 1899, p. 366).

death inevitable and are therefore contrary to the 'humane idea . . . of finding means of putting enemies out of action without putting them out of the world'.[7] Secondly, they can 'endanger the existence of a large number of noncombatants, for instance, in case of a siege';[8] 'if directed against a besieged city, they would perhaps hit more harmless inhabitants than the ordinary projectiles'.[9]

A second prohibition which, however, is no longer in force, was based to a very great extent on the indiscriminate nature of the weapons. In 1899 the Hague Conference adopted a Declaration forbidding the discharge of projectiles and explosives from balloons, though only for a term of five years. While one delegate opposed that method of combat because it was to his mind 'perfidious',[10] most supporters of the Declaration pointed out that at that time the throwing of projectiles from balloons could 'make victims among the noncombatants';[11] it is impossible 'to foresee the place where the projectiles or other substances discharged from a balloon will fall and . . . they may just as easily hit inoffensive inhabitants as combatants, or destroy a church as easily as a battery'.[12] It was felt, however, that aerial navigation was likely to be perfected in such a way that the defects of balloons, in particular the indiscriminateness of projectiles launched from them, might be done away with; it was precisely to take account of these possible future developments that the prohibition was limited to a definite period of time.[13]

Another international treaty whose stipulation was motivated, at least in part, by the desire to avoid the indiscriminate striking of noncombatants is the Convention on the laying of automatic submarine contact mines, adopted by Hague Conference II, in 1907. It is well known that by its provisions the Convention embodied the principle that while enemy men-of-war can lawfully be destroyed, noncombatants are to be spared. More precisely, the basic ideas behind the Convention were first that enemy 'merchantmen are entitled to immunity from attack without warning'[14] and secondly that neutral commerce on the high sea must be safeguarded. This is clearly demonstrated by the debates that took place at the Hague Peace Conference. Although one delegate hinted, at one point, at the treacherous character of the submarine contact mines,[15] several delegates

[7] Delegate of Russia (*ibid.*, p. 283).
[8] Delegate of the Netherlands (*ibid.*, p. 283).
[9] Delegate of Denmark (*ibid.*, p. 366).
[10] Delegate of the Netherlands (*ibid.*, p. 342 and p. 288).
[11] Delegate of France (*ibid.*, p. 280).
[12] Delegate of the United States of America (*ibid.*, p. 280). See also *ibid.*, p. 354.
[13] Delegate of the United States of America (*ibid.*, p. 354).
[14] Oppenheim-Lauterpacht, *International Law, a Treatise,* vol. II, p. 471.
[15] The Chairman of the III Commission of the Conference, the Italian Delegate Tornielli stated as follows: 'Of all the engines of modern war, there is none comparable, in the horror it inspires or the devastation it inflicts, to automatic mines. There is something infernal about these apparatus which, hidden like traitors under the water, spread destruction and death without any risk to those who have laid them, without presenting a common danger to the combatants, which seems to take away from war the aspect of murder, where the assassin stabs his victim suddenly and

supporting the Convention stressed that it aimed at guaranteeing 'the interests and safety of peaceful navigation'.[16] As was stated by the Chairman of the Third Commission of the Conference 'the horror (of submarine contact mines) is augmented when the mine floats at the pleasure of wind and wave, a menace not only to belligerents but to all voyagers . . .'[17] A further reason behind the elaboration of the Convention was the need not 'to expose neutrals to the dangers' to which only belligerents 'should be exposed'.[18] These two basic reasons were often combined. Thus, in the Report submitted by the *ad hoc* Subcommission to the Third Commission of the Peace Conference, it was pointed out that:

'No one dreams of contesting the legitimacy of these weapons (submarine mines) from the viewpoint of existing law; likewise, no one has thought of forbidding their use completely—especially a use for the purpose of injuring the armed forces of the enemy. But the employment of this weapon, in itself allowable, carries danger for peaceful shipping . . . The purpose of assuring to pacific commerce an effectual protection has constituted the point of common departure of all the discussions of the Subcommission and the Committee'.[19]

Two other treaties were concluded for the purpose of banning weapons whose effects cannot be confined to limited targets: the 1925 Geneva Protocol prohibiting the use in war of asphyxiating, poisonous or other gases and of bacteriological methods of warfare, and the 1972 Convention on the prohibition of the developments, production and stockpiling of bacteriological (biological) and toxin weapons and on their destruction, which supplemented, developed and improved the Geneva Protocol so far as biological warfare is concerned. Suffice it to quote here the statement made by the Polish delegate to the 1925 Geneva Conference that 'it is impossible to limit the field of action of bacteriological factors once introduced into warlike operations. The consequences of bacteriological warfare will thus be felt equally by the armed forces of the belligerents and the whole civilian population, even against the desire of the belligerents, who would be unable to restrict the action of the bacteriological weapons to an area decided upon beforehand'.[20] A pronouncement of the UN General Assembly is also worth quoting. In the second preambular paragraph of Resolution 2603 A (XXIV) the

in the dark. It is pitiable to think of the mass of courage marching on the foe, as sang the English poet, of men thrilling with patriotism and ready to fight, who are crushed, annihilated, and overwhelmed by a muderous agency laid by an absent enemy' (*ibid.*, p. 451).

[16] Delegate of Germany (*Proceedings of The Hague Peace Conferences*, edited by J.B. Scott, The Conference of 1907, vol. III, p. 380 and 385). See also the statements by the delegate of Russia (*ibid.*, p. 387). See also the Report of the *Ad Hoc* Subcommission to the III Commission (*ibid.*, p. 404).

[17] *Ibid.*, p. 451.

[18] Delegates of Great Britain (*ibid.*, p. 383; see also p. 382), of Germany (*ibid.*, p. 385), Japan (*ibid.*, p. 386), USA (*ibid.*, p. 388).

[19] *Ibid.*, pp. 399–400. See also the Report of the III Commission to the Conference (*ibid.*, p. 459 and vol. I, p. 282).

[20] League of Nations, *Proceedings of the Conference for the Supervision of the International Trade in Arms and Ammunition and Implements of War* (1925) p. 340.

General Assembly stated that chemical and biological methods of warfare 'are inherently reprehensible because their effects are often uncontrollable and unpredictable and may be injurious without distinction to combatants and noncombatants, and because any use would entail a serious risk of escalation'.

By and large, the above prohibitions have been complied with by States. Although on some occassions a few States have disregarded them (e.g., Italy used poison gas in Ethiopia, in 1935;[21] and, allegedly, Egypt used the same weapon in Yemen, in 1967)[22] one can fairly conclude that these treaty rules have satisfactorily met the test of time and still prove to be valid and effective. What is needed at present is their extension to new agencies of destruction which are no less cruel and 'blind'.

4. Practice of States Concerning Weapons Other than those Prohibited by Specific Bans

Two main elements emerge from State practice: first, a string of pronouncements concerning the use of both atomic weapons and some new conventional arms; secondly, the statements of a great number of States calling for the enactment of treaty bans on the use of some specific conventional weapons. I propose to analyze these trends briefly and to indicate what conclusions can be drawn therefrom.

The inherent incapability of hitting combatants only has been relied upon for labelling *atomic and nuclear weapons* as unlawful. In a protest of August 10, 1945, the charge of indiscriminateness was levelled by the Imperial Government of Japan against the United States for the atomic bombing of Hiroshima. After recalling the 'principles' of wartime international law whereby the belligerents have not an unlimited right as to the choice of means of combat and must not employ weapons, projectiles and other materials causing unnecessary suffering, it was stated in the protest that 'the bomb in this case, which the United States used this time, far exceeds, in its indiscriminate performance and in its atrocious character, poisonous gases and other weapons which hitherto have been banned because they possess these performances';[23] in the opinion of Japan, therefore, the US Government had disregarded 'the fundamental principles of international law and humanity'.[24] The reasoning of this protest is quite original and could give rise to important developments. In short, the idea behind the Japanese Government's protest is that a new weapon is unlawful if it causes indiscriminate effects which exceed those of weapons which have already been banned precisely because of

[21] Cf. Ch. Rousseau, *Le conflit italo-éthiopien devant le droit international,* Paris, 1938, p. 169ff.
[22] See the relevant documents in Whiteman, 10 *Digest of International Law* (1968) pp. 474–477.
[23] Text in Whiteman, *cit.,* at p. 502.
[24] *Ibid.,* p. 252.

their indiscriminateness. In other words, the Japanese Government held that, in applying the general principle on indiscriminate weapons, resort must be made to a test of 'unlawfulness by analogy': the standards by which new weapons must be gauged are the effects of already prohibited weapons.

The reaction by other concerned parties to that protest reveals strong disagreement on the legal characterization of the atomic bombing. It is well known that Truman,[25] Stimson,[26] and Churchill[27] regarded that bombing as lawful in that it was justified by the need to avoid greater losses both to the Allies and to the Japanese. In addition, they stressed that both Hiroshima and Nagasaki contained a great many important military targets;[28] furthermore, precautions had been taken for allowing civilians to leave the towns before the bombing.[29] Truman emphasized as well that the Japanese had on many occasions violated international law, thus implying that the atomic bombing was to some extent made in reprisal for the enemy's violations.[30] Another reason why the Japanese protest remained an isolated event without important legal repercussions is that the Japanese Government itself subsequently retracted its previous statement by maintaining in 1962 and in 1963, that no rules of international law cover atomic bombs.[31]

The characterization of the bombing of Hiroshima and Nagasaki made in the Japanese protest was taken up to some extent by the Tokyo District Court in the *Shimoda* case. In its judgment delivered on December 7, 1963[32] the Court did not hold the atomic bombing unlawful *per se*. For the purpose of assessing its lawfulness, the Court preferred to regard atomic bombing as a special category of 'blind' aerial bombardment. Put another way, the Court did not take into account and evaluate the atomic weapon as a *means* of combat, but referred to it as a *method* of warfare. The Court held that in certain instances the use of the bomb, though it produces indiscriminate effects, may be lawful. More specifically the Court held that one of the reasons why that bombing was a violation of international law was that the two Japanese cities, being 'undefended',

---

[25] See Truman's declaration of August 9, 1945, *Keesing's Contemporary Archives*, 1945, p. 7407.

[26] Stimson, 'The Decision to Use the Atomic Bomb', 194 *Harper's Magazine* (Febr. 1947) No. 1161 pp. 98, 101, 102, 105, 106.

[27] See the statement made by Churchill on August 16, 1945 in the House of Commons, in *Keesing's Contemporary Archives,* 1945, p. 7383. See also *Churchill,* The Second World War, vol. VI, *Triumph and Tragedy,* pp. 552–553.

[28] Stimson, op cit, p. 100, 104, 105; Truman, declaration quoted above, p. 7407; Idem, *Memoirs,* vol. I, pp. 530–533.

[29] Churchill, statement quoted above, p. 7383.

[30] In his declaration, of August 9, quoted above, he said: 'Having found the bomb, we have used it against those who attacked us without warning at Pearl Harbour, against those who have starved, beaten and executed American prisoners, against those who have abandoned all pretence of obeying international laws of warfare' (*Keesing's Contemporary Archives,* 1945, p. 7407).

[31] See 8, *Japanese Annual of International Law,* (1964) pp. 225–226 and 10, *Japanese Annual of International Law,* (1966) p. 91.

[32] Text in Friedman (ed.), The *Law of War, A Documentary History,* vol. II, 1972 pp. 1690–1694.

were bombed indiscriminately. The Court thus qualified its terming atomic bombardments unlawful, in that it implied that indiscriminate aerial bombardment (hence also atomic bombing) is permitted when a city is 'defended', i.e. resists any possible occupation attempt by land forces and is not far from the battlefield. The fallacy of the Court's reasoning lies in its relying on the notion of 'undefended town' as well as on the basic principles of the Hague Draft Rules on Air Warfare of 1923. Had the Court more correctly discarded both that notion and those principles, and based its decision on the law applicable at the time of the atomic bombing, it would have relied on the principle of proportionality. As a result, no distinction between 'defended' and 'undefended' towns would have been drawn, and the lawfulness of the atomic bombardments, whatever the nature of the target town, would have been assessed by the following standard: did the bombed town contain military objectives? If so, was the killing and wounding of civilians proportionate to the direct military advantage gained by the destruction of military targets? It is apparent from the relevant documents that the answer to this last question must be in the negative. In particular, the civilian casualties brought about by the atomic bombing were not justified by the need to avoid greater losses by inducing the Japanese to surrender. As B.V.A. Röling rightly stressed, 'it is a myth that the Japanese surrendered because of the atomic bombs'.[33] And he goes on to say: 'As a judge in the I.M.T.F.E. I have seen all the records of the sessions of the Japanese Imperial Council and other governmental councils during the war, and it is clear that Japan was prepared to capitulate before the atomic bombs were dropped, on the sole condition that the imperial system would be maintained and that the emperor might keep his position'.[34]

A more significant and authoritative declaration that atomic weapons are unlawful because they are indiscriminate is Resolution 1653 (XVI) adopted on November 24, 1961 by the General Assembly. In the fourth preambular paragraph the General Assembly states that:

. . . The use of nuclear and thermonuclear weapons would bring about indiscriminate suffering and destruction to mankind and civilizations to an even greater extent than the use of those weapons declared by the aforementioned international declarations and agreements (namely those of St. Petersburg of 1868, of Brussels of 1874, of the Hague of 1899 and 1907 and the Geneva Protocol of 1925) to be contrary to the laws of humanity and a crime under international law.

Then, in the first operative paragraph the General Assembly goes on to declare that:

...b) The use of nuclear and thermonuclear weapons would exceed even the scope of war and cause indiscriminate suffering and destruction to mankind and

---

[33] B.V.A. Röling, 'The Significance of the Laws of War', in A. Cassese (ed.), *Current Problems of International Law*, (1975) p. 143.
[34] *Ibid.*, pp. 143–144.

civilization and, as such, is contrary to the rules of international law and to the laws of humanity;

. . . c) The use of nuclear and thermonuclear weapons is a war directed not against an enemy or enemies alone but also against mankind in general since the peoples of the world not involved in such a war will be subjected to all the evils generated by the use of such weapons;

Any State using nuclear and thermonuclear weapons is to be considered as violating the Charter of the United Nations, as acting contrary to the laws of humanity and as committing a crime against mankind and civilization.[35]

The value of this resolution has been played down by a number of States and scholars. It has been contended that, like all recommendations of the General Assembly, it has no legally binding value; that in addition, it was not adopted by an overwhelming majority; that furthermore, it was 'indiscriminate' itself, for it did not take into account and except from the ban resort to nuclear weapons for self-defense under Art. 51 of the Charter or for collective enforcement under Chapter VII, nor did it make provision for 'tactical nuclear weapons', which are assertedly not indiscriminate in character. It has further been contended that that resolution did not acquire any legally binding value either by being acquiesced in by States (thus becoming binding as a result of its acceptance), or by being tantamount to an important element of a general process for the creation of a customary rule. It has also been argued that the very fact that the resolution calls for the conclusion of a treaty on the subject[36] demonstrates that no legal value can be attributed to the condemnation of atomic and nuclear weapons made in the resolution itself.[37]

Whatever the soundness of these arguments, it cannot be denied that the afore-mentioned resolution is very significant at least in two respects. First, it brings out that a great number of States (with the exception, however, of most 'nuclear powers') consider atomic and nuclear weapons to be contrary to international law in that they are indiscriminate. It is worth adding that the reference to the future conclusion of a treaty on the matter does not detract from the value of the resolution as an indicator of the conviction held by the majority of States as to the existing law. If those very States which espoused the view that the weapons at issue were already violative of international law, at the same time called for the elaboration of a treaty on the subject, this merely shows that in their view a prohibition stemming from the general principles of the law of warfare is not

---

[35] The resolution was adopted by 55 votes to 20, with 26 abstentions. The States voting against the resolution included France, the United Kingdom and the United States.

[36] Operative para. 2 of the resolution requests 'the Secretary General to consult the Governments of Member States to ascertain their views on the possibility of convening a special conference for signing a convention on the prohibition of the use of nuclear and thermonuclear weapons for war purposes and to report on the results of such consultation to the General Assembly at its seventeenth session'.

[37] For these arguments see the UN doc.: *Respect for Human Rights in Armed Conflicts, Existing Rules of International Law Concerning the Prohibition or Restriction of Use of Specific Weapons*, Study prepared by the Secretariat, vol. I (A/9215-I), p. 148*ff.*

sufficient (a treaty is clearly needed to regulate manufacturing, stockpiling, international supervision, etc.).[38]

A second important feature of the resolution is that the indiscriminateness of nuclear weapons is assessed by *comparing* the effects of atomic or nuclear arms with the effects of weapons which through treaty provisions were proscribed in the past for their indiscriminateness. The General Assembly thereby took up the important test used by the Japanese Government in its 1945 protest.

It is apparent from the above remarks that State practice concerning atomic and nuclear weapons is far from proving that all States consider those weapons to fall under the general rules proscribing indiscriminate means of warfare. Only a segment—albeit a vast one—of the international society takes this view.

Even more fragmentary is the practice of States concerning modern conventional weapons. In recent international armed conflicts many protests were lodged by one of the belligerents against the use of certain arms by the adversary. Thus, Syria protested in 1973 the alleged use by Israel of delayed-action weapons;[39] charges were made against the United States for resorting to the same weapons (as well as to flechettes, cluster bombs and electronic warfare) in Vietnam.[40] In 1975 South Vietnamese authorities were accused of using particularly cruel and indiscriminate cluster bombs.[41] As normally happens in these cases, the States accused never took a stand on the legality of the weapons at issue; they either refrained from commenting on the charges made against them, or claimed that they had not actually used the weapon. More protests were aroused by the use of napalm. In April 1965, in a joint Soviet-Vietnamese communiqué the two parties condemned 'the use of barbarous weapons of annihilation, including napalm

---

[38] The above remarks hold to a great extent true for all other resolutions adopted by the General Assembly in the matter: see above all Resolution 2936 (XXVII) of November 28, 1972. For a list of all resolutions, see the UN document cited at note 37, p. 148 ff.

[39] 'Among the cruel weapons used by the Israeli Air Force [in air raids against Damascus and other Syrian cities during the 1973 Middle East war] against those persons [civilians], were incendiary and fragmentation weapons, flechette warheads and delayed action weapons, whose purpose was to create an atmosphere of terror among civilians' (statement made by the delegate from Syria in the General Assembly's Sixth Committee, Dec. 1973, A/C.6/SR. 1454, pp. 2–3). The Israeli representative replied that: 'It was wrong to claim, as the representative of Syria had done, that Israel had deliberately attacked civilian targets. Unlike Syria, Israel had never had anything but military targets and had not used delayed-action bombs' (*ibid.*, p. 5). On June 26, 1967, the King of Jordan had protested in the General Assembly 'the widespread use of napalm and fragmentary bombs' by the Israeli military authorities. Cf. UN Doc. A/6740.

[40] See e.g. the charges made in the General Assembly by the delegate of Cuba in 1972 (A/C.1/PV.1889, pp. 31–35) and in 1973 (A/C.6/SR. 1449, pp. 5–7). See also the accusations made in the Geneva Diplomatic Conference, in 1975, by the representative of the Democratic Republic of Vietnam (CDDH/III/SR. 26, pp. 141–144).

[41] On April 24, 1975, the Provisional Government of South Vietnam and the Democratic Republic of Vietnam protested the use by the Saigon authorities of CBU 55 bombs. They claimed that these weapons were contrary to international law because they were inhumane, indiscriminate and terrorized the population; they therefore warned South Vietnam that they would bring to trial as war criminals those pilots who did not refuse to use such weapons. Is seems that after this stern warning, the Saigon authorities discontinued resort to CBU bombs (*L'Unità*, April 25, 1975, p. 20; cf. *Le Monde*, February 5, 1975, p. 6 and April 24, 1975, p. 3).

bombs, against the peaceful population'.[42] In a message of January 24, 1966, the President of the Democratic Republic of Vietnam condemned the use of napalm to destroy the countryside and annihilate the civilian population.[43] The Member States of the Warsaw Pact declared, in a joint statement of July 6, 1966, their condemnation of napalm.[44] It is to be noted that the bulk of these statements do not seem to be inconsistent with statements in the military manuals of some Western countries (such as those of the United States and the United Kingdom),[45] that the use of napalm is lawful provided it is made against military targets.[46] It should be recalled that in 1972 the UN General Assembly adopted Resolution 2932 A (XXVII), where it noted that 'the massive spread of fire through incendiary weapons is largely indiscriminate in its effect on military and civilian targets' and that such weapons posed a threat to 'the long upheld principle of the immunity of the 'noncombatant'; the General Assembly therefore *deplored* 'the use of napalm and other incendiary weapons in all armed conflicts'. As was stressed in a study of the UN Secretary-General, 'those delegations speaking in support of the resolution did so in terms suggesting that the use of napalm…ought to be forbidden but was not yet prohibited by general international law'.[47]

To sum up the above survey of State practice, three main conclusions can be drawn.

First, that practice is indicative of the fact that in the view of a number of States some weapons are contrary to international law because they cause indiscriminate suffering. As even those States that opposed this view did not go as far as to reject the general rules prohibiting indiscriminate weapons, the clear inference is that all States have upheld those general rules. The importance of this conclusion is somewhat belittled, however, by the second and third conclusions to be drawn from State practice. The second conclusion is that when it was contended by a State that a certain weapon ran counter to those general rules, in no case did the State against which that contention was made acknowledge the violation. This is only natural, because no State is ready to openly admit violating international law. What, however, is lacking, at least in the case of conventional weapons, has been the *repetition of protests by a great number of States* and the affirmation *by some international body representative of the world community* that the weapons at issue are contrary to international law. Criticisms and protests against the use of certain weapons have remained therefore 'unilateral' moves

---

[42] See the Study prepared by the UN Secretariat on 'Respect for Human Rights in Armed Conflicts—Existing Rules of International Law Concerning the Prohibition or Restriction of Use of Specific Weapons', A/9215, vol. I, p. 142.

[43] *Ibid.*

[44] *Ibid.*

[45] See respectively 'The Law of Land Warfare' (1956), para. 36 and 'The Law of War on Land' (1958), para. 1110, note 1.

[46] It must by noted, however, that the US Military Manual uses a very vague expression, for it considers lawful the use of napalm and similar weapons 'against targets requiring their use'.

[47] See the UN Study quoted above, note 42, p. 141.

and have not been able to elicit the agreement of a vast number of States. Thirdly, no State has thus far discontinued the use of any weapon as a result of allegations by other States that that weapon is illegal because of its indiscriminateness. If in a few instances, as in the case of South Vietnam referred to above, charges resulted in the State accused dropping the use of the weapon, this was mainly due to the surrounding circumstances of the war (i.e., the State accused was about to lose the war) and to the warning that military personnel using those weapons would be tried as war criminals, if captured.

In short, a survey of State practice proves that while no State denies the existence and the binding value of the general rules banning indiscriminate weapons, no agreement (outside treaty stipulations) has as yet evolved on the concrete application of that principle to specific weapons. This amounts to saying that the prohibitory intent of those rules has proved scarcely effective.

These conclusions must be borne in mind when considering some States' recent pronouncements. At the UN General Assembly, in 1973, and at the First Session of the Geneva Diplomatic Conference on Humanitarian Law, in 1974, when the question was raised of the prohibition or restriction of conventional weapons having indiscriminate effects, only a few States—namely Switzerland,[48] the Ukraine,[49] Romania[50] and (in rather contradictory terms) Cuba[51]—contended that those weapons are *already prohibited* by present customary international law, the Swiss delegate specifying that the proposals put forward by some States with a view to elaborating conventional rules on the subject were therefore 'merely executing rules' for they 'were not aimed at creating new law, but at clarifying and illustrating the rules already in force'.[52] By contrast, the overwhelming majority of States, including such States as USSR, USA, UK, Sweden and Canada, stated either specifically or by implication, that their task and goal was to create new rules. They all maintained that the purpose of the conventional rules

---

[48] *Geneva Diplomatic Conference*, Doc. CDDH/IV/SR. 1, pp. 9–10.

[49] *UN General Assembly's Sixth Committee*, Doc. A/C.6/SR. 1450, 13 ('The Secretariat's study (A/9215) showed clearly that the use of weapons of mass destruction was prohibited by contemporary international law. That prohibition also applied to some types of particularly destructive weapons, such as napalm and incendiary, chemical and biological weapons'). See also 14.

[50] *Geneva Diplomatic Conference*, Doc. CDDH/IV/SR. 3, p. 6. 'The use of weapons of mass destruction, nuclear, bacterial and chemical weapons, was prohibited by international law and by the legal conscience of peoples'. See, however, the statement of the Roumanian representative in the *UN General Assembly's Sixth Committee*, Doc. A/C.6/SR. 1451, pp. 4–5.

[51] *UN General Assembly's Sixth Committee*, Doc. A/C.6/SR. 1449, p. 6. After stating that napalm, phosphorous and antipersonnel weapons 'should be absolutely prohibited' he noted that 'that technical escalation' (of 'imperialist industrial technology', which had created 'increasingly cruel and refined methods of inflicting suffering') 'was in conflict with the old Hague principles'.

[52] *Geneva Diplomatic Conference*, Doc. CDDH/IV/SR. 1, p. 9. The Swiss Representative went on to say that: 'It was a question of the codification of existing law rather than the creation of new legal norms, of removing all possible doubts and rendering the practical effects of the general principles intelligible to all . . . To establish rules governing the use of certain weapons or prohibiting others would be of the greatest value in eliminating possible disputes concerning the interpretation of the general principles' (*ibid.*, p. 10). See also the statement of the Swiss observer in the UN General Assembly's Sixth Committee: UN Doc. A/C.6/SR. 1450, p. 10.

to be evolved was to put a ban on, or restrict, the use of certain conventional weapons.[53] Furthermore, they agreed that all modern weapons which are indiscriminate are either to be banned or their use restricted. In other words, there was agreement that the indiscriminateness of arms amounts to a general criterion for assessing which arms should be outlawed. This latter convergence of views was however qualified, for no agreement was reached on the actual scope and significance of the standard of indiscriminateness. Must we infer from the stand taken by the majority of States that they took the view that those modern conventional weapons which have indiscriminate effects are not as yet prohibited and will only be banned when treaty provisions to this effect are enacted? If this were the right interpretation, it would be tantamount to saying that States consider the general principle on indiscriminate weapons to have become valueless. This, however, would run counter to the attitude previously taken by many States including those forming the majority at the General Assembly in 1973, and at the Geneva Diplomatic Conference in 1974. It is hard to believe that a State which voted in 1961 and 1972 for the General Assembly resolutions on atomic and nuclear weapons (thereby upholding the general prohibition of indiscriminate weapons) subsequently denied any significance whatsoever to that prohibition when conventional weapons were at stake. In addition, some of the States forming the 1973 and 1974 majorities had previously gone on record as denouncing the illegality of some conventional weapons because of their indiscriminate character.[54] The logical conclusion is not that States were whimsical and inconsistent, but that they felt the general prohibition to be insufficient. They were aware that that prohibition lacks precision and certainty and leaves much room for opposing arguments on the legality of the use of a specific weapon.[55] They therefore felt that

[53] E.g., Syria protested in 1973 the use of indiscriminate weapons by Israel as being violative of existing international law (see *supra,* note 39). As to the general stand on new weapons taken by Syria in the General Assembly, see infra, note 54.

[54] Several States pointed out, at the 1974 Geneva Diplomatic Conference, that the standard of indiscriminateness, being vague and open to different interpretation, needed to be clarified. See the statements by: Canada (CDDH/IV/SR. 1, p. 12: 'The question of indiscriminate effects remained open to varying interpretations, since all weapons might be deemed indiscriminate by their very nature'); UK (CDDH/IV/SR. 2, p. 4); India (*ibid.,* p. 5); the Netherlands (*ibid.,* p. 9); USSR (*ibid.,* p. 11).

[55] This stand was taken by many States in 1973 both in the First and the Sixth Committee of the General Assembly. As to the First Committee, the following States can be quoted: Sweden (A/C.1/PV.1941, pp. 58–67; PV.1947, pp. 12–16); Kenya (A/C.1/PV.1941, p. 76); Ecuador (A/C.1/PV.1947, p. 37); the Netherlands (A/C.1/PV.1948, pp. 31–32); Brazil (PV.1948, pp. 49–51); New Zealand (A/C.1/1949, pp. 68–70); Afghanistan (PV.1950, p. 47); Tunisia (PV.1951, p. 51); USSR (PV.1968, pp. 57–60). The following States took the same view in the General Assembly's Sixth Committee: Yugoslavia (A/C.6/SR. 1448, pp. 13–14: 'new rules must be formulated to prohibit the use of weapons and methods of warfare indiscriminately affecting civilians and combatants', p. 13); the Netherlands (A/C.6/SR. 1449, pp. 8–9); Denmark (*ibid.,* p. 14); Finland (A/C.6/SR. 1450, pp. 4–5); Sweden (*ibid.,* p. 6: the decision to pay attention to the problem of prohibiting or restricting the use of specific conventional weapons reflected 'a desire to move on from theoretical condemnation to the adoption of legal norms'); Mexico (A/C.6/SR. 1451, p. 3); Federal Republic of Germany (A/C.6/SR. 1452, pp. 13–14); Soviet Union (*ibid.,* p. 18: 'It was also necessary to prohibit

the generic prohibition should be *strengthened* and *elaborated* by treaty provisions regarding certain specified categories of weapons.[56]

5. Trends in the Current Development of New Law

In the works now in progress at Geneva in the Diplomatic Conference on the International Humanitarian Law Applicable in Armed Conflicts five major tendencies are discernible.

First, the idea of merely reaffirming the general rules has been discarded by the vast majority of States. Some States had insisted on the need to restate the general principles banning indiscriminate weapons. Amendments to this effect had been tabled by a Third World and a socialist country, respectively Pakistan[57] and the German Democratic Republic.[58] The Democratic Republic of Vietnam, on its part, had submitted an amendment designed to prohibit *inter alia* the employment of such means of combat which cause mass extermination.[59] None of these amendments, however, was accepted by the Conference, although a few of them rallied some support.[60] Although the reasons for their rejection were not given, it seems likely that the primary ground for their not being adopted was the one

certain particularly cruel methods of warfare, and the USSR had always supported United Nations efforts to that end. However, the question of deciding which types of weapons should be prohibited on the grounds that they caused unnecessary suffering or affected civilians and combatants indiscriminately should be resolved within the framework of the question of arms limitation and disarmament . . . '); Kenya (A/C.6/SR. 1453, p. 3: 'It was to be hoped that that Conference (the 1974 Geneva Diplomatic Conference) would be guided by the realization that modern warfare, sophisticated weapons and the effects thereof were by no means covered by existing law and would devote special attention to developing the rules of humanitarian law contained in the 1899 and 1907 Hague Conventions, the 1949 Geneva Conventions and other pertinent instruments'); German Democratic Republic (*ibid.,* p. 8); Syrian Arab Republic (A/C.6/ SR. 1454, p. 3); Venezuela (*ibid.,* p. 4). The following States took the same view in 1974, at the Geneva Diplomatic Conference: Norway (CDDH/IV/SR. 1, p. 3); Finland (*ibid.,* p. 4); Federal Republic of Germany (*ibid.,* p. 5, despite some doubts as to the *advisability* of elaborating specific prohibitions); Sweden (*ibid.,* p. 7; see also CDDH/IV/SR. 6, pp. 2–3) Poland (*ibid.,* pp.10–11); Canada (*ibid.,* pp. 12–13); Togo (*ibid.,* p. 15); Austria (CDDH/IV/SR. 2, p. 2); New Zealand (*ibid.,* pp. 2–3); Brazil (*ibid.,* pp. 3–4; see also CDDH/IV/SR. 6, p. 6); Nigeria (*ibid.,* p. 6); USA (*ibid.,* p. 6; see also CDDH/ IV/SR.5, p. 10); the Netherlands (*ibid.,* p. 9); France (*ibid.,* p. 9); Tanzania (*ibid.,* p. 9); Italy (*ibid.,* p. 10); Mongolia (CDDH/IV/SR. 3, p. 2); Morocco (*ibid.,* p. 3); Sri Lanka (*ibid.,* p. 3); Japan *ibid.,* p. 6); Mexico (CDDH/IV/SR. 4. p. 7; see also SR 5, p. 8); Norway (CDDH/IV/SR 5, p. 4); Egypt (CDDH/IV/SR. 6, p. 5).

[56] It is worth recalling the statement made by the representative of Sweden in 1973, in the General Assembly. He observed that 'In one sense the wish for early action might be thought to be satisfied by a resolution by the General Assembly condemning the use of specific types of weapons and declaring the opinion of the Assembly to be that such weapons fall under the existing general legal prohibitions of weapons. Such action would hardly be effective, however—we know that—and my delegation would not propose it' (A/C.1/PV.1941, pp. 53–65).

[57] See doc. CDDH/III/11.
[58] See doc. CDDH/III/225.
[59] See doc. CDDH/III/238.
[60] See CDDH/III/SR. 26, pp. 145–149; SR.27, pp. 151–155.

adduced by the Brazilian representative when he opposed them. He stated that 'the question of weapons with indiscriminate effects had perhaps been sufficiently discussed during the consideration of Article 46, para. 3 (dealing with indiscriminate attacks), which the Committee had already adopted'.[61] It was probably felt that the adoption of a provision specifically determining the characteristics of indiscriminate attacks, and thus covering also indiscriminate means of warfare, made any generic prohibition of indiscriminate weapons superfluous. This possible argument has much value, because elaborating the general rules is no doubt more useful than merely restating them.

A second trend consists precisely in the *developing, specifying* and *expanding* of the general rules. To this end, a major breakthrough was achieved by the adoption of a provision, Art. 46, para. 3, which covers *inter alia* indiscriminate weapons. It is worth quoting this rule *in extenso*:

Indiscriminate attacks are prohibited. Indiscriminate attacks are those which are not directed at a specific military objective; or those which employ a method or *means of combat* which cannot be directed at a specific military objective, or the effects of which cannot be limited as required by this Protocol and consequently are of a nature to strike military objectives and civilians or civilian objects without distinction. Among others, the following types of attacks are to be considered as indiscriminate:

(a) An attack by bombardment by any methods or *means* which treats as a single military objective a number of clearly separated and distinct military objectives located in a city, town, village or other area containing a concentration of civilians or civilian objects; and

(b) An attack of the type prohibited by Article 50 (2) iii [under this provision, in conducting military operations, those who plan or decide upon an attack, 'shall refrain from deciding to launch any attack which may be expected to cause incidental loss of civilian life, injury to civilians, damage to civilian objects, or a combination thereof, which would be excessive in relation to the concrete and direct military advantage anticipated'].

This rule among other things elaborates the prohibition of indiscriminate weapons, in two respects: (1) by specifying what must be understood by 'blind' weapons; (2) by developing the rule of proportionality. As far as the first point is concerned, the provision is no doubt a great improvement over the existing law, for *litt.* (*a*) specifies in clear and unambiguous terms the circumstances under which a means of combat is illegal for its indiscriminateness. The first and clearest inference from this provision is that non-'tactical' atomic and nuclear weapons (provided of course that 'tactical' ones are capable of hitting military objectives only) are prohibited. There could, however, be some elements pointing to a contrary conclusion.[62]

---

[61] CDDH/III/SR. 26, 148.

[62] In its introduction to the Draft Additional Protocols, the ICRC states: 'It should be recalled that, apart from some provisions of a general nature, the ICRC has not included in its drafts any rules governing atomic, bacteriological and chemical weapons. These weapons have either been the subject of international agreements such as the Geneva Protocol of 1925 or of discussions within intergovernmental organizations'; ICRC, *Draft Additional Protocols to the Geneva Conventions of August 12, 1949, Commentary,* Geneva, October 1973, p. 2.

Less felicitous appears to be the second part of the provision, which elaborates the rule of proportionality. It seems that the main focus is placed on the *subjective evaluation,* by belligerents, of the destructive effects of attacks or of the use of means of warfare. For it is stated there that a belligerent must refrain from launching attacks which *may be expected* to cause damage to civilians disproportionate to the military advantage *anticipated* by that belligerent. Instead of establishing that the possible disproportion must be *objective* (i.e. that the actual incidental damage to civilians must not be out of proportion to the military advantage actually gained), the provision hinges on how a belligerent perceives and anticipates the effect of its attack. It would seem that the provision therefore lends itself to subjective interpretations. Thus, for instance, faced with a glaring disproportion of civilian loss to the military advantage, a belligerent could claim that when he planned the attack he did not expect or anticipate such a great disproportion. How could one assess the decision-making process of belligerents and the manner by which they weigh the various alternatives and make the final choice? The difficulty of looking into such imponderable elements to determine whether a belligerent *should have expected* disproportionate damage to civilians could result in rendering the practical application of that rule very difficult.

Besides developing and specifying the general rules on indiscriminate weapons, the Geneva Diplomatic Conference has taken another significant step. Aware of the fact that in modern wars belligerents (or, more appropriately, technologically advanced belligerents) tend to use weapons which eventually affect civilians in that they bring about severe damage to the environment, the States assembled at Geneva adopted Article 33, para. 3, a provision which prohibits, *inter alia,* means of ecological warfare.[63] It reads as follows:

It is forbidden to employ methods or means of warfare which are intended or may be expected to cause widespread, long-term, and severe damage to the natural environment.

This provision is of necessity rather vague. Especially the time element ('long-term . . . damage') can lend itself to subjective interpretations. Some light is shed, however, by the debates preceding its adoption. As is stated in the Report submitted by Committee III to the Conference,

It was generally agreed that battlefield damage incidental to conventional warfare would not normally be proscribed by this provision. What is proscribed, in effect, is such damage as would be likely to prejudice over a long-term the continued survival of the civilian population or would risk long-term major health problems for it.[64]

---

[63] While the ICRC had made no proposals on the matter, some States put forward at Geneva proposals aimed at strengthening the protection of the environment from the damages of war: see the amendments by Finland (CDDH/III/91), by Egypt, Australia, Czechoslovakia, Finland, GDR, Hungary, Ireland, Norway, Yugoslavia, Sudan (CDDH/III/222) and by the Democratic Republic of Vietnam (CDDH/III/238).

[64] CDDH/III/286, p. 9.

A third trend is apparent from the works of Geneva. The vast majority of States strongly believes that a very close link exists between general rules on indiscriminate weapons and the working out of *conventional rules dealing with specified categories of weapons.* It was felt that though the elaboration of general principles is important, it is not sufficient, and that States should endeavor to agree upon a list of weapons whose use must be prohibited because they could prove indiscriminate. These specific bans would strengthen and make more effective the general rules. To overcome the numerous difficulties existing in this field, the ICRC promoted several meetings and conferences of government experts. The primary aims of these gatherings were to collect and discuss information of a military, technical or medical nature on new weapons, and to endeavor to narrow differences among government experts from various countries. Legal criteria for the banning of certain uses of weapons were also discussed.[65] While so far the area of possible agreement has not proved very large, substantial progress has been reached in these conferences, at least with respect to some weapons such as mines, booby-traps and fragmentation bombs, so that one can share the view expressed in 1976 at the end of the Lugano Conference by Mr. J. Pictet, that 'en dépit des difficultés et des divergences de vues, l'on s'achemine vers la conclusion d'un Acte diplomatique sur l'interdiction de certaines armes et la limitation de leur emploi'.[66]

A fourth trend is discernible in the Geneva debates. States have become increasingly aware that, even assuming that it is possible to arrive at the enactment of specific bans, such bans could easily be dodged by manufacturing new and even more inhuman weapons. A growing number of States therefore suggest that national as well as international mechanisms be set up for the purpose both of keeping new developments in conventional weapons under review and of assessing new weapons in the light of humanitarian principles. Such machinery should thus ensure that States do not devise new weapons capable of bypassing existing bans. So far only a national review mechanism has been set up. In 1975 Committee III of the Geneva Diplomatic Conference adopted a provision which provides as follows:

In the study, development, acquisition, or adoption of a new weapon, means, or method of warfare a High Contracting Party is under an obligation to determine whether its employment would, under some or all circumstances, be prohibited by this protocol or by any other rule of international law applicable to the High Contracting Party.

Under this provision, contracting States are not bound to disclose anything about the new weapons they are studying or developing. They are therefore not required to assess publicly the legality of new weapons. It follows that other contracting States have no possibility of verifying whether the obligation laid down there is

---

[65] See ICRC, Conference of Government Experts on the Use of Certain Conventional Weapons, Lucerne, 24 September–18 October, 1974, *Report,* Geneva, 1975, as well as the Report of the 1976 Lugano Conference (COLU/Rep./1).

[66] ICRC, Lugano Conference of Government Experts, *Déclaration finale* de M. J. Pictet, p. 1.

complied with. It could be argued, however, that Article 34 actually imposes both the duty to set up domestic procedures for exploring the issue of legality of new weapons and the duty to use concretely these procedures with respect to each new means of combat. While compliance with the former duty can be made subject to international scrutiny by other contracting States (which could request to be informed about these procedures), implementation of the latter duty is left—in actual practice—to the discretion of the contracting State which studies or elaborates a new means of warfare.

In addition to this national procedure, several States have also proposed an international review mechanism. In an important proposal submitted by a group of States the need for such a continuous scrutiny was forcefully spelled out, although no actual mechanisms for review were suggested.[67] In the course of the debates in Committee IV, in 1975, the Austrian delegate put forward some very interesting suggestions. He proposed that all States parties to Additional Protocol III (on weaponry) should be entrusted with the task of collecting the necessary information concerning scientific and technological developments in the field of conventional weapons. The study of this information for the purpose of determining whether any new weapon causes superfluous injuries or has indiscriminate effects should be entrusted to a Conference of government experts. Subsequently, a plenipotentiary conference—to be convened at the request of one-third of the parties to the Protocol or after a specified number of years has passed—could enact provisions for the banning of any new weapon found to be contrary to the aforementioned basic requirements.[68] This suggestion received wide support in the *Ad Hoc* Committee[69] and it is not unrealistic to believe that, after being improved, it can eventually be adopted by the Conference.[70]

A fifth trend characterizing the works at Geneva is the attempt at extending to non-international armed conflicts the rules on indiscriminate weapons applicable in international armed conflicts. Thus, the Draft Protocol II prepared by the ICRC contains a provision (Art. 26) which *inter alia* prohibits indiscriminate means of warfare, by taking up the provisions proposed with respect to Protocol I (and to a great extent already adopted by the III Committee of the Conference). It is to be hoped that these draft provisions will eventually be adopted, if only because the 'threshold' of application of Protocol II agreed upon by Committee I

---

[67] See the Working Paper submitted to the Geneva Conference by Algeria, Austria, Egypt, Lebanon, Mali, Mauritania, Mexico, Norway, Sudan, Sweden, Switzerland, Venezuela and Yugoslavia (doc. CDDH/IV/201, p. 6 of the annexed 'Explanatory Memorandum').

[68] See CDDH/IV/SR. 15, pp. 79–81.

[69] See in particular the statements by the representatives of Sweden (CDDH/IV/SR. 15, pp. 81–83), Venezuela (*ibid.*, p. 84), Sudan (*ibid.*, p. 89), Egypt (SR. 16, p. 93), Sri Lanka (*ibid.*, pp. 94–95), the Netherlands (*ibid.*, pp. 99–100). Cf. also the cautious remarks of the Soviet delegate (SR. 15, pp. 87–89).

[70] See also the 'informal proposal' on a review mechanism submitted by the Austrian experts to the 1976 Lugano Conference of Government Experts (doc. COLU/GG/LEG/201). This proposal was discussed at Lugano by the Working Group on General and Legal Questions (see the Report of this Group, COLU/GG/LEG/Rep.) 1 Rev. 1, pp. 6–8).

is so high that that Protocol will only apply to 'classical' civil wars.[71] It would therefore be illogical and contrary to humanitarian demands not to apply rules on indiscriminate means of combat to strife that in so many respects resembles international armed conflict. If these rules are adopted, a great advance will be made in this matter. Suffice it to notice that the only treaty rules concerning civil wars presently in force, namely Article 3 common to the four 1949 Geneva Conventions, do not cover the behavior of combatants. This matter is only governed by a few rules of customary international law which evolved during the Spanish Civil War (1936–1939).[72] Such rules, however, are mainly concerned with the protection of civilians, and do not directly affect the use of means of warfare. Although on a few occasions some States have recently claimed that the use of cruel and indiscriminate weapons in civil strife is prohibited by international law,[73] it would seem that so far no general practice has developed on the matter. Therefore, if the aforementioned provisions proposed by the ICRC are adopted by the Diplomatic Conference, for the first time international rules will cover an important area of non-international armed conflicts.

6. Concluding Remarks

All five trends of the Geneva works identified above are highly commendable from a humanitarian viewpoint. The majority of States have chosen the right approach for making war—both international and civil—less inhumane. In short, they have realized that the battle, as it were, must be fought on several fronts: what is needed is both to restate and develop general prohibitory rules and to enact new bans concerning specific weapons; by the same token, it is necessary to set up supervisory machinery to ensure that such bans are not evaded and

[71] See text of Art. 1 of Draft Protocol II, adopted by Committee I, in 1975 (in UN doc. A/10195, Annex I, pp. 9–10).

[72] May I refer to my paper 'The Spanish Civil War and the Development of Customary Law Concerning Non-International Armed Conflicts', in Cassese (ed.), *Current Problems of International Law,* 1975, p. 298 ff. Also published in this volume.

[73] In 1973, a report of an *Ad Hoc* Working Group of Experts on gross violations of human rights of Southern Africa was submitted to the UN Human Rights Commission. This report (E/CN.4/1111) referred *inter alia* to massacres committed in Angola and Mozambique by Portuguese military forces, in particular to bombardments of inhabited villages and the use of chemical weapons (*ibid.,* paras 408–413). Strong condemnation of such practices was expressed by the delegates of Chile (E/CN.4/SR. 1232, p. 262), Zaire (*ibid.,* SR. 1233, pp. 269–270), Tanzania (*ibid.,* pp. 272–273), Philippines (*ibid.,* pp. 273–274), Senegal (*ibid.,* pp. 274–275). The delegate of Italy stated that 'If the allegations concerning aerial bombardment and the use of chemical weapons were fully substantiated, such occurrences must be considered very grave breaches of Article 3 which was common to the four Geneva Conventions of 1949, as well as of the general principles of international law governing the protection of the civil population—principles which undoubtedly applied also to non-international armed conflicts, such as those taking place in the Portuguese territories' (E/CN.4/SR. 1233, p. 271). See also the important statement made by the delegate of Jamaica in the First Committee of the General Assembly, in 1973: A/C.1/Pv. 1953, p. 37.

furthermore to extend the bans to internal armed conflicts, to take account of the fact that these conflicts are more and more widespread in international society.

The choice of the right path does not necessarily mean, however, that it will be easily trodden: it remains to be seen, for instance, if it will be possible to achieve satisfactory restraints on the use of some specific weapons and if, in addition, review mechanisms will actually be established. Many States still resist any major limitation on their military strength. It will be useful to recall what was tellingly stated in 1973 by the head of the US delegation to the Geneva Conference, Mr. G.H. Aldrich: 'States which rely more on massed manpower for military strength than on firepower and mobility would be likely to see security advantages in prohibiting many weapons'. However, 'many governments—and particularly those of the technologically most advanced States—hesitate to submit questions of fundamental importance to their national security to negotiations designed to supplement and improve the 1949 Red Cross Conventions'.[74] Although some major States seem now less reluctant to discuss weaponry in international fora other than the Conference of the Committee on Disarmament, there is still much opposition to the enactment of new bans. It is therefore to be hoped that those countries which more strenuously advocate the need to strengthen and expand the outlawing of indiscriminate weapons will persevere in their efforts, however difficult their task may be.

---

[74] Statement made by Mr. G.H. Aldrich in the House of Representatives: see 'Hearings before the Subcommittee on International Organizations and Movements of the Committee on Foreign Affairs', House of Representatives, Ninety-third Congress, First Session, Washington 1974, p. 99.

2. Weapons Causing Unnecessary Suffering: Are They Prohibited?*

1. The Increasing Use of Cruel Weapons in Modern Wars

Owing to technological progress, belligerents in modern warfare increasingly use extremely cruel weapons which inflict agonizing and terrible suffering. One need only think of nuclear weapons, whose radiation causes either death or awesome diseases; incendiary weapons, containing napalm and phosphorus, which produce dreadful burnings; and fragmentation and cluster bombs, the latest generation of which consists of bombs containing pellets of plastic, which, having penetrated the human body, cannot be traced by X-ray. Just to give a general idea of how frightful these new weapons can be, one of the latest types of incendiary weapons has been described in the following terms:

This is a bouncing 'pop-up' anti-personnel mine filled with fifteen pounds of plasticized white phosphorus. When activated, the main part of the mine is propelled about four meters into the air where it explodes, 'spewing' burning white phosphorus in all directions. The radius effect is said to be about 25 meters. The phosphorus has the quality of gluing to the body when burning and cannot be scraped off, but must be cut out, leaving frightful wounds. Furthermore, it is said to be highly toxic, poisoning the liver, the kidneys and the nervous system after absorption through the wound.[1]

Furthermore, there are the atrocious wounds caused by hypervelocity rifles, whose bullets become completely unstable on impact, tumbling in the wound and producing a large cavity.[2] Suffice it to quote here two cases illustrating the effects of bullets fired by the U.S. rifle M-16, which were published by an Australian surgical team:

Case 1: A Vietnamese civilian was brought in dead after receiving a single projectile from an M-16 in the right thigh. Autopsy showed that the bullet had torn its way through the

---

* Originally published in *Riviste di diritto internazionale* (1975) 12.
  [1] Statement by the Swedish delegate H. Blix, in the general debate in the II Conference of Government Experts on the Reaffirmation and Development of International Humanitarian Law Applicable in Armed Conflicts, Geneva, May 4, 1972 (text provided by the Swedish Delegation), p. 15.
  [2] See SIPRI, *Working Papers on International Law and the Prohibition of Unnecessary Injury,* Stockholm, 1974, Section III, p. 12 ff.
  On the various modern weapons likely to cause unnecessary suffering see also *International Committee of the Red Cross, Weapons that may Cause Unnecessary Suffering or have Indiscriminate Effects,* Report on the Work of Experts, Geneva, 1973; Swedish Working Group, *Conventional Weapons. Their Deployment and Effects from Humanitarian Aspect,* 1973.

obturator foramen and disintegrated in the abdomen, only fragments of about 0.5 mm being recovered. Within the abdomen it had wrenched the whole small bowel from its mesentery and had perforated the pancreas, stomach and spleen. Such an injury is comparable to that produced by an explosive missile.

Case 2: A Vietnamese civilian running away from an American received seven shots in the leg, the buttock, the chest and the arm. The injuries outside the abdomen were minor, but several bullets must have penetrated the buttock, leaving a hole in the sacrum which accepted a fist. The rectum was transected and the small bowel perforated in eight places. Once more no trace of the projectiles could be found at laparotomy.[3]

How does international law face these and other no less inhumane agencies of destruction? It is the purpose of this paper to point to the efforts so far made by international legislators in order to cope with modern progress of large-scale, industrialized cruelty, as well as to the basic deficiencies of the regulation that States have hitherto achieved.

2. Existing Legal Restraints on Inhuman Weapons

Up to now legal restraints have been imposed on several *specific* categories of cruel weapons, while one general and sweeping *principle* has been laid down covering an unspecified class of weapons. These bans either developed as rules of customary law, or they were formulated in the form of treaty provisions but have later passed into customary international law: they are therefore binding at present on all members of the international community.

The specific prohibitions motivated by the cruel character of weapons[4] are to be found first in some customary rules developed in early 1800, specifying that such arms as poisoned bullets, projectiles filled with glass and caustic lime, minced lead, and chain-bullets, were proscribed because they caused needless suffering.[5] Other specific prohibitions are embodied in the St. Petersburg

---

[3] DUDLEY et al., *Civilian Battle Casualties in South Vietnam*, in *British Journal of Surgery*, 1968, No. 5, quoted in SIPRI, op cit, p. 13.

[4] It seems that the prohibition of weapons other than those listed in the text above was effected not because they were cruel, but for different reasons. Thus, for instance, bacteriological weapons are forbidden by the Geneva Protocol of June 17, 1925 and the Convention of April 10, 1972 on bacteriological (biological) and toxic weapons, primarily because they affect indiscriminately military personnel and objectives, and the civilian population. More exactly, they are 'unpredictable in their effects, affecting the forces using them and civilians, as well as enemy personnel' (BAXTER, *Criteria for the Prohibition of Weapons in International Law, in Festschrift für Scheuner*, Berlin 1973, p. 48). Tear gas and irritant chemicals were outlawed by the 1925 Geneva Protocol (cp. BAXTER and BUERGENTHAL, *Legal Aspects of the Geneva Protocol of 1925*, in *American journal of Int. Law*, 1970, pp. 856–866) for a different reason. States feared that the use of chemicals which although they cause only a temporary inconvenience, have nevertheless a toxic action on the human organism, could touch off an *escalation* resulting in resort to chemicals causing serious sufferings or permanent disabilities, or even death.

[5] Suffice it to recall two notes sent in 1868 by the Governments of Portugal and of Prussia, respectively, to the Russian Emperor, who had proposed to outlaw explosive bullets. The Portuguese

Declaration of 1868 on explosive projectiles under 400 grammes weight, in Article 23(a) of the 1899 and 1907 Hague Regulations on Land Warfare, prohibiting poison or poisoned weapons,[6] in the 1899 Hague Declaration on expanding (so-called dum-dum) bullets, and in the 1899 Hague Declaration on asphyxiating and deleterious gases (supplemented by the 1925 Geneva Protocol).[7] The general principle is laid down in Article 23(e) of the 1899 and 1907 Hague Regulations on Land Warfare, stating that 'it is especially forbidden... to employ arms, projectiles or material which are such as to cause superfluous injury' (in the official translation of the authentic French text: '... material *calculated* to cause unnecessary *suffering*').[8] While the specific bans referred to above have not raised any significant questions as to their interpretation and application, Article 23(e) of the Hague Regulations is one of the most unclear and controversial rules of warfare. That is why I shall concentrate on its construction. Yet, before turning to considering it at length, it is well to underscore the basic approach which differentiates this provision from the aforementioned sets of rules proscribing the use of specific means of combat.

The latter rules put a ban on certain weapons by indicating their objective characteristics: they envisage projectiles weighing 'less than 400 grammes which

note, in complying with the Russian proposal, stated that explosive bullets 'amènent une mort certaine avec des souffrances horribles chez tous ceux qu'elles blessent et souvent même dans des cas où les autres balles mettent seulement hors de combat. Par conséquent elles sont comme les balles envenimées, celles remplies de verre et de chaux et d'autres armes ou moyens de combat, qui causent des douleurs inutiles, des blessures difficiles à guérir, et qui, selon l'opinion des publicistes les plus accrédités, ont effectivement été et doivent être prohibées par toutes les nations civilisées' (text in *Nouveau Recueil Général de Traités... continuation du Grand Recueil de G. Fr. Martens,* by SAMWER and HOPF, tome XVIII, Gottingue 1873, p. 464). The Prussian Government, after speaking of 'certains principes... proclamés depuis longtemps par le droit des gens, reconnus parfois dans des traités conclus entre telle et telle puissance et mis plus ou moins généralement en pratique', pointed out: 'Telle est par exemple la prohibition des projectiles enduits ou imprégnés d'une substance vénéneuse, du plomb haché, du verre, des boulets à chaîne ou à bras' (*ibid.,* p. 465).

On the prohibiton of these weapons see KLUBER, *Droit des gens moderne de l'Europe,* Paris 1861, p. 315; BLUNTSCHLI, *Le droit international codifié³,* Paris 1881, p. 326; NEUMANN, *Grundriss des heutigen Europäischen Völkerrechtes³,* Wien 1885, p. 45; LUEDER, *Krieg und Kriegsrecht im Allgemeinen,* in VON HOLZENDORFF, *Handbuch des Völkerrechts,* 1, Hamburg 1889, pp. 391–392; BONFILS, *Manuel de droit international public,* Paris 1905, pp. 608–610.

[6] Although such a great authority as SCHWARZENBERGER, *The Legality of Nuclear Weapons,* London 1958, p. 29 (cp. also STONE, *Legal Controls of International Conflict,* New York 1954, pp. 353–354 and TUCKER, *The Law of War and Neutrality at Sea,* Washington 1957, p. 52, note 15) takes a contrary view, it seems that many official pronouncements hold that the use of poison is proscribed in war because it has *cruel* effects, and causes unnecessary suffering. See, e.g., the two statements quoted above, at note 5, as well as many modern military manuals, such as the Netherlands *Rules of the Law of War* (VR 2—1120/11, Ministerie van Oorlog, Voorlopige Richtlijnen nr. 2–1120, Velddienst-Deel 11—*Oorlogsregelen,* 1958), Ch. III, para. 14 (p. 7), as well as the Netherlands *Manual for the Soldier* (VS 2–1350, Koninkijke Landmacht, *Handboek voor de Soldaat,* 1974), Ch. 7, para. 10 (p. 7/3).

[7] Of course, relevant to our purposes, in the Geneva Protocol, are the provisions concerning asphyxiating and deleterious gases, which no doubt are now part of customary international law.

[8] On the relevance of the difference between the French and English text see ICRC, *Report on the Work of the Conference of Government Experts on the Use of certain Conventional Weapons,* p. 7.

are either explosive or charged with fulminating or inflammable substances', 'bullets which expand or flatten in the human body', etc., 'projectiles the sole object of which is the diffusion of asphyxiating or deleterious gases'. Their *rationale,* as clearly stated in the preamble to the St. Petersburg Declaration, is to outlaw means of combat which are too cruel, in that they inflict on combatants pains which are out of proportion to the object of disabling them. *In Article 23(e) this rationale has been turned into a rule.* Mention is no longer made of the objective characteristics that a weapon must possess for being prohibited. What in the 'specific' provisions lay behind the prohibitions, that is to say the motives which prompted States to agree upon such prohibitions, is now elevated to the rank of a purportedly self-sufficient rule of international law.

We shall consider in the following paragraphs whether and to what extent this approach to the banning of means of combat has yielded any positive results.

3. The Interpretation Proposed on the Basis of the Hague Debates

The only point of Article 23(e) which is clear and undisputable is that the rule does not provide a complete and self-sufficient regulation: it does not list, for instance, the weapons it proscribes, nor does it indicate, not even in general terms, the positive features making a weapon unlawful. Article 23(e) indicates forbidden weapons by using a test (their causing unnecessary suffering), which, to say the least, is very vague. Indeed, under Article 23(e) a weapon is unlawful or permissible according to whether it causes unnecessary suffering or not. But how can we determine whether in a given instance suffering is necessary?

The preparatory works are of little avail, for the draftsmen of Article 23(e) confined themselves to taking up, in substance, the similar provision contained in the 1874 Brussels Declaration.[9] The only conclusion that can be drawn from the discussions taking place at Brussels is that the provision was inspired by the St. Petersburg Declaration of 1868.[10] Article 23(e) therefore must be viewed in the light of the preparatory work and the preamble of the St. Petersburg Declaration. As a result, 'suffering' must be considered necessary when it is caused in order to achieve 'the only legitimate object which States should endeavour to accomplish during war' namely 'to weaken the military forces of the enemy' and, for this purpose, 'to disable the greatest possible number of men'. On the contrary, 'suffering' is superfluous when aggravating the injuries of disabled men or rendering their death inevitable offer no real advantage for achieving the 'direct object' of war.[11]

---

[9] See *The Proceedings of the Hague Conference,* Translation of the Official Texts prepared under the Supervision of J.B. Scott, *The Conference of 1899,* New York, 1920, pp. 474, 491.

[10] *Actes de la Conférence de Bruxelles (1874),* Bruxelles 1874, pp. 32, 198–199.

[11] In a note of May 4, 1868, which after being fully endorsed by the Russian Emperor, was sent to all Governments with a view to urging them to agree upon a conventional prohibition of explosive projectiles, the Russian War Minister, Milutine, stated: 'Si la guerre est un mal inévitable, on doit

By reaching this conclusion, however, we do no make much headway. When can it be said that a weapon in addition to disabling the enemy causes him excessive sufferings or makes his death needlessly inevitable? How can we concretely establish at which point cruelty ceases to be necessary for the achievement of the 'direct object' of war, and becomes unwarranted?

It is submitted that some light is shed on this point by the debates which in 1899 led to the elaboration of two treaties, the Declaration prohibiting the use of expanding bullets and the Declaration banning asphyxiating gases. Both these agreements were concluded for the purpose of implementing, with specific reference to two types of weapons, the general principle laid down in Article 23(e). It is therefore fully justified to draw on the debates concerning those Declarations with a view to grasping what States gathered at The Hague had in mind, when they proclaimed the principle on 'unnecessary suffering'.

Two points of the Hague debates deserve to be particularly stressed.

First, mention must be made of a statement by the delegate of the Netherlands, in the course of the discussion on the Declaration on expanding bullets. The Netherlands delegate, who proposed the prohibition which was subsequently laid down in the Declaration, and was also the Rapporteur of the Subcommission entrusted with drawing up the Delaration, motivated the prohibition of the arms at issue as follows:

The dum-dum bullet whose point is very soft, whose projectile covering is very hard, and whose interior is formed of a softer substance, makes, by exploding at the slightest resistence, enormous ravages in the body, its entrance being very small, but its exit very large. *It is sufficient to disable an armed man for the rest of the campaign, and such ravages are not necessary.*[12]

It follows from this authoritative statement, which went unopposed, that the Hague legislators took the view that weapons causing 'incurable wounds',[13] namely wounds remaining unhealed even after the cessation of war, are unlawful, while weapons are permitted that disable combatants for the (foreseeable) length of belligerent hostilities.

The second point to be underscored concerns the Declaration prohibiting projectiles spreading asphyxiating or deleterious gases. The delegate of the United

---

cependant chercher à en diminuer les cruautés autant que possible, et c'est pourquoi il n'y a pas lieu d'introduire des armes meurtrières qui ne peuvent qu'aggraver les calamités sans avantage pour le but direct de la guerre' (text in *Nouveau Recueil Général de Traités,* cit., tome XVIII, p. 460). At the outset of the St. Petersburg Conference, the Chairman (the same Milutine) said *inter alia:* 'Il y a là d'abord une question de principe sur laquelle nous sommes tous d'accord, un principe d'humanité qui consiste à limiter autant que possible les calamités de la guerre et à interdire l'emploi de certaines armes, dont l'effet est d'aggraver cruellement les souffrances causées par les blessures, sans utilité réelle pour le but de la guerre' (*ibid.,* p. 451).

[12] *Proceedings,* cit., p. 286. This statement is related in the Report of the First Subcommission to the First Commission, made by the Dutch delegate himself. The same statement, as reproduced in the summary records of the First Subcommission, is less accurate (see *ibid.,* p. 332).

[13] *Ibid.,* p. 332.

States opposed this prohibition by observing that those gases were not more inhumane than submarine torpedo boats (on which there was agreement that they should not be forbidden). He stated that:

> ...From a humane standpoint it is no more cruel to asphyxiate one's enemies by means of deleterious gases than with water, that is to say by drowning them, as happens when a vessel is sunk by the torpedo of a torpedo-boat.[14]

This remark was rejected by the proponent of the ban on gases, the Russian delegate, who pointed out that:

> ...No comparison can be made between the effect produced by torpedoes and that of asphyxiating gases. The latter may as a matter of fact be compared rather to the poisoning of a river, which Mr. Mahan (the U.S. delegate) did not wish to allow. Many persons may be saved even if they have been wounded or placed out of action, in case a vessel is sunk by a torpedo. *Asphyxiating gases, on the contrary, would exterminate the whole crew. This procedure would therefore be contrary to the humane idea which ought to guide us, namely, that of finding means of putting enemies out of action without putting them out of the world.*[15]

A basic idea can be inferred from this most important statement: weapons are to be deemed unlawful when they are such as to produce death whenever and in whatever manner they hit the enemy. Put it another way, a weapon is legitimate if, by striking the adversary, it can either kill or wound him, depending on the circumstances. By contrast, it is not in keeping with international law if it *always* results in *killing all* persons who in some way happen to be struck by it.

The above quotation, it is submitted, throws some light also on the scope of the first of the two facets of the notion of 'unnecessary suffering', namely on the concept of 'uselessly aggravating the suffering of disabled men'. Rendering enemies disabled until even long after the war cannot, as such, be considered unlawful. Otherwise even the bullets of ordinary rifles, which sometimes mutilate, blind, cripple or anyhow injure combatants forever should be deemed unlawful. Rather, what is important is the inevitability or the high degree of probability for a weapon to incapacitate men with lasting effects. Ordinary bullets have among their possible effects the one consisting in disabling an enemy for the rest of his life; but this is neither their typical nor their usual effect. If on the contrary a weapon by its very nature produces the normal effect of putting men out of action for a period largely exceeding the length of a war, that weapon could be regarded as illegal.

Despite these clarifications, the notion of 'unnecessary suffering' remains, however, very vague. To be sure, the test we have been trying to enunciate *is not subjective,* for it does not hinge on the degree of pain experienced by combatants. Nevertheless, it is not a fixed and stable test; rather, it is likely to change depending on the special circumstances of each war. As a rule, one cannot say that a

---

[14] *Ibid.,* p. 283.
[15] *Ibid.,* p. 283.

weapon, as such, 'uselessly aggravates the sufferings of disabled men' or 'renders their death inevitable'. Since account must be taken of various factors for the purpose of making such assessment, labelling a weapon lawful or unlawful will vary according to the varying of those factors. It is plain that one of the most important of such factors is the degree of development of the medical resources of the belligerent against whom a weapon is used. The chances of survival of patients or of their not becoming permanently incapacitated often depend on the quality and accessibility of medical treatment. Wounds that in normal circumstances are likely to result in death or in permanent deformities and disabilities may not produce such effects if medical services of a very high professional standard are available. Hence, the use of a weapon against a belligerent lacking sophisticated medical facilities can prove unlawful, while the use of the very same weapon against another belligerent, who is instead equipped with modern medical services, can be perfectly legal. Of course, the most important factor to be taken into account is whether the injury caused by a weapon, although cruel, is warranted by the need to weaken (the military forces of) the enemy. Yet, this is the area in which one encounters the greatest difficulties, for balancing the degree of suffering against military effectiveness cannot but be extremely subjective.

Still another factor which must be taken into account in order to establish whether a weapon uselessly aggravates the suffering of a disabled adversary, is the length of wars. It was pointed out above that the disabling of enemies should not exceed the (foreseeable) length of belligerent hostilities. Yet, unlike previous wars which were usually very long, modern wars tend to be either very short (think of the Middle East armed conflicts of 1967 and 1973 or of the India-Pakistan war of 1972) or to drag on a long time (think of the 1968–1973 Vietnam war). How then can one assess the legality of a weapon, from the viewpoint under consideration, before the end of the hostilities?

It is apparent from the above that Article 23(e) provides a test which is not generally and uniformly applicable. This test, in particular, has two drawbacks. First, it can be applied only *ex post,* after a weapon has been used and all the aforementioned factors have clearly emerged. It does not possess therefore the value of a safe standard of action for belligerents; more exactly, it lacks 'deterrent' effects, for it is not capable of dissuading combatants from using a weapon for the first time in a certain war.

The second deficiency of the test at issue is that, even *ex post,* it is mainly applicable to exceptional cases, where the effects of a certain weapon are so clear-cut and glaring as to be indisputably deemed contrary to Article 23(e). There is however a wide range of weapons, whose effects are not so well-defined as to be safely classified as falling under that prohibition. Article 23(e) provides no helpful indication for such borderline cases.

4. The International Legislators Gathered at The Hague were Themselves Aware of the General Principle

The States gathered at the Hague were fully aware that a general ban on weapons causing unnecessary suffering is too sweeping and loose and, therefore, cannot but be unworkable. This is apparent from the debates which took place at the Peace Conference in 1899, with respect to the Declaration on expanding bullets. It is appropriate to dwell at some length on this point.

In the course of the discussions on arms which took place in the First Subcommission, it turned out that several delegates agreed on the prohibition of dum-dum bullets because they considered those bullets to be contrary to the principle endorsed at St. Petersburg in 1868.[16] At the request of the Chairman, some concrete proposals were put forward, among which that of the Russian delegate, who suggested a precise wording (which to a great extent corresponded to that subsequently taken up in the Declaration). Faced with this situation, the delegate of Austria proposed that the provision to be elaborated should not enter into details but prohibit in general terms 'the use of bullets which produce uselessly cruel wounds'.[17] This suggestion was supported by the representatives of Great Britain[18] and the United States,[19] although the motives behind their attitudes somewhat differed from the reasons invoked by the Austrian delegate. The idea of leaving aside any reference to 'technical details of construction' and only affirming the principles enunciated in the St. Petersburg Declaration, though it was vigorously advocated by the British delegate,[20] met with strong objections. The delegates of the Netherlands and Russia objected that should the British proposal be accepted 'the prohibition would no longer have any scope'.[21] The Chairman (who was the Belgian delegate) noted that he did not see 'what would remain of the article if they were to accept the modifications' proposed by the British delegate.[22] A somewhat less general wording suggested by the American delegate ('The employment of bullets which inflict uselessly cruel wounds, such as explosive bullets and in general every kind of bullet which exceeds the limit necessary in order to put a man *hors de combat* at once, is forbidden')[23] aroused similar objections. The delegates of the Netherlands, Russia and Belgium observed that that wording was 'far too vague',[24] the representative of Belgium adding that the St. Petersburg Declaration 'is more precise, since it prohibits the use of any projectile

---

[16] *Ibid.*, pp. 332, 347, 491; see also pp. 278, 79–80, 83.
[17] *Ibid.*, p. 343.
[18] *Ibid.*, pp. 343–344 (First Subcommission) and 276–278 (First Commission).
[19] *Ibid.*, p. 278.
[20] *Ibid.*, p. 278.
[21] *Ibid.*, p. 278.
[22] *Ibid.*, pp. 278–279.
[23] *Ibid.*, p. 279.
[24] *Ibid.*, p. 279.

under four hundred grams which is either explosive or loaded with fulminating or inflammable substance'.[25] Their view was adhered to by the majority of delegates, who eventually adopted the Russian draft.[26]

When the issue was subsequently taken up in the plenary and the American delegate again put forward his proposal, the delegate of the Netherlands strongly opposed it, repeating that it was 'too vague' and did not have 'sufficient range'.[27] The general stand of the majority of delegates emerged very clearly from the statements of the representatives of the Netherlands and Russia. The Netherlands delegate stated:

It is a question of a general statement of a neccessary limit. Now what is understood by this necessary limit or by needlessly cruel wounds? We do not know; a criterion would be necessary in order to be able to determine it. We must be able to say: here is a bullet entirely different from that which has been adopted heretofore. *There must be a specified limit and not a general limit. Otherwise, no result will be reached.*[28]

For his part, the Russian delegate, in rejoining to the representative of the United States, who had criticized the Russian draft stating that 'in the effort to catch a single detail of construction' it 'left the door open to everything else which ingenuity may be able to suggest',[29] observed:

At St. Petersburg in 1868, something already in existence was under contemplation. It was desired to prohibit bullets which really existed. *We desire to do the same here: to prohibit the use of a certain category of bullets which have already been manufactured. We do not know what is going to be invented. The inventions of the future will perhaps render a new prohibition necessary.*[30]

The opposite positions of the American and Russian representatives were even more clearly defined in a subsequent exchange between the two delegates which is well worth recalling. The American delegate observed that ultimately the question could be summed up as follows: 'In order to reach an end that we all approve, is it better to adopt a general principle or to vote on a few details that tend only toward a certain point?' The Russian representative replied that

As to bullets, the accepted formula has in view the general principle: prohibition of bullets which expand and flatten. *But it is necessary to define the details that are well known, otherwise it would not be a formula but a phrase.*[31]

I have been expatiating on the Hague debates of 1899—whose results were confirmed in 1907[32]—for they prove beyond any doubt that those very States which

[25] *Ibid.*, p. 279.
[26] *Ibid.*, pp. 279–280.
[27] *Ibid.*, p. 82.
[28] *Ibid.*, p. 82.
[29] *Ibid.*, p. 81; see also pp. 85–86.
[30] *Ibid.*, p. 83; see also p. 84.
[31] *Ibid.*, p. 86.
[32] In 1907 the US Delegation proposed, in the form of an amendement to the 1899 Declaration on expanding bullets, the same text that the US delegate had suggested in 1899 (see *The Proceedings*

proclaimed in Article 23(e) the prohibition of weapons causing unnecessary suffering, when they came to discuss concretely questions of weapons, clearly showed that they considered a general affirmation of the St. Petersburg principle to be almost pointless. This, to my mind, demonstrates that Article 23(e) was not given much normative value by its very drafters.

Why, then, did they include that provision in the Regulations they adopted? It can be argued that they probably did so for two main reasons. First, they took up rather automatically the wording of Article 13 (e) of the Brussels Declaration, without questioning its significance and impact. This is a phenomenon of 'viscosity' of legal notions and phrases, that frequently occurs in legislative drafting. Secondly, the States gathered at The Hague probably believed that anyway the proclamation of a general principle could serve some useful purpose in future; they did not ask themselves what this purpose might be, but possibly thought that it was better to have some general concept than nothing at all.

5. The Practice of States Concerning the Implementation and Interpretation of the General Principle of Article 23(e)

Article 23(e) of the Hague Regulations, as stated above in paragraph 3, sets such a vague and obscure standard that States can hardly act upon it. That rule could ultimately apply only to extreme cases.

The question must now be considered whether the practice of States has given flesh and blood to that skeleton. To put it in less inaccurate words, we must establish whether the subsequent conduct of States can evidence the reaching of an agreement regarding the interpretation of the rule in point.

First and foremost, attention must be drawn to the fact that in very few instances States relied on Article 23(e) when protesting the use of weapons not covered by existing specific prohibition. This provision was explicitly invoked by Germany, in 1918, when it lodged a protest against the use of *shotguns*[33] by the armed forces of the United States. In this case no great elaboration was given on why the weapon was contrary to Article 23(e).[34] In another instance, it was asserted by the

---

of the Hague Peace Conferences, translation of the Official Texts, prepared under the Supervision of J.B. Scott, *The Conference of 1907,* vol. III, New York 1921, p. 251). This proposal, however, was not taken into account in the First Subcommission of the IInd Commission (*ibid.,* pp. 154 and 29), for the Chairman considered that the modification or abrogation of the Declaration on dum-dum bullets did 'not appear in the program'. The American delegate protested in the II Commission (*ibid.,* pp. 15–16), but this was to no avail. The Chairman did not allow any discussion of the proposal, by remarking *inter alia* that 'The text proposed is identical with that which Captain Crozier first offered in 1899 and which was unanimously rejected as insufficient' (*ibid.,* p. 16).

[33] See the German note of September 19, 1918 and the reply of the U.S. Secretary of State in *Papers relating to the Foreign Relations of the United States, 1918, Supplement No. 2, The World War,* Washington, 1933, pp. 785–786.

[34] The German Government, in its protest confined itself to pointing out that 'this protest is based upon Article 23(e)' (*loc. cit.,* p. 785). The U.S. Secretary of State, in his reply, only stated that

French Inquiry Commission on the violations of the laws of war in World War I that Germans had used *saw-edged bayonets* and that those weapons caused horrible wounds, thus being contrary to 'international conventions'.[35] Also a military manual considers this weapon contrary to Article 23(e).[36] *Irregular-shaped bullets* are another weapon which was regarded as causing unnecessary sufferings. The use of these bullets by Austrians in World War I was protested by an Italian Inquiry Commission on the violations of the laws of war[37] and is also condemned in some modern military manuals.[38] A further instance is the protest addressed in 1945 by the Imperial Government of Japan to the United States for its atomic bombing of Hiroshima. In that protest Japan claimed in terms that the American Government by resorting to the *atomic bomb* had violated the principle embodied in Article 23(e), because this bomb was no less atrocious than poisonous gases and other prohibited weapons.[39]

These cases, in addition to being scarce[40] are not very relevant for they give no conclusive evidence as to the legal conviction of States on the legality or illegality of the weapons to which they refer. Both in the case of shotguns and atomic

'the Government of the United States has to say that the provision of the Hague Convention, cited in the protest, does not in its opinion forbid the use of this kind of weapon. Moreover, in view of the history of the shotgun as a weapon of warfare, and in view of the well-known effects of its present use, and in the light of a comparison of it with other weapons approved in warfare, the shotgun now in use by the American Army cannot be the subject of legitimate or reasonable protest' (*ibid.*).

[35] 'Un certain nombre de militaires allemands sont armés de baïonnettes dont le dos est garni d'encoches en dents de scie, depuis la poignée jusqu'aux deux tiers environs de la longueur de la lame... Il est incontestable... qu'elles sont de nature à causer des blessures horribles' (*République française, Documents relatifs à la guerre 1914-'15'-16, Rapports et procès-verbaux d'enquête de la Commission instituée en vue de constater les actes commis par l'ennemi en violation du droit des gens,* III-IV, Paris, 1916, p. 10). The account of the use of those weapons has the heading 'Emploi de projectiles et d'armes interdits par les Conventions internationales' (*ibid.,* p. 9).

[36] See the Netherlands *Rules of the Law of War* quoted above, at note 6, Ch. III, para. 14 (p. 7) and the *Manual for the Soldier* of the same country (quoted in the aforementioned note), Ch. 7, para. 10 (p. 7/3).

[37] *Reale Commissione d'inchiesta sulle violazioni del diritto delle genti e delle norme di guerra e sul trattamento dei prigionieri di guerra, Relazioni preliminari sui risultati dell'inchiesta fino al 31 marzo 1919,* vol. I, Roma, 1919, p. 216. The Report explicitly stated that the use of those weapons was contrary to Article 23(e): *ibid.,* pp. 215–216.

[38] See the United States Field Manual (FM 27–10, Department of the Army Field Manual, *The Law of Land Warfare,* 1956, para. 34 *B,* p. 18), the British Manual (The War Office, *The Law of War on Land,* being *Part III of the Manual of Military Law,* 1958, para. 110, p. 41).

[39] Text in WHITEMAN, *Digest of International Law,* vol. 10, Washington, 1968, p. 502.

[40] Article 23(e) was also invoked in another instance, in connection however with Article 23(a), prohibiting the use of poison or poisoned weapons. On February 6, 1918 the International Committee of the Red Cross transmitted to belligerents an appeal calling upon them not to use poisonous or asphyxiating gases. It was stressed in the appeal that such gases were violative both of Article 23(a) and of Article 23(e) (text in *Papers Relating to the Foreign Relations of the United States,* cit., pp. 780–781). The French, British and American replies did not contain any reference to Article 23(e) (*ibid.,* pp. 782–784). The German reply contained instead such a reference (*ibid.,* pp. 787–788).

In this instance, however, the reference to Article 23(e) was primarily made for the purpose of strengthening the impact of the prohibition following from Article 23(a). In other words, it was pointed out that the weapons in question, in addition to violating Article 23(a), also caused unnecessary suffering.

bombs, the claim that those means of combat are illegal was rejected by the adversary and no precise reason was given as to why these weapons were considered as not being contrary to Article 23(e).[41] As to saw-edged bayonets and irregular-shaped bullets, so far as is known, there was no follow-up to the conclusion of the Commissions of Inquiry that they were unlawful.

Let us now turn to see how States have *interpreted* Article 23(e) in national legislation, in military manuals, or in other manifestations of State practice. A survey of these materials leads one to conclude that, far from arriving at some agreed-upon interpretation of that provision, States have taken very divergent views of what is prescribed by it.

For one thing, most national legislations on war or military manuals confine themselves to repeating the words of Article 23(e) without adding anything.[42]

[41] As to the American reply to the German protest concerning shotguns, see *supra,* note 34. The Japanese protest concerning the atomic bombing of Hiroshima was indirectly given a reply by Truman and Churchill. The former, in his statement of August 9, 1945 (*Keesing's Contemporary Archives,* 1943–1945, p. 7407), justified that bombing on three main grounds (which seem to be somewhat contradictory): first, the bomb struck a military objective ('The first atomic bomb was dropped on Hiroshima, a military base, because we wished in this first attack to avoid, so far as possible, the killing of civilians'); secondly, it was used in reprisal ('Having found the bomb, we have used it against those who attacked us without warning at Pearl Harbour, against those who have starved, beaten, and executed American prisoners, against those who have abandoned all pretence of obeying international laws of warfare'); thirdly, the bomb was justified by the military advantage it offered ('We have used it in order to shorten the agony of the war, in order to save the lives of thousands of young Americans').

As to Churchill, he advanced two main reasons, in the statement he made on August 16, 1945 in the House of Commons: first, the bomb saved 1,000,000 Americans and 250,000 British lives (*Keesing's Contemporary Archives,* 1943–1945, p. 7383); secondly all precautions were taken to save civilians ('In addition to my repeated warnings an endeavour was made to secure the evacuation of the Japanese from the threatened cities', *ibid.*).

See also Truman, *Memoirs—Year of Decision,* vol. I, New York, 1955, pp. 419–420; Churchill, *The Second World War,* vol. VI, London, 1960, pp. 551–554; and Stimson, *The Decision to Use the Atomic Bomb,* in *Harper's Magazine,* 1947, vol. 194, No. 1161, pp. 98, 100–102, 104–107.

It is common knowledge that the US Army and Navy Manuals consider the use of nuclear weapons against military objectives to be lawful. See *The Law of Land Warfare,* cit., para. 35 (p. 18); *Law of Naval Warfare,* para. 613 (in Tucker, *The Law of War and Neutrality at Sea,* Washington, 1955, p. 410). See to the same effect the British Field Manual, *The Law of War on Land,* cit., para. 113 (p. 42). See also the statement by the US delegate in the General Assembly, concerning resolution 2936 (XXVII) of November 29, 1972, in *American Journal of Int. Law,* 1973, p. 330.

[42] See e.g.: Article 11 *a* of the Russian Instructions to the Army Respecting the Usages and Customs of Continental War, issued on July 14, 1904 (Text in Hershey, *The Russo-Japanese War,* p. 274); Article 57, para. 8, of the French Military Manual by Jacomet (*Les lois de la guerre continentale,* Paris, 1913, p. 58); Article 18 of the Military Manual of Switzerland (*Manuel des lois et coutumes de la guerre,* 1963, p. 5); Article 34, para. 2, of the French Decree of October 1, 1966 on military law ('Décret portant règlement de discipline générale dans les armées'); Ch. III, para. 14 of the Dutch *Rules of the Law of War* (*Oorlogsregelen*) cit. (p. 7), and Ch. 7, para. 10 of the *Manual for the Soldier* (*Handboek voor de Soldaat*) cit. (p. 7/3). See also the *Rules of Warfare under International Law* contained in the 'Manual of Military Principles' issued to members of the armed forces of the German Democratic Republic (*Handbuch Militärisches Grundwissen,* NVA-Ausgabe, Berlin 1974, p. 47). After quoting Article 23(e), this Manual adds, however, the following: 'Der Einsatz jeglicher Massenvernichtungswaffen, einschließlich Napalm und solcher Mittel, die die natürlichen Lebensbedingungen für Menschen, Tiere und Pflanzen vernichten oder diese selbst schädigen, ist völkerrechtswidrig. Der Einsatz von Kernwaffen ist, sofern er nicht als unumgängliche

In all likelihood, this widespread attitude is motivated both by the inherent difficulty of pointing to any conclusive interpretation of Article 23(e) and by the desire to avoid being somewhat bound by a certain construction, which in the future could be turned by any adversary against the very State advocating it.

Be that as it may, three principal constructions of Article 23(e) emerge from the practice.

A first interpretation can be found in the Army Field Manual of the United States (1956), according to which the 'practice of States' represents the test for determining whether a weapon is permissible under Article 23(e) of the Hague Regulations. Commenting upon this article, paragraph 34 (b) of the Manual states:

> What weapons cause 'unnecessary injury' can only be determined in light of the practice of States in refraining from the use of a given weapon because it is believed to have that effect. The prohibition certainly does not extend to the use of explosives contained in artillery projectiles, mines, rockets, or hand grenades. Usage has, however, established the illegality of the use of lances with barbed heads, irregular-shaped bullets, and projectiles filled with glass, the use of any substance on bullets that would tend unnecessarily to inflame a wound inflicted by them, and the scoring of the surface or the filing off of the ends of the hard cases of bullets.[43]

Similar but somewhat less elaborate provisions have been laid down in the 1958 British Field Manual,[44] as well as in the 1963 Israeli War Manual.[45] These provisions explicitly or by implication take the practice of States as a standard for evaluating the legality of weapons. Therefore, they do not attach, in the end, any great importance to the prohibition of Article 23(e). According to them that provision merely indicates a reason why weapons can *become unlawful,* provided States *evolve a practice to that effect.*

Erwiderung auf eine imperialistische Kernwaffenaggression erfolgt, ebenfalls völkerrechtswidrig'. (It is not clear whether or not the Manual, in drawing these conclusions, relies on Article 23(e); in other words, whether modern weapons of mass destruction are regarded in the Manual as prohibited by Article 23(e), or by some other principle).

One can also quote some military manuals which, although issued prior to the 1899 Hague Regulations, already made reference to the notion of unnecessary suffering, without however clarifying it. See, for example, paras 6 and 10 of the *Instructions concerning the Application of the Geneva Convention of August 22, 1864 and of the Rules of the Law of War,* issued by the Ministry of War for the Principality of Serbia on December 1, 1877. In para. 6 reference is made to the 'general rule that in time of war the depth of suffering and the extent of the losses inflicted upon the enemy should not be in excess of that which is necessary to defeat his forces and that all persons should abstain from cruel and inhumane acts' (text in *International Review of the Red Cross,* 1974, no. 157, p. 172). See also para. *b* of the Preamble, and Article 718 para. 2, of the Italian Regulations of November 26, 1882 ('Regolamento per servizio delle truppe italiane in guerra'); these provisions clearly took over the notion of 'superfluous injury' from the Brussels Declaration of 1874 (text in FIORE, *Trattato di diritto internazionale pubblico*³, Torino 1891, vol. 3, pp. 643 and 645).

[43] FM 27–10, *Department of the Army Field Manual, The Law of Land Warfare,* Department of the Army, July 1956, p. 18.

[44] *The War Office, The Law of War on Land, being Part III of the Manual of Military Law,* London, 1958, Article 100 (p. 41).

[45] *The Laws of War,* No. 446–17-002, 1963 [in Hebrew], Ch. III, para. 8, No. 2 (p. 11).

A second way of interpreting and applying the 'unnecessary suffering' criterion consists in relying upon the notion of 'proportionality to the military advantage' for assessing whether the effects of a weapon are lawful. In this connection, mention must be made of the Military Manual of the Federal Republic of Germany (1961), which in commenting on Article 23(e), states:

Unnecessary is any suffering which bears no relation to this object [the object of war enunciated in the St. Petersburg Declaration] or exceeds it. Yet in addition suffering is also unnecessary when it is out of proportion to the military advantage which is pursued by the belligerent activity causing such suffering.[46]

Along the same lines, the Austrian Military Manual (1965) states in Article 39 that:

Prohibited are means of combat that cause unnecessary suffering and injury, and whose employment is not absolutely necessary for the suppression of the enemy, or inflicts suffering which is out of proportion to the military advantage to be gained by those means.[47]

These Manuals suggest two concrete tests. One makes reference to the St. Petersburg principles; it is the traditional criterion which was also upheld in the debates of the 1899 Hague Conference. The other test is that of 'proportionality'. The position of the German and Austrian Military Manuals was taken up and elaborated by the Swedish delegate in the 1974 Diplomatic Conference on Humanitarian Law. Unlike the Manuals, however, he did not consider that each of those two tests is self-sufficient. It would seem that he rather took the view that the proportionality test must *supplement* the other criterion.[48]

---

[46] 'Unnötig sind Leiden, die mit diesem Zweck nicht im Zusammenhang stehen oder über ihn hinausgehen. Unnötig sind weiter aber auch Leiden, die ausser Verhältnis zu dem militärischen Vorteil stehen, der mit der Kriegshandlung erstrebt wird, durch die diese Leiden zugefügt werden' (*Kriegsvölkerrecht, Allgemeine Bestimmungen des Kriegsführungsrechts und Landkriegsrecht*, März 1961, p. 46).

[47] 'Kampfmittel, die unnötige Leiden und Schäden verursachen und deren Anwendung nicht unbedingt zur Niederwerfung des Feindes nötig ist oder Leiden hervorruft, die in keinem Verhältnis zum militärischen Vorteil des Kampfmittels stehen, sind verboten (zum Beispiel Dumdumgeschosse)': *Bundesministerium für Landesverteidigung, Truppenführung* (TF), Anhang B, *Grundsätze des Kriegsvölkerrechts*, Wien, Juli 1965, p. 253.

[48] See *Statement* by H. Blix in the General debate of the Ad Hoc Committee on the Question of Prohibition or Restriction of Use of Specific Categories of Convention Weapons, March 13, 1974 (text provided by the Swedish Delegation to the Geneva Diplomatic Conference on Humanitarian Law, 1974) pp. 5–6. A summary can be found in CDDH/IV/SR. 1, pp. 7–8.
According to the Swedish delegate 'the philosophy which underlies the concept "unnecessary suffering" may perhaps be said to be that if two means or methods of weakening the adversary's military forces are roughly equal to the attacker for the purpose of assuring that the adversary is placed *hors de combat,* that which is least injurious must be chosen. Furthermore, "to conciliate the necessities of war with the laws of humanity"—in the words of the St. Petersburg Declaration— would also seem to call for the use of the least injurious of two means available where the additional injury or suffering inflicted by a more injurious means are out of proportion to the advantage which may be gained by it' (pp. 5–6 of the full text).

Sometimes only the criterion of proportionality is used as a decisive test for applying Article 23(e). Thus, in a paper submitted to the 1974 Lucerne Conference of Government Experts on the Use of Certain Conventional Weapons, a British expert stated:

The correct criterion at present is whether the weapon is calculated to cause (propre à causer) injury or suffering greater than that required for its military purpose; and in this regard a weapon which in practice is found inevitably to cause injury or suffering disproportionate to its military effectiveness would be held to contravene the prohibition. In deciding the legality of a specific weapon under this rule, therefore, one must assess first its proven effects in battle; secondly the military task which it is called upon to perform; and thirdly, the proportion between these two factors.[49]

Without wishing to enter into the question of whether the 'proportionality' and the 'military imperativeness' tests have each an autonomous standing or whether they are in fact two facets of the same criterion, I submit that they shed some light on the notion of 'unnecessary suffering'. Needless to say, they leave a very ample margin of discretion to the only subjects who are ultimately called upon to apply them—belligerents.

A third way of determining whether a weapon causes unnecessary suffering has also been suggested. This test, which consists in a comparison of the effects of a certain weapon with those of weapons which are already under a specific ban, has been advanced primarily in some pronouncements relating to the atomic bombing of Hiroshima and Nagasaki (a short reference to it, however, had already been

[49] *Legal Criteria for the Prohibition or Restriction of Use of Categories of Conventional Weapons*, p. 6 (paper submitted to the Lucerne Conference by the British expert Colonel Sir David Hughes-Morgan). It is appropriate to note that it is added in the paper that 'of course, even if a weapon is "acquitted" under the above procedure, this does not mean that its use on certain occasions may not be such as to contravene the basic general rule' (*ibid.*).

It would seem that the Italian Law on war (enacted by Royal Decree on July 8, 1938), considers 'unnecessary suffering' to mean any suffering which is not justified by 'military necessity' (paras 1 and 2 of Article 35 of that law state: 'L'uso della violenza in guerra è lecito sempre che sia contenuto nei limiti, in cui è giustificato dalle necessità militari e non contrario all'onore militare. Non si devono arrecare al nemico sofferenze superflue o danni e distruzioni inutili').

The gross imbalance between the military result (or the military necessity for the use of a weapon) and the injury caused is regarded as the decisive test for applying Article 23(e) by a number of authors. See, for example: Spaight, *War Rights on Land*, London, 1911, pp. 76–77; Hall, *International Law*, 8th edn, Oxford, 1924, pp. 636–637; Hyde, *International Law*, 2nd edn, vol. III, New York, 1945, p. 1814; Baxter, *The Role of Law in Modern War*, in *Proceedings of the American Society of Int. Law*, 1953, pp. 91–92; Balladore Pallieri, *Diritto bellico*, 2nd edn, Padova, 1954, p. 170; Schwarzenberger, *The Legality of Nuclear Weapons*, London, 1958, pp. 43–44; McDougal and Feliciano, *Law and Minimum World Public Order*, New Haven and London, 1961, pp. 616–617; Meyrowitz, *Les juristes devant l'armée nucléaire*, in *Revue générale de droit int. public*, 1963, pp. 844–848; Idem, *Les armes biologiques et le droit international*, Paris, 1968, p. 93; Aldrich, *Remarks on Human Rights and Armed Conflicts*, in *Proceedings of the 67th Annual Meeting of the American Society of Int. Law*, 1973, p. 148.

Cf. also Fleck, *Völkerrechtliche Gesichtspunkte für ein Verbot der Anwendung bestimmter Kriegswaffen*, in *Beiträge zur Weiterentwicklung des Humanitären Völkerrechts für bewaffnete Konflikte*, Hamburg, 1973, pp. 14–15 of the offprint, and Kalshoven, *The Law of Warfare*, Leiden, 1973, pp. 95, 99.

made in 1918 by the United States, in replying to the German protest concerning the use of shotguns).[50] In the previously mentioned protest lodged on August 10, 1945 with the US Government, the Imperial Government of Japan charged the US with violating international law. After quoting Article 23(e) of the Hague Regulations, it stated that:

The bomb in this case [bombardment of Hiroshima], which the United States used this time, far exceeds, in its indiscriminate performance and in its atrocious character, poisonous gases and other weapons which hitherto have been banned because they possess these performances... The United States has used the new bomb in this case which has indiscriminate and cruel character beyond comparison with all weapons and projectiles of the past...[51]

The basic test underlying the protest rested on a comparison of the suffering caused by already prohibited weapons with those brought about by the new weapon. The same test was applied in the judgment delivered on December 7, 1963 by the District Court of Tokyo in the *Shimoda* case. The test, however, was on the one hand rendered more specific by the Court, in that this stated that 'besides poison, poison-gas and bacterium the means of injuring the enemy which causes *at least the same or more injury* is prohibited by international law'.[52] The test was, on the other hand, substantially qualified, for the Court stressed the need to take account of the 'military effectiveness' of a weapon, when considering its effects and comparing them with the inhumane effects of already proscribed weapons. For, 'however great the inhumane result of a weapon may be, the use of the weapon is not prohibited by international law, if it has a great military efficiency'.[53] Applying these two conflicting tests, the Court concluded that the bombing of Hiroshima and Nagasaki was illegal. For it took the lives of many civilians and 'among the survivors there are people whose lives are still imperilled owing to the radial rays, even today 18 years later'. Besides 'it is doubtful whether atomic bombing really had an appropriate military effect at that time and whether it was necessary'.[54]

To sum up this survey, it can be said that States either have refrained from suggesting any concrete test for applying Article 23(e) or have advanced criteria which widely differ. Furthermore, in the few cases where the contention was made that the use of a certain weapon in a specific situation was contrary to that provision, such contention was implicitly rejected by the other States concerned.

International practice having fallen far short of agreement on the interpretation of Article 23(e), no light is shed by the subsequent conduct of States on how the principle on 'unnecessary suffering' should be construed and applied.

[50] See *supra*, note 34.
[51] WHITEMAN, *Digest*, cit., p. 502.
[52] Text in *The Japanese Annual of Int. Law*, 1964, vol. 8, p. 241.
[53] *Ibid.*, p. 241.
[54] *Ibid.*, p. 241.

6. The Negative Stand as to the Normative Value of Article 23(e)

As shown above, State practice does not offer any *positive* contribution to pin-pointing the meaning and the scope of the principle embodied in Article 23(e). Rather, *negative* conclusions can be drawn from it, in particular the conclusion that there exist such wide differences of views among States as to the meaning of that principle that one can reasonably doubt whether it is at all applicable. Indeed, how can it be said of a principle that it is capable of guiding the conduct of States if no common agreement on its meaning underlies it within the international community?

This negative conclusion is borne out and even enhanced by some recent pronouncements of States in the UN General Assembly in 1973 and in the 1974 Diplomatic Conference on Humanitarian Law. Since they shed much light on the very restrictive view States currently take of Article 23(e), it will be appropriate to consider them closely.

Both in the General Assembly and in the Geneva Diplomatic Conference the question at issue was the legal status to be accorded to some so-called neo-conventional weapons, i.e. modern weapons other than the atomic, chemical or biological ones, which are very cruel and produce inhuman effects on combatants and civilians alike (e.g., incendiary weapons such as napalm, cluster bombs, delayed-action weapons, high-velocity bullets etc.). In the course of lengthy debates on this subject, as well as in the Governments' comments on the UN Secretary General's report on napalm, only a few States maintained that since such weapons—or at least some of them—cause unnecessary suffering they are *already prohibited* under international law,[55] and, as a result, any treaties to

---

[55] This was stated in the Sixth Committee of the UN General Assembly by the delegates of Ukraine (A/C.6/SR. 1450, p. 13. The view expressed by the Ukrainian representative in the 1974 Diplomatic Conference seems however to be different: see CDDH/IV/SR. 3, p. 4), and of Cuba (A/C.6/1449, p. 6). The Cuban delegate, however, contradicted himself, for he stated on the one hand that 'that technical escalation (of modern 'imperialist... technology', especially in Vietnam) was in conflict with the old Hague principles', and on the other hand he pointed out that 'napalm and phosphorus were weapons of extreme cruelty *which should be absolutely prohibited* and the same held true of anti-personnel weapons' (emphasis added). In the Geneva Diplomatic Conference, in 1974, the same position was taken by the representative of Switzerland (CDDH/TV/SR. 1, pp. 9–10).

In its comment on the report of the UN Secretary-General on napalm, Australia made the following remark: 'Australia is a party to international agreements to prohibit the employment in war of weapons calculated to cause unnecessary suffering. Australia *reaffirms the principles in those agreements and their application to the use of all classes of weapons, particularly napalm*' (A/9207, p. 41, emphasis added). The same view was expressed by the Australian representative in the First Committee of the General Assembly, in 1973 (A/C.1/PV. 1949, pp. 21–22).

Lastly, it is worth mentioning that in 1973 the representative of New Zealand in the First Committee of the General Assembly stated as follows: 'The early part of this century saw the development of a norm of international law which prohibited the use of weapons calculated to cause unnecessary suffering. However, *that principle has been seriously eroded by developments in technology and recent military practice*, which appears to have placed the pursuit of military advantage ahead of the dictates of humanity. The New Zealand Government finds these developments gravely

be elaborated on the subject would set 'merely executing rules...not aimed at creating new law but at clarifying and illustrating the rules already in force'.[56] The vast majority of States took instead the opposite view. They argued that the use of weapons which might be deemed to cause unnecessary suffering *must be proscribed* or *restricted* and that *new rules* are to be formulated to that end.[57]

disturbing. There now exists an urgent need *to update and strengthen the existing norm of international law by new and specific prohibitions,* including rules relating to incendiary weapons...We consider that the present draft resolution [A/C. 1/L.650/Rev.2; reference is made to it *infra,* note 58] opens the way towards restoring the original efficacy of an accepted principle of international law...' (A/C.1/PV.1949, pp. 68–70; emphasis added). Cf. the statement of the delegate of New Zealand in the Sixth Committee (A/C.6/SR. 1453, pp. 2–3). See however the statements that the delegate of the same State had made in 1972, in the First Committee of the General Assembly (A/C.1/PV.1887, p. 26 and PV.1894, p. 37).

[56] This was stated by the representative of Switzerland (CDDH/IV/SR. 1, p. 9), who furthermore observed that 'It was a question of the codification of existing law rather than the creation of new legal norms, of removing all possible doubts and rendering the practical effects of the general principles intelligible to all...To establish rules governing the use of certain weapons or prohibiting others would be of the greatest value in eliminating possible disputes concerning the interpretation of the general principles' (*ibid.,* p. 10).

[57] This view was taken both in the First and in the Sixth Committee of the General Assembly, as well as in the comments made by States on the Secretary-General's report on napalm. In the First Committee the view was expressed by the delegate of Sweden (A/C.1/PV.1941, pp. 58–67). The Swedish delegate stated *inter alia:* 'In one sense the wish for early action might be thought to be satisfied by a resolution of the General Assembly condemning the use of specific types of weapons and declaring the opinion of the Assembly to be that such weapons fall under the existing general prohibitions of weapons. Such action would hardly be effective, however—we know that—and my delegation would not propose it. If "instant legislation" is not the best method, the same can be said of the opposite method, i.e. allowing the question of prohibitory legislation to disappear in the distance' [by referring it to the CCD; the best method was instead to have specific prohibitions or restrictions agreed on by the Geneva Diplomatic Conference]; see also the very important statement the Swedish delegate had made in the same Committee, in 1972 (A/C.1/PV.1882, pp. 32–33). The same view was shared by the delegates of Kenya (*ibid.,* p. 76), Ecuador (PV.1947, p. 37), Netherlands (PV.1948, pp. 31–32), Brazil (*ibid.,* pp. 49–51), Cyprus (PV.1949, p. 48), Afghanistan (PV.1950, p. 47), Tunisia (PV.1951, p. 61), and the USSR (PV.1968, pp. 57–60: 'The Soviet Union has always supported and continues to support the United Nations efforts to prohibit the use of particularly cruel...weapons', p. 57). It is worth recalling that in 1972, in the same First Committee, the representative of Ireland had taken the same stand: after pointing out that in the view of his Government the principle laid down in Article 23(e) is part of customary international law, he argued however, that napalm and other incendiary weapons likely to cause unnecessary suffering must be proscribed through treaty stipulations (A/C.1/PV.1883, p. 44).

In the Sixth Committee this position was taken by the following States: Yugoslavia (A./C.6/SR. 1448, pp. 13–14: 'New rules must be formulated.. for the prohibition or restriction of the use of specific weapons deemed to cause unnecessary suffering', p. 13), Netherlands (SR. 1449, pp. 8–9), Denmark (*ibid.,* p. 14), Finland (SR. 1450, p. S), Sweden (*ibid.,* p. 6), Mexico (SR. 1451, p. 3: '...The Conference...should prepare new rules which would take account of contemporary methods of warfare...'), the Federal Republic of Germany (SR. 1452, pp. 13–14: 'There was a need, however, for other rules concerning the prohibition or restriction of the use of specific weapons which might cause unnecessary suffering...', p. 14), the USSR (SR. 1452, p. 18: 'It was also necessary to prohibit certain particularly cruel methods of warfare, and the USSR had always supported United Nations efforts to that end. However, the question of deciding which types of weapons should be prohibited on the grounds that they caused unnecessary suffering...should be resolved within the framework of the question of arms limitation and disarmament...'), Kenya (*ibid.,* p. 3: 'It was to be hoped that that Conference would be guided by the realization that modern warfare, sophisticated weapons

They even adopted in the UN General Assembly a resolution to that effect.[58] By taking such a stand, those States clearly intended to signify that in their opinion the new weapons at issue are not as yet prohibited by the principle

and the effects there of were by no means covered by existing law...'), the German Democratic Republic (*ibid.,* p. 8), Madagascar (*ibid.,* p. 13), and Venezuela (SR.1454, p. 4).

In the comments on the Secretary-General's report on napalm, the view was expressed by the following States: Denmark (A/9207, p. 6), Guatemala (*ibid.,* p. 8), India (*ibid.,* p. 9), Iran (*ibid.,* p. 10), Mexico (*ibid.,* p. 11), Netherlands (*ibid.,* p. 13), Norway (*ibid.,* p. 15), Poland (*ibid.,* p. 17) and Sweden (*ibid.,* p. 18). The stand taken by Netherlands is particularly illuminating. This State on the one hand pointed out that the use of incendiaries 'inasmuch as it affects human beings could come within the purview of Article 23(e)...'. It observed, on the other hand, that restrictions on the use of incendiary weapons should be achieved though international agreements, since 'one of the principal aims of international law applicable in armed conflicts is to prohibit or to limit the use of means of warfare which tend to cause unnecessary suffering...' (*ibid.,* p. 13).

In the 1974 Diplomatic Conference the view under consideration was expressed by the following States: Poland (CDDH/IV/SR. 1, pp. 10–11), Canada (*ibid.,* pp. 12–13; the Canadian representative pointed out *inter alia* that 'agreement was lacking on standards by which "unnecessary suffering"...could be measured', p. 12), Togo (*ibid.,* p. 15; the delegate of this country said *inter alia* that 'his delegation could not accept the concept of "unnecessary" suffering. It considered that suffering could not be divided into categories'), Austria (SR. 2, p. 2); New Zealand (*ibid.,* pp. 2–3), the United Kingdom (*ibid.,* pp. 4–5), India (*ibid.,* p. 5), Nigeria (*ibid.,* pp. 5–6), the United States (*ibid.,* p. 6; see also SR. 5, p. 10), Netherlands (*ibid.,* p. 9), France (*ibid.,* p. 9), the USSR (*ibid.,* p. 11), Mongolia (SR. 3, p. 2), Morocco (*ibid.,* p. 3), Sri Lanka (*ibid.,* p. 3), Sudan (*ibid.,* p. 4: 'The Declaration of St. Petersburg had been a great step forward in the promotion of humanitarian law. *The agreement reached between the Powers of that time to work together to prohibit the use of inhumane weapons should be implemented'* [emphasis added]) Japan (*ibid.,* p. 6), Mexico (SR. 4, p. 7: 'This Government considered that the use of certain weapons which caused unnecessary suffering, should be prohibited without further delay, category by category'; see also SR. 5, p. 8), Norway (SR. 5, p. 4), Sweden (SR. 6, pp. 2–3), and Egypt (*ibid.,* p. 5).

[58] Resolution 3076 (XXVIII), adopted on December 6, 1973, by 103 votes in favour, 18 against, and no abstention.

Preambular paras 4, 9 and 10, as well as operative para. 1 are of special relevance. They read as follows:

'... *Convinced* that the widespread use of many weapons and the emergence of new methods of warfare that may cause unnecessary suffering or are indiscriminate call urgently for efforts by Governments to seek through possible legal means the prohibition or restriction of the use of such weapons and of indiscriminate and cruel methods of warfare and, if possible, through measures of disarmament, the elimination of specific, especially cruel or indiscriminate weapons,...

Welcoming as a basis for discussion at that conference [the 1974 Diplomatic Conference] proposals elaborated by the International Committee of the Red Cross and aiming, *inter alia,* at a reaffirmation of the fundamental general principles of international law prohibiting the use of weapons which are likely to cause unnecessary suffering and means and methods of warfare which have indiscriminate effects,

Considering that the efficacy of these general principles could be further enhanced if rules were elaborated and generally accepted prohibiting or restricting the use of napalm and other incendiary weapons, as well as other specific conventional weapons which may cause unnecessary suffering or have indiscriminate effects,...

1. *Invites* the conference on the reaffirmation and development of international humanitarian law applicable in armed conflicts consider—without prejudice to its examination of the draft protocols submitted to it by the International Committee of the Red Cross—the question of the use of napalm and other incendiary weapons, as well as other specific conventional weapons which may be deemed to cause unnecessary suffering or to have indiscriminate effects and to seek agreement on rules prohibiting or restricting the use of such weapons.'

laid down in Article 23(e), although at least some of them may be regarded as inflicting unnecessary suffering. In other words, those States expressed the conviction that the principle under consideration has no legal impact on new weapons causing unnecessary suffering. In short, to all those States Article 23(e) does not amount to a prohibitory rule. At most it indicates a ground upon which States should endeavour to ban individual weapons through specific rules.[59]

It is worth stressing that some of the States in question implicitly hinted at the main reason for their holding that Article 23(e) does not lay down a veritable standard of action. They underscored that the notion of 'unnecessary suffering' is still imprecise and open to varying interpretations; its exact meaning, therefore, still needs to be clarified and agreed upon.[60]

7. Concluding Remarks

To sum up the main conclusions of the present paper, the contention can be made that the principle laid down in Article 23(e) is to a great extent couched in such vague and uncertain terms as to be barren of practical results. Even if it is construed in the light of the debates which took place at the Hague in 1899 and 1907, it does not provide any safe and fixed standard. As was shown above (paragraph 3), the test for determining whether a weapon causes unnecessary suffering is whether in its normal use, such weapon inevitably (i.e. in whatever circumstances) inflicts

---

It would not be correct to infer from the words used in above quoted preambular para. 10 ('the efficacy of these general principles could be further enhanced' etc.) that in the opinion of the General Assembly the general principle laid down in Article 23(e) has *per se* any great efficacy. It is quite apparent from the statements of the sponsors of that resolution, as well as from all the debates concerning it (see especially A/C.1/PV.1941, p. 57 ff.; PV.1947, p. 12 ff.; PV.1968, p. 32 ff.) that States attributed a decisive value to the elaboration of *new* rules prohibiting or restricting the use of incendiary weapons, and that therefore in their view Article 23(e) amounted only to a very general guideline for their legislative action. The aforementioned words must be considered an over-emphasized expression of this position. Res. 3255 (XXIX), adopted by the General Assembly on December 9, 1974, is couched in very similar terms.

[59] It can be interesting to note that even the legal and military governmental experts who met in 1974 in Lucerne to specifically discuss *inter alia* the possible legal criteria for prohibiting the use of new weapons were not able to reach any agreement on the legal significance that should be given to this principle. In the British paper submitted to the Conference, and referred to above (note 49), the view had been expressed that a weapon which in practice would be found inevitably to cause injury or suffering disproportionate to its military effectiveness could be held to contravene the existing prohibition. At the Conference 'some experts supported the correctness of this view, while others questioned the correctness of the word "inevitably" in this statement; in their view, it was not a true statement of the law that only those weapons were forbidden which caused, without exception, disproportionate injury or suffering. The true test, according to these experts, was whether a given weapon would normally, or typically, entail such disproportionate effects. Other experts however considered that concepts like 'normally' or 'typically' were too vague a guide because what was the normal or typical use of a given weapon would vary from campaign to campaign and from one party to a conflict to another' (ICRC, *Report,* cit., p. 9).

[60] Canada (CDDH/IV/SR. 1, p. 12), the United Kingdom (SR. 2, p. 4), India (*ibid.,* p. 5), Netherlands (*ibid.,* p. 9), and the USSR (*ibid.,* p. 11).

on persons who are struck by it either death or disabilities which are permanent (or at any rate exceed the length of belligerent hostilities) and are not strictly justified by military demands. It is plain that in order to concretely apply this test account should be taken of a wide range of factors such as the military effectiveness of a weapon, the medical resources of the belligerent against whom the weapon is used, the development of his relief organizations, the probable length of the armed conflict, etc. Two main consequences follow from this. First, the test could normally be applied only *ex post,* namely after a weapon has been used in a certain conflict between certain specific belligerents. Secondly, the application of the test calls for a wide range of different examinations (military, medical, etc.).

What, then, is the normative value of the principle under consideration? I submit that two answers are possible. One could argue that the aforementioned practice of States and especially the stand recently taken by most States in the United Nations General Assembly and in the 1974 Geneva Diplomatic Conference are conclusive evidence that for States, Article 23(e) has no legal value whatever: it does not amount to a binding standard of conduct; at most, it can represent a moral source of inspiration.

A different conclusion could be reached on the basis of the principle of interpretation expressed in the maxim *ut res magis valeat quam pereat,* which is also referred to as the 'principle of effectiveness' or 'of the maximum effect'. Under this principle, when a rule is obscure, it should be given an interpretation which can, at least to some extent, enable it to have effects, rather than deprive it of any value. Relying on this principle, one could argue that Article 23(e) works as a legal standard at least *in exceptional cases,* namely in cases where there is conclusive evidence that the use of a weapon unquestionably meets the test described in paragraph 3 above, and referred to at the outset of this paragraph. Thus, it could be argued that in the light of the abundant material available on the various effects of the atomic bombing of Hiroshima and Nagasaki as well as on the medical and relief services and defense organization of Japan at that time, the atomic bomb used on that occasion violated the principle on unnecessary suffering. For it produced terrible injuries and diseases such as cataracts, leukemia, retarded development of children *in utero* at the time of exposure to the nuclear radiation, genetic mutations, etc., which appeared some years after exposure to nuclear radiation.[61] In addition, it could be contended that any use of the *same* bomb in conditions

[61] On the effects of the bombing of Hiroshima and Nagasaki see: GLASSTONE (ed.), *The Effects of Nuclear Weapons,* prepared by the U.S. Department of Defense, Washington, 1957, pp. 308–327, 455–502; *United Nations, Report of the Secretary-General on the Effects of the Possible Use of Nuclear Weapons and on the Security and Economic Implications for States of the Acquisition and Further Development of these Weapons,* A/6858, pp. 6–10.

Various authors consider that the use of atomic bombs is contrary to Article 23(e): see, for example, SPAIGHT, *Air Power and War Rights,* 3rd edn, London, 1957, p. 276; SPETZLER, *Luftkrieg und Menschlichkeit,* Göttingen, 1956, p. 373; SCHWARZENBERGER, *The Legality of Nuclear Weapons,* cit., pp. 43–44; SINGH, *Nuclear Weapons and International Law,* London, 1959, pp. 75, 149; MENZEL, *Legalität oder Illegalität der Anwendung von Atomwaffen,* Tübingen, 1960, pp. 47–50; MEYROWITZ, *Les juristes devant l'armée nucléaire,* cit., pp. 844–848; BROWNLIE, *Some Legal Aspects*

similar to those obtaining in Japan in 1945 would be contrary to international law—a contention, to be sure, open to the criticism that these circumstances are unlikely to ever occur again.

Whichever of these two conclusions one might prefer, it seems difficult to hold that such modern weapons as napalm, cluster bombs, high-velocity bullets, etc.—which have already been used in modern wars and have been the subject of accurate scientific reports[62]—are contrary to Article 23(e). For, as pointed out above, quite recently most States took the view that those weapons are not outlawed as yet and could possibly, or should, be banned through conventional stipulations.[63]

In any event, it deserves to be stressed that, even assuming Article 23(e) has some normative value, its very limited prohibitory scope would be further eroded by the present condition of enforcement procedures in the international community. When there exists no authority capable both of stating with binding effect that the use of a weapon in a certain instance is contrary to Article 23(e), and of enforcing such statement, scant practical value can be attributed to any contention that a specific means of combat inflicts unnecessary suffering. This is confirmed by what happened precisely with respect to the atomic bombing of Hiroshima and Nagasaki. As recalled above (paragraph 5), the United States and Great Britain rejected the Japanese claim that the bombing was unlawful; subsequently those States went so far as to embody in their military manuals a provision to the effect that atomic and nuclear bombs are not forbidden;[64] in the end the Japanese Government itself retracted what it had asserted in 1945 and took the same position as her former enemy countries.[65] In the light of all this, the contention (which could be regarded as correct) that the atomic bombing of Hiroshima and Nagasaki was unlawful cannot but carry very little weight.

These remarks are borne out by State practice: as mentioned above (paragraph 5) Article 23(e) has been invoked very rarely; in addition, the few instances where it was relied upon did not lead to any convergence of views as to the legality or illegality of the weapons at issue. This prompts us to share the view expressed by most States in 1973 and 1974 (see *supra* paragraph 6), that the general principle of weapons causing unnecessary suffering cannot provide any safe standard for assessing whether any given modern weapon is illegal, and therefore any such weapon can be outlawed only through *new, conventional rules*. Those States were aware of how pointless Article 23(e) is. They rightly preferred another approach,

---

of the Use of Nuclear Weapons, in *Int. and Comp. Law Quarterly,* 1965, pp. 441, note 14 and 450; BINDSCHEDLER-ROBERT, *A Reconsideration of the Law of Armed Conflicts,* New York, 1971, p. 19.

[62] See the Report of the Secretary General of the United Nations on *Napalm and Other Incendiary Weapons and all Aspects of their Possible Use,* A/8803/Rev.1; *Weapons that may Cause Unnecessary Suffering,* etc., cit.; SIPRI, *Working Papers* etc., cit.

[63] See *supra,* para. 6 and notes 57–60.

[64] See *supra,* note 41.

[65] This stand was taken by the Japanese Government both in 1962, in the trial on the *Shimoda* case (*The Japanese Annual of Int. Law,* 1964, pp. 225–226), and in 1964, in the Japanese House of Representatives (*The Japanese Annual of Int. Law,* 1966, p. 91).

the very approach that in 1868 and 1899 had led up to the banning of explosive and expanding bullets as well as of asphyxiating and deleterious gases.

What, then, is left of Article 23(e)? It is the author's view that this rule serves as a very significant source of inspiration inasmuch as it sets forth the general humanitarian ground on which States should endeavour either to refrain from developing new weapons or at least to ban them. This is most clearly confirmed by the stand taken in 1973 and 1974 by a number of States, which agreed that one of the reasons for forbidding through conventional rules new weapons was their causing unnecessary suffering.[66] From this point of view, then, Article 23(e) constitutes but a reiteration of what was already spelled out in the St. Petersburg Declaration (which, even in this respect, still remains the best illustration of the right approach to the question of weapons). The last paragraph of the Declaration embodied an undertaking of the contracting parties to endeavour to agree, in the future, upon restrictions or prohibitions of new weapons, on the same grounds which had prompted the banning of explosive projectiles weighing under 400 grammes.[67]

It is well known that efforts are currently being made by several States with a view to proscribing *inter alia* incendiary weapons as well as so-called neo-conventional weapons. For this purpose some States favour the general-principle approach— which, in this case, is tantamount to a reiteration of Article 23(e)—while other States strongly argue for the specific-ban approach. It may be asked whether either approach is the only sound one and should therefore be selected to the exclusion of the other. If not, a further question arises, namely whether a sort of compromise solution can be reached in order to take account of the number of conflicting demands which come into play in this matter.[68]

As to the specific-ban approach, no one can deny that it is a realistic and fruitful one. It has three major advantages. First, as a result of drawing up precise rules which prohibit specific weapons by pointing to their objective features, a high degree of *certainty* is provided about the kind of weapon which is outlawed. Secondly, certain instruments of destruction are proscribed *in any circumstance,* regardless of the quality and quantity of the medical or relief resources of the belligerents or of the degree of their technological development. Thirdly, thanks

---

[66] See *supra,* para. 6, notes 57–60.

This stand was most clearly spelled out in the comments made by the Netherlands on the UN Secretary-General's report on incendiary weapons. As already mentioned above, at note 57, that State, after pointing out that incendiary weapons, inasmuch as they effect human beings 'could come within the purview of Article 23(e)', stressed the need to work out an international agreement for banning, or restricting, the use of such weapons; it then recalled that 'one of the principal aims of international law applicable in armed conflicts is to prohibit or to limit the use of means of warfare which tend to cause unnecessary suffering...' (A/9207, p. 13).

[67] The Declaration stated: 'The Contracting or Acceding Parties reserve to themselves to come hereafter to an understanding whenever a precise proposition shall be drawn up in view of future improvements which science may effect in the armament of troops, in order to maintain the principles which they have established, and to conciliate the necessities of war with the laws of humanity.'

[68] On the various practical difficulties which one faces when an attempt is made to implement by legislation the 'unnecessary suffering' criterion, see in general BAXTER, *Criteria for the Prohibition of Weapons in International Law,* cit., pp. 46–48.

to its specific and precise formulation which makes reference to objective connotations of the forbidden weapons, the prohibition is capable of providing a safe
normative guidance which is effective *even though any enforcement authority is
lacking:* this is clearly evidenced by the fact that the existing prohibitions of specific weapons have been normally respected even though they were at times violated by one of the belligerents.[69]

The drawbacks of this approach, however, are no less apparent than its merits. As already pointed out, specific bans can be easily by-passed by elaborating
new and more sophisticated weapons which, while they are no less cruel than the
proscribed ones, do not fall under the prohibition owing to their new features. It
was rightly noted that 'since we cannot always predict context and technological
change, the effort to ban specific weapons is an effort geared to the past'.[70] What
can turn out to be more important is that the States more likely or capable of
dodging the ban are the more industrialized ones, for they possess the technological resources which are needed to manufacture more sophisticated weaponry.
As a result, the gap between technologically developed States and less advanced
countries would be enhanced also in this field.[71]

It seems therefore that in order to obviate these shortcomings at least to some
extent, the drawing up of lists of specific weapons whose use is forbidden should
go hand in hand with the elaboration of a general standard 'geared to the future',
that is to say a principle capable of covering at least the most blatant cases of
inhuman weapons that States are likely to devise. Needless to say, for this purpose the mere reiteration of Article 23(e) would serve no use for, as I have tried to
demonstrate, that provision as it now stands has very little value.

What is needed is a principle which, being couched in not too vague terms,
could provide some standard of conduct, however general it may be. The major
role of such principle should be to fill the gaps of existing specific prohibitions,
by at least covering extreme cases of new weapons which while they are patently
cruel do not fall under specific bans.

The task of drawing up such a principle is no doubt very arduous; it calls for the
combined skill of draftsmen specializing in different fields (legal, military, medical, etc.). Suggestions stemming from a single viewpoint are therefore bound to
be unsatisfactory. Subject to this *caveat,* the following tentative suggestions can be
put forward with a view to contributing to the elaboration of the general principle.

---

[69] On the violations during World War I of international prohibitions of specific weapons,
and the protest that they evoked, see GARNER, *International Law and the World War,* London,
1920, pp. 262–292; FAUCHILLE, *Traité de Droit international public,* II, Paris, 1921, pp. 121–124;
MÉRIGNHAC, and LEMONON, *Le droit des gens et la guerre de 1914–1918,* Paris, 1921, pp. 143–164.

[70] See PAUST, *Remarks on Human Rights and Armed Conflicts,* in *Proceedings of the 67th Annual
Meeting of the American Society of Int. Law,* 1973, p. 163.

[71] In a Working Paper submitted by six States (Egypt, Mexico, Norway, Sweden, Switzerland,
Yugoslavia) to the 1974 Geneva Diplomatic Conference on Humanitarian Law, it is suggested,
in addition to elaborating prohibition of specific weapons, *to provide for periodic reviews* of these
prohibitions (CDDH/DT/2, p. 5). The objection can be easily made, that *pacta de contrahendo* are
very unlikely to work.

First of all, it could prove helpful to spell out what, to my mind, is the true meaning of Article 23(e), a meaning that—as noted above (paragraph 3)—is at present somewhat hidden behind the laconical wording of the provision and can be brought out only by means of an interpretative process. In addition to such spelling out, some improvement could also be introduced. In particular it could prove worth doing away with any reference to the foreseeable length of belligerent hostilities (it may be recalled that this reference served the purpose of proscribing weapons which inflict sufferings lasting even beyond the close of war). Since a major drawback of this element is that it causes the principle on unnecessary suffering to work primarily *ex post,* it may be helpful to use instead the concept of 'permanent' disabilities. Thus, it could be stated in the rule that 'it is prohibited to use weapons, methods or materials causing unnecessary injury, i.e. weapons etc. which by their nature, or in their normal use, either inevitably cause death or permanent disablement or incapacitation'. This wording, which of course should be viewed in the light of what was stated *supra* (at paragraph 3), would have at least the merit of ruling out one of the abovementioned constructions of Article 23(e), namely that relying upon the notion of 'military advantage' (to the effect that suffering is 'necessary' whenever it is not out of proportion to the military gain obtained by the use of a weapon). Given the highly subjective character of the test advocated by this interpretation and its consequent effect of eventually disrupting the whole scope of Article 23(e), its exclusion could be instrumental in making less pointless the provision at issue. A further advantage of that wording is that it would dispense with any reference to the length of war, thereby making the working of the principle on unnecessary suffering somewhat less uncertain.

This being said, it is necessary to add that admittedly the suggested formulation is far from precise. The objection could be raised that it is difficult to prove that a weapon by its very nature or in its normal use is such as to inevitably inflict on belligerents, in whatever the way they are struck by it, permanent disabilities or death. In a number of instances this test indisputably cannot work satisfactorily. The fact remains, however, that it can prove useful at least with respect to extreme cases. Thus, for instance, laser beams which are now in the process of being perfected as highly effective weapons, if used against personnel 'are capable of damaging the human eye at ranges of up to some thousands of meters'.[72] If, as it seems likely, the blinding effects of such beams will affect any person who is exposed to the laser radiation, then one could safely conclude that this weapon comes within the purview of the prohibition under consideration. Furthermore, the prohibition would at least cover atomic weapons producing effects as cruel and inhumane as those of the bombs dropped at Hiroshima and Nagasaki.

In order both to remedy to some extent the indisputable deficiencies of the wording so far suggested and to expand as much as possible the prohibitory ambit of the principle, a further element should be included in it. In addition to the prohibition

---

[72] See ICRC, *Weapons that may Cause Unnecessary Suffering,* cit., p. 67.

which has just been referred to, the principle should provide that also those weapons are deemed to cause unnecessary suffering and are therefore forbidden which bring about sufferings that are equal to or greater than the pains caused by weapons which were specifically banned because they were thought to be contrary to the 'unnecessary suffering' standard. In other words, the principle should also incorporate the 'comparison' test. It is worth recalling that such test was relied upon in 1918 by the United States, with respect to shotguns,[73] in 1945 by Japan, with regard to the atomic bombing of Hiroshima,[74] and in 1963 by the Tokyo District Court in the *Shimoda* case.[75] This test can prove very useful, because it permits in substance to extend to new weapons an existing prohibition, which as such could not apply to weapons other than those specifically envisaged in it, owing to the general principle of law whereby the analogical application of prohibitory rules is inadmissible. Thus, for instance, the prohibition laid down in the 1899 Declaration on dumdum bullets could be extended to the hypervelocity bullets fired by the M-16 rifle: since it has been demonstrated that the disrupting effects of such bullets are very much akin to, and even more cruel than, those of dum-dum bullets,[76] a strong case could be made for outlawing them. The rewording of Article 23(e) referred to above would be the only means of reaching this result: indeed, it would be neither correct nor appropriate to apply by analogy the 1899 Declaration on expanding bullets.

A major advantage of the test is that it permits doing away with the possibility that an existing specific prohibition be dodged by States having recourse to new weapons which differ from the banned ones only for technical details although they produce the same, or even more cruel, effects. The test could therefore ensure that the *ratio legis* behind the prohibition of specific weapons keeps operating with regard to new weapons as well. It is worth stressing that the test would of course also work with respect to *future specific bans;* accordingly, it would automatically prohibit any new weapons causing the same or even graver effects than those of the weapons which *will fall* under such future specific restraints. The normative value of the principle embodying the test would therefore have a great 'force of expansion', amounting to a steadily working safeguard against possible circumventions of new bans through the development of more modern devices.

In conclusion, whatever the value of the suggested rewording of Article 23(e), it is to be hoped that States will not confine themselves to enacting specific prohibitions of individual weapons, but will also restate Article 23(e), provided of course that by so doing they will elaborate its meaning and expand its ambit.

---

[73] See *supra,* notes 33–34.
[74] See *supra,* note 39.
[75] See *supra,* notes 52–54.
[76] Cp. SIPRI, *Working Papers on International Law,* quoted *supra,* note 2, Section III, p. 77 ff. *Weapons that may Cause Unnecessary Suffering,* cit., p. 30 ff.; Swedish Working Group, Conventional Weapons, quoted *supra,* note 2, pp. 117–119.

10. Means of Warfare: The Traditional and the New Law*

1. The Traditional Law

A. Two Approaches. The General Principle Approach

So far States have adopted two different approaches to the banning of weapons. They have either laid down general principles concerning broad and unspecified categories of weapons, or they have agreed upon restraints on the use of specific weapons.[1]

The former approach is the less satisfactory one. It has led to the formulation of three main principles prohibiting weapons.

Article 22 of the Hague Regulations, which has passed into customary international law, provides that 'Belligerents have not got an unlimited right as to the choice of means of injuring the enemy'. At first sight this rule can appear to be pointless, for it does not give any indication as to the weapons which cannot be 'chosen'. It cannot be presumed, however, that international legislators intended to lay down in an international treaty a provision devoid of any significance. The interpretative principle of effectiveness ('ut res magis valeat quam pereat'), must induce us to try to give some meaning to that article. According to a learned author Article 22 'imposes on the belligerents the general obligation to refrain

---

* Originally published in A. Cassese (ed.), *The New Humanitarian Law of Armed Conflict* (Napoli: Editoriale Scientifica, 1979) 161.

[1] On the prohibition of weapons in international law, see above all: ZORN, *Kriegsmittel und Kriegsführung im Landkriege nach den Bestimmungen der Haager Conferenz 1899,* 1902, 4–34; MCDOUGAL and FELICIANO, *Law and Minimum World Order* 1961, 614ff.; MALLISON, 'The Laws of War and the Juridical Control of Weapons of Mass Destruction in General and Limited Wars', *George Washington Law Review* 1967–68, 308ff.; BINDSCHEDLER-ROBERT, D., 'A Reconsideration of the Law of Armed Conflicts', in *The Law of Armed Conflicts* (Carnegie Endowment for International Peace) 1971, 28–37; FARER, 'The Laws of War 25 Years After Nuremberg', 583 *International Conciliation* 1971, 18ff.; BAXTER, R.R., 'Criteria of the Prohibition of Weapons in International Law', in *Festschrift fur U. Scheuner* 1973, 41–52; HARRIS, 'Modern Weapons and the Law of Land Warfare', 12 *Revue de Droit penal militaire et de Droit de la guerre* 1973, 9ff.; FLECK, 'Völkerrechtliche Gerichtspunkte für ein Verbot der Anwendung bestimmter Kriegswaffen', in FLECK (ed.), *Beiträge zur Weiterentwicklung des Humanitären Völkerrechts für Bewaffnete Konflikte* 1973, 43ff.; SIPRI, *The Problem of Chemical and Biological Warfare,* vol. III, *CBW and The Law of War* (1973); MALINVERNI, 'Armes conventionnelles modernes et droit international' 30. *Annuaire suisse de Droit international* 1974, 23ff.; BLIX, 'Current Efforts to Prohibit the Use of Certain Conventional Weapons', 4 *Instant Research on Peace and Violence* 1974, 21ff.; TROOBOFF (ed.), *Law and Responsibility in Warfare, The Vietnam Experience,* 1975; RÖLING and SUKOVIE, *The Law of War and Dubious Weapons,* Sipri (1976).

from cruel or treacherous behaviour'.[2] Neither in the preparatory works[3] nor in the subsequent practice of States is there any evidence corroborating this view. A more correct view seems to be that Article 22 must be construed to the effect that it rules out any *argumentum a contrario;* it excludes the inference that weapons which are not prohibited by the Hague Regulations are *ipso facto* allowed. Such weapons are banned or permitted according to whether or not they are prohibited by *other* rules of international law. This interpretation is also supported by some Military Manuals.[4]

Another general principle is the one laid down in Article 23(e) of the Hague Regulations, whereby 'it is particularly forbidden . . . to employ arms, projectiles or material apt to cause unnecessary suffering'. This provision aims at turning into an autonomous rule the rationale behind the specific prohibition of some means of combat (explosive projectiles weighing less than 400 grammes, dum-dum bullets and asphyxiating and deleterious gases). While those specific bans hinged, as it were, on the indication of the objective properties weapons must possess for being prohibited, mention is no longer made in Article 23(e) of these objective properties. The focus is instead on a test (whether or not the injury caused is 'necessary'), for the use of which the Article itself provides no indication whatsoever. Taken on its face value, the provision is couched in such vague and uncertain terms as to be barren of practical effects. Furthermore, as I have tried to demonstrate elsewhere,[5] neither the preparatory works nor the subsequent practice of States shed any light on the purport of the rule. Also, the way States have attempted to implement Article 23(e), either in military manuals or in the few cases where the rule was invoked, shows that no common consent has ever evolved among States as to the actual normative value of the principle. Each State has interpreted

---

[2] BINDSCHEDLER-ROBERT, D., 'A Reconsideration of the Law of Armed Conflicts', cit. 28.

[3] Art. 22 was substantially taken over, without any discussion or comment, from Article 12 of the Brussels Declaration of 1874: see *The Proceedings of the Hague Conferences,* prepared under the Supervision of J.B. Scott, *The Conference of 1899,* 491, 424, 58 (1920). In Brussels the participating States had substantially accepted the wording proposed in the Russian draft (*Actes de la Conférence de Bruxelles, 1874,* 4 (1874) which stated in Article 11 that 'Les lois de la guerre ne reconnaissent pas aux parties belligérantes un pouvoir illimité quant aux choix des moyens de se nuire réciproquement' and went on to say in Article 12 that 'D'après ce principe, sont interdits: A) l'emploi d'armes empoisonnées', etc. In the discussion on draft Article 11 the Italian delegate pointed out that it was useful to insert at the beginning of Article 12 the word 'notamment' (especially), otherwise one could have thought that the list in Article 12 was exhaustive and no other means of combat was prohibited by Article 11 ('L'article 11 combiné avec l'article 12, semble indiquer que les seules limites imposées aux pourvoirs des belligérants sont celles signalées dans le second de ces articles. Il croit qu'il serait préférable de poser comme principe général qu'il y a des moyens que la civilisation réprouve, puis d'indiquer quels sont *notamment* les moyens interdits aujourd'hui', *ibid.,* 198). The Italian suggestion was supported by the Belgian delegate (who stated that 'on pourrait croire, sans cela [scil. l'insertion du mot *notamment*] que tout ce qui n'est pas compris dans l'énumération est licite' *ibid.*). Consequently, the word 'notamment' was added in draft Article 12 (*ibid.* 199).

[4] See e.g. the *British Manual* (*The Law of War on Land* (1958), 40 para. 107); the *U.S. Manual* (*The Law of Wand Warfare* 17, para. 33 *b* (1956)).

[5] See my paper 'Weapons Causing Unnecessary Suffering: Are They Prohibited?', *Rivista di Diritto Internationale,* 1975, p. 16ff. Also published in this volume.

the principle in its own way and international disagreement over whether a given weapon fell under the prohibition of the principle has never resulted in the reaching of a common view. It is therefore my opinion that Article 23(e) as it stands now plays in practice a normative role only in extreme cases (such as cases where the cruel character of a weapon is so manifest that nobody would deny it, or where evidence can be produced of gross, repeated and large-scale violations of the principle). It stands to reason that Article 23(e) can also play a role as a moral and political standard by which world public opinion assesses how belligerent States behave or misbehave. This meta-legal value of the principle under consideration should not be underestimated; it could turn out to be more important than the merely legal value, for the impact that public opinion can have, through mass-media, on governments. Furthermore, Article 23(e) can serve as a very significant source of inspiration inasmuch as it sets forth one of the general humanitarian grounds on which States should endeavour either to refrain from developing new weapons or to ban their use. This is most clearly borne out by the stand taken in 1973–1975, both in the U.N. General Assembly and at the Geneva Diplomatic Conference on Humanitarian Law of Armed Conflicts, by a number of States which agreed that one of the reasons for forbidding through conventional rules new weapons was their causing unnecessary suffering.[6] Even from this point of view, then, Article 23(e) constitutes but a reiteration of what was already spelled out in the 1868 St. Petersburg Declaration (which, even in this respect, still remains the best illustration of a proper and realistic approach to the question of weapons).[7]

A third general prohibition on weapons follows from the general principle whereby 'distinction must be made at all times between persons taking part in the hostilities and members of the civilian population to the effect that the latter be spared as much as possible' from the horrors of war.[8]

The argument can be made that a belligerent who knowingly makes use of a weapon which by its very nature cannot but cause injuries both to combatants and civilians, intended to hit civilians or at any rate consciously brought them under his attack. This belligerent would thus be violating the rule forbidding deliberate attack on civilians, a rule that significantly specifies the aforementioned general principle. As I have tried to demonstrate elsewhere, this argument can hold true only for extreme cases.[9]

---

[6] Cp. my paper quoted at n. 5, 30ff.

[7] See on this Declaration *infra*. Sect. I, C.

[8] The words quoted above were used by the U.N. General Assembly in its resolution 2444 (XXIII), adopted unanimously on December 18, 1968. In 1972 the General Counsel of the U.S. Department of defense stated that the U.S. regards this principle 'as declaratory of existing customary international law' (67 'American Journal of International Law', 1973, 122).

See also the G.A. resolution 2675 (XXV), adopted on December 9, 1970 ('Basic Principles for the Protection of Civilian Population in Armed Conflicts').

[9] See in this volume, 'The Prohibition of Indiscriminate Means of Warfare', Sect. II.

Far more relevant and frequent is the case of weapons that are not so 'blind' and, while they also hit civilians, are primarily aimed at military objectives. The use of these means of warfare necessarily falls under the rule whereby if belligerents resort to methods or means of warfare which result in incidental civilian losses, such losses must not be out of proportion to the military advantage gained.[10]

B. Merits and Inadequacies of General Principles

The principal advantage of general principles lies in their covering vast categories of weapons. They do not affect only those agencies of destruction existing at the time when they were laid down, but can work also with respect to future means of combat. Consequently, they have a continuing force of espansion and a reach that can broaden with the passage of time. Two elements, however, go hand in hand to erode the value of general principles. First, they are couched in very vague terms; accordingly, they do not amount to safe standards of conduct but are susceptible to divergent interpretations. Their implementation calls for the existence of international bodies capable of verifying impartially whether a given weapon falls within their prohibitory scope, and of enforcing them. It is common knowledge that at present such bodies do not exist in international society. This is precisely the second element eroding the normative force of the principles under consideration. Their application is left to the belligerents concerned. The resulting picture is distressing. When a belligerent considers that the adversary is using weapons violative of one of the aforementioned principles, he can stop the enemy from such use either by resorting to reprisals or by announcing that he will prosecute as war criminals all those involved in the employment of the weapon. Needless to say, whether this kind of reaction can produce any real effect actually depends on how strong the belligerent resorting to it is. Ultimately, therefore, the implementation of the general principles on weapons turns on the military strength of belligerents: strong States can dodge the bans without fear. The only 'sanction' against them is to resort to world public opinion.

C. Specific Bans. Their Rationale

So far specific weapons have been prohibited, either through the evolving of customary international rules or by international agreements, for one or more of the following grounds: *a*) they have been considered cruel or such as to cause unnecessary suffering; *b*) they have been deemed treacherous; *c*) they have been regarded as indiscriminate, in that they affect combatants and civilians alike. These three humanitarian grounds on which weapons have been prohibited have never been accurately defined. It is however possible to find some general

---

[10] *Ibid.* [Some parts of the original text have been omitted.]

descriptions of them. Thus, the *'unnecessary suffering'* criterion was set out in the 1868 St. Petersburg Declaration, where it is stated that for the purpose of achieving the legitimate object of war it is sufficient to disable the greatest possible number of enemies; consequently 'this object would be exceeded by the employment of arms which uselessly aggravate the sufferings of disabled men or render their death inevitable'.[11] A similar general formulation can be found in the 1877 Serbian Instructions, where mention is made of 'the general rule that in time of war the depth of suffering and the extent of the losses inflicted upon the enemy should not be in excess of that which is necessary to defeat his forces and that all persons should abstain from cruel and inhumane acts'.[12]

The criterion of *treachery* has never been defined in terms. Military manuals, however, give numerous illustrations[13] from which one can infer that combatants behave perfidiously or treacherously whenever they abuse the good faith of the enemy. More exactly, acts of treachery or perfidy are those which invite 'the confidence of the adversary with intent to betray that confidence'.[14]

Finally, as to the criterion of *indiscriminateness,* it is at first sight self-evident, and seems to need no explanation. On closer consideration, though, it also proves to be uncertain, for it is not clear whether a weapon is considered indiscriminate for the mere fact of not being selective (i.e. capable of hitting combatants only) or because it can entail civilian losses which are out of proportion to the military advantage gained through the use of the weapon.

One must not believe, however, that *any* means of combat exhibiting one or more of these features has been banned. In fact, only those weapons have been proscribed which, in addition to having one or more of those characteristics, have not been regarded as *decisive* from a military point of view. In deciding whether

---

[11] Text in SCHINDLER and TOMAN, *The Laws of Armed Conflicts* 96 (1973).

[12] Para. 6. Text in 14 *International Review of the Red Cross* (n. 157) 173 (1974).

[13] See e.g. the British Manual (*The Law of War on Land*): para. 311 n. 1 ('For example, by calling out "Do not fire, we are friends" and then firing: or shamming disablement or death and then using arms . . . '); para. 314 ('In general, it is contrary to modern practice to attempt to obtain advantage of the enemy by deliberate lying, for instance, by declaring than an armistice has been agreed upon when in fact that is not the case . . .'); para. 316 ('To demand a suspension of arms and then to break it by surprise, or to violate a safe conduct or any other agreement, in order to obtain an advantage, is an act of perfidy and as such forbidden'); see also paras 317 and 318. See furthermore the examples given in the *Swiss Manuel des lois et coutumes de la guerre* (under para. 36) and in paras 50 and 493 of the *U.S. Manual* (*The Law of Land Warfare*). Interesting examples are also given in older manuals or military instructions: see e.g. para. 13 of the 1877 *Serbian Instructions* and para. 57, subparas 9 and 10 of the French *Lois de la guerre continentale* (1913).

[14] See Art. 35 para. 1 of the ICRC Draft Additional Protocol to the four Geneva Conventions. In the final version of Protocol I, Art. 37 deals with 'perfidy' and contains, in para. 1, a definition of it.

It is stated in para. 307 of the British Manual (*The Law of War on Land*) that 'Belligerent forces must be constantly on their guard against, and prepared for, legitimate ruses, but they should be able to rely on their adversary's observance of promises and of the laws of war'. Para. 308 then lays down that 'Good faith, as expressed in the observance of promises, is essential in war, for without it hostilities could not be terminated with any degree of safety short of the total destruction of one of the contending parties'.

to prohibit a given weapon account has always been taken of their military effect-iveness. And this factor has indeed always overriden humanitarian grounds. Whenever it has turned out that a means of destruction was really effective, States have refrained from outlawing it. The interplay of humanitarian and military demands was tellingly spelled out in 1899 by the delegate of the United States to the Hague Peace Conference. Speaking in the Subcommission of the Conference concerned with means of warfare, he stated:

The general spirit of the proposals that have received the favourable support of the Subcommission is a spirit of tolerance with regard to methods tending to increase the efficacy of means of making war and a spirit of restriction with regard to methods which, without being necessary from the standpoint of efficiency, have seemed needlessly cruel. It has been decided not to impose any limit on the improvements of artillery, powders, explosive materials, muskets, while prohibiting the use of explosive or expanding bullets, discharging explosive material from balloons or by similar methods. If we examine these decisions, it seems that, when we have not imposed the restriction, it is the *efficacy* that we have wished to safeguard, *even at the risk of increasing suffering, were that indispensable*.[15]

The same idea had already been expressed in 1868, at St. Petersburg, when several States met in order to ban explosive projectiles.[16] The St. Petersburg Declaration is also the best illustration of how humanitarian demands are balanced against mili-tary exigencies. Explosive projectiles were banned at the request of the Russian Emperor, who thought that such weapons cause inhumane sufferings when they hit men, whereas they are militarily useful to destroy ammunition cars ('caissons d'artillerie', 'voitures à cartouches et munitions d'artillerie').[17] Although some States advocated a general and complete ban,[18] the Russian proposal was eventually adopted and it was therefore decided to outlaw explosive projectiles only insofar as they are fired by rifles and machine-guns ('fusils ordinaires, mitrailleuses, mitraille à canon'),[19] and are thus aimed at hitting combatants individually.[20] The same pro-jectiles were instead allowed if fired by artillery. The weight of 400 grams was cho-sen as 'a minimum for artillery projectiles and as a maximum for the projectiles to be prohibited'.[21] Plainly, the fact that an explosive artillery projectile by hitting a

---

[15] *Proceedings on the Hague Peace Conference*, cit. 354 (emphasis added).

[16] See the statements to this effect made by various delegates at St Petersburg, 'Protocoles des Conférences tenues à St-Pétersbourg', in *Nouveau recueil général de traités*, continuation du *Grand recueil* de G. Fr. de Martens par SAMWER, CH., et HOPF, J., 452ff. (1873).

[17] See the Russian 'Mémoire sur la suppression de l'emploi des balles explosives en temps de guerre' (*ibid.*, 458ff.).

[18] See e.g. the statements made by the representatives of Austria (*ibid.*, 455) and France (*ibid.*). Cp. also the statement of the delegate of Prussia (*ibid.*, 454), who, however, subsequently took a different stand (*ibid.*, 456ff.).

[19] See the remarks made by the Russian representative (*ibid.*, 455 and cp. 462).

[20] 'Il s'agit de proscrire seulement ceux (projectiles) qui ont pour but d'atteindre isolément les hommes et non des projectiles d'artillerie' (statement by the representative of Prussia, *ibid.*, 455).

[21] The Russian delegate observed that 'l'essentiel lui paraît être de tracer une ligne de démarca-tion nette entre les projectiles d'artillerie et ceux affectés aux armes portatives. Le chiffre de 400 grammes a été choisi parce qu'il peut être considéré comme le minimum pour les premières et le

man or a group of combatants can inflict horrible wounds on them, was not considered so decisive as to outweigh the military importance of those projectiles.

A few weapons were banned on one ground only. The 'unnecessary suffering' criterion was the only rationale behind the prohibition, in 1868, of *projectiles weighing less than 400 grams* which are either explosive or charged with fulminating or inflammable substances;[22] and of the prohibition, in 1889, of 'bullets which expand or flatten easily in the human body, such as bullets with a hard envelope which does not entirely cover the core, or is pierced with incisions'.[23] Furthermore, the desire 'to safeguard the life and interests of neutrals and noncombatants' lay behind some basic provisions of the VIII Hague Convention of 1907, on the laying of *automatic submarine contact mines*.[24]

Most weapons, instead, were banned on several grounds. Thus some means of combat were prohibited both because they affect combatants and civilians alike and because they were regarded as perfidious. This applies, in particular, to the 1899 and 1907 Hague Declaration on the *discharge of projectiles from balloons*.[25] *Poison and poisoned weapons* were prohibited because they were regarded as perfidious[26] and cruel,[27] as well as—according to the 1877 Serbian

maximum pour les secondes. Toutes les pièces d'artillerie de moins d'une livre doivent être reconnues inefficaces' (*ibid.,* 469 and cp. also 457).

[22] See the 'Mémoire sur la suppression de l'emploi des balles explosives en temps de guerre' sent by the Russian Emperor to the States invited to the St. Petersburg Conference, *ibid.,* 458–467, as well as the statements made at St. Petersburg by the various States (*ibid.* 451ff.), in particular the statement by the Russian representative (*ibid.,* 451): 'Il y a là d'abord une question de principe sur laquelle nous sommes tous d'accord, un principe d'humanité qui consiste à limiter autant que possible les calamités de la guerre et à interdire l'emploi de certaines armes, dont l'effect est d'aggraver eruellement les souffrances causées par les blessures, sans utilité réelle pour le but de la guerre').

[23] For the pertinent citations see my paper *Weapons Causing Unnecessary Suffering* etc., cit., 16ff.

[24] See the statement by the British delegate in the I Subcommission of the III Commission, in *The Proceedings of the Hague Peace Conferences,* edited by J.B. Scott, *The Conference of 1907,* vol. III, 523 (1921). See also, *inter alia,* the statement of the Italian delegate (who spoke of the need to eliminate from the use of 'these terrible contrivances' all the fatal consequences that they could have 'for the peaceful commerce of neutrals and for fishing', *ibid.,* 522). See also the report submitted by the I to the III Commission (*ibid.,* 459: emphasis is placed on 'the very weighty responsibility towards peaceful shipping assumed by the belligerent that lays mines', as well as on 'the principle of the liberty of the sea').

[25] See the statements made at The Hague, in 1899, by the representative of the United States, who insisted on the fact that those weapons hit combatants and non-combatants alike (*Proceedings of the Hague Peace Conferences, The Conference of 1899,* cit., 354, 280), and the statement by the delegate of the Netherlands, who stressed instead that the launching of explosives from balloons was 'perfidious' (*ibid.,* 341–342; see also 288).

[26] See e.g. the statements made at The Hague, in 1899, by the representative of the United States (*Proceedings of the Hague Peace Conferences* etc., cit., 356) and of The Netherlands (*ibid.,* 356 and 296). See also para. 40 of the Austrian Military Manual ('Grundsätze des Kriegsvölkerrechts', in *Bundesministerium für Landesverteidigung, Truppenführung 253* (1965)).

[27] See e.g. the diplomatic notes sent in 1868 by the Government of Portugal and Prussia, respectively, to the Russian Emperor (who had proposed to outlaw explosive bullets). Text in *Nouveau recueil général de traités,* etc. cit., 464 and 465. See also the statements made in 1899 at The Hague by the delegate of Russia (*Proceedings of the Hague Peace Conferences,* cit., 366 and 296) and of the United States (*ibid.,* 366). See furthermore many modern military manuals, such

Instructions—because 'the employment of poison . . . is not only dishonourable but is also a double-edged weapon that can easily turn against those who resort to it'.[28] *Asphyxiating gases* were banned in 1899 because they were considered cruel,[29] indiscriminate[30] and because they cause unnecessary suffering.[31] *Bacteriological means of warfare* were banned in 1925 and then in 1972 for two reasons: they are 'savage' and 'horrible',[32] 'so revolting and so foul that (they) must meet with the condemnation of all civilised nations';[33] furthermore, they are indiscriminate: as was put by the Polish delegate to the 1925 Geneva Conference, 'it is impossible to limit the field of action of bacteriological factors once introduced into warlike operations. The consequences of bacteriological warfare will thus be felt equally by the armed forces of the belligerents and the whole civilian population, even against the desire of the belligerents, who would be unable to restrict the action of the bacteriological weapons to an area decided upon beforehand'.[34]

D. Merits and Inadequacies of the Specific-Ban Approach

This approach has three major advantages. First, as a result of drawing up precise rules which prohibit specific weapons by pointing to their objective features, a high degree of *certainty* is provided about the kind of weapon which is outlawed. Secondly, certain instruments of destruction are proscribed *in any circumstance*, regardless of the quality and quantity of the medical or relief resources of the belligerents or of the degree of their technological development.[35] Thirdly, thanks to its specific and precise formulation which makes reference to objective connotations of the forbidden weapons, the prohibition is capable of providing a safe normative guidance which is effective *even though no enforcement authority exists:* this is clearly evidenced by the fact that the existing prohibitions of specific weapons have been normally respected even though they were at times violated by one of the belligerents.

as The Netherlands *Rules of the Law of War* (VR 2-1120/11, Ministerie van Oorlog. Voorlopige Richtlijnen nr 2-1120. Velddienst-Deel 11—*Oorlogsregelen*. Chapt. III, para. 14, at 7 (1958)) as well as The Netherlands *Manual for the Soldier* (VS 2-1350. Koninklijke Landmacht, *Handboek voor de Soldaat,* Chapt. 7, para. 10, at. 7/3 (1974)).

[28] Para. 12, in *International Review of the Red Cross,* cit. 174.

[29] See e.g. the statements made in 1899 at The Hague by the representatives of Russia and of Austria-Hungary (*Proceedings of the Hague Peace Conferences,* cit. 366).

[30] See e.g. the statement made in 1899 at The Hague by the representative of Denmark (*ibid.,* 366) and by the delegate of the Netherlands (*ibid.,* 283).

[31] See e.g. the statement made in 1899 at The Hague by the representative of Russia (*ibid.,* 283).

[32] See the statement made by the delegate of Poland in the 1925 Geneva Conference: League of Nations, *Proceedings of the Conference for the Supervision of the International trade in Arms and Ammunition and in Implements of War,* 340.

[33] See the statement made in 1925 by the delegate of the United States, 1925 *Geneva Conference Proceedings,* cit., 341.

[34] *Ibid.,* 340.

[35] May I refer to my paper on *Weapons Causing Unnecessary Suffering* etc. cit., 18ff.

The drawbacks of this approach, however, are no less apparent than its merits. Specific bans can be easily by-passed by elaborating new and more sophisticated weapons which, while they are no less cruel than the proscribed ones, do not fall under the prohibition owing to their new features. It was rightly noted that 'since we cannot always predict context and technological change, the effort to ban specific weapons is an effort geared to the past'.[36] What can turn out to be more important is that the States more likely or capable of dodging the ban are the more industrialized ones, for they possess the technological resources which are needed to manufacture more sophisticated weaponry. As a result, the gap between technologically developed States and less advanced countries could be widened also in this field.

E. State Practice

On many occasions States have claimed, in recent years, that some weapons used by the adversary, or at any rate by other States, were unlawful as violative of general principles of the laws of war. As in this paper I cannot enter into details,[37] I shall confine myself to pointing to some general conclusions which can be drawn from a survey of practice.

First, State practice is indicative of the fact that in the view of a number of States some weapons are contrary to international law, because they are indiscriminate or perfidious, or cause unnecessary suffering. As even those States that opposed this view did not go as far as to reject the general principles on weapons, the clear inference is that all States have upheld those general principles. The importance of this conclusion is somewhat belittled, however, by the second and third conclusions to be drawn from State practice. The second conclusion is that when it was contended by a State that a certain weapon ran counter to a general principle, in no case did the State against which that contention was made acknowledge the violation. This is only natural, because no State is ready to openly admit violating international law. What, however, is lacking, at least in the case of conventional weapons, has been the *repetition of protests by a great number of States* and the affirmation *by some international body representative of the world community* that the weapons at issue are contrary to international law. Criticism and protests against the use of certain weapons have remained therefore 'unilateral' moves and have not been able to elicit the agreement of a vast number of States. Thirdly, no State has thus far discontinued the use of any weapon as a result of allegations by

---

[36] PAUST, 'Remarks on Human Rights and Armed Conflicts', in *Proceedings of the 67 Annual Meeting of the American Society of International Law* 1973, 163.

[37] For the practice of States concerning the application of the principle on unnecessary suffering, see my paper *Weapons Causing Unnecessary Suffering: Are they Prohibited?* For the practice relating to the principle on indiscriminate weapons, see my paper 'The Prohibition of Indiscriminate Means of Warfare' (also published in this volume).

other States that a given weapon is illegal. If in a few instances,[38] charges resulted in the State accused dropping the use of the weapon, this was mainly due to the surrounding circumstances of the war (e.g. the State accused was about to lose the war) and to the warning that military personnel using those weapons would be tried as war criminals, if captured.

In short, a survey of State practice proves that while no State denies the existence and the binding value of the general principles, no agreement (outside treaty stipulations) has as yet evolved on the concrete application of those principles to specific weapons. This amounts to saying that the prohibitory intent of those principles has proved scarcely effective.

2. The New Law

A. General

The present legal situation is no doubt very unsatisfactory. Since the last World War, States have constantly been developing and occasionally using new and very cruel weapons: suffice it to mention incendiary weapons containing napalm and phosphorus, which produce dreadful burnings, and other conventional weapons such as fragmentation and cluster bombs, as well as hypervelocity bullets, which become completely unstable on impact, tumbling in the wound and producing a large cavity. In addition, States have steadily been perfecting nuclear weapons of various sizes and have been manufacturing new chemical weapons of increasing effectiveness. The existing rules of international law are obviously inadequate to cope with these new agencies of destruction. It is therefore legitimate to ask what the ICRC and the international community are doing to outlaw or at least to curb the use of such weapons.

Various major trends are discernible. First, a wide tendency has emerged to *reaffirm and develop* the existing general principles referred to above (*supra,* Sect. 1.A.) and, by the same token, to broaden their scope. Secondly, most States have expressed doubts about whether conventional means of warfare, such as incendiary weapons, delayed-action weapons, fragmentation bombs, high-velocity bullets etc., come under the purview of the existing general principles proscribing weapons. Consequently, a large majority of States have strongly pressed for the formulation of *specific bans* on some of these weapons. Yet, despite

---

[38] Thus, it may be recalled that on April 24, 1975, the Provisional Government of South Vietnam and the Democratic Republic of Vietnam protested the use by the Saigon authorities of CBU 55 bombs. They claimed that these weapons were contrary to international law because they were inhumane, indiscriminate and terrorized the population; they therefore warned South Vietnam that they would bring to trial as war criminals those pilots who would not refuse to use such weapons. It seems that after this stern warning, the Saigon authorities discontinued resort to CBU bombs (*L'Unità,* April 25, 1975, at 20; cf. *Le Monde,* February 5, 1975, at 6 and April 24, 1975 at 3).

generous efforts on the part of several small and middle-sized Powers, no concrete results have been achieved in this field. Nor has the Geneva Diplomatic Conference on Humanitarian Law succeeded in making headway in two other areas: (a) the criminal repression of violations of international rules concerning the use of means of warfare, and (b) the extension of prohibitions or restrictions on the use of weapons to non-international armed conflicts.

In the following pages I shall expatiate on each of these trends.[39]

B. The Reaffirmation and Development of General Principles

Most States have deemed it advisable to reiterate the existing general prohibition on weapons causing unnecessary suffering. Consequently, Protocol I includes a provision to that effect (Article 35 para. 2).[40] The reaffirmation of the general rule restricting the choice of means of combat has also been regarded as appropriate, and to this end a provision was included in the same Protocol (Article 35 para. 1).[41] Both provisions were adopted by consensus.[42]

This approach, however, was not considered sufficient. The aforementioned provisions were eventually adopted after being supplemented *in two ways*. First, they were expanded so as to include other general prohibitions, namely the prohibition of *indiscriminate* means of warfare and of means of *ecological warfare*. As for the first category, the ICRC proposed a provision (Article 46 para. 3) stipulating that:

the employment of means of combat, and any methods which strike or affect indiscriminately the civilian population and combatants or civilian objects and military objectives, are prohibited.

[39] On the current efforts to enact new international rules on weapons see in general: BLIX, 'Human Rights and Armed Conflicts, Remarks', *Proceedings of the 67 Meeting of the American Society of International Law* 1973, 152ff.; BAXTER, 'Perspective: The Evolving Laws of Armed Conflicts', *Military Law Review* 1973, 99ff.; BAXTER, 'Criteria of the Prohibition of International Law', cit. 46ff.: KALSHOVEN, 'Human Rights and Armed Conflicts, Remarks', *Proceedings of the 67 Meeting of the American Society of International Law* 1973, 160–162; KALSHOVEN, *The Law of Warfare. A Summary of its recent History and Trends in development* 1973, 87ff.; BLIX, 'Current Efforts to Prohibit the Use of Certain Conventional Weapons', *Instant Research on Peace and Violence* 1974, 21ff.; CASSESE, 'Current Trends in the Development of the Law of Armed Conflicts', in this volume and in *Rivista Trimestrale di Diritto Pubblico* 1974, 1426–1429; MALINVERNI, 'Armes conventionnelles modernes et droit international', cit. 39ff.; BAXTER, 'Humanitarian Law or Humanitarian Politics? The 1974 Diplomatic Conference on Humanitarian Law', *Harvard International Law Journal* 1975, 22–24; BIERZANEK, 'Protection of Civilians and Belligerents Against the Effects of Modern Conventional Weapons', *Studies on International Relations*, no. 4 (Warsaw) 1975, p. 60ff.; DE MULINEN, 'A propos de la Conférence de Lucerne et Lugano sur l'emploi de certaines armes conventionnelles', *Annales d'études internationales*, 1977, p. 111ff.

[40] 'It is prohibited to employ weapons, projectiles and material and methods of warfare of a nature to cause superfluous injury or unnecessary suffering'.

[41] 'In any armed conflict, the right of the Parties to the conflict to choose methods or means of warfare is not unlimited'.

[42] CDDH/SR. 39, p. 10. See, however, the various statements made before and after the adoption (*ibid.*, pp. 9–10).

This suggestion received wide support, and elicited proposals for improvements by various States.[43] After lengthy debates, the Conference adopted, in 1977,[44] a text (Article 51 paras 4–5), which reads as follows:

4. Indiscriminate attacks are prohibited. Indiscriminate attacks are:

   (a) those which are not directed at a specific military objective;

   (b) those which employ a method or means of combat which cannot be directed at a specific military objective; or

   (c) those which employ a method or means of combat the effects of which cannot be limited as required by this Protocol; and consequently, in each such case, are of a nature to strike military objectives and civilians or civilian objects without distinction.

5. Among others, the following types of attacks are to be considered as indiscriminate:

   (a) an attack by bombardment by any methods or means which treats as a single military objective a number of clearly separated and distinct military objectives located in a city, town, village or other area containing a similar concentration of civilians or civilian objects; and

   (b) an attack which may be expected to cause incidental loss of civilian life, injury to civilians, damage to civilian objects, or a combination thereof, which would be excessive in relation to the concrete and direct military advantage anticipated.

This rule among other things elaborates the prohibition of indiscriminate weapons, in two respects: (1) by specifying what must be understood by 'blind' weapons;[45] (2) by developing the rule of proportionality. As far as the first point is concerned, the provision is no doubt a great improvement over the existing law, for para. 4 and para. 5 (a) specify in clear and unambiguous terms the circumstances under which a means of combat is illegal for its indiscriminateness. The first and clearest inference from these provisions is that non 'tactical' atomic and nuclear weapons (provided of course that 'tactical' ones are capable of hitting military objectives only) are prohibited. There could, however, be some elements pointing to a contrary conclusion.[46]

---

[43] See above all CDDH/III/8, CDDH/III/27 and CDDH/III/43.

[44] Art. 46 (now 51) was adopted by 77 votes in favour, one against (France) and 16 abstentions (CDDH/SR. 41, p. 29).

[45] It should not be passed over in silence, however, that after the adoption of Art. 46 (the present Art. 51) some States have entered reservations or suggested interpretations which greatly weaken the interpretation set forth in the text above. Thus, the U.K. delegation stated that 'it considered that the definition of indiscriminate attacks given in that paragraph was not intended to mean that there were means of combat the use of which would constitute an indiscriminate attack in all circumstances. The paragraph did not in itself prohibit the use of any specific weapon, but it took account of the fact that the lawful use of any means of combat depended on the circumstances' (CDDH/SR. 41, pp. 29–30). The same interpretation was propounded by the delegation of Italy (*ibid.,* p. 30), of the Federal Republic of Germany (*ibid.,* Annex, p. 1) and of Canada (*ibid.,* Annex, p. 4).

[46] In its introduction to the Draft Additional Protocols, the ICRC stated: 'It should be recalled that, apart from some provisions of a general nature, the ICRC has not included in its drafts any rules governing atomic, bacteriological and chemical weapons. These weapons have either been the subject of international agreements such as the Geneva Protocol of 1925 or of discussions within

Less felicitous appears to be paragraph 5 (b), which elaborates the rule of pro-portionality. It seems that the main focus is placed on the *subjective evaluation,* by belligerents, of the destructive effects of attacks or of the use of means of war-fare. For it is stated there that a belligerent must refrain from launching attacks which *may be expected* to cause damages to civilians disproportionate to the mili-tary advantage *anticipated* by that belligerent. Instead of establishing that the possible disproportion must be *objective* (i.e. that the actual incidental damage of civilians must not be out of proportion to the military advantage actually gained), the provision hinges on how a belligerent perceives and anticipates the effect of its attack. It would seem that the provision therefore lends itself to subjective interpretations.[47]

Thus, for instance, faced with a glaring disproportion of civilian loss to the mili-tary advantage, a belligerent could claim that when he planned the attack he did not expect or anticipate such a great disproportion. How could one assess the decision-making process of belligerents and the manner by which they weigh the various alternatives and make the final choice? The difficulty of looking into such imponderable elements to determine whether a belligerent *should have expected* disproportionate damages to civilians could result in rendering the practical application of that rule very difficult.[48]

It thus appears that, along with very important elements, the provisions of Article 51 under consideration show features which are open to abuse or lend themselves to interpretations which could go so far as to stultify the significance of the Article. Furthermore, in formulating a general assessment of Article 51, it should not be overlooked that some States, including France, stressed at Geneva that the Article could not be interpreted as limiting in any way 'a nation's right of self-defence'.[49] This means that, for those States, Article 51 of the Protocol

intergovernmental organizations' (ICRC, 'Draft Additional Protocols to the Geneva Conventions of August 12, 1949, Commentary', Geneva, October 1973, at 2).

On the signature of Protocol I, the U.S. stated that its signature was subject to the understand-ing that 'the rules established by this Protocol (I) were not intended to have any effect on and do not regulate or prohibit the use of nuclear weapons' (Department politique fédéral de la Suisse, *Notification aux Etats parties aux Conventions de Genève,* 17 janvier 1978). Also the U.K. signed the Protocol on the same understanding (*ibid.*).

[47] In commenting on Art. 46. after its adoption, the U.K. delegate pointed out that 'It was clear . . . that military commanders and others responsible for planning, initiating or executing attacks had to reach decisions on the basis of their assessment of the information available to them from all sources at the relevant time' (CDDH/SR. 41, p. 30).

[48] The value and significance of the rule in question can be further belittled by certain inter-pretations suggested after its adoption. Thus, the U.K. delegation stated that in its view 'the ref-erence in sub-para. 5 (b) and in Article 50 to "military advantage anticipated" from an attack was intended to refer to the advantage anticipated from the attack as a whole and not only from isolated or particular parts of the attack' (CDDH/SR. 41, p. 30).

The same interpretation was placed on Art. 46 by the delegates of the Federal Republic of Germany (*ibid.,* Annex, p. 1) and of the Netherlands (*ibid.,* Annex, p. 13).

[49] Before the adoption of the Article, the delegate of France said he would vote against it because 'his delegation, while agreeing with the fundamental purpose behind Article 46, felt that it went beyond the scope of humanitarian law and tended, in particular, to limit a nation's right of

shall not apply to combat actions considered necessary for 'self-defence'. This would manifestly restrict to a very great extent the range and the scope of the Article.

Besides developing and specifying the general principles on indiscriminate weapons, the Geneva Diplomatic Conference has taken a very significant step. Aware of the fact that in modern wars belligerents (or, more appropriately, technologically advanced belligerents) tend to use weapons which eventually affect civilians in that they bring about severe damage to the environment, the States assembled at Geneva adopted Article 35 para. 3, a provision which prohibits means of ecological warfare.[50] It reads as follows:

It is forbidden to employ methods or means of warfare which are intended or may be expected to cause widespread, long-term, and severe damage to the natural environment.

This provision is of necessity rather vague.[51] Especially the time element ('long-term . . . damage') can lend itself to subjective interpretations. Some light is shed, however, by the debates preceding its adoption. As is stated in the Report submitted by Committee III to the Conference.

It was generally agreed that battlefield damage incidental to conventional warfare would not normally be proscribed by this provision. What is proscribed, in effect, is such damage as would be likely to prejudice over a long-term the continued survival of the civilian population or would risk long-term, major health problems for it.[52]

---

self-defence. His delegation especially objected to paras 4, 5 and 6, which, in its opinion, were too complex and likely to hamper defensive operations in any country' (CDDH/SR. 41, p. 28). France actally voted against Art. 46 (*ibid.,* p. 29).

A declaration similar to that of France was made by Cameroon (CDDH/SR. 41, p. 34) and, although in different terms and with different reasons, by Romania (*ibid.,* Annex, pp. 18–19).

[50] While the ICRC had made no proposals on the matter, some States put forward at Geneva proposals aimed at strengthening the protection of the environment from the damages of war: see the amendments by Finland (CDDH/III/91), by Egypt, Australia, Czechoslovakia, Finland, GDR, Hungary, Ireland, Norway, Yugoslavia, Sudan (CDDH/III/222) and by the Democratic Republic of Vietnam (CDDH/III/238).

[51] Protection of the natural environment against damages of warfare is also provided in Art. 48 *bis* (now Art. 55) which reads as follows: '1. Care shall be taken in warfare to protect the natural environment against widespread, long-term and severe damage. Such care includes a prohibition of the use of methods or means of warfare which are intended or may be expected to cause such damage to the natural environment and thereby to prejudice the health or survival of the population. 2. Attacks against the natural environment by way of reprisal are prohibited'.

[52] CDDH/III/286, at 9.

After the adoption by consensus, in plenary, of the Article, on 26 May 1977 (CDDH/ SR. 39, p. 10), the delegation of the Federal Republic of Germany put on the record the following declaration: 'Bearing in mind the special scope of application of Additional Protocol I, it is the understanding of the Federal Republic of Germany that the interpretation of the terms 'widespread', 'long-term' and 'severe' has to be consistent with the general line of thought as it emerged from the deliberations on this article in Committee III, as reflected in its report CDDH/215/Rev. 1.

In no case should it be interpreted in the light of the respective terminology of other instruments of environmental protection that have a different scope of application altogether' (CDDH/SR. 39, Annex, p. 1).

The second way of making general principles effective lies in imposing on States the duty of *verifying* whether new weapons, that they develop or manufacture, are in keeping with international standards. To this end, the ICRC proposed a new rule, Article 34, which provided that 'In the study and development of new weapons or methods of warfare, the High Contracting Parties shall determine whether their use will cause unnecessary injury'.

After considering various amendements, the Conference adopted by consensus, in 1977[53] the following text (Article 36):

In the study, development, acquisition, or adoption of a new weapon, means or method of warfare, a High Contracting Party is under an obligation to determine whether its employment would, under some or all circumstances, be prohibited by this Protocol or by any other rule of international law applicable to the High Contracting Party.

Under this provision contracting States are not bound to disclose anything about the new weapons they are studying or developing. They are therefore not required to assess publicly the legality of new weapons. It follows that other contracting States have no possibility of verifying whether the obligation laid down there is complied with. It could be argued, however, that Article 36 actually imposes both the duty to set up domestic procedures for exploring the issue of legality of new weapons and the duty to concretely use these procedures with respect to each new means of combat. While compliance with the former duty can be made subject to international scrutiny by other contracting States (which could request to be informed about these procedures),[54] implementation of the latter duty is left—in actual practice—to the discretion of the contracting State which studies or elaborates a new means of warfare.[55]

Surprisingly, a point in Article 36 which aroused disagreement, notwithstanding the clarity and the precision of the wording, is the range of activities covered by the provision. The delegate of the Soviet Union, after the adoption of Article 36, rightly pointed out that it 'covered not only the manufacture

---

[53] CDDH/SR. 39, p. 11.

[54] It can be mentioned that some States have already set up procedures for verifying whether new weapons comply with international standards (see e.g. the US Department of Defense *Instruction* n° 5500 15 of October 16, 1974 on 'Review of Legality of Weapons under International Law'. Reference to such instruction was made by the US delegate in 1975 at Geneva: CDDH/IV/SR. 15, at 14). Other States could always request a certain State to disclose in general terms what procedures it has set up.

In 1977 the U.K. delegate pointed out, after the adoption of Art. 36, that 'the drawing up of the Additional Protocols had provided the United Kingdom with an opportunity for the codification of existing practice and his country was at present establishing a review procedure to ensure that future weapons would meet the requirements of international law' (CDDH/SR. 39, p. 11).

[55] After the adoption of Art. 36 the delegate of the Soviet Union stressed the importance of this provision and said that he was gratified at its adoption, stressing *inter alia* that by its adoption 'the Conference strengthened humanitarian law in the matter of the sovereignty of States, which were not obliged to apply to a supranational control organization' (CDDH/SR. 39, p. 11).

of . . . weapons but also their purchase abroad . . . '.[56] The Italian delegate said, by contrast, that his delegation could not 'conceal its perplexity about the wording of those provisions, which could not be interpreted as introducing a specific prohibition operative in all circumstances attendant on the study, development, acquisition or adoption of particular weapons and methods of warfare'.[57] A somewhat similar statement was made by the delegate of France.[58] In my view, these interpretations should be rejected, for they cleary run counter to the plain wording of Article 36 as well as to its intent and purpose.

C. The Failure to Adopt Specific Bans

i. *The link between general principles and specific bans*

The best way of supplementing and strengthening the existing general principles consists in *linking them with the enactment of specific bans.* This link was stressed by various States, which pointed out that the reformulation and expanding of general principles would be of little value without their being implemented through the elaboration of specific bans. Many States therefore underscored the close relationship existing between the works of Committee III of the Diplomatic Conference on Humanitarian Law (concerned *inter alia* with the general principles on means of combat) and the *Ad Hoc* Committee on Conventional Weapons, of the same Conference. By taking such a stand, States intended to bring out that specific bans are the indispensable corollary of general principles—or, to put it differently, that general principles *per se* can primarily serve as guidelines for outlawing single weapons through specific provisions, This position is illustrated, *inter alia,* by a statement of the delegate of Mauritania, made in 1975. His delegation considered that the provisions of Article 22 and 33 (e) of the Regulations respecting the Laws and Customs of War on Land, which appeared in The Hague Conventions of 1899 (II) and 1907 (IV) and were to be found in the Preamble to the Saint Petersburg Declaration of 1868, as well as the report of the Secretary-Generay of the United Nations, clearly showed that the use of certain categories of weapons *should be generally prohibited* for the well-being of all mankind.[59]

---

[56] CDDH/SR. 39, p. 11. The delegate of Switzerland later associated himself with the statement of the representative of Soviet Union (*ibid.,* p. 12).

[57] CDDH/SR. 39, pp. 11–12.

[58] The French delegate said that 'although the provisions of Article 34 (now Art. 35) had been drawn up for a humanitarian purpose, they were by their nature connected with the general problem of disarmament. His delegation had always maintained that the Diplomatic Conference on the Reaffirmation and Development of International Humanitarian Law Applicable in Armed Conflicts was not an appropriate forum for dealing with such problems. That was why the French delegation, although it had not opposed the consensus on the adoption of Article 34, wanted to make it clear that it would have abstained if a vote had been taken' (CDDH/SR. 39, p. 12).

[59] CDDH/IV/SR. 11 at 4 (emphasis added).

Another statement which is worth citing was made in 1975 by the delegate of Algeria, who observed in the *Ad Hoc* Committee on Conventional Weapons that:

while other committees were trying to draw up provisions which would take account of the legitimate requirements of the international community with respect to humanitarian law in situations of modern armed conflicts, it was natural that Committee IV should be given the task of harmonizing the use of certain weapons with those requirements. Would it not, in fact, be useless to include such provisions as those contained in Article 33 about the prohibition of unnecessary injury and in Article 34 about new weapons if the Committee proved to be too hesitant in taking a concrete approach to those provisions? The Committee had an exceptional opportunity to carry out a truly humanitarian task in the tradition of the St. Petersburg Declaration of 1868 and the Hague Rules of 1907, which had resulted in the prohibition of the dum-dum bullet and poison gases.[60]

The same stand was taken in 1977, even after it had become apparent that no specific ban on weapons would be enacted by the Conference. After the adoption of Article 33 (the present Article 35 laying down the general principle which prohibits weapons causing superfluous injury or unnecessary suffering), the representative of Yugoslavia pointed out that:

paragraph 2 of Article 33 [on prohibited weapons] stated a general rule which would have to be put into concrete form. It should specify which were the weapons which caused superfluous injury, for otherwise the rule would be of very limited value. Unfortunately, the *Ad Hoc* Committee on Conventional Weapons which had been dealing with the matter had failed to achieve its objective . . . .[61]

After the adoption of Article 34 (the present Article 36, concerning obligations of States with respect to the study, development etc. of new weapons), the representative of Switzerland said that:

Article 34 was especially important since it had not been possible to specify in Article 33 the Conference's proposals for the restriction of certain weapons . . . .[62]

The same delegate restated the position of his Government when Article 86 *bis* (concerning the setting up of a Committee for recommending specific bans: see below para. 3 *b, in fine*) was discussed in plenary. He said that:

[60] CDDH/IV/SR. 16, at 6. See also the statement made by the delegate of New Zealand ('According to those principles (*seil.* certain long-established principles of law)—which were also being considered in the Third Committee—the use of weapons apt to cause unnecessary suffering or to have indiscriminate effects was prohibited. The concept of perfidy or treachery must also, however, be borne in mind. The elaboration and application of those principles required a process of a particular kind: a dialogue in which there was a close assessment of the effects and advantages of the categories of weapons. The New Zealand Delegation . . . welcomed the fact that dialogue was now well under way' (CDDH/IV/SR. 10, at 4). See also the statement by the representative of Sudan (CDDH/IV/SR. 15, at 21).
[61] CDDH/SR. 39, p. 10.
[62] CDDH/SR. 39, p. 12.

the Swiss delegation was in favour of Article 86 *bis* because Article 33 was too general. The serious and urgent problem of the banning or restriction of the use of certain conventional weapons called for much more specific provisions.[63]

A similar position was taken by the representative of Syria. He said:

Article 86 *bis* was the logical consequence of the adoption by the Conference of Article 33. If the use of weapons causing unnecessary suffering or having indiscriminate effects was to be prohibited, the conclusion must be the establishment of an appropriate mechanism for providing information concerning the list of such weapons. The provisions currently in force on the matter were out of date and no longer answered the humanity's needs.[64]

To sum up, it can be said that, while no State challenged at Geneva the binding force of the existing general principles on weapons, many States tended to believe that such principles need to be concretely implemented by specific prohibitions. Furthermore, many States tended to consider that modern conventional weapons such as incendiary or anti-personnel fragmentation weapons, etc., do not fall as of now under the prohibitory scope of those principles. They maintained that, at the most, those general principles could point to the criteria for enacting new and specific prohibitions. Consequently, for many States, the only realistic and proper approach to such weapons should consist in considering whether it is feasible to elaborate new rules forbidding or restricting their use.

ii. The (meagre) achievements of the conference

Despite the keen awareness on the part of most participants in the Geneva Conference of the need to specify the general principles by agreeing upon specific bans, and despite lengthy discussions which stretched over 4 years (in the *Ad Hoc* Committee of the Conference, and in two Conferences of Governments Experts held under the auspices of the ICRC), the labours of the Geneva Conference ended up, in this area, in an almost complete failure. Actually, only the following results were achieved:

1) it was agreed that efforts should be made to prohibit or restrict the use of those weapons which prove not to be in keeping with either of the following criteria: a) that they should not cause unnecessary suffering; b) that they should not hit indiscriminately combatants and civilians alike;
2) the Conference reached a general agreement on the desirability of prohibiting the use of conventional weapons the primary effect of which is to injure by fragments not detectable by X-ray;
3) the Conference concluded that many States agree that land-mines and booby-traps should be banned or restrictions should be placed on their use;

[63] CDDH/SR. 47, p. 11.
[64] CDDH/SR. 47, p. 14.

4) it was agreed to recommend the holding, not later than 1979, of a Conference of Governments on conventional weapons which may be deemed to be excessively injurious or have indiscriminate effects.[65]

[65] On 9 June 1977, the Conference adopted by consensus (CDDH/SR. 57, p. 21) the following resolution (Res. 22):

'*The Diplomatic Conference on the Reaffirmation and Development of International Humanitarian Law Applicable in Armed Conflicts, Geneva, 1974–1977*

Having met at Geneva for four sessions, in 1974, 1975, 1976 and 1977, and having adopted new humanitarian rules relating to armed conflicts and methods and means of warfare,

Convinced that the suffering of the civilian population and combatants could be significantly reduced if agreements can be attained on the prohibition or restriction for humanitarian reasons of the use of specific conventional weapons, including any which may be deemed to be excessively injurious or to have indiscriminate effects,

Recalling that the issue of prohibitions or restrictions for humanitarian reasons of the use of specific conventional weapons has been the subject of substantive discussion in the *Ad Hoc* Committee on Conventional Weapons of the Conference at all its four sessions, and at the Conferences of Government Experts held under the auspices of the International Committee of the Red Cross in 1974 at Lucerne and in 1976 at Lugano,

Recalling, in this connexion, discussions and relevant resolutions of the General Assembly of the United Nations and appeals made by several Heads of State and Government,

Having concluded, from these discussions, that agreement exists on the desirability of prohibiting the use of conventional weapons, the primary effect of which is to injure by fragments not detectable by X-ray, and that there is a wide area of agreement with regard to land mines and booby-traps,

Having also devoted efforts to the further narrowing down of divergent views on the desirability of prohibiting or restricting the use of incendiary weapons, including napalm,

Having also considered the effects of the use of other conventional weapons, such as small calibre projectiles and certain blast and fragmentation weapons, and having begun the consideration of the possibility of prohibiting or restricting the use of such weapons,

Recognizing that it is important that this work continue and be pursued with the urgency required by evident humanitarian considerations,

Believing that further work should both build upon the areas of agreement thus far identified and include the search for further areas of agreement and should, in each case, seek the broadest possible agreement,

1. *Resolves* to send the report of the *Ad Hoc* Committee and the proposals presented in that Committee to the Governments of States represented at the Conference and to the Secretary-General of the United Nations;
2. *Request* that serious and early consideration be given to these documents and to the reports of the Conferences of Government Experts of Lucerne and Lugano;
3. *Recommends* that a Conference of Governments should be convened not later than 1979 with a view to reaching:
    (*a*) agreements on prohibitions or restrictions on the use of specific conventional weapons including those which may be deemed to be excessively injurious or have indiscriminate effects, taking into account humanitarian and military considerations; and
    (*b*) agreement on a mechanism for the review of any such agreements and for the consideration of proposals for further such agreements;
4. *Urges* that consultations be undertaken prior to the consideration of this question at the thirty-second session of the United Nations General Assembly for the purpose of reaching agreement on the steps to be taken in preparation for the Conference;
5. *Recommends* that a consultative meeting of all interested Governments be convened during September/October 1977 for this purpose;
6. *Recommends further* that the States participating in these consultations should consider *inter alia* the establishment of a Preparatory Committee which would seek to establish the best possible basis for the achievement at the Conference of agreements as envisaged in this resolution;

No agreement whatsoever was reached on the mere desirability of restricting the use of such cruel weapons as small-calibre projectiles, fuel-air explosives and incendiary weapons. Similarly, the Conference rejected a proposal for a new Article (86 *bis*), aimed at establishing a Committee responsible for both determining weapons contrary to accepted criteria (and therefore to be subjected to prohibition or restriction) and for recommending the convening of special conferences to conclude agreements on the matter.[66]

iii. Reasons for the failure. The opposing arguments

It is apparent from the Geneva debates that the primary reason for the failure to achieve major results in this area lies in the non-cooperative attitude and the delaying tactics of two groups of States: those of NATO (minus Norway) and those of the Warsaw Pact (minus Romania). This strong coalition succeeded in nullifying all the generous efforts of a group of States, made up of some

7. *Invites* the General Assembly of the United Nations at its thirty-second session, in the light of the results of the consultations undertaken pursuant to para. 4 of this resolution, to take any further action that may be necessary for the holding of the Conference in 1979.'

On 25 November 1977 the U.N. General Assembly adopted, by 84 votes to none, with 21 abstentions, a resolution by which, in operative para. 2, it decided to convene a U.N. Conference in 1979 'with a view to reaching agreements on prohibitions or restrictions on the use of specific conventional weapons, including those which may be deemed to be excessively injurious or have indiscriminate effects'.

[66] See CDDH/SR. 47, pp. 3–27.

It must be stressed that a general trend is discernible in the Geneva debates. States have become increasingly aware that, even assuming that it is possible to arrive at the enactment of specific bans, such bans could be easily dodged by manufacturing new and even more inhuman weapons. A growing number of States therefore suggested that machinery should be set up for the purpose both of keeping new developments in conventional weapons under review and of assessing new weapons in the light of humanitarian principles. Such machinery should thus ensure that States do not devise new weapons capable of by-passing existing bans. In the working document CDDH/IV/201 the need for such a continuous scrutiny was forcefully spelled out, although no actual mechanisms for review were suggested. In the course of the debates in Committee IV, in 1975, the Austrian delegate put forward some very interesting suggestions. He proposed that all States parties to Additional Protocol III (on weaponry) should be entrusted with the task of collecting the necessary information concerning scientific and technological development in the field of conventional weapons. The study of this information for the purpose of determining whether any new weapon causes superfluous injuries or has indiscriminate effects should be entrusted to a Conference of government experts. Subsequently, a plenipotentiary conference—to be convened at the request of one-third of the parties to the Protocol or after a specified number of years has passed—could enact provisions for the banning of any new weapon found to be contrary to the aforementioned basic requirements. See CDDH/IV/SR. 15, at 2–6. See also the 'informal proposal' on a review mechanism submitted by the Austrian experts to the 1976 Lugano Conference of Government Experts (doc. COLU/GG/LEG/201). This proposal was discussed at Lugano by the Working Group on General and Legal Questions (see the Report of this Group. COLU/GG/LEG/Rep/I Rev/I, at 6–8).

This suggestion received wide support in the *Ad Hoc* Committee: see in particular the statements by the representatives of Sweden (CDDH/IV/SR. 15, at 7–10), Venezuela (*ibid.*, at 11–13), Sudan (*ibid.*, at 21), Egypt (SR. 16, at 3), Sri Lanka (*ibid.*, at 3), the Netherlands (*ibid.*, at 13–14), Cp. also the cautious remarks of the Soviet delegate (SR. 15, at 19).

Unfortunately, as is pointed out in the text above, all these proposals and suggestions were subsequently thwarted by the East-West coalition of military powers.

238 *The Human Dimension of Wars*

Afro-Asian countries, a few Latin American countries and some Western States such as Sweden and Norway. These States strongly advocated that the Geneva Conference or an *Ad Hoc* Diplomatic Conference should ban at least some incendiary and other conventional weapons.[67] They were primarily moved by humanitarian considerations. It should not be thought, however, that they disregarded military considerations. That the traditional intent to reconcile humanitarian demands with military effectiveness is constantly borne in mind by States as much now as it was in the past, is *inter alia* demonstrated by several declarations of States. It is worth quoting here a statement by the delegate of Sweden, which is all the more significant because this neutral State is among the most outspoken advocates of strict and wide bans on conventional weapons. The Swedish delegate stated in 1975 that:

where a weapon could cause a high degree of suffering and was shown to be of relatively little military value, the case for a ban on use was obviously strong.[68]

And the Swiss delegate pointed out:

As to weapons not subject to the prohibition (para. B. 1) . . . smoke-producing weapons contained white phosphorus, which caused extremely painful burns; there could be no question of banning them, however, since to do so would place small armies at a disadvantage to large ones.[69]

The States in question did take military demands into consideration, but they concluded that these demands were not so imperative in the case of such inhuman or indiscriminate weapons as incendiary weapons, booby-traps, flechettes, etc., and therefore proposed that they be banned or that their use be restricted.

What were the arguments put forward by the States opposing any restriction or prohibition? They were basically two. First, the East-West coalition argued that the Geneva Diplomatic Conference was not the appropriate forum for enacting new bans or restrictions on the use of weapons. They contended that the matter should be discussed by a disarmament forum, such as the Geneva Conference of the Committee for Disarmament (CCD). The reason for this choice lay, in their view, in the fact that any action concerning modern conventional weapons should also cover their production, stockpiling, etc; and moreover, that a disarmament forum was needed for balancing strategic and military demands as well as economic problems.[70] The second argument was based on the technical

---

[67] At the 1974 Session of the Geneva Diplomatic Conference six States, namely Egypt, Mexico, Norway, Sweden, Switzerland and Yugoslavia, submitted a working paper proposing that the use of some of those arms be restricted or prohibited, because they are either indiscriminate in their effects or cause unnecessary suffering, and also because they have no great military value. See CDDH/DT/2, at 311. This document was revised and updated in 1975 (see doc CDDH/IV/201).

[68] CDDH/IV/SR. 9, p. 12.

[69] CDDH/IV/SR. 10, p. 17.

[70] See e.g. the Comment by Canada and Denmark on the Reports of the UN Secretary-General on Respect for Human Rights in Armed Conflicts, U.N. Doc. A/8313 (15 June 1971), respectively at 13 and 22, 24–25. The same stand was taken in 1974 by some Latin American countries, such as

difficulty of assessing whether or not a specific weapon meets one of the afore-mentioned criteria for banning or restricting the use of means of combat. Major Western countries as well as the Soviet Union have consistently emphasized that more study and thought should be devoted to each specific weapon to ascertain whether it is really cruel or indiscriminate.[71]

The best reply to the first argument (that relating to the 'competence' of the Geneva Diplomatic Conference) was given, in plenary, by the delegate of Pakistan, Mr. Hussain. He said:

> The banning or restriction of the use of weapons that caused a certain type of injury, were already dealt with, in a general way, in Article 33. Moreover, for the past four years the Conference had included the *Ad Hoc* Committee, for which it had provided legal and secretarial assistance. Moreover, special conferences of experts on the matters in question had been convened, in conjunction with the Conference, at Lucerne and at Lugano. Nobody had ever raised any objection to the existence of the *Ad Hoc* Committee or to the holding of the Lucerne and Lugano Conferences. Indeed, the very delegations which were now disputing the Conference's competence to deal with those matters had played an active part in those discussions. The two attitudes were totally incompatible; either the Conference was competent to deal with the possibility of prohibiting or restricting the use of certain weapons, or the *Ad Hoc* Committee and the Lucerne and Lugano Conferences should have been ruled out of order from the start.[72]

Also the argument centring on the alleged need for further research on the technical data was dismissed by the advocates of specific bans on weapons. They contended that the argument did not hold water. Indeed, those very States which had advanced it had not put forward any constructive suggestion nor given any major technical contribution on the matter over the past four years. The argument, in the opinion of Third World countries, served only to hide the substantial unwillingness of the States bound by military alliances to achieve any real humanitarian progress on the matter.[73]

D. The Failure to Extend the Elaborate Repressive System Provided for in the 1949 Conventions to Violations of Rules on Means of Warfare

It is well known that the 1949 Geneva Conventions made a distinction between simple breaches and 'grave breaches' of the Conventions. While both categories

---

Brazil (CDDH/SR. 10, at 11). See also Ukraine (CDDH/SR. 11 at 19), Hungary (*ibid.,* 22), USSR (*ibid.,* SR. 12, at 8), Byelorussia (*ibid.,* SR. 14, at 14).

See also USSR (CDDH/SR. 47, pp. 6–7), France (*ibid.,* pp. 15–16), Italy (*ibid.,* Annex, p. 9).

[71] See e.g. the statements of the representative of Italy (CDDH/IV/SR. 25, pp. 38–39), of Spain (CDDH/IV/SR. 26, p. 43), Italy (*ibid.,* pp. 49–50), Soviet Union (CDDH/IV/SR. 29, p. 77), Austria (CDDH/IV/SR. 31, p. 103), U.S. (*ibid.,* p. 107), Italy (CDDH/IV/SR. 32, p. 114).

[72] CDDH/SR. 47, p. 13.

[73] See e.g. the statement that representative of Mexico made on 24 May 1977, in plenary (CDDH/SR. 37, p. 11).

of violations can be regarded as war crimes, the latter entails special obligations for Contracting States. With respect to 'grave breaches' of the Conventions each Contracting party is under various obligations: to enact legislation providing effective penal sanctions for persons committing or ordering the commission of such breaches; to search for those persons; and the obligation to bring them before its own courts—regardless of their nationality and of the place where the breach was committed—or to hand them over for trial to another Contracting State concerned.

At the Geneva Diplomatic Conference the question arose whether violations of the provisions of the Protocol governing means and methods of combat should be labelled 'simple breaches' or 'grave breaches' (in the latter case all the afore-mentioned obligations following from the Geneva Conventions concerning 'grave breaches' would have applied to those violations). In the course of the discussions two trends emerged: a group of States (mainly Western countries) suggested to proceed with great caution and to exclude from the category of 'grave breaches' breaches committed on the battlefield;[74] another group of States (the socialist countries, various Arab States plus a few Western countries)[75] proposed to broaden the concept of 'grave breaches' by including *inter alia* violations of combat rules.

The former group of States put forward two arguments to oppose any widening of the category of 'grave breaches'. First, they contended that the provisions of the Protocol governing combat action were not free from ambiguity: some of them were so imprecise as 'to create the risk that any soldier involved in the conduct of warfare would without intentional violation of the Protocol's provisions, be open to charges of war crimes'.[76] Secondly, it would have been very difficult to find reliable evidence concerning alleged violations of combat rules: the very nature of combat situations made it difficult to collect first-hand and convincing proof of the breaches. Therefore, if universal jurisdiction was provided for such breaches, 'some countries would undoubtedly find it very difficult to mount an enquiry into events which had occurred in a remote part of the world and to qualify certain acts as grave breaches when the situation was confused and evidence was lacking'.[77]

---

[74] See, e.g., Canada (CDDH/I/SR. 43, p. 17), U.S. (*ibid.*, pp. 18–20), U.K. (*ibid.*, pp. 24–25), Belgium (CDDH/I/SR. 44, pp. 35–36), Federal Republic of Germany (CDDH/I/SR. 45, p. 46). Cf. also Korea (*ibid.*, p. 44).

[75] See e.g. Byelorussia (CDDH/I/SR. 43, p. 17), German Democratic Republic (*ibid.*, pp. 20–21), Soviet Union (*ibid.*, p. 23), Italy (CDDH/I/SR. 44, pp. 28–30), Romania (*ibid.*, pp. 31–32), Yugoslavia (*ibid.*, pp. 32–33), Ukraine (*ibid.*, pp. 33–34), Syria (*ibid.*, pp. 37–38), Norway (*ibid.*, p. 44), Finland (CDDH/SR. I/45, p. 44), Philippines (*ibid.*, pp. 48–51), Egypt (*ibid.*, pp. 53–54), Poland (CDDH/I/SR. 46, p. 56), Jordan (*ibid.*, p. 57), Mexico (*ibid.*, p. 57). Cf. also Netherlands (CDDH/I/SR. 45, p. 47) and Switzerland (*ibid.*, p. 53).

[76] U.S. (CDDH/I/SR. 43, p. 19).

[77] U.K. (CDDH/I/SR. 43, pp. 24–25).

States belonging to the other group answered these arguments. To the contention that combat rules of the Protocol did not offer sufficiently precise standards for combatants some of these States replied that it was possible to specify the nature of the prohibited acts in appropriate texts.[78] As to the argument concerning the difficulty of producing proof of the breaches committed on the battlefield or at some remove from the armies concerned, a State replied that:

That argument, if accepted, would result in totally excluding battlefield crimes from the category of breaches of the Protocol. It was difficult to think that anyone would wish to go that far if only because those violations were already crimes under customary international law. The same problems of proof would arise if the aim was to make them simple breaches of the Protocol. That being so, he could not see why such violations should not fall under the category of 'grave breaches'. Some of the penal provisions relating to grave breaches might even facilitate the search for evidence. Article 79 relating to mutual assistance in criminal matters was a case in point.[79]

It was further pointed out against the thesis of the other group of States that only wrongful acts committed against persons in the hands of the enemy should be regarded as grave breaches that:

it had to be recognized that violations committed against persons in the power of the enemy such as the maltreatment of prisoners of war or civilians in occupied territory were much easier to conceal than air attacks against civilian objectives for instance.[80]

The outcome of the discussions was the elaboration, in a Working Group, of a text which to some extent took account of the views of those who advocated the broadening of the category of 'grave breaches'. Thus, the violation of various provisions relating to combat situations was included among 'grave breaches'.[81] The

[78] The representative of Egypt, speaking of the argument whereby 'many of the prohibitions in Parts III and IV were loosely formulated—their violations could not be sufficiently defined to entail personal criminal responsibility for their perpetrators, according to the fundamental principle *nulla poena sine lege*' pointed out 'that objection raised a technical question of drafting, which could be taken into consideration in the Drafting Committee, but it could not place an obstacle in the way of the sanctioning of some of the most serious violations of Protocol I' (CDDH/I/SR. 45, p. 54).

[79] Statement of the representative of Italy (CDDH/I/SR. 44, p. 29).

[80] Statement of the representative of Egypt (CDDH/I/SR. 45, p. 54).

[81] Paras 3 and 4 of Art. 85 provide as follows:

3. In addition to the grave breaches defined in Article 11, the following acts shall be regarded as grave breaches of this Protocol, when committed wilfully, in violation of the relevant provisions of this Protocol, and causing death or serious injury to body or health:

(*a*) making the civilian population or individual civilians the object of attack;

(*b*) launching an indiscriminate attack affecting the civilian population or civilian objects in the knowledge that such attack will cause excessive loss of life, injury to civilians or damage to civilian objects, as defined in Article 57, para. 2 (*a*) (iii);

(*c*) launching an attack against works or installations containing dangerous forces in the knowledge that such attack will cause excessive loss of life, injury to civilians or damage to civilian objects, as defined in Article 57, para. 2 (*a*) (iii);

(*d*) making non-defended localities and demilitarized zones the object of attack;

(*e*) making a person the object of attack in the knowledge that he is *hors de combat;*

text agreed upon, however, did not go so far as to regard as a grave breach violations of rules prohibiting the use of *means* of warfare.[82]

At a later stage[83] and subsequently in plenary, the Philippine delegation tabled an amendment (CDDH/418) in which it was proposed to consider as a 'grave breach' of the Protocol:

the use of weapons prohibited by international conventions, namely: bullets which expand or flatten easily in the human body; asphyxiating, poisonous or other gases, and all analogous liquids, materials or devices; and of bacteriological methods of warfare.[84]

> (*f*) the perfidious use, in violation of Article 37, of the distinctive emblem of the red cross, red crescent or red lion and sun or of other protective signs recognized by the Conventions or this Protocol.
> 4. In addition to the grave breaches defined in the preceding paragraphs and in the Conventions, the following shall be regarded as grave breaches of this Protocol, when committed wilfully and in violation of the Conventions or the Protocol:
> > (*a*) the transfer by the occupying Power of parts of its own civilian population into the territory it occupies, or the deportation or transfer of all or parts of the population of the occupied territory within or outside this territory, in violation of Article 49 of the Fourth Convention;
> > (*b*) unjustifiable delay in the repatriation of prisoners of war or civilians;
> > (*c*) practices of *apartheid* and other inhuman and degrading practices involving outrages upon personal dignity, based on racial discrimination;
> > (*d*) making the clearly-recognized historic monuments, works of art or places of worship which constitute the cultural or spiritual heritage of peoples and to which special protection has been given by special arrangement, for example, within the framework of a competent international organization, the object of attack, causing as a result extensive destruction thereof, where there is no evidence of the violation by the adverse Party of Article 53, sub-para. (*b*), and when such historic monuments, works of art and places of worship are not located in the immediate proximity of military objectives;
> > (*e*) depriving a person protected by the Conventions or referred to in para. 2 of this Article of the rights of fair and regular trial.

[82] Actually, under Art. 85 para. 3 (*b*), the use of a means of combat cannot amount to a grave breach *per se* but only insofar as such use amounts to an 'indiscriminate attack'. See to this effect the statement made by the representative of Egypt after the adoption of Art. 74 (the present Art. 85). He said that, although the Philippine amendment had been rejected 'the effects of using prohibited weapons came within the scope of the Article as adopted. In that respect, he associated his delegation with the comments of the Greek representative' (CDDH/SR.44, p. 21). For the statement of the Greek delegate see *ibid.,* p. 15.

[83] In 1976 the Philippines had submitted to Committee I, in a slightly different form, the amendment referred to above (CDDH/I/SR. 60, p. 258). This amendment, submitted orally, proposed to consider as 'grave breaches' 'the use of weapons prohibited by the law of war, such as asphyxiating, poisonous or other gases and analogous liquids, materials or devices, bullets which expand or flatten easily in the human body, and those weapons that violate the traditional principles of international law and humanitarian rules, such as biological weapons, blast and fragmentation weapons'. After a full discussion it was suggested that no decision should be taken on this proposal at the 1976 session, 'it being understood that the question of including in Protocol I a provision for the treatment of such violations as grave breaches could be taken up at the Fourth Session. With this understanding the proposal was not pressed to a vote' at the Third session (CDDH/234/Rev. 1, p. 16, para. 71).

[84] Introducing his proposal, the representative of the Philippines said that 'its purpose was to reaffirm and restore faith in the principles of humanitarian law and to give new force to the Hague Declaration of 1899 and the Geneva Protocol of 1925 by providing some recourse in the event of their violation. Most of the countries represented at the Conference had ratified the Declaration and Protocol. Furthermore, the Conference had recently adopted Article 33 of Protocol I,

As it is apparent from its wording, this amendment did not consider as 'grave breaches' the violations of the Protocol's provisions on weapons, but any violation of prohibitions or restrictions laid down in *other* rules of international law (practically, treaty provisions turned into rules of customary law). It was therefore designed to set a very important link between the Geneva system for the criminal repression of 'grave breaches' and the pre-existing law of warfare. Having said this, it must be added that the Philippine amendment was undoubtedly far from perfect. It could have been greatly improved by a joint effort of delegates willing to arrive at a real progress. Regretfully, opposing positions hardened and an unbridgeable gulf manifested itself. On the one side, Western and—surprisingly—socialist countries lined up to decidedly oppose the amendment, arguing that it was too imprecise, vague and ambiguous;[85] it could therefore 'give rise to differing interpretations. The result might be that innocent people would be persecuted'.[86] On the contrary side, Afro-Asian States, together with some Western countries firmly held that the amendment was the logical consequence of other provisions of the Protocol and 'a perfectly reasonable text'.[87] When a vote was taken, it

laying down basic rules on the methods and means of warfare, which in para. 2 prohibited the use of weapons, projectiles and materials and methods of a nature to cause superfluous injury or unnecessary suffering. It was thus difficult to understand the attitude of those delegations which at earlier stages had resolutely opposed the Philippine proposal.

The Conference's main objective had always been to ensure that, if war could not be avoided, the suffering it caused should be reduced to the minimum. All intolerable forms of cruelty had frequently been denounced. The *Ad Hoc* Committee, however, had not adopted any of the many proposals aimed at prohibiting or restricting certain weapons, and the only provisions approved on the matter were those in Article 33. The Philippine proposal was therefore designed to fill that gap. Para. 3 of Article 74, made various acts against the civilian population grave breaches of Protocol I, while para. 4 did the same for such acts as attacks on historic monuments. Surely, by the same token, some protection was needed for the fighting soldier too?

He appealed to all who opposed the proposal to adopt a realistic and objective attitude and to be guided by the dictates of justice and conscience. Even if the delegations concerned were to concede that the use of the weapons prohibited under the Hague Declaration of 1899 and the Geneva Protocol of 1925 constituted a grave breach, their countries would still have at their disposal stockpiles of more sophisticated and lethal weapons, which were not prohibited or restricted under any international agreement.

If the Conference sincerely wished to reaffirm and develop humanitarian law, political considerations should be set aside in favour of an impartial rule, for true humanitarianism did not countenance double standards' (CDDH/SR. 44, pp. 2–3).

[85] See the statements of the representatives of the U.S. (CDDH/SR. 44, pp. 3–4), of the Soviet Union (*ibid.,* pp. 4–5), of the German Democratic Republic (*ibid.,* p. 5), of the U.K. (*ibid.,* pp. 6–7), of Italy (*ibid.,* p. 9), of Finland (*ibid.,* pp. 10–11), of Cuba (*ibid.,* p. 14).

[86] Statement of the delegate of the Soviet Union (CDDH/SR. 44, p. 4).

[87] This was said by the representative of Syria (CDDH/SR. 44, p. 8). Other delegations favorable to the Philippine amendment were: Mexico (*ibid.,* p. 3), Switzerland (*ibid.,* p. 4), Pakistan (*ibid.,* p. 5), the Holy See (*ibid.,* p. 6), Iraq (*ibid.,* pp. 7–8), Algeria (*ibid.,* p. 11). The delegate of Pakistan made the following comments on the view that the Philippine amendment lacked clarity and precision: 'It had been said that the word "easily" was not sufficiently precise. But one might also ask what exactly was to be understood by "indiscriminate" and "non-defended localities" in paras 3 (b) and (c) of Article 74. Words could be understood or misunderstood at will; if the intention was to misunderstand them, any legal provision, no matter how sacrosanct, could be subverted.

turned out that the majority of States did not support the amendment: the result of the vote was 41 in favour, 25 against, with 25 abstentions.[88] The amendment was rejected, for it had failed to obtain the necessary two-thirds majority.

Although the Protocol as presently drafted to some extent covers—albeit indirectly—the use of at least one category of prohibited weapons (the use of *indiscriminate* weapons can be considered a 'grave breach' in so far as such use amounts to an 'indiscriminate attack') the fate of the Philippine amendment shows that States are not yet ready to draw the logical consequences which should follow from the existing prohibitions or restrictions on the use of weapons. This demonstrates that the international law of warfare still finds itself in a stage where the prohibitions or restrictions in question are not fully operative.

E. The Failure to Extend General Principles to Non-International Armed Conflicts

The text of the Draft Protocol proposed by the ICRC (Protocol II) contained several provisions extending the application of general principles on the use of weapons to civil strife: Art. 20, on the 'prohibition of unnecessary injury', and Art. 26 para. 3, on indiscriminate means of combat.[89]

The time had come for the Conference to decide once and for all whether it wished to save mankind from the cruelties inflicted in time of war. As stated in the explanatory note to the amendment (CDDH/418), the aim was simply to reaffirm the Hague Declaration of 1899 and the Geneva Protocol of 1925. It was therefore regrettable that those who opposed the amendment should claim to be acting in the name of principle. If the amendment were not included in the Protocol, the Conference would have failed to take a decisive step at a turning point in the affairs of mankind' (CDDH/SR. 44, p. 5).

[88] CDDH/SR. 44, p. 13.

[89] Art. 20 was worded as follows:

1. The right of parties to the conflict and of members of their forces to adopt methods and means of combat is not unlimited.
2. It is forbidden to employ weapons, projectiles, substances, methods and means which uselessly aggravate the sufferings of disabled adversaries or render their death inevitable in all circumstances.

Art. 26, para. 3, stated:

The employment of means of combat, and any methods which strike or affect indiscriminately the civilian population and combatants, or civilian objects and military objectives, are prohibited. In particular it is forbidden:

(a) to attack without distinction, as one single objective, by bombarment or any other method, a zone containing several military objectives, which are situated in populated areas and are at some distance from each other;

(b) to launch attacks which may be expected to entail incidental losses among the civilian population and cause the destruction of civilian objects to an extent disproportionate to the direct and substantial military advantage anticipated.

Two States (Finland and Brazil) submitted amendments primarily aimed at a technical improvement of those provisions (CDDH/III/91 and CDDH/III/215, respectively). The German Democratic Republic, on its part, proposed an amendment (CDDH/III/87) that would greatly expand the scope of the Article, by adding three prohibitions: 1) of 'other particularly cruel means and methods' of warfare; 2) of indiscriminate weapons; and 3) of means of war that 'destroy

The importance of these provisions should not be underestimated. The only treaty rules concerning civil strife at present in force, namely Article 3 common to the four 1949 Geneva Conventions, do not cover the behaviour of combatants. This matter is only governed by a few rules of customary international law which evolved during the Spanish Civil War (1936–1939).[90] Such rules, however, are mainly concerned with the protection of civilians, and do not affect *directly* the use of means of warfare. If the two aforementioned provisions proposed by the ICRC had been adopted by the Diplomatic Conference, for the first time treaty rules would have covered an area of civil strife which so far has not been directly governed by international law. However vague and general these rules may be, their extension to internal armed conflicts would no doubt have constituted a step forward, in this area.

Yet, as is well known, Protocol II suffered a very strange fate. Most of the provisions proposed by the ICRC, including those on combat, were adopted in Committee, but were subsequently deleted, either in the 'simplified draft' worked out by Judge Hussain of Pakistan (CDDH/427),[91] or in plenary.

Art. 20, in a version slightly different from that proposed by the ICRC, was adopted by consensus on 4 June 1976 by Committee III.[92] It was deleted, by 25 votes to 19, with 33 abstentions, in plenary on 3 June 1977.[93] It is apparent from the debates that to most States that provision constituted an unwarranted restriction on State sovereignty and, consequently, an undue extension to internal conflicts of rules governing the conduct of international armed conflicts. There was, however, also some confusion about the real value and meaning of that provision, as is proved by the following declaration that the delegation of Saudi Arabia considered fit to put on record after the rejection of the Article:

Article 20 . . . was rejected in a vote. I should like to show that our attitude was natural, since the legitimate party to an internal conflict is the *de jure* State. Obviously it will never try to exterminate its nationals or to damage its environment. We therefore considered that the article was merely a repetition in contradiction with Protocol II.

---

natural human environmental conditions'. This amendment was strongly supported by the Soviet Union (CDDH/III/SR. 32, p. 6).

[90] May I refer to my paper 'The Spanish Civil War and the Development of Customary Law Concerning International Armed Conflicts', in CASSESE (ed.), *Current Problems of International Law* 1975, 298ff. Also published in this volume.

[91] See on the 'Hussain draft' the paper by A. Eide on 'The New Humanitarian Law in Non-International Armed Conflicts', in A. Cassese (ed.), The New Humanitarian Law of Armed Conflict (Napoli: Editoriale Scientifica, 1979) 277.

[92] CDDH/III/SR. 49, p. 107.
Art. 20 read as follows:
1. In any armed conflict to which this Protocol applies, the right of the parties to the conflict to choose methods or means of combat is not unlimited.
2. It is forbidden to employ weapons, projectiles, and material and methods of combat of a nature to cause superfluous injury or unnecessary suffering (CDDH/236/Rev. 1).

[93] CDDH/SR. 51, p. 10.

It should be taken into consideration that Islamic legislation is generally opposed to war as such. In Islamic society war is always defensive, merciful and humanitarian. Its sole aim is to repel aggressors without exposing either civilians, cultural objects or the environment to danger. This is a well-known aspect of Islamic history. This text therefore has no place in Protocol II.[94]

The Conference, at the Committee stage, had also adopted Art. 26, para. 3, on indiscriminate means of combat.[95] This provision had been approved by 44 votes to none, with 22 abstentions, on 4 April 1975.[96] It was deleted by consensus, in plenary, on 6 June 1977.[97] No delegation considered it opportune either to raise its voice against this serious mutilation of Protocol II, or to endeavour to give a justification of this further erosion of the Protocol.

At the Committee stage the Conference had even gone farther than the ICRC Draft Protocol. On 10 April 1975, it had adopted in Committee III, by 49 votes to 4, with 7 abstentions, an important provision (Art. 28 *bis*) on the protection of the natural environment, which *inter alia* prohibited means of combat which cause damage to the natural environment.[98] This provision was luckily spared the misfortune of being rejected in plenary: it was dropped, beforehand from the 'Hussain draft', and thus disappeared without even troubling the plenary.

The reasons for this major setback are not difficult to discover. As early as 1974, the Canadian delegation had insisted on the need to eliminate from Protocol II 'all wording which fell under the laws of war'.[99] Canada contended in general that 'rules based on moral principles would be unworkable' and should be omitted 'to avoid the danger of adopting a code which could not be respected'.[100] With particular reference to combat rules, Canada pointed out that in civil strife, the governmental forces could not but use means of combat which could prove indiscriminate, or in any event affect civilians along with rebels. The very nature of combat in civil wars (street battles, armed actions against rebels hiding among civilians, etc.) would render it difficult for the Government to avoid using indiscriminate means

[94] CDDH/SR. 51, Annex, p. 1.
See, however, the explanation of vote of two States which had voted in favour of Art. 20: Ireland (*ibid.*, p. 2) and Portugal (*ibid.*, p. 4).
[95] It read as follows:
'The employment of means of combat, and any methods which strike or affect indiscriminately the civilian population and combatants, or civilian objects and military objectives are prohibited.
An attack by bombardment by any methods or means which treats as a single military objective a number of clearly separate and distinct military objectives located in a city, town, village or other area containing a concentration of civilians or civilian objects is to be considered as indiscriminate.'
[96] CDDH/III/SR. 37, p. 297.
[97] CDDH/SR. 47–59.
[98] CDDH/III/SR. 38, p. 314.
Art. 28 *bis* read as follows:
It is forbidden to emply methods or means of combat which are intended or may be expected to cause widespread, long-term and severe damage to the natural environment.
[99] CDDH/III/SR. 4, p. 32, para. 71.
[100] CDDH/III/SR. 9, pp. 70–71, paras 11–13.

or methods of combat. Rebels, on their part, would be likely to resort to actions against civilians siding with the Government. Hence, it would prove illusory to enact prohibitions that none of the parties would have complied with.[101] This view did not gain much support at the Committee stage: actually, as I have said above, the majority of States gathered at Geneva took a contrary view. In 1977, however, the opposition to Draft Protocol II gained momentum, because of the increasing fear that this Protocol could pave the way to unwarranted interference in internal affairs of States. The head of the Pakistan delegation, Mr. Hussain, became the most strenuous spokesman of the growing number of opponents to the Protocol. In submitting his simplified draft to the plenary, in 1977, he pointed out that most States were dissatisfied with the 'length' of the text adopted in Committee 'as well as with the fact that it ventured into domains which they considered sacrosanct and inappropriate for inclusion in an international instrument'.[102] He then presented his 'simplified draft' pointing out that:

It was based on the following theses: its provisions must be acceptable to all and therefore of obvious practical benefit; the provisions must be within the perceived capacity of those involved to apply them and, therefore, precise and simple; they should not appear to affect the sovereignty of any State Party or the responsibility of its Government to maintain law and order and defend national unity, nor be able to be invoked to justify any outside intervention; nothing in the Protocol should suggest that dissidents must be treated legally other than as rebels; and, lastly, there should be no automatic repetition of the more comprehensive provisions, such as those on civil defence, found in Protocol I.[103]

It goes without saying that the provisions on means of combat were among those which turned out to be at odds with the criteria that the Protocol should meet in the view of the delegate of Pakistan and of the growing majority behind him. They were therefore among the first provisions to fall beneath the guillotine.

The deletion of these provisions contributes, in my view, to rendering Protocol II as something of a 'legal ectoplasm'—to use the strong words of the representative of the Holy See.[104] This label may appear excessive. The fact remains, however, that the dismantling in plenary of Protocol II actually deprived it of those very rules which are more urgently needed in civil wars—including the rules which

---

[101] Cf. the remarks by A. Eide in the paper on 'The New Humanitarian Law in Non-International Armed Conflict', cit., para. 4 *b*.

[102] CDDH/SR. 49, p. 4.

[103] CDDH/SR. 49, pp. 4–5.

[104] In plenary, in opposing the attempt at deleting Art. 27 (protection of objects indispensable to the survival of the civilian population), the representative of the Holy See said *inter alia*:

'When the Conference had decided to delete any reference to "Parties to the conflict" in Protocol II, it had, as it were, abandoned attempts to draft a real legal instrument and instead had restricted itself to a statement of good intentions which in terms of humanitarian law came down to a "legal ectoplasm", for the text would be devoid of any real humanitarian substance and of any mandatory character. Yet, its creators were daring to claim that it would serve to control internal conflicts, a euphemism for civil wars which, as everybody was aware, were the cruellest and most pitiless of all conflicts' (CDDH/SR. 52, p. 17).

aim at restricting the use of armed violence against combatants, and at imposing that armed force not be used against civilians.

3. Concluding Remarks

The present international law on means of warfare no doubt greatly benefits *major powers*. It includes only a few general principles, which are so vague that they have little value as a yardstick for the assessment of the conduct of belligerents. In addition, the limited number of specific bans at present in force only covers minor weapons, or arms (such as bacteriological weapons) which were prohibited mainly because they could also affect the belligerent using them. Instead, really important weapons such as nuclear bombs or new conventional weapons do not fall—in the opinion of most States—under any prohibitory rule of international law.

Can it be argued that the tendency of favouring, in this area of the laws of war, major powers, is in the process of being reversed? Small and medium-sized States are no doubt stronger now than before, if only because they are very vocal in international gatherings and passionately advocate new and more sweeping bans. They are, however, aware that any new treaty in this area would be pointless if it were not endorsed by major military powers. These powers, on their part, still resist any major limitation on their military strength. It will be useful to recall what was tellingly stated in 1973 by the head of the U.S. delegation to the Geneva Conference, Mr. Aldrich: 'States which rely more on massed manpower for military strength than on firepower and mobility would be likely to see security advantages in prohibiting many weapons'. However, 'many governments— and particularly those of the technologically most advanced States—hesitate to submit questions of fundamental importance to their national security to negotiations designed to supplement and improve the 1949 Red Cross Conventions'.[105] Faced with this opposition, small and medium-sized States are necessarily compelled to narrow the range of their demands. In addition, all those States which are dependent for their military security on arms supplied by great powers are not eager to see possible bans imposed on those very arms they need for their self-preservation. Furthermore, some Third World countries consider that new prohibitions or restrictions on the use of means of combat would only play into the hands of major powers, for a number of reasons.[106]

---

[105] Statement made by Mr. G.H. Aldrich in the U.S. House of Representatives: see *Hearings before the Subcommittee on International Organizations and Movements of the Committee on Foreign Affairs,* House of Representatives, Ninety-third Congress, First Session, Washington 1974, at 99.

[106] It is worth citing in this respect the statement made at Geneva, in 1977, by the representative of the Socialist Republic of Vietnam. After the adoption of the Resolution on weapons (see *above*, note 65), he said the following:

He considered it pointless to contemplate prohibiting or restricting the use of certain conventional weapons. In practice, the technical criteria were not such as could be verified on the battlefield, and as emerged clearly from the report of the conferences of Lucerne and Lugano, the

It is against this general background that the achievements and failures of the Geneva Conference can be rightly assessed. Undoubtedly, it is very significant that a large group of States (mainly consisting of small and medium-sized countries) have chosen the right approach for making international wars less inhumane. In short, they have realized that the battle, as it were, must be fought on several fronts: what is needed is both to restate and develop general prohibitory rules and to enact new bans concerning specific weapons; by the same token, it is necessary to set up supervisory machinery to ensure that such bans are not evaded and furthermore to extend the bans to internal armed conflicts, to take account of the fact that these conflicts are more and more widespread in international society.

While this mere fact is in itself very positive (it represents a significant precedent and a good starting-point), it cannot be gainsaid that, all in all, the results of the Geneva Conference in the area of means of combat are disappointing. To be sure, the restatement of general principles and their development and supplementation referred to above (2.B), are indisputable improvements on the existing law. The balance is, however, offset by the failure to enact specific bans or restrictions on the use of certain conventional weapons, by the failure to extend the system for penal repression set up by the 1949 Geneva Conventions to violations of existing prohibitions or restrictions on the use of weapons (see above 2.D), and by the failure to extend combat rules to non-international armed conflicts (see *supra* 2.E).

In view of this disquieting evaluation, one cannot but express the hope that the Conference of Governments to be held in 1979 under the auspices of the United Nations may prove capable of achieving better results.

---

experts themselves had failed to agree either in the laboratory or round the conference table. On the other hand standard criteria such as superfluous injury and the absence of discrimination were both more readily accessible to the public at large, and more effective, as had been shown by the world-wide outburst of indignation which had stigmatized the use of criminal weapons in Vietnam. The mobilization of world opinion had proved its worth by staying the hand of the aggressor.

There were several drawbacks to the prohibition and restriction of the use of certain weapons. In the first place, an aggressor who unleashed a neocolonial war—and such conflicts were those which were the most likely to occur in the future—would not lay himself open to reprisals and would elude all forms of control, especially as no check was possible on the battlefield; on the contrary, such controls would be a constraint on the Party which was on the defensive—always the weaker, the less well-armed and, essentially, the most inclined to obey the law. Then again, prohibition and restriction would give the impression that only weapons which were listed were dangerous, whereas in fact an aggressor would have at his disposal authorized means of combat and industrial equipment, such as bulldozers, capable of producing effects no less dangerous and no less cruel (CDDH/SR. 57, pp. 21–22).

D. Military Occupation

11. Powers and Duties of an Occupant in Relation to Land and Natural Resources*

1. Introduction

Before considering the subject of this chapter, it may prove useful briefly to touch on a preliminary issue: what legal rules govern a military occupation such as that of Israel over the Arab territories invaded in 1967?

It has been contended by a distinguished scholar,[1] and was also suggested in an official Israeli document,[2] that the long duration of that occupation makes it quite unique; as a consequence, not all the legal constraints concerning 'normal' belligerent occupation could apply in the case of the Israeli 'administration' of the Arab territories.

This view has already been authoritatively criticized by von Glahn.[3] I see two basic objections to it. First, it fails to specify which of the customary and conventional rules on belligerent occupation should be set aside, and which should continue to apply to the Israeli occupation. It is plain that in a matter so delicate and controversial as the one with which we are here concerned, one cannot rest content with vague and loose suggestions.

Second, it is true that the existing body of law proceeds from the assumption that belligerent occupation is, or should be, of short duration. But in order to establish whether instances of prolonged occupation are governed by different rules from the traditional ones, one should inquire into whether new rules have evolved through the traditional law-making processes of international law: custom and treaty. Can we argue that *new rules* of customary or treaty law have recently emerged for the specific purpose of regulating prolonged military occupations? As is apparent from the attitude of all states *vis-à-vis* the Israeli occupation

---

* Originally published in E. Playfair (ed.), *International Law and the Administration of Occupied Territories* (Oxford: Clarendon Press, 1992) 419.

[1] Y.Z. Blum, quoted in S.V. Mallison and W.T. Mallison Jr., *The Palestine Problem in International Law and World Order* (Harlow, 1986), 260.

[2] Memorandum of Law, in *ILM* 17 (1978), 432–3.

[3] See Ch. 11 E. Playfair (ed.), cit. and also Chs 1 and 7.

of the Arab territories, states have consistently taken the view that customary law as embodied in the 1907 Hague Regulations, as well as the Fourth Geneva Convention of 1949, apply to that situation. Attempts by Israel to propound the idea that her occupation does not fit into those rules have been firmly and consistently rejected by states as well as by the United Nations. In these circumstances it was impossible for new customary rules to evolve in the matter: unilateral statements by one state are not sufficient to form a customary rule.

It follows that, however unique and new its features may be, the Israeli occupation remains subject to the body of law to which I have just made reference. On the other hand, I shall show, in part 4, that it is possible to make allowance for the novelty of the Israeli occupation, without departing from the legal framework offered by traditional international law. This 'adjustment', as I shall show, can be made on the strength of an 'evolutive' interpretation of the existing rules. (By an 'evolutive' interpretation I mean a dynamic one, which takes account of the changing context in which the rules operate).

2. General Principles Governing Belligerent Occupation

Before examining the legal principles governing the use of natural resources in occupied territories, it is fitting to point to the general context in which they must be viewed, that is, the general principles governing belligerent occupation. The latter principles ought always to be borne in mind when considering specific problems. In many instances they may prove of great help in reaching the right solution.

Belligerent occupation, as is well known, is based on four fundamental principles. First, the occupant does not acquire any sovereignty over the territory; it merely exercises *de facto* authority. Second, occupation is by definition a provisional situation. The rights of the occupant over the territory are merely transitory and are accompanied by an overriding obligation to respect the existing laws and rules of administration. Third, in exercising its powers, the occupant must comply with two basic requirements or parameters: fulfilment of its military needs, and respect for the interests of the inhabitants. International rules strike a careful balance between these two (often conflicting) requirements: while military necessities in some instances may gain the upper hand, they should never result in total disregard for the interests and needs of the population. Fourth, the occupying Power must not exercise its authority in order to further its own interests, or to meet the needs of its own population. In no case can it exploit the inhabitants, the resources or other assets of the territory under its control for the benefit of its own territory or population. Linked with this is the principle that the occupying Power cannot force the occupied territory—both its inhabitants and its resources—to contribute to, or in any way assist, the occupant's war effort against the displaced government and its allies.

3. Principles Governing the Use of Land and Other Natural Resources in Occupied Territories

Customary rules governing the powers and duties of the occupant in the field of economic activities are fairly simple. The occupant must respect *private property.* Thus, Article 46(2) of the Hague Regulations provides that 'private property may not be confiscated'. This is, however, subject to Article 53(2), whereby all kinds of privately-owned war materials may be seized, 'but must be restored at the conclusion of peace, and indemnities must be paid for them'. Private property may only be requisitioned 'for the needs of the army of occupation', upon payment in cash or the provision of a receipt, with payment as soon as possible (Article 52). Alternatively, private property may be expropriated in the public interest of the whole of the inhabitants of the occupied territory (ex. Article 46). The property of local authorities, as well as that of institutions dedicated to public worship, charity, education, science, and art, is assimilated to private property (Article 56(1)). As for *public property,* that is, assets belonging to the state, the occupant can seize movables 'which may be used for military purposes' (Article 53), whereas it can only use immovables as 'administrator and usufructuary' (Article 55: it can benefit from the use of these assets, but 'must safeguard the capital').

Two general remarks are called for. First, as has been noted by a few authorities,[4] and also stressed by the Supreme Court of Israel in a judgment in 1984,[5] this legal regulation reflects the approach to economic organization prevailing in the nineteenth century. Private property was sacred. As was pointed out in 1921 by the US Arbitrator W.D. Hines in the *Cession of vessels and tugs for navigation on the Danube* case: '[T]he purpose of the immunity of private property from confiscation is to avoid throwing the burdens of war upon private individuals, and is, instead, to place those burdens upon the States which are the belligerents'.[6] On the other hand, since, in that period, state involvement in economic activity was still limited, no account was taken of possible forms of state intervention in the economic sphere (which have become so widespread and multifarious this century).

My second remark relates to the limits within which the occupying Power can exercise the rights and fulfil the duties deriving from customary law. In my view it follows from the provisions of the Hague Regulations referred to above that the occupant can interfere in the economic activity of the territory under its control (by requisitioning private property, seizing public movables, or using state-owned immovables) only for the following purposes: (*a*) to meet its own military

---

[4] E. Feilchenfeld, *The International Economic Law of Belligerent Occupation* (Washington DC, 1942), 87; J. Stone, *Legal Controls of International Conflict* (New York, 1959), 729.

[5] HC 393/82, *A Teachers' Housing Cooperative Society v. The Military Commander of the Judea and Samaria Region et al.,* excerpted in *IYHR* 14 (1984), 301, esp. 306–7.

[6] *UN Reports of International Arbitral Awards,* 1, 107.

or security needs (i.e. the exigencies posed by the conduct of its military operations in the occupied territory); (*b*) to defray the expenses involved in the belligerent occupation; (*c*) to protect the interests and the well-being of the inhabitants.

These are indeed very strict limitations upon the powers of the occupant. Any interference with enemy private or state-owned property must be effected for one of these purposes. It is strictly forbidden for the occupant to resort to one of the aforementioned measures for other purposes, e.g. with a view to drawing economic benefits for himself (that is, for his inhabitants, or for the national economy, etc.).

The above view is borne out by recent state practice, which tends to uphold a *strict* approach to the rights of belligerent occupants. The opposition of the British Government to the projected building by Israel of a canal between the Mediterranean and the Dead Sea illustrates this kind of approach and provides support for a number of the limitations noted above. On 18 November 1981, replying in writing to a question in the House of Commons, the British Minister of State, Foreign and Commonwealth Office, stated that:

[T]he project as planned is contrary to international law, as it involves unlawful works in occupied territory and infringes Jordan's legal rights in the Dead Sea and neighbouring regions. No official support will be given by Her Majesty's Government in respect of the project.[7]

On 4 December 1981, in the UN General Assembly, the British representative, speaking also on behalf of the European Community, restated the opposition to the Israeli project, because, among other things,

the plan as announced by the Israeli Government would involve construction work across the Gaza Strip. The [at the time] Ten consider that under general international law, and with reference to the Fourth Geneva Convention, *such construction and alteration of property would exceed Israel's right as an occupying power.* Under international law an occupant exercises only a temporary right of administration in respect of territory occupied by it. *The proposed canal can in no way be considered an act of mere administration.* In addition, the Ten believe that the project as planned could serve to prejudice the future of Gaza which should be determined as part of a general peace settlement. In the circumstances the Ten wish to reiterate their opposition to the project.[8]

The canal project has, in the event, been scrapped, but the statement nevertheless shows that the (then) ten member states of the European Community adhered to the general concept that alterations to property carried out by an occupant in the territory under his control (1) must not have permanent effects and (2) must not be undertaken to the detriment of the displaced government or, at any rate, the local population.

---

[7] See *BYIL* (1981), 515.
[8] *Ibid.* 516 (emphasis added).

4. Should Traditional Customary Law on Belligerent Occupation be Construed in Light of Present Circumstances (the So-Called 'Evolutive Interpretation')?

I now wish to raise a general question, which has some impact on the specific issues addressed in this paper. I mentioned before that the Hague Regulations were drafted in a period when state intervention in the economy was minimal, whereas private property was regarded as sacred. In addition, those rules were conceived on the assumption that the belligerent occupation of foreign territories should be of short duration. It is obvious that things have greatly changed since then. State authorities have become more and more 'interventionist' in the realm of the economy; at present it is often hard to distinguish in many countries between the 'private' and 'public' sector of the economy. In addition, the financial requirements of modern occupants have increased at a staggering pace, on account of the growing demands of modern armies. This became particularly apparent during World War II. On top of all this, one may mention that one of the most conspicuous instances of modern belligerent occupation is the prolonged occupation begun by Israel in 1967.

The question therefore arises whether one should interpret the body of traditional customary rules on occupation in the light of the present circumstances surrounding belligerent occupation. This sort of interpretation has been upheld by the Supreme Court of Israel in at least two cases.[9] In the first, Judge Shamgar stated that the scope of an occupant's authority is influenced by the time factor; hence, a prolonged occupation cannot be totally governed by rules envisaging an occupation of short duration. In the second case, Judge Barak ruled that the High Court, though bound to apply the Hague Regulations, ought to consider the tasks and duties of an occupant according to the prevailing norms present among civilized countries. As he put it with reference to a specific customary rule:

[T]he concrete content that we shall give to Article 43 of the Hague Regulations in regard to the occupant's duty to ensure public life and order will not be that of public life and order in the nineteenth century, but that of a modern and civilized State at the end of the twentieth century.[10]

The same judge stated that one should also make allowance for the duration of the belligerent occupation. According to him, although the Hague Regulations were adopted against the background of a short duration occupation,

---

[9] Case HC 69/81, *Abu Aita et al. v. The Military Commander of the Judea and Samaria Region*, excerpted in *IYHR* 13 (1983), 348; HC 393/82, *A Teachers' Housing Cooperative Society v. The Military Commander of the Judea and Samaria Region et al., IYHR* 14 (1984), 301.
[10] *Ibid.* 307.

nothing prevents the development—within their framework—of rules defining the scope of a military government's authority in cases of prolonged occupation.

He drew the following specific conclusion:

Long-term fundamental investments [made by the occupant] in an occupied area [in the course of a prolonged occupation] bringing about permanent changes that may last beyond the period of the military administration are permitted if required for the benefit of the local population—provided there is nothing in these investments that might introduce an essential modification in the basic institutions of the area.[11]

I submit that both the 'evolutive' interpretation advocated by the Supreme Court of Israel, and the practical inference the Court drew from that interpretation, are correct. The following considerations are intended to support and expand them.

That in certain instances international rules should be interpreted so as to take account of current circumstances, has been pointed out by the International Court of Justice, in the advisory opinion delivered in 1971 on *Legal Consequences for States of the Continued Presence of South Africa in Namibia (South West Africa)*. The Court held that: '[A]n international instrument has to be interpreted and applied within the framework of the entire legal system prevailing at the time of the interpretation.'[12] The Court inferred from that, that the concept of 'sacred trust' embodied in Article 22 of the Covenant on the League of Nations (1919) was to be interpreted in the light of the current situation. As the Court put it:

[V]iewing the institutions of 1919, the Court must take into consideration the changes which have occurred in the supervening half-century, and its interpretation cannot remain unaffected by the subsequent development of law, through the Charter of the United Nations and by way of customary law.[13]

This principle of interpretation entails for our purposes that the relevant international rules (the Hague Regulations) can be somewhat 'adjusted' both to the present legal system and to current political and historical realities. This process of 'adjustment' should not, however, result in thwarting the underlying objectives of the rules at issue. It should rather aim at applying the rules in a flexible way, adapting their scope and purpose to the new general context in which they now operate. Two consequences follow. First, the Hague Regulations should be viewed in the light of developments in international law since 1907 (and particularly since the adoption of the UN Charter). Second, they should be so construed in the light of factual developments since 1907, particularly cases of prolonged occupation.

From the first vantage point, it is appropriate to mention an argument advanced by the US State Department in the legal memorandum concerning the

[11] *Ibid.* 310.
[12] ICJ *Reports* (1971), 31–2 (para. 53).
[13] *Ibid.*

alleged right of Israel to develop new oilfields in Sinai and the Gulf of Suez. One may recall that it was stated there that the Hague Regulations should be taken to mean that the occupant can use the economic resources of the enemy state, in particular state-owned immovables, within the limits of what is required for the army of occupation and the needs of the local population. The legal memorandum goes on to state that:

[T]hese limitations are entirely consistent with, if not compelled by, the limited purposes for which force may be used under the UN Charter. It is difficult to justify a rule that the use of force in self-defence may, during any resulting occupation, give the occupant rights against the enemy sovereign not related to the original self-defence requirement, or not required as concomitants of the occupation itself and the occupant's duties. A rule holding out the prospect of acquiring unrestricted access to the use of resources and raw materials, would constitute an incentive to territorial occupation by a country needing raw materials, and a disincentive to withdrawal.[14]

It is submitted that this view is illustrative of the right way to interpret the Hague Regulations in the light of the general legal principles currently prevailing in the world community.

Aside from the prohibition on the use of force except in self-defence referred to in the above-mentioned US legal memorandum, another recent legal development which has an important impact on the interpretation of the Hague Regulations (and particularly those provisions relating to state-owned immovable property) is the notion of 'permanent sovereignty over natural resources'.

This principle, which has been established by, *inter alia,* a series of resolutions of the United Nations,[15] as well as by the International Covenants on Human Rights adopted in 1966,[16] recognizes the universal right fully and freely to use and exploit the natural wealth and resources of one's own territory for one's own ends. This is seen as both an 'inalienable right of all States'[17] (that is, an aspect of state sovereignty), and, at the same time, an 'inherent right of all peoples'[18] (that is, an aspect of the right of peoples to self-determination).

In the context of belligerent occupation, this, of course, tends to support a restrictive interpretation of the occupant's powers to exploit and dispose of

[14] Memorandum of Law, *ILM* 16 (1977), 745–6.
[15] See, *inter alia,* GA Res. 626 (VII) of 21 Dec. 1952, Res. 1803 (XVII) of 14 Dec. 1962 (the so-called 'landmark resolution' on permanent sovereignty over natural resources), Res. 2994 (XXVII) of 15 Dec. 1972 (noting with satisfaction the Report of the UN Conference on the Human Environment, Stockholm, 5–16 July 1972, UN Doc. A/CONF.48/14; see esp. Princ. 21), Res. 3171 (XXVIII) of 17 Dec. 1973, Res. 3021 (S–VI) of 1 May 1974 ('Declaration on the Establishment of a New International Economic Order'; see esp. para. 4(e)), Res. 3281 (XXIX) of 12 December 1974 ('Charter of Economic Rights and Duties of States'; see esp. Art. 2). See also SC Res. 330 (1973) of 21 Mar. 1973.
[16] See common Art. 1(2) of the International Covenant on Economic, Social, and Cultural Rights (ICESCR) and the International Covenant on Civil and Political Rights (ICCPR), adopted by the UNGA on 16 Dec. 1966. See also Art. 25 of the first-mentioned Covenant.
[17] GA Res. 1803 (XVII) of 14 Dec. 1962 (preamble).
[18] ICESCR, Art. 25.

immovable property. Even if the occupant has reservations about the 'statehood' of its enemy, this principle should serve to restrain the occupant from exploiting resources in contravention of the rights of an alien people in occupied territory.

Customary rules should also be construed so as to take account of new practical developments. The long duration of the Israeli occupation is a fact that cannot but impinge upon the relevant rules. But what is its precise impact on those legal rules? To my mind, the right approach was suggested by Dinstein[19] and the Israeli Supreme Court[20] when they stated that the prolongation of military occupation makes it increasingly necessary to take into consideration the social and economic needs of the local population. Indeed, as a result of a drawn-out occupation, the provisional nature of the administration by a military authority tends to fade away, and the occupying force tends to turn into a fully-fledged administrative entity, without there being any of the safeguards of ordinary government (political representation, etc.). Consequently, to avoid frustrating the purpose and the spirit of the Hague Regulations, one should give pride of place to those limitations upon the powers of the occupant that are explicitly or implicitly set out in the Hague Regulations. The strengthening of these limitations is the only safeguard against the turning of the occupant (a transitory military administration) into a political and administrative government in disguise.

It is suggested that the view propounded by Dinstein and the Israeli Supreme Court should be upheld and should be applied to, *inter alia,* uses by the occupant of enemy state-owned movables or immovables. The use of locally-owned property during a prolonged occupation is obviously particularly susceptible of producing permanent—and potentially detrimental—effects.

5. The Occupant's Use of Enemy State-owned Immovable Property

The general proposition stated in part 3 above, concerning the limited purpose for which the occupant is allowed to use the resources of the territory under his control, is based on the text of a number of provisions of the Hague Regulations, including those relating to the levying of taxes and other 'money contributions' (which, under Article 49, can only be done for 'the needs of the army or of the administration of the territory') and those relating to requisitions in kind, services and contributions (which, under Article 52(1), can be demanded from local authorities or inhabitants only 'for the needs of the army of occupation').

---

[19] Y. Dinstein, quoted in *IYHR* 14 (1984), 307, and also his article, The International Law of Belligerent Occupation and Human Rights', *IYHR* 8 (1978), 112.
[20] See HC 337/71 The *Christian Society for the Holy Places* case, *ibid.* 112, and HC 393/82, *Teachers' Housing Cooperative Society* case, *IYHR* 14 (1984), 307–9; and see also discussion of both cases in Chs 1, 2 and 6, in E.Playfair (ed.), cit.

That proposition also follows from the provisions relating to movable property belonging to the enemy state, although it must be acknowledged that the matter is not without controversy. A number of learned commentators (including Dinstein)[21] take the view that the expression 'which may be used for military operations' in Article 53(1), refers to all goods susceptible of military use; the actual use to which the occupant puts them is seen as immaterial and may be non-military. To put it differently, according to those commentators the proviso '[movable property] which may be used for military operations' is only intended to identify the class of property of which the occupying army can take possession (the army is allowed to seize only property susceptible of use for military operations). The expression at issue is not intended—so they argue—to demand that the occupant should actually use that property solely for military operations. However, reading Article 53 in the context of the other provisions to which reference has already been made, it seems clear to me that such *potential* military use is not sufficient to justify a taking under that Article.

The principal provision relating to the power of the occupant to exploit the resources of the occupied territory is Article 55 (concerning 'immovable property belonging to the hostile State'). This contains no such explicit reference to purpose. Should one infer from this omission that, acting as the 'usufructuary' of those assets, the occupant is allowed to use the fruits of all state-owned immovable property *for any purpose whatsoever,* provided only that it does not want only to dissipate them? In particular, should one infer that the occupant is allowed to sell those 'fruits' with a view to boosting the home economy, or even to transfer them to the national territory of the occupying state? This is precisely the view taken by a few distinguished scholars (von Glahn, McDougal and Feliciano, Gerson, Dinstein)[22] as well as by the Israeli authorities.[23] Other scholars (for example, Oppenheim–Lauterpacht and Greenspan) merely state[24] that the produce of public immovables belonging to the enemy state may be appropriated by the occupant, without adding any restriction as to purpose. However, the fact that those authors point out that the occupant, being only a 'usufructuary', 'is prohibited from exercising his right in a wasteful or negligent way so as to decrease the value of the stock and plant'[25] indicates that, in their view, no other restriction is imposed on the use of the 'fruits' of the immovables at issue.

This view is clearly based on a *textual* or *literal* interpretation of Article 55. Admittedly, such an interpretation may have been appropriate at the time the

---

[21] Dinstein, 'The International Law of Belligerent Occupation', 131.

[22] G. Von Glahn, *The Occupation of Enemy Territory* (Minneapolis, 1957), 177; M. McDougal and F.P. Feliciano, *Law and Minimum World Public Order* (New Haven, Conn., 1961), 812–13; A. Gerson, 'Off-shore Oil Exploration by a Belligerent Occupant—the Gulf of Suez Dispute', *AJIL* 71 (1977), 730–1; Dinstein, 'The International Law of Belligerent Occupation', 129–30.

[23] Memorandum of Law, in *ILM* 17 (1978), 432–3.

[24] L. Oppenheim, *International Law: A Treatise,* ii: *Disputes, War and Neutrality,* ed. H. Lauterpacht, 398; M. Greenspan, *The Modern Law of Land Warfare* (Berkeley, 1959), 288.

[25] Oppenheim, *International Law,* 398.

Hague Regulations were drafted, in spite of what today can turn out to be an inconsistency with other provisions of the same Regulations. Indeed, the textual or literal interpretation of Article 55 can appear illogical if one considers that this interpretation leads to *greater* limitations being imposed on the use of that class of property (movables) which the occupant can go as far as to appropriate, than are imposed on the use of that class of property (immovables) which the occupant can only administer as 'usufructuary'. Why demand that a certain use be made of assets of which the occupant can take possession, while leaving that occupant free to do whatever he pleases with respect to property over which he holds only limited rights? This illogicality probably stems from the historical origin of the provisions at issue. It should be borne in mind that, when the provision under consideration was drafted (and indeed Article 55 takes up Article 7 of the Brussels Declaration of 1874), immovable property owned by states was of limited relevance compared to state-owned movables; in particular, state-owned factories were almost non-existent. In short, at that stage seizure of movables was far more important than the exercise of rights of use over state-owned immovables. If that was so, the fact that those limitations upon the occupant concern only the more important category can be easily understood.

Today, however, the illogicality is glaring. This was graphically shown, of late, with reference to a specific case. In the US legal memorandum referred to above, it was pointed out, that:

certainly there would be no basis for arguing that an occupant had greater freedom regarding the use or disposition of oil found in the ground (public immovable property) than of oil he found already lifted (public movable property).[26]

This reasoning is compelling: would it make sense to claim that the same resource (oil) could in one case be sold or used only for the military operations of the occupant, while in the other case it could be sold for any purpose, including that of enriching the occupant's home economy?

While a distinction between the two classes of property would be illogical from the particular vantage point we are discussing, resort to *systematic interpretation* and the consequent extension to immovable property of the same restrictions required for state-owned movables render the whole legal regulation of this matter fully coherent. The occupant cannot appropriate immovables belonging to the enemy state, for to do so would run counter to the provisional nature of belligerent occupation. It can, however, enjoy their fruits to the extent that this is made permissible by other provisions concerning the exploitation of enemy natural resources by the occupant.

As indicated above (part 4), the textual interpretation of Article 55 has, in any event, been overtaken by a number of very significant legal and factual developments. These developments call for a new 'evolutive' interpretation that limits an occupant's rights to exploit and dispose of the resources of the occupied territory.

---

[26] Memorandum of Law, *ILM* 16 (1977), 742.

In addition to the developments already referred to in part 4, mention should be made, in this regard, of a series of cases that point in what I consider to be the correct direction. I shall first of all refer to the judgment delivered in 1947 by the International Military Tribunal at Nuremberg in the case *Goering et al.* The Tribunal, after quoting Articles 49 and 52 of the Hague Regulations, stated that:

[T]hese articles, together with Article 48, dealing with the expenditure of money collected in taxes, and Articles 53, 55, and 56 dealing with public property, make it clear that under the rules of war, the economy of an occupied country can only be required to bear *the expenses of the occupation,* and these should not be greater than the economy of the country can reasonably be expected to bear.[27]

A similar view was taken in 1948 by the US Military Tribunal at Nuremberg, in the *Flick, Krupp,* and *Krauch* cases.[28] The same view was also taken in 1956 by the Court of Appeal of Singapore in the famous *N.V. De Bataafsche Petroleum Maatschappij v. The War Damage Commission* case.[29] Equally, the US and the British manuals on the law of land warfare, as well as the aforementioned legal memorandum of the US State Department, submitted in 1976,[30] contain the same overriding requirement.

This authoritative body of legal opinion, which should be taken to reflect the right interpretation of Article 55, is corroborated by legal authors. In this connection reference may be made to the resolution adopted in London on 12 July 1943 by the International Law Conference[31] (a resolution that, according to von Glahn, 'can be said to represent the latest word on the problem, comprising as it did the considered opinion of outstanding jurists'),[32] and to the views of such authorities as Capotorti, Balladore Pallieri, and Stone.[33]

6. Applicability of the Previous Considerations to Land, Water, and Oil

The comments so far enunciated apply in particular to such natural resources as land, water, or oil.

---

[27] *Trial of the Major War Criminals Before the International Military Tribunal,* 1 (1947), 238–9 (emphasis added).

[28] These cases are quoted in the case mentioned in the following note.

[29] Text in *AJIL* 51 (1957), 808.

[30] See US Dept. of the Army, *Field Manual FM 27–10, The Law of Land Warfare* (Washington, 1956), para. 364, and UK War Office, *Manual of Military Law,* iii: *The Law of War on Land,* para. 526, as well as the US Memorandum of Law, *ILM* 16 (1977), 742–6.

[31] Text reproduced in von Glahn, *Occupation,* 194–6 (the relevant passage is para. 3, at 194).

[32] Ibid. 194.

[33] F. Capotorti, *L'occupazione nel diritto di guerra* (Naples, 1949), 118–19, 126–7, and 166–7; G. Balladore-Pallieri, *Diritto bellico* (Padua, 1954), 325–32, and *Diritto internazionale pubblico* (Padua, 1962), 662–5; Stone, *Legal Controls of International Conflict,* 697.

In the next section I shall consider in some detail some problems that arise concerning land. At this juncture, I shall confine myself to the following remark. The prohibition on using land belonging to the occupied state or to its inhabitants for purposes other than those referred to above (military needs of the occupant, etc.), is strengthened by Article 49(6) of the Fourth Geneva Convention of 1949, which provides that 'the Occupying Power shall not deport or transfer parts of its civilian population into the territory it occupies'. This provision is but the logical corollary of the requirement of customary international law whereby the occupant is not allowed to use the property of the occupied country, or of its inhabitants, for the furtherance of its own economic or other interests. Plainly, the transfer of civilians from the occupying state into the occupied territory cannot but serve economic, social, or 'strategic' needs of the occupying state as such. To this extent it is strictly prohibited.

Similar principles to those applying to land apply also to water. Water sources (rivers, wells, other natural springs) constitute assets that can be either private or public depending on the legal classification made in each particular state. In any case, water usable for drinking or irrigation purposes should be regarded as immovable property, like all 'appurtenances to real estate'. This seems to be the better view, and it is confirmed by the provisions of the civil code of a number of countries.[34] Reliance on these codes is warranted in view of the fact that the Hague Regulations are largely based on Roman law concepts ('usufruct', Article 55; 'movable property', Article 53; 'landed property'—'immeubles' in the original French—Article 54) and it is common knowledge that these concepts, in turn, have been taken up in many civil law countries.

A different view might be reached if one were to apply to water, by analogy, what has been stated by a distinguished scholar[35] with reference to oil: that unlike coal, which 'must be literally extracted from rock, namely carved out of it', oil 'is in a liquid state within a natural pocket underground, and drilling from it merely means that it is made possible for the oil to gush—or to be drawn up—on to the ground'. Whatever the value of these considerations concerning oil, the better view, as stated above, is that water is to be regarded as immovable property.

In the case of state-owned water, the occupant has therefore the legal position of a 'usufructuary': it has the right to use the fruits of the property without any right of ownership (including the right of disposal). The exercise of this right of use is, however, clearly restricted in that it can only serve the military needs of the occupying army, or the needs of the population. It follows that the occupant is not allowed to use water to promote its own economy or to pump it into the home country.

---

[34] See e.g. Art. 812 of the Italian Civil Code; Art. 2119 of the French Civil Code; Art. 526 of the Belgian Civil Code.

[35] Dinstein, 'The International Law of Belligerent Occupation and Human Rights', 130.

Mention should now be made of the particular problem of the use of water in the Arab territories occupied by Israel. According to a reliable document on water resources in the West Bank and Gaza, a large part of the West Bank's water resources is utilized by the Israeli settlements:

The Israeli settlements of the Jordan Valley and North Dead Sea utilize over 30,646 million cu.m. Most of this water is pumped from boreholes. The total demand for water by the Arab villages of the valley is 44 million cu.m. (1983 consumption levels). In the region, the consumption of water for the irrigation of one dunam measures 1,342 million cu.m. in the Israeli settlements and 712 million cu.m. in the Arab villages. These figures reveal the contrasting levels of intensity of water use.[36]

I have pointed out above that the numerous civilian settlements established by Israel in the West Bank are illegal, for they are not intended to meet the military needs of the occupant but are designed to expand the economic and political penetration of Israel in the occupied territories. Consequently, the use by these settlements of a large quantity of the (limited) water resources available in the West Bank and the Gaza Strip cannot but confirm and accentuate the unlawful character of those settlements.

Similar considerations also apply to state-owned oil in the occupied territory. If oil is regarded as movable (the view taken by such scholars as Dinstein),[37] then it is obviously bound by the restrictions laid down in Article 53(1), and it can only be used for the purposes of the military operations of the occupying army. However, even if the better view is taken that at least oil in the ground should be regarded as immovable, the same limitations apply, for the reasons set forth above (part 5). Consequently, use of oil by the occupant for the general benefit of its own economy, or its sale for commercial or military use, is prohibited.[38]

7. Case Law on the Use of Land in the Occupied Arab Territories

I propose at this point to make some observations about a number of decisions of the Israeli Supreme Court relating to the use of land in the West Bank. The reason why I shall concentrate on decisions concerning land use is that, to my knowledge, the Supreme Court has not, so far, dealt with other natural resources in the Occupied Territories. I am not familiar with all the recent jurisprudence of

---

[36] D. Kahan, *Agriculture and Water Resources in the West Bank and Gaza (1967–1987),* (Jerusalem, 1987), 113. See generally p. 110–14. See also Ch. 15 in E. Playfair (ed.), cit.

[37] Dinstein, 'The International Law of Belligerent Occupation and Human Rights' 130.

[38] On the question of oil, in addition to the memoranda of law of the US and Israel quoted before, see Gerson, 'Off-shore Oil Exploration by a Belligerent Occupant', and B.M. Claggett and O.T. Johnson Jr., 'May Israel as a Belligerent Occupant Lawfully Exploit Previously Unexploited Oil Resources of the Gulf of Suez?', *AJIL* 72 (1978), 558ff.; J. J. Paust, 'Oil Exploitation in Occupied Territory: Sharpening the Focus of Appropriate Legal Standards', *Houston Jnl. of Int. Law* 1 (1979), 147ff.; and *Procs. of the ASIL* (1978), 118–42.

the Israeli Supreme Court and certainly do not propose any complete survey of its judgments on this matter. Rather, I shall confine myself to first drawing attention to some important features of the Court's pronouncements, and then raising doubts about some other points made in those pronouncements.

A. The Importance of the Supreme Court's Judicial Review

The Court's judicial review of decisions of the military authorities in the West Bank and Gaza deserves to be praised in many respects. I shall begin by briefly underscoring some points of general interest, although they do not relate directly to the subject of this paper.

First, the Court has rightly upheld its power of judicial review over official measures taken with respect to the Occupied Territories, '[T]he ground for this review being that the Military Commander [in the Occupied Territories] and his subordinates are public officials exercising public functions by virtue of law.'[39] Clearly, resort to judicial safeguards against abuses by the occupant should be regarded as an important step taken in the interests of the inhabitants of the Occupied Territories.

Second, the Court has consistently stated (contrary to the position of the Israeli political and military authorities) that the occupation of the Arab territories is a *belligerent occupation* governed by the Hague Regulations (which are seen to reflect customary international law) and by the Fourth Geneva Convention of 1949 (to which Israel and the relevant Arab States are parties). Admittedly, on a number of occasions the Court has ruled that the Geneva Convention cannot be relied upon by individual petitioners.[40] This, however, appears to be due to the particular legal system of Israel, where international treaties for which no implementing legislation has been passed are not incorporated into national law and cannot therefore be invoked or relied upon by individuals before domestic courts. While, of course, disregard for this treaty amounts to an international wrong *vis-à-vis* the other contracting states, the failure of the Court to apply the Convention cannot *per se* be regarded as an international wrong—contrary to what has been recently stated.[41] And at any rate one should not downplay the importance of the ruling by the Court that,

---

[39] See the various cases quoted in *IYHR* 14 (1984), 312.

[40] See, for instance, case HC 500/72, *Abu el-Tin v. Minister of Defence et al.*, excerpted in *IYHR* 5 (1975), 376; HC 606/78 and 610/78, the *Beit El* case, jointly reproduced in Mallison and Mallison, *The Palestine Problem*, 371, at 388; HC 390/79, the *Elon Moreh* case, *PYIL* 1 (1984), 134 at 156, and excerpted in *IYHR* 9 (1979), 345; and HC 629/82, *Mustafa et al. v. The Military Commander of the Judea and Samaria Region*, excerpted in *IYHR* 14 (1984), 313 at 315. See also Ch. 2 in E. Playfair (ed.), cit.

[41] *PYIL* 2 (1985), 134–5 (editor's note).

...towards the international community of States, an Occupying State in an occupied territory must observe and apply both the rules of customary international law and the rules embodied in international conventions to which it is a party.[42]

I shall now move on to my third remark, which, like following ones, has a more direct connection with the subject of this paper. The Court must be commended for having rightly stressed the *restrictions* imposed by international law on the occupant: *dicta* appear in two judgments, observing that:

the Military Commander [of the Israeli forces in the Arab territories] is not allowed to consider any national economic or social interests of his own State; not even national security interests, but only his own military needs and those of the local population.[43]

The Court has also pointed out that an occupied territory is not an 'open field for economic or other exploitation' and has consequently held that, for example, it is forbidden for a military administration to impose taxes on the inhabitants of an occupied territory in order to fill the coffers of the occupying State.[44] It would seem that this interpretation supports the construction of Article 55 of the Hague Regulations put forward above (see part 5).

Fourth, the Court appears to have adopted an evolutive interpretation of the Hague Regulations, for the purpose of taking account of a prolonged occupation such as that of Israel. To this effect the Court has stated that the occupant can plan and carry out fundamental investments likely to produce permanent modification in the occupied territory on condition that this be to the benefit of the inhabitants of the territory.[45] In other words, the Court appears to be applying, as a basic test, the *protection of the interests of the local population,* to the exclusion of any other criteria.

At the same time, it should be mentioned in this context that the Court has also used this 'evolutive' approach to permit the establishment of 'permanent' settlements in occupied territory; that is, settlements apparently intended to remain in existence after the occupation has ended. Given the already prolonged occupation and the fact that 'the prospect of a comprehensive peace with all [Israel's] neighbours still lies hidden in the unknown future', the Court has held that 'the word 'permanent' must be taken in a relative sense'.[46]

Fifth, it should be emphasized that in at least one case (the famous *Elon Moreh* case),[47] the Court has declared null and void the measures taken by the occupying army (namely the creation of a Jewish settlement not justified by military needs).

---

[42] See HC 393/82, the *Teachers' Housing Cooperative Society* case, *IYHR* 14 (1984), 303.

[43] See HC 390/79, and HC 393/82, 304.

[44] *Ibid.*

[45] See HC 393/82, 309–13; see also Ch. 6 in E. Playfair (ed.), cit.

[46] See HC 606/78 and 610/78, the *Beit El* case, jointly reproduced in Mallison and Mallison, *The Palestine Problem*, 371.

[47] HC 390/79, the *Elon Moreh* case, *PYIL* 1 (1984), 134 at 156, excerpted in *IYHR* 9 (1979), 345.

B. Issues and Findings in the Supreme Court's Case Law on which Doubts Can Be Raised

Along with important and innovative interpretations that deserve full commendation, one can however also discern rulings that may give rise to misgivings. I shall refer to some of them.

i. Disregard for the Fourth Geneva Convention

First, one may wonder whether the Court could not have gone beyond its 'Pontius Pilate' attitude with regard to the question of the applicability, in the Israeli legal system, of the Fourth Geneva Convention of 1949. It is clear that in Israel, as in many other countries, treaties ratified but not 'incorporated' by dint of implementing legislation do not become part and parcel of Israeli law; consequently, they cannot be relied upon by individuals in Israeli courts. Yet this would not seem to preclude the Court from taking account of the Convention in the course of interpreting and applying the customary rules of international law on belligerent occupation, as reflected particularly in the Hague Regulations.

Thus, the Court could have taken into consideration Article 49(6) of the Fourth Geneva Convention (prohibiting the transfer of parts of the occupant's civilian population into the occupied territory) for the purpose of restricting the use of land in the Arab territories by the Israeli military authorities. Whenever the requisition of private land or seizure of public land had been carried out by the occupying army for military needs, the Court could have demanded that those needs be met, to the consequent exclusion of any civilian Jewish settlement in the areas; only the use of land by members of the army should have been allowed.

By contrast, the Court's approach when dealing with petitions regarding civilian settlements in occupied areas has been generally to exclude Article 49 from consideration and even give to the Hague Regulations a rather 'loose' interpretation as regards the occupant's rights to use land in occupied territory. (In at least one case—the *Beit El* case—the court upheld the lawfulness of certain civilian settlements in the West Bank on the basis, *inter alia,* that their existence contributed 'to security in that territory and [made] it easier for the army to carry out its task'.[48] Thus the Court characterized the function of the settlements (admittedly for the purposes of certain domestic law) as military.)

The method of relying upon international treaties, particularly when applying customary rules of international law, is certainly not unusual. Suffice it to recall, first, that, as pointed out by a learned author, Ruth Lapidoth,[49] Israeli courts have long applied treaties ratified by Israel but not attended by any

---

[48] See HC 606/78 and 610/78, the *Beit El* case, jointly reproduced in Mallison and Mallison, *The Palestine Problem,* 377.

[49] R. Lapidoth, *Les Rapports entre le droit international public et le droit interne en Israel* (Paris, 1959), 118–27.

implementing legislation. Indeed, in other countries with the same system as Israel, treaties which have not been incorporated by means of national legislation are regularly applied by domestic courts—usually for the purpose of interpreting national statutes consistently with the relevant state's international obligations. (In England, the rule whereby treaties are not part of English law if no enabling Act of Parliament has been passed exceptionally does not apply to treaties relating to the conduct of war or treaties of cession).[50]

If this approach is well established with respect to a state's national legislation, there seems to be no reason in principle why resort to it should not also be had for the purpose of interpreting other rules of international law (which form part of the state's domestic law) as well. Were one then to object that the application of Article 49(6) goes further than mere interpretation of the relevant customary rule, I would rebut that this is not correct. As was pointed out above (part 6), Article 49(6) of the Fourth Geneva Convention is simply a corollary or a necessary implication of the general principle laid down in the Hague Regulations, whereby the occupant is not allowed in the territory under its control to further economic, social, or political interests of its own state. In other words, the Fourth Geneva Convention in this respect merely specifies this general principle. For reasons of security for the occupying army, the occupant can establish military camps or military installations. It is not allowed, however, to move a great number of its own civilians into the occupied territory, for due to their presence, the military or security grounds would be considerably outweighed by other (economic, political, etc.) considerations.

I shall add that, should one consider the above observations as unsound, or inapplicable to the Israeli legal system, due to the particularities of that system, the Court could perhaps have taken a different step. That is, it could have urged the Knesset to take the necessary measures for passing implementing legislation. It is not unusual for Supreme Courts to call upon other state agencies to take measures that, although beyond the province of the judiciary, are strictly required by international law.

The Court has rightly held that the Fourth Geneva Convention is applicable to the Israeli occupation. It has also stated that 'enforcement [of the Convention] is a matter for the States parties to the Convention'.[51] By themselves, these holdings may be seen as a clear reprimand to the Israeli Government, which has consistently denied the applicability of the Convention. And yet, this sort of implicit criticism would seem insufficient. I would submit that the Court should have gone further and made it clear to the Israeli Government that it does not make sense to ratify a treaty and then leave it in abeyance or, even worse, totally disregard some of its basic provisions.

[50] See I. Brownlie, *Principles of Public International Law* (Oxford, 1979), 49; and see Ch. 2 in E. Playfair (ed.), cit.

[51] HC 606/78 and 610/78, the *Beit El* case, jointly reproduced in Mallison and Mallison, *The Palestine Problem*, 389.

There are also moral reasons for complying with the Convention: after all, it was a distinguished Israeli scholar, H. Klinghoffer, who remarked that whatever legal reasons may justify the non-application of unincorporated treaties, from a moral point of view a court should not refuse to take account of a treaty regularly signed and ratified by the Government.[52]

ii. *The presumption that enemy property in the occupied territories is public*

In the case of *Al-Nawar v. The Minister of Defence et al.,* the Supreme Court stated that: '[W]hen doubt arises concerning whether a given property [in an occupied territory] is governmental or private, it is presumed to be governmental until the contrary is proved.'[53] Although the case at issue related to an enterprise which manufactured plastic products, situated near the village of Damur in South Lebanon, the ruling made by the Court might be taken to have a general import, so as to apply to property in the West Bank as well.

I submit that this ruling is questionable. I am aware that some authors (for example, von Glahn)[54] take the same view as the Court, and that support for it can be found in the US and UK military manuals currently in force.[55] One fails to see, however, the justification for this view. Indeed, the only argument in its support is suggested by the British Military Manual, where it is recalled that, in many instances, when an enemy belligerent occupation is impending, governments transfer public property to private individuals, in order to shelter it from any take-over by the occupant. If this were to be the only sound justification for such presumption, it would be correct to rely upon the presumption only when there is sufficient evidence of abuses committed before the occupation. Whenever no such legal expedients have been resorted to, one fails to see why, by propounding the presumption referred to, one should in fact broaden the powers of the occupant.

It appears from the *al-Nawar* judgment that in that case the parties concerned had indeed resorted to a legal expedient for the transfer of ownership. According to Judge Shamgar, the enterprise seized by the IDF belonged to the PLO but had been sold to an individual after its seizure by the occupying force. In that case the presumption might therefore have been justified, were PLO property to be deemed, for the purposes of the Hague Regulations, property belonging to the hostile state. In fact, however, Judge Shamgar was equivocal in his characterization of the status of PLO property for this purpose.[56]

---

[52] H. Klinghoffer, *Administrative Law* (in Hebrew), quoted by Lapidoth, *Les rapports,* 131–2.
[53] HC 574/82, excerpted in *IYHR* 16 (1986), 326.
[54] Von Glahn, *Occupation,* 179.
[55] *US Field Manual,* para. 394(c); *British Manual,* para. 614. (According to this manual, 'cases of Government property being transferred to private ownership to avoid seizure have occurred in various wars'.)
[56] Characterizing the PLO as 'a comprehensive organization engaged in terrorist and military activity', he held that the property of its economic arm should be treated as either 'property of a

In any case, what seems dubious is the possible extension of this presumption to other instances. It is to be hoped that the Court's above-mentioned ruling will be applied in the light of the particular circumstances of each case.

iii. The presumption in favour of the occupant's appraisal of the military necessity justifying requisition of privately-owned property

Another ruling by the Supreme Court which is open to doubt is that in the *Amira et al. v. Minister of Defence et al.* case.[57] The Military Commander in the West Bank had requisitioned privately-owned land situated in the Ramallah District. In the opinion of the occupying authority, the requisition was necessary for military needs. The land was designed to form part of a defensive line, based on three settlements, which together would constitute a system protecting the Ben Gurion International Airport. The statement of the military commander was disputed by the petitioner, who produced an affidavit submitted by a military expert to the effect that the needs of the military did not warrant the requisitioning.

The Court held that it was faced with a 'factual and professional' issue, and then stated the following:

In a dispute such as this, involving questions of a military-professional character in which the Court does not have its own founded knowledge, it will presume that the professional arguments ... of those actually responsible for security in the occupied areas and within the Green Line [the border dividing Israel from the West Bank] are valid. This presumption may only be rebutted by very convincing evidence to the contrary.[58]

Again, one fails to see the legal justification for such a presumption. In order to establish it, one has to proceed from the assumption that in principle the allegations of the occupant are right, unless refuted by the petitioner on the strength of strong evidence. But why should one proceed from this assumption? Arguably, the presumption should be *inverted* to the effect that it is incumbent on the *occupying army* convincingly to prove that military requirements justify the requisitioning of private land. This proposition rests on the following reasons. Since, as pointed out above (part 5), in a prolonged occupation the necessity of safeguarding the needs and interests of the civilian population becomes more imperative than before, one should place severe limitations on the power of the occupant to requisition privately-owned land or to use public land for military needs.

Whereas in a short occupation, taking place during a fully-fledged war, international law can be less demanding on the occupant, in the case of a prolonged occupation greater restraint should be exercised in allowing the occupant to take measures tampering with property in the occupied territory. In a drawn-out

belligerent enemy state *or*...private property serving the enemy' (my emphasis). See HC 574/82, excerpted in *IYHR* 16 (1986), 327–8.

[57] HC 258/79, excerpted in *IYHR* 10 (1980), 331ff.
[58] *Ibid.* 332.

occupation the occupant is tempted to expand the concept of 'military needs' so as to cover a wide range of actions which fall more in the province of the military activity of an *ordinary government* than in the field of the *provisional administration, by a military force,* of a foreign territory.

iv. The court's power to determine whether or not certain actions of the occupant serve the interests of the local population or are at any rate beneficial to such population

I have mentioned above the rulings of the Supreme Court to the effect that a prolonged occupation such as that of Israel in the Arab territories entails among other things the following consequence: greater care must be taken in ascertaining whether or not the actions of the occupant are either justified by military exigencies or are designed to meet the needs of the inhabitants.

In a very important case (*A Teachers' Housing Cooperative Society v. The Military Commander of the Judea and Samaria Region et al.*),[59] the Court was called upon to pass judgment on the lawfulness of the requisition of private lands for the purpose of constructing a network of metropolitan highways. In view of the permanent modifications in the occupied territory these works would entail, the Court asked itself whether they were lawful, and answered in the affirmative, on the basis of the 'test of the benefit for the local population'.

Resort to this test is undoubtedly correct, and the Court must be praised for making use of it. It appears, however, that in the view of the Court the test must be applied by the Court itself; so the Court remains the only body to pronounce on whether or not certain measures benefit the inhabitants of the Occupied Territories. Is this conclusion warranted? I respectfully submit that it is not.

It seems to me that the Court is not the best-placed body for determining whether or not certain measures of the occupant meet the needs of the local population. In a democratic country such a determination would naturally fall on the various representative bodies of the community concerned. In the Occupied Territories, local administrations run by the inhabitants or their representatives would seem to be the most appropriate bodies for making this sort of decision. These administrations could be requested to provide—ideally at the stage when the measures are being considered by the occupation authorities but, if not then, at least when they are being challenged in Court—a statement as to whether in their view the measures in question serve their interests, meet their needs. This statement would then (save in exceptional circumstances involving, for instance, bad faith) be treated as conclusive on the matter. In any case, whatever local body may be selected and however its views may be elicited, what should be surely ruled out is the power of the Court to decide on behalf of, or in lieu of the local population, in cases where there may be conflicting values, patterns of judgement, psychological approaches, and so on.

[59] HC 393/82, excerpted in *IYHR* 14 (1984), 301ff.

That such conflicts can and do arise, is apparent from the facts of the case referred to above. The Israeli occupying forces claimed that the highways project was intended to serve the needs of the local population, for it would considerably facilitate transportation between populated settlements, towns, and villages of the West Bank. The occupant conceded that the highways would also facilitate connection between the West Bank and Israel, but drew attention to the fact that thousands of Arab workers employed in Israel travelled daily to their places of work and back to their homes in the West Bank. The occupying forces also pointed out that if they were to refrain from improving the existing outdated roads, they surely would be blamed for 'freezing' the development of the West Bank and of its population. These allegations should be contrasted with those of the petitioning Arab co-operative society, which saw the highways project—developed in Israel and partly financed by it—as one which would exclusively serve the transportation requirements of Israel. In its view the West Bank did not need such a 'luxurious and showy' highways scheme.[60]

I should like to add that the test concerning the interests of the local population cannot be applied by the Court on its own, not even if it is supplemented by some sort of fairly 'objective' standard. One such standard or yardstick was suggested by Dinstein.[61] In his view, although:

there is no objective criterion in practice for drawing a distinction between sincere and insincere concern [by the occupant] for the civilian population, in most cases the criterion may be simple enough, namely whether or not the occupant is equally concerned about his own population. In other words, if the occupant enacts, for example, a law for the prevention of cruelty to animals in an occupied territory, the proper question is whether there is a similar (not necessarily an identical) law in his own country. If the answer is affirmative, there can usually be no objection to the legislation under Article 43 [of the Hague Regulations]; if it is in the negative, an objection is definitely in order.

It is apparent that his criterion can only work in extreme cases; in normal situations, the comparison with the home state of the occupant may prove misleading, on account of the possible huge differences in social and economic conditions, in psychological outlook, customs, etc. Thus, for example, with reference to the case brought before the Court and discussed in this section, Dinstein's criterion would have been of little consequence.

C. Concluding Remarks on the Case Law Previously Surveyed

Undoubtedly the judicial review of the occupant's acts, undertaken by the Israeli Supreme Court, has had a restraining impact and has also served to delineate the parameters within which the occupant is allowed to operate. It seems, however,

[60] *Ibid.* 301–2; and see generally Chs 2 and 6 in E. Playfair (ed.), cit.
[61] Dinstein, 'The International Law of Belligerent Occupation and Human Rights', 113.

that, in spite of its important contribution to the scrutiny of military action by Israel in the Occupied Territories, the Court has frequently shown excessive self-restraint towards the other Israeli authorities, or has indulged in some sort of legal formalism that ultimately diminishes its bearing on the action of the occupying forces. Very often, the Court has made great strides towards the abstract affirmation of the need to respect the interests of the local population, while *in concreto* it has refrained from actually catering for those interests.

One can only hope that the Court will take a more incisive approach by being less deferential to the political and military authorities of Israel.

12. Legal Considerations on the International Status of Jerusalem*

1. Introductory Remarks

It is not the purpose of this paper to review all the thorny questions relating to the international status of Jerusalem. I shall confine myself to discussing three points, which appear to be worthy of particular interest. They are: (i) the question of whether after the 1948–49 hostilities Israel and Jordan acquired sovereignty over Western and Eastern Jerusalem respectively; (ii) the legal status of Jerusalem after Israel occupied the whole city following the 1967 Arab-Israeli war, and (iii) the question of whether the United Nations is still legally responsible for deciding upon the status of the city, or whether authority on the matter has devolved upon the states concerned.

In briefly discussing these three issues I shall adopt a legal approach and shall only deal with *lex lata.* It is not within my province to look into *lex ferenda,* and make proposals for a change in the present situation. The choice of this approach raises two distinct problems. First, is it possible to make an unbiased legal assessment of the present situation in Jerusalem (or, for that matter, in the whole area)? Secondly, assuming that an even-handed approach is feasible, does international law have any role to play in this intricate and politically loaded subject, or is its role merely peripheral to any political settlement?

As for the first question, it is common knowledge that two schools of thought exist among jurists: one showing strong pro-Israeli leanings,[1] the other manifestly supporting Arab demands.[2] Save for rare exceptions[3] it would seem that one

* Originally published in 3 *The Palestine Yearbook of International Law* (1986) 13.

[1] See, *e.g.* E. Lauterpacht, *Jerusalem and the Holy-Places* (1968), (hereinafter 'Lauterpacht'); Stone, *No Peace No War in the Middle East* (1969); Schwebel, *What Weight to Conquest?,* 64 Am. J. Int'l L. 344 (1970), (hereinafter 'Schwebel'); Blum, *The Juridical Status of Jerusalem* (1974), (hereinafter 'Blum'); Stone, *Israel, the United Nations and International Law—Memorandum of Law,* UN doc. A/35/316 (1980).

[2] See, *e.g.,* Cattan, *Palestine and International Law* (1973), (hereinafter 'Cattan'); Hassan Bil Talal, *A Study on Jerusalem* (1979) (This study was written with the collaboration of G.I.A.D. Draper), (hereinafter 'Hassan Bin Talal'); Mallison & Mallison, *The Palestine Problem in International Law and World Order* (1986), 207–275, (hereinafter cited as 'Mallison & Mallison').

[3] See, *e.g.,* Akehurst, *The Arab Israeli Conflict and International Law,* 5 New Zealand Univ. L. Rev. 231 (1973); Draper, *The Status of Jerusalem as a Question of International Law,* in Kochler (ed.), *The Legal Aspects of the Palestine Problem with Special Regard to the Question of Jerusalem* (1980), 154.

As for scholarly contributions which, although they do not specifically deal with the question of Jerusalem, take an original and unbiased stand, I shall mention, by way of illustration, Gerson, *Trustee—Occupant: The Legal Status of Israel's Presence in the West Bank,* 14 Harv. Int'l L. J. (1973); Weiler, *Israel and the Creation of a Palestinian State—A European Perspective* (1985).

cannot avoid being decidedly influenced by political feelings. Nevertheless, international scholars should at least try to be as little conditioned as possible by political prejudice. The idea that even the jurist must perforce adhere to one of the two camps would not only be contrary to the scholarly function but—and this is even more important—would make true dialogue, and compromise, impossible in this area. This I will not accept, if only because it would be contrary to the whole spirit of the fundamental principles governing international relations[4] and to the basic aspiration to the peaceful settlement of disputes laid down in the U.N. Charter.

Efforts should be made to look beyond the crystallized juridical positions of the two camps. The aim is thus not to present a partisan solution to the problem, but to show one possible way in which recourse to rules of international law may help to circumvent political obstacles. The fact that in considering each particular issue I will start from an examination of the legal views advanced by the pro-Israeli jurists should not be seen as contradicting the above; in fact, these views tend to be better argued and usually bolstered by sophisticated juridical reasoning.

We now turn to the second question, that is, the role law could play in this problem-area. Before embarking upon an analysis of the various legal issues relating to Jerusalem, one might be tempted to think that in this, as in all similar questions with a high political and military element, law inevitably plays a marginal role; at best it is used as a weapon in the hands of the opposing factions to buttress their respective political demands. Instead, I shall start from the assumption that even where international law has reached its 'vanishing point'[5] in matters directly impinging upon force, one should not *a priori* discount the possible role of legal standards. In particular, one ought to shun generalizations, for everything depends on the way the legal framework of the world community responds to the strains of the specific situation. To put it differently, one should enquire, case by case, whether or not law is a remote and pointless entity, or whether it provides the guidelines for a feasible political settlement. One of the purposes of this paper is precisely this: to ascertain to what extent legal precepts—as they have evolved in the international community and are currently upheld by the majority of states—help in the search for peace in the Middle East.

2. The Israeli and Jordanian Commitment Not to Change the Legal Status of Jerusalem Without U.N. Consent

It is not disputed that from 1517 to 1917 Jerusalem was part of the Ottoman Empire and therefore under its exclusive sovereignty. Similarly, no one questions the fact that in the period from 1917 to 1948 Jerusalem was actually controlled by the United Kingdom, first as a military occupant (during and after the first World

---

[4] On these principles, see Cassese, *International Law in a Divided World*, (1986), at 126–165.
[5] As used by H. Lauterpacht, *The Problem of the Revision of the Law of War*, 29 Brit Y. B. Int'l. (1952), at 360.

War) then, after 1922, as the mandatory power under the League of Nations system. During these thirty-one years the United Kingdom did not, however, possess sovereign rights over the city. Although opinions on the general question where sovereignty over mandated areas lay differ widely,[6] in the case of Jerusalem the best view seems to be that 'if the test of sovereignty rests in determining who had the power to dispose of any part of a territory under Mandate, the answer is that sovereignty lay in the League and the administering authority acting jointly'.[7]

Who held sovereignty over Jerusalem after the Arab countries had refused the U.N. Partition Plan and a war erupted between Israel and the Arab countries is a matter of great controversy.[8] In particular, once the hostilities had ceased and the Armistice Agreement was signed by Israel and Jordan on 3 April 1949,[9] did Israel and Jordan gradually acquire a legal title over Western and Eastern Jerusalem respectively?

To answer this question it is necessary to determine who had the power to dispose of Palestine after the British had withdrawn from the area.

It is well known that before the League of Nations was dissolved on 18 April 1946 the last League Assembly adopted a resolution which took note of the 'expressed intentions' of the League Members, then administering territories under mandate, to continue to administer them for the well-being and development of the peoples concerned 'until other arrangements' had been 'agreed between the United Nations and the respective mandatory Powers'.[10] All the

---

[6] See *e.g.*, I. Oppenheim–Lauterpacht, *International Law, a Treatise* at 222, note 5. (Eighth ed., 1955).

[7] Lauterpacht, at 13–14.

[8] After the demise of the League of Nations, the question of Palestine was discussed by the U.N. General Assembly on the question of initiative of the United Kingdom which, in a letter dated April 2, 1947, had requested the convening of a special session of the Assembly; this body was called upon to make recommendations under Article 10 of the Charter. In operative para. 3 of Resolution 181 (II) A, containing the Partition Plan, adopted on November 29, 1947, the General Assembly *recommended* 'to the United Kingdom, as the Mandatory Power for Palestine, and to all other Mambers of the United Nations the adoption and implementation, with regard to the future Government of Palestine, of the Plan of Partition with Economic Union', 2 U.N. GAOR, Resolutions, 131–132, U.N. Doc. A/519 (16 Sept.–29 Nov. 1947). Part III of the Partition Plan related to the City of Jerusalem provided that: 'The City of Jerusalem shall be established as a *corpus separatum* under a Special International Regime and shall be administered by the United Nations. The Trusteeship Council shall be designated to discharge the responsibilities of the Administering Authority on behalf of the United Nations'.

The Resolution was substantially accepted by the United Kingdom, but rejected by the Arab States. The U.K., although it abstained from voting, declared that it would not obstruct the implementation of the Partition Plan, while Saudi Arabia, Pakistan, Iraq, Syria and Yemen denounced the Plan as being against the Charter, illegal and immoral, and stated that they did not feel bound by the Resolution.

What was the legal value of the Resolution? I submit that, since the General Assembly had special powers on mandated territories, its recommendations on the matter bore more weight that any ordinary resolution. In actual fact, they were *proposals* concerning the legal status of a territory. If accepted by the parties concerned, they would have given rise to an *international agreement* binding on the parties.

[9] 42 U.N.T.S. 303 No. 656, Apr. 4,1949.

[10] U.N.Y.B., 1946–47, at 575.

The resolution, adopted unanimously (with Egypt abstaining) stated among other things the following:

parties concerned therefore agreed that the mandatory powers were not free to dispose of mandated areas as they thought fit; the United Nations was to play a major role in the matter, in that it was to authorize any change of status for the areas. This authority did not flow from the U.N. Charter, but rather from an *agreement* reached outside the Charter. The agreement had been concluded by all the Member States of the League of Nations when they adopted the resolution referred to above. It should be stressed that it is not unusual for a group of states to enter into an internationally binding agreement by passing a resolution within an international organization;[11] plainly, to ascertain whether the resolution is merely an ordinary recommendation or amounts to an international agreement one should look both into the intentions of the states concerned, as they are shown in their statements, and into the actual terms of the resolution. By virtue of this agreement, the Member States of the League of Nations administering mandated territories undertook not to relinquish their control over those areas without the consent of the United Nations; the remaining Member States of the League acquired a right to claim from the former compliance with the obligation just referred to. Besides, the United Nations was granted the right to authorize any transferral of power over the territories under mandate. This authority, it should be added, was tacitly accepted by the United Nations by its decision to deal with those territories, and, in the case of Palestine, by its decision to propose a settlement of the matter by means of the Partition Plan.

It is worth emphasizing that later on both Israel and Jordan tacitly 'joined' the agreement. Israel did so as early as 1948. On 15 May 1948, Mr. Moshe Shertok, the Israeli Foreign Minister, sent a cable to the U.N. Secretary-General in which he recalled the proclamation issued by the National Council for the Jewish State declaring *inter alia* that 'the State of Israel will be ready to co-operate with organs and representatives of the United Nations in the implementation of the resolution of [The General] Assembly of 29 November 1947' laying down the so-called 'Partition Plan'. He went on to state:

Accordingly I beg [to] declare on behalf [of the] Provisional Government of [the] State of Israel its readiness to sign [the] declaration and undertaking provided for respectively in part I C and part I D of [the] resolution of [the] Assembly.[12]

---

3. [The Assembly] Recognizes that, on the termination of the League's existence, its functions with respect to the mandated territories will come to an end, but notes that Chs XI, XII and XIII of the Charter of the United Nations embody principles corresponding to those declared in Art.22 of the Covenant of the League;

4. Takes note of the expressed intentions of the Members of the League now administering territories under mandate to continue to administer them for the well-being and development of the peoples concerned in accordance with the obligations contained in the respective mandates, until other arrangements have been agreed between the United Nations and the respective mandatory Powers.

[11] 11. See, *e.g.*, Castaneda, *Valeur juridique des resolutions des Nations Unies*, 129 Hague Recueil (1970-I), at 302–312; Conforti, *Le rôle de l'accord dans le système des Nations Unies*, 142 Hague Recueil (1974-II), at 271–288.

[12] U.N. Doc. S/747.

These Israeli commitments made it clear that Israel implicitly recognized the authority of the United Nations to propose a plan for Palestine which included Jerusalem. It seems that, in addition, Israel accepted, by implication, that decisions on Jerusalem should be initiated by the United Nations or, in any event, had to receive its consent.

After the rejection of the Partition Plan by the Arab States, the Israeli stand was reiterated and expressed in even clearer terms by the Israeli representative to the United Nations, Mr. Abba Eban, in the statement he made on 5 May 1949, before the *Ad Hoc* Political Committee of the General Assembly, on the occasion of the discussion of Israel's application for admission to membership of the U.N. In the part of his lengthy statement concerning Jerusalem, Mr. Eban made the following points: (a) Israel 'had cooperated to the fullest extent with the Statute drawn up in November 1947', in an effort to implement the section of the General Assembly Resolution concerning Jerusalem;[13] (b) the failure of the United Nations scheme was therefore not to be blamed on Israel but on the Arab States and on the 'refusal of United Nations organs to assume the obligations necessary for the fulfilment of the Statute';[14] (c) in spite of the failure of the Partition Plan, Israel recognized that competence to decide on the status of Jerusalem still rested with the United Nations, and believed that a satisfactory solution of the question could only be reached 'by international consent' within the United Nations. Indeed, the hostilities that ensued thereafter had created a new situation; in particular, they had brought about a 'process of integration of the life of Jerusalem into the life of the neighbouring States which now exercised the *functions of administration* [of Jerusalem]'.[15] However, although Western and Eastern Jerusalem had therefore been placed under the 'administration' of Israel and Jordan respectively, and Israel suggested as the best proposal for a settlement a 'functional internationalization' (i.e., an international regime for the Holy Places only—situated in the area under Jordanian control), nevertheless, Israel was ready to bow to an international decision on the matter if it was agreeable to her. As Mr. Eban put it:

The statement contained in the Lebanese draft resolution that the New City of Jerusalem [i.e., West Jerusalem] had been proclaimed as part of the State of Israel was false and malicious. The most salient feature of the Government of Israel's present attitude to the Jerusalem problem was its earnest desire to see the juridical status of the city satisfactorily determined by international consent.[16]

He later on stated the following:

The Government of Israel would continue to seek agreement with the Arab interests concerned in the maintenance and preservation of peace and the reopening of blocked access

---

[13] 3 U.N. GAOR, *Ad Hoc* Political Committee, Summary Records, 45th Meeting, at 235.
[14] *Idem.* at 236.
[15] *Idem.* at 232.
[16] *Idem.* at 233.

into and within Jerusalem. Negotiations on that subject would not, however, affect *the juridical status of Jerusalem, to be defined by international consent.*[17]

In particular, as for Israel's suggestions for a 'functional internationalization' of Jerusalem, Mr. Eban pointed out as follows:

[I]t was for the Committee [i.e., the *Ad Hoc* Political Committee of the General Assembly] to decide whether it endorsed or did not endorse the views of the Government of Israel on the future status of Jerusalem.[18]

It is apparent from Mr. Eban's statement that although it no longer felt bound by the Partition Resolution, Israel still recognized—quite explicitly—the *authority of the United Nations* in any decision concerning Jerusalem acceptable to the parties concerned, and that consequently, no final settlement of the matter could be reached without the approval or the endorsement of the United Nations. Thus Israel undertook to refrain from seeking any settlement of the question without United Nations consent.[19]

One could infer from the Israeli stand that she eventually joined the agreement concluded within the League of Nations on 18 April 1946. One could even see it as a 'tacit accession' to that agreement, brought about by the statement made by Israeli representatives to the United Nations. Should this view appear formalistic or somewhat farfetched, the suggestion could be made that Israel undertook a commitment vis-à-vis the United Nations parallel to the 1946 agreement. It is worth noting that the Israeli commitment was very similar to that undertaken— in the view of the International Court of Justice—by the Union of South Africa vis-à-vis the United Nations, on the question of the status of South West Africa. It is well known that in its Advisory Opinion on the *Status of South West Africa* (1950), when the Court tackled the question whether the Union of South Africa had the competence to modify unilaterally the international status of South West Africa, it denied this competence. Among other things, it noted that on 9 April 1946, before the Assembly of the League of Nations, the South-African representative had recognized the competence of the United Nations to consent to any change of status for South West Africa. The Court thus inferred from the commitment made by the Union of South Africa before the U.N. that the authority to

---

[17] *Idem.* at 236.

[18] *Idem.* at 234.

[19] It should however be pointed out that Israel somewhat hardened its stand in November 1949. See for instance the statement made on Nov. 2, 1949, in the General Assembly *Ad Hoc* Political Committee by the Israeli representative, Mr. Sharelt, GAOR *Ad Hoc* Political Committee, Forty-Fourth Meeting, at 261–264, and by Mr. Eban, *Idem.* Forty-Ninth Meeting, Nov. 29, 1949 at 293–300. Nevertheless, Israel still upheld the U.N. authority to consent to any definitive settlement. Thus, for instance, Mr. Sharett stated the following: 'As to the function of supervision in the area controlled by Israel, his delegation believed that the best way to ensure its effective discharge was through an agreement solemnly to be concluded, by virtue of a special resolution of the General Assembly, between the United Nations and the Government of Israel, providing for the obligations of that Government and for the prerogatives of the United Nations in that regard' *Idem.* at 264, para. 72. As for the statement by Mr. Eban, see for example, *Idem.* paras 41 at 297; 54 at 299; and 56.

determine and modify the international status of South West Africa rested 'with the Union of South Africa acting with the consent of the United Nations'.[20]

Whichever of these legal configurations seems preferable, what really matters is the ultimate result: the Israeli statements precluded Israel from making any decision on the status of Jerusalem without the approval of the United Nations. In particular, Israel was barred from acquiring sovereignty over Western or Eastern Jerusalem without United Nations approval.[21]

Jordan adopted a rather ambiguous attitude toward the United Nations 1947 scheme for Jerusalem in 1947–48.[22] Later on, by holding on Eastern Jerusalem, it manifested its rejection of the scheme. However, on 26 November 1949, in the *Ad Hoc* Political Committee of the U.N. General Assembly, the Jordanian representative, while insisting on the importance it attached to Jordanian control over the Eastern part of Jerusalem, bowed to U.N. authority on the general issue of Jerusalem; he indeed used words that should not be labelled as a merely hypocritical homage to U.N. prestige, but can be construed as conveying the idea that Jordan would answer to the U.N. for its control over Eastern Jerusalem.[23] Although the attitude of Jordan was rather ambiguous and unclear for many years, once this country became a member of the United Nations, in 1955, it voted in favour of the various resolutions of the General Assembly on Jerusalem, particularly after 1967. It stands to reason that by supporting all the General Assembly resolutions calling upon Israel to rescind the measures adopted in Eastern Jerusalem after 1967, Jordan implicitly assented to the U.N.'s authority to determine—in agreement with the parties concerned—whether changes in the status of Jerusalem are internationally lawful. It follows that, like Israel, Jordan undertook an obligation vis-à-vis the United Nations along the lines of the 1946 agreement referred to above. Like Israel, Jordan was then barred from acquiring any title over Jerusalem without United Nations consent.

3. Who Wielded Sovereignty Over Jerusalem Between 1948 and 1967?

The rejection of the Partition Plan by most of the parties concerned and the consequent fighting in Palestine, left the General Assembly Resolution embodying

[20] *International Status of South Africa*, Advisory Opinion of 11 July 1950, [1950] I.C.J. 128 at 143.

[21] See also *infra*, Section 5.

[22] For an examination of Jordan's stand see Safaer, *The Political Status of Jerusalem in the Hashemite Kingdom of Jordan, 1948–1967*, Middle Eastern Studies (1978–79) at 75–77.

[23] The Jordanian representative stated among other things that 'The Government of the Hashemite Kingdom of the Jordan... had the greatest respect for the wishes for the international community represented in the United Nations' GAOR *Ad Hoc* Political Committee, 46th Meeting, November 26, 1949, para. 73, at 276. He also stated, while insisting on the fact that 'the existing system of control and protection in Jerusalem could [not] be modified in any way', that his Government 'hoped that the Committee would duly consider and appreciate the arguments it had submitted'. *Idem.* para. 77, at 277.

the Plan a dead letter. However, although it was not implemented, it was never formally repealed by the General Assembly.

Can the contention be made that the actual occupation of Jerusalem by Jordan and Israel meant they acquired sovereign rights over Eastern and Western Jerusalem respectively?

A learned author has argued that, after 1952, both the General Assembly and the Security Council gradually abandoned any idea of internationalizing Jerusalem, although the 'Secretariat and various individual Members of the U.N. continued, on occasion, to pay lip service to the idea';[24] this was so much so that, in his view, one could safely contend that 'the U.N. by its unconcern with the idea of territorial internationalization, as demonstrated from 1952 to the present date [1968], effectively acquiesced in the demise of the concept'.[25] The whole complex situation that developed in Jerusalem was described by the same author as follows: since Jordan's occupation of Eastern Jerusalem in 1948 was in breach of Article 2 (4) of the U.N. Charter, it lacked any legal justification; consequently, Jordan was unable to acquire a legal title to sovereignty over the area. It merely performed a 'prolonged *de facto* occupation' from 1948 to 1967. By contrast, Israel's occupation of Western Jerusalem was prompted by Jordan's attack; Israel acted in self-defence, under Article 51 of the U.N. Charter. Her occupation of Western Jerusalem, being lawful, allowed Israel to acquire a legal title to that area. Acquisition of sovereignty was also possible because the United Nations did not challenge it; it acquiesced in the new legal situation.[26]

I shall not make a detailed analysis of the lawfulness of Jordan's invasion of Eastern Jerusalem—for the purposes of this paper it is sufficient to note that the better view is that the invasion was contrary to Article 2 (4) of the U.N. Charter and to the general principle arising out of it. As regards Israel, it seems that both assumptions on which the view quoted above rests, namely that Israel became the lawful sovereign of Western Jerusalem, and that the U.N. acquiesced in her sovereignty are questionable.

First, although Israel acted in self-defence under Article 51, this did not authorize her to annex territories under a 'sovereignty vacuum'[27]. Indeed the view referred to above seems to rest on a misconception of self-defence. Self-defence only entitles states to use force to repel an unlawful armed attack; it does not legitimize the acquisition of territory.[28] The authors under consideration actually stretch the concept and the substance of self-defence to such an extent as to distort this notion substantially. To be sure, the victim of an 'armed attack' could go so far as to occupy, temporarily, a territory in order to forestall the

---

[24] Lauterpacht, at 23. See also at 23–36.

[25] *Idem.* at 36.

[26] To this effect see also Blum, *The Missing Reversioner, Reflections on the Status of Judea and Samaria*, 3 Isr. L. Rev. 279, (1968); Schwebel.

[27] Lauterpacht, at 41, 45.

[28] Jennings, *The Acquisition of Territory in International Law*, 55 (1963).

recurrence of armed attacks which might seriously jeopardize its territorial integrity and political independence. This occupation should, however, discontinue as soon as the United Nations steps in, and in any event does not entail acquisition of sovereignty over that territory. The situation cannot but be provisional; pending the cessation of the wrongful behaviour or a final settlement, the occupying power is only authorized to exercise *de facto* control over the territory.[29] At least since 1945, sovereignty cannot be acquired through military conquest, not even when the territory was previously unlawfully controlled by another state, or when force is resorted to in order to repel an unlawful attack. The ban on the use of force and military conquest, laid down in the Charter,[30] is too sweeping and drastic to make allowance for such qualifications. Cogent arguments would be necessary to demonstrate that these qualifications are permissible. So far no international lawyer has advanced any.[31] By contrast, a great authority, Professor Robert Jennings (as he then was), wrote in 1963 that 'conquest as a title to territorial sovereignty has ceased to be a part of the law' whether or not force used for the purpose of seizing territory was lawful or unlawful under the U.N. Charter'.[32] In my view, a careful examination of the Charter system and its general purposes, as restated among other things in the 1970 Declaration of Friendly Relations[33] leads us to believe that 'acquisition' of sovereignty as a result of military force *might perhaps* be allowed, but only on very strict conditions: (i) it must be *undisputed* that prior to the use of force *sovereignty* over the territory belonged to the same state which used force to expel the unlawful occupant; (ii) all possible means for a peaceful settlement of the dispute have been used before resorting to armed violence and,

---

[29] See Articles 42–56 of the Regulations annexed to the Hague Convention IV Respecting the Laws and Customs of War on Land, 1907, 36 US Stat. 2227.

[30] Article 2(4) of the U.N. Charter.

[31] Schwebel, at 345, has argued that the notion that 'defensive conquest' and 'the taking of territory which the prior holder held [unlawfully]' legitimize the acquisition of sovereign rights over a territory 'must be read in particular cases together with other general principles, among them the still more general principle of which it is an application, namely, that no legal right shall spring from a wrong, and the Charter principle that the Members of the United Nations shall refrain in their international relations from the threat or use of force against the territorial integrity or political independence of any state'. With all due respect, it is submitted that this view is unsound. In the case at issue, the fact that Jordan unlawfully attacked Israel in 1948 and then in 1967 and that after the first conflict Jordan acquired control over Eastern Jerusalem, simply means that its resort to force was in breach of Article 2(4) of the Charter as well the corresponding general principle and that it did not acquire any sovereign rights over that territory. It does not follow at all from that premise that 'Israel has better title in the territory' in hand. I cannot see why the fact that Jordan violated international Law and only gained *de facto* control over a territory could result in Israel acquiring a right over the same territory simply because of her acting in self-defence. The only logical and sound inference from the aforementioned premise is that neither Jordan nor Israel ever acquired sovereignty over Jerusalem.

[32] Jennings, at 56, and see generally at 52–68.

[33] Principle I, para. 10 of the Declaration (adopted on October 24, 1970 by consensus), provides that 'No territorial acquisition resulting from the threat or use of force shall be recognized as legal'. For the full text of the *Declaration on Principles of International Law Concerning Friendly Relations and Co-Operation among States in Accordance with the Charter of the United Nations*, see U.N. General Assembly, 25th Sess., Doc. ARES/2625(XXV).

in particular, recourse has been made to the appropriate U.N. bodies, but they have failed to dispossess the *unlawful* occupant of the territory; and (iii) the use of force has not gone beyond the limited goal of restoring sovereign rights over the territory (it is apparent from these conditions that in the case under consideration it would be more correct to speak of 'reacquisition' of territory).

If one looks at the question in the light of these conditions, it becomes clear that at least one of them is missing: before 1948 Israel could not claim to hold *sovereign rights* over Western Jerusalem.

The second criticism of the view referred to above is predicted upon the premise that it does not seem that after 1952 the U.N. ever endorsed Israeli (and, for that matter, Jordanian) alleged sovereignty over Jerusalem. It should be pointed out that U.N. silence on the question between 1952 and 1967 cannot amount, as such, to acquiescence in their acquisition of a legal title. U.N. inaction, clearly motivated by an inability to overcome the political impasse, can only mean that the world organization accepted and acquiesced in *de facto* control of Jerusalem by Jordan and Israel. The granting of a legal title or, to be more precise, the turning of *de facto* authority into fully-fledged sovereignty, could not be brought about by mere silence. In view of the enormous importance of the question at issue and of the impact that a solution could have on the very tricky problems of the Middle East, the issue of consent should not be taken lightly. How could one assume that the U.N. expressed its consent on such a complex and explosive matter by merely *keeping silent?* At least *a tacit manifestation of consent through conclusive acts* would have been necessary.

What has just been pointed out is corroborated by the action taken over the years by several prominent members of the United Nations, including the states more directly concerned. Thus, for instance, the United Kingdom, after granting in 1950 and 1951, *de facto* recognition only of Israel's and Jordan's control of Jerusalem, in contradistinction to its *de jure* recognition of Israel and Jordan,[34] did not appear to modify its position over the years. In addition, the U.S. Government consistently emphasized the need for Jerusalem to be given an international regime proving that it did not intend to recognize any sovereignty over Jerusalem. Suffice it to mention here a few U.S. statements. On 22 July 1952, in response to the proposed move of the Israeli Foreign Ministry from Tel Aviv to Jerusalem, the American Embassy stated:

The Government of the United States has adhered and continues to adhere to the policy that there should be a special international regime for Jerusalem which will not only provide protection for the holy places but which will be acceptable to Israel and Jordan as well as the world community.

---

[34] See *Arab Bank v. Barclays Bank*, L.R. [1954] A.C. 495, 498, reported in I. Whiteman, *Digest of International Law*, at 699 (hereinafter 'Whiteman'). See also the statement made in 1950 by Lord Hendersen in the House of Lords and reported in *Hassan Bin Talal*, at 25 and n. 41.

Since the question of Jerusalem is still of international importance, the U.S. Government *believes that the United Nations should have an opportunity to reconsider the matter* with a view to devising a status for Jerusalem which will satisfactorily preserve the interests of the world community and the States directly concerned. Consequently, the U.S. Government would not view favorably the transfer of the Foreign Office of Israel to Jerusalem.[35]

On 30 December 1958, in a despatch to the Secretary of State, the American Consul General at Jerusalem stated:

The majority of U.N. member nations, including the United States and the Soviet Union, have continued to respect the United Nations resolutions despite the *de facto* occupancy of the city of Jerusalem part by Israel and part by Jordan. As a result, an anomalous situation exists today embodied, in the case of the United States, by a Consulate General whose district is the 'international city' and certain adjacent areas on the Jordanian side. Other nations which maintain similar establishments are the United Kingdom, Turkey, Italy, Spain, Greece and Belgium. Many other countries mark their respect for the internationalization resolutions by establishing embassies in Tel Aviv thus avoiding recognition of Jerusalem as the capital of Israel and, by implication, as Israel's *de facto* sovereign territory.[36]

This stand was reaffirmed in 1960. On 5 April of that year the U.S. Ambassador at Amman, in a despatch to the Secretary of State, pointed out, *inter alia,* that:

The Government of the United States of America has adhered and continues to adhere to a *policy which respects the interest of the United Nations in the status of Jerusalem.* The United States Government therefore cannot recognize or associate itself in any way with actions which confer upon Jerusalem the attributes of a seat of government of a sovereign State, and are thus *inconsistent with this United Nations interest in the status of that city.*[37]

As late as 1967 the U.S. reiterated its attitude. In a statement made on 28 June, the Department of State made it clear that:

The United States has never recognized such unilateral actions by any of the States in the area as governing the international status of Jerusalem.[38]

Another important pronouncement was made in 1958 by the Italian Council of State (*Consiglio di Stato*), the supreme body of 'administrative justice' responsible for reviewing the legality of executive acts either in contentious proceedings or at the request of other Italian State agencies. In an advisory opinion delivered on 9 December 1958 following a request of the Foreign Ministry, the Council had to pronounce upon the following issue: whether the Italian Consulate in Western Jerusalem had to pay rent to the Arab owner of the premises, who did not live in the city, or to the Israeli Custodian—the only entity authorized to receive the

---

[35] Whiteman, at 595 (emphasis added).
[36] *Id.* at 594.
[37] *Id.* (emphasis added).
[38] *Dep't. St. Bull.*, July 17, 1967, at 60.

money under Israeli law.[39] The Italian Council held that since the Israeli law was applicable in Western Jerusalem, the Italian Consul was to conform to it and pay the rent to the Custodian. However, before reaching this conclusion the Council stated, *inter alia,* the following on the status of Jerusalem:

> The situation of the territory of Jerusalem is not at all clear from the point of view of public international law. To be sure, there exists an international law convention (*convenzione*) providing that the territory should be internationalized. However, it seems that this convention has not yet been implemented and sovereignty is *de facto* exercised by the State of Israel, although this state of affairs has not been legally recognized by the Member States of the United Nations, which are duty bound to abide by that convention.[40]

Thus the Italian *Consiglio di Stato* clearly pointed out that Israel had not acquired full sovereignty over Western Jerusalem. Also very significant appear the Council's remarks on the duty of all the Member States of the U.N. to comply with the General Assembly pronouncements on the matter by withholding recognition of the Israeli claim to sovereignty over Western Jerusalem.[41] Although the *Consiglio di Stato's* point on this issue was merely an *obiter dictum,* it can be considered indicative of the views of Italian State authorities, not only because the Foreign Ministry (which, as emphasized above, had requested the Council's advisory opinion) eventually upheld it but also because it is in line with other pronouncements by Italian authorities on the matter.[42]

It is apparent from all these statements that a great number of U.N. members did not intend to recognize any asserted acquisition of sovereignty either by Israel or by Jordan over Jerusalem; in addition, some of them strongly believed that the city should enjoy an international status. This being so, how could it be claimed that the United Nations acquiesced in the alleged transfer of sovereignty over Jerusalem? It is indeed difficult to dissociate the U.N. stand from that of the majority of its members. The attitude taken by the aforementioned states only confirms that U.N. inaction cannot be taken to mean a tacit acceptance of Israeli or Jordanian sovereignty over Jerusalem.

4. What Exactly Has the Legal Status of Jerusalem Been Since the 1967 War?

In 1967 Israel occupied Eastern Jerusalem in the course of armed hostilities started by Jordan, whereas during the conflict with Egypt and Syria, she had

---

[39] On the authority of the Custodian under Israeli law, see 4 *Laws of the State of Israel,* (LSI) at 68 (1950), in particular, see Art. 2. See also *Israel Government Yearbook* (1958) at 235.

[40] Text (in Italian) in *Rivista di diritto internazionale,* at 321–322 (1960).

[41] On the advisory opinion of the *Consiglio di Stato* see Sereni, *La situazione giuridica di Gerusalemme,* Foro italiano, 1960, IV, 205 ff (who, however, takes a different view from this writer).

[42] For the stand of Italian authorities on the question of the Middle East, see the statement quoted *infra,* note 54 as well as the various statements adopted by the Foreign Ministers or the Head of State of the EEC countries (see for example the one quoted *infra,* note 72).

acted in 'anticipatory self-defence'.[43] On 27 June 1967, the Israeli Parliament (the Knesset) passed a law as a result of which in July of the same year the Israeli Government decreed that the whole of Jerusalem was incorporated into the municipal and administrative spheres of its government.[44] The administrative incorporation of Jerusalem into Israel was upheld by various Israeli courts in the following years[45] and completed by a 'Basic Law' passed on 30 July, 1980 by the Knesset.[46] On the strength of this law the whole of Jerusalem was actually made an integral part of the State of Israel, and indeed became her capital city.

It is submitted that the annexation of Jerusalem is contrary both to *conventional* and *general* international law. As to conventional law, it has already been emphasized before[47] that by implicitly joining the agreement concluded in 1946 within the last League of Nations Assembly, or at any rate by entering into a distinct but parallel agreement with the United Nations, both Israel and Jordan formally recognized the need for U.N. authorization or consent to any change in Jerusalem; they accordingly undertook to refrain from doing anything that would impinge upon the legal status of that city without prior U.N. approval. It is common knowledge that both in 1967 and in the following years, in particular in 1980, the Security Council, as well as the General Assembly, strongly condemned the Israeli annexation of Jerusalem and declared all the acts accomplished by Israel are null and void.[48] It should be stressed that the refusal to acknowledge the legality of Israeli action in Jerusalem was reiterated, both within and outside the United Nations, by various Western countries—normally more friendly, or at least less hostile to Israel than socialist and developing states. Thus, for instance, mention can be made of the U.S.,[49] the United

---

[43] On this issue, see Malawer, *Anticipatory Self Defence Under Article 51 of the United Nations Charter and the Arab–Israeli War, 1967* in *Problems,* vol. VIII, no. 1–2 at 14 (June 1970). For the general legal criteria of anticipatory self defence, see McDougal & Feliciano, *Law and Minimum World Orders* at 231 (1961).

[44] See text of the Law and Administrative Ordinance (Amendment No-11) Law, 21 *LSI* at 75 (1967). Other Israeli Legislation affecting Jerusalem are Municipalities Ordinance (Amendment No.6) Law, *Id.* Protection of Holy Places Law, *Id.* at 76.

[45] See, *e.g.,* the judgment delivered on March 10, 1969 by the Supreme Court of Israel in the *Hanzalis'* case (French translation in 98 *Journal de Droit International*, 1971 at 345). See also the comments by Shaki, *Id.* at 356–357.

[46] Basic Law: Jerusalem, Capital of Israel in 34 *LSI* at 209 (1980).

[47] See *supra,* Section 2.

[48] For a survey of these resolutions, see Jones, *The Status of Jerusalem: Some National and International Aspects* in Moore (ed.), *The Arab–Israeli Conflict Readings and Documents* at 223 (1973); Cattan; at 202 and *passim;* Plaff, *Jerusalem: a Keystone of an Arab–Israeli Settlement; Id.* at 273 and *passim;* Mallison & Mallison, at 211–228; Reddaway, *Jerusalem and International Organizations* (reneotyped), at 7 and *passim* (1979); Rostow, *Palestinian Self-Determination: Possible Futures of the Unallocated Territories of the Palestine Mandate,* Yale Studies in World Public Law, at 162 and *passim* (1980).

[49] See, for example, 57 *Dep't St. Bull.* July 31, 1967 at 148; *Id.* July 28, 1969, at 76; *Digest of United States Practice in International Law* 1976, at 634–635; 1977, at 922–925; 1978, at 1557, 1579–1580; 1979 at 258.

Kingdom,[50] France,[51] the Federal Republic of Germany,[52] Belgium,[53] Italy,[54] the Netherlands,[55] Canada[56] and Japan.[57] All these pronouncements make it clear that the United Nations as a whole, as well as its individual member states, expressly withheld recognition of the Israeli annexation of Jerusalem. It follows that the consent required by the multilateral or bilateral agreements referred to above was not given; consequently Israel never acquired a valid legal title.

Let us now consider whether such a title was acquired under customary international law. Can we maintain that Israeli sovereignty stems from a different source than treaty law, a more flexible source and which *ex hypothesi* could override treaty obligations? To put it differently, can we hold that—unlike treaty law, by definition better geared to the specific circumstances of individual cases—customary law, being more traditional and general, takes account of, and legitimates, the physical taking of Jerusalem by Israel coupled with her intention to annex it?

Two points need to be made. First, under customary international law, actual control over a territory attended by *animus possidendi* can only create a legal title to areas belonging to no one.[58] However, it would be both unsound and contrary to all evidence to suggest that Jerusalem became *terra nullius* after the British withdrawal. Hence, a legal title other than the one required for the acquisition of 'territories without master' is necessary. In the case at issue, the legal title should be granted by the previous holders of sovereignty, i.e. the League of Nations (after 1946 by its successor, the U.N.) and the United Kingdom, as the former Mandatory State. Such transferral, however, has not been made, either through formal international instruments, or by implication (i.e. by the acquiescence of the U.K. and the U.N. in the alleged sovereignty of Israel and Jordan, or of Israel only).[59] Can acquisition of territory derive from a different title, namely 'unlawful

[50] See Brit, *Y.B. Int'l. L.* at 481 (1980); *Id.* at 514–517, (1981); *Id.* at 366, 531–534 (1982); *Id.* at 459, 538–539, (1983).

[51] See, *e.g., 26 Annuaire francais de droit international, at 919–920, (1980), Id.* at 256, (1983).

[52] See 44 *Zeitschrift fur auslandisches offentliches Recht and Volkerrecht,* at 503 (1984).

[53] See 15 *Revue Belge de droit international,* at 616 (1980).

[54] See 3 *The Italian Y.B. Int'l L.* at 418 (1977); 4 at 224–227, (1978–79); 5 at 301, (1980–81).

[55] See, *e.g., Netherlands Y.B. Int'l L.* at 151, (1970) as well as *The Times,* Feb. 11, 1981.

[56] See 15 *The Canadian Y.B. Int'l. L.* at 346 (1977); 17 at 340–341 (1979).

[57] See Oda and Owada (eds) 1982, *The Practice of Japan in International Law 1961–1970,* at 6–7 (1982).

[58] See the *Island of Palmas* case (U.N., *Reports of International Arbitral Awards,* II, 838–856) the *Clipperton Island* case (*Id.* at 1108–111), and the *Eastern Greenland* case (P.C.I.J., Ser. A/B, no.53. In general, on this subject see the classical work by R. Ago, *Il requisito dell'effetività dell'occupazione in diritto internazionale* (Roma, 1934)).

[59] In addition, as I have already pointed out above (Section 2), the undertaking of Israel and Jordan serves to exclude the possibility of their acquiring sovereignty without U.N. assent, should the mistaken theory of Jerusalem as *terra nullius* be upheld. Indeed, assuming that Jerusalem became a 'territory without sovereign' after the British authorities relinquished it, Israel and Jordan could not acquire sovereignty simply by meeting the requirements of general international law. For they had both assumed the *conventional* obligation vis-à-vis the United Nations and its Member States to refrain from changing the legal status of Jerusalem without the U.N. assent. This obligation would of necessity overrides customary international law to their advantage.

conquest'? It has been suggested that between 1948 and 1967 Eastern Jerusalem was under the unlawful control of Jordan and in 1967 occupied by Israel acting in self-defence against the wrongful attack by Jordan. According to various distinguished jurists[60] the lawful conquest of a territory illegally occupied by a state in breach of Article 2 (4) of the U.N. Charter creates a sovereign title in favour of the conquering state. Arguments advanced with respect to the status of Jerusalem in the period between 1948 and 1967[61] could be repeated in this instance. General international law on territorial sovereignty has undergone a major change, at least since 1945: whenever a state appropriates a territory by using force (whether in breach of Article 2 (4) or by acting in self-defence under Article 51 of the U.N. Charter), no legal title over the territory can be acquired. The classical elements for transferral of sovereignty are no longer sufficient. Authority over the territory is internationally illegal (except as a belligerent occupant), until such time as the overwhelming majority of states (or the competent organs of the United Nations) decide legally to recognize the change of status of the territory.[62] However, U.N. approbation or consent have been refused in the case at issue.

In sum, while treaty law excludes any acquisition of sovereignty by Israel over Jerusalem, one cannot even fall back on customary law for the purpose of validating Israeli claims to sovereignty. As pointed out above, at present, general international law has departed markedly from the *principle of effectiveness*: *de facto* situations brought by force of arms are no longer automatically endorsed and sanctioned by international legal standards. At present the principle of legality is overriding—at least at the normative level—and effectiveness must yield to it. As it has already been emphasized, this is the consequence of a whole range of major changes that occurred in the world community after the adoption of the U.N. Charter.

5. Does the United Nations Still Have a Role in Deciding Upon the Future of Jerusalem?

It is apparent from the above that the United Nations, although it has no 'real' power of disposition over Jerusalem (certain *de facto* situations cannot be obliterated by merely legal means) it does, however, have a decisive say in the matter and no international settlement can be lawfully reached without its approval. Admittedly, Israel has shown much reticence on this matter and at present in actual practice it denies the United Nations the authority to legalize any settlement acceptable to the parties concerned by its approbation. Nevertheless, Israel's refusal is contrary to her previous commitments vis-à-vis the United Nations—a commitment never nullified on any of the grounds for rendering agreements null and void (in particular, the clause *rebus sic stantibus* cannot validly be invoked,

---

[60] See, for instance, the works by Schwebel and Blum.

[61] See *supra*, Section 3.

[62] It stands to reason that this recognition cannot be granted at whim, but should be motivated by special circumstances fully warranting an exception to the ban on acquisition of sovereignty by force.

for, as stated above, Israel accepted U.N. authority even after the Partition Plan had been rejected by Arab countries). In addition, the Israeli refusal referred to above cannot produce any legal effects under customary international law, for the latter requires a set of conditions for the acquisition of a valid legal title to sovereignty that Israel does not fulfil.

However deep the cleavage between Israel on the one side, and the world community on the other, a settlement sanctioned by law must require the assent of the world community, as expressed by its representative body, the United Nations.

6. Has the Idea of Territorial Internationalization Been Abandoned by the United Nations?

Let us now briefly look into the question of whether the U.N., given its authority over any settlement of the Jerusalem issue, has yet proposed a definite scheme, or whether it has refrained from taking any initiative on the matter.

One of the authors referred to above has suggested that recent U.N. resolutions do not reflect any intention on the part of the United Nations 'to resurrect the idea of the territorial internationalization of Jerusalem' and in particular that the 'status of the city', about which some of these resolutions expressed concern, was not the status chosen by the General Assembly in 1947 for internationalization.[63] This contention rests on two elements: first, in the discussion before the passing of those resolutions, no mention was usually made of internationalization; second, no reference whatsoever to internationalization is to be found in the language of the resolutions itself. The conclusion is accordingly drawn that the United Nations now accept that Jerusalem should be divided into two parts: one under Israeli sovereignty, the other in a sort of legal vacuum as to sovereign rights—although, in the opinion of the author under consideration, after 1967, Israel may have come lawfully to exercise the powers of a belligerent occupant over Eastern Jerusalem,[64] while other authors take the view that Israel lawfully acquired sovereignty over the whole of Jerusalem.[65]

Admittedly, the various resolutions passed by the United Nations since 1967 only refer, in terms, to the duty of Israel to cancel the measures it has taken in Eastern Jerusalem and, consequently, to withdraw to Western Jerusalem. Taken at their face value, they seem to indicate that the United Nations has abandoned any idea of internationalization. Indeed, a few authorities[66] have spoken of the 'apparent ambiguity' or 'lack of clarity' of these resolutions. Can we infer from their text that the United Nations has now come to accept a city divided into two parts, each under the sovereignty of a different state?

---

[63] Lautetpacht, at 34–36.
[64] *Id.* at 47–51.
[65] See, for example, the works by Schwebel and Blum.
[66] Mallison and Mallison, at 228; Reddaway at 8–13.

The somewhat obscure character of the resolutions and their deliberate openness to various interpretations, as well as the whole context of the United Nations' stand on the question of Jerusalem, point to the following conclusions.

First, the world organization never intended to endorse the occupation of Eastern Jerusalem by Israel, much less the alleged acquisition of sovereignty by that state.

Secondly, the United Nations never proposed a definite scheme for the final settlement of the question; it has neither insisted on the idea of *internationalization,* nor has it favoured the *splitting* of the city into two parts, each under the sovereignty of a different state. The organization has preferred to take a very cautious stand by leaving either solution open. In particular, it has avoided pronouncing both on the legal title required for either solution, and on which state would have a better title to sovereignty over all or part of Jerusalem.

Thirdly, the organization has clearly shown its intention of retaining full power of disposition over the territory or, to put it in more accurate terms, to maintain its right to authorize, or consent to, any legal change in the status of Jerusalem.

This stand, which at first sight might appear ambiguous, hence open to criticism, is instead realistic and flexible. By not crystallizing its position in one rigid formula, the United Nations has left all the options open, thus showing its desire to take account of the evolving political and military realities in the area. It has adopted a wise and balanced course of action, by only insisting on one crucial point—the principle of United Nations authority over any final settlement.

It should be noted that the United Nations' attitude ultimately represents *a synthesis* of the differing views of some of its members. A number of Member States still believe that the idea of *a corpus separatum* should be revived; suffice it to mention the statements made in Parliament by the Belgian Government in 1969[67] and again in 1971[68] and by the Philippines in 1980 in the Security

---

[67] In 1969, during the discussion on the Foreign Ministry's budget which took place in the Belgian Senate, the official position of the Belgian Government on the question of Jerusalem was set out as follows: 'Dans son discours prononcé lors de la session extraordinaire de l'Assemblée générale des Nations Unies en 1967, le ministre des Affaires étrangères a exprimé la préoccupation du governement belge quant au sort de Jerusalem. Il demeure favorable à l'établissement d'un statut international des lieux saints qui en garantirait le libre accès aux fidèles de toutes les religions'. Report in *Revue Belge de Droit International,* at 278 (1971).

[68] In 1971, replying to a question from a Senator, the Belgian Foreign Minister declared in the Senate the following; 'Je voudrais rappeler au Senat que la Belgique demeure fidèle à la décision du 29 novembre 1947 de l'Assemblée générale des Nations Unies qui prévoyait un territoire international pour Jerusalem *corpus separatum.* L'Assemblée générale des Nations Unies, en juillet 1967, c'est-à-dire après la reprise des conflits, et le Conseil de sécurité, le 21 mai et le 23 juillet 1969, ont invité l'Etat d'Israel à renoncer à l'annexion de Jerusalem et à s'abstenir de toute disposition visant à modifier le statut de la ville. La Belgique a approuvé ces dispositions du Conseil de sécurité et de l'Assemblée générale des Nations Unies.

Des lors, les principaux pays occidentaux: les Etats-Unis, la Grande-Bretagne, la France, l'Italie, l'Espagne, la Grèce et la Turquie maintiennent à Jerusalem des consuls généraux.

Respectant le principe du *corpus separatum,* l'exequatur n'est demandé ni aux Israeliens, ni aux Jordaniens. Les autorités israeliennes ne sont guere favorables au maintien de ces consuls dans cette situation, mais qui est conforme à l'attitude que la plupart des gouvernements occidentaux, y

Council.[69] The same stand had already been taken in 1967 within the United Nations, following the Israeli occupation of Eastern Jerusalem, by 20 Latin American States, as well as by Spain.[70] A different view was expressed in 1979 by the British Foreign Minister, who proposed that 'there should be an Arab Jerusalem and an Israeli Jerusalem, each exercising full sovereignty within its own territory, but with no barriers between them and no impediment in freedom of movement between them'.[71] A looser formula was suggested by the EEC members. On 13 June 1980 the European Council, meeting in Venice, stated that the Nine (as they then were) did not accept any unilateral initiative aimed at changing the status of Jerusalem, and that any agreement on the status of the city should guarantee free access for all to the Holy Places.[72] The apparent implication is that the EEC members do not intend to recognize the alleged sovereignty of Israel over Eastern Jerusalem, and take the view that only through an international agreement can a final settlement be reached. It should he added that in 1980, in the Security Council, Cuba, Jordan and Turkey loosely referred to an international regime for Jerusalem under the aegis of the United Nations. Clearly, the existence of disparate or even opposed viewpoints among the member states of the United Nations helps to explain why the organization has deemed it advisable since 1967 to shun any clear-cut scheme for the city, as long as the political situation remains fraught with danger and no solution acceptable to all the parties concerned is in sight.[73]

compris le gouvernement belge, ont prise. Cette situation particulière explique le caractère délicat des fonctions de consul général à Jerusalem, puisque le titulaire doit entretenir des relations avec les autorités locales, qui sont israeliennes, sans pour autant reconnaître l'annexion de la ville' Report in *Revue Belge de Droit International*, at 266 (1973).

[69] See *U.N.Y.B* at 40 (1980).

[70] On the occasion of the debate in the U.N. on the occupation of Eastern Jerusalem resulting from the June War, several States suggested that Jerusalem should be placed under permanent international administration, as a *corpus separatum*, with special guarantees for the protection of the Holy Places. This stand was taken by Argentina, Brazil and Spain (*U.N.Y.B.* at 210 (1967), which explicitly referred to G.A. Resolution 181 (II) of 29 November 1947, as well as by Uruguay and Venezuela, *Id.* Furthermore, 20 countries (Argentina, Barbados, Bolivia, Brazil, Chile, Colombia, Costa Rica, Dominican Republic, Ecuador, El Salvador, Guatemala, Guyana, Honduras, Jamaica, Mexico, Nicaragua, Panama, Trinidad and Tobago and Venezuela) put forward a proposal (draft resolution A/L. 523 Rev. 1) which among other things reaffirmed, as in earlier recommendations, the desirability of establishing an international regime for the City of Jerusalem, for the consideration of the Assembly at its next session. True, this draft was not adopted because it failed to obtain the required two-thirds majority (it received 57 votes in favour, 43 against with 20 abstentions: *Id.,* at 220). Although it did not acquire the status of a General Assembly Resolution, that draft is of great importance at least in the following respect: it shows that the 20 co-sponsors, as well as other states which voted in favour of it, *clung to the idea of the internationalization of Jerusalem.*

[71] See *The Guardian*, 27 August 1979 as quoted by Hassan Bin Talal, at 49 and n. 86.

[72] See *EEC Bulletin*, 1980, no. 6, para. 1.1.6 sub-para. 8.

[73] See *U.N.Y.B.* at 401 (1980).

7. Final Remarks

A. Conclusions of the Foregoing Analysis

Under current international law it is ultimately for the United Nations, Israel and Jordan to make arrangements for the international status of Jerusalem.[74] However, by virtue of the general principle on the self-determination of people, these arrangements cannot be validly made without the participation of the legitimate representatives of the Palestinian people, who must be allowed to take part in the decision-making process, and express the aspirations of the Palestinians. Until such time as a general agreement is reached with the United Nations on the matter, Israel's present claim to sovereignty cannot produce any legal effects. Under international law, Israel only exercises *de facto* control over Jerusalem. And, as for her control over Eastern Jerusalem, it is clearly a breach of the international rules on military occupation, because it goes far beyond the limits assigned to the powers of a military occupant.[75]

In concluding this study, one may try to advance a few general remarks on the role of law. It is submitted that current international law does not 'freeze' the existing *de facto* situation in Jerusalem; it does not give it its 'blessing'. In the case of Jerusalem, we come face to face with a striking phenomenon: a *de facto* situation, brought about by force of arms and now solidly implanted in the daily life of the city, is not recognized by any other member of the world community, and consequently is not validated either under general international law or conventional law.[76] The principle of *effectiveness* is overriden by that of *legality*, although the United Nations—creator of and spokesman for international legality— is unable to enforce it. This schizophrenic state of affairs forces international

---

[74] It seems that this position was to some extent adumbrated by the U.S. representative to the U.N. in the statement he made on September 25, 1971, in the U.N. Security Council. He said the following: '... In our view, the ultimate status of Jerusalem should be determined through negotiation and agreement between the Governments of Israel and Jordan in the context of an overall peace settlement, taking into account the interests of its inhabitants, of the international religious communities who hold it sacred, and of other countries in the area'. *Dept. St. Bull* at 469 (1971).

[75] The legal consequences of the illegality of the Israeli annexation of Eastern Jerusalem were also drawn on the domestic plane. Thus, for instance, a Dutch Bill on naturalization was changed in the Netherlands Parliament to take account of the legal situation existing in Jerusalem. The Bill mentioned the place and date of birth of an applicant for naturalization as follows: 'Jerusalem (Israel), June 20, 1923' (it actually concerned Eastern Jerusalem).

In this connection the following observation was made in Parliament, 'Since this annexation has never been formally recognized, it is hardly possible to state that, under international law, this zone belongs to Israel. In connection with this application for naturalization the Bill mentions that Jerusalem is situated in Israel. How this is to tally with the Minister's statement that these indications are based upon the present status under international law of the area concerned?' The Government shared this view and the Bill was changed to the effect that 'Jerusalem (Israel)' was replaced by 'Jerusalem (old city, Jordan), presently under Israeli administration'. See *Netherland Y.B. Int'l. L.* at 151, (1970).

[76] See *supra*, Section 3.

law to confine itself to an essentially negative stand, that is to withholding its endorsement of the *de facto* situation. Subject to what shall be suggested later, by and large international law does not seem to provide a solution in *positive* terms. Although a huge gap separates law from reality, law at least accomplishes the useful function of indicating *how* a solution can be reached. Under international law a definitive settlement can only be achieved by dint of agreement between the parties concerned and subject to the consent of the United Nations. In other words, although international law does not furnish a *fully-fledged substantive* settlement, at least it enjoins the *procedure* to be followed. It calls for a process of negotiation involving the two states of the area, the legitimate representatives of the Palestinian people, as well as the other members of the world community. It is a process that will necessarily require a number of mutual concessions by the parties concerned. It will also have to take account of the keen interest of the whole international community in the safeguarding of the holy places in Jerusalem. It seems that only on these conditions can a solution acceptable to the world community be achieved.

B. Substantive Guidelines for a Possible Settlement, Stemming From International Law and Practice

One could object that a peaceful settlement along the procedural lines suggested above is a chimera, like that house mentioned by Swift: so perfectly built in accordance with all the rules of symmetry and equilibrium that if a sparrow were to alight on it, it would immediately collapse. Indeed, considering the present rift between Israel and most Arab States, the tensions or dissensions both among the Arab countries and within the Palestine Liberation Organization, the deadlock at the U.N., the political inability of the organization to smooth out the conflicts, a prompt solution through mutual concessions and trade-offs becomes highly problematical. This being so, it would seem all the more urgent to delve among the legal norms to see if one could at least postulate a *general scheme.* This, of course, could not impose itself by legal fiat until it had been embodied in an agreement. Nevertheless, its mere existence would provide a *substantive* blueprint for action, thereby *facilitating* the achievement of a compromise.

It is submitted that international law and practice tend to suggest the following solution. In the first place, international practice seems to regard as feasible the possible granting to Israel of sovereign rights over Western Jerusalem. Indications to this effect can be drawn from three sets of circumstances. First, at the end of hostilities in 1948 the armistice line dividing Jerusalem corresponded more or less to the demographic situation of Arabs and Jews in Jerusalem: the Western sector of the city included the highest number of Jewish inhabitants. Second, after 1967, the U.N. has repeatedly called upon Israel to withdraw from the 'occupied territories'; this expression could be taken to cover only those territories occupied in 1967. By implication, one might infer that since Western Jerusalem is not among such territories, the U.N. might be ready to accept that *de facto* control over the Western sector be turned into sovereign rights proper. Third, when concluding the Camp David Agreement,[77] Egypt made a unilateral declaration on Jerusalem, whereby it implicitly accepted Israeli control over Western Jerusalem while rejecting any acquisition by Israel of rights over the Old City.

One could object that foreign embassies have been withdrawn from Western Jerusalem with ever-increasing frequency after 1967, and particulary after 1980, when the whole of Jerusalem was annexed by Israel. However, this was primarily done in protest at the illegal incorporation of Jerusalem into the Israeli political, administrative and legal system. This seems to he the best way of accounting for the seeming contradiction between the probably implicit acceptance of Israeli control over the Western sector of the city after 1967 and the withdrawal of foreign embassies.

In the second place, international law seems to point in a different direction as far as sovereign rights over Eastern Jerusalem are concerned. They should be granted to the legitimate representative of the Palestinian people for three reasons. First, in 1948 the ethnic majority in Eastern Jerusalem was Arab. Second, Jordanian control over Eastern Jerusalem in the period 1948–67 was never accepted as definitive by the world community, nor, indeed, by the Arab League which, as early as 12 April 1948, stated that Jordanian control in Palestine was temporary and that the country 'should be handed [over] to its owners so that they may rule as they please'.[78] Third, the right of people to self-determination requires that a home be granted to the Palestinian people,[79] and this could be brought about, amongst other things, by entrusting the Palestinians with full authority over Eastern Jerusalem. Of course, such authority should be made conditional on full enjoyment by everyone of the rights of access and worship in the Holy Places.

This substantive settlement may, or may not, be considered realistic. Be that as it may, one can say, in conclusion, that international law, faced with this highly complex political problem, can allow a flexible and constructive 'response'; a response which is neither preposterous and overbearing nor blind to political realities. It points to one of the few paths that can lead to peaceful settlement. It is incumbent upon the parties concerned, and the international community at large, to tread one of these paths and, through a process requiring patience and reasonable trade-offs, bring about a compromise acceptable to all.

[77] See text of the *Agreements in The Camp David Summit,* U.S. Dept. St. Pub. 8954, Sept. 1978).
[78] See M. Khalil (ed.), (1962) *The Arab States and the Arab League—A Documentary Record,* at 166.
[79] There are many U.N. Resolutions confirming this right. See, *e.g.,* Resolution 2672 C on Dec. 8, 1970 in U.N. GAOR. Supp. 28 at 73–74; Res. 39/17, November 23, 1984.

PART II

OUR COMMON RIGHTS

A. Torture and Inhuman or Degrading Treatment

13. Prohibition of Torture and Inhuman or Degrading Treatment or Punishment*

1. General

Article 3 of the European Convention on Human Rights states: 'No one shall be subjected to torture or to inhuman or degrading treatment or punishment' and is one of its most important provisions. This is borne out by the fact that—along with Articles 2, 4(1) and 4(7)—it is a rule from which no derogation is allowed, not even in times of war or other public emergencies threatening the existence of a Contracting State (see Article 15(2)). By the same token, it is also one of the most difficult norms of the Convention to interpret and apply, for two main reasons. First, it prohibits, in very strong terms, torture and, in the same breath, two other classes of misbehaviour: inhuman treatment or punishment and degrading treatment or punishment. Second, it provides no clue as to the meaning and purport of the proscribed actions. Admittedly, other provisions of the Convention also fall short of a clear explanation of the precise meaning of what it is they are prohibiting. Those provisions can, however, be interpreted fairly easily, either because of the clarity of the expressions used (for example, 'respect to private and family life' in Article 8 or 'right to marry and found a family' in Article 12), or because of the technical nature of the expressions used, these being supported by a whole tradition of legal practice and legal thinking (for example, 'right to a fair and public hearing within a reasonable time by an independent and impartial tribunal established by law' in Article 6, 'right to freedom of expression' in Article 10 or 'right to freedom of peaceful assembly and to freedom of association with others' in Article 11).

By contrast, it is particularly difficult to pinpoint the exact scope and meaning of the bans enshrined in Article 3 regarding the notion of 'inhuman' and

* Originally published in R. St. J. Macdonald et al. (eds), *The European System for the Protection of Human Rights,* (Dordrecht: Kluwer Int., 1993), 225–261.

'degrading' treatment or punishment. For although one can contend that, as far as torture is concerned, a whole body of municipal legislation, case law and legal scholarship on which contracting States and the European Commission and Court could draw was already in existence by 1950 (the year the Convention was adopted), no comparable definition or interpretation of the concepts of 'inhuman' and 'degrading' treatment or punishment can be found even in municipal bodies of law.

It is therefore very clearly and immediately apparent how arduous a task the Commission and Court faced when called upon to construe and apply Article 3. Thus it was that these two bodies came ultimately to be endowed with wide powers of interpretation, bordering on 'judicial legislation': it stands to reason that the looser the purport of legal rules, the greater is the power of supervisory bodies to authoritatively lay down what those legal rules aim to provide.

In the following sections I shall first of all establish whether any useful indications can be drawn from the preparatory works; I shall then examine how the two bodies have interpreted Article 3 in their case law; and finally, I shall endeavour to suggest possible avenues for further developments in the application of Article 3.

2. Preparatory Works

Even a cursory glance at the preparatory works (*travaux préparatoires*) enables one to see that very little can be deduced from them.

The provision first proposed by the Consultative Assembly in its draft text of a Convention explicitly referred to Article 5 of the Universal Declaration of Human Rights, whereby 'no one shall be subjected to torture or to cruel, inhuman or degrading treatment or punishment': Article 2(1) of the draft provided that the Member States undertook to ensure the security of persons, 'in accordance with Articles 3, 5 and 8 of the United Nations Declaration.' In the first session of the Consultative Assembly, in 1949, the British representative, Mr. Cocks, moved that the following text should be added to Article 1, to become Article 2(1):

The Consultative Assembly takes this opportunity of declaring that all forms of physical torture, whether inflicted by the police, military authorities, members of private organizations, are inconsistent with civilized society, are offences against heaven and humanity and must be prohibited.

It declares that this prohibition must be absolute and that torture cannot be permitted for any purpose whatsoever, either for extracting evidence, to save life or even for the safety of the State.

The Assembly believes that it would be better even for society to perish than for it to permit this relic of barbarism to remain.[1]

---

[1] See *Travaux Préparatoires* 2, pp. 2–4 and 36.

Mr. Cocks also proposed that the following text should be added at the end of Article 2(1):

In particular no person shall be subjected to any form of mutilation or sterilization or to any form of torture or beating. Nor shall he be forced to take drugs nor shall they be administered to him without his knowledge and consent. Nor shall he be subjected to imprisonment with such an excess of light, darkness, noise or silence as to cause mental suffering.[2]

It is clear that these two amendments were cast in lofty and eloquent language, better suited for a political or moral declaration than for a legal text. One should not, however, pass over the important novelties of Mr. Cocks's proposals in ailence. First, they stated that torture is to be regarded as a crime against humanity. Second, they proclaimed that torture is never justified, not even when it is practised for the safety of the State. Third, they encompassed any kind of torture, even that carried out by 'members of private organizations.' Fourth, they extended the prohibition to beating, to 'imprisonment with such an excess of light, darkness, noise or silence as to cause mental suffering,' as well as to mutilation, sterilization and the administration of drugs without the knowledge and consent of the persons concerned.

In the eloquent presentation of his drafts, Mr. Cocks emphasized that his proposals were intended as a barrier against a return to barbarism such as that experienced by Europe on account of Nazi atrocities: in his view, the Consultative Assembly must 'condemn in the most forthright and absolute fashion this retrogression into barbarism.'[3] However, misgivings about the advisability of adopting Mr. Cocks's first proposal were expressed by the British (Mr. Maxwell-Fyfe) and the French (Messrs Philip, Lapie and Teitgen). Mr. Teitgen, besides supporting the critical comments made by the previous speakers, compounded the objections in forceful terms by stating, in substance, that Mr. Cocks's proposals were dangerous, for what was not stated explicitly there would be taken as allowed; hence, at the end of the day those proposals would eventually weaken the text as it stood, instead of strengthening it.[4] Clearly, Mr. Teitgen, and the majority of

---

[2] *Ibid.*, p. 4.

[3] See *ibid.*, pp. 36–40. The words cited in the text are on p. 40.

[4] 'If we add a commentary on these statements [the wording of Article 5 of the Universal Declaration, referred to in Article 2(1)], whose terms have been carefully weighed, we shall limit their scope to the comments which we make. For example, I shall shortly tell our very dear colleague that if, in our Resolution, he enumerates a certain number of means of torture which he wishes to have prohibited, he risks giving a wholly different interpretation from that which he hopes to make, namely that the other processes of torture are not forbidden. And this is certainly the opposite of what he intends. I really think that the best way of stating the fundamental principle which he expressed a short while ago, and behind which every man of heart and conscience will immediately and entirely take his stand, is simply to state that all torture is prohibited. When this is stated in a legal document and in a diplomatic Conference, everything has been said. It is dangerous to want to say more, since the effect of the Convention is thereby limited' (*ibid.*, pp. 44–46). For the statements of the preceding speakers, see *ibid.*, pp. 40–44.

the Assembly, did not object to the banning of the classes of torture suggested by Mr. Cocks, but only feared that spelling out particular instances of torture would undermine the general scope of the ban; in short, they wisely favoured the old maxim *omnis definitio periculosa est.* As a result of these criticisms, Mr. Cocks withdrew his amendments.[5]

Subsequently, it was decided that the text of Article 5 of the Universal Declaration should be taken up as an autonomous provision.[6] Later on, for reasons which are not recorded, the word 'cruel' was deleted, and the provision became the present Article 3.[7]

What can we infer from the preparatory works? The main lesson to be learned is that Article 3 was conceived of as *a very sweeping ban,* so broad as to embrace all the forms of torture or inhuman treatment also included by Mr. Cocks in his proposals (to the extent, of course, that this was compatible with other provisions of the Convention: take, for example, the ban on torture by private groups, which in the light of Article 1 of the Convention can clearly apply only to those instances of torture which involve some sort of liability of a Contracting State).[8]

3. The Case Law of the Strasbourg Bodies

A. General

A careful investigation of the huge case law of the Commission and the Court shows—as might well have been expected—that after some initial hesitation, and even disagreements between them, the two bodies have gradually expanded their interpretation of Article 3 so as to make the purport of the provision as broad as possible. They have pursued this goal in two ways: first, they have gradually enlarged the *areas* to which Article 3 should apply; second, they have specified the criteria for establishing whether or not Article 3 is breached, and by the same token have in real terms broadened the *contents* of the proscriptions laid down in that provision.

---

[5] See *ibid.*, p. 46. A compromise was agreed upon, whereby Mr. Cocks's ideas were to constitute the substance of a motion, to be voted upon as a text separate from the text of the Convention. However, when subsequently Mr. Cocks submitted the text of a draft resolution (*ibid.*, p. 238), this text too drew much criticism (*ibid.*, pp. 240–44), so much so that it was agreed to ask a Committee to re-examine the text and submit a new report to the following session of the Assembly (*ibid.*, p. 244). It would seem that a new draft was never proposed, and the matter was laid to rest.

[6] The British member of the Committee of Experts charged with preparing a draft proposed in the second meeting of this Committee that at the end of Article 2 the following articles should be added: 'No one shall be subjected to torture or to cruel, inhuman or degrading treatment or punishment' and 'No one shall be subjected to any form of physical mutilation or medical or scientific experimentation against his will' (*ibid.*, vol. 3, pp. 204–6). Subsequently, it was ostensibly agreed to drop the second proposed provision and to retain only the first (see *ibid.*, pp. 222 and 236; no official record exists of a discussion on the deletion of the second provision).

[7] See *ibid.*, vol. 3, pp. 282, 314 and 320; vol. 4, pp. 24, 32, 52, 58, 184 and 218.

[8] Cf. the judgment of the Court.

B. Areas to which Article 3 Has Been Applied

Initially the Commission and the Court applied Article 3 with regard to the conditions of detention of persons deprived of their liberty (usually in prisons, police custody or mental institutions). From the 1960s, they also examined the question whether extradition, expulsion or deportation to a country where an individual is likely to be subjected to torture or to inhuman or degrading treatment was contrary to Article 3. In addition, the Commission examined whether racial discrimination can be said to amount—in some instances at any rate—to inhuman or degrading treatment. Subsequently, the Commission and the Court dealt with alleged cases of inhuman or degrading treatment in educational institutions. Finally, the Commission has considered a few cases where it was alleged that very poor economic or social conditions actually amounted to inhuman treatment by the authorities responsible for such conditions.

C. Definitions and Case Law of the Commission and the Court

i. *Inhuman treatment or punishment*

Almost immediately the two Strasbourg bodies began to feel the need to formulate a definition of the various concepts mentioned in Article 3. Although in some instances they then disagreed on the concrete application of such definitions, they have not made any fundamental departures from them. It may therefore prove useful to summarize these briefly here.

The Commission or the Court first of all stated that the category of inhuman treatment (or punishment) is more general than that of torture: torture constitutes but one instance—a particularly serious and aggravated one—of inhuman treatment or punishment. While these two classes can in a way be grouped together, degrading treatment or punishment constitutes a category by itself, as will be shown.

What is meant by inhuman treatment? On several occasions the Commission has stated that 'the notion of inhuman treatment covers at least such treatment as deliberately causes severe suffering, physical or mental, which in the particular situation is unjustifiable.'[9] Thus, at least three elements are required for there to be a breach of Article 3: the *intent* to ill-treat, a *severe suffering* (physical or psychological), and the *lack of any justification* for such suffering.[10]

---

[9] Op. Com., 5 November 1969, *Greek* case, *Yearbook* 12, p. 186, para. 2; Op. Com., 7 December 1978, *Guzzardi* case, p. 31, para. 80; Dec. Adm. Com., Application no. B706/79, 5 October 1981 (unpublished); Dec. Adm. Com., Application no. 11701/85, 7 March 1988, DH(88)2, Appendix IV, p. 17.

[10] To them one should probably add a fourth one: the *imputability* of the misbehaviour to one of the Contracting States. This element, which is general in nature in that it applies to any misconduct proscribed by the Convention, should never be neglected. In actual fact, in a few cases the Commission has had an opportunity to pass on it. In the *Greek* case the Commission was obliged

As the existence of these elements in specific instances is a delicate matter calling for an accurate evaluation of all the contributing factors, the Court has hastened to state that each case must be assessed on its own merits. In the *Ireland v. The United Kingdom* case, the Court stated that 'ill-treatment must attain a minimum level of severity if it is to fall within the scope of Art. 3. The assessment of this minimum is, in the nature of things, relative; it depends on all the circumstances of the case, such as the duration of the treatment, its physical or mental effects, and, in some cases, the sex, age and state of health of the victim.'[11]

Let us now see how the Commission and the Court have applied this notion in specific instances. Given the multitude of cases available, for the sake of brevity only a few have been selected.

Cases where the Commission or the Court found a breach of Article 3

In this category mention should first be made of the famous case of *Denmark, Norway, Sweden and The Netherlands v. Greece.* The Commission found in 1969 that, in addition to numerous cases of torture, inhuman treatment or punishment had also been inflicted by the Greek authorities in some instances. It held in particular that in the Athens Security Police premises in Bouboulinas Street, the conditions of detention in the basement—where persons arrested for political reasons were held—were contrary to Article 3;[12] that the bad conditions of detention

---

to deal with the preliminary question of the imputability of the practice of torture alleged by the applicant Governments to the Greek State. It first dwelt on the notion of 'an administrative practice of torture and ill-treatment' (this examination was rendered necessary because, in the view of the Commission, whenever one is confronted with such a practice, the local remedies, the exhaustion of which is imposed by the Convention, 'will of necessity be sidestepped or rendered inadequate'). In dealing with the 'administrative practice of torture or ill-treatment,' the Commission stated that 'acts prohibited by Article 3 of the Convention will engage the responsibility of a Contracting State only if they are committed by persons exercising public authority' (*Yearbook* 12, p. 195) and went on to state that these acts can be imputed to a State also when there is 'official tolerance' by the State authorities of ill-treatment ('by *official practice* is meant that, though acts of torture or ill-treatment are plainly illegal, they are tolerated in the sense that the superiors of those immediately responsible though cognisant of such acts, take no action to punish them or prevent their repetition; or that higher authority, in face of numerous allegations, manifests indifference by refusing any adequate investigation of their truth or falsity, or that in judicial proceedings, a fair hearing of such complaints is denied' (*ibid.*, p. 196). The Commission subsequently dwelt on the concepts of State responsibility and 'official tolerance' in relation to alleged cases of torture, in the *Ireland v. UK* case, *Yearbook* 19, p. 758 ff.

Furthermore, in the *Cyprus v. Turkey* case the Commission, when dealing among other things with instances of alleged rape of female inhabitants of Cyprus by Turkish soldiers or officers, stated the following: 'The evidence shows that rapes were committed by Turkish soldiers and at least in two cases even by Turkish officers, and this not only in some isolated cases of indiscipline. It has not been shown that the Turkish authorities took adequate measures to prevent this happening or that they generally took any disciplinary measures following such incidents. The Commission therefore considers that the non-prevention of the said acts is imputable to Turkey under the Convention.' Rep. Com., 10 July 1976, Application no. 6780/74 and Application no. 6950/75, para. 373.

[11] Judgment of 18 January 1978, Series A no. 25, p. 65, para. 162. See also Dec. Adm. Com., Application no. 11701/85 (*E. v. Norway*), 7 March 1988, DH(88)2, Appendix IV, p. 17.

[12] The Commission stressed in particular the lack of hygiene; the lack of natural light; overcrowding; the lack of access to elementary sanitary facilities; the fact that when detained in 'strict

of political prisoners in Averoff Prison were also unjustifiable and amounted to a breach of Article 3;[13] and that in addition the harsh manner of the separation of detainees from their families and the gross overcrowding in the camps on Leros Island were inhuman.[14]

The well-known case of *Ireland v. United Kingdom* should also be mentioned. The applicant alleged, and the Commission held, that the use by British police in Northern Ireland, in 1971, of five 'techniques' as an aid to the interrogation of fourteen persons amounted to torture. These 'techniques' consisted basically of hooding the detainees, subjecting them to a continuous loud, hissing noise, depriving them of sleep, subjecting them to a reduced diet, and making them stand for periods of some hours against a wall in a painful posture. The Court held instead that the five techniques constituted inhuman treatment. It stated that they 'were applied in combination, with premeditation and for hours at a stretch. They caused, if not actual bodily injury, at least intense physical and mental suffering to the persons subjected thereto and also led to acute psychiatric disturbances during interrogation. They accordingly fell into the category of inhuman treatment within the meaning of Art. 3.'[15]

Another interesting case is *Cyprus v. Turkey*. The Commission had among other things to deal with allegations of rape and physical ill-treatment inflicted by Turkish soldiers on the inhabitants of Cyprus in 1974. It concluded that the incidents of large-scale rape amounted to inhuman treatment; similarly the fact that in a considerable number of cases prisoners had been severely beaten or otherwise ill-treated by Turkish soldiers, and that these acts of ill-treatment had caused considerable injuries and in at least one case the death of the victim, also amounted to inhuman treatment. The same definition was given to the 'withholding of an adequate supply of food and drinking water and of adequate medical treatment in a number of cases'.[16]

Cases where the Commission and the Court indicated, in abstract terms, a possible breach

In other cases the Commission and the Court, while holding that in the specific instance under consideration there had been no breach of Article 3, left the

---

solitary confinement,' detainees were deprived of any food; the fact that repeatedly during the first days of their detention inmates were forced to sleep in their clothes, without blankets, on the bare cement floor; the insufficient medical care; the lack of contact with the outside world; the lack of recreation and exercise, particularly for those held in solitary confinement cells. See *Yearbook* 12, pp. 468–80, for the report of the Sub-Commission and p. 505 for the conclusion of the plenary Commission.

[13] The Commission stressed in particular the complete absence of heating in winter, the lack of hot water, the poor lavatory facilities, the unsatisfactory dental treatment and the tight restriction on letters and visits to prisoners (see *ibid.*, pp. 482–89 and p. 505).

[14] See *ibid.*, pp. 489–97 and p. 505.

[15] Judgment of 18 January 1978, Series A no. 25, p. 66 (*Yearbook* 21, p. 602).

[16] Rep. Com., 10 July 1976, paras 373–414.

door open, as it were, to other possible violations, in that they indicated other instances where it could be concluded that a breach had occurred. In the case of *Campbell and Cosans* the Commission and the Court held that the use of corporal punishment as a disciplinary measure in school did not amount to a breach of Article 3. However, the Court pointed out that 'provided it is sufficiently real and immediate, a mere threat of conduct prohibited by Article 3 may in itself conflict with that provision. Thus, to threaten an individual with torture might in some circumstances constitute at least inhuman treatment.'[17] Furthermore, in a number of cases relating to harsh conditions of detention in prison, the Commission, while dismissing the application, has stated that 'complete sensory isolation [of a detainee] coupled with total social isolation, can destroy the personality and constitutes a form of treatment which cannot be justified by the requirements of security or any other reason.'[18] In addition, the Commission has often stated that failure to provide adequate medical treatment may be contrary to Article 3.[19] Finally, in numerous cases the Commission and the Court have pointed out that a person's deportation, expulsion or extradition may give rise to an issue under Article 3 'where there are serious reasons to believe that the individual will be subjected, in the receiving State, to treatment contrary to that Article.'[20]

Cases where no breach of Article 3 was found

Let us now turn to the most significant cases where the Commission or the Court held that allegations of inhuman treatment or punishment were ill-founded. These cases refer primarily to the following areas: the conditions of prison detention, in particular, solitary confinement; compulsory medical treatment of detainees; life imprisonment as such; the handcuffing of prisoners in public; the claim of persons released from prison, following a criminal conviction, to economic and social measures designed to ensure a minimum subsistence payment or employment; the cutting off of electricity to a family living in a social welfare centre. I shall focus briefly on the most revealing cases.

---

[17] Judgment of 25 February 1982, Series A no. 48, p. 12, para. 25.

[18] Rep. Com., Application no. 5310/71, *Ireland v. United Kingdom*, p. 379; Dec. Adm., Application nos 7572/76, 7586/76 and 7587/76, *Ensslin, Bander, Raspe v. FRG*, DR 14, p. 109; Dec. Adm., Application no. 8317/78, *McFeeley and others v. UK*, DR 20, p. 82.

[19] See, e.g., Dec. Com. 6 May 1978, Application no. 7994/77, *Kotalla v. The Netherlands*, DR 14, p. 238; Com. Rep. 7 October 1981, Application no. 6870/75, *B. v. UK*, DR 32, p. 5; Com. Rep. 8 December 1982, Application no. 9044/80, *Chartier v. Italy*, DR 33, p. 41; Com. Rep. 1 March 1991, Application no. 10533, *Herczegfalvy v. Austria*, p. 48, para. 242.

[20] See Dec. 3 May 1983, Application no. 10308/83, *Altun v. FRG*, DR 41, pp. 209–35; Dec. 13 December 1984, Application no. 10078/82, *M. v. France*, DR 41. p. 103; Dec. 12 March 1984, Application no. 10479/83, *Kirkwood v. UK*, DR 37, pp. 158–91; Rep. 19 January 1989, Application no. 14038/88, *Soering v. UK*, pp. 16–27, paras 94–154. As for the Court, see the judgment of 20 March 1991 in the *Cruz Varas* case, Series A no. 201, paras 69–70, as well as the judgment of 30 October 1991 in the *Vilvarajah and others* case (no. 45/1990/236/902–6, paras 102–16). For the *Soering* case, see section 5(A) below.

An important case concerning *conditions of detention* is *B. v. UK,* decided by the Commission in 1981. The applicant had been detained for more than three and a half years in Broadmoor Hospital, a 'special hospital' where detainees requiring treatment under conditions of special security on account of their dangerous, violent or criminal propensities are held. The applicant claimed that he was held there in 'extremely slum conditions.' He alleged, in particular, that (i) Broadmoor was grossly overcrowded and lacking in sanitary facilities (he referred in particular to the filthy condition of toilets and lack of washing facilities; (ii) he had to live constantly with murderers, rapists, arsonists, sexual perverts and other lunatics and that there was a constant atmosphere of violence (in particular, he alleged that in the dormitories the beds were only six to twelve inches apart, that observation lights were kept on all night, that seriously disturbed patients occasionally went on the rampage at night, shouting and screaming, and that the atmosphere in the dormitories was foul and airless since the majority of the windows were screwed shut); (iii) he had received no medical treatment whatever since being in Broadmoor; (iv) he was not kept sufficiently occupied, found the daily routine boring, received no preparation for return to the world outside and was afraid of vegetating. The Commission examined these allegations one by one and dismissed them all. Since the reasoning of the Commission is indicative of its attitude concerning Article 3, it may prove apposite to quote some relevant passages. Regarding overcrowding, the Commission stated the following:

The Commission notes, firstly, that the applicant has a tendency to exaggerate the inadequacy of conditions in Broadmoor Hospital partly because of his uncooperative and negative attitude towards the institution where he considered he should never have been detained.

Nevertheless certain of the applicant's complaints have some basis, particularly that concerning overcrowding. There is no doubt that there was deplorable overcrowding in the dormitory accommodation in which the applicant slept from February 1974 to December 1976. Particularly unpleasant must have been the dormitories in Kent and Cornwall Houses between February and August 1974. This serious overcrowding is borne out by official reports of the Parliamentary Estimates Committee and the Butler Committee. Moreover, although major improvements have been carried out by the time of the [Commission's] Delegates visit to Broadmoor in July 1977, the dormitory accommodation still appeared cramped and bleak. However by that time the applicant had been located to a single room.

Although the overcrowding obviously led to a lack of privacy and the applicant's fear of attack by other patients, the Commission finds that the applicant's fears were exaggerated and that hospital staff maintained an adequate degree of control over patients.[21]

This argument is indeed surprising. It seems that one of the reasons for dismissing the applicant's complaints was his tendency to exaggerate the harshness of conditions of detention. The Commission also attached importance to the fact

---

[21] Dec. 7 October 1981, Application no. 6870/75, DR 32, pp. 29–30, paras 175–77.

that, although for two and a half years the applicant had suffered from over-crowding, when the Commission's Delegates visited Broadmoor, he had been located in a single room. It is submitted that the fact of getting a single room at the time of the Delegates' visit can in no way reduce the importance of, let alone cancel, the previous conditions of overcrowding. One is left with the feeling that the Commission deliberately avoided passing judgment on whether or not over-crowding—to the extent that the applicant had suffered from it for a long period of time—amounted to inhuman treatment.

Let us now move on to the way the Commission tackled the question of alleged lack of sanitation and hygiene. It stated the following:

As regards the applicant's complaints about sanitary conditions, contrary to the appli-cant's assertions, there were toilet facilities in Kent and Cornwall Houses. It is true, however, that there were no such facilities in the small dormitory on Ward II of Dorset House during the applicant's stay there from October 1974 to about the late summer of 1975. There were only chamber pots and a commode. The toilet, which was subse-quently installed, appears not to have been screened by a curtain at first. Moreover, it was accepted by hospital staff during the Delegates' visit in July 1977 that, outside the dormi-tories, the sanitary conditions, washing facilities and toilets were less than satisfactory. It appears that the applicant unduly and obsessively magnified his complaint concerning the absence of toilet paper.

The applicant also seems to have exaggerated his complaint of a lack of hygiene in the hospital. It appears that many patients were employed on ward cleaning, although for a limited time, but that, given the nature of the institution, facilities could rapidly become soiled. However the Commission finds no reason to doubt that regular cleaning was car-ried out during the applicant's detention in Broadmoor. The Commission . . . concludes that, although facilities in Broadmoor Hospital at the material time were extremely unsatisfactory, nevertheless, in all the circumstances of the case, they did not amount to inhuman or degrading treatment contrary to Art. 3 of the Convention.[22]

Again, one cannot but express dissatisfaction with the Commission's reason-ing. Regarding the sanitary conditions, one of the principal reasons for the Commission's rejection of the applicant's complaints was his so-called obsession with the absence of toilet paper. The Commission did not, however, investigate whether the lack of sanitation and the consequent necessity for detainees to com-ply with the needs of nature in the presence of other detainees, together with the poor washing facilities and toilets outside the dormitories, amounted to inhuman or degrading treatment. The Commission simply ducked the issue.

Let us now consider how the Commission dealt with the applicant's complaint about the alleged total lack of adequate employment and occupation. It rejected the complaint with the following words:

The Commission notes that during the assessment period (December 1973–February 1974) in Norfolk House, when the applicant was first admitted to Broadmoor, he was

---

[22] *Ibid.*, p. 30, paras 178–79 and 181.

not given any employment as he underwent the routine tests given to new arrivals. From February 1974 to December 1975 the applicant was employed on cleaning chores which would have only lasted a short time each, probably not more than one hour . . . This work lasted an average of about five hours a day, five days per week. The applicant had not been willing to take advantage of other offers of employment off the ward, such as in the workshops, for fear of assault by other patients. It is true that the applicant had requested a much demanded job in the hospital garden, but in view of his uncooperative attitude, the time he required off work for his visits, etc. and the privileged (reward) nature of the employment, the request was refused. In the circumstances, the Commission does not find that the applicant was treated unfairly vis-à-vis other patients in this respect.

The Commission also finds that the applicant's complaints of a lack of recreational and occupational facilities were unfounded. He refused to take advantage of educational facilities, up to Open University level, which the hospital could offer, even though he was an intelligent person, with quite advanced educational qualifications already. Weather permitting, he was able to play cricket and football and receive visits on the terrace. He was a member of the classical film club and could make use of the library, albeit small.[23]

Although here the Commission's arguments appear to be more plausible, one may still wonder why it did not take into account that, since the applicant suffered from paranoid schizophrenia, it was fairly natural for him to refuse employment in the workshops or to take advantage of education facilities for fear of assault by other patients. One may also wonder why the Commission did not question the suitability of the British authorities' decision not to give the applicant the gardening job he so strongly requested. It can be reasonably concluded that, although probably not inhuman, the attitude of the British authorities as regards the applicant's employment and occupation had nevertheless been, at the very least, highly questionable.

Let us now come to the final point raised by the applicant, that concerning his medical treatment. The Commission first of all pointed out that three different issues were to be examined, namely, the necessity for the applicant to be confined at Broadmoor Hospital, the surveillance of his mental health, and the actual medical treatment he had been given. It then disposed of the first two issues with sound arguments. As for the question of psychiatric treatment, the Commission stressed that the applicant had been given none, for he had always refused any such treatment. While expressing reservations about the attitude of the medical officer in charge of the applicant, the Commission concluded that the behaviour of the medical staff did not amount to a breach of Article 3.[24]

In addition to the questionable way in which the Commission dealt with specific points concerning the applicant's complaints, the Commission's decision lends itself to a more general criticism: it deals with each issue *per se*, without considering a possibly cumulative effect, that is to say, without tackling the question whether each aspect of the British authorities' alleged misconduct, although

---

[23] *Ibid.*, p. 31, paras 183–85.
[24] *Ibid.*, pp. 31–35, paras 187–202.

not very serious in itself, collectively added up to a general standard of inhuman treatment. This sort of criticism was voiced by a member of the Commission, Mr. Opsahl, in his dissenting opinion (which was shared in this respect by another member, Mr. Melchior). Mr. Opsahl also added another objection: in his view the Commission should have considered the question of proportionality, namely whether there was a 'lack of proportionality between the applicant's past behaviour (offence) and its adverse consequences for him.'[25] I submit that this criterion is, however, too broad to be workable as a standard for gauging whether or not national authorities infringe upon Article 3 with regard to conditions of detention.

Another significant case where the findings of the Commission are open to objection is *Chartier v. Italy,* decided in 1982. The applicant, a French national detained in Italy as a result of a conviction for murder, was very ill: he suffered from hereditary obesity and from various respiratory troubles, as well as hypertension and pancreatic diabetes. He claimed that his detention amounted to inhuman treatment, for in the detention centre for the physically handicapped where he was held, he was unable to get the medical treatment necessary for his condition. He also pointed out that the medical authorities of the detention centre had requested the Italian Ministry of Justice to authorize his hospitalization in a centre specializing in the treatment of obesity. The applicant therefore asked to be released on parole, in order to be able to be treated at this kind of highly specialized medical institution. The Commission rejected the application, with a tortuous argumentation. It first stated that the medical records produced showed that the applicant had been given the necessary medical treatment in prison; it added, however, that it was true that, given his serious health problems, detention for Mr. Chartier was a 'particularly painful experience.' In this context the Commission made two remarks: first, it was gratified to see that the Italian authorities had undertaken to hospitalize the applicant whenever this should prove necessary; second, the Commission 'would be sensitive to any measure the Italian authorities might take with a view to either attenuating the effects of his detention or to terminating it.' It is submitted that the reasons that the Commission brought to bear were not compelling enough to demonstrate that the detention of the applicant did not amount to inhuman treatment. It is striking that the Commission did not find it necessary to make use of the three aforementioned criteria for the application of Article 3 (intent, suffering, lack of justification). In this connection it can be argued that at least two of these criteria—precisely those two which in my view are decisive (see further discussion below)—may lead to a belief that Italy was indeed in breach of Article 3: the degree of suffering caused by detention to the applicant was very high, and at the same time the security requirements justifying detention were not so compelling as to outweigh the necessity that the applicant should not suffer. It is also striking that the Commission

---

[25] *Ibid.*, pp. 41–44.

indulged in suggestions or appeals to the respondent Government; although the making of such appeals probably comes within the Commission's province, it would have been more straightforward to opt neatly for a breach, or a lack of breach, of Article 3.

Let us now consider the numerous cases concerning *solitary confinement*. As pointed out above, in a large number of Commission decisions a difference is drawn between two situations: the first, where a detainee is subjected to total social and sensory isolation, and the second, where a detainee is removed from association with other prisoners for security, disciplinary or protective reasons. According to the Commission, in the first case isolation can destroy the detainee's personality or cause severe mental or physical suffering; it is therefore contrary to Article 3. By contrast, the other form of segregation is not normally to be regarded as inhuman treatment or punishment, depending of course on the circumstances surrounding each particular instance.[26] With regard to the second category the Commission has often added that 'prolonged solitary confinement is undesirable, especially where the person is detained on remand.'[27]

With all due respect, it should be emphasized that, by so doing, the Commission has chosen a fairly easy way out. For, by saying that total social and sensory isolation undoubtedly amounts to inhuman treatment, it has stated the obvious: this sort of isolation would be equivalent to being placed in a kind of tomb; who could therefore deny that it would be in breach of Article 3? It is no coincidence that so far the Commission has never come across any cases of this kind; without going to the lengths of saying that such treatment can only exist as a figment of the imagination, it is at least probable that it is not ever carried out—at any rate not among Council of Europe Members. Indeed, this isolation, as envisaged by the Commission, would presuppose a combination of a medieval dungeon, where the prisoner would not even be able to speak to the jailer and where food and water would be passed through a small slot, and a highly sophisticated modern cell, equipped with soundproofing and permanent electrical lighting. Having ruled out the compatibility of this extreme sort of isolation with Article 3, the Commission has opted for the admissibility—in principle, and subject to the circumstances of each case—of what we may call 'ordinary' solitary confinement. It then has hastened to add a caveat: 'it is undesirable.' Now, it is precisely

[26] See, e.g., Dec. Application no. 1392/62, *X. v. FRG*, CD 17, p. I; Dec. Application no. 5006/71, *X. v. UK*, CD 39, p. 91; Dec. Application no. 2749/66, *Kenneth Hugh De Courcy v. UK, Yearbook* 10, p. 382; Dec. Application no. 6038/73, *X v. FRG*, CD 44, p. 115; Dec. Application no. 4448/70, Second *Greek* case, CD 34, p. 70; Dec. Application no. 7854/77, *Sergio Bonzl v. Switzerland*, DR 12, p. 185; Dec. Application no. 8317/78, *McFeeley and others v. UK*, DR 20, p. 441; Dec. 10 July 1980, Application no. 8158/78, *X v. UK*, DR 21, p. 99; Rep. 16 December 1982, Application no. 8463/78, *Kroecher and Moeller v. Switzerland*, Report, p. 53; Dec. 7 March 1988, Application no. 11701/85, *E. v. Norway*, DH(88)2, pp. 17–18.

[27] See, e.g., Dec. Application no. 6948/73, *X v. FRG*, CD 44, p. 115; Rep. 16 December 1982, Application no. 8463/78, *Kroecher and Moeller v. Switzerland*, Rep. p. 53; Dec. 7 March 1988, Application no. 11701/85, *E. v. Norway*, pp. 17–18.

this latter category of isolation that constitutes the typical deprivation of social intercourse in prisons—witness the fact that it is with precisely this issue that the Commission has had to deal any time it has been presented with the question of solitary confinement. On this typical form of isolation, the Commission has uttered pronouncements that often appear questionable. I shall mention only three cases here.

In the *X v. UK* case the applicant had been held in solitary confinement for approximately 760 days. According to the respondent Government, the restrictions on the applicant's freedom to associate with other prisoners were due to his being classified as 'category A' (a high security risk), to his being on the escape list, and also to various disciplinary punishments. The Commission noted that, on the one hand, the applicant's confinement was justified by security reasons, while on the other, his conditions in prison did not resemble social and sensory isolation; he was allowed normal visits, received a daily exercise period of one hour (on some occasions with other 'category A' prisoners), was able to borrow books from the prison library, had access to writing materials and newspapers, could work in his cell and was allowed to attend chapel service, albeit segregated from the rest of the congregation. The Commission therefore concluded that, although the applicant had been 'segregated for an unusual and undesirable length of time,' his isolation was neither arbitrary nor of such severity as to fall within the scope of Article 3.[28]

Two objections can be made. First, it is highly questionable whether a comparison between the situation at issue and an abstract case of total social and sensory deprivation is of any value. Once one takes as a standard of evaluation an extreme (and, to my mind, entirely theoretical) situation of this type, it clearly follows that any condition falling short of it becomes admissible. To put it another way, what is fallacious, in the Commission's reasoning, is its point of departure, namely the abstract situation referred to. Second, when comparing the security reasons warranting segregation and the ill-effects of segregation for the detainee, one should weigh up security considerations against not only the possible physical or mental harm caused by isolation, but also *two basic requirements concerning imprisonment* (both laid down in the European Prison Rules): (a) the requirement that deprivation of liberty be the only penalty meted out to detainees, that is, that no further suffering be inflicted on them as a result of very poor prison conditions, harsh disciplinary measures and the like; and (b) the requirement that imprisonment be geared as much as possible to rehabilitation, so as to enable prisoners to return to normal life after detention. This means that, when faced with a case of solitary confinement, one should in particular ask oneself whether it may not jeopardize the detainee's chances of attaining social reinsertion after prison, or, at the very least, whether it may aggravate his or her psychological conditions. In this respect it is worth citing a passage from the Explanatory Memorandum to the Recommendation (No. R(82)17) on the custody and treatment of dangerous

---

[28] Dec. 10 July 1980, Application no. 8158/78, DR 21, pp. 98–100.

prisoners, adopted by the Committee of Ministers of the Council of Europe on 24 September 1982:

Human dignity is to be respected notwithstanding criminality or dangerousness and if human persons have to be imprisoned in circumstances of greater severity than the conventional, every effort should be made, subject to the requirements of safe custody, good order and security and the requirements of community well being, to ensure that living environment and conditions offset the deleterious effects—decreased mental efficiency, depression, anxiety, aggressiveness, neurosis, negative values, altered biorhythms—of the severer custodial situation. In the most serious instances prisoners regress to a merely vegetative life. Generally the impairment may be reversible but if imprisonment, especially in maximum security, is prolonged, perception of time and space and self can be permanently and seriously impaired—'annihilation of personality' (para 43).

Similar considerations can also be put forward for the other two cases. One is very famous: *Kroecher and Moeller v. Switzerland*. In this case the conditions of detention were so extreme that even by the Commission's own standards it should have been easy to find that Article 3 had been infringed upon by the Swiss authorities. Indeed, isolation was even harsher than in the *X v. UK* case, although only in the first month of the two German terrorists' detention: their cells were located on a floor which was empty at the time (the occupants of the other cells had been removed); the cells' windows had frosted glass panes, and even the small rectangle in the window which was usually of transparent glass had been painted over; there was continuous artificial lighting. Nevertheless, the Commission held that this was not contrary to Article 3, for there was no acoustic isolation from the other floors, not were the cells equipped with any special form of soundproofing. Similarly, there was no total social isolation, for the detainees could have regular medical examinations (presumably by prison doctors), could read books and write letters, and had a right (which they did not exercise) to talk to the chaplain or to representatives of the Prisoners' Aid Committee (the detainees were allowed to have contact with their lawyers and families only after the first month of isolation). The reasoning of the Commission once again brings to the fore the artificiality of its taking as a point of reference 'total sensory and social isolation.' If one considers the conditions of the two German terrorists in their first month of isolation, one cannot help thinking that were one to apply the Commission's standards, a breach of Article 3 could have been found only if they had been literally walled in. One is at a loss to see how being able to hear some noise from other prison floors can be regarded as sensory communication. Similarly, one cannot see how being visited by a prison doctor, being able to send and receive (presumably censored) letters, and being able to read books can be regarded as tantamount to human communication. It is therefore not surprising that four members of the Commission expressed their disagreement in a forceful and thoroughly convincing dissenting opinion.[29]

---

[29] See the opinion of Commissioners Tenekides, Melchior, Sampaio and Weitzel, *ibid.*, pp. 97–98.

No less disquieting is the other case, *E. v. Norway*. The applicant had spent approximately eight years in various Norwegian prisons, placed in 'preventive detention' after receiving various sentences for a number of violent crimes. Of these eight years he had spent approximately five in solitary confinement, including a total of 118 days in security cells. It appeared from medical records that, although not insane, he was extremely aggressive and had an 'underdeveloped and impaired mental capacity.' The Commission made a series of remarks, some of them contradictory. It stressed, first, that the applicant's segregation was to a large extent related to his aggressive behaviour. It then pointed to the features of his segregation: apart from when he was placed in security cells, he had access to radio and, to a certain extent, television; he could read newspapers and borrow magazines and books from the prison library; every day he spent one hour in the exercise yard (presumably by himself); and several times a day he had contact with prison staff. Third, the Commission noted that in his most recent stay at Ullersmo prison, the applicant had been subjected to a system which was quite different from that of the other prisoners in solitary confinement: among other things he had been allowed to go home for short periods approximately once every three months and had also been released from prison under protective surveillance, although these attempts had failed due to the applicant's own behaviour. Fourth, the Commission emphasized that it was not convinced that 'the applicant's placement in prison was suitable to counteract [his] aggressive tendency.' But then it immediately hastened to point out that 'the care and treatment which the applicant received while in detention does not reveal to the Commission any indications which could lead to the conclusion that the applicant was not looked after as well as prison conditions allowed. Further, . . . the prison authorities appear to have done what was possible under their competence, including working out programmes which could increase the applicant's contact with the outside community.' Fifth, the Commission then added a remark that appears to be contradictory both with what it had already stated and within itself:

The Commission has not overlooked the statements of the Norwegian courts . . . from which it appears that the applicant should have received treatment for his mental deficiencies in a hospital rather than being placed in preventive detention where he obviously could not receive any such treatment. The Commission can only support these views. Furthermore, the Commission has noted with concern that the authorities, under the court authorisation given to them, obviously failed for a regrettable period of time to implement the measures appropriate to the applicant's needs. Nevertheless, having regard to the case law of the Commission and the Court of Human Rights and to the circumstances of the applicant's detention, in particular in the light of his distinct dangerousness, the Commission must conclude that the stringency of the measures, when compared to the objective pursued and the effects on the applicant, did not attain the level of seriousness which would make the treatment inhuman or degrading within the meaning of Art. 3 of the Convention.[30]

---

[30] Dec. Adm., 7 March 1988, Application no. 11701/85, DH(88)2, pp. 17–18.

My short summary of the Commission's considerations, as well as the passage just quoted, clearly show, I believe, that the ultimate reason for the Commission's holding that in the case at issue there was no breach of Article 3 was its intent to stick to its own case law. For it clearly appears from the Commission's recital of the facts and the law that the applicant had indeed been kept in total social isolation for a very long period of time, that the prison authorities had failed to implement the measures appropriate to his needs and—what is even more important—his mental problems would have been better addressed in a hospital. The conclusion that seems to me to be inescapable is that in this case solitary confinement was an utterly inadequate response to the detainee's aggressive behaviour; instead of improving his mental condition, such treatment was bound simply to aggravate it. The balancing of security requirements against the rights and needs of the applicant should, in fact, have led to the conclusion that the respondent Government had disregarded Article 3.

ii. Torture

The Commission and the Court have consistently stated that torture is an aggravated form of inhuman treatment and is characterized by its purpose, which may be the obraining of information or confessions, or the infliction of punishment.[31] The Court has also pointed out that Article 3, by using the term torture, intended 'to attach a special stigma to deliberate inhuman treatment causing very serious and cruel suffering.'[32] Thus, it is clear that the two organs distinguish torture from inhuman treatment or punishment in two respects: torture is *more serious or grave,* in that it causes greater suffering; and torture is always carried out for a *purpose* (which may be one of those just mentioned, or also that of intimidating or coercing the tortured or a third person or that of discriminating against the tortured or a third person, to make use of the definition enshrined in Article 1 of the 1984 UN Convention Against Torture). This entails that for the Commission and the Court the intent to cause severe mental or physical suffering (which, as we saw above, is one of the constitutive elements of 'inhuman treatment or punishment') is not sufficient: in addition to this intent there must also be a specific purpose, that is, one of the purposes just referred to.

It goes without saying that the appraisal of the circumstances of each case, in order to establish if the requisite conditions are met, is a matter of judicial discretion, as in the case of 'inhuman treatment or punishment.' This is indeed borne out by the fact that in at least one instance the Commission and the Court widely

---

[31] See Op. Com., 5 November 1969, *Greek* case, *Yearbook* 12, p. 186, para. 2; Dec. Adm, Com., 3 February 1971, Application no. 4220/69, CD 37, p. 59 (*Yearbook* 14, p. 276); Op. Com., 25 January 1976, *Ireland v. UK, Yearbook* 19, p. 794; Op. Com., 14 December 1976, *Tyrer v. UK,* p. 13, para. 29; *Ireland v. UK* judgment of 18 January 1978, Series A no. 23, pp. 66–67 (*Yearbook* 21, p. 602); *Tyrer v. UK* judgment of 25 April 1978, Series A no. 26, p. 131; *Campbell and Cosans v. UK* judgment of 25 February 1982, Series A no. 48, p. 12.

[32] See *Ireland v. UK* judgment of 18 January 1978, Series A no. 25, pp. 66–67, para. 167. This statement has since been taken up by the Court in subsequent pronouncements.

differed on the characterization of the relevant facts: as is well known, in the
Ireland v. UK case, the Commission held that the five 'techniques' used by the
British police in Northern Ireland for 'aiding' interrogation constituted a form of
torture, while the Court found instead that they were not tantamount to torture
but to 'inhuman treatment.'

Let us now consider the cases where the Commission or the Court have found
a State responsible of having inflicted torture. While the Court so far has not
made such a finding (in the *Ireland v. UK* case it disagreed with the Commission),
the Commission has made a finding of torture in two cases: the *Greek* case and
the *Ireland v. UK* case. Given that I have already recalled the main elements of
the latter, I shall here refer briefly to the former. The Commission investigated
30 instances of alleged torture by the Greek authorities and was satisfied that in
at least 11 of them torture had been practised beyond any doubt. Torture took
mostly the form of *falanga* ('the beating of the feet with a wooden or metal stick
or bar which, if skilfully done, breaks no bones, makes no skin lesions, and leaves
no permanent and recognisable marks, but causes intense pain and swelling of
the feet'), and severe beatings of all parts of the body. But it also included the
application of electric shock, mock execution or threats to shoot or kill the victim,
squeezing of the head in a vice, pulling out of hair from the head or pubic region,
kicking of the male genital organs, dripping water on the head and intense noise
to prevent sleep.[33]

iii. Degrading treatment or punishment

The Commission and the Court have consistently argued that a treatment or
punishment is degrading when it grossly humiliates an individual before himself or others, or drives him to act against his conscience or will.[34] The Court
has also emphasized that, for a punishment to be 'degrading,' the humiliation or
debasement involved must exceed a particular level and must in any event be different from the normal humiliation involved in being criminally convicted.[35] In
addition, it need not be necessary that the humiliating treatment or punishment
cause severe or long-lasting physical effects or adverse psychological effects; while
these are likely to occur, they are not indispensable—or, at any rate, crucial—
elements of this notion.[36] What matters is that the treatment or punishment
should constitute an assault on precisely that which is one of the main purposes
of Article 3 to protect, namely a person's 'dignity and physical integrity.'[37] As is

[33] Com. Rep., 18 November 1969, *Yearbook* 12, pp. 499–500.
[34] See in particular Op. Com., 5 November 1969, *Greek* case, *Yearbook* 12, p. 186; Op. Com.,
25 January 1976, *Ireland v. UK Yearbook* 19, p. 748; *Tyrer v. UK* judgment of 25 April 1978, Series
A no. 26, p. 15 (*Yearbook* 21, p. 612); *Guzzardi v. Italy* judgment of 6 November 1978, Series A no.
39, p. 31, para. 80; *Campbell and Cosans v. UK* judgment of 25 February 1982, Series A no. 48, p.
13.
[35] *Tyrer v. UK* judgment of 25 April 1978, Series A no. 26, p. 15, para. 30.
[36] *Ibid.*, p. 16, para. 33.
[37] *Ibid.*

apparent in the *Campbell and Cosans v. UK* case, the physical or mental suffering may, however, prove important as evidence of whether or not the alleged victim of debasement felt humiliated in his own or others' eyes.[38]

The Court has also stated that the assessment is, in the nature of things, relative: it depends on all the circumstances of the case and, in particular, on the nature and context of the treatment or punishment itself and the manner and method of its execution.[39]

It is apparent from the above that in the opinion of the Commission and the Court the concept of degrading treatment or punishment does not hinge on the three elements propounded by the Strasbourg organs for the notion of 'inhuman' treatment or punishment (that is, intent, severe mental or physical suffering, and lack of justification), nor, *a fortiori*, does it require the elements of gravity and purpose necessary for establishing the existence of torture. Instead, degrading treatment or punishment means severe humiliation (in either the victim's own or others' eyes) or severe debasement, driving the victim to act against his will or conscience.

Let us now briefly consider the major cases where the Commission and the Court have pronounced on this issue. In the *Tyrer v. UK* case, the Commission and the Court found that the applicant, who had been sentenced to three strokes of the birch in accordance with the penal legislation of the Isle of Man, had been subjected to a judicial corporal punishment that was degrading and hence fell short of the demands of Article 3. The Court, in particular, used forceful arguments to reach this conclusion and phrased its reasoning in lofty language that is worth quoting:

The very nature of judicial corporal punishment is that it involves one human being inflicting physical violence on another human being. Furthermore, it is institutionalized violence, that is in the present case violence permitted by the law, ordered by the judicial authorities of the State and carried out by the police authorities of the State... Thus, although the applicant did not suffer any severe or long-lasting physical effects, his punishment—whereby he was treated as an object in the power of the authorities— constituted an assault on precisely that which it is one of the main purposes of Art. 3 to protect, namely a person's dignity and physical integrity. Neither can it be excluded

---

[38] Judgement of 25 February 1982, Series A no. 48, pp. 13–14, paras 30–31. This case concerned the corporal punishment of two school children. One of them had not even been threatened with the punishment, while the other had been threatened with the punishment but had never actually been subjected to it, for he refused the disciplinary measure and was suspended from school. The Court, after excluding that the alleged victim felt humiliated in the eyes of others on account of his being threatened with corporal chastisement, also ruled out that he was debased in his own eyes, because he had not actually been subjected to the punishment and in addition it had not been shown 'by means of medical certificates or otherwise' that either he or the other child 'suffered any adverse psychological or other effects.' The Court added that the pupil on whom the disciplinary measure had been imposed but not executed 'may well have experienced feelings of apprehension or disquiet when he came close to an infliction' of the corporal punishment, 'but such feelings are not sufficient to amount to degrading treatment within the meaning of Art. 3.'

[39] *Ibid.*, p. 15, para. 30.

that the punishment may have had adverse psychological effects. The institutionalised character of this violence is further compounded by the whole aura of official procedure attending the punishment and by the fact that those inflicting it were total strangers to the offender.

Admittedly, the relevant legislation provides that in any event birching shall not take place later than six months after the passing of sentence. However, this does not alter the fact that there had been an interval of several weeks since the applicant's conviction by the juvenile court and a considerable delay in the police station where the punishment was carried out. Accordingly, in addition to the physical pain he experienced, Mr. Tyrer was subjected to the mental anguish of anticipating the violence he was to have inflicted on him . . .

Accordingly, viewing these circumstances as a whole, the Court finds that the applicant was subjected to a punishment in which the element of humiliation attained the level inherent in the notion of 'degrading punishment'. . . The indignity of having the punishment administered over the bare posterior aggravated to some extent the degrading character of the applicant's punishment but it was not the only or determing factor.[40]

Other important cases where the Commission found that a degrading treatment or punishment had been inflicted, or could be regarded as having been meted out, are the *East African Asians v. UK* case[41] and the *M. and K. Warwick v. UK* case. In the latter a school headmaster, after seeing two young females students smoking cigarettes in the street outside the school, had given a stroke with a cane on the left hand of one of them, in front of the deputy headmaster and the other girl. The Commission found that considering the circumstances of the case as a whole, 'the corporal punishment inflicted upon the second applicant [the first was her mother] caused her humiliation and attained a sufficient level of seriousness to be regarded as degrading within the meaning of Art. 3 of the Convention.'[42]

---

[40] Series A no. 26, pp. 16–17, paras 33 and 35.

[41] The applicants, who were citizens of the UK and Colonies or had an equivalent status, and were holders of UK passports, had been denied entry or permanent residence in the UK. They claimed that this refusal amounted to treating them as second-class citizens and was a degrading treatment. In its decision on admissibility of 10 October 1970, the Commission stated the following: '[D]iscrimination based on race could, in certain circumstances, of itself amount to degrading treatment within the meaning of Art. 3 of the Convention . . . [T]he Commission considers that it is generally recognised that a special importance should be attached to discrimination based on race, and that publicly to single out a group of persons for differential treatment on the basis of race might, in certain circumstances, constitute a special form of affront to human dignity . . . [T]herefore, differential treatment of a group of persons on the basis of race might be capable of constituting degrading treatment in circumstances where differential treatment on some other ground, such as language, would raise no question' (*Yearbook* 13, p. 994). As is well known, following the adoption by the UK of measures intended to facilitate the entry of UK passport holders from East Africa, on 21 October 1977 the Committee of Ministers decided that no further action was called for with regard to Article 3. However, it did not authorize the publication of the Commission's report.

[42] Com. Rep., 18 July 1986, Application no. 9471/81, para. 88. Five members of the Commission (Schermers, Batliner, Vandenberghe, Hall and Soyer) dissented from the Commission on the application of Article 3. On the issue relating to Article 3 the Committee of Ministers was unable to attain the required two-thirds majority (see Resolution DH(89), Application no. 9471/81, of 2 March 1989). The Commission had subsequently the opportunity to pronounce upon corporal

By contrast, no breach of Article 3 was found by the Commission or the Court in the *Campbell and Cosans v. UK* case (the child of one of the two applicants had merely been threatened in a Scottish school, as a disciplinary measure, with being struck on the palm of his hand with a leather strap or 'tawse'; the child of the other applicant had not been even threatened);[43] nor was a breach found in the *Guzzardi v. Italy* case (concerning the detention in cramped quarters of a member of the Mafia on the small island of Asinara).[44] Similarly, the Commission held that Article 3 was not breached by the penalty of being struck off the roll of the Medical Association and being prohibited from practising medicine,[45] nor by the imposition on a detainee, as a disciplinary measure, of a restricted diet coupled with confinement in a cell,[46] nor by the 'close body search' of detainees by prison officers,[47] nor by the disadvantages that a transsexual experienced as a result of the discrepancy between her appearance and her identity papers, which recorded that she was male at birth.[48]

4. A Critical Assessment of the Concept of 'Inhuman Treatment or Punishment' as Laid Down by the Commission and the Court

I have mentioned above the various criteria set out by the two Convention institutions for applying the three concepts enshrined in Article 3. While the notion of torture and degrading treatment or punishment, propounded by the Commission and the Court, and the relative criteria for establishing whether in specific cases Article 3 is breached, are quite persuasive, the same does not hold true for the notion offered by the two bodies of 'inhuman treatment or punishment.'

As I have already pointed out, according to the case law of the Commission and the Court, three elements are required for the existence of 'inhuman treatment or punishment': intent, severe mental or physical suffering, lack of justification. I submit that while the first element (intent) is not indispensable, the third (lack of justification for the measures impugned) needs to be drastically revised.

punishment in other cases, in which a friendly settlement was reached (see *Three Members of the A. Family v. The UK*, Rep. of 16 July 1987, Application no. 10592/83 and *X v. The UK*, Dec. of 11 May 1988, Application no. 10172/82), or the Commission held the application inadmissible (see *W. and J. Costello-Roberts v. The UK*, Dec. of 13 December 1990, Application no. 13134/87, and *X and Y v. The UK*, Dec. of 13 December 1990, Application no. 14229/88).

[43] Com. Rep., 16 May 1980, Application nos 7511/76, 7743/76 and 7819/77; Judgment of 25 February 1982, Series A no. 48.

[44] Com. Rep., 7 December 1978, Application no. 7367/76; judgment of 6 November 1980, Series A no. 39.

[45] Op. Com., 14 December 1981, *Albert and Le Compte* case, pp. 24–25, paras 54–57.

[46] Dec. Adm. Com., 15 May 1980, Application no. 8317/78, DR 20, p. 89.

[47] Dec. Adm. Com., 13 May 1980, Application no. 8317/78, *McFeeley et al. v. UK*, DR 20, p. 85.

[48] See *B. v. France*, Rep. of 6 September 1990, Application no. 13343/87. See at pp. 21–23 the dissenting opinion of three members of the Commission.

A. Intent

The Commission and the Court have repeatedly stated that inhuman treatment or punishment must be 'deliberate' for it to be against Article 3; that is, it must 'deliberately cause' severe and unjustifiable suffering.[49] Furthermore, in a number of cases both the Court and the Commission have gone even further, for they have—surprisingly—contended that 'premeditation' is needed.[50] I suggest that I although the intention to cause suffering *may* be one of the constituent elements of inhuman treatment or punishment, *it is not indispensable.* In other words, it ought not to be regarded as one of the factors the absence of which warrants the conclusion that no inhuman treatment or punishment is meted out.

Proof that the above proposition is tenable can be found precisely in those cases where the Commission soundly, if contradictorily, held that the respondent Government was guilty of a breach of Article 3 without requiring the intention to cause suffering. A case in point is the Commission's decision in the *Cyprus v. Turkey* case, where the Commission held among other things that there was a 'withholding of food and water and of medical treatment, in a number of cases' from detainees in the hands of Turkish troops. The Commission rightly concluded that this behaviour was in breach of Article 3 as amounting to inhuman treatment, without looking into whether or not the Turkish forces which had so acted had intended to cause severe and unjustifiable sufferings.[51] The same applies to the Commission's dicta whereby 'failure to provide adequate medical treatment may be contrary to Art. 3.'[52] Clearly, what matters here is not the possible intention of the persons failing to provide medical treatment to wilfully inflict suffering on those deprived of that treatment, but the *objective fact* that the treatment was not provided. Furthermore, in the *Greek* case the Commission held that in certain cells the conditions of detention of persons arrested for political reasons were contrary to Article 3, without asking itself whether or not the Greek authorities had purposefully caused the ensuing suffering.[53] In the same case the Commission also held that 'the extreme manner of the separation of detainees from their families and the conditions of gross overcrowding in the camps on Leros' constituted a breach of Article 3.[54] Again, the Commission rightly refrained from asking itself whether the separation of families and overcrowding had been caused by the Greek authorities with the purpose of bringing about distress and anguish in the detainees.

---

[49] See, e.g., Op. Com., 5 November 1969, *Greek* case, *Yearbook* 12, p. 186; Op. Com., 7 December 1978, *Guzzardi v. Italy* case, p. 31, para. 80; Judgment of 6 November 1980, Series A no. 39.

[50] See, e.g., *Ireland v. UK* judgment of 18 January 1978, Series A no. 25, p. 66 (*Yearbook* 21, p. 602); *Soering v. UK* judgment of 7 July 1989, Series A no. 161, p. 39, para. 100; Rep. Com., 11 December 1990. *Felix Tomasi v. France,* Application no. 12850/87, p. 18, para. 91.

[51] See *ibid.*, paras 395–405.

[52] See the cases cited in note 7 above.

[53] See Rep. Com., 18 November 1969, *Yearbook* 12, p. 505.

[54] *Ibid.*

The truth of the matter is that in many cases a treatment or punishment is *objectively* inhuman, regardless of the intention of the relevant authorities to cause serious harm. The Commission and the Court should therefore endeavour to be consistent and drop from their definition of 'inhuman' treatment or punishment the element of intent—subject to the exception of the absolutely involuntary causing of suffering (that is, suffering resulting from an act not involving any culpable negligence or recklessness).

In short, my proposition has, it is submitted, three merits. First, it allows instances of ill-treatment to be covered which otherwise—should one rigorously stick to the definition set out by the Commission and the Court—could not be regarded as breaches of Article 3. Secondly, it would make the case law of the two Strasbourg bodies consistent: that is, it would do away with the contradictions currently existing in this case law. Thirdly, and more importantly, it would bring the definition of 'inhuman treatment or punishment' in line with that of 'degrading treatment or punishment,' for both concepts would hold without any intent to cause suffering, and both would be geared to objective circumstances.

In this way, the general picture resulting from a correct interpretation of Article 3 would be as follows: (a) neither in the case of 'inhuman treatment or punishment' nor in that of 'degrading treatment or punishment' would any intent to cause suffering be required; (b) in the formet case, however, a certain level of mental or physical suffering would be necessary and, in addition, would need to be out of proportion to the security and other considerations behind the 'inhuman' measure or behaviour; (c) in the case of 'degrading treatment or punishment,' a high level of debasement or humiliation would be needed; (d) as for torture proper, it would be markedly distinct from the other two categories, as it would hinge on a specific purpose (that of extracting information or a confession, of punishing, intimidating or coercing, or of wilfully discriminating) and would in addition require a degree of mental or physical suffering higher than that needed for 'inhuman treatment or punishment.'

B. The Absence of Justification for Inhuman Measures

I have already mentioned that the Commission has dwelt on this element particularly in cases concerning conditions of detention. In these, it has weighed up the security considerations behind measures such as harsh conditions of detention or solitary confinement, against the suffering caused thereby. To my mind the standards of reference to be taken into account against the demands of security should not lie simply in the need for a detainee to be immune from suffering or anguish. Rather, one should take as a reference point, besides the dignity of the detainee and the whole corpus of his rights, something no less important: the extent to which the allegedly inhuman measures jeopardize the basic purpose of imprisonment, namely the rehabilitation of the detainee with a view to his possible reinsertion into society after release.

If the approach is broadened in such a way, one can then try to establish—according to a criterion akin to (but less loose than) that suggested by Mr. Opsahl in his dissenting opinion referred to above (see note 25)—whether there is proportionality between, on the one hand, security or other considerations, and, on the other, the demands of persons deprived of their liberty.

I shall add that the remarks I have made above could prove particularly useful in such cases as prolonged solitary confinement or repeated infliction of disciplinary measures, or failure to provide an adequate regime (work, training, association, exercise, and so forth) for convicted detainees or for prisoners on remand who spend fairly long periods in prison before trial.

5. New Trends in the Case Law of the Commission and the Court

Recently the two Strasbourg bodies have started taking a broader approach to Article 3, in particular to the notion of 'inhuman treatment or punishment.' While not departing from their definition of such proscribed treatment or punishment formally, the two Convention institutions have in many respects made innovations in their case law by propounding a more liberal construction of Article 3. I shall briefly consider the new direction taken by the Commission and the Court in three different cases.

A. The Notions of 'Extraterritorial Reach' of the Convention and of Liability for Potential Breaches (the *Soering* Case)

I have already mentioned above the Commission's copious case law stating that extradition or expulsion to a country where an individual is likely to be tortured or seriously persecuted for political reasons or to be subjected to inhuman or degrading treatment might give rise to issues relating to Article 3. Strikingly, whenever the Commission has formulated this dictum, it has in actual fact dismissed the application. One might have therefore thought that this case law was a sort of keg full of wet powder, for the Commission seems to confine itself to issuing to Governments a serious warning, without ever finding a breach of Article 3. Luckily, in the *Soering v. UK* case the Court has recently applied that dictum and held that the respondent Government was in breach of Article 3 because it intended to extradite to the US a German national who had allegedly committed a crime in the US, for which he was there liable to capital punishment after spending many years on 'death row.' The judgment of the Court is important not only because it sets an exceedingly important precedent, but also because the Court has enunciated two important notions.

Let us first examine what we could call, in non-technical terms, the 'extraterritorial reach' of the Convention. The respondent Government contended that

Article 3 should not be interpreted so as to impose responsibility on a Contracting State for acts which would occur outside its jurisdiction (both the possible infliction of capital punishment on a person who was only 18 years old at the time of his crime and in addition suffered from 'an abnormality of mind,' and the likely stay of this individual on 'death row' for many years before eventual execution). Indeed, a literal construction of Article 3, read in conjunction with Article 1 ('The High Contracting parties shall secure to *everyone within their jurisdiction* the rights and freedoms defined in Section 1 of this Convention'), could well lead to the belief that the contention of the UK was right. The Court has instead held that the obligation not to extradite a person to a country where he could be subjected to torture or inhuman or degrading treatment or punishment 'is inherent in the general terms of Art. 3,' for it 'would be hardly compatible with the underlying values of the Convention, that "common heritage of political traditions, ideals, freedoms and the rule of law" to which the Preamble refers, were a Contracting State to knowingly surrender a fugitive to another State' where he could be subjected to the aforementioned treatment or punishment. 'Extradition in such circumstances [the Court proceeds] while not explicitly referred to in the brief and general wording of Article 3, would plainly be contrary to the spirit and the intendment of the Article'.[55] Clearly, the Court, by privileging a teleological interpretation over a literal and logical construction, has greatly extended the scope of Article 3. Indeed, it has stated that the basic values enshrined in Article 3 must be respected *not only in Europe* (within the circle of the States Parties to the Convention), but also *abroad,* whenever a State Party to the Convention gets involved in some sort of action which may extend its effects beyond the confines of Europe.

Let us now move to the other considerable merit of this case. The respondent Government had submitted that, even assuming that one might apply Article 3 to extradition cases, this application must be limited to those occasions in which the treatment or punishment abroad was certain, imminent and serious. In its view, the fact that by definition the matters complained of were only anticipated, required a very high degree of risk that ill-treatment would actually occur. The Court to a large extent met this point by the following remarks: 'It is not normally for the Convention institutions to pronounce on the existence or otherwise of potential violations of the Convention. However, where an applicant claims that a decision to extradite him would, if implemented, be contrary to Art. 3 by reason of its foreseeable consequences in the requesting country, a departure from this principle is necessary, in view of the serious and irreparable nature of the alleged sufffering risked, in order to ensure the effectiveness of the safeguard provided by that Article.'[56]

---

[55] Judgment of 7 July 1989, para. 83.
[56] *Ibid.*, para. 90.

It is apparent from this ruling that again the Court has placed a liberal interpretation on the Convention, by resorting to the principle of effective interpretation (the so-called *principe de l'effet utile*). The Court has thus—rightly—broadened the scope of the Convention's prescriptions.[57]

B. The Presumption of Ill-treatment of Persons in Police Custody (the *Tomasi v. France* Case)

Recently the Commission had to pronounce on a case of injuries allegedly caused by police officers to a person being held in police custody. The respondent Government objected that, first, there was no evidence that the injuries were attributable to police officers and, second, in any case they were light and therefore did not reach the threshold of severity required by Article 3.

As regards the first point, the Commission emphasized, on the one hand, that it was apparent from various medical reports that the applicant had bruises and ecchymoses when he left the police station, and, on the other, that the respondent Government had not claimed that he already had such bruises and ecchymoses before entering the police station, nor had it claimed that he caused the injuries to himself or that they resulted from an attempted escape. From these considerations the Commission drew the following inference: the injuries to the applicant were sustained while he was in police custody, and were caused by police officers.[58]

With regard to the question of the nature of the injuries, the Commission noted that, however light they might appear to be, they were the result of physical force used against a person deprived of his liberty and hence vulnerable and in a state of inferiority (the Commission emphasized in this respect that the applicant had been held 48 hours in police custody without any contact with the outside world, not even with his family or lawyer). This kind of treatment, the Commission said, could not be justified and therefore, in the circumstances of the case, appeared to be both inhuman and degrading.[59]

---

[57] Recently the Commission reached a friendly settlement in some cases of expulsion (see *Leila Sami El-Makhour v. FRG*, Rep. of 10 July 1989, Application no. 14312/88; and *Abdel-Quader Hussein Yassin Mansi v. Sweden*, Rep. of 9 March 1990, Application no. 15658/89), whereas in another case the application was rejected by a vote of seven to seven, with a casting vote of the President (see *Nadarajah Vilvarajah et alii v. The UK*, Rep. of 8 May 1990, Application no. 13163/87; see at pp. 43–44 the dissenting opinion of the seven members in favour of the application of Article 3); on 30 October 1991, by eight votes to one, the European Court too held that the UK had not breached Article 3 (judgment no. 45/1990/236/302–6).

[58] Rep. Com. 11 December 1990, Application no. 12850/87, pp. 19–20, paras 97–104.

[59] Rep. Com. 11 December 1990, Application no. 12850/87, p. 20, para. 105. One member of the Commission, Mr. Soyer, appended a dissenting opinion concerning both issues discussed above (*ibid.*, pp. 30–37). More recently the Commission declared admissible the application of a Colombian who allegedly had been ill-treated by Swiss police officers during and after his arrest (see *X v. Switzerland*, Application no. 17549/90, decision of 3 April 1992, unpublished).

There can be no doubt that this decision marks a turning point in the Commission's case law, in two respects. First, because the Commission ingeniously suggested that in cases where no witnesses are available to check the veracity of a detainee's allegations, resort can be had to a *presumption:* one should presume that injuries to a person held in police custody have been caused by those who detained him, if the respondent Government does not prove that these injuries existed before or were self-inflicted (the onus of proof is thus reversed, for it falls to the respondent Government to prove that the injuries were not caused by its authorities). Second, undoubtedly the Commission has lowered the threshold of suffering previously required for a finding of inhuman treatment. Although the reasoning of the Commission on this issue is perhaps too succinct, arguably the reasons for such lowering lie chiefly in the fact that ill-treatment of suspects held for interrogation by police officers lacks any justification whatsoever. The element of lack of justification is so strong in this case, that one may accept that the other element—the mental or physical suffering—be made less stringent. It should be added that the Commission rightly found that the ill-treatment in question, in addition to being inhuman, was degrading. There is clearly an element of debasement in the fact that representatives of the State's enforcement bodies profit from their position of superiority vis à vis persons held in custody by ill-treating them: at the very least the dignity of that person is lowered and he is humiliated both in his and their own eyes. The fact that ill-treatment is thus regarded as also degrading strengthens the conclusion reached by the Commission, for, as I pointed out above, in the case of degrading treatment the mental or physical suffering involved plays a lesser role than that required for inhuman treatment.

C. The Criterion of the Cumulative Effects of Various Forms of Ill-treatment (the *Herczegfalvy v. Austria* Case)

So far the Commission and the Court, when dealing with Article 3, have gone into the various individual facets of ill-treatment by considering each issue *per se* and not as part of a global picture. In other words, they have considered in isolation each aspect of the conduct or measures allegedly contrary to Article 3; they have scrutinized these on their own merits, to determine if they passed the stringent test to be administered under Article 3. To use a well-known metaphor, they have looked at every single tree one by one, and neglected to establish if the combination of various trees added up to a forest. Recently, and for the first time, the Commission has chosen to resort to a new standard for gauging the conformity of States' behaviour to Article 3: the possible cumulative effect of various factors, each of which, taken by itself, would not amount to inhuman treatment.

In the case where the Commission has taken this innovative approach (*Herczegfalvy v. Austria*), the applicant, a Hungarian refugee living in Austria, complained among other things that when detained in a psychiatric hospital in the period 1978–1984, he had been subjected to treatment falling foul of

Article 3, as he had been subjected to compulsory medical treatment, to artificial feeding and had been held in isolation. The Commission examined each of these three issues.

Regarding the compulsory medical treatment, it noted that the complaint concerned both the use of force on the occasion of an incident which occurred on 15 January 1980, and the measures taken thereafter by the hospital authorities. On 15 January the applicant, who was on a hunger strike and therefore very weak, became extremely agitated about the compulsory treatment which the medical authorities intended to administer to him. He fell into a rage; the staff of the hospital were unable to control him and an emergency squad was called in. After the incident the applicant collapsed and developed pneumonia and nephritis. Following this incident he was fettered continuously to his bed for several weeks, including a period when he was unconscious. The Commission pointed out, with regard to the incident just mentioned, that the use of force seemed to have contributed to the applicant's state of agitation and his complete physical breakdown. Although the medical authorities could not have foreseen this development when the compulsory treatment was started, they should 'have reconsidered the appropriateness of the measures taken to overcome the applicant's physical resistance once their effect on his state of health became apparent.' As for the use of physical restraint resorted to after the incident, the Commission noted that 'even if fettering may have been unavoidable in order to secure his [the applicant's] effective treatment, the manner in which it was carried out and the period during which it was maintained appear disproportionate.' The Commission concluded that although the applicant's compulsory medical treatment was not, as such, contrary to Article 3, the particular manner in which it had been administered amounted to a breach of that provision.[60]

As regards the applicant's compulsory feeding, the Commission noted that the 'medical authorities' margin of appreciation' had not been overstepped: the feeding was necessary and the methods applied (infusions and artificial feeding through a tube) corresponded to the standards of medical science. However, 'the maintenance of artificial feeding through a tube during a long period of time when such acute danger [for the applicant's health resulting from his hunger-strike] no longer existed was . . . unusual from the medical point of view, even if it may have had a therapeutical purpose in the context of the simultaneous psychiatric treatment of the applicant'.[61]

Finally, with respect to isolation in the psychiatric hospital, the Commission noted that the applicant, apart from short periods, was relatively free to move around in the ward and was able to have contact with other mental patients in the ward when he was not the only inmate there; he also had contact with the medical staff and other staff, besides receiving visits from outside. In addition, the

[60] Rep. Com. 1 March 1991, Application no. 10533/83, pp. 48–49, paras 242–48.
[61] *Ibid.*, p. 49, paras 248–50.

Commission emphasized that his isolation was partly a result of his own conduct. It is thus apparent that this sort of segregation was not the kind of total social and sensory deprivation which under the Commission's case law could amount to a breach of Article 3. Nevertheless—and here comes the breakthrough in the Commission's attitude—this body held that, 'insofar as imposed on him by the hospital, it [the isolation] constituted, together with the compulsory artificial feeding and medical treatment, a further element to be considered under Article 3.'[62]

The Commission wound up its handling of the case from the viewpoint of Article 3 with a finding that 'the applicant's compulsory medical treatment and the way in which it was administered, combined with its artificial feeding and isolation, amounted to inhuman and degrading treatment.'[63] The criterion of the cumulative effect of various factors, some of which by themselves would not reach the requisite threshold, could not have been set out more forcefully.

6. Prospects for the Future

We have just seen that recently the Commission and the Court have taken a more dynamic approach to Article 3. They are now increasingly placing a liberal interpretation on that all-important provision, thus contributing to a better safeguard of some fundamental values in Europe. One should not, however, underrate some possible pitfalls in this case law, as well as the harsh criticisms which the new trends have aroused. Furthermore, there are areas of human rights where the Commission and the Court could make more headway by gradually revising the bulk of their interpretation of Article 3. I now propose to deal briefly with these issues.

A. Is There a Need to Resort to Sociological Standards?

It is possible to see in the case law of the two Convention institutions a certain tendency to refer to the attitude of the community of a given country vis à vis the behaviour of States' authorities, as a sort of acid test to appraise whether or not that behaviour is admissible. This approach first came to the fore in the Commission's report in the *Greek* case. The Commission stated the following:

It appears from the testimony of a number of witnesses that a certain roughness of treatment of detainees by both police and military authorities is tolerated by most detainees and even taken for granted. Such roughness may take the form of slaps or blows of the

---

[62] *Ibid.*, p. 50, paras 251–53.
[63] *Ibid.*, p. 50, para. 254.

hand on the head or face. This underlines the fact that the point up to which prisoners and the public may accept physical violence as being neither cruel nor excessive, varies between different societies and even between different sections of them. However, the allegation raised in the proceedings generally concern much more serious forms of treatment which, if established, clearly constitute torture or ill-treatment.[64]

Although the Commission did not go into the various instances of this 'rough treatment,' for it considered the allegations of torture as more important, it nevertheless propounded a test which is open to criticism: the test of the extent to which public opinion and the persons concerned (the detainees) consider some sort of treatment as admissible. This test, it is submitted, is very dangerous, for it could lead to a difference of treatment among various Member States of the Council of Europe, depending on the attitude of the population there, and even among various social groups in each country. This would open a Pandora's box likely to lead to preposterous results: for instance, manhandling of academics or judges by police officers might be regarded as inhuman or degrading, whilst it might be acceptable if practised against petty criminals or uneducated people from the lower classes. It is instead imperative that the Strasbourg bodies should uphold a set of standards valid for all the Contracting Parties to the European Convention, whatever their economic and social background and their cultural traditions.

Luckily, in a later judgment, the Court put things in the right perspective. In the *Tyrer v. UK* case, concerning the fact that Mr. Tyrer, a British citizen living on the Isle of Man, had been sentenced by a local juvenile court to three strokes of the birch in accordance with the legislation of the island, the Court stated the following:

The Attorney-General for the Isle of Man argued that the judicial corporal punishment at issue in this case was not in breach of the Convention since it did not outrage public opinion in the Island. However, even assuming that local public opinion can have an incidence on the concept of 'degrading punishment' appearing in Art. 3, the Court does not regard it as established that judicial corporal punishment is not considered degrading by those members of the Man population who favour its retention: it might well be that one of the reasons why they view the penalty as an effective deterrent is precisely the element of degradation which it involves. As regards their belief that judicial corporal punishment deters criminals, it must be pointed out that a punishment does not lose its degrading character just because it is believed to be, or actually is, an effective deterrent or an aid to crime control. Above all, as the Court must emphasise, it is never permissible to have recourse to punishments which are contrary to Art. 3, whatever their deterrent effect may be.

The Court must also recall that the Convention is a living instrument which, as the Commission rightly stressed, must be interpreted in the light of present-day conditions. In the case now before it, the Court cannot but be influenced by the developments and

---

[64] Com. Rep. 18 November 1969, *Yearbook* 12, p. 501. This passage was then quoted by the Commission on the *Ireland v. UK* case (*Yearbook* 19, pp. 388–89).

commonly accepted standards in the penal policy of the member States of the Council of Europe in this field.[65]

It is difficult to find a more balanced and judicious appraisal of the role that social standards and public opinion can play in this matter. As the Court rightly emphasized, what counts in the field of application of Article 3 are present-day conditions and, even more importantly, the commonly accepted standards in the penal policy of the Council of Europe, as reflected in the European Prison Rules.

It should be added that the Court, in a subsequent judgment, while reaffirming that public opinion should not be a decisive factor for evaluating the conformity of State measures with Article 3, did nevertheless make allowance for some sort of a role for public opinion. In the *Campbell and Cosans v. UK* case, the applicants had assailed corporal punishment practised as a disciplinary measure in Scottish schools. As I mentioned before, the Court held that there had been no degrading punishment within the meaning of Article 3, among other things because no punishment had actually been inflicted. Before reaching this conclusion the Court stated the following:

Corporal chastisement is traditional in Scottish schools and, indeed, appears to be favoured by a large majority of parents . . . Of itself, this is not conclusive of the issue before the Court, for the threat of a particular measure is not excluded from the category of 'degrading,' within the meaning of Art. 3, simply because the measure has been in use for a long time or even meets with general approval . . . However, particularly in view of the above-mentioned circumstances obtaining in Scotland, it is not established that pupils at a school where such punishment is used are, solely by reason of the risk of being subjected thereto, humiliated or debased in the eyes of others to the requisite degree at all.[66]

It is submitted that to the limited extent underscored by the Court, public opinion or the views prevailing in a social group may be taken into account. (Indeed, in the case at issue, the crucial point for determining whether the punishment was degrading was different: it revolved around the question whether the punishment was debasing or humiliating in the pupil's own eyes.) However, as was soundly reaffirmed by the Court, the important point is that generally speaking no importance should be attached to social perceptions of certain measures in a given State. Except for the very limited role they can play in cases such as that just referred to, these social perceptions may be taken into account only for pre-legal purposes, that is, for the purpose of better understanding the historical and social reasons why certain conducts or measures are widespread in some countries or are tolerated by some social groups there.

---

[65] Judgment of 25 April 1978, Series A no. 26, pp. 16–17, para. 31.
[66] Judgment of 25 February 1982, Series A no. 48, p. 13, para. 29.

B. Is There Any Likelihood that the Prescriptions of Article 3 Will Be Trivialized?

In their partially dissenting opinion in the *Warwick v. UK* case, four members of the Commission, Schermers, Batliner, Vandenberghe and Hall, together with another member, Soyer, stated that the corporal punishment inflicted on one of the applicants by her school headmaster was not so severe as to be in breach of Article 3, and then warned the Commission against a possible weakening of the protection afforded by this provision. They stressed that:

> There might be to some extent two dangers in weakening the protection of Art. 3. The one would be to interpret it too flexibly in following changing social and political conditions which would result in the adverse effect that in difficult times the Article might lose a great deal of its protection. The other risk consists in overloading the content and of amplifying the Article with matters of a lesser degree of severity and thus weakening the very serious nature of a breach of Art. 3.[67]

The same point was forcefully taken up by Mr. Soyer in his dissenting opinion in the *Tomasi v. France* case. After attacking the majority's decision to consider as a breach of Article 3 the ill-treatment of a person in police custody by police officers—an ill-treatment that in his view was not so severe as to reach the threshold required by Article 3—Mr. Soyer again sternly cautioned against an overstretching of the bans laid down in Article 3. He warned that the majority's decision would result in a trivialization of inhuman or degrading treatment which would be far from constituting a better prevention against it ('une banalisation du traitement inhumain et dégradant qui n'en constitue pas la meilleure prévention, loin s'en faut'). He went on to say the following:

> Aujourd'hui, un État qui reconnaît la prééminence du Droit peut redouter la condamnation du chef de l'Art. 3, jusqu'ici largement synonyme de manquement majeur, d'infamie internationale, parce qu'elle n'est retenue qu'à titre exceptionnel et dans des situations de particulière gravité.
>
> Mais si la gravité majeure n'est plus requise, la barrière psychologique s'abaisse, la dissuasion morale s'affaiblit. S'agit-il là d'une bonne politique jurisprudentielle? . . . Pense-t-on que si l'Art. 3 peut s'appliquer à des lésions relativement légères, l'Art. 15 conservera son sens d'ultime sauvegarde devant les convulsions de l'histoire? Et pense-t-on que cet Art. 3, ainsi dévalué, pourra continuer de faire obstacle aux extraditions, aux expulsions qu'il empêchait jusqu' à présent?[68]

With all due respect, I submit that this view is wrong. Four arguments can be adduced against it. First, although admittedly breaches of Article 3 carry an aura of infamy and dishonour for the responsible State, there is no legal justification for contending that Article 3 must be applied exceptionally and with regard

---

[67] Com. Rep., 18 July 1986, p. 21.
[68] Rep, Com., 11 December 1990, Application no. 12850/87, p. 37, paras 32–33.

to extremely grave situations. The upgrading of Article 3 to such a special and unique status is not warranted by any sort of interpretation—literal, logical or teleological. What can be deduced from the wording of Article 3 and the general context of this provision is simply that it aims to ban unacceptable practices against human dignity, and for this reason has been elevated to the rank of a nonderogable norm, on a par with the ban on unlawful deprivation of life, on slaverly or servitude and on the retroactivity of criminal legislation (see Article 15, paragraph 2). Furthermore, the text of the provision establishes a sort of hierarchy between different categories of outrages, in that it regards torture as the most serious, whilst it admits that inhuman or degrading treatment may take the form of a less damaging injury.

Second, the proposition that the broadening of the scope of Article 3 will entail that in times of emergency its impact is lessened, and that therefore the Article 'may lose a great deal of its protection' is begging the question. It is difficult to see why the impact of the prescriptions of Article 3—if these were to be endowed with a broader content than that conceived of by the aforementioned five members of the Commission—should diminish in times of emergency. What matters is that Article 3 should be strictly complied with. Why should a State, on the one hand, abide by this provision in times of emergency if it prohibits only the most extreme forms of inhuman or degrading treatment, and, on the other hand, fail to observe it if it bans less appalling manifestations of outrageous conduct too? Not too great an importance should be attached to the psychological attitude of States. They are at liberty to believe what they want to believe; the fact remains that what ultimately matters is that they must obey international imperatives as authoritatively interpreted by the Commission and the Court, be it in normal or in exceptional conditions. If they fail to comply with these prescriptions, the supervisory bodies will take the appropriate measures.

These first two points have been argued from an essentially negative point of view; I shall now set forth two positive reasons for upholding the view of the Commission's majority. My third point is that the opinion to which I am taking exception is probably based to some extent on an old idea of torture and inhuman or degrading treatment, one that dates back to forms of treatment carried out in medieval times (dislocation of a person's limbs by straining them by cords and levers on a rack, chaining detainees to a wall and depriving them of food and drink until they starve to death, and so forth). A quick view of the various instruments exhibited in the Museum of Torture at Prinsegracht at The Hague is enough to give us a clear idea of the forms this took in the past.

Today, however, in Europe we are no longer confronted with either these atrocious and extreme practices or with the modern, sophisticated but no less appalling methods obtaining in other continents—witness Amnesty International's reports. Allegations usually relate to more subtle and inconspicuous forms of ill-treatment: beating detainees on the head with telephone directories; hanging them by their wrists for short periods of time after padding the wrists; giving electrical shocks for short periods of time with a low-intensity voltage; beating the soles of the feet with sticks, again for short periods of time; hosing naked detainees with pressurized cold water; beating prison inmates with rubber truncheons; and so on. The essential feature of these practices is that normally they do not leave any physical marks or scars. Often, officials are said to use a combination of various methods to break a detainee's will without leaving physical evidence of ill-treatment. In addition to these form of 'trivial' or 'petty' torture, there is said to be frequent resort to sometimes unintentional forms of inhuman or degrading treatment, such as deprivation of medical care or treatment, very poor living conditions in prison cells, overcrowding coupled with poor sanitation, protracted solitary confinement and the like. These trends should be seen against their general historical and political background: at present a number of States feel that, in order to cope with increasing criminality (often linked to terrorism and drug-trafficking), harsh methods of interrogation and detention may help both to achieve the required results quicker, and to produce markedly deterrent effects. This political philosophy, combined with the increased 'professionalism' of law enforcement officials, often results in a change in the modes of ill-treatment, which are now less dramatic, less conspicuous and less painful (at least at the physical level). If this is so, international law should adjust itself to these new developments. Since, as the Court rightly stated in the *Tyrer v. UK* case, the Convention is a *living instrument* which, as the Commission also stressed in dealing with the same case, must be interpreted in the light of present-day conditions, one fails to see why the Commission and the Court should not lower the threshold of Article 3, precisely to take account of these new manifestations of ill-treatment.

Fourth, a further consequence follows from the need—just referred to—to interpret the Convention in the light of present-day conditions. It is a fact that there is increasing opposition in the world, and in Europe in particular, to ill-treatment. As for Europe, tangible and official proof of this opposition can be seen in the adoption in 1987, by the Council of Europe, of the Convention for the prevention of torture and inhuman or degrading treatment or punishment, and the subsequent working of the Committee set up in this regard. The increased awareness about the adverse effects of ill-treatment means that public opinion and Governments alike have become more sensitive to the need to protect human dignity; it also means that they have become alert to classes of misconduct that previously went either unnoticed or were to some extent taken for granted.[69] *The area of unacceptable misbehaviour by State agencies has thus greatly broadened.*

---

[69] What is stated in the text does not of course imply that one should underrate the tension existing between the requirement that the prison be 'une maison de guérison,' as Clemenceau put it as early as 1906, and the claims by some segments of public opinion, and even some national authorities, that it should instead be a place where exemplary punishment is meted out under such harsh conditions as to deter future crime. On this tension see the apposite remarks by R. Badinter, *La prison républicaine* (Paris: Fayard, 1992), pp. 387–92.

Important evidence of this new trend can also be found in decisions handed down by national courts, which pay increasing attention to precisely these new forms of ill-treatment.[70] If this is so, why should the Commission and the Court refrain from taking account of this increasing awareness and sensitivity when interpreting and applying Article 3? Taking a fresh look at Article 3 and placing a broader interpretation on its scope and purport can only be beneficial to human dignity and more conducive to a better implementation of the aims set out in the Preamble of the Convention.

7. Possible Further Developments

It stands to reason that the Commission and the Court, which have already made so much headway in interpreting and applying Article 3, can easily strengthen and widen the scope of their case law. This, in particular, can be achieved if they first of all avoid making decisions that offer no substantial reasoning, as has happened in some cases.[71] What is even more important, they should endeavour

[70] By way of illustration, mention can be made of a number of recent decisions delivered by courts of some European States. Thus, for instance, various Spanish courts have applied Article 204 *bis* of the Spanish Penal Code prohibiting torture (this provision was introduced into the Penal Code in 1978; in 1989 a new para. 2 was added which provides a harsher penalty for some categories of torture). See for instance the following judgments of the Supreme Tribunal: 10 May 1985, in *Repertorio de Jurisprudencia* (1985), pp. 2098–90 (a police officer was sentenced to eleven years in prison for ill-treating a suspect, whose death he also accidentally caused after a scuffle); 5 July 1985, *ibid.*, pp. 3326–33 (some prison officers were sentenced to light penalties for beating a group of detainees on the occasion of their transfer to prison); 25 September 1989, *ibid.* (1989), pp. 7810–13 (police officers had allowed other, unidentified, police officers to cause injuries to a suspect in police custody, by making burns on the soles of his feet; they were sentenced to four months in prison plus suspension from service); 26 October 1989, *ibid.*, pp. 9019–20 (a prison officer was sentenced for placing a detainee in solitary confinement into a 'blind cell' which was unfit and was not to be used); 23 January 1990, *ibid.* (1990), p. 533 (a police officer caused injuries to a suspect during interrogation in order to obtain a confession; he was sentenced to one month and one day in prison); 24 February 1990, *ibid.*, pp. 2129–33 (a police officer was sentenced to a penalty of two months in prison and suspension from service for one year for causing injuries to a suspect); 23 April 1990, *ibid.*, pp. 4269–76 (police officers who had allowed other officers to cause injury to a suspect were sentenced to four months in prison; a fine; disqualification for six years, presumably from active and passive voting rights; and suspension from service for one month); 18 May 1990, *Ibid.*, pp. 5475–77 (a police officer was sentenced for ill-treatment and threats against a person suspected of drug-trafficking).

[71] As a telling illustration of a regrettable lack of reasoning one may mention the *van Volsen v. Belgium* case (Com. Dec. Adm. 9 May 1990, Application no. 14641/89, published in 2 *Rev. Universelle des Droits de l'Homme* (1990), 384–85). See on this decision the comments by F. Sudre (*ibid.*, pp. 349–53) and C. Pettiti (*Droit social* (1991), pp. 87–88), as well as my note in 2 *European J. of Int. Law* (1991), pp. 141–45. Another illustration of a lack of reasoning can be found in the *Wilson and others v. UK* case (13 April 1989, Application no. 13004/87, unpublished), where some of the applicants complained about their conditions of detention on remand (they had been subjected to rigorous surveillance). The Commission confined itself to stating that the level of severity of the measures complained of did not attain the requisite level of severity, without spelling out why this was the case.

to do away with the element of 'intent' on the one hand, and to make use of the criterion of proportionality between proper terms of reference in the case of 'inhuman treatment or punishment,' on the other (see discussion above). It would also be helpful if the Commission or the Court could spell out that the concept of 'degrading treatment or punishment' as envisaged by Article 3 does not require, as an indispensable element, a severe level of physical or mental suffering, and that humiliation and debasement may also consist in a state of anxiety which does not necessarily bring with it intense suffering (for instance, a prison inmate's being obliged, because of overcrowding and lack of sanitation, to comply with the needs of nature in the presence of other detainees in the same cell could be regarded as degrading, without there being any intense physical or mental suffering). Significant results can also be attained if the two bodies continue to use the criterion of the 'cumulative effect' of different factors which individually may appear to be below the requisite threshold, a criterion propounded by the Commission in the *Herczegfalvy v. Austria* case, as well as the presumption of ill-treatment set forth by the Commission in the *Tomasi v. France* case. It may well also prove very helpful if the Commission and the Court made greater use of the European Prison Rules, as a valuable set of standards which may help shed light on the applicability of Article 3.[72]

As for the areas where the two institutions might explore the possibility of applying Article 3, these include general socio-economic conditions, and health and living conditions in prisons (for instance, the impact of overcrowding and lack of sanitation on individual detainees, forced feeding of detainees on a hunger strike or of mentally impaired inmates, as well as extreme cases of such stringent measures as protracted and harsh solitary confinement). Furthermore, it may well be useful for the Commission and the Court to explore the possibility of applying Article 3 as much as possible to instances of ill-treatment inflicted by private groups (such as terrorist groups) when some sort of State responsibility is involved, for example, for failure to take adequate preventive measures.[73]

---

[72] In some cases the Commission has already made reference to the Rules. Mention can be made of the *X v. FRG* case (11 July 1977, Application no. 7408/76, in Dec. 10, pp. 221–23). The applicant complained about the harshness of the disciplinary sanction to which he had been subjected. With regard to the applicability of Article 3 the Commission stated that 'in this respect . . . [it] had regard to the Standard Minimum Rules for the Treatment of Prisoners (Council of Europe Resolution 73–5) which forbid corporal punishment, detention in a dark cell, as well as brutal, inhuman and degrading punishment for disciplinary offences. These Rules reflect the efforts of the Council of Europe Member States generally to improve the conditions of prisoners and in this context the Commission notes with interest that under the revised version of the Prison Rules for Prisoners on Remand of 15 December 1976 the FRG has abolished the possibility of making the disciplinary detention more severe by hard bed and reduction of food' (*ibid.*, p. 222).

[73] So far the Commission has already raised the eventuality of some sort of *Drittwirkung*. For instance, in the *G.M. v. FRG* case (14 May 1987, Application no. 12437/86, unpublished), the applicant complained that his expulsion to Lebanon involved serious dangers to his life, arising not from Government authorities but from 'autonomous groups,' The Commission recalled 'its previous case law in which it left open the question whether, in examining a case of this kind from the standpoint of Art. 3, it may take into account an alleged danger arising not from public authorities,

Certainly, in these and similar areas the Commission and the Court ought to tread warily, lest the delicate balance established by the Convention between States' requirements, on the one hand, and demands of human dignity on the other, should be jeopardized. The wisdom shown so far by these two institutions, however, bodes well for the future of the protection of human rights in Europe.

but from autonomous groups (see no. 8481/79, D.R. 29, p. 48).' It added that 'even assuming that in the present case an alleged danger arising from autonomous groups may be taken into account,' in any event the German authorities had issued an indefinite stay of execution for the applicant's expulsion. See also *X v. Switzerland,* Dec. of 1 October 1990, Application no. 14912/89, p. 5. It should be added that recently the Commission found that a Contracting State is bound under Article 1 of the Convention to prohibit corporal punishment contrary to Article 3 in independent schools: see *W. and J. Costello-Roberts v. The UK,* Dec. of 13 December 1990, Application no. 13134/87, pp. 6–7.

14. Can the Notion of Inhuman and Degrading Treatment be Applied to Socio-Economic Conditions?*

1. In a number of cases the European Commission and Court of Human Rights have applied Article 3 of the European Convention on Human Rights, whereby 'No one shall be subjected to torture or to inhuman or degrading treatment or punishment'. It is in the area of civil rights that the two Strasbourg bodies have relied primarily upon this Article: the bulk of the applications dealt with by the two supervisory bodies relate to the conditions of detention of persons deprived of their liberty (usually in prisons, in police custody or in mental institutions). Other applications raise the question whether corporal punishment in educational institutions can be regarded as inhuman and degrading, or whether extradition or deportation to a country where an individual is likely to be subjected to inhuman treatment is contrary to Article 3. In addition, the question has also been raised whether—at least in some instances—racial discrimination can be said to amount to inhuman or degrading treatment.[1]

Recently, the European Commission has been given the opportunity of looking into the possibility of extending the notion of inhuman and degrading treatment to the area of social and economic rights: *Francine van Volsem v. Belgium* (decision of 9 May 1990, application No. 14641/89).[2]

2. Francine van Volsem, a Belgian national born in 1950, obtained the custody of her two children following her divorce. Being depressive and suffering from near-chronic respiratory problems, she was unable to hold a stable job. She therefore relied for her living on the alimony paid by her former husband. In addition, she lived on the social security provided by a social welfare centre (C.P.A.S.: 'Centre public d'aide sociale'). With the help of this Centre she had managed to obtain accommodation in a half-empty block of council flats. In these, everything, and

* Originally published in 2 *European Journal of International Law* (1991) 141.

[1] For concise and up-to-date accounts of the case law of the European Commission and Court of Human Rights on Article 3, see J.Ab. Frowein, 'Freiheit von Folter oder grausamer, unmenschlicher oder emiedrigender Behandlung und Strafe nach der Europäischen Menschenrechtskonvention', in F. Matscher (ed.), *Folterverbolt sowie Religions- und Gewissensfreiheit im Rechtsvergleich* (1990) 69–79, and G. Cohen-Jonathan, *La Convention Européenne des Droits de l'Homme* (1990) 286–310.

[2] The decision has been published in 2 *Revue Universelle des Droits de l'Homme* (1990) 384–385, and commented upon by F. Sudre (ibidem, pp. 349–353) and C. Pettiti (in *Droit social* (1991) 87–88).

particularly the heating, ran on electricity; in addition, as the flats had been badly built, the consumption of electricity was very high, and in any case disproportionate to the low income of most of the inhabitants. The use of any other source of energy was prohibited.

It should therefore come as no surprise that between 1981 and 1983 Mrs van Volsem was unable to meet the cost of her electricity bills. The C.P.A.S. took no notice of a request by Mrs van Volsem to provide financial help, or to at least support her case with the electricity company, S.A. Unerg. Thus the company cut off the electricity on 9 December 1983 (a very inappropriate period indeed). Mrs van Volsem took legal proceedings against this measure. The Brussels Tribunal of First Instance upheld her case (and the electric power was restored), but subsequently, on 25 February 1988, the Brussels Court of Appeal authorized S.A. Unerg to cut off the power. The company acted immediately upon this judicial order, in spite of the fact that meanwhile—it was now 14 May 1988—Mrs van Volsem was caring for her grandchild and a doctor had issued a medical certificate stating that owing to respiratory problems the child needed a minimum level of heating. In the event, thanks to the intervention of a bank (the C.P.A.S. had refused any help), Mrs van Volsem was able to comply with the request of the company to pay the arrears and promised to pay future bills regularly: on 15 September 1988 the company reconnected her power, although at very low intensity (only two Amperes, producing a power of 440 Watts).[3]

In the application lodged with the European Commission of Human Rights, Mrs van Volsem claimed, among other things, that: 1) the electricity company was not a private enterprise; indeed, it was a public utility ('service public') and acted as representative ('mandataire') of the association of district councils, which in turn were to be regarded as representatives of the Belgian State; consequently, the measures taken by the company were to be imputed to the Belgian State; 2) the cutting off of electricity in a very cold period and subsequently the supply of a low power voltage amounted to inhuman and degrading treatment, proscribed by Article 3 of the European Convention on Human Rights. In this respect, the applicant drew the European Commission's attention to two points. First, she had never demanded free electricity; she had merely been unable to cover all the high electricity expenses regularly. Secondly, the company itself had conceded in its brief before the Brussels Court of Appeal that 'the provision of gas and electricity must be regarded in our State as based on the rule of law and in our community as indispensable to human dignity'.[4]

The petitioner concluded that, since the European Convention 'guarantees in Article 3 the right for everybody to have the basic goods indispensable for

---

[3] The decision to supply a low voltage of electric power—so low that it can be regarded as absolutely inadequate for the needs of three persons living in a flat where everything runs on electricity— had already been taken as early as 1985.

[4] 'L'alimentation en gaz et l'électricité doivent être considerée dans notre Etat de droit et notre collectivité, comme indispensable à la dignité humaine, ce que l'intimée (la S.A.Unerg) ne conteste pas et que le premier juge au demeurant ne contestait pas non plus', in *Requête,* p. 5.

ensuring human dignity'[5] the Belgian authorities had meted out inhuman and degrading treatment, by cutting off the electric power in the past and by threatening to do so in the future.[6]

3. It is well known that the European Commission of Human Rights is overburdened with hundreds of petitions and finds it difficult to deal quickly with them. The recent establishment of a new procedure was considered, then, as a way of solving this problem. This procedure is provided for in a new rule of procedure included in Protocol 8 to the Convention. Under the rule, now constituting Article 20 paragraph 3 of the Convention, 'The Commission may set up committees, each composed of at least three members, with the power, exercisable by a unanimous vote, to declare inadmissible or strike from its list of cases a petition submitted under Article 25, when such a decision can be taken without further examination'. On the strength of this provision, a Committee of three members of the Commission pronounced upon the case at issue and unanimously held that the application was inadmissible. It may be noted that resort to the new rule made it possible for the Commission to handle the case expeditiously: the application had been lodged on 5 December 1988, and the Commission delivered its decision on 9 May 1990.

As regards the question relating to Article 3, the Committee of three confined itself to making two points. First, it stressed that the question could arise of whether the severing of electric power should be imputed to the Belgian State. However, there was no need to delve into this issue, for in any event the petition was to be rejected on other grounds. Second, regarding the allegation that the measure complained of amounted to an inhuman or degrading treatment, the Committee stated that 'in the case at issue, the cutting off or the threat of cutting off electricity did not reach the level of humiliation or debasement needed for there to be inhuman or degrading treatment'.[7]

4. It is apparent from this decision that the Committee did not rule out the possibility of applying Article 3 to a case where social and economic conditions rather than alleged misbehaviour of public authorities impinging upon the area of civil rights were at stake. In other words, the Committee did not dismiss out of hand the contention that Article 3 also bans any social and economic treatment of persons that is so humiliating as to amount to inhuman treatment.

[5] 'La Convention garantit en son article 3 le droit de chacun à bénéficier des biens de première nécessité indispensables à la dignité humaine.'

[6] The applicant also invoked Article 8 protecting family life and in addition complained of having been unable to benefit from legal aid in Belgium for the purpose of bringing her case before the Court of Cassation.

[7] 'La question peut se poser de savoir si la suspension des fournitures d'électricité peut être considerée comme un acte imputable à l'Etat défendeur. La Commission n'estime cependant pas nécessaire de procéder à l'examen de cette question, le grief devant être rejeté pour d'autres motifs.

En ce qui concerne l'allégation de traitement inhumain et dégradant, la suspension ou les menaces de suspension des founitures d'électricité n'atteignaient pas le niveau d'humiliation ou d'avilissiment requis pour qu'il y ait un traitement inhumain ou dégradant', ECHR, décision 14641/89, p. 3.

On this score the decision of the Committee cannot but be approved. It stands to reason that the scope of Article 3 is very broad; nothing could warrant its possible limitation to only physical or psychological mistreatment in the area of civil rights. Plainly, the concept of human dignity underpinning Article 3 and the prohibition of any treatment or punishment contrary to humanitarian principles embrace any measure or action by a public authority, whatever the specific field to which this measure or action appertains. Article 3 could therefore constitute an appropriate means for the Commission and the Court to make, if only in extreme cases, the protection of economic and social rights more incisive. It could constitute the bridge between the area traditionally covered by the Convention, hence guaranteed by the Commission and the Court—that of civil and political rights—and the broad field of social and economic rights.

The Committee's decision is however disappointing in two other—closely intertwined—respects.

First, it does not tackle an admittedly complex and intricate issue: that of the circumstances under which one can conclude that practical measures bearing on social life and the daily living conditions of a person may amount to inhuman or degrading treatment. This was a relatively new issue for the Commission,[8] and one which was in addition not easy to solve. It therefore required careful examination and in-depth analysis. Indeed, a ruling that the poor quality or insufficiency of public social services may be tantamount to inhuman or degrading treatment, would have far-reaching ramifications. For, if it were to be true that Article 3 guarantees the right of everybody to have their most basic social needs met, this would imply that Contracting States are duty-bound to provide basic social benefits to everybody under their jurisdiction. This would also give rise to a number of crucial problems, such as the question of whether the notion of democratic State underlying the European Convention bears the stamp of neo-liberalism or comes instead closer to that of the Welfare State.

Given the great number of intricate and closely related problems raised by this petition, it would have been appropriate for the Committee of three to have submitted it to the plenary Commission, where the various complex facets of the question could have been better explored and discussed (Article 20 paragraph 4 of the Convention envisages such an eventuality, for it provides that a committee 'may at any time relinquish jurisdiction in favour of the plenary Commission').

The second ground for disappointment, and indeed dissatisfaction, is that the Committee made its ruling without offering any insight into its reasoning. It

---

[8] In a decision of 4 July 1979, Applic. No. 8247/78 (unreported), the Commission hinted that in some circumstances the lack of a pension could lead to inhuman or degrading treatment in breach of Article 3. (See A. Clapham, *The Fight against Poverty and Marginalisation: The Human Rights Dimension,* unpublished manuscript, p. 1). It is worth recalling that in the *Cyprus v. Turkey* case the Commission held that the fact that the Turkish authorities had withheld from detainees 'an adequate supply of food and drinking water and adequate medical treatment' amounted to inhuman treatment in the sense of Article 3 (Report of 10 July 1976, para. 405).

did not motivate its decisions in any way: as pointed out above, the Committee merely stated that the cutting off of electricity 'did not reach the level of humiliation or debasement' needed for it to be considered as degrading or inhuman. No details were provided on the reasons for which that level was not reached in the case at issue. One is therefore at a loss to understand by what standards one can gauge whether or not practical measures of the type at hand or of a similar type exceed the threshold required.[9]

To be sure, it is very difficult to spell out clear-cut standards for appraising whether the kind of conduct under discussion attained the 'minimum level of severity' needed for treatment to be regarded as inhuman or degrading. When pronouncing on these difficult cases international bodies must perforce retain a large measure of discretion. Nevertheless, they ought at least to set out the 'indicators' they actually take into account when assessing a certain situation. In the case at issue, one may well wonder whether the Committee of three turned its attention to the economic conditions of the applicant, to her mental and physical state (in particular, to her being depressive and suffering from near-chronic respiratory troubles), to her having charge of two children and a grandchild, or to the attitude of the social welfare centre (the C.P.A.S.). Did the Committee ask itself whether in the area where Mrs van Volsem lived it was easy for a person in her conditions, or for her elder daughter, to find a job? Did it consider that the measures taken by the electricity company (cutting off of the power, and consequent supply of a derisory power flow coupled with the threat of a further cut-off) may have a different psychological or moral impact on persons, depending on their physical and psychological conditions? In addition, did the Committee attach any importance to the intent, or lack of intent, of meting out inhuman and degrading treatment?

One should assume that, in ruling the way it did, the Committee of three took into account most of these issues, perhaps others also. One may wonder why it refrained from indicating its methodology concerning its balancing of all the relevant circumstances.

---

[9] In the past the European Commission has held that the notion of 'inhuman treatment' includes at least such treatment as deliberately causes severe suffering, whether mental or physical (see *Ireland v. the United Kingdom,* Commission's Report of 25 January 1976, in *Yearbook of the European Conv. of Human Rights,* 19, pp. 745 and 752). According to the Commission, 'treatment or punishment of an individual may be said to be degrading if it grossly humiliates him before others or drives him to act against his will or conscience' (*Greek* case, in Report of the Commission of 18 November 1969, *Yearbook,* cit., vol. 12, p. 186). In the view of the Court treatment is degrading when it is such as to arouse in a person 'feelings of fear, anguish and inferiority capable of humiliating and debasing him and "possibly breaking" his physical or moral resistance' (*Ireland v. the United Kingdom,* Judgment of 18 January 1978, Series A No. 25, para. 167).

However, the Court has stressed that 'ill-treatment must attain *a minimum level of severity* if it is to fall within the scope of Article 3' (*ibid.,* para. 162; italics added). According to both the Court and the Commission, the assessment of this minimum is, in the nature of things, relative: it depends 'on all the circumstances of the case, such as the duration of the treatment, its physical or mental effects and, in some cases, the sex, age and state of health of the victim' (*ibid.,* para. 162 as well as, for the Commission, *McQuiston et al. v. the United Kingdom,* dec. of 4 March 1986, p. 17).

5. Had the European Commission considered the application lodged by Mrs van Volsem in greater detail, it could have broken new ground, even if it eventually were to conclude that the application was inadmissible. It is a matter of regret that the Commission has missed this significant opportunity.

One of the consequences of the Commission's failure to make a searching examination of the case should be emphasized: the Commission has left all those who might be interested in invoking Article 3, owing to their dire economic or social conditions, without any yardstick by which to appraise whether or not they are entitled to benefit from that all-important provision.

15. A New Approach to Human Rights: The European Convention for the Prevention of Torture*

1. Introduction

A review of the current state of legal regulation in the field of human rights is likely to give the disappointing impression that international legislation is unequal to the task of checking widespread disregard for human dignity. Despite the vast proliferation of instruments setting standards on human rights, imposing obligations as regards the observance of those standards and establishing procedures to deal with breaches of those obligations, violations of human rights continue, their perpetrators apparently undeterred.

The proliferation has mainly been of instruments dealing with particular kinds of rights[1] or with particular groups of people requiring special treatment.[2] This approach is clearly justified by the need to give more specific content to the generalized terms of the 'core' documents, particularly the United Nations Charter, the Universal Declaration of Human Rights of 1948 and the International Covenants of 1966. The recent instruments thus attempt, on the one hand, to achieve and preserve consensus on how the general standards are to apply in concrete situations and, on the other, to ensure that no room is left for loopholes or disingenuous interpretations of those standards.

These instruments clearly have important educational value; in setting standards on human rights, they serve both to raise the level of people's expectations as to how they should be treated and, to some extent, to raise the level of treatment of individuals by governments. Those instruments that establish some enforcement machinery can also have some effect, at least in the long term, in discouraging gross violations of human rights. Following judicial or quasi-judicial decisions confirming violations, national laws and practices may eventually be changed for

---

* Originally published in 83 *American Journal of International Law* (1989) 128.
[1] *See, e.g.,* Convention on the Political Rights of Women, Mar. 31, 1953, 27 UST 1909, TIAS No. 8289, 193 UNTS 135; and Convention on the Elimination of All Forms of Racial Discrimination, Mar. 7, 1966, 660 UNTS 195.
[2] *See, e.g.,* Convention Relating to the Status of Refugees, July 28, 1951, 189 UNTS 137; and Declaration of the Rights of the Child, GA Res. 1386, 14 UN GAOR Supp. (No. 16) at 19, UN Doc. A/4354 (1959).

the better. Further, a number of such instruments offer at least some possibility for recompense to those who fall victim to human rights violations.[3]

Yet all these instruments lack machinery capable of enforcing compliance in any systematic or rigorous way with the obligations they create. All too frequently, they simply cannot stop violations; those international implementing and remedial measures which do exist do not appear to have a sufficiently strong and direct deterrent effect. Plainly, in a sphere such as human rights, where violations are in large measure irremediable, in the sense that nothing can ever efface the victim's memory of suffering—and, in many cases, its scars, physical or psychological—the key is prevention.

The European Convention for the Prevention of Torture and Inhuman or Degrading Treatment or Punishment (the Convention),[4] concluded in 1987 under the aegis of the Council of Europe, marks a fresh, preventive approach to the handling of human rights violations of a sort acutely in need of containment. The Convention establishes a European Committee for the Prevention of Torture and Inhuman or Degrading Treatment or Punishment (the Committee);[5] this body will have the right to conduct visits to any place within the jurisdiction of the states parties where persons are deprived of their liberty by a public authority, with a view to protecting such persons from torture and from inhuman or degrading treatment or punishment.[6] Both regular and ad hoc visits are envisaged.[7]

2. Drafting History

The origins of the Convention[8] can be traced back to a proposal in 1976 by Jean-Jacques Gautier, founder of the Swiss Committee against Torture. Gautier, in

[3] For instruments providing a right of individual complaint, see, e.g., Optional Protocol to the International Covenant on Civil and Political Rights, Dec. 16, 1966, GA Res. 2200, 21 UN GAOR Supp. (No. 16) at 59, UN Doc. A/6316 (1966); European Convention for the Protection of Human Rights and Fundamental Freedoms, Nov. 4, 1950, 213 UNTS 221, Art. 25 [hereinafter ECHR]; American Convention on Human Rights, Nov. 22, 1969, *reprinted in* ORGANIZATION OF AMERICAN STATES, HANDBOOK OF EXISTING RULES PERTAINING TO HUMAN RIGHTS IN THE INTER-AMERICAN SYSTEM, OEA/Ser.L/V/II.65, doc. 6, at 103 (1985), Art. 44.

[4] *Opened for signature* Nov. 26, 1987, Council of Europe Doc. H (87) 4, *reprinted in* 27 ILM 1152 (1988). *See generally The European Draft Convention against Torture*, 31 REV. INT'L COMM'N JURISTS 50 (1983); Wickremasinghe, *A radical step in the crusade against torture: the European Convention*, 2 INTERIGHTS BULL. 30 (1987); and Decaux, *La Convention européenne pour la prévention de la torture et des peines ou traitements inhumains ou dégradants* ([...] in 34 ANNUAIRE FRANÇAIS DE DROIT INTERNATIONAL (1988)); Vigny, *La Convention européenne de 1987 pour la prévention de la torture et des peines ou traitements inhumains ou dégradants*, 43 ANNUAIRE SUISSE DE DROIT INTERNATIONAL 62 (1987). See also, concerning the Convention's approach to the problem of torture, SWISS COMMITTEE AGAINST TORTURE, HOW TO COMBAT TORTURE: REPORT OF THE INTERNATIONAL COLLOQUIUM, GENEVA, 1983 (1984).

[5] Convention, Art. 1.

[6] *Id.*, Art. 2.

[7] *Id.*, Art. 7, para. 1.

[8] *See also* Explanatory Report, *id.*, App. II, paras 1–11.

turn, was inspired by the long-standing activities of the International Committee of the Red Cross (the ICRC) in conducting visits to places where prisoners of war are detained and, if necessary, making recommendations for the improvement of conditions there. The ICRC carries out these visits on a confidential basis. The element of trust and cooperation between the ICRC and the local authorities is seen as essential to their success. However, the ICRC has the right to conduct such visits only when there is an international armed conflict between states parties to the Geneva Conventions of August 12, 1949.[9] In all other cases, the ICRC gains access to places of detention only through special agreements concluded with the state concerned[10] or, in case of internal armed conflicts, with each of the parties to the conflict;[11] these agreements may generally be terminated at any time.

Gautier's proposal was to broaden this system of visits to encompass all other places where persons are deprived of their liberty such as prisons, police stations, psychiatric institutions and remand centers. This proposal subsequently formed the basis of a draft Optional Protocol to the (then) draft International Convention against Torture and other Cruel, Inhuman or Degrading Treatment or Punishment (the UN Convention).[12] The draft was prepared jointly by the Swiss Committee against Torture and the International Commission of Jurists and was submitted in April 1980 by the Government of Costa Rica for eventual consideration by the Commission on Human Rights, the body called upon to draft the UN Convention.[13]

[9] *See* common Art. 10/10/10/11, Geneva Conventions for the Protection of Victims of War, Aug. 12, 1949, 75 UNTS 31, 85, 135 and 287, respectively. Where both parties to the conflict are also parties to the Protocol Additional to the Geneva Conventions of 12 August 1949, and Relating to the Protection of Victims of International Armed Conflicts (*opened for signature* Dec. 12, 1977, ICRC, PROTOCOLS ADDITIONAL TO THE GENEVA CONVENTIONS OF 12 AUGUST 1949, at 3 (1977)) [hereinafter Protocol I], the ICRC's powers will apply in the context of a war of national liberation regarding which a declaration under Article 96, para. 3 of that Protocol has been made. Note also in this connection Article 81 of Protocol I.

[10] This applies in particular to visits made by the ICRC to political detainees (in peacetime). *See, e.g.,* Sandoz, *La Notion de protection dans le droit international humanitaire et au sein du Mouvement de la Croix-Rouge,* in STUDIES AND ESSAYS IN HONOUR OF J. PICTET 985 (1984).

[11] *See* common Art. 3, Geneva Conventions, *supra* note 9. The minimum standards of protection in non-international armed conflicts set forth in common Article 3 are amplified in Article 4 of Protocol Additional to the Geneva Conventions of 12 August 1949, and Relating to the Protection of Victims of Non-international Armed Conflicts (*opened for signature* Dec. 12, 1977, ICRC, *supra* note 9, at 89) [hereinafter Protocol II], at least with respect to the restricted category of internal conflicts to which Protocol II applies (*see* Art. I). However, a proposal to reiterate in Article 4 of Protocol II that an impartial humanitarian body such as the ICRC 'may offer its services to the Parties to the conflict' (the so-called right of initiative provided for in common Article 3 of the Geneva Conventions) was defeated at the 1977 Diplomatic Conference that adopted the Protocol.

[12] GA Res. 39/46 (Dec. 10, 1984), *draft reprinted in* 23 ILM 1027 (1984), *substantive changes noted in* 24 ILM 585 (1985).

[13] For the text of the draft Optional Protocol, see UN Doc. E/CN.4/1409 (1980). *See also* INTERNATIONAL COMMISSION OF JURISTS & SWISS COMMITTEE AGAINST TORTURE, TORTURE: HOW TO MAKE THE INTERNATIONAL CONVENTION EFFECTIVE (2nd edn 1980). The draft was submitted 'for use as a basis for consideration by the Commission on Human Rights when once [*sic*] the

With the fate of the Costa Rican draft extremely uncertain,[14] steps were in the meantime set in train within the Council of Europe to realize Gautier's idea, at least at the regional level. The initiative came from the Legal Affairs Committee of the Council's Consultative Assembly,[15] acting on the strength of the support for Costa Rica's Optional Protocol that had earlier been expressed by the Assembly itself.[16] In June 1983, a report was produced on behalf of the Legal Affairs Committee by its rapporteur, Noël Berrier, with a draft European Convention on the Protection of Detainees from Torture and from Cruel, Inhuman or Degrading Treatment or Punishment appended.[17] The draft had been prepared at Berrier's request by the International Commission of Jurists and the Swiss Committee against Torture and was closely modeled on their earlier draft Optional Protocol for the UN Convention. In September 1983, the report was accepted by the Consultative Assembly, which proceeded to issue a recommendation[18] that the Committee of Ministers adopt a convention incorporating the terms of the Legal Affairs Committee's draft.[19]

There followed almost 4 years of debate over the draft Convention within the subordinate organs of the Committee of Ministers. That committee first referred the matter to the Steering Committee for Human Rights,[20] which in turn referred it to the Committee of Experts for the Extension of the Rights Embodied in the

Convention has been adopted.' This was done to avoid any further delay in submitting the already long-debated UN Convention to the Economic and Social Council. Given its novel approach, the draft Optional Protocol was thought likely to prove controversial.

[14] In the event, the UN Convention was adopted by the General Assembly on Dec. 10, 1984; it entered into force on June 26, 1987; and the first members of the Committee against Torture were elected at a meeting of the parties to the UN Convention held in Geneva on Nov. 26, 1987. Costa Rica's draft Optional Protocol has yet to be considered by the Commission on Human Rights. On Mar. 13, 1986, that Commission deferred consideration of the draft to its 45th session in 1989. At the same time, it recommended that states consider adopting regional conventions along the same lines as Costa Rica's draft. *See* H.R. Comm'n Res. 1986/56, UN Doc. E/CN.4/1986/L.11/Add.10, at 5.

[15] The Consultative Assembly is a consultative organ comprising members of the national legislatures of each of the 22 member states of the Council of Europe. Its function is to provide recommendations to the Committee of Ministers, the Council's decision-making organ. The Committee of Ministers is composed of the Foreign Ministers (or their deputies) of each of the member states.

[16] *See* Eur. Consult. Ass., 32d Sess., Recommendation No. 909, especially paras 7 and 8 (1981).

[17] *See* Eur. Consult. Ass., 35th Sess., Doc. No. 5099 (1983). An opinion on the Legal Affairs Committee's report was also sought from the Assembly's Political Affairs Committee, whose rapporteur, Claude Dejardin, concluded by endorsing the Legal Affairs Committee's proposals. *See id.,* Doc. No. 5123 (1983).

[18] *See id.,* Recommendation No. 971 (1983).

[19] On Assembly recommendations, see note 15 *supra.*

[20] The Steering Committee for Human Rights is a body of government experts on human rights from member states of the Council of Europe, responsible directly to the Committee of Ministers. The relevant terms of reference were conferred on it at the 366th meeting of the Ministers' Deputies, in January 1984.

European Convention on Human Rights (Committee of Experts).[21] The labors of the Committee of Experts occupied seven successive sessions,[22] during which it also sought and considered the views of the European Commission and Court of Human Rights, the European Committee for Legal Co-operation and the European Committee on Crime Problems,[23] and held hearings with representatives of the Swiss Committee against Torture, the International Commission of Jurists and the ICRC, as well as two psychiatric experts. An agreed draft of the Convention was finally conveyed to the Steering Committee for Human Rights in June 1986. Annexed to the report of the Committee of Experts was an Explanatory Report, amplifying upon and explaining the provisions of the Convention itself. In the course of debate on the text of the Convention, numerous compromises were reached on the basis of agreement to insert particular clarifications or observations into this Explanatory Report. Accordingly, the report was seen by the drafting bodies as having great importance for the eventual interpretation of the Convention, and almost as having a kind of 'binding force' of its own.[24]

Following further consideration by the Steering Committee at two meetings in late 1986, the draft Convention and Explanatory Report were transmitted to the Committee of Ministers, which ultimately adopted it on June 26, 1987, after final consultation with the Consultative Assembly.[25] Opened for signature on November 26, 1987, the Convention has been signed by all of the then 21 member states of the Council of Europe.[26] As of the date of writing, it has been ratified by the requisite seven states,[27] and consequently will enter into force on February 1, 1989.

---

[21] The Committee of Experts is a body of government experts from member states of the Council of Europe, specifically concerned with measures to achieve the fullest possible implementation of the ECHR. The Committee is responsible to the Steering Committee. The relevant terms of reference were conferred on it by the latter Committee at its 15th meeting, in March 1984.

The subject was seen as falling within the expertise of the Committee of Experts because the Convention was perceived as an elaboration or specification of the provisions of Article 3 of the ECHR: 'No one shall be subjected to torture or to inhuman or degrading treatment or punishment.' However, as will be indicated later, the precise relation between the Convention and Article 3 proved in the end to be one of the major points of controversy.

[22] The Convention was debated at its 19th to 25th meetings (May 1984–June 1986), under the chairmanship initially of the Swiss expert Krafft, and later of the Norwegian expert Mase. As these meetings are confidential, no minutes exist.

[23] These are two other subordinate bodies responsible to the Committee of Ministers.

[24] In one of its reports, the Steering Committee for Human Rights drew the attention of the Committee of Ministers to the 'great importance which should be attached to the explanatory report in relation to the interpretation of the Convention by the Parties and the new Committee.'

[25] *See* Eur. Consult. Ass., 39th Sess., Opinion No. 133 (1987) (on draft European Convention for the Prevention of Torture and Inhuman or Degrading Treatment or Punishment).

[26] It was signed by all member states except Turkey and Ireland on Nov. 26, 1987. Turkey signed it on Jan. 11, 1988, and Ireland on Mar. 14, 1988.

[27] Turkey, Ireland, Malta, Sweden, the United Kingdom, Luxembourg and Switzerland. The Convention has subsequently been ratified by the Netherlands.

3. Utility Questioned

An early question faced by the various committees charged with elaborating the Convention was whether any international instrument of the kind envisaged was needed at all. This question soon resolved itself into two.

First, was such a Convention needed in *Western Europe* where the rate of torture and inhuman or degrading treatment or punishment is relatively low? There can be little doubt that it was. According to various respectable non-governmental organizations (NGOs) (including Amnesty International and the International Commission of Jurists), inhuman and degrading treatment, as well as, in some isolated cases, torture itself, has been practiced in several member states of the Council of Europe, particularly in relation to persons held on suspicion of terrorist or other politically motivated offenses.[28] Even with respect to states not then known to be engaging in human rights violations of this type, the Convention would serve a useful purpose because they, too, were at risk. Torture and inhuman and degrading treatment are social diseases whose only permanent cure is the complete eradication of the conditions that give rise to them, an important, but long-term, goal indeed. In the meantime, no state can remain complacent or count itself immune.

A further rationale for the Convention was that it could serve as a prototype for testing the validity and practicality of the system at the regional level before it came to be implemented at the more difficult universal level pursuant to Costa Rica's draft Optional Protocol. This was the answer to those who expressed concern that the Convention might slow down or even jeopardize Costa Rica's efforts within the United Nations. There were—and remain—grounds for treating this as a matter better regulated, or at least more easily regulated, at the regional level than at the world level. Thus, if successful, it was hoped that the Convention could also serve as a model for similar conventions in other regions.[29] The committees and NGOs involved in the elaboration of the Convention were acutely conscious of this pioneering human rights mission of the Council of Europe, a mission that had begun in 1950 with the adoption of the European Convention for the Protection of Human Rights and Fundamental Freedoms. Accordingly, great importance was attached to setting a valuable precedent and the Convention

---

[28] The Federal Republic of Germany, Italy, Spain, the United Kingdom and Turkey were the main targets of NGO criticism. *See, e.g.,* AMNESTY INTERNATIONAL, REPORT ON TORTURE (1973); AMNESTY INTERNATIONAL, TORTURE IN THE EIGHTIES (1984). *See also* C. HUMANA, THE ECONOMIST WORLD HUMAN RIGHTS GUIDE (1986).

[29] Efforts to supplement the Inter-American Convention to Prevent and Punish Torture (Dec. 9. 1985, *reprinted in* 25 ILM 519 (1986)) with a mechanism for preventive visits are currently in progress. Similar work may also be expected in relation to the African Charter on Human and Peoples' Rights of June 1981 (OAU Doc. CAB/LEG/67/3/Rev.5 (1981), *reprinted in* 21 ILM 59 (1982) (entered into force Oct. 21, 1986)).

should therefore be read with an eye to its application outside the member states of the Council of Europe.

The second question raised about the utility of the Convention was: would the Convention simply *duplicate* activities undertaken pursuant to other conventions or arrangements? Four possibilities were mentioned: the activities of national authorities in pursuance of the Standard Minimum Rules for the Treatment of Prisoners drawn up under the aegis of the United Nations and the penal rules established by the Council of Europe,[30] as implemented in national legislation; the activities of the ECRC; the functions of the organs of the ECHR, the European Commission and Court of Human Rights (the Commission and Court, respectively); and, finally, the activities undertaken under the umbrella of the United Nations, both by the Committee against Torture[31] and by the UN Special Rapporteur on Torture.[32]

First, as regards national measures undertaken on the basis of the various sets of rules concerning the treatment of prisoners, experience has shown that these have not provided a sufficient guarantee against torture and inhuman and degrading treatment in European institutions. When left entirely in the hands of national authorities, human rights standards appear to be all too easily overborne by 'conflicting' considerations.

Second, so far as the ICRC is concerned, it was plain from the outset that the Convention was intended to supplement, rather than duplicate, its work.[33]

---

[30] The UN rules were adopted by the First UN Congress on the Prevention of Crime and the Treatment of Offenders, Aug. 30, 1955, and then approved by ESC Res. 663C (XXIV) (July 31, 1957). They were later amended by ESC Res. 2076 (LXII) (May 13, 1977). The Council of Europe's European penal rules were recommended by the Committee of Ministers on Feb. 12, 1987, Recommendation No. R (87) 3. *See also* Draft Body of Principles for the Protection of all Persons under any Form of Detention or Imprisonment, Sub-Comm'n on Prevention of Discrimination and Protection of Minorities Res. 5C (Sept. 13, 1973); Declaration on the Police, Appendix, Eur. Consult. Ass., 31st Sess., Res. 690 (May 8, 1979); Code of Conduct for Law Enforcement Officials, GA Res. 34/169 (Dec. 17, 1979); Principles of Medical Ethics Relevant to the Role of Health Personnel, particularly Physicians, in the Protection of Prisoners and Detainees against Torture and other Cruel, Inhuman or Degrading Treatment or Punishment, GA Res. 37/194 (Dec. 18, 1982). See further, in relation to the treatment of involuntary psychiatric patients in European institutions, Recommendation No. R (85) 3 of the Council of Europe's Committee of Ministers, on the legal duties of doctors.

[31] *See* note 14 *supra*.

[32] The Special Rapporteur on Torture was established pursuant to Commission on Human Rights Res. 1985/33 of Mar. 13, 1985, UN Doc. E/CN.4/1985/SR. 55, paras 50, 62. This resolution was ratified on May 30, 1985, by the ECOSOC by Decision 1985/144, 1985 UN ESCOR Supp. (No. 1) at 44, UN Doc E/1985/85. For an account of the background to this resolution and a description of the rapporteur's functions, see N. Rodley, The Treatment of Prisoners Under International Law 120–25 (1987).

[33] On the work of the ICRC, see generally the *Annual Reports* of the ICRC. As to its practice in relation to non-international conflicts, see J. Moreillon, Le Comité International de la Croix-Rouge et la protection des détenus politiques (1973); Veuthey, *Implementation and Enforcement of Humanitarian Law and Human Rights Law in Non-International Armed Conflicts: The Role of the International Committee of the Red Cross*, 33 Am. U. L. Rev. 83 (1983); T. Meron, Human Rights in Internal Strife: Their International Protection 105–17 (1987).

However, to the extent that the ICRC's efforts, particularly in relation to political detainees, may be restricted or hampered or in any other way not totally adequate, there seems to be no reason in principle that the new Committee should not intervene. Thus, the Convention provides that the Committee is not to visit places 'effectively' visited 'on a regular basis' by the ICRC by virtue of the Geneva Conventions and Additional Protocols thereto.[34] Peacetime visits by the ICRC, falling entirely outside the ambit of the Geneva Conventions and Additional Protocols, accordingly remain unaffected by this provision. Nevertheless, there can be little doubt that the new Committee will establish liaison with the ICRC and will not seek to duplicate effective, regular visiting arrangements the ICRC already has in place in time of peace.

The third area of possible overlap—the competence of the Commission and of the Court pursuant to the ECHR—was the one of greatest concern. It was feared that the efficacy of the ECHR protection machinery would be diluted through the concurrent activities of an autonomous third body. In particular, the new Committee might adopt an interpretation of Article 3 of the ECHR[35] that conflicted with the Court's jurisprudence on the matter, undermining the authority of the Court and creating undesirable confusion. In addition, a person whose case had been examined by the Committee might actually be left in a worse position, in that he or she could be barred from lodging a petition with the Commission under the ECHR,[36] on a basis similar to *res judicata*.[37] Finally, attention was drawn to the fact that provision for on-the-spot fact-finding visits and for action of a preventive nature was already made in the Commission's Rules of Procedure.[38]

To allay these fears, the Convention explicitly provides that it is not to be construed as limiting or derogating from the competence of the ECHR organs.[39] The Explanatory Report adds that the Committee is to respect the established competence of the Commission and the Court and is not to intervene in proceedings pending before them or formulate interpretations of the ECHR, particularly Article 3.[40] The report also states that the right of individual petition remains unaffected.[41]

[34] *See* Convention, Art. 17, para. 3; and Explanatory Report, *supra* note 8, para. 93.

[35] *See* note 21 *supra*.

[36] *See* note 3 *supra*.

[37] ECHR Art. 27, para. 1 provides: 'The Commission shall not deal with any petition submitted under Article 25 which . . . (b) is substantially the same as a matter which has already been examined by the Commission or has already been submitted to another procedure of international investigation or settlement and if it contains no relevant new information.'

[38] European Commission of Human Rights, Rules of Procedure (rev. text brought up-to-date on May 15, 1983), 1983 Y.B. Eur. Conv. on Hum. Rts., ch. II, at 7. Concerning on-the-spot fact-finding visits, see *id.*, Rule 14 para. 2, and Rule 28, para. 2. *See also* ECHR Art. 28(a). Concerning preventive measures, see Rules of Procedure, *supra*, Rule 28, para. 1, and Rule 36.

[39] Convention, Art. 17, para. 2.

[40] Explanatory Report, *supra* note 8, paras 17, 27 and 91. Although the Committee will not intervene in proceedings brought under the ECHR, there have been suggestions that it may assist individual petitioners of whose circumstances it has become aware, particularly in relation to the exhaustion of local remedies.

[41] *Id.*, para. 92.

However, even absent these provisions, the Committee's work will not inter-fere with that of the Commission and the Court, which are charged with enfor-cing legal rules and redressing legal wrongs. The Committee will be concerned only with fact-finding investigations carried out in a humanitarian and practical manner and leading only to non-binding recommendations. Its aim will be to enlist the cooperation of national authorities in protecting persons deprived of their liberty, rather than to make legal assessments of those authorities' conduct or accuse them of violations of the relevant rules.

In consequence, there is little reason to expect any adverse effect on the activ-ities of the Commission and the Court. On the contrary, the new Committee can only supplement the valuable—but complex, hence unfortunately slow—procedures of these bodies, which in any case come into play ex post facto, indeed not until all domestic remedies have been exhausted. Even though the Commission's rules provide for fact-finding visits, they can only be undertaken when an application before the Commission under the ECHR has been declared admissible.[42] Preventive measures can be indicated prior to the Commission's decision on admissibility, but still only in the context of a particular application. Thus, unlike the new Committee, the Commission has no jurisdiction to investi-gate the human rights situation in the territory of a state party otherwise than in connection with pending judicial or quasi-judicial proceedings.

Similar considerations apply to the fourth suggested area of duplication, the activities of the UN Committee against Torture.[43] Its functions are essentially to monitor compliance with,[44] and deal with complaints of breaches of,[45] the UN Convention. It may also undertake visits[46] but only once it is in possession of 'well-founded indications that torture is being systematically practised in the ter-ritory of a State Party' and, significantly, only 'in agreement with that State Party.'

---

[42] For an account of the fact-finding powers of the Commission and of the very few occasions on which they have been used, see Ramcharan, *Introduction,* in INTERNATIONAL LAW AND FACT-FINDING IN THE FIELD OF HUMAN RIGHTS 1, 19–20 (B. Ramcharan ed. 1982); and Krüger, *The Experience of the European Commission of Human Rights,* in *id.* at 151, 151–59.

[43] Several Council of Europe member states are parties to the UN Convention and hence are potentially subject to the competence of the Committee against Torture. As of Oct. 31, 1987, Sweden, France, Norway, Switzerland, Denmark, Austria, Luxembourg and Spain had ratified the Convention, each at the same time making a declaration under Articles 21 and 22 that it accepted the competence of the Committee to receive and consider 'communications' from states and indi-viduals concerning violations of the Convention. In addition, none of them made the reservation envisaged by Article 28 whereby a state can exclude the competence of the Committee to undertake, *proprio motu,* investigations, including fact-finding visits, under Article 20. *See* MULTILATERAL TREATIES DEPOSITED WITH THE SECRETARY-GENERAL, STATUS AS AT 31 DECEMBER 1987, UN Doc. ST/LEG/SER.E/6, at 174–77 (1988); and UN Doc. A/43/519 (1988).

[44] UN Convention, *supra* note 12, Art. 19.

[45] A specific declaration recognizing the UN Committee's competence in this regard is required. *See id.,* Arts 21 and 22; and note 43 *supra.*

[46] UN Convention, *supra* note 12, Art. 20. A specific right of reservation is conferred in respect of this provision, *id.,* Art. 28; *see also* note 43 *supra.*

Such visits will probably be relatively infrequent, as compared to the regular and occasionally ad hoc, but always compulsory, visits of the new Committee.

The mandate of the UN Special Rapporteur on Torture[47] is to 'examine questions relevant to torture' and report on 'the occurrence and extent of its practice.'[48] These provisions certainly do not seem to exclude his making visits to places where persons are deprived of their liberty but, again, any such visits would require the specific consent of the state concerned[49] and clearly could not be undertaken on any regular basis.

Admittedly, each of the four categories of organs and authorities mentioned does operate in the same sphere as the new Committee, even if their respective functions and orientation are different. The Convention itself implicitly recognizes this by stating that it shall not prejudice the provisions of any domestic law or international agreement which provide greater protection to persons deprived of their liberty.[50] Thus, the new Committee will contribute one means among many of combating ill-treatment of detainees. Any precise appreciation of its relation to existing bodies, that is, of its proper niche, will, of course, need to await the Committee's actual practice.

4. Legal Basis

Just as the Committee does not operate entirely in a 'practical' vacuum, there was concern to ensure that it should also not operate in a legal vacuum. Since the Convention was designed to provide a new mechanism for securing respect for human rights of a particular kind but not to set new standards as regards those rights, some foundation for the activities of the Committee under preexisting legal standards needed to be provided.

From the outset, it was clear that the relevant legal standard was the prohibition on torture and inhuman or degrading treatment or punishment contained in a variety of legal instruments, including, for the purposes of 'European' law, Article 3 of the ECHR.[51] As a result, Article 1 of the original draft of the

---

[47] As the special rapporteur is appointed by resolution of the UN Commission on Human Rights (*see* note 32 *supra*) rather than by agreement, his competence extends to all UN member states, and hence to all member states of the Council of Europe with the exception of Switzerland.

[48] *See* Commission on Human Rights Res. 1985/33, *supra* note 32, paras 1 and 7.

[49] The special rapporteur's first report makes no mention of any visits having been undertaken. *See* UN Doc. E/CN.4/1986/15.

[50] Convention, Art. 17, para. 1. Correlative provisions are made in the ECHR (Art. 60) and the UN Convention, *supra* note 12 (Art. 1, para. 2, Art. 14, para. 2, and Art. 16, para. 2).

[51] *See* note 21 *supra*. *See also* Universal Declaration of Human Rights, GA Res. 217A, UN Doc. A/810, at 71 (1948), Art. 5; International Covenant on Civil and Political Rights, GA Res. 2200, *supra* note 3, Supp. (No. 16) at 52, Art. 7; American Convention on Human Rights, *supra* note 3, Art. 5, para. 2; African Charter on Human and Peoples' Rights, *supra* note 29. Art. 5; as well as the specific instruments concerning torture mentioned in notes 14 and 29 *supra*.

Convention,[52] began: 'In order better to ensure respect for and observe Article 3 of the [ECHR].'

However, precisely how Article 3 was to be referred to in the final version was a delicate question; although it was to be the standard justifying and underlying the Committee's activities, the Committee was not actually going to 'apply' it. As already noted, the Commission and the Court have exclusive jurisdiction to apply Article 3 in the sense of construing it and then measuring existing circumstances against it. By contrast, the Committee's charge was to appraise itself of a broad range of circumstances among which would undoubtedly be some that did not fall afoul of Article 3 but which, if allowed to continue or develop, might do so. On the basis of this factual appraisal, it was to make recommendations for alleviating the latter type of circumstances.

Thus, there was resistance to the sort of reference to Article 3 that had been included in the original draft, as it seemed to imply that the Committee would be involved in the 'application,' or even enforcement, of the article. The solution eventually adopted was a symbolic one: reference to Article 3 was deleted from the text of the Convention and moved instead to its Preamble and to the Explanatory Report.[53] The latter explains that Article 3 is to provide the Committee with a 'point of reference,' the case law of the Court and the Commission[54] on the article providing it also with a 'source of guidance.'[55] In practice, however, fine definitional distinctions concerning the provisions of Article 3 are not likely to be of much concern to the Committee, given the preventive nature—hence relatively wide compass—of its activities. On the other hand, the reference to Article 3 does not rule out the possibility of recourse by the Committee both to other international instruments dealing with torture (e.g., the 1966 International Covenant on Civil and Political Rights,[56] the 1984 UN Convention on Torture[57]

---

[52] The draft appended to Recommendation 971, *supra* note 18, will be referred to as the 'original draft.'

[53] Explanatory Report, *supra* note 8, paras 22, 26 and 27.

[54] For a summary of the voluminous case law on Article 3, together with references to the relevant cases, see 1 COUNCIL OF EUROPE, DIGEST OF STRASBOURG CASE-LAW RELATING TO THE EUROPEAN CONVENTION OF HUMAN RIGHTS 89–235 (1984) [hereinafter STRASBOURG CASE-LAW]. For academic commentary on the subject, see Doswald-Beck, *What does the Prohibition of 'Torture or Inhuman or Degrading Treatment or Punishment' mean? The interpretation of the European Commission and Court of Human Rights,* 25 NETH. INT'L L.R. 24 (1978); Duffy, *Article 3 of the European Convention on Human Rights,* 32 INT'L & COMP. L.Q. 316 (1983); Sudre, *La Notion de 'peines et traitements inhumains ou dégradants' dans la jurisprudence de la Commission et de la Cour européennes des droits de l'homme,* 88 REVUE GÉNÉRALE DE DROIT INTERNATIONAL PUBLIC 825 (1984).

[55] The Convention facilitates reference to the jurisprudence on Article 3 by exactly reproducing the formula used in Article 3 ('torture and inhuman or degrading treatment or punishment'). By contrast, the origiral draft employed the formula used in the UN Convention and elsewhere, which incorporates 'cruel' treatment or punishment as well, though it is doubtful that this actually reflects any substantive difference.

[56] *See* note 51 *supra.*

[57] *See* note 12 *supra.*

and the 1969 American Convention on Human Rights[58]) and to the 'case law' developed by the relevant international bodies under those instruments (e.g., the UN Human Rights Committee, the UN Committee against Torture and the Inter-American Commission and Court of Human Rights). Reliance on this outside 'legislation' and practice might prove of some help in a few difficult areas, such as that covered by the concept of 'inhuman or degrading treatment or punishment.' Although the Committee will not need to delve into sophisticated legal considerations, it might find it useful in some cases to draw inspiration from what has been said or done in related international forums.

5. Visits

A greater practical concern for the Committee will be the legal parameters that circumscribe its rights to make visits. On what basis may the Committee decide upon a visit? What places can it visit? Must it give notification and, if so, when? On what grounds, if any, may it be excluded from, or restricted in, carrying out visits? How extensive are its powers of investigation? I shall consider each of these five questions in turn.

In deciding to carry out an ad hoc visit, the Committee is entitled to act on *information* received from any sources (including individual Communications, allegations from NGOs and press reports). On the other hand, the Committee is not obliged to act on information it receives.[59]

Especially in relation to periodic visits, the Committee is also clearly dependent on receiving information as to the existence of places of detention in the various contracting states. In addition to the information it may receive from individuals and private organizations, the Committee obviously requires assistance in this respect from the states themselves. On its request, the latter are bound to provide a list of places under their jurisdiction where persons deprived of their liberty are being held and to indicate the nature of each establishment (e.g., police station, prison, hospital, military barracks, mental health institution).[60] In planning its periodic visits, the Committee is at liberty to decide which institutions in a particular state it wishes to visit, since it will generally not be practicable for it to see, on every visit, all the places in the state that fall within the ambit of Article 2. Thus, the Committee is accorded a useful margin of discretion in relation to its visits. The only requirement is that periodic visits be made to states parties on a roughly 'equitable' basis.[61]

---

[58] *See* note 3 *supra*.
[59] *See* Convention, Art. 7, para. 1; and Explanatory Report, *supra* note 8, para. 49.
[60] *See* Convention, Art. 8, para. 2(b): and Explanatory Report, *supra* note 8, para. 62.
[61] *See* Explanatory Report, *supra* note 8, para. 48.

As for the second of the five questions posed, Article 2 of the Convention provides that the Committee *may visit any place* within the jurisdiction of states parties 'where persons are deprived of their liberty by a public authority.' Some elaboration of this provision is given in the Explanatory Report: as few as one person need be detained in the place to be visited; no formal decision of the public authority need have been made (hence, de facto detention is also covered by the Convention); civilian and military, penal and 'medical,' and administrative and 'educational' detentions of all kinds are included; and public and private institutions are equally covered, provided the deprivation of liberty is the result of action by a public authority.[62] Deprivation of liberty in private institutions with which a public authority has nothing whatever to do is thus excluded, as is voluntary confinement.

On its face, the Convention therefore seems not to cover, among other things, the 'voluntary' committal of a person to a psychiatric hospital carried out at the request of the family, without the intervention of a public authority and without the consent of the person concerned, which is permitted under the legislation of a number of European countries. Yet it stands to reason that the commitment of healthy persons to a mental hospital can amount to inhuman or degrading treatment. Accordingly, the Explanatory Report stresses that, in the case of 'voluntary' patients, the Committee is authorized 'to satisfy itself that [the confinement] was indeed the wish of the patient concerned.'[63] Alternatively, if the patient is unable to 'express his wish,' the Committee also seems to have the power to investigate whether the committal was warranted by his medical condition and does not amount to inhuman treatment.

A further question arises: who has the final say as to whether a particular place falls within the ambit of Article 2? This question has both a factual and a legal dimension: must the Committee accept a state's assertion as to the factual circumstances obtaining in a particular place or can it act on its own information about the circumstances there? The issue will doubtless be resolved within the framework of Article 3: 'In the application of the Convention, the Committee and the competent national authorities of the Party concerned shall co-operate with each other.' Cooperation in regard to the Committee's right to visit appears to mean that an exaggeratedly strict application of Article 2 which moreover denies the Committee the possibility of verifying a party's assertions, is inappropriate. Thus, it could well be argued that in doubtful cases the Committee should be permitted to make whatever visits it chooses, especially as a mechanism for postponing visits to a 'sensitive' place or person is available to parties with valid objections to them.[64]

---

[62] *Id.,* paras 28–32.
[63] *Id.,* para. 32.
[64] *See* Convention, Art. 9 (and text at n. 70 *infra*).

Let us now consider the third question: what is meant by *'deprivation of liberty'?* The Explanatory Report states that this notion is to be 'understood within the meaning of Article 5 of the [ECHR], as elucidated by the case law of the . . . Court and . . . Commission.'[65] Article 5, paragraph 1, of the ECHR sets forth the basic proposition that 'everyone has the right to liberty and security of person.' It then lists six situations in which the deprivation of a person's liberty will exceptionally be lawful when carried out in accordance with a procedure prescribed by law. Most of the relevant case law involves these six exceptions. Thus, there was serious concern that the reference to Article 5 case law might give the misleading impression that this distinction between lawful and unlawful deprivations of liberty was somehow relevant to the Convention or, worse still, might suggest that the Convention should only apply in relation to places where persons were 'lawfully' deprived of their liberty. To overcome these concerns, the Explanatory Report, in its final draft, states that the distinction between lawful and unlawful deprivations of liberty arising in connection with Article 5 is immaterial as regards the Committee's competence.[66]

Notification of visits by the Committee is provided for in Article 8.[67] The Committee is required to notify the government concerned of its 'intention to carry out a visit' and may then visit 'at any time' any place in the relevant state's jurisdiction that falls within the ambit of Article 2. The national authorities are required to provide the Committee with the facilities needed to carry out its tasks, including full information on places where persons deprived of their liberty are held, free access to all such places and private interviews with persons held there, and such other information as the Committee might require.[68]

Underlying Article 8 is a tension between two conflicting objectives. On the one hand, it is obviously desirable for the Committee's visits to be unannounced, so that national authorities cannot engage in anticipatory cover-ups. To be effective, the Committee must form a true picture of the conditions in the places it visits. On the other hand, some prior notification is needed to enable national authorities to provide the necessary facilities to the Committee and to make its visits effective. A prison is unlikely to open its doors to the Committee without some advance notice of its arrival; a prison governor may not be available to speak to the Committee if he does not know when it will be visiting. Special arrangements

---

[65] *See* Explanatory Report, *supra* note 8, para. 24. For a summary of the case law on this aspects of Article 5, together with references to the relevant cases, see I STRASBOURG CASE-LAW, *supra* note 54, at 271–306; and M.-A. EISSEN, CASE-LAW ON ARTICLE 5 OF THE CONVENTION FOR THE PROTECTION OF HUMAN RIGHTS AND FUNDAMENTAL FREEDOMS (1986).

[66] *See* Explanatory Report, *supra* note 8, para. 24.

[67] *See also id.,* paras 55–59.

[68] *See* Convention, Art. 8, para. 2; and Explanatory Report, *supra* note 8, paras 60–65. To meet concerns regarding the data protection implications of this provision, it is specifically stated that parties are to have regard to relevant national laws and professional (particularly medical) ethics. Convention, Art. 8, para. 2(d).

will also be needed for visits to high-security prisons and certain psychiatric institutions.

The issue was resolved by not specifying any particular periods of notice to be given (3 months, 6 months, 24 hours and 48 hours were among those suggested) and, instead, leaving notification flexible. When an urgent ad hoc visit is called for, notice may presumably be as short as a few hours. On the other hand, a periodic visit or an ad hoc visit that is not urgent may be proposed and notification given without specifying the date and place of arrival of Committee members. In this situation, the Committee may be expected, in keeping with the principle of cooperation laid down in Article 3, to give the states concerned sufficient *further notice* to enable them to make the arrangements necessary to ensuring the effectiveness of the visit.

The fourth aspect of its right to visit that will be of vital importance to the Committee is the *grounds for restricting visits.* The original draft of the Convention contained no provision for parties to prevent, or secure the postponement of, a visit to which they objected. This was a particularly significant omission because, at the same time, the draft precluded reservations to the Convention. The bar on reservations was retained in the final version,[69] but a new provision allowing for the postponement of visits on certain grounds was included. What led to this change?

In the drafting process, two major problems were raised in this respect. First, it was pointed out that if persons are being detained in *military installations* (particularly nuclear plants), compelling considerations of national security may prompt a state to regard a visit by the Committee as inappropriate (e.g., fear that defense secrets may be revealed to the Committee). Second, attention was drawn to the case of *detainees presenting a high security risk,* in particular, those held because of acts of terrorism or espionage; their place of detention might have to be kept secret. Further, circumstances may arise that warrant at least a temporary postponement of visits by the Committee: epidemics in the area to be visited, outbreaks of serious disorder where detainees are being held and similar situations in which the health or personal safety of members of the Committee would be at risk.

While these considerations seemed relevant and important, a number of draftsmen stressed that they should not prevent the Committee from fulfilling its task. If a contracting state were given the right to rely upon one of those grounds to avoid being visited, this right might easily lend itself to abuse and thwart the Committee's function.

A balance between these two opposing needs was struck in Article 9.[70] It provides that in exceptional circumstances a party may make representations to the Committee against a visit at the time or to the particular place proposed, on the

---

[69] Convention, Art. 21.
[70] *See also* Explanatory Report, *supra* note 8, paras 71–72.

grounds only of 'national defence, public safety, serious disorder in places where persons are deprived of their liberty, the medical condition of a person or that an urgent interrogation relating to a serious crime is in progress.' Following the representations, the party and the Committee 'shall immediately enter into consultations in order to clarify the situation and seek agreement on arrangements to enable the Committee to exercise its functions expeditiously.' In the meantime, the Commission is to be kept fully informed about the persons deprived of their liberty in the place concerned.

Plainly, this provision, although it makes allowance for the compelling needs of the contracting states, *does not* grant states the power to impede a visit of the Committee altogether, or to remove particular places from its supervisory authority. First, it specifically provides that there must be 'exceptional circumstances.' Second, while some grounds are couched in very loose terms ('national defence,' 'public safety') and consequently confer some leeway on states in their interpretation and application, other grounds lend themselves to a less subjective appraisal and will not be difficult for the Committee to evaluate ('serious disorder' in places of detention, 'the medical condition' of detainees, the fact that 'an urgent interrogation relating to a serious crime is in progress'). Third, the state concerned and the Committee are duty bound to reach a mutually acceptable settlement for *postponing* the visit or for *carrying it out in accordance with special arrangements.*[71] Fourth, the state concerned is obliged to keep the Committee informed about any person concerned 'until the visit takes place.' Finally, the Committee is provided with a 'sanction' in case the state is uncooperative: it can make a 'public statement on the matter.'[72]

There will clearly be occasions when state concerns will constitute entirely proper grounds for seeking the postponement of a visit or for making alternative arrangements for one. On the other hand, it should not be possible to postpone visits for too long or even indefinitely, with the result that the Committee would be effectively prevented from carrying out visits in situations where they are often most needed. (Experience has shown that most torture occurs during interrogations and is inflicted on political suspects and those in 'secret' military or quasi-military establishments.) In this way, the parties' obligations could easily be rendered illusory.

---

[71] These arrangements might include, in the case of military installations, confining the Committee's visit solely to the place where persons deprived of their liberty are being detained. In addition, the Committee might be accompanied on its visit by an official of the state concerned (who, however, should not be allowed to be present at the interview of detainees). In the case of high-security prisons, to keep from revealing the whereabouts of detainees presenting a high-security risk, the state concerned might be required to supply the Committee with two different lists, one of places of detention and one of persons deprived of their liberty. Should the Committee wish to interview a particular person, the interview might be held in a place other than the place of detention (however, this procedure should be exceptional, for it is generally important for the Committee to visit the place where a detainee is actually held, to get an idea of how he is being treated).

[72] *See* Convention, Art. 10, para. 2.

Article 9, then, was a compromise that seeks to meet the concerns referred to above, without providing an actual escape clause. The article must be read in the light of other provisions of the Convention: Articles 2, 8, 10 and, especially, 3. The latter, which states the obligation of the parties and the Committee to cooperate with one another, was seen as the linchpin of Article 9. Thus, Article 9 permits parties to propose the postponement of a visit on the basis of their willingness to cooperate with the Committee in reaching agreement on alternative arrangements so that the visit can be carried out as soon as possible. At the same time, it is implicitly incumbent on the Committee to cooperate with the parties in maintaining an appropriate degree of sensitivity to any valid practical or other objections to a proposed visit and in finding acceptable means of overcoming those objections.

One could perhaps envisage the danger that Article 9 may weaken the Convention, at least where good faith in its application is lacking. Although the article does not allow a visit to be postponed indefinitely, it does provide a mechanism by which a visit may be delayed on vague, and perhaps easily manufacturable, grounds. A government intent on practicing torture and 'getting away with it' might find this advantageous, since even a short delay may be sufficient for the physical signs of ill-treatment—frequently the victim's only corroborative evidence—to disappear. The most subjective grounds mentioned above—those relating to 'national defence' and 'public safety'—might be cause for particular concern in this regard.

Much will depend on whether, in the event, the Committee is successful in fostering a spirit of cooperation in relation to the Convention. If it is, parties will come to trust the Committee and rely on its discretion. For the Committee's part, it will clearly have no interest in facilitating escapes by prisoners or in learning military secrets. Its sole interest will be in examining, and, if necessary, securing it improvements in, the treatment of persons deprived of their liberty; in this endeavor, it can only profit from a cooperative, understanding attitude.

Let us now turn to our fifth question, the *powers of investigation* of the Committee. This body, by its very nature (not being a judicial organ, as noted above), cannot conduct formal hearings similar to those of a court of law. In particular, it cannot oblige persons to give evidence under oath or to produce documents. Indeed, it cannot oblige persons to communicate with it at all. Of course, under Article 3, representatives of national authorities—including staff members of places of detention such as prison officers, employees of mental hospital's and the police—have a duty to cooperate with the Committee and therefore cannot, in practice, refuse to communicate with it. By contrast, detainees themselves, as well as their families, lawyers, doctors, nurses, and the like (those unconnected with their place of detention), may be interviewed by the Committee in private, but only if they agree.[73] Anticipating the possibility that a person deprived of his

---

[73] *See id.,* Art. 8; and Explanatory Report, *supra* n. 8, paras 66–69.

liberty may refuse to communicate with the Committee following pressure from his national authorities, the Explanatory Report stresses that the Committee must be given an opportunity to satisfy itself that the decision not to communicate was in fact freely made.[74]

A further illustration of its broad powers of investigation is the fact that the Committee is not limited to visiting the places of detention specified in its original notification. If it appears, during the course of a visit to one establishment, that important evidence as to the treatment of certain detainees may be found in another establishment in the same state, the Committee is free to visit that second establishment notwithstanding its omission from the Committee's original notification.[75]

Finally, it should be recalled that the Committee's mandate is couched in relatively wide terms; the thrust of its activities is generally to strengthen the protection of detainees from torture and inhuman or degrading treatment or punishment. Thus, its investigations will be concerned not only with adverse treatment by the authorities themselves, but also with ill-treatment of detainees by their fellow detainees. In relation to the latter, the Committee will no doubt consider what measures could be taken by the relevant authorities to prevent, or at least minimize, such abuses.

6. The Committee

In setting up the Committee, the Convention largely follows the model of the ECHR for the establishment of the Commission. It provides, first, that the number of members of the Committee is to equal that of the parties,[76] with no two members being nationals of the same state.[77] However, members are to serve in their individual capacity.[78] Obviously, the Committee's activities should be as apolitical and impartial as possible. There was some debate as to whether the qualifications of members should be spelled out; ultimately, only general indications—high moral character, competence in human rights, professional experience in the areas covered by the Convention—were given.[79] Although the members will not have to be lawyers, at least some of them will need practical experience in fields such as prison administration, and perhaps even the care of psychiatric patients, so as to enable the Committee to make useful recommendations to national authorities. An appropriate blending of professionals and persons with experience in the legal field of human rights will no doubt be required

[74] *See* Explanatory Report, *supra* note 8, para. 67.
[75] *See* Convention, Art. 8; and Explanatory Report, *supra* note 8, para. 58.
[76] Convention, Art. 4, para. 1. The corresponding provision of the ECHR is Article 20.
[77] Convention, Art. 4, para. 3. The corresponding provision of the ECHR is Article 20.
[78] Convention, Art. 4, para. 4. The corresponding provision of the ECHR is Article 23.
[79] Convention, Art. 4, para. 2. *See also* Explanatory Report, *supra* note 8, para. 2.

if the Committee's members are to carry out in-depth investigations and, in addition, negotiate on a high level with national authorities.

The Convention provides that the members of the Committee are to be elected
by the Committee of Ministers of the Council of Europe from among candidates
proposed by the Bureau of the Council's Consultative Assembly.[80] This mode of
election is modeled on that stipulated in the ECHR for the election of members of
the European Commission on Human Rights. The ECHR, however provides for
a different system for members of the Court: they are elected by the Consultative
Assembly from a list of persons nominated by member states of the Council of
Europe. Thus, in the case of the Court, the last word lies with a representative
body, while in the case of the Commission, a political body (the Committee of
Ministers) makes the final decision. The Consultative Assembly had proposed
in its original draft of the Convention on Torture that the system for electing
members of the Court be adopted as well for the new Committee. However, considerations relating to sovereignty prevailed in the end over demands more geared
to respect for human rights.[81]

In contrast to members of the European Commission on Human Rights,
Committee members are elected for a period of 4 years and may be re-elected
only once.[82] Considering the difficult and delicate nature of the Committee's
activities, one may wonder why the term of its members was not made longer
so they could profit from the experience gained in fact-finding techniques. The
reason behind the brevity of these terms of office can be found in the 'legislative
history' of the Convention.

The original draft prepared by the Consultative Assembly did not provide
that the Committee would consist of as many members as there were parties to
the Convention; it set the number at only five.[83] Subsequently, in the course of
hammering out a final draft, it was proposed in the Committee of Experts that
the membership be brought to 7 to ensure balanced geographical distribution

---

[80] Convention, Art. 5, para. 1. The corresponding provision of the ECHR is Article 21, para. 1.

[81] It should be emphasized, however, that other considerations were adduced to support the
system eventually adopted. At one stage of the drafting process, it was envisaged that states should
be allowed to refuse entry to a member of the Committee. It was then argued that states parties to
the Convention would be less likely to reject a particular member of the new Committee if it was
elected by the Committee of Ministers rather than by the Consultative Assembly (the idea being
that states would be estopped from objecting to a particular Committee member after his election by such an authoritative political body, on which all member states of the Council of Europe
sit). Accordingly, election by the Committee of Ministers was to be preferred to election by the
Consultative Assembly.
  Another reason supporting the system at issue was the fact that the Committee of Ministers
would be in a better position than the Consultative Assembly to ensure both that there was a geographical balance within the Committee and that all members had the requisite qualifications.

[82] Convention, Art. 5, para. 3; cf. ECHR, *supra* note 3, Art. 22. The original draft (*see* note 52
supra) followed the model of ECHR Article 22, providing for a 6-year term, indefinitely renewable
(Art. 5, para. 2).

[83] Original draft, *supra* note 52, Art. 4.

(with the Convention entering into force upon ratification by 7 states); it was later proposed that the number be increased to 11 after ratification by 15 states. Thus, in spite of this change in figures, the draftsmen still held to the idea that there should be no correlation between the number of ratifying countries and the number of members of the Committee. This, however, prompted some members of the Committee of Experts to point out that it was only fair to ensure some rotation in membership so as to allow all contracting states the opportunity to have a national serve on the Committee. Accordingly, it was proposed that the terms of office be relatively short and that members not be allowed to sit on the Committee for more than a total of 8 years. Subsequently, concern for state sovereignty came to prevail, with the consequence, among other things, that each contracting state was permitted to have a national (or a person linked to it) on the Committee, making the total number of members equal to that of the parties. After making this important change, however, the draftsmen neglected to change the rules on duration of membership and we are now left with a somewhat contradictory, or at any rate unsatisfactory, legal regime of membership.

Decisions of the Committee are to be taken by a simple majority of the members present,[84] subject to one exception to which I shall refer later. The Committee is to draw up its own rules of procedure to deal with such matters as the election of a chairman, arrangements for meetings, the organization of visits and the storage of information.[85]

An early question that arose in connection with the Committee was precisely *who would carry out the visits* contemplated in the Convention. The original draft provided that the visits would be carried out by 'delegates chosen from among its members or other persons'.[86] It was envisaged that these delegates would be experts, with experience particularly in visiting places of detention, assessing levels of respect for human rights and administering prisons. The 'other persons' to be chosen as delegates were thought likely to be individuals with some past experience in the ICRC or other NGOs, such as Amnesty International, or other professionals in prison and psychiatric administration.

During the hearings before the drafting bodies, the International Commission of Jurists, the ICRC and the Swiss Committee against Torture argued strongly that the visits should be carried out by *experts,* not by members of the Committee. They reasoned that visits are time-consuming, call for a great deal of personal availability and demand much practical experience in the field of prisons and similar institutions. They therefore suggested that outside experts be engaged to carry out all visits, after receiving advanced special training similar to that of the ICRC's delegates. The experts would visit places of detention, establish facts and

---

[84] Convention, Art. 6, para. 1. By contrast, ECHR Article 34 provides that the Commission is to take its decisions by a majority of the members present and voting. The original draft of the Convention, *supra* note 52, followed this model (Art. 6).

[85] Convention, Art. 6, para. 2.

[86] Original draft, *supra* note 52, Art. 8, para. 1.

report them to the Committee; this body would then be responsible for contacts with the national authorities and for drawing up the final report.

As in other cases, however, considerations of state sovereignty came to the fore here. States felt more comfortable with the idea of a Committee that would have the necessary expertise to perform the bulk of its functions itself. They perceived, in other words, that their national interests would be less threatened by opening up their places of detention to an international, institutionalized committee in whose composition they at least would have a say (in that the choice of members would be made by a political body, the Committee of Ministers), than to a group of private, possibly antagonistic, individuals, selected not by the states themselves or by a political body, but by the Committee.

Nevertheless, it was recognized that there may be occasions when some reliance on experts is called for. Thus, the final draft provides that visits are generally to be carried out by 'at least two members of the Committee'[87] and that these members may, if necessary, be 'assisted by experts and interpreters.'[88] The possibility of delegating a visit entirely to 'other persons' who are not members of the Committee is accordingly excluded, although the Committee may authorize a visit by only one of its members where the urgency of a case or some other circumstance so requires. The Committee is also left free to choose the most appropriate assistants to supplement its own expertise.[89]

---

[87] Convention, Art. 7, para. 2. *See also* Explanatory Report, *supra* n. 8, paras 50, 52 and 53. One reason that only two Committee members are required to take part in visits is that the drafting bodies were aware of the great number of places that could potentially be visited. Figures provided to the drafting bodies indicated that the number of penal establishments alone was extremely high in the various European states: 130 in France, 166 in the Federal Republic of Germany, 240 in Italy, 83 in Spain, 150 in Switzerland, 125 in the United Kingdom and 639 in Turkey.

As regards the nationality of the two Committee members who would take part in a visit, the notion emerged during the drafting process that, if possible, one of them should have the nationality of the state to be visited. A number of drafters, as well as the NGOs consulted by the Committee of Experts, disagreed on this point, on the ground that members might prove biased or feel psychologically constrained from making a dispassionate assessment in their own country. The majority, however, took the view that the national member, in addition to knowing the language, would have firsthand knowledge of the national setting and would therefore be able to contribute to a balanced appraisal of the conditions of the place visited. The ECHR opts for this system in regard to the formation of Chambers of the Court. Article 43 of the ECHR, *supra* note 3, provides:

For the consideration of each case brought before it the Court shall consist of a Chamber composed of seven judges. There shall sit as an *ex officio* member of the Chamber the judge who is a national of any State party concerned, or, if there is none, a person of its choice who shall sit in the capacity of judge. . . .

[88] Convention, Art. 7, para. 2; *see also* Explanatory Report, *supra* n. 8, para. 51.

[89] At the initial stage of the drafting process, it was suggested that the Committee should have available a 'panel' of experts to draw upon on each particular occasion. However, other drafters expressed the fear that in this way a new structure would be institutionalized alongside the Committee and that the experts would be given undue weight. In their view, recourse to outside experts should be exceptional. In the end, no provision was made covering this admittedly very important issue. It is for the Committee, once established, to decide how and on what basis to draw upon experts.

The extent to which the Committee actually makes use of such outside assistance will naturally depend partly on whether gaps exist in the expertise of its own members and partly on its eventual workload. Interpreters, at least, will probably need to be engaged relatively frequently, especially if, as was suggested by the International Commission of Jurists, the members of the Committee conducting visits do not include a national of the state visited.[90]

To allay any remaining fears of states concerning outside experts, it is provided that experts act 'on the instructions and under the authority of the Committee.'[91] Moreover, parties may resist the participation in visits of particular experts or interpreters to whom they object.[92] Objection to a person assisting the Committee may be made both as soon as the state is notified about who will participate in a visit and during the visit itself. The reasons envisaged by the draftsmen for such an objection (which are also reflected in the Explanatory Report) are the manifestation of a biased attitude against the relevant state, the breaking of the rule of confidentiality on a previous occasion or in the course of the visit, and the making of political or similar public statements during the visit. Two safeguards against abuses by states were laid down: (1) resort to objections must be had 'exceptionally'; and (2) the Committee is entitled to ask the state for the reasons behind the objection, 'on the understanding that the enquiry and any response shall be confidential.'

Finally, in discharging the functions of the Committee, both its members and those assisting them are protected by a comprehensive set of privileges and immunities.[93]

7. Reporting and Confidentiality

After each visit, the Committee is required to draw up a report setting forth the facts found during its visit, as well as any recommendations for improvement it considers necessary to protecting persons in the place visited from torture and inhuman or degrading treatment or punishment. The report, together with the recommendations, if any, is then transmitted to the state concerned.[94] Both the report and all the information gathered by the Committee in relation to the visit, as well as its follow-up activities, are required to be kept strictly confidential.[95] However, publication of an annual summary report of the Committee's activities,

---

[90] See, however, n. 87 *supra.*
[91] Convention, Art. 14, para. 2.
[92] *Id.,* Art. 14, para. 3; and Explaratory Report, *supra* n. 8, paras 83–86.
[93] Convention, Art. 16 and Annex.
[94] *Id.,* Art. 10, para. 1.
[95] *Id.,* Art. 11, para. 1; and Explanatory Report, *supra* n. 8, para. 76. *See also* Convention, Art. 13; and Explanatory Report, para. 80.

which will entirely respect the confidentiality of information concerning its vis-its, is envisaged.[96]

Special emphasis is placed by the Convention on confidentiality not only to 'protect' States as much as possible from undue attacks and to gain their trust, but also to protect the detainees involved. Thus, it is provided that, in seeking information about persons deprived of their liberty, the 'Committee shall have regard to applicable rules of national law and professional ethics';[97] for example, medical records, prison files and police records must not be disclosed and per-tinent domestic legal restrictions on the disclosure of information relating to criminal investigation must be observed. The duty of confidentiality is further strengthened by the provision in the Convention that 'no personal data shall be published [by the Committee] without the express consent of the person concerned.'[98]

As the success of the Committee depends substantially on its gaining the trust and confidence of the governments concerned, and in particular on its gaining access to 'restricted' places and information, this principle of confidentiality is clearly a key element in the structure of the Convention. Indeed, it even applies vis-à-vis the European Commission and Court of Human Rights: the Court's suggestion in 1985 that the Commission and the Court be provided, where appropriate, with copies of the Committee's reports for the performance of their own functions was not accepted by the relevant drafting bodies.

The strict confidentiality of its report and of the information collected by the Committee can only be set aside at the request of the party concerned,[99] or if the prospects of the Committee's gaining a party's trust and confidence are considered no longer 'realistic': that is, when the party has consistently failed to cooperate with the Committee or has refused to take steps to improve the situ-ation in the light of the Committee's recommendations.[100] In the latter event, the Convention provides that the Committee, acting exceptionally by a two-thirds majority, may make a public statement, but only after giving the party in ques-tion an opportunity to explain why it has failed to cooperate or take the steps recommended.

This power to make a public statement will undoubtedly be perceived as a kind of sanction to be applied to recalcitrant governments, or at least as a deterrent to refusals to cooperate. Be that as it may, the Committee will need to adopt an extremely cautious approach to its use. The whole point of the Convention is that, as regards the matters it covers, more can be achieved by discreet contacts than by public exposure and denunciations, which tend to produce denials rather than

---

[96] Convention, Art. 12. The annual report is to be submitted to the Committee of Ministers and then transmitted to the Consultative Assembly and made public.

[97] *See id.,* Art. 8, para. 3.

[98] *See id.,* Art. 11, para. 3.

[99] *Id.,* Art. 11, para. 2; and Explanatory Report, *supra* n. 8, para. 77.

[100] Convention, Art. 10, para. 2; and Explanatory Report, *supra* n. 8, paras 74–75.

improvements. Caution will also be called for, to avoid giving parties the correlative impression that confidentiality is a reward for cooperation.

8. Concluding Observations

While a considered appraisal of the Convention will obviously need to await its actual implementation, some general comments can be made.

First, the Convention is unique among treaties on human rights in that, as already noted, it contains no substantive, standard-setting provisions; its *sole* function is to establish a mechanism for international supervision[101] of compliance with preexisting standards. This is not to suggest, however, that the aims of the Convention are modest. On the contrary, the mechanism it establishes takes the element of supervision substantially further than it had previously been taken in relation to peacetime human rights. Previous instruments have sought to monitor compliance with the obligations they create by requiring states to submit reports at predetermined intervals for examination by international bodies,[102] or by providing for a contentious procedure enabling other parties to the treaty or individuals to make complaints to such bodies.[103] With the exception of those under the ECHR and the American Convention on Human Rights, these procedures are exclusively nonjudicial and lead to a nonbinding recommendation or report. States have not generally been willing to accept compulsory judicial review in this—only recently 'internationalized'—sphere. Where they have accepted it, international adjudication has proved valuable but, for reasons already indicated, not totally effective in securing respect for human rights obligations.

This should probably not surprise us. It is common knowledge that human rights obligations are substantially non-reciprocal—that is, states are *not* induced to comply with them for fear that other states might otherwise feel at liberty to disregard them. Even when the right to initiate ex post facto adjudication is given to individuals and international bodies and not just to states, we should not expect that it will compel compliance to the same extent as more reciprocal obligations, where the inherent incentives to comply are stronger. The prospect of an adverse human rights judgment is simply not as fearful to states as the continuing threat of retaliatory economic disadvantage that may follow from the breach

[101] For a discussion of the rationale for, and the various methods of, international supervision, see A. CASSESE, INTERNATIONAL LAW IN A DIVIDED WORLD 208–11, 304–06 and 310–11 (1986).

[102] *See, e.g.,* Supplementary Convention on the Abolition of Slavery, the Slave Trade and Institutions and Practices Similar to Slavery, Sept. 7, 1956, 18 UST 3201. TIAS No. 6418, 266 UNTS 3, Art. 8; Convention on the Elimination of All Forms of Racial Discrimination, *supra* note 1, Art. 9; the International Covenant on Civil and Political Rights, *supra* note 51, Art. 16; and the International Covenant on Economic, Social and Cultural Rights, GA Res. 2200, *supra* note 3, Supp. (No. 16) at 49, Art. 40.

[103] *See, e.g.,* the instruments referred to in note 3 *supra*.

of a commercial treaty. In the field of human rights, some form of continuous monitoring or supervision pervision by an autonomous body is called for.

The Convention responds to this need for supervision of the obligations of states regarding torture and inhuman or degrading treatment and, moreover, applies to those obligations the most advanced and penetrating form of supervision so far devised. Having an international body actually *inspect* places within the jurisdiction of states so as to ascertain their conduct is clearly much more far-reaching than providing for it merely to examine data submitted by states themselves or inquire into specific complaints. This technique also has the advantage of affording an effective method not only of checking whether a state is respecting or disregarding its international obligations, but also of forestalling violations, at least before they occur on any significant scale.

Prior to the adoption of the Convention, this method of supervision had largely been confined to the field of peaceful uses of nuclear energy,[104] where the special nature of the subject matter—in particular, the need to avoid the diversion of nuclear material to military use—induced states to accept an especially rigorous method of international scrutiny. As noted, it had also been applied to certain humanitarian obligations in wartime, as well as in other fields (with other modalities).[105] The Convention represents a major innovation in that it applies the technique of supervisory and preventive inspection to peacetime human rights protection.[106] By means of its visits, the Committee will be able to bring relief—not just consolation or moral support—to otherwise helpless victims and potential victims of torture and other forms of ill-treatment.

The Convention is also a significant step forward in the ongoing process of 'internationalization' of human rights. By ratifying the Convention, states agree to allow the Committee into their prisons, police stations, juvenile detention centers, psychiatric institutions and all other places where persons are deprived of their liberty; they agree to expose to the scrutiny of an international body many

---

[104] *See, e.g.,* Statute of the International Atomic Energy Agency, Oct. 26, 1956, 8 UST 1093, TIAS No. 3873, 276 UNTS 3, Art. XII(A)(6); and Convention on the Establishment of a Security Control in the Field of Nuclear Energy, Dec. 20, 1957, 351 UNTS 235. Art. 5(a). Regarding inspection for the purpose of avoiding the release of excessive levels of radioactivity, see, e.g., Treaty Establishing the European Atomic Energy Community (EURATOM), Mar. 25, 1957, 298 UNTS 167, Art. 35.

[105] *See* notes 9, 10 and 11 *supra.* A similar method of supervision, where the 'supervisor' is not an international body but the other party or parties to the relevant treaty, is even more widely used. *See, e.g.,* Antarctic Treaty, Dec. 1, 1959, 12 UST 794, TIAS No. 4780, 402 UNTS 71, Art. 7; Treaty on Principles Governing the Activities of States in the Exploration and Use of Outer Space, Including the Moon and other Celestial Bodies, Jan. 27, 1967, 18 UST 2410, TIAS No. 6347, 610 UNTS 205, Art. 12; and Treaty on the Elimination of Intermediate-Range and Shorter-Range Missiles, Dec. 8, 1987, USSR-U.S., S. TREATY DOC. 11, 100th Cong., 2d Sess. (1988), *reprinted in* 27 ILM 90 (1988), Art. 11.

[106] However, as noted above (see the section 'Utility Questioned' and note 34 *supra*), the Convention, although primarily concerned with peacetime situations, can also apply in time of war or during civil strife, to the extent that the ICRC does not 'effectively' visit 'on a regular basis' places where people are deprived of their liberty, *see* Art. 17, para. 3).

sensitive, indeed painful, spheres of national activity. In doing so, they affirm their conviction that 'expressions of concern at violations of [human] rights cannot be considered interference in the domestic affairs of a State.'[107]

Finally, the Convention—seen in the light of its drafting history—affords a revealing insight into the increasingly valuable role of both NGOs and the Council of Europe's Consultative Assembly in stimulating governments to move forward in protecting human rights. This is a field where governments are in particular need of prodding, or at least of being set concrete challenges to greater and greater achievements, as other priorities tend to monopolize their attention. Moreover, the role of these bodies has not ended with the adoption of the Convention. It is likely that they will continue to monitor its implementation and, to the extent that they consider any aspect of the Committee's practice unsatisfactory, to press for improvements.

On its face, the Convention appears tightly drawn (subject, as indicated, to a possible concern regarding Article 9), but with flexibility where appropriate. Like all international instruments for the protection of human rights, it is the outcome of rigorous negotiations between those favoring the progressive development of legal rules designed to safeguard human dignity as much as possible, and those more concerned with the demands of state sovereignty. The final result shows that the former eventually got the upper hand, although in a number of instances they had to accommodate to some extent the requests of the other group. (Some of these instances were mentioned above: the rules on the composition of the Committee, on its election and on the role of professional experts.)[108]

The text of the Convention, as it now stands, is a courageous attempt at a novel approach to human rights. Those concerned with human dignity will no doubt hope that this new European system for preventing torture and ill-treatment will fulfill a pioneering role by stimulating the establishment of similar systems elsewhere in the world, so that eventually visits by international committees to all kinds of detainees will come to be as normal, as accepted and as effective in raising the level of respect for human rights as ICRC visits to prisoners of war are today.

---

[107] *See* Declaration on Human Rights, adopted by the Foreign Ministers of the Council of Europe on July 21, 1986, in COUNCIL OF EUROPE, INFORMATION SHEET, No. 20, May-October 1986, at 118.

[108] To highlight the importance of the Convention, one should also recall that in the course of its drafting, a number of proposals were made with a view to qualifying or seriously limiting the action of the Committee, or, more generally, to lessening the smoothness of application of the Convention in comparison to the system eventually agreed upon. Even before the actual drafting started, it was suggested that instead of working out a Convention, a simple recommendation should be adopted. The following are some of the proposals made at different stages: that the entering of reservations to the Convention be allowed; that the Committee be under the control of the Council of Europe's Committee of Ministers; that the outside experts to be used by the Committee be proposed by the contracting states; that certain classes of national institutions be excluded from the application of the Convention; and that under certain circumstances, the contracting parties be relieved of their obligations under the Convention.

16. The European Committee for the Prevention of Torture and Inhuman or Degrading Treatment or Punishment Comes of Age*

1. Introduction: A Brief Reminder of the Essential Characteristics of the European Committee for the Prevention of Torture and Inhuman or Degrading Treatment or Punishment

The main features of the Council of Europe Committee for the Prevention of Torture and Inhuman or Degrading Treatment or Punishment (CPT)[1] are by now well known.[2] The Committee is an international body of inspectors charged with visiting all places in contracting states in which persons are deprived of their liberty by a public authority. Unique traits of the CPT are first of all its composition (it consists of persons coming from a variety of professions: medical doctors, psychiatrists, experts in penitentiary systems, criminologists, experts in human rights, former members of parliament, etc.). Second, its powers (it has the right to visit, without hindrance, any of the places referred to above—i.e. police stations, prisons, detention centres for foreigners, hospitals, psychiatric institutions, etc—to freely move around within those places as well as to privately interview persons deprived of their liberty and to speak freely with any person who might

---

* Originally published in N. Blokker et al. (eds), *Towards More Effective Supervision by International Organizations* (Dordrecht: Nijhoff, 1994) 115.

[1] Although the official name of the CPT, based on Article 1 of the 1987 Convention, is the 'European Committee for the Prevention of Torture and Inhuman or Degrading Treatment or Punishment', it is commonly called the 'Committee for the Prevention of Torture' (CPT). I believe that this is a misnomer, for the role of the CPT is broader: its aim is to prevent inhuman or degrading treatment or punishment. In its Second Annual Report, the CPT stated the following: 'it is noteworthy that in some countries visited by the CPT, police and prison officers have expressed surprise that an 'anti-torture' Committee should consider it necessary to examine the way in which they treat persons in their custody. This is perhaps an unfortunate result of the CPT's rather long title, attention inevitably focussing on the term 'torture' to the detriment of that of 'inhuman or degrading treatment'. Of course, the subject of torture is central to the CPT's mandate. However, (. . .) the concerns of the Committee are not restricted to preventing that particularly atrocious form of human rights violation: they extend to any form of ill-treatment of persons deprived of their liberty. Hopefully, as knowledge of the CPT's activities spreads, this will become apparent to all', (para. 63).

[2] *See* in particular my paper *in* A. Cassese (ed.), The International Fight Against Torture 135 ff. (1991), and M. Evans & R. Morgan, *The European Convention for the Prevention of Torture: Operational Practice*, 41 ICLQ 590 ff. (1992).

be able to supply relevant information). Third, its primary objective (which is to prevent any inhuman or degrading treatment or punishment including torture, besides of course putting a stop to any such treatment or punishment, whenever the CPT is satisfied that ill-treatment is being inflicted by state authorities on persons deprived of their liberty). Fourth, its means of action (the Committee's findings and recommendations must be sent confidentially to the relevant state, and can only be made public at the request of such state; the CPT can only 'go public' when a state fails to co-operate or to comply with its recommendations).

2. The First Stage of the Development of the CPT

The 1987 Convention setting up the Committee was ratified relatively quickly by 23 of the 28 member states of the Council of Europe (Bulgaria, Hungary, Poland, the Czeck and the Slovak Republics are not yet parties to the Convention).

The Committee commenced operations in November 1989, and in its first two years of activity established the organizational and procedural framework for the proper conduct of its mission. It adopted (and revised several times) its Rules of Procedure, elaborated a set of 'common working tools' (consisting of a host of documents concerning each type of place of detention coming within the purview of its activity: prisons, police stations, etc.), held a series of training sessions for its members, worked out how visits would be conducted and followed up, established relations with other international bodies specializing in this area (e.g. the International Committee of the Red Cross, the UN Committee against torture).

In formulating the framework for its activities, the CPT sought to act upon three basic principles. Firstly, that its work should have a collegiate direction. Whereas in other bodies the main task of conducting business (particularly when the body is not in session) is often conferred upon the President, the CPT decided (on the proposal of its President) to assign the task of directing its work to its Bureau, which consists of the President and the two Vice-Presidents. This approach has been consistently adhered to, with undisputably positive results.

The second principle that the CPT has consistently laid down as one of the bases of its action is that of impartiality. The Committee has constantly (and successfully, in my opinion) striven to be absolutely even-handed and unbiased in its action. More importantly, it has adopted various measures designed to ensure this impartiality at the institutional level. I shall only mention here the method used in order to select the countries to be periodically visited (for the first two years they were chosen by the drawing of lots) and the role assigned to the 'national' member (he may not take part in visits to his own country and should not take part in the vote on the visit report concerning his country).

The third principle the CPT decided to act upon was that of effectiveness. To try and ensure that its work was as fruitful and efficacious as possible, the Committee adopted a number of measures designed to enhance its inspecting role. In particular, it devised a kind of 'warning procedure'; upon receiving disturbing information about certain cases or situations in a country, and if this information is deemed not to warrant an immediate ad hoc visit, the CPT can request the state concerned to report forthwith on those cases or situations as well as any remedial action taken. Another important measure adopted was to provide for a system whereby after each visit to a country, its authorities, upon the receipt of the Committee's visit report, are bound to 'report back' all measures adopted to comply with the CPT recommendations.[3]

3. The Second Stage

After two years of carrying out visits, the CPT entered the second phase of its life. In this second phase the bulk of the CPT's activities have been devoted to carrying out visits, with all the attendant chores: preparations of visits, making of notes and comments by members of each visiting delegation, drafting of the report by the delegation, discussion and the adoption of the report by the plenary Committee. This phase will be drawn to a close by the end of 1993, when all the 23 contracting states will have been visited at least once.

In addition, in this stage, the CPT has concentrated on the examination and discussion of states' reports (states visited by the CPT are normally requested to send in an interim report within six months of their receiving the CPT visit report, and thereafter a final report within the next six months). This process has become part of an ongoing dialogue between the CPT and each contracting. state visited. Indeed, the key to a gradual resolution of the problems for which the CPT was set up lies in a standing and fruitful co-operation between the CPT and each contracting state. For this purpose, it is proving increasingly useful for the CPT to engage in a dialogue with the authorities of each state. This dialogue goes through various stages. First, a CPT delegation visits a state and sends a visit report, then the state sends its interim and final reports; subsequently the CPT comments on these reports and sends the state its observations and suggestions or, if need be, makes a further visit and so on.

In this second phase of its activity the Committee has also had occasion to apply, for the first time, Article 10(2) of the Convention, whereby if a state party 'fails to co-operate or refuses to improve the situation in the light of the Committee's recommendations, the Committee may decide, after the Party has had an opportunity to make known its views, by a majority of two-thirds of its members to make a public statement on the matter'. After two ad hoc visits and one periodic visit to Turkey, the Committee felt that, despite the acknowledged efforts on behalf of the Turkish authorities in order to comply with the Committee's

---

[3] For further details, *see* the CPT First General Report covering the period of November 1989 to December 1990, Council of Europe Doc. CPT(91) 3, paras 23–33.

requests and notwithstanding the improvements introduced in some areas, Turkey had failed to adequately tackle the continued and wide-spread existence of torture. Accordingly, on 15 December 1992, the CPT adopted a public statement.[4] However, even in making this statement the CPT was eager not to depart from its basic principle of co-operation with contracting states, upon which all its activities depend. In other words, the Committee did not intend in any way to put Turkey in the dock, let alone break off relations with it. The CPT, whilst feeling that it had no choice but to publicly expose Turkey's failure to comply with its recommendations, conceived and drafted its public statement as merely but one element—albeit undisputedly an element at first sight unfavourable to Turkey—of its ongoing and indispensable dialogue with the Turkish authorities. To put it differently, the statement was never conceived as a final or breaking point, after which there could be no further co-operation between the CPT and Turkey. This intention was spelled out in the final paragraph of the statement, where it was pointed ont that it had been issued 'in a constructive spirit. Far from creating an obstacle, it should facilitate the efforts of both parties— acting in co-operation—to strengthen the protection of persons deprived of their liberty from torture and inhuman or degrading treatment or punishment' (paragraph 37).

4. A Tentative Stock-taking

Now that the CPT is gradually reaching a 'cruising speed' of seven or eight visits per year and is about to complete its first round of visits to all contracting states, it is perhaps possible to hazard a sort of overall assessment of its performance.

A. Major Achievements

To my mind, a general appraisal of the Committee's action would be by and large positive. Among its merits the following stand out.

First, it has been able to fully exercise its right of investigation in the countries visited. Admittedly, on a few occasions there have been clashes with local authorities, both in police and prison establishments. On these occasions, access to a place that the CPT delegation wished to visit was delayed. However, this was normally due to inadequate knowledge about the CPT on the part of the authorities in question and not to a deliberate attempt to hinder its activities. More importantly, the CPT delegation always managed eventually to enter the place and carry out its visit (on one occasion only did the CPT delegation deem it necessary to enter a formal protest to the Minister of Foreign Affairs of the

---

[4] For the text of the statement *see* 4 *European Journal of International Law* (1993) 119–127. *See also ibid.*, 115–118, the comment by A. Tanca.

country concerned, but it was subsequently allowed to freely move around within the premises to which the protest related). More disturbing is the fact that in a few instances the CPT delegation was satisfied that just prior to its visit to certain places, persons detained there had been moved out so as to leave those places either empty or with only one or two detainees. On these occasions the CPT issued a severe warning to the state concerned to the effect than any repetition of such behaviour would be regarded as a serious breach of co-operation. Again, what matters is that these instances of misconduct by some of the authorities of certain states were not of such a magnitude as to distort the overall picture of the conditions of detention in those countries and that the CPT was able to get through its visit. In other words, in spite of these endeavours by some authorities, the CPT was always able to ascertain the conditions of detention in those countries, by dint of careful investigation in other localities or in other establishments of those countries.

The second merit of the CPT lies in its sagacious interpretation of its primary task: prevention. The Committee wisely decided that for the purpose of preventing inhuman or degrading treatment it needed to investigate a wide spectrum of conditions and situations. In so doing, its objective is to ascertain whether they are inhuman or degrading or whether they might degenerate into inhuman or degrading conditions or treatment. In other words, the CPT has decided to also investigate all those situations where a risk is present, in that they may eventually develop into serious ill-treatment or inhuman behaviour. Thus, for example, as regards police custody, the CPT carefully explores such matters as notification of custody to a family member or friend, access of detained persons to a lawyer and to a medical doctor, information about one's own rights while in police custody, the conduct of questioning, physical conditions within police holding areas, etc. As for prisons, CPT delegations look, among other things, into the physical environment of detention, the extent of activity programmes (work, education, sport, etc.), solitary confinement practices, relations between prisoners and staff, grievance or disciplinary and inspection procedures and so on.

A third merit of the CPT is its imaginative and thoughtful formulation of a follow-up system. This system enables the visit reports the CPT sends to states to become part and parcel of a permanent monitoring of the conditions of detention in each contracting party. In addition, that system enables the Committee to satisfy itself as to whether or not each of these Parties has introduced the changes or ameliorations recommended.

A fourth merit is that the CPT has started, from its inspections and related activities, a gradual distilling of a kind of corpus of standards on which it bases its assessment of specific situations. The CPT has wisely decided to gradually make public these standards, by including them in its Annual Report. Thus, in its Second Annual Report it included its basic criteria of appraisal concerning police stations and prison establishments, while in its Third Annual Report it has included basic standards on medical services in prisons. The setting down and publication of these general, if tentative, criteria will no doubt prove beneficial to national authorities; they will be able to draw inspiration from them in the planning and carrying out of any possible changes or reforms. Hopefully, the gradual publication of these standards by the CPT will lead to the building up of a set of general guidelines on conditions of detention, able to effectively supplement and enrich the European Prison Rules.

That all the steps taken by the CPT, which I have just underlined, constitute major achievements is, in my view, borne out by three elements.

First, so far the response of contracting states to CPT visits and reports has been by and large positive. In spite of the wealth of critical findings, stern comments and strong recommendations made by the CPT with the aim of improving national conditions of detention, states have not protested or resented the CPT's action. On the contrary, while sometimes expressing doubts about the sweep of the CPT activities, most states visited so far have willingly taken in hand changes and improvements in their conditions of detention. What is even more striking, whenever a CPT delegation has decided to make 'immediate observations' at the end of a visit as to the need to introduce, forthwith, improvements in some specific areas, states have abided by these recommendations and made the necessary changes. To recall just two instances (they can be mentioned because the relevant states published the CPT report and their own preliminary comments), Switzerland and France took immediate action to comply with 'observations' made on the spot by the visiting delegation.

The second element that bears testimony to the impartiality, professionalism and effectiveness of the CPT is the fact that so far almost all the states visited have decided to make the CPT report concerning them public. This courageous step shows that contracting states have taken their obligations under the Convention so seriously as to go beyond what is required by the Convention, in that they do not insist on the confidential nature of CPT reports. It also shows that states by now have confidence in the work of the Committee and appreciate its evenhandedness, meticulousness and expertise.

The third factor confirming the importance of the Committee's work is the fact that, acting in consultation with the CPT, the Council of Europe Committee of Ministers is considering extending the geographical scope of the Committee's action in two ways. First, by opening up the Convention to states participating in the Conference on Security and Co-operation in Europe that are not members of the Council of Europe (this would be effected by way of an Amending Protocol to be drafted by the Council of Europe Steering Committee on Human Rights). Second, by envisaging the possibility of third states making ad hoc arrangements with the Council of Europe designed to authorize the CPT to visit them on an ad hoc basis; that is to say without formally becoming a contracting party to the Convention.

That such possibilities are under consideration no doubt bears witness to the importance that the CPT is gradually acquiring.

B. Some Possible Deficiencies

One should not, however, pass over in silence some weaknesses of the Committee.

First of all, it would seem that not all of its members possess the required competence in at least one of the specific fields of investigation of the CPT, nor do they have the requisite experience in the area of human rights. It follows that for the purpose of carrying out visits, sometimes the Committee needs to rely heavily on the contribution of experts on an ad hoc basis. Admittedly, experts are always necessary, if only to bolster or supplement the competence of the Committee members making up the various visiting delegations. In some cases, however, their participation becomes crucial because no Committee member in the visiting delegation possesses the necessary competence in the area (e.g. penitentiary establishments, psychiatric institutions) that is particularly important in the country at issue. This might prove unsatisfactory, in view of the fact that, after a visit, experts—unlike Committee members—only take part in the drafting of the visit report, and do not participate in the discussion in the plenary Committee on the draft report, nor in the discussion on the interim and final reports subsequently sent by the visited state.

A second weakness might be seen in the lack of an exhaustive panel of experts on which to draw for each visit, in the light of the specific needs of the visit. So far the CPT has been able to draw up a list of experts and has consistently relied on some of them. The list, however, is far from satisfactory and in particular does not include experts from all the countries of the Council of Europe. As a consequence, hitherto the CPT has tended to primarily use experts from two or three countries and this may prove objectionable. To be sure, the CPT itself should not be blamed for this drawback; it is merely a fact of life that it is quite difficult to draw up a panel of highly competent experts, familiar with one of the two working languages of the CPT (English and French). Nevertheless, hopefully the CPT will resolve this situation in the not too distant future.

A further deficiency perhaps lies in the failure of the CPT to make a greater effort to publicize its activity at the international level and especially within the contracting states. For the sake of avoiding any breach of the basic principle of confidentiality, the Committee has so far tended to eschew public exposure and the giving of greater information about its action to the media. By the same token, it has relied heavily upon the contracting states, urging them to disseminate as much information as possible about its activities to national authorities and detainees. Quite a few states have not, however, lived up to this request and this has resulted in difficulties and misunderstandings with national officials in the course of some visits. Probably it is now high time for the Committee itself to make its action better known at the national and international level; this could have important spin-offs in connection with future visits to contracting states.

5. Prospects for the Future

Undisputedly, various factors are bound to result in the stepping up and intensifying of the CPT action. First, the largely favourable response of contracting states to the first round of CPT visits will consolidate and strengthen the Committee's role. Second, the follow-up process, or ongoing dialogue between states and the CPT, that has already started, will, of necessity, become more and more significant but also increasingly complex and time-consuming. Third, the impending extension of the CPT action to numerous other states (the newly arrived members of the Council of Europe, those members of the CSCE that intend to become parties to the Convention, plus the other European states that plan to enter into ad hoc arrangements with the Committee) will pose serious strains on the CPT and its staff.

To adequately cope with these new tasks, the Committee will soon need to become a 'semi-permanent' body in the sense that its members must be asked to devote two-thirds of their time to the CPT. One of the possible consequences is that they will need to be adequately remunerated (a 'retainer system' and appropriate home-work allowances could be provided for, similar to that which currently applies for the European Commission of Human Rights). By the same token, the CPT staff should be strengthened considerably.

A second development that could prove useful is the CPT's concentration on areas that, so far, it has little or insufficiently explored: for example, administrative detention of aliens, especially asylum seekers; confinement of the mentally ill; confinement of the elderly; detention of minors; deprivation of liberty in military establishments; the condition of sentenced persons, etc. In the second round of its visits, the CPT might think it fit to confine itself to only visiting some classes of establishments, depending of course on the individual country to be visited. It would thus take the opportunity to reach out in order to investigate new areas, or to focus on areas that it has so far considered only briefly.

Thirdly, the Committee might wish to consider the advisability of making 'targeted visits'. It is apparent from the present practice of the CPT that it is increasingly encountering a major problem during its visits. On occasion the police stations it visits, in particular those which have been the subject of notification, are empty. An examination of custody records has often shown that the absence of detainees was exceptional. This bears out the suspicion that the premises have been vacated to prevent the CPT visiting delegation from interviewing detainees. One possible way of surmounting this obstacle could lie in undertaking impromptu visits. These visits should (i) be targeted on the police stations of one or two cities, (ii) be short (two or three days) and (iii) be carried out by a delegation that should split into three or four sub-groups, so as to be able to undertake simultaneous inspections of a number of establishments. Of course, to make a surprise visit presupposes that, contrary to the present practice, no prior notice should be given a few weeks in advance of the visit, except for a general notification, to be given a year before ('Next year your country will be visited by a CPT delegation'). However, the state to be visited should be put in a position to exercise its right under Article 14(3) of the Convention ('A Party may exceptionally declare that an expert or other person assisting the Committee may not be allowed to take part in a visit to a place within its jurisdiction'). To this end, the notification of the visit should also include the names of the persons making up the visiting delegation.

The undertaking of 'targeted visits' is not contrary to, and indeed is permitted by, Article 8(1) of the Convention ('The Committee shall notify the Government of the Party concerned of its intentions to carry out a visit. After such notification, it may at any time visit any place referred to in Article 2'). By contrast, it would not be in keeping with paragraphs 56–58 of the Explanatory Report on the Convention (whereby 'it is expected' that the CPT, before the visit takes place, will provide details concerning 'the date and place of arrival' of the delegation) as well as Rule 35 paragraphs 3 and 4 of the Rules of Procedure (which restate the provisions of the Explanatory Report just referred to). However, it would not be too arduous to bypass these legal obstacles by reason of a new interpretation of the Convention and the Explanatory Report and the amending of the Rules of Procedure. One could point out that ultimately the basic 'constitution' of the CPT is the Convention, while the Explanatory Report has only a secondary and subsidiary role. Consequently, in case of doubt or conflict, one should lay emphasis on the Convention and disregard the Explanatory Report.

It ought to be added that, should the CPT decide to undertake these 'targeted visits', of course they would by no means replace the 'ordinary visits' (be they periodic, ad hoc, or follow-up visits) to large institutions such as prisons, psychiatric establishments, detention camps for foreigners, etc. Plainly, it is difficult for national authorities to alter overnight the objective conditions prevailing in such large institutions; consequently, there would be no need for 'targeted visits' there. Both classes of visits could thus be usefully undertaken by the CPT, and the choice would depend on the circumstances of each country and the attitude taken by national authorities.

Fourthly, the CPT might wish to consider drawing up a body of standards concerning both the basic safeguards for detainees and the requisite behaviour of state officials in establishments coming within the purview of the Committee. As I pointed out before, the CPT has already taken this path, by distilling in each of its Annual Reports some general guidelines on specific matters. It should probably step up and enhance this formulation of general standards, so as to build up a corpus of norms that national authorities could usefully rely upon.

6. Concluding Remarks

The CPT is no doubt a unique body in the international community. Its tasks and the way it has so far gone about them clearly show that *prevention* and *inspection* are the key to the handling of human rights questions in the international community. Norm-setting and even *ex post facto* implementation procedures (be they judicial, quasi-judicial or merely supervisory in nature) are not sufficient.

The CPT's activities also show that this international body has been able to make deep and important inroads into states' domestic jurisdictions. Once contracting states have agreed at the international law level (by ratifying the Convention) to be visited by the Committee, this body can override domestic jurisdiction in two ways. First, it freely enters places that so far had been regarded by states as their *sancta sanctorum,* as their sacred penetralia in which no outsider, let alone a group of international inspectors, could set foot. In doing so, the Committee has shown that by now even the innermost recesses of state practices are open to international scrutiny. The barrier of state sovereignty has been torn down, at least in this area (to be sure, this has occurred as a result of the free choice of the contracting states; however, once they have made this choice, it is extremely difficult—politically and psychologically—to go back on it).

The Committee pierces the veil of domestic jurisdiction in a second way. This happens *after* its visits to states have been carried out. As I have pointed out above, following its visits the CPT makes a host of recommendations and suggestions for improvements, that range from legislative to judicial and administrative matters. These recommendations often impinge upon delicate areas of the state machinery, and in addition may entail financial burdens for the national authorities. The state concerned is duty bound to first send an interim report and then a final report describing the way in which it has complied with the CPT recommendations. These CPT recommendations, unlike similar acts of other international bodies (e.g. those of the UN General Assembly), are not couched in loose terms, nor are they deprived of the means designed to monitor their application. The CPT's recommendations are specific, precise, worded in technical language and their addressees must report on their implementation. If the recommendations are not complied with, or are insufficiently implemented, the CPT can not only insist on their application, but also carry out a follow-up visit to the same state, in order to exert stronger pressure towards compliance. If the relevant state is still reluctant to abide by the CPT's requests, this body can apply Article 10(2) and make a public statement. Thus, the CPT's recommendations, although they are not legally binding, possess a force and an authority that are unique in the international community.

What I have just emphasized demonstrates that the setting up of the Committee marked a turning point in the international fight for human dignity. It is to be hoped that soon other international organizations will institute similar bodies in the field of human rights, so as to shift the struggle for the protection of these rights increasingly from the area of normativity to that of actual realization.

B. Economic Assistance and Human Rights

17. Foreign Economic Assistance and Respect for Civil and Political Rights: Chile—A Case Study*

1. Introduction

The question of whether foreign economic assistance to states grossly disregarding human rights has an impact on the enjoyment of civil and political rights in those states is undoubtedly very complex. The nexus between economic assistance and human rights is often indirect and subtle. In addition, there arises the thorny question of evidence: upon what elements can one show the multifaceted yet elusive nexus between foreign economic aid and various forms of human rights that on the surface appear to have few economic implications?

Without attempting to address all problems that fall within the purview of the subject-matter, I have limited the discussion to five questions that appear crucial:

1) Have human rights violations within a state discouraged governments, international agencies, or private institutions from sending economic assistance to that state?
2) Might a state's human rights violations actually attract foreign economic assistance in some situations?
3) Have restrictions on civil and political rights caused inefficiencies in or had an adverse consequence on the utilization of foreign economic aid?
4) Do the benefits of foreign economic assistance reach those persons who have been victims of human rights violations, particularly the families of persons arbitrarily detained or imprisoned?
5) To what extent has foreign economic assistance supported the recipient state's social and economic policies which have an adverse impact on the enjoyment of civil and political rights?

* This paper is based on a revised version of a section of a report prepared by the author for the United Nations in 1976. Notes 2, 4 *infra*. Originally published in *Texas International Law Journal* (1979) 251.

2. A Case Study: Chile

This article will briefly address these five questions specifically in regards to Chile. The reasons for this choice stem from the fact that there is sufficient documentation available, both from the Chilean authorities and from the United Nations, to analyze the relationship between foreign economic assistance and civil and political rights in that nation.

This analysis assumes that the various pronouncements of the U.N. General Assembly regarding Chile's poor human rights record are indeed correct.

A. Violations of Civil and Political Rights in Chile and the Withholding of Foreign Economic Assistance

The first of the five questions referred to above can be broached on the basis of replies of various governments to information requests sent in 1977 by the Secretary-General of the United Nations[1] and by the Rapporteur on Chile of the Sub-Commission on Prevention of Discrimination and Protection of Minorities.[2] Reference is made here only to the official comments of a few Western governments concerning their economic relations with Chile since the military *golpe de estado* of September 11, 1973.

In its reply to the Secretary-General's information request, the Federal Republic of Germany stated that as a consequence of the disregard for human rights in Chile, '[T]he Federal Government has not provided Chile with any more development aid. It has discontinued supplies of weapons and military equipment. In negotiations for the rescheduling of debts, harder terms have been imposed. University partnerships have not been continued.'[3]

The government of Italy, in response to the request for information of the Rapporteur on Chile, stated:

Economic, financial, cultural and technical cooperation between Italy and Chile have been strongly influenced since September 1973 up to the present—both at the multilateral and the bilateral level—by the attitude adopted by our country towards the military Government [*sic*] headed by General Pinochet. In keeping with the unequivocal positions it has taken at the political level, Italy has gradually broken off all forms of collaboration, so that it can now be said that official aid by Italy to the Chilean Government is virtually non-existent.

---

[1] G.A. Res. 31/124, 31 U.N. GAOR, Supp. (No. 39) 104–05, U.N. Doc. A/31/39 (1976).

[2] The Sub-Commission on Prevention of Discrimination and Protection of Minorities directed the Rapporteur to undertake a study on the 'Impact of Foreign Economic Aid and Assistance on Respect for Human Rights in Chile.'

[3] Report of the Economic and Social Council: Protection of Human Rights in Chile, Report of the Secretary General, 32 U.N. GAOR (Agenda Item 12) 9, U.N. Doc. A/32/234 (1977) [hereinafter cited as Report of the Secretary General].

As to economic and financial co-operation within the competent multilateral organizations in regard to loans granted to Chile . . . Italy's position has always been negative; in particular, [in the World Bank] Italy voted against the grant of a loan to Chile in January 1974 and in May 1975 ($20 million for an agricultural reorganization programme), and it abstained from voting on the decision concerning three other loans to Chile in February ($33 million) and December 1976 ($25 million and $35 million).

In the Inter-American Development Bank . . . , the position adopted with regard to the grant of two loans to Chile . . . was as follows: abstention on an integrated technical assistance progamme which also includes Bolivia and Peru, and a vote against the grant of a loan of $20 million exclusively to Chile.

With regard to multilateral technical co-operation . . . Italy has not failed to express reservations concerning programmes for Chile, in view of the non-observance by the Chilean Government of the resolutions adopted by various United Nations bodies which call for respect for human rights and the restoration of fundamental freedoms in that country.

As regards the consideration of economic and financial relations on a bilateral basis, it must be pointed out that, during the period in question, Italy suspended the privileges enjoyed by Chile under the Insurance and Export Credit Law and that, consequently, no request concerning that country has been considered by the competent organizations.

A similar attitude has been adopted in regard to bilateral technical co-operation. In September 1973, various programmes were being executed in fields such as occupational training, university education and building, together with volunteer programmes, chiefly in education. Today, there is only one volunteer programme (nine persons), for occupational retraining of personnel of the Curanilahve coal mines, which has not been discontinued because of its distinctly social character. . . .

This consistent over-all attitude . . . is also reflected in the refusal by our authorities to take part in multilateral talks held within the Club of Paris with a view to restructuring Chile's external debt.[4]

The government of the Netherlands responded to the information requests by declaring that it had taken 'a number of concrete steps which it hopes will contribute to the restoration and safeguarding of human rights and fundamental freedoms in Chile. Financial assistance in the framework of development co-operation has been suspended. Aid is provided only in respect of certain small welfare projects, directly benefiting the poorest section of the population. This aid is channelled through non-governmental organizations. . . . In the field of trade, credit guarantees by governmental bodies for export transactions by Dutch companies have been discontinued as from 1973.'[5] In a note to the United Nations on December 21, 1977, the Government of the Netherlands informed that body that it had not provided any bilateral aid to the Chilean Government since the *golpe de estado* of 1973, but that '[t]hrough some non-governmental organizations funds

---

[4] Study of the Impact of Foreign Economic Aid and Assistance on Respect for Human Rights in Chile, 31 Sub-Commission on Prevention of Discrimination and Protection of Minorities (provisional Agenda Item 13) para. 407, U.N. Doc. E/CN.4/Sub.2/412 (1978) [hereinafter cited as Foreign Economic Aid Study].

[5] Report of the Secretary General, *supra* note 3, at 12–13.

are supplied for activities which are directly benefiting the most distressed groups of the Chilean population.'[6]

Norway, in a note to the United Nations dated November 25, 1977, stated that as a result of the suppression of democratic institutions in Chile,

Bilateral aid given to Chile from Norway has been suspended. Together with the Governments of the other Nordic countries the Norwegian Government has voted against loans to Chile from the World Bank. At the twenty-third session of the Governing Council of UNDP, held in January 1977, the Norwegian representative and those of the other Nordic Governments in a joint statement made clear that the land programme of Chile did not enjoy their support because of the failure of Chilean authorities to concur with past United Nations resolutions to improve the human rights condition in Chile.[7]

The degradation of human rights in Chile since the 1973 military *golpe de estado* has also severely strained relations between Chile and the United States. A recent study submitted to the United Nations Ad Hoc Working Group on the situation of human rights in Chile stated:

Since 1974, Congressional critics of United States Chilean policy have legislated limitations on military and economic aid to Chile on the grounds of its human rights violations. . . . Thus far, when all military aid and most forms of bilateral economic aid have been denied to Chile by the United States Congress and it has become increasingly evident that very little aid would be available, the Chilean Government has responded by renouncing any United States bilateral assistance. The complete rejection of this aid came in response to the State Department's decision to delay for 30 to 60 days $9.3 million of the $27.5 million economic assistance package for 1977 to express disapproval of human rights violations by the Chilean Government of President Augusto Pinochet. . . . The Chilean junta issued a note which formally spurned the proposed $27.5 million economic aid package [and] angrily react[ed] against the Carter Administration's attempt to use human rights as a factor in considering foreign aid distibution.[8]

However, economic relations between Chile and the United States improved somewhat in 1978. According to press reports, on April 24, 1978, the Commodity

---

[6] Foreign Economic Aid Study, *supra* note 4, at para. 409.

[7] *Id.* para. 410. In its reply of 5 December 1977 to a request for information sent by the Rapporteur on Chile, the Government of Sweden stated the following:

The Swedish Government extends no aid to the present Chilean authorities. The Swedish policy in this regard is illustrated by the following facts: On 31 August 1973, an Agreement, called the Development Co-operation Agreement of 1973, was signed in Santiago de Chile between the Government of Sweden and the Government of the Republic of Chile. The preamble of this Agreement states that the objective of the Agreement is to enable the respective Governments to continue 'their co-operation for the purpose of economic development and social and economic justice in Chile as envisaged in the Development Plan of Chile for 1971–76.' The resources made available by Sweden according to the Agreement were intended to contribute to the achievement of these goals as stated in the Plan.

Id. para. 412.

[8] CENTER FOR INTERNATIONAL POLICY, CHILE: AN ANALYSIS OF HUMAN RIGHTS VIOLATIONS AND UNITED STATES SECURITY ASSISTANCE AND ECONOMIC PROGRAMMES 1–2 (July 1978).

Credit Corporation, a private corporation under the auspices of the Department of Agriculture, approved thirty-eight million dollars in commercial export credits to farmers and ranchers in Chile. The *Washington Star* reported:

State Department officials confirmed . . . that approval of the credits was delayed for some time, but they denied that the credits reflect a departure from the administration's emphasis on human rights.

Officials emphasized that the credits were for private parties rather than the Chilean Government, and were intended primarily to aid American farmers. They also stated that the credits reflected approval of what was described as 'encouraging political developments' within Chile's military Government [*sic*].

One State Department official cited the recent amnesty for many political prisoners in Chile and the government's decision to turn over to United States authorities Michael Vernon Townley, the 35-year-old American who has been charged with conspiracy in the murder of former Chilean Ambassador Orlando Letelier in 1976.[9]

Senator Edward Kennedy, however, felt that the credit would have been more appropriately used if allocated specifically to the improvement of human rights in Chile.[10]

From the above, it is clear that most of the States that have commented on their economic relations with Chile after the *golpe* have either discontinued or substantially decreased their economic assistance to Chile as a direct consequence of its suppression of civil and political rights. Thus the introduction of a repressive system has resulted in much of the international community denying economic aid to Chile in the hopes of using such pressure to force the present Chilean authorities to restore human rights.

Although the aforementioned change recently occurred in United States policy, this change has been justified primarily by emphasizing that the Chilean authorities are in the process of improving the human rights situation in that country. While I do not pass judgment on the United States assessment of the Chilean situation, one must recognize that even this new stand reveals that a close link exists between foreign economic assistance and respect for human rights in Chile.

---

[9] Washington Star, May 5, 1978, at A-5.

[10] In a speech from the Senate floor, Senator Kennedy said:

I am disturbed by the Administration's recent approval of $38 million in Commodity Credit Corporation credits for Chile. [I]t would have been much wiser for the United States to loan this much money on the basis of substantial human rights movement in Chile.

I am now consulting with the Administration to ensure that this action will not be misunderstood, or repeated in the absence of further progress. Let us not lose this opportunity to make a critical difference in the lives of the Chilean people—and to demonstrate that the United States can be an effective force for human rights in Latin America.

124 Cong. Rec. S6,983 (daily edn May 4, 1978) (remarks of Sen. Kennedy).

B. Repression of Human Rights as a Means of Attracting Foreign Economic Assistance

The relationship between foreign economic assistance and the economic policy of the present Chilean Government on the one hand, and Chile's current repression of civil and political rights on the other, is quite visible. Gross violations of human rights, particularly of trade union rights, have become an important factor in attracting foreign economic investment to Chile.

Chilean authorities regard attracting foreign investment as a 'central economic principle.'[11] Among the most important aspects of this effort to attract foreign capital are the offer of cheap labour and the strict enforcement of industrial discipline. Immediately after the military takeover, editors of the highly influential *El Mercurio* began to advocate 'the perfecting of the labour market,' suggesting, among other things, that 'the cost of hiring labour should be reduced substantially in relation to that of capital.'[12] The elimination of virtually all trade union rights, including the rights to elect trade union representatives freely, to bargain collectively, and to strike, have put Chilean workers in a position of impotence with few means of asserting their rights to decent living and working conditions. This distressing situation has been amply documented in reports by the International Labor Organization (ILO) and the United Nations Commission on Human Rights, which have urged the Chilean Government to 'promulgate new trade union legislation as soon as possible and to repeal Legislative Decree No. 198 in order to ensure the normal functioning of trade union activities.'[13] Minister of Economy Sergio de Castro explained in a seminar on the Chilean policy on foreign investment: 'We think that foreign investors take their capital from one place to the other, looking for the highest profitability. This is why they have to periodically evaluate the most important variables for their companies' profits, such as wage-levels, taxes and customs tariffs.'[14] Thus Chilean authorities offer foreign investors the economic benefits derived from violating the rights of Chilean workers—rights that have been universally agreed upon at the United Nations. Foreign investors are openly invited to translate the transgression of these human rights into increased profitability.

[11] El Mercurio (Santiago), *Informe Económico,* Aug., 1976, at 16.

[12] El Mercurio (Santiago), 1973.

[13] Report of the Ad Hoc Working Group to Inquire into the Situation of Human Rights in Chile, 34 U.N. ESCOR Annex (provisional Agenda Item 5) 66, U.N. Doc. E/CN.4/1266 (1978) [hereinafter cited as Human Rights Study].

[14] El Mercurio (Santiago), Sept. 22, 1975, at 6, (int'l ed.). This is a recurrent theme in the Chilean Government's attempts to attract foreign investment. An advertisement in the Wall Street Journal entitled 'Chile: safety zone for foreign investors,' pointed out 'Tranquillity and stability in all sectors of the labor force, plus a high standard of technical and professional skills [are] readily available,' and assured readers that, 'It is safe to invest in Chile.' Wall Street Journal, June 8, 1977, at 16, cols. 1–6 (eastern edn).

C. Impact of the Restrictions on Civil and Political Rights on the Utilization of Foreign Economic Assistance

The serious violations of human rights that are still occurring in Chile have adverse consequences on the actual use of the foreign economic aid flowing into Chile. Grave restrictions on freedom of expression, freedom of association and trade union rights prevent most Chilean people from taking part in the decision-making process. The government can request and use foreign economic assistance without close scrutiny by the Chilean population. This lack of freedom of expression and the existence of a ruling group which makes all the basic decisions affecting the lives of the people permits neither a free exchange of ideas nor the introduction of improvements or corrections in the execution of economic policies, including the utilization of foreign economic assistance.

The Permanent Committee of the Episcopal Conference of Chile, in a statement issued on March 25, 1977, has forcefully analyzed this situation. After stressing that 'for many families, especially those who are unemployed or earning a minimum wage, the extremely precarious and difficult conditions in which they are living are becoming almost intolerable' and that 'the peasants, workers and settlers appear to be bearing an excessive and disproportionate burden,' the Permanent Committee said:

Economic development depends on decisions taken at the national level, and the right of participation defended by the Catholic social doctrine is also applicable to the economy. In the economic sphere it is easy to create a technocratic élite which aspires to make all the decisions itself. . . . To maintain that economic problems have only one solution, without any alternative, is to establish the rule of science and the scientific élite over human responsibilities. It is also to assume that the decisions made are based only on scientific reasons and that no part is played in them by reasons of dogma or group interest. But this is not the case: doctrinal positions and group interests often play a part in making decisions, though somewhat unconsciously.

In the name of human rights and of the right of participation, the Church asks that *the various economic options should be the subject of open discussion, and that access to decisions and the possibility of exerting influence should not be reserved to a single scientific school or to a few more privileged economic groups.* Without a great national debate, the reasons given by the specialists lack full credibility. There is usually more wisdom in the discussion of differing opinions than in a single opinion which is affirmed dogmatically and without contradiction (emphasis added).[15]

Workers feel this same need to participate in the economic decision-making process. In a letter dated April 29, 1977, to the President of the Republic of Chile, a group of trade union leaders cited the 'historical failure of private enterprise,' and

---

[15] El Mercurio (Santiago), March 26, 1977.

called for worker participation in the development of a new national 'investment plan.'[16]

The views expressed in general terms by the Permanent Committee of the Episcopal Conference and by trade union leaders also apply to the subject of this article. Since the junta allows no political parties or political groups in Chile, and strictly controls trade unions, only members of the ruling group participate in the decisions concerning the type of economic assistance to be requested abroad; the choice of the states, international institutions or private groups which may furnish economic assistance; the conditions under which such assistance can be accepted; and the social or economic areas targeted for foreign assistance. Fresh ideas and perspectives from excluded groups could correct the major defects in foreign assistance schemes which at present greatly limit the beneficial influence foreign economic assistance could have.

D. Foreign Economic Assistance and the Condition of Those Suffering from the Present Disregard of Civil and Political Rights in Chile

In its February 1, 1978 report, the United Nations Ad Hoc Working Group on the Situation of Human Rights in Chile, established by the Commission on Human Rights, pointed out that Chilean authorities 'continue to refuse to respect the liberty and security of persons believed to be opposed to the present régime. The system of intimidation through arrests, detention, torture or ill-treatment and harassment continues to be used to repress those sectors of the Chilean population.'[17] According to the Ad Hoc Working Group, 'Persons detained by the security agencies continue to disappear, though at a rate significantly less than in the past.'[18]

The fate of political detainees and of relatives of missing persons or political detainees raises particularly serious problems. Their lot has been aptly described by the representative of Amnesty International. In a statement before the Commission on Human Rights on February 24, 1978, he pointed out:

Often, the victims of arbitrary arrest and imprisonment were from the poorer sectors of society. They could be divided into four different groups. The first consisted of prisoners charged with political offenses, the greatest number of whom were in the three major prisons of Santiago, and their families. Where the prisoner has been the chief breadwinner, the family lived in the utmost need and poverty. The second category comprised political prisoners charged with and tried for a common law offense. That was a phenomenon particularly noticed in recent months and which Amnesty International had only recently begun to investigate, and it had not always been possible to ascertain beyond all reasonable

---

[16] Report of the Economic and Social Council: Protection of Human Rights in Chile, Note by the Secretary General, 32 U.N. GAOR, LII Annexes (Agenda Item 12) 286, U.N. Doc. A/32/227 (1977) [hereinafter cited as Human Rights Report].

[17] Human Rights Study, *supra* note 13, at 73.

[18] *Id.*

doubt that there were political reasons behind the arrest. The third category was composed of former political prisoners and former detainees who had been held without trial under the provisions of the state of seige. On release they faced common problems and underwent extreme hardship. Finally, there were the families of missing persons, possibly the most tragic group, who suffered severe psychological disruption and often serious financial stress. It was estimated that over 10,000 persons had been affected.[19]

In 1978 the Ad Hoc Working Group received the report of a mission that visited Chile in 1977 under the auspices of the World Council of Churches. According to the Ad Hoc Working Group, this report stated that 'the mental and physical health of the families, especially the children, of persons who have disappeared has been severely affected. The information provided to the Group in this report concerning 145 specific cases of children revealed somatic disorders, psychological problems, and retardation of development. . .'[20]

It appears that medical doctors detained for political reasons often lose their right to work when released.[21] In addition, the families of the 'disappeared' frequently undergo hardship even in the field of education.[22] No less serious is the fate of persons who oppose the government's social policy or who are regarded by the authorities as potential opponents. Thus trade union leaders and members often lose their jobs or encounter great difficulty in obtaining employment.[23]

Up to now relief agencies have aided relatives of missing persons, or political detainees and opponents.[24] These groups have also received financial and other forms of support from some governments and private institutions. It seems, however, that the financial means available to these people are not sufficient. Sources of foreign economic assistance do not design their programs to help the victims of political detention, and the Chilean government does not direct aid to this group.[25] The conclusion therefore seems warranted that at present foreign economic assistance provided to the Chilean authorities does not benefit those people who suffer directly or indirectly from deprivation of liberty for political reasons (i.e., detention, disappearance). These persons receive assistance from relief agencies operating in Chile through *direct funding* from foreign governments or private organizations.

---

[19] 34 Commission on Human Rights (1456th mtg.) 4–5, U.N. Doc. E/CN.4/SR. 1456 (1978) (remarks of Mr. Rodley).

[20] Human Rights Report, *supra* note 16, at 111.

[21] Foreign Economic Aid Study, *supra* note 4, at para. 172.

[22] *Id.* at para. 238.

[23] *Id.* at para. 171.

[24] Relief has been provided by the Vicaria de la Solidaridad, the Fundación de Ayuda Social de la Iglesia Cristiana (FASIC), and the Ayuda Cristiana Evangélica (ACE), as well as by the Intergovernmental Committee for European Migration, the Office of the United Nations High Commissioner for Refugees and the International Committee of the Red Cross.

[25] *See* Foreign Economic Aid Study, *supra* note 4, chs. III and IV.

E. Socio-Economic Policies Adopted in Chile: Repression of Civil and Political Rights and Foreign Economic Assistance

Chilean authorities seek the following social and economic goals: (a) enhancement of the role of private enterprise in the national economy; (b) opening of the Chilean market to imported products and reducing customs tariffs and duties; (c) removal of present price controls; and (d) drastic reduction of state expenditure, including the reduction of staff wages and salaries.[26] These socio-economic policies have had certain consequences for the Chilean people, including: (a) increase in unemployment; (b) reduced income of wage earners; (c) decreased purchasing power of wage earners; (d) bankruptcies of small and medium-sized national enterprises; (e) serious deterioration of public services such as the health services; (f) food shortages for the poor; and (g) reduction of categories of persons economically eligible for admission to university education.[27]

Discontent and a profound sense of dissatisfaction are byproducts of these policies. Actually, some groups in Chile have voiced strong protests. Recall the important statement issued on March 25, 1977, by the Permanent Committee of the Episcopal Conference of Chile,[28] and the letter sent to the President of the Republic of Chile by Chilean trade union leaders.[29]

Significantly, the Government has not prevented public expression of dissent or criticisms by prominent groups. In more democratic societies, however, when governmental authorities draw up and implement economic and social measures that disadvantage the interests and needs of the less privileged strata, usually trade unions oppose those measures through strikes, walk-outs, public protests, and so forth. Lack of freedom of assembly, association, and, in particular, trade union rights, prevent this reaction in Chile. A close link apparently exists between the kind of policies carried out by the present authorities in the socio-economic field, and repression in the field of civil and political rights. In short, without suppression of or serious restrictions on civil and political rights, the military government could not impose and enforce its economic and social policies.[30]

---

[26] *Id.* at paras 88–112.

[27] *Id.* at paras 113–248.

[28] See text *supra*, C.

[29] See text *supra*, C.

[30] It is necessary to point out that this view does not constitute a novelty. Actually, as early as 1970, Jorge Cauas, one of the main economic policy-makers in Chile, who was Minister of Finance to the military government and is now Ambassador to the United States, showed himself to be aware that only political repression can allow a free market system to survive in such a society as that of Chile. In 1970 he described the political measures that should accompany the implementation of his economic theories and of the monetary policy he advocated (control of the money supply through restriction of domestic credit, a single exchange rate and a balanced budget, etc.), warning that serious problems were to be faced in applying that policy, most of them deriving from the need for discipline to ensure that the measures would be respected. 'The main pressure factors to be taken into account are the actions of organized groups of workers in connection with wage policy and the ambitious governmental programmes which must be financed by non-inflationary

Foreign economic assistance to a great extent serves to prop up the present governmental authorities in Chile.[31] The assistance, through design or implementation, supports the policy that the authorities choose and carry out in the field of socio-economic relations. The economic policy fosters repression of basic human rights because implementation is only possible without dissent.

It follows from the above considerations that foreign economic assistance, to the extent that it reinforces the present government in Chile and its socio-economic strategy, contributes to consolidating and perpetuating the repressive system which to a great extent is a counterpart of the socio-economic policies of the Chilean authorities.[32]

3. Concluding Remarks

The present gross violations of human rights in Chile are related to economic assistance in two respects. First, and most apparently, the bulk of this assistance

means.' He concluded that 'in a democratic system . . . , there are obviously both conceptual and practical difficulties' in applying the proposed scheme, but these disappear as soon as it is agreed to use 'other measures, *in the form of the establishment of a centralized system, with the consequent loss of freedom.*' Cauas Lama, *Política Económica de Corto Plazo,* in 2 Banco Central de Chile: Estudios Monetarios 25, 41–42, 44–45 (1970) (emphasis added).

[31] *See* Foreign Economic Aid Study, *supra* note 4, chs. I and II.

[32] It is necessary to underscore that this conclusion has already been reached by other persons who have dealt with the problems of Chile. In this connection, it is worth citing a statement made April 29, 1976, before the Sub-Committee on International Organizations of the Committee on International Relation of the United States House of Representatives by Mr. Leonard C. Meeker, a prominent lawyer and former Legal Adviser to the United States Department of State. Although Mr. Meeker refers only to the economic assistance furnished to Chile by the United States, his conclusions can also apply to the assistance provided by other states. After surveying the various forms of economic assistance provided by the United States to Chile, he stressed that this assistance did not go to those who are most in need, and concluded, 'Under present programs, U.S. Government assistance is simply shoring up and easing the problems of a brutally repressive régime.' *Chile: the Status of Human Rights and its Relationship to U.S. Economic Assistance Programs: Hearings before the Sub-comm. on Int'l Organizations of the House Comm. on Int'l Relations,* 94th Cong., 2d Sess. 7 (1976) (statement of Leonard C. Meeker). Replying to a question by United States Representative A.T. Moffet, Mr. Meeker said:

The U.S. Government needs to make it clear in its own statements to the Government of Chile that it is deeply offended by the treatment that that government is meting out to human beings, that it is a kind of treatment that we simply cannot condone. We will not support that government in its policies, and we will not give it the practical sinews to continue its repression through grants of foreign aid that go to the government to be dispensed by the government at its discretion.

Id. at 12.

On May 4, 1978, Senator Edward M. Kennedy, speaking on 'Challenges to Human Rights in Chile,' stated before the United States Senate that:

The economic assistance tragically continues which, in so many instances, is being used to perpetuate in power those particular forces and those particular interests which we state are alien to our own traditions and our own basic and fundamental principles.

124 Cong. Rec. S6,987 (daily edn May 4, 1978) (remarks of Sen. Kennedy).

helps to strengthen and maintain power in a system which pursues a policy of large-scale violations of human rights. This applies to some forms of economic assistance concerned with development as well as to most forms of economic assistance that show no concern either with human rights or with development. The same holds true for many cases of assistance directly related to human rights (assistance given with the specific aim of improving the situation of the population in the fields of housing, sanitation, hospitals, health centers, and so forth).[33] Often the government uses this assistance to replace national resources, which are diverted to other ends, including that of financing the repressive system. In all these cases economic assistance often appears instrumental in perpetuating or at least maintaining the current situation of gross violations of human rights.

The second aspect is no less important. In order to obtain the assistance which it seeks abroad, the government has to ensure a favorable presentation of the indices by which an economy is normally held to be 'healthy.' It must appear to be 'creditworthy' (i.e., it must have, among other things, a favorable balance of payments, controlled or diminishing inflation, a reduction of public expenditure). This domestic policy does not take into account the human factor and, in fact, creditworthiness can only be obtained by a redistribution of income which is unfavorable to the vast majority of the population. Furthermore, to the extent that it is not only foreign economic assistance in the form of loans (bilateral or multilateral), but investment that the government wants to attract, the state of poverty or backwardness of the working sector of the population does not appear as a negative factor. Instead, it appears as a positive element that may lead foreign enterprises, attracted by cheap labor and the low cost of production in the country, to make the decision to invest. In this respect, a deterioration in the benefits that workers and their families receive in other than monetary form also plays a major role in investment decisions. The absence of social unrest and restrictions on trade unions are important added advantages of a regressive system to foreign investors.

If the two aspects of the relationship between economic assistance and the violation of human rights are considered, one can see that in the second aspect the causal relationship is inverted: repression encourages investment. Thus, together, they make up a closed circle of 'cause' and 'effect': economic assistance to a very great extent permits the perpetuation of violations of human rights, and such violations, in turn, bring about the necessary conditions to obtain economic assistance.

---

[33] For details on this form of economic assistance, see Foreign Economic Aid Study, *supra* note 4, at paras 472, 476.

18. A 'Contribution' by the West to the Struggle against Hunger: The Nestlé Affair*

1. The Facts

The fight to make the fundamental right to life a reality in the world is a truly titanic one, often enough to make the bravest despair. This is highlighted by an episode which, though very well-known, seems to me so important as to call for a brief reminder.

In 1974, a British charity, *War on Want* (founded in the early 1950s with the main aim of providing information on the problems of poverty in the world), published a brief study, *The Baby Killer*,[1] edited by Mike Muller, examining the pernicious effects produced in the Third World from the promotion and sale of powdered milk for infants. In brief it asserted that the increasingly widespread distribution of powdered milk, encouraged and organized by large food industries in the West, was producing devastating effects. Why? For the very simple reason that all the hygienic and sanitary conditions, and more generally conditions of social progress, that may make replacement of mother's milk by powdered milk useful do not exist in most developing countries. For that milk to have beneficial effects, the baby's bottle must be sterilized, there must be drinkable water, and the accompanying instructions for using the bottle must be followed rigorously. But in many of those countries, none of this happens. Let us consider in more detail why.

'Wash your hands carefully, using soap, every time you prepare the child's feed'. That is how, according to *The Baby Killer,* the instructions for bottle feeding in the Nestlé pamphlet *Mother Book* start. But, the study continues, '66% of housewives in the capital of Malawi do not have running water. 60% do not have a kitchen inside their home.' 'Put the bottle and teat in a pan with enough water to cover them. Bring to the boil and boil for ten minutes', says another pamphlet, *Cow and Gate*, prepared by another large multinational and aimed at West Africa. In this pamphlet, the instructions I have just quoted are accompanied by a picture of a shining aluminium pan on top of an electric cooker. 'But,' observes *The Baby Killer,* 'the great majority of mothers in West Africa do not have electric cookers. They cook on three stones that support a pot heated over a wood fire.

* Originally published as Ch. 8 of A. Cassese, *Human Rights in a Changing World* (Oxford, Polity Press, 1990) 138.
[1] See M. Muller, *The Baby Killer*, a study sponsored by a *War on Want* (London, 1974).

The pot for sterilizing the baby's bottle also has to be used to cook the family meal; sterilization and boiling water are likely to be forgotten.'

The *Cow and Gate* babycare pamphlet for Africa says: 'If you have a refrigerator, it is more convenient for you to prepare enough for baby for the whole day.' But how many African families, especially in rural areas, have access to a refrigerator?

In addition to the negative effects I have just pointed out, there is another one: the explanations for using powdered milk are of course in writing, and are contained in the pamphlets distributed along with the powdered milk. But the very great majority of Third World mothers are illiterate.

Another problem is the cost of artificial feeding, which is very high in developing countries. In 1973 the cost of feeding a three-month-old child was approximately equal in Burma to 10.6 per cent of the minimum working wage, in India 22.7 per cent, in Nigeria 30.3 per cent, in Pakistan 40.3 per cent and in Egypt 40.8 per cent. These percentages go up considerably when it comes to calculating the cost of artificial feeding for a six-month-old child, which needs more.

What are the consequences of all these concomitant factors? The answer is clear. The bottle is not sterilized and so becomes a breeding ground for dangerous germs; the instructions for use are not understood so that the milk is wrongly used; to make the milk go further it is diluted with water, often heavily polluted. The result is that the children are less resistant to infection and easily fall victim to gastric or intestinal complaints like gastro-enteritis; the malnutrition resulting from the use of diluted powdered milk often causes physical or mental damage, followed in many cases by serious illnesses and even death.

In short, the distribution of powdered milk in the Third World, instead of being a factor for progress, has brought deleterious effects; instead of raising the standard of life and nourishment of children, it has contributed to causing illnesses and malnutrition, the prelude to death. Who is primarily at fault?

The *War on Want* study laid the blame principally on the big foodstuffs multinationals. Indeed, an annual report from Nestlé itself helps us to understand why. Here is what it says: 'In general, sales [of infant feeding products] are developing satisfactorily, though the birth-rate in countries with a higher standard of living is continuing to fall, slowing down the increase in our sales. The result is increasing competition and an ever broader choice of products for the consumer. But in developing countries our products continue to sell well, thanks to population growth and the rise in standard of living.' Accordingly, the best market, on which the multinationals have to concentrate, is in the poor countries. The *War on Want* study specifically accused large-scale Western companies of using a host of questionable methods to sell their products: from recourse to mass-media repetition of slogans on the enormous advantages of artificial feeding ('your children will be more intelligent', and the like), to the use of 'saleswomen' (who, in the guise of nurses, 'counsel' mothers in dispensaries and hospitals, 'pushing' the various products under the pretext of giving advice on feeding), to the free distribution of 'samples' or of baby bottles to those who buy tins of powdered milk. The *War on Want* study concluded with an appeal directed at both the companies themselves and the governments of developing countries. It urged a return to breast-feeding, as not only healthier but above all more suited to Third World conditions; the multinationals were asked to stop publicizing their products in poor countries or carrying out sales campaigns, and instead to collaborate with intergovernmental organizations such as the World Health Organization (WHO) that are specially involved with problems of infant feeding in poor countries. The governments of those countries, it was suggested, should exercise effective control, and in particular ensure access to industrial products for those who really need them—infants who cannot be fed by their mothers, such as some twins or orphans.

2. The Case Brought in Switzerland by Nestlé

One of the multinationals mentioned in the English document was Nestlé, an enormous firm with its headquarters in Switzerland, with an annual budget higher than the Swiss Federal Government's (in 1974 its budget was 16.6 billion Swiss Francs as against 13.9 billion for the budget of the Swiss Confederation).[2] A group of individuals concerned with Third World issues, the 'Swiss Working Groups for Development Policy' (*Schweizerische Arbeitsgruppen für Entwicklungspolitik,* SAFEP), translated the pamphlet from English to German, entitling it *Nestlé tötes Babies* ('Nestlé Kills Babies'). This led to an enormous furore. But still greater furore was provoked in Switzerland and abroad by the charge against SAFEP brought on 2 July 1974 by Nestlé in the Bern Criminal Court (and the Court of Zug, another small Swiss town with an active SAFEP group). Nestlé invoked the Swiss Penal Code: in its opinion, the 'Working Groups' had defamed it by repeatedly disseminating through the press, in bad faith, allegations that 'injured' its 'reputation' (*Ehre*). In particular, according to the Swiss company, the 'Working Groups' had defamed it for four reasons: they had claimed in the title of the pamphlet that the company 'killed babies'; they had said that the activity of Nestlé and other multinationals operating in the sector was 'contrary to the principles of ethics, and immoral'; they had asserted that Nestlé was responsible for the death or permanent mental or physical impairment of thousands of children because of its advertising practices (i.e. the fact that it publicized powdered milk using unacceptable expedients); they had accused Nestlé of camouflaging its commercial representatives in the Third World as 'nurses', thereby deceiving mothers in those countries.

---

[2] See Arbeitsgruppe Dritte Welt Bern, *Flaschenpost* (Information zum Ehrverletzungsprozess Nestlé Alimentena SA gegen Arbeitsgruppe Dritte Welt), no date, p. 4. For more up-to-date information see P. Harrisson, *L'Empire Nestlé* (Editions Favre, Paris, 1983); J.C. Buffle, *N. . . . comme Nestlé* (Editions A. Moreau, Paris, 1986).

The trial dragged on for two years (from 1974 to 1976) before the President of the Bern Criminal Court, Sollberger, acting as sole judge. The two parties to the dispute of course made wide use of 'forensic' arguments, the one side to cut down the 'Groups', the other to refute the accusations decisively. Before sentence was pronounced, specifically at the third hearing (22 June 1976), Nestlé took a step that aroused much surprise and confirmed the impression that it felt rather weak in its legal action: it withdrew three of the four accusations referred to, leaving only the first one, that the 'Working Groups' had defamed it by having used as title for the German translation of the pamphlet an unproven, unfounded accusation: that Nestlé killed children. The 'Working Groups', in a periodical bulletin, hastened to underline the importance of this decision, noting that by virtue of it the three allegations against Nestlé covered by the part of the action withdrawn could now legitimately be levelled against Nestlé 'without being punishable or prohibited'.[3]

3. The Verdict

Judgment was pronounced on 24 June 1976[4] and as was foreseeable, amounted to running with the hare and hunting with the hounds. In brief, the thirteen members of the 'Working Groups' were found guilty not of *defamation* (*Verleumdung*), but of the less serious offence of *'false accusation'* (*üble Nachrede*) (I shall explain why presently); with the consequence that each of them was condemned to a modest fine (300 Swiss Francs) with no jail sentence.

Before describing Judge Sollberger's reasoning, I wish to highlight one important point. When complex human affairs with manifold political and social implications are brought before the courts, a peculiar phenomenon not infrequently occurs: they become subsumed and, as it were, absorbed into the aseptic, impassive world of the law; they are stripped of their human dimension and translated into 'legal facts', that is, into facts with abstract, timeless connotations; facts described in rigid technical terminology: offences, lawful acts, powers, rights, obligations, and so on. It is for the magistrate concerned to obstruct this process of rarefaction of life. He may do so either by 'reading' the laws with modern eyes and a modern sensitivity, or by inserting into the formal parameters offered by those laws the real situation, warts and all.

---

[3] See Schweizerische Arbeitsgruppen für Emtwicklungspolitik (SAFEP), *Nestlé-Prozess beendet-Auseinandersetzung geht weiter*, no. 3 (Bern, December 1976), p. 6.

I should like to express my gratitude to the Swiss Justice Department for providing me with all the issues of these periodicals, as well as other documents relating to the Nestlé case.

[4] See the typescript of the unpublished text, in German, of the judgment (the pagination is unclear; the text of the decision and of the reasons runs to 35 pages). The translation is mine.

I should like to thank Dr K. Schnyder, Vice-President of Nestlé for providing me with the original text of the judgment.

On the facts surrounding the trial see also *Nestlé contre les bébés? Un dossier réuni par le Groupe de Travail Tiers Monde de Berne* (Editions F. Mespéro and Presses Universitaires de Grenoble, Paris, 1978).

What happened at the Bern trial? Judge Sollberger sought to take cognizance of the complex issues of the case and go beyond the rigid standards and formal choices imposed by law. He sought to be a rigorous jurist, and at the same time open to the moral arguments of the accused. But he did not have the courage to opt decisively for the thesis of one or other of the parties, and ended up saying that in some ways both were right, and in others both wrong—even if in the end the party in whose favour judgement was given was Nestlé. The result was a clumsy, vacillating verdict, a mixture of legal formalism and hypocritical moralism.

Let us see how this conclusion was arrived at. In doing so, I shall seek to review the reasoning adopted by the Swiss magistrate step-by-step.

As I mentioned earlier, Nestlé had withdrawn three of the four charges. Accordingly, the magistrate had to ascertain only whether, by asserting that 'Nestlé Kills Babies', the 'Working Groups' had defamed it. I should say straight away that the magistrate could easily have resolved the issue by noting that the German title of the pamphlet ('Nestlé tötet Babies') did not in any way reflect the pamphlet's content. The pamphlet did express criticisms of, and grave objections against, the advisability and 'ethics' of the conduct of various multinationals, but did not specifically accuse any one of them of 'killing'. The judge could have noted that the title in question, albeit unfortunate, inappropriate and out of place, was however to be read *in conjunction with* the pamphlet to which it referred; he could then have concluded that the 'Working Groups' had not intended to accuse Nestlé literally of 'killing' Third World children; the charge could have thus been dismissed.

Judge Sollberger preferred instead to proceed with the maximum formalism, and give the accusations against Nestlé the full weight attributed to them by the Swiss company.

The judge began by observing that the assertion that someone kills children, whether intentionally or negligently, has ethical implications and injures the person's reputation (*Ehre*) (by which is understood the 'respect to which the bearer of the reputation may lay claim, from an ethical and social point of view'). He then asked whether this injury to Nestlé's reputation constituted defamation (for which in Swiss law bad faith is required, namely full awareness that the charge levelled against somebody else is false and unfounded), or mere 'false accusation' (for which, by contrast, a lack of due diligence in ascertaining the truth is sufficient and neither awareness of the untruth of the utterance nor a special intention to insult or offend, i.e. the so-called *animus injurandi,* are required). The judge found that the 'Working Groups' had not acted 'in bad faith' (*wider besseres Wissen*):

To be sure, they were above all concerned to make the public attentive to the problem at issue through as effective as possible a title. They wished to denounce the firm of Nestlé, as a Swiss firm, for its advertising practices for baby milk powder in developing countries, termed unethical and immoral. The defendants [i.e. the 'Working Groups'] saw these advertising practices as the basic cause of mothers being turned away from breast feeding and towards artificial nourishment of their babies, with the consequence, from hygienic and financial reasons, that babies fed in this way are more likely to fall ill and die than breast-fed babies. The causal chain constructed by the accused, with at the beginning the advertising methods of the firm of Nestlé for artificial infant nutrition and at the end danger to health, or death, of infants fed on dried milk, shows that subjectively the accusation of killing was meant specifically morally. The accused believed that they could draw this conclusion from the information and documents available to them, in particular the English original brochure, and believed they ought to concentrate on the firm of Nestlé because they, as members of a Swiss organization for development policy (see the object of the Association) felt themselves morally obliged to exert themselves on behalf of the infants concerned in underprivileged strata in developing countries, and to draw the attention of the public, and particularly the Swiss public, to the business practices of this Swiss firm.

The judge therefore noted that in any case the offence of defamation ought to be ruled out, since the accused could not 'be reproached with having made the accusation of killing in bad faith (*gegen besseres Wissen*) and at any rate they were not aware of the untruthfulness of their allegation'.

In this way, the Swiss judge resolved the first problem (i.e. assuming that the defendants were guilty, were they guilty of defamation or 'false accusation'?) in favour of the accused. At this point another problem arose. Nestlé had sought the application of the provisions of Article 173 of the Swiss Penal Code, so as to deny the accused the possibility of bringing evidence in exculpation. This Article of the Swiss Penal Code lays down, in paragraph 2, that persons accused of having injured someone else's reputation are not punished if they can prove either that their statements are in conformity with the truth, or that 'they had serious reason to regard them, in good faith, as true'. Paragraph 3 adds that the accused *is not allowed to furnish such proof* and is hence punishable, 'if the statements have been uttered or disseminated without taking account of the public interest or otherwise without justified cause, primarily with the aim of accusing someone of evil, especially when such affirmations relate to private life or family life'. Nestlé asked the judges to apply this last paragraph and therefore bar the 'Working Groups' from producing evidence in exoneration.

On this point too the judge found against Nestlé: the defendants had taken account of the public interest, there being a public 'right to information about the business methods of a firm of the size and importance' of the company that had brought the charge. The immediate consequence of this decision by the judge was important: the accused had the right at the trial to demonstrate the truth of their assertions, or at least their reasonable belief in their truth, that is, that they had 'done everything that could be expected of them to convince themselves of the truth of their allegations'.

We thus come to the crux of the matter, the pivotal issue around which the verdict turned: had the defendants told the truth in their pamphlet or had they not? With almost pedantic logic, acting on Article 173, paragraph 2 of the Swiss

Penal Code quoted above, the judge then dwelt first on whether the 'Working Groups' had during the trial demonstrated the truth of their assertions. Having concluded in the negative, he then went into the question whether the 'Working Groups' had nevertheless acted with due diligence and in good faith 'by taking all reasonable steps to convince themselves of the truth of their utterances'.

On the first point, the judge's reasoning was as follows:

The evidence taken has shown that incompetent use of milk powder can lead to the death or severe illness of infants. In the poor suburbs and also in the country, in developing countries the hygienic conditions for preparing bottled milk in accordance with the dried milk manufacturer's instructions are often lacking. The use of dirty, unboiled bottles and teats, and of dirty, unboiled water may lead to infections and to the death of infants. It is also known that milk powder is sometimes 'stretched' for economic reasons. The administration of over-diluted powdered milk may cause marasmus, a wasting disease resulting from lack of protein and calories, and this, along with other diseases to which the weakened infant is more susceptible, may have the consequence of death [...] The quality of Nestlé milk powder is undisputed. An insufficient amount of the product, dirty water and lack of hygiene in the preparation of the bottle are the causes of the death or severe debilitation of infants. It is not therefore the product itself that leads to the death of infants in developing countries.

Up to this point the judge seemed to be reasoning in a way favourable to the 'Working Groups': they had clearly never meant to say that Nestlé powdered milk in itself and by itself kills; they had only, asserted that artificial milk produced that result *in the particular social conditions of backward countries.*

Let us, now, look at how the Swiss magistrate's reasoning proceeded. He asked whether in its illustrative pamphlets on the use of powdered milk Nestlé adequately indicated the dangers of its use in poor countries. He stated:

No answer could be secured from the Private Prosecutor's representative [i.e. legal counsel for Nestlé] to the question whether the Nestlé company used the same advertising methods in developing countries as in Europe. The judge is of the opinion, following the taking of evidence, that they go considerably further there than in Europe. The advertising takes place, as far as has become known in this case, through posters in hospitals, and through coloured brochures which are distributed and lay the emphasis, as regards nutrition, on the bottle. The reference to breast feeding in these brochures may be sufficient for the state of knowledge in the West, but for mothers in developing countries it is by no means sufficient.

It is taken as proven that the Nestlé company employs nurses on advertising contracts, who advertise its products through their work. The witness Dr Ebrahim has impressively demonstrated this by referring to the so-called gift package, an advertising method that he terms most appalling, in which, along with a box of 'NAN' milk powder, a baby bottle with teat and an illustrated brochure are given free. The inducement towards artificial feeding instead of breast feeding could according to Dr Ebrahim have the consequence that, after only three days, the breast may fail as a source of milk owing to lack of sucking and disruption of hormonal stimulation, leaving the mother dependent on bottled milk.

The judge then goes on to consider publicity for artificial milk by radio, press and posters, and notes that in poor countries, this is aimed at mothers with little education, who are 'not in a position to differentiate and are susceptible to propaganda slogans'. On this point, the judge concludes as follows:

To sum up, it may be taken as proven that powdered milk, the quality of which is not disputed, is necessary as a substitute or supplementary food for infants that cannot, or cannot sufficiently, be breastfed. Certainly, these products should be administered only where instruction, supervision and hygienic requirements are available. These preconditions for the use of powdered milk in developing countries are repeatedly mentioned in the documentation submitted [. . .]. It is accordingly incumbent on the Nestlé company completely to rethink their advertising practices for bottle feeding in developing countries, since their advertising practice adopted so for can transform a life-saving product into a dangerous, life-destroying one. If the Private Prosecutor wishes in the future to avoid the accusation of immoral, unethical conduct, it must alter its advertising practices.

After this thrust against Nestlé, one might think that the judge had completely embraced the thesis of the accused party. Not so. He hastened to add that nevertheless the accused had not succeeded in proving the fact that supply of powdered milk constituted homicide. For, so the judge reasoned,

This does not, however, constitute evidence of negligent or deliberate killing. The adequate causal connection [*Kausalzusammenhang*] between the purchase or other supply of milk powder and the death of infants fed on these products is interrupted by the action of third parties [*durch das Tun von Drittpersonen*] for which the plaintiff [Nestlé] cannot be held criminally responsible. In this sense, then, there is no, negligent, far less deliberate, killing.

At this point the reader will be jumping up or rubbing his eyes, at the sudden apparition of figures (third persons), equipped with the magic power to break the 'causal chain' that would lead to finding against Nestlé. Who are these 'third persons'? The verdict itself does not say, but fortunately the judge clarified this in his oral explanation of his judgment given the same day it was handed down: they are 'the mothers using the bottle'. Nestlé could not be regarded as responsible for the actions of mothers; as the magistrate put it 'it is not the product but the circumstances that kill [*Nicht das Produkt sondern die Umstände töten*]'.[5]

At this point we cannot complain of mere legal formalism. What we have here is downright aberration. The judge began by accepting that Nestlé's publicity is misleading, since it induces mothers in poor countries to use a commodity which, though useful in industrialized countries, may become lethal in backward areas. He even rebuked the Swiss company, urging it to 'rethink' its methods of commercial penetration in the Third World. At this point it would seem logical to draw the consequence that Nestlé's conduct in poor countries, even if

---

[5] Schweizerische Arbeitsgruppen für Entwicklungspolitik (SAFEP), *Rundbrief, Sondernummer zum Nestlé-Prozess* (Bern, August, 1976), p. 11.

not undertaken with ill-intentions, in fact leads to the most pernicious effects. Conclusion: Nestlé is in breach of the obligations of diligence imposed both by legal standards and by the *de facto* circumstances; in short it—unintentionally— kills the infants to whom its powdered milk is administered. Nestlé's culpability (or more precisely, its managers' culpability) results from the cumulative effect of a whole set of actions, that is, it is the outcome of a complex of commercial operations and practices. And yet the judge, instead of arriving at this conclusion, introduced a *deus ex machina* to break the 'causal chain': the mothers themselves. But these mothers are in fact the *object* of Nestlé's conduct; they, along with their children, are the victims of that conduct. Assigning them the role of 'third persons' who in some way intervene between the 'agent' causing the damage and the direct victim of the damage (the children), means ignoring a fundamental fact (one even previously admitted by the judge himself): these mothers are not in a position to decide freely whether to use Nestlé's powdered milk and, if so, how, because they are misled both by their ignorance and the backward conditions in which they live, and by Nestlé's deceptive publicity (deceptive in that it is totally inappropriate to the conditions of those poor countries). The 'intervention' of the 'mothers' thus comes to appear as a mere expedient to wipe out the blame and guilt of the Swiss company. At this point, all the judge's previous considerations against Nestlé, the rebukes of lack of seriousness and so forth, appear as a sort of alibi to justify the final conclusion, which is, surprisingly, in favour of the multinational.

Having found that the allegations of the defendants against Nestlé were untrue, the judge moved on to the question whether nevertheless the defendants were to be acquitted on account of their having acted in good faith. He pointed out that a defendant would have to show that:

he believed in the truth of his utterances after having conscientiously taken all reasonable steps to convince himself of its correctness

And added that:

the issue is whether the perpetrator made the utterance contrary to care (*sorgfaltswidrig*) or not [. . .] The proof of good faith is based on the idea that anyone making utterances to the detriment of a third party is duty-bound to check those utterances.

After a detailed examination of the way in which this proof of good faith can be administered, the judge concluded that in the case at issue the defendants had not met the relevant requirements, on the following grounds:

The duty of care must be all the greater the more burdensome is the accusation and the more widely it has been disseminated. The accusation of killing is without doubt a serious one and the range of addressees was very wide, since the pamphlet met with a wide response, in particular in the press. And the defendants were just not any Tom, Dick or Harry thoughtlessly bringing the calumnious utterances into the world. On the contrary, they are people with a generally high level of education, with a high ethical estimate of their activity in development policy research and information, who accordingly wish to be taken seriously. By the fact that as wide a public as possible was addressed by using as spectacular and sensational as possible a wording, the duty of diligence [*Sorgfaltspflicht*]—on which in this case very high requirements must be placed on account of the serious accusation of killing—was neglected. If a sufficient extent of diligence or care had been applied, this wording would have been avoided [. . .] The defendants applied too small an amount of diligence when they decided on the wording 'Nestlé kills babies'. On the basis of the documentation available to them when making up the title, they ought not simply to have plumped for this wording.

If, then, the, accused were in the wrong, the proper penalty had to be meted out to them. The penalty turned out to be a moralistic homily in which the judge displayed understanding for the youthful ardour of the thirteen accused and at the same time pointed them in the direction of the proper path of moderation. Do criticize, yes—he says—since it is right that that should happen in a democratic society; but do not get hot-headed, do not let yourselves be led astray by immoderation or by polemical fits. Let us read his own words:

The people in the 'Bern Third World Working Group' find themselves in isolation in their endeavours, and have difficulty reaching the public; they stay within a small circle. Here lies the cause for their great leap forward. Through the exaggerated, unjustified heading [of the pamphlet] they secured publicity they would otherwise not have achieved. At any rate for the majority of them, their concern is honourably meant. They recognize the problem and seek in their own way to solve it. The way they chose is unfortunate, but that alters nothing as to the motives.

The accused are all of good reputation. Major previous offences are not recorded. Even though in the case of some of the accused a desire for social change and revolution may have played a part in the wording of the heading, it is not appropriate to dismiss the accused *en bloc* as left-wing revolutionaries. What comes from the left need not necessarily be evil in itself [*was von links aussen kommt, muss nicht as sich schlecht sein*). Development work is necessary and information more necessary than ever. Factual criticism must exist and may indeed be aggressive, but it must remain within limits. That limit has been overstepped by the accused in their choice of title for their pamphlet.

In this way the judge demonstrated his 'openness'. He deigned to admit that being to the left of the political spectrum does not necessarily mean being a messenger of evil. And he showed 'indulgent' understanding for those who wish to change society: but these changes must come about in conditions of respect for established rules and forms. No dressing up as ragamuffins and going to the barricades. Things have to be changed wearing collar and tie and speaking politely.

Reading the final words of the judgment and thinking over the substance of the verdict one hardly knows whether to be angry or discouraged. This judgment constitutes an astonishing mixture of basic deference to the 'high and mighty', of pedantic formalism in applying legal standards, and of pharisaical respect for the rules of democracy. And yet, in the end, one cannot escape the fact that the machinery of the law has been used to make strength prevail over justice.

4. A Defeat for the 'Working Groups'?

Despite all the criticisms, albeit circumspect, directed at Nestlé, Judge Soliberger's verdict clearly went against the accused. The latter came away from the trial beaten. To be sure, they immediately lodged an appeal (in accordance with the rules of penal procedure in force in Bern, appeals must be made within ten days). Later, however, they withdrew it, for three reasons: going on with the trial would have meant rather considerable financial expense; there was little hope that the Court of Appeal would alter the interpretation of the concept of 'homicide' upheld by the trial judge when dealing with the alleged negligent killing of infants by Nestlé; and in any case, a battle in the glare of public opinion would be more fruitful than prolonged legal proceedings, the outcome of which would be uncertain.

How did Nestlé react? Shortly after the verdict, on 2 July 1976, the Managing Director, A. Führer, sent all staff a letter applauding the result of the legal action undertaken against the 'Working Groups', and confirming the effectiveness of Nestlé's commercial penetration in the Third World, in conformity with advertising methods used by other companies too. He then undertook—though in rather generalized terms—to ensure that in the future these methods are better suited to the needs and conditions of poor countries.[6] In essence, Nestlé remained fixed in its positions.

Was the whole affair, then, an utter defeat for the 'Working Groups'? Not if we look a bit further than the trial. The furore aroused, by the legal case and the campaign waged by the 'Groups' in the sphere of public opinion slowly began producing some of the results they sought, at three levels; in some of the poor countries directly concerned; within some industrialized countries; and within intergovernmental bodies concerned with such matters, particularly the World Health Organization (WHO).

As for Third World countries directly concerned, the Government of Guinea Bissau, on 15 April 1976, adopted restrictive measures on the feeding of children with artificial milk and similar measures were adopted in Malaysia in September 1976 and in Algeria in 1977.[7]

No less important was the impact of the 'Groups' campaign in industrialized countries. As early as 1974 various firms, including Nestlé, decided to adopt an 'ethical code' to regulate their business activities in the Third World: this comprised a set of non-binding and also rather bland rules (for instance, there were no restrictions on advertising); but it was at least one step in the right direction.

---

[6] The letter of Dr Führer is reproduced as Annex B to *Nestlé-Prozess beendet-Auseinandersetzung geht weiter.*

[7] For the information given in the text see *Nestlé-Prozess beendet-Auseinandersetzung geht weiter*, pp 4–5; *Solidarisme* (January, 1979), pp. 31–3; J.C. Buffle, *N. . . .comme Nestlé*, pp. 87 ff.

The 'Code' was updated several times and gradually made more far-reaching in subsequent years.

Still more important was the action that was taken at government level. In the Netherlands the Ministry for Development Aid decided to review its whole policy regarding food aid. In the United States, in 1978, Senator Edward Kennedy initiated a series of hearings before a Senate Committee in the course of which strong criticisms were directed at multinationals operating in the food sector in poor countries. Again in the United States, a Catholic group, the 'Sisters of the Precious Blood', owners of 500 shares in an American company, the Bristol-Myers Company, presented a proposal to the shareholders' meeting which would have required the company's managers to submit a written report on advertising and commercial practices of the company in the infant feeding sector in the Third World. Unfortunately, this proposal was defeated by the majority of shareholders, winning only 3.5 per cent of votes. Subsequent legal proceedings brought by the Catholic group before the New York State District Court were dismissed, in a judgment of 11 May 1977. More effective was the boycott of Nestlé begun in the United States, again in 1977, by a pressure group, the 'Infant Formula Action Coalition', involving hundreds of consumer associations, trade unions, women's groups and religious movements, and gradually spreading to other countries as well.

Also significant, for better or worse, were the responses of intergovernmental organizations. In 1974, the World Health Organization Assembly approved a resolution inviting member states to review their policies regarding commercial promotion of infant feeding products. Subsequent resolutions culminated in the most significant document, adopted in 1981: the 'Code on international marketing of substitutes for mother's milk'. This 'Code' contains important rules on advertising of products and on the practice of giving mothers free samples (though it is ambiguous as regards information and education). It has, however, one serious, basic flaw: it is not binding, but purely exhortatory. States were not inclined to bind themselves in a field where enormous economic interests were involved. Moreover, despite its relative weakness, the 'Code' met with opposition from some states: the United States voted against it, and Argentina, Japan and the Republic of Korea abstained. The United States delegate, Elliot Abrams, noted that the 'Code' raised many problems for the Americans; in particular, it conflicted with certain freedoms established in the United States (freedom of speech and association), by forbidding certain commercial practices such as advertising, and also with American antitrust laws (by forbidding association among consumers and producers).[8] These criticisms clearly reflect the objections raised by the large multinationals, namely, that the WHO 'Code' is unrealistic

---

[8] See E. Helsing and J. Cartwright Taylor, 'WHO and the Right to Food: Infant Nutrition Policy as a Test Case', in A. Eide, W.B. Eide, S. Goonatileke et al. (eds), *Food as a Human Right* (the UN Library, Tokyo, 1984), pp. 223–32.

and contrary to infants' health needs, and is, moreover, an attack on the market economy and on freedom of speech. Some representatives of those multinationals went so far as to assert that groups in favour of the 'Code' (often led or supported by religious associations) were 'Marxists marching under the banner of Christ'.

5. What Are the Lessons To Be Learnt?

In the long, impassioned campaign by private groups against Nestlé and other companies in the infant nutrition sector, darkness unfortunately ends up prevailing over light. Even though in 1983 Nestlé officially agreed to regulate advertising for its infant feeding products, we are still a long way from the demands of the 'Working Groups'. And there remains in any case one striking figure: in 1986 sales of substitutes for mother's milk in the Third World exceeded 2000 million dollars, as against 600 million dollars in 1978. The multinationals are omnipotent, we know, and they often have judges, governments, newspapers and television channels on their side. Furthermore, as recently demonstrated by a Tunisian research chemist,[9] they 'pollute' the Third World not only with milk powder, but also with pesticides and more generally with all sorts of chemicals. These produce lethal effects both on human beings (every year between 10,000 and 20,000 people die in the Third World as a result of exposure to pesticides) and on the ecosystem at large. All too often the fight against multinationals is therefore an unequal one: in front of them, we cannot but look like Chaplin's little man, so terribly unprotected and powerless. Ought we therefore to despair? I think not. Just like that little man, we can use the weapon of our intelligence. The persevering action against Nestlé of so many private groups and organizations has achieved something. And as for the broader problem of pollution caused by the North in the South, we ought to behave like the Tunisian chemist: we should do research and disseminate the results of our investigations as much as possible, we should publicly discuss those results and we should also propound constructive proposals.

[9] M.L. Bouguerra, *Les poisons du Tiers Monde* (Editions La Découverte, Paris 1985).

PART III

FIGHTING STATE AND INDIVIDUAL CRIMINALITY

A. State 'Criminality' v. Individual's Criminal Liability

19. Remarks on the Present Legal Regulation of Crimes of States*

1. General

The purpose of this paper is briefly to comment on the extent to which *current international practice* upholds the concept of international crimes of States.

It is apparent from Art. 19 of the (International Law Commission) ILC Draft Convention on State Responsibility (adopted in first reading by the ILC in 1996) as well as the ILC Commentary, that the concept of crimes of States hinges on three basic elements: first, the existence of a special class of rules that are designed to protect fundamental values and consequently lay down obligations *erga omnes;* second, the granting of the right to claim respect for those rules not only to the State that may suffer a damage from a breach but also to other international subjects; third, the existence of a 'special régime of responsibility' for violations of those obligations; in other words, the fact that the legal response to breaches is not merely a request for reparation, but may embrace a wide range of 'sanctions' or 'remedies'. Although Art. 19 of the ILC draft does not specify the kind of sanctions, it seems logical that they should be commensurate to the gravity of the breach; hence, they should be at least as serious and far-reaching as the violation to which they are a response. However, the ILC has taken great pains to underscore that the régime of responsibility for crimes of States *may vary* from one breach to another. In other words to different classes of crimes there may correspond different classes of enforcement measures.

A survey of State practice shows that as regards the first two elements underlying the concept of crimes of States there has undisputedly been a departure from the traditional approach to State responsibility; under the 'old' law the consequences of international delinquencies were only a 'private business' between the tortfeasor and the claimant and no distinction was made as regards the importance of the primary rule breached. Today, however, many customary and treaty rules lay down

* Originally published in *International Law At the Time of Its Codification, Essays in Honour of Roberto Ago*, vol. III (Milano: Giuffrè, 1987) 49.

obligations that States regard as being of fundamental importance; in addition those rules confer on broad categories of international subjects the right to demand their observance. Thus, the breach of one of them has become a 'public affair' involving not only the two parties directly concerned but also the world community at large. As far as the third element of the concept, that is to say the kind of legal reaction to 'international crimes', is concerned, international practice *prima facie* appears to be less clear and homogeneous and, what is more important, less advanced.

A survey of State practice in the light of the four categories set forth in Art. 19 para. 3 leads to the following conclusion. While gross violations of the rules protecting the 'human environment' have not been regarded, so far, as 'crimes of States' proper, breaches of the other primary rules referred to in Art. 19 (that is to say, the ban on the use of force, the principle on self-determination and the standards on human rights) have been considered by States as delinquencies warranting a legal response different from that typical of international delicts. However, a different reaction for each of the three categories of wrongdoings has been adopted or considered permissible. The strongest reaction has been allowed for breaches of the ban on force. A similar but less far-reaching response has been allowed for violations of the right to self-determination; a very different response has been given to gross infringements of standards on human rights.

It is proposed here briefly to examine the practice of States concerning two of the classes mentioned in Art. 19 para. 3 of the ILC draft, i.e. infringements of obligations concerning self-determination and violations of human rights (whether in time of peace or war). By contrast, I shall not go into the two other classes, namely breaches of rules concerning environment (I have just pointed out that these breaches are not regarded as crimes of States) and non-fulfilment of obligations concerning peace and security (States practice on the matter is well known and need not be elaborated).

Before undertaking the proposed survey, a preliminary point should be made. The various measures adopted by the UN with regard to *apartheid* warrant the conclusion that the latter has been treated as a crime of State. However, international sanctions against South Africa have been urged by the UN not so much on account of massive violations of human rights, but insofar as *apartheid* constitutes a *threat to the peace* (Security Council Resolution 418 of 1977 stated that 'the policies and acts of the South African Government are fraught with danger to international peace and security' and then invoked Chapter VII of the Charter) or amounts to a grave manifestation of *forcible denial of self-determination*. Hence, ultimately *apartheid* has been regarded as an instance of gross disregard for the ban on the use or threat of force, or for the rules on self-determination, or both.

2. Response to Gross Violations of the Right to Self-Determination

It is widely held that forcible denial of the right to self-determination accruing to peoples subjected to colonial domination, racist régimes or foreign occupation, entitles such peoples to use force and to seek the aid of third States. I shall not go into the question whether these peoples have an international right proper (the so-called *jus ad bellum*) or rather may *de facto* resort to force without their action amounting to an international wrong.[1] What is indisputable is that third States are authorized to lend assistance to liberation movements, in derogation from the customary rule forbidding any help to rebels fighting against the central authorities. It is thus apparent that gross infringements of the rule conferring the right to self-determination legitimize—in one form or another—the use of force by the oppressed people and of measures by third States that would otherwise be prohibited. The authorization to respond in this exceptional manner to egregious

---

[1] The legality of the use of force by the three categories of peoples referred to above has been consistently advocated by socialist and developing countries in the UN The initial opposition of Western countries has gradually dwindled, but it seems difficult to assert that the West has totally relinquished its initial objections. The adoption by consensus of the 1970 Declaration on Friendly Relations and, in 1974, the Definition of Aggression, was taken by some scholars to indicate that Western countries had relaxed their stringency. However, the objections made by various Western States in 1974 suggest that one should proceed very gingerly when assessing States' legal views. It is therefore worth dwelling on those objections, to see to what extent one may infer from them whether or not an international rule on the right of peoples to use force has evolved.

The discussion centered in 1974 on Art. 7 of the General Assembly's Definition of Aggression, which reads as follows: 'Nothing in this Definition, and in particular Art. 3, could in any way prejudice the right to self-determination, freedom and independence, as derived from the Charter, of peoples forcibly deprived of that right and referred to in the Declaration on Principles of International Law concerning Friendly Relations and Co-Operation among States in accordance with the Charter of the United Nations, particularly peoples under colonial and racist régimes or other forms of alien domination; nor the right of these peoples to struggle to that end and to seek and receive support, in accordance with the principles of the Charter and in conformity with the above-mentioned Declaration'.

According to the *Yearbook of the United Nations* (vol. 28), 1974, pp. 845–846, a number of representatives, including those of Algeria, China, Egypt, Ghana, Kenya, Senegal, the USSR and Yugoslavia, maintained that this article recognized that the armed struggle of the peoples listed in the provision was an instance of the legal use of force. With that principle established, they said, Art. 7 set out the corollary that any State had the right, or even the duty, to provide support of all kinds to ensure the exercise of that right. However, several representatives, in particular those of Canada (G.A.O.R., XXIXth Session, VIth Committee, 1473rd Mtg., para. 15), Belgium (1476th Mtg., para. 11), the UK (1477th Mtg., para. 24) and the US (1480th Mtg., para. 73) stated that Art. 7 could not be interpreted as justifying the use of armed force by oppressed peoples (cf. also the statements by the delegates of the Netherlands (1473rd Mtg., para. 5), of the FRG (1478th Mtg., para. 19), of Portugal (*ibidem,* para. 22), as well as Italy (1472nd Mtg., para. 27), Israel (1480th Mtg., para. 60). The reference to struggles of those peoples could only be interpreted as meaning struggle by peaceful means, and not as a condonation of the use of force contrary to the Charter. Art, 7, they contended, when read in conjunction with Art. 6 (whereby 'Nothing in this Definition shall be construed as in any way enlarging or diminishing the scope of the Charter, including its provisions concerning cases in which the use of force is lawful'), did not and could not legitimize acts of force which would otherwise be illegal.

To my mind, the aforementioned views of Western countries show that no *general* rule on the *right* of liberation movements to use force has evolved. This however does not mean that the attitude of the majority of member States of the UN should be discarded out of hand or neglected. Possibly, a way of taking account of both the majority and the minority opinion may consist in saying that, although liberation movements have not a right proper, their use of force does not however amount to a breach of the international ban on the use of force. In other words, liberation movements' use of force could be equated to that of insurgents in civil strife: both categories have neither a right to use force nor a duty to refrain from using it.

instances of disregard for the right to self-determination warrants the view that gross violations of self-determination amount to an international crime proper, although the class of enforcement measures allowed in this case does not coincide with, and is less sweeping than, the measures allowed in response to breaches of the ban on the use of force.

According to a distinguished Italian author, V. Starace,[2] infringements of the right to self-determination amount to international crimes because international rules assimilate them to violations of the ban on the use of force. Consequently, the forcible denial of self-determination would be but one category of the unlawful use of force.

This view, I submit, is unsound. In laying down the obligation for States to respect the right to self-determination and in granting to organized peoples (i.e. to liberation movements) what developing and socialist countries label 'the right to use force' the 1970 Declaration on Friendly Relations, the 1974 Definition of Aggression and other international documents do not make the latter 'right' conditional on the use of military force by the oppressing State. They merely provide that liberation movements may respond to any forcible action of the oppressive State designed to deprive them of their right to self-determination. 'Forcible action' ('toute mesure de coercition' in French) means the establishment of a repressive régime which does not allow the oppressed people to choose its lot by free means. That expression does not necessarily entail that the State should continuously use military violence against the oppressed people: the existence of institutionalized violence (such as that obtaining in South Africa) is sufficient to establish the right of the people to resort to force.

That the possibility for liberation movements to resort to force does not follow from the use of military force by the colonial, racist or foreign Power, is borne out by the fact that the relevant international instruments do not grant liberation movements a right *to individual self-defence.*

Finally, we should remember that in commenting upon Art. 19 para. 3, the ILC pointed out that in the provision labelling crimes of States as serious breaches of 'an international obligation of essential importance for safeguarding the right of self-determination of peoples, such as that prohibiting the establishment or maintenance by force of a colonial domination' the expression 'by force' 'should be understood as meaning *against the will of the subject population,* even if that will is not manifested, or has not yet been manifested, by armed opposition'.[3]

To conclude on breaches of the right to self-determination, let me point out that here the enforcement measures allowed by law are no doubt less farreaching than those authorized in the case of violations of the ban on force. First, only the oppressed people may use force without breaking the international prohibition

---

[2] V. STARACE, *La responsabilité résultant de la violation des obligations a l'égard de la communauté internationale, Hague Recueil,* vol. 153, 1976-V, p. 299.

[3] *Yearbook of the International Law Commission,* 1976, II, Part II, p. 121 (emphasis added).

on resort to force. Secondly, third States can only lend various forms of help; they may not use force themselves (the attempt made by certain States to transfer the concept of collective self-defence to this area has not been endorsed by the world community at large). The right 'to lend support' should not, however, be underrated; if it were not legitimized by a general rule, such 'support' would run counter to the ban on non-interference in internal affairs. Furthermore, being entitled to give assistance to liberation movements entails the right for a 'third State' not to comply with commercial, military and other treaties previously made with the State against which the liberation movement is struggling; in short, 'third States' have the right to resort to 'peaceful counter-measures' against the oppressing State. Thirdly, normally international organizations such as the UN only resort to a condemnation of the oppressing State or call upon third States to lend assistance to the liberation movement fighting for self-determination; or else they can, and often do, grant international legitimation to the liberation movement by giving it the status of observer or other forms of access to international political and diplomatic fora.

3. Reactions to Gross Breaches of Human Rights in Times of Peace

A number of States are currently trampling upon human rights in various areas of the world. The UN has reacted *to some instances* only of gross violations: Chile, Guatemala, El Salvador, Bolivia, Kampuchea, Morocco, Equatorial Guinea, Iran, Poland.

The UN General Assembly, when it has decided to pass a resolution on a specific country, has normally *deplored* the serious violations and *called upon* the country concerned to put an end to them. Only exceptionally has the UN taken a further step and started an *investigation* into the alleged violations. In one particular case, that of the massacre of Sabra and Chatila, the General Assembly (by res. 37/123 D, adopted on 16 December 1982) merely 'condemned' 'in the most vigorous terms' the slaughter in the two Palestinian camps, and 'decided' that it was an act of genocide. The General Assembly might have requested the States concerned (Israel and Lebanon) to endeavour to punish the phalangist militias who materially perpetrated the genocide, or it might have called upon all States to search for and bring to trial those militias. Instead, the Assembly confined itself to a verbal condemnation, the real import of which one is at a loss to grasp.[4]

---

[4] Various Western countries (Spain, Denmark on behalf of the to EEC countries, Israel, the US, Finland, Sweden, Turkey, Canada) plus Singapore and the Philippines expressed misgivings about the resolution: they argued that it was not proper for the General Assembly to characterize the massacre of Sabra and Chatila as 'genocide' and that in any event it should have proceeded with great caution when embarking upon an assessment of complex and controversial situations; it was also

By and large, international practice shows that in case of very serious and systematic breaches of human rights the response of the international community boils down to a *formal pronouncement* by a collective body (such as the UN General Assembly or the Commission on Human Rights) to the effect that a certain country is showing serious disregard for the basic international standards on human rights, and is followed by an *invitation* to the delinquent State to discontinue its wrongdoings.

Of course, this sort of 'enforcement' may, to some extent, be regarded as an advance on the traditional practice whereby matters concerning human rights fell exclusively under domestic jurisdiction. While not denying that much headway has been made here, one should not however pass over in silence that the current response to infringements of human rights proves utterly inadequate and, one might even say, without consequences.

4. Economic 'Sanctions' against Certain States Violating Human Rights

In legal literature a few recent instances of so-called economic sanctions taken against some countries have been greatly extolled. I shall refer here only to the 'sanctions' resorted to against Iran (for the maltreatment of US diplomats) and to those against Poland (for the suppression of certain basic human rights). Other instances, such as the sanctions against the USSR (for the invasion and occupation of Afghanistan) and those against Argentina (for her resort to force against the UK) do not relate to violations of human rights proper and will consequently be left out.

The importance of these 'sanctions' is far less than is commonly contended, for three reasons. First, they normally have not amounted to sanctions proper, namely violations of international rules vis-à-vis the delinquent State, warranted by the previous wrongdoing of the latter States. Legally speaking, the economic measures taken jointly by various State have been more akin to retorsions, for they did not involve a breach of international obligations by the sanctioning States vis-à-vis the wrongdoer, but were merely unfriendly measures taken to 'punish' the delinquent party (however, unlike retorsions proper, they responded to a previous breach, whereas in the case of retorsion no violation of legal rules is committed by either party).

Secondly, it is no coincidence that these so-called economic sanctions have so far been taken by Western countries against socialist States (Poland) or Third World nations (Iran). The inference might be drawn that one segment only of the world community considers them appropriate. In addition, not only the target

objected that the language used in that resolution was too loose and inaccurate from a legal point of view. See A/37/PV.108, pp. 33–101.

State, but also States of other political and ideological areas have protested against this sort of sanction. It follows that 'the international community as a whole' is far from considering this sort of response to gross disregard of human rights as warranted.

Thirdly, even assuming that these instances prove that members of the world community intended to punish the delinquent State by sanctions proper, one cannot fail to be struck by their paucity, as compared with the immense number of cases where similar gross violations have occurred. The isolated and sporadic character of those 'sanctions' and the other features I have just mentioned above, might lead one to believe that States were actually motivated by political considerations and that the taking of 'economic sanctions' cannot be regarded as indicative of a real trend in the international community.

5. Response to Gross Infringements of Obligations Laid Down in International Treaties for the Protection of War Victims

A bit more needs to be said about the consequences of the breach of these obligations, for two reasons: first, they are less well-known than normal UN practice; second, in this area States have had greater opportunity to state their views.

Let me start by quoting the basic provision common to the four Geneva Conventions of 1949, a provision taken up almost *verbatim* in the 1st (Additional) Protocol of 1977. It stipulates that 'The High Contracting Parties undertake to respect and ensure respect for the present Convention in all circumstances'. According to the view and the practice of the International Committee of the Red Cross (ICRC) and the opinion of a number of States, this provision clearly implies that any contracting State is entitled to request that the other contracting parties involved in an international armed conflict live up to the provisions of the Conventions and the Protocol. It is important to note that the right accrues to any contracting State from the mere fact of being a party to the Conventions or the Protocol: it is not necessary for it to prove that it has a specific and direct interest in the observance of the rules violated. In other words, the obligations laid down in the Conventions and the Protocol are *erga omnes contractantes* and consequently each of the latter is endowed with the corresponding right to demand their fulfilment, irrespective of any damage it may have suffered from the wrongful action.

One might of course object that consideration of the way in which this provision has been implemented by States does not prove of decisive importance for the purpose of enquiring into crimes of States, for the provision—so might the objection go—merely lays down that the obligations of the 1949 Conventions and the 1977 Protocol are not reciprocal but *erga omnes contractantes*. The objection would be unsound, however. This feature of the obligations at hand constitutes *the necessary precondition* for the possible characterization of *gross breaches* of the Conventions and the Protocol as international crimes of States. If a contracting

State has the general right to demand compliance with the Geneva rules, this means that it also has the right to adopt measures to impel a belligerent who has grossly disregarded those rules to live up to them. If one shares the broad concept of responsibility upheld by the ILC, as embracing all the legal relationships consequent upon a wrongful act, it follows that when States parties to these humanitarian treaties react to gross breaches, their actions might come within the purview of the concept of 'legal régime of responsibility' for international delinquencies.

In view of the loose wording of Art. 1, it is crucial to see what kind of action States consider authorized by the Article in the face of gross violations by a belligerent. Luckily, we have at our disposal an important document of the ICRC. In 1972, the International Committee sent out to States parties to the 1949 Conventions a 'Questionnaire concerning measures intended to reinforce the implementation' of the Conventions. Question no. 2 was as follows: 'Can and should the States Parties to the Geneva Conventions exercise supervision collectively, pursuant to Art. 1 common to those Conventions? If so, what procedure might be envisaged?' Clearly, although the question was put in terms of 'supervision', it also embraced steps to be taken in case of violation, for the broad concept of 'supervision' covers both 'preventive action' and 'reaction to breaches'. In surveying the replies given by States, I shall differentiate between those concerning the question whether individual or collective action was authorized, and the question what concrete action States could take.

A. Individual v. Collective Action

If one looks at the answers to the ICRC Questionnaire[5] it appears that the majority of States took the view that both classes of action are possible. This view is indeed the more consonant with the literal text of the provisions. That both categories of action are permitted was unambiguously stated by such States as Belgium, the FRG, Canada, Denmark, Italy, Monaco, the Netherlands, the UK, as well as Austria (albeit with certain qualifications). Other countries merely stated that collective démarches are permissible, without however giving an opinion upon the question of whether action by individual States is also authorized by the rules at issue. A limited number of States (Brazil, the US, Israel, Switzerland) insisted that only individual action is envisaged by Art. 1 common to the Geneva Conventions; it seems, however, that this view is more dictated by expediency (i.e. it is less advisable to resort to collective steps than to make individual démarches), than reasons of legal feasibility. Finally, a group of States excluded the admissibility of collective action, again primarily on grounds of practical feasibility and on the basis of a realistic assessment of the present international situation, rather than on legal grounds.

---

[5] ICRC, *Questionnaire*, Geneva 1973, *passim*.

Thus, although the views were divided, the majority of States seemed favourable to both classes of action. This interpretation is more in keeping with the tenor of the provisions: they do not place any restriction on the sort of activity that contracting parties can carry out in order to demand respect for the Conventions and the Protocol by other contracting parties.

B. To What Concrete Actions Can States Resort?

Is seems that a wide spectrum of actions is available to States wishing to act individually or jointly for the purpose of ensuring respect for the Geneva Conventions or the Protocol. The only limitation is that they cannot resort to forcible measures; otherwise they can take political or other steps, either bilaterally, jointly or in international fora. To give an illustration of the various measures possible, it may be useful to mention the opinion of a few States that answered the aforementioned ICRC Questionnaire. Thus, for instance, Belgium pointed out that contracting States could make individual or joint representations with a view to inducing a belligerent to live up to its obligations; resort to the UN could also be had: through the appropriate UN body States could jointly urge a belligerent to comply with its duties.[6] Denmark, in its turn, stressed 'the right of the contracting parties to protest, individually or collectively'.[7] Italy drew attention to the importance of diplomatic *démarches,* either public or confidential.[8] By contrast, the UK took a somewhat restrictive attitude, for it pointed out that in its view contracting States would be unable 'to go beyond exhortation and statement of

---

[6] Belgium stated the following: '*Ce principe posé, il en découle que chaque Etat individuellement et, par voie de conséquence, la collectivité des Etats, parties aux conventions, ont pour obligation de veiller, autant qu'il est en leur pouvoir, à ce que les dispositions des conventions soient appliquées indistinctement par toutes les Parties au conflit. La procédure qui vient ici tout naturellement à l'esprit est celle du* recours éventuel à des représentations par la voie diplomatique *auprès des deux Parties engagées au conflit ou auprès de l'une d'elles s'il y a lieu de supposer qu'elle ne respecte pas certaines dispositions de la convention. Ces représentations peuvent être le fruit d'une initiative propre à un seul Etat. Elles peuvent être également accomplies—et sans doute avec plus de chances de succès—par plusieurs Etats conjointement. Enfin, l'Organisation des Nations-Unies, saisie de la question à la requête d'un ou de plusieurs Etats participant aux conventions de Genève, est certainement habilitée à rappeler, comme elle l'a déjà fait, aux Parties belligérantes l'obligation qui leur incombe de respecter les dispositions desdites conventions. En tout état de cause, il y a lieu de constater que les dispositions de l'article I ne sont guère explicites quant aux moyens que les Etats, tierces puissances par rapport à un conflit armé, ont à mettre en oeuvre en vue de faire respecter les conventions par les Parties belligérantes*' (ICRC, *Questionnaire,* cit., p. 21, emphasis added).

[7] Denmark pointed out that: 'The only supervisory mechanism that with any certainty can be inferred from this basic obligation is *the right of the contracting parties to protest,* individually or collectively, against non-compliance by another contracting party. Each contracting party is free to decide whether and in what form it wants to protest against violations' (*ibid.,* p. 24, emphasis added).

[8] Italy said that: '*La procédure à envisager pourrait être constituée par une* action diplomatique secrète ou publique *auprès des Etats en conflit et même, le cas échéant, auprès des Puissances protectrices*' (*ibid.,* p. 26, emphasis added).

general principles'.[9] By and large it is apparent from the replies of the various States that none of them contended that the reaction to gross violations of the Geneva rules could go beyond entering a protest, taking diplomatic steps or making public representations to the delinquent State.

Let us now take a quick look at State practice. It confirms the view that *States have been tremendously cautious in reacting to serious breaches of the Geneva rules.* In spite of various appeals by the ICRC, contracting parties to the Geneva Conventions and the Protocol have avoided taking individual steps and have greatly preferred to impel international bodies to make appeals to the belligerents concerned. To mention just a few examples, appeals were made at the regional level by the 'Contadora Group' in the case of the civil strife in El Salvador, while both the UN General Assembly and the Commission on Human Rights have adopted several resolutions calling upon the belligerents or the occupying Power to respect humanitarian law (e.g. in the case of Israel, Lebanon, Kampouchea, Iran-Iraq, South Africa, El Salvador). In the case of the Iran-Iraq war, the Foreign Ministers of the EC countries made two appeals, one in February, the other in March 1984,[10] calling upon the two belligerents to comply with the relevant rules of humanitarian law. After conducting an investigation on the spot, the UN Secretary-General appealed to the belligerents to refrain from using prohibited weapons.

What is striking is that, in spite of the reported gross violations of humanitarian rules and principles, the States gathered in the international bodies just mentioned confined themselves to *verbal condemnations* and *appeals.*

C. Other Implementation Mechanisms Provided for in Protocol I of 1977

It may prove apposite to see whether implementation mechanisms other than those adumbrated in Art. 1 could be used to react against large-scale violations of humanitarian rules.

A provision of Protocol I of 1977 should be mentioned here: Art. 89. It grants tasks of supervision to the United Nations. It provides that 'In situations of serious violations of the [1949 four] Conventions or of this Protocol, the High Contracting Parties undertake to act, jointly or individually, in co-operation with the United Nations and in conformity with the United Nations Charter'.

---

[9] The UK stated the following: 'If States Parties determine upon collective action during or after hostilities, they would presumably be unable to go beyond *exhortation* and *statement of general principles.* It would be inappropriate for them to conduct anything in the nature of an enquiry into the actions of particular States. Any collective effort to enforce respect for the Conventions would be outside the scope of the Conventions and would be a proper matter for discussion by the Security Council' (*ibid,* p. 31, emphasis added).

[10] See the *European Communities Bulletin,* 1984, no. 2, p. 95, and no. 3.

Art. 89 did not command general support. It was adopted by 50 votes to 3, with 40 abstentions.[11] Many Western and developing countries expressed misgivings about the ambiguity and the inadequacy of the provision: Spain, Canada, France and Italy put their doubts and dissatisfaction on record, as did Cameroon, Vietnam, Ecuador, India, Indonesia and Peru.[12] By way of example let me quote the statement made by India after the vote: The Indian delegation abstained in the voting on Article 70 [present Art. 89] as the sponsor of the proposal himself admitted that it was vague and imprecise and could be interpreted in different ways by different delegations.[13]

Some light on the scope and meaning of the provision was shed by the Syrian delegate (the main proponent of the rule) in two different statements. First, he pointed out that 'there was absolutely no question of resorting to the threat or use of force, as stated in Art. 2 para. 4 of the United Nations Charter'.[14] Second, he stressed that 'as for the nature of the action proposed, there was no need to spell it out. It was, in fact, the action prescribed by the United Nations Charter and could not be undertaken without the consent of the General Assembly or the Security Council'.[15]

It would therefore seem that, in case of serious violations of the Conventions or the Protocol, contracting parties could take advantage of Art. 89 by asking the General Assembly or the Security Council to pass a resolution calling upon the delinquent State to discontinue the wrongful act. Arguably, a UN resolution might even authorize members of the United Nations to take individual or joint (peaceful) countermeasures against the delinquent State. This, however, seems unlikely in point of fact, if only for reasons of policy (eventually the sanctioning States might get involved in the armed conflict).

Everything considered, even the special mechanism provided for in the Protocol of 1977 is unlikely to lead to reactions against gross breaches of humanitarian rules that differ conspicuously from the other sort of response considered above.

D. Reaction by Individual States

If one contrasts the daily perpetration of gross violations of human rights during armed conflicts with the legal reaction of other States, the impression is exceedingly dispiriting. Only in very unique and exceptional circumstances do third States publicly react to them. They normally prefer to keep aloof or, at most, they approach the delinquent State via diplomatic channels when they wish to request that it discontinue the wrongdoing.

[11] *Official Records,* vol. VI, p. 348, para. 53.
[12] *Ibidem,* pp. 345–349 and 368–382.
[13] *Ibidem,* p. 374.
[14] *Ibidem,* p. 346, para. 37.
[15] *Ibidem,* p. 347, para. 46.

Let us now take a quick glance at those exceptional instances in which States have taken action. In the case of the Geneva Conventions and Protocol, in spite of the repeated appeals of the ICRC that other contracting States should demand compliance with the Geneva rules by the belligerents, so far either no action or only confidential action has been taken by third States. However, according to a learned author[16] in 1984 Switzerland and Austria made public appeals to Iraq and Iran to abide by the Conventions. On 27 March 1984, in a letter to the ICRC another Western country replied to the appeal made by the Committee pointing out that it 'would have pursued its action [for the respect of humanitarian principles] both in the various multilateral fora and in direct contacts with the parties to the conflict'.

6. Concluding Remarks

I emphasized, at the outset, that the legal régime of responsibility for the three classes of crimes of States to which I have referred (breaches of the ban on force, of general rules on self-determination and of general standards on human rights in times of peace or armed conflict) is strikingly diverse. The legal response to the unlawful use of force is fairly proportionate, and reactions to instances of forcible denial of the right to self-determination are sufficiently congruous with the gravity of such a breach. By contrast, the way in which States have responded to gross disregard for some basic rules on human dignity is surprisingly disproportionate to the seriousness of the violations. It is thus apparent that there is a *quantitative and qualitative difference* between the international response to other gross breaches of fundamental obligations *erga omnes* and violations of human rights. The conclusion is therefore warranted that such response does not come within the purview of the legal régime of responsibility for crimes of States. For the time being, only gross breaches of the prohibition of force and of the right to self-determination amount to crimes of States proper. In the case of massive disregard for human rights the violation of obligations *erga omnes* only gives rise to the right of international subjects other than the one directly injured (if any), to claim cessation of the international delinquency.

Plainly, in the field of human rights the world community has not made the same headway as in a few other areas: the 'Westphalian model', that is the traditional pattern of world community, has not been completely supplanted by the 'UN Charter model'. State sovereignty still tenaciously dominates the international community and solidarity relationships as well as the feeling that certain basic values concerning human dignity must be respected, emerge only amidst

---

[16] M. VEUTHEY, *Pour une politique humanitaire*, in *Studies and Essays on International Humanitarian Law and Red Cross Principles in Honour of J, Pictet*, Geneva-The Hague, 1984, p. 1002.

very great resistance. The passage from the old to the new law proves slow and laborious in this as much as in other crucial areas of international law.

The striking inadequacy of current international legislation is of course a matter of deep regret. Indeed, it seems utterly absurd that even in the case of such heinous breaches of human rights as *genocide* or *large-scale torture,* the world community has not gone so far as to regard them as crimes of States proper and to respond accordingly. It is my belief that in this area there is much room for a *progressive development* of international law and that an attempt should therefore be made to suggest appropriate means of improving the present legal régime.

20. On the Current Trends towards Criminal Prosecution and Punishment of Breaches of International Humanitarian Law*

1. Introduction: International Criminal Prosecution as a Means of Enforcing International Humanitarian Law

As is well known, various means are available for enforcing international humanitarian law. First, there is the traditional, but controversial, method of reprisals, whereby a belligerent employs illegal means of warfare in response to violations of the laws of war by its adversary. Reprisals are resorted to in order either to induce the adversary to terminate its unlawful conduct or to 'punish' the adversary for the purpose of deterring any further breach. This method of enforcement has been criticized on the ground that it more often than not leads to an escalation of conflict and, it is argued, it often proves to be ineffective.[1] Further, the 1949 Geneva Conventions and Additional Protocol I[2] severely limit the scope of this enforcement method. In addition, reprisals can under no circumstances take the form of violations of human rights, genocide or 'crimes against humanity'.[3]

Second, respect for international humanitarian law can be sought through specific mechanisms agreed upon by the parties to a conflict, such as the designation of a Protecting Power to secure the supervision and implementation by the belligerents of their international obligations.[4] Granted, the Protecting Power aims

---

* Originally published in 2 *European Journal of International Law* (1998).

[1] See. e.g., P. Kalshoven. *Belligerent Reprisals* (1971).

[2] See Geneva Convention for the Amelioration of the Conditions of the Wounded and Sick in Armed Forces in the Field of August 12, 1949 ('First Geneva Convention'). Article 46: Geneva Convention for the Amelioration of the Conditions of the Wounded, Sick and Shipwrecked Members of Armed Forces at Sea of August 12, 1949 ('Second Geneva Convention'). Article 47: Geneva Convention Relative to the Treatment of Prisoners of War of August 12, 1949 ('Third Geneva Convention'). Article 13(3); Geneva Convention Relative to the Protection of Civilian Persons in Time of War of August 12, 1949 ('Fourth Geneva Convention'). Article 33(3) and 46: Protocol Additional to the Geneva Conventions of August 12, 1949, and Relating to the Protection of Victims of International Armed Conflicts ('Protocol I'). Article 5 (the four Geneva Conventions will hereinafter collectively be referred to as '1949 Geneva Conventions'). These bans on reprisals against protected persons/objects can be said to have become part of customary international law.

[3] On the illegality of reprisals pursuant to a developing 'principle of humanity' and non-derogable human rights norms, see R. Provost. 'Reciprocity in Human Rights and Humanitarian Law', BYbIL (1994) 383, at 413.

[4] This mechanism is provided for in Article 8 of the First, Second and Third Geneva Conventions, and Article 9 of the Fourth Geneva Convention, and also in Article 5 of Protocol I.

to protect the interests of the parties, but it is a mechanism that may be activated in order to contribute to the enforcement of international humanitarian law. This method, however, has proved to be a relative failure, as it has only been resorted to in three cases since the entry into force of the 1949 Geneva Conventions.[5]

A further means of promoting compliance with international humanitarian law is the utilization of fact-finding mechanisms, such as the 'Fact Finding Commission' provided for in Additional Protocol I. One of the advantages of fact-finding is that it enables the creation of a public 'record' of violations of international humanitarian law, which can assist in war crimes trials, thereby contributing to enforcement.[6] The Commission of Experts set up by the Secretary-General of the UN at the request of the Security Council pursuant to Resolution 780 (1992) to investigate and report on evidence of grave breaches of the 1949 Geneva Conventions and other violations of international humanitarian law in the former Yugoslavia falls within this category. With the establishment of the Commission of Experts, the Security Council was seeking to deter the parties from violating their obligations under international humanitarian law.[7] It was subsequent to the findings of this Commission of Experts that the Security Council decided to establish the International Criminal Tribunal for the Former Yugoslavia (ICTY).

This brings us to the next level of enforcement of international humanitarian law, through criminal jurisdiction: that is, through the prosecution and punishment by national or international tribunals of individuals accused of being responsible for violations of international humanitarian law. This article will focus on the problems of, and prospects for, this method of enforcement. This method distinguishes itself from the others described above in that it is concerned with individual criminal responsibility as opposed to state responsibility. Its aim is to enforce the obligations of *individuals* under international humanitarian law, whereas the preceding methods concentrate on the enforcement of the obligations of *states*. However, as I shall demonstrate later in this paper, the principal problem with the enforcement of international humanitarian law through the prosecution and punishment of individuals is that the implementation of this method ultimately hinges on, and depends upon, the goodwill of states.

---

[5] Protecting Powers were resorted to in three cases: in 1956 in the Suez conflict (only, however, between Egypt on the one hand and France and the UK on the other): in the short conflict between India and Portugal over Goa in 1961: and in the Indo-Pakistani war in 1971, although India soon withheld its consent. In relation to war crimes prosecution, one author posits that '[I]f the task of the Protecting Powers, and of the substitute humanitarian organisation such as the ICRC, includes that of scrutiny, might it not also include that of gathering evidence of violations of the Conventions for use in subsequent prosecutions? Any such overt action by a Protecting Power might well lead one of the belligerents to declare it non grata and terminate its functions. The consequences for the Protecting Power are not far-reaching. But for the ICRC the assumption of a scrutiny role involving the collection of evidence poses great dangers.' See Shearer, 'Recent Developments in International Criminal Law Affecting Enforcement of International Humanitarian Law', in Australian Defence Studies Centre, *Selection of Papers Delivered to the Second Regional Conference on International Humanitarian Law,* 12–14 December 1994, at 72–73.

[6] *Ibid,* at 75 *et seq.*

[7] See SC Res. 780 (1992).

2. The Failure of Prosecution through National Jurisdiction

The obligation of states to prosecute and punish persons accused of serious viola-tions of international humanitarian law through their respective *national* juris-dictions arises out of their treaty obligations,[8] most notably those under the 1949 Geneva Conventions.[9]

As is commonly known, the jurisdiction provided by the 1949 Geneva Conventions is universal in that those suspected of being responsible for grave breaches come under the criminal jurisdiction of all states parties, regardless of their nationality or the *locus commissi delicti*. In addition, Article 88 of Protocol I requires that states parties provide mutual assistance with regard to criminal pro-ceedings brought in respect of grave breaches to the 1949 Geneva Conventions or to Protocol I, including cooperation in the matter of extradition.

However, these provisions on *national* jurisdiction over grave breaches have been, at least until recent years, a dead letter. In situations of armed conflict abroad, a state is generally reluctant to prosecute its own personnel, especially when it is on the 'winning side'. In such cases, a state may also be disinclined to prosecute enemy personnel because such legal actions carry the risk of exposing war crimes committed by the state's own personnel. As for crimes committed in an armed conflict in which a state has not participated, both political and diplo-matic considerations and the frequent difficulty of collecting evidence normally induce state authorities to refrain from prosecuting foreigners.

---

[8] While it is doubtful, in the absence of clear state practice and opinio juris, that states have a duty under customary international law to enforce international humanitarian law through crim-inal jurisdiction, states have jurisdiction to prosecute in the absence of a treaty pursuant to prin-ciples such as the universality principle and the passive personality principle. The principles on suppression of war crimes in the 1949 Geneva Conventions are said to be 'declaratory of the obliga-tions of belligerents under customary international law to take measures for the punishment of war crimes committed by all persons, including members of a belligerent's own armed forces': United States, *The Law of Land Warfare, Department of the Army Field Manual*, July 1956, at 181, para. 506 (b). The obligation to prosecute is also said to arise by corollary with the right to an effective remedy; the obligation on the state to provide effective remedies to persons within its jurisdiction is complemented by the obligation to prosecute persons responsible for such violations, whether occurring in conflict or otherwise.

[9] See also the Convention on the Prevention and Punishment of the Crime of Genocide (1948) (Genocide Convention) at Articles V and VI and the International Convention on the Suppression and Punishment of the Crime of Apartheid (1973) (Apartheid Convention) at Articles IV and V. Both conventions contain clear obligations on states parties to introduce and take the necessary measures to prosecute and punish perpetrators. With respect to 'grave breaches' of their provisions, the 1949 Geneva Conventions and Protocol I require states:

(i) to enact legislation necessary to provide effective penal sanctions for persons committing or ordering the commission of grave breaches, and
(ii) to search for the persons alleged to have committed or ordered the commission of grave breaches and to try such persons before their own courts, or alternatively to hand them over to another contracting state that has made out a *prima facie* case.

Both in the context of international conflicts and civil wars, political motivations may often lead states to prefer amnesty to prosecution.[10] As Bishop Desmond Tutu, Head of the Truth and Reconciliation Commission of South Africa, put it, referring to gross violations of human rights, political leaders choose 'reconciliation' over 'justice and ashes'.[11] Leaving aside the question of the political advisability of this choice, granting amnesty to persons responsible for grave breaches of international humanitarian law and mass violations of human rights raises serious moral and legal objections. Moral because, as Justice Robert Jackson commented in relation to the trial at Nuremberg, letting major war criminals live undisturbed to write their 'memoirs' in peace 'would mock the dead and make cynics of the living'.[12] And legal because the validity of such amnesty is doubtful. Arguably, the prohibition of such crimes and the consequent obligation of states to prosecute and punish their authors should be considered a peremptory norm of international law (*jus cogens*): hence, states should not be allowed to enter into international agreements or pass national legislation foregoing punishment of those crimes. Furthermore, the Human Rights Committee has held that:

Amnesties are generally incompatible with the duty of States to investigate such acts: to guarantee freedom from such acts within their jurisdiction; and to ensure that they do not occur in the future. States may not deprive individuals of the right to an effective remedy including compensation and such full rehabilitation as may be possible.[13]

Until very recently, the few trials that had been held within national criminal jurisdictions in respect of violations of norms of international humanitarian law related to crimes committed during the Second World War. The trials in France of Barbie, Touvier and Papon for crimes against humanity are prominent examples. However, following the establishment of the International Criminal Tribunal for the Former Yugoslavia, and plausibly as a result of the incentive created by that initiative, national courts in Denmark, Germany, Austria and Switzerland, among others, have begun to try and prosecute persons accused of committing atrocities in the former Yugoslavia. In 1994, for example, Danish courts

[10] As occurred in several South American countries for gross violations of human rights. For discussion on the validity of amnesty/impunity for gross violations of human rights in international law, see N. Roht-Arriaza (ed.), *Impunity and Human Rights in International Law and Practice* (1995) and Orentlicher, 'Setting Accounts: The Duty to Prosecute Human Rights Violations of a Prior Regime', 100 *Yale LJ* (1991) 2537.

[11] See Woollacott, 'Reconciliation, or Justice and Ashes?'. *The Guardian,* 1–2 February 1997, quoting Bishop Desmond Tutu in relation to the choice faced by law-makers in South Africa after Apartheid. In this regard, for many countries facing such a 'choice', an international criminal court may be the only feasible means of ensuring that justice is done, to the extent that amnesty under national criminal jurisdiction has no effect on individual criminal responsibility in the eyes of international humanitarian law.

[12] R.H. Jackson, *The Nürnberg Case, as Presented by Robert H. Jackson* (1947), nt 8.

[13] United Nations Human Rights Committee General Comment No. 20 in relation to Article 7 of the international Covenant on Civil and Political Rights.

exercised universal jurisdiction to try and convict Refik Sarić, a Bosnian refugee in Denmark, for atrocities committed in Dretell camp, Bosnia-Herzegovina.[14]

3. The Failure of Prosecution through International Jurisdiction Prior to 1993

While the 1949 Geneva Conventions do not expressly provide for the prosecution of offenders before an international tribunal, neither do they exclude 'handing over the accused to an international criminal court whose competence has been recognised by the Contracting Parties'.[15] This mechanism is expressly provided for in Article VI of the Genocide Convention and Article V of the Apartheld Convention.[16]

Nevertheless, the Cold War in international relations from the 1960s until the beginning of the 1990s made it impossible for international humanitarian law to be enforced through such international judicial institutions. This paralysis, characterized by the mutual suspicion and distrust of the Western and Eastern blocs, also triggered an obsession with non-interference in domestic affairs. In this climate, the likelihood of establishing an international criminal court was very remote.

4. The Turning Point: The New World Order

With the end of the Cold War, the animosity that had dominated international relations for almost half a century dissipated. In its wake, a new spirit of relative optimism emerged, stimulated by the following factors:

(i) there has been a clear reduction in the distrust and mutual suspicion that frustrated friendly relations and cooperation between the Western and Eastern blocs;

(ii) the successor states to the USSR—Russia and the other states participating in Confederation of Independent States—are coming to accept and respect some basic principles of international law;

[14] *Tribunal,* January/February 1996, no. 2. at 7.

[15] J. Pictet, *The Geneva Conventions of 12 August 1949: Commentary on Article 129,* vol. III, at 624. This interpretation is supported by Röling, 'Aspects of the Criminal Responsibility for Violations of the Laws of War', in A. Cassese (ed.), *The New Humanitarian Law of Armed Conflict.* vol. 1 (1979), at 200–201, Draper disagrees: 'The modern system of penal repression of "grave breaches" has reduced the competent jurisdiction exclusively to the Courts of the Detaining Power'. See Draper, 'The implementation and Enforcement of the Geneva Conventions of 1949 and of the Two Additional Protocols of 1978 [sic]', 164 R*d*C (1979-III) 38, at 41–42.

[16] Article VI of the Genocide Convention, which provides that 'Persons charged with genocide...shall be tried...by such international penal tribunal as may have jurisdiction with respect to those Contracting Parties which shall have accepted its jurisdiction'.

(iii) there is unprecedented agreement in the Security Council and increasing convergence in the views of its five permanent members, with the consequence that this institution is able to fulfil its functions more effectively.

It is common knowledge that, despite the obvious problems of the Cold War era, the two power blocs did guarantee a modicum of international order to the extent that each of the superpowers acted as policeman and guarantor of order in its respective bloc. The collapse of this structure of international relations ushered in a wave of negative consequences. It has entailed a fragmentation of international society and intense disorder which, coupled with rising nationalism and fundamentalism, has resulted in a spiralling of (mostly) internal armed conflict, with much bloodshed and cruelty. The ensuing implosion of previously multi-ethnic societies, such as the former Yugoslavia and Rwanda, has led to gross violations of international humanitarian law on a scale comparable to those committed during the Second World War, which have shocked the conscience of the world. To be sure, the Cold War era witnessed many such excesses,[17] but it is only now with the new 'harmony' among the Big Five, together with intense media coverage of such events, that unprecedented opportunities have been created for the prosecution and punishment of those responsible for serious violations of international humanitarian law.

In this context, it should not come as a surprise that the end of the Cold War brought with it a revival of proposals for the establishment of a permanent international criminal court, an idea first mooted in the aftermath of the First World War and, as discussed above, envisaged in the Genocide and Apartheid Conventions. To quote the Final Report of the Commission of Experts set up under the terms of Resolution 780 (1992) of the Security Council, 'since the nations are expecting a new world order based on international public order, there is a need to establish permanent and effective bodies to dispense international justice'.[18] In other words, a new world order based on the rule of international law.

5. The Post-Cold-War Twin-Track: The Establishment of Ad Hoc International Tribunals and Work on the Establishment of a Permanent International Criminal Court

In response to major violations of international humanitarian law since the end of the Cold War, the Security Council has set up ad hoc Tribunals pursuant to its power to decide on measures necessary to maintain or restore international

---

[17] For example, the Vietnam War, Cambodia under Pol Pot, civil wars in Guatemala, El Salvador, Afghanistan, Angola and Mozambizque.
[18] UN Doc. S/1994/674.

peace and security: in 1993 the International Criminal Tribunal for the Former Yugoslavia (ICTY), and in 1994 the International Criminal Tribunal for Rwanda (ICTR). Moves towards the establishment of an international tribunal to prosecute and punish war crimes committed by Iraqi forces in Kuwait, an idea first mooted in the autumn of 1990,[19] seem once more to be gaining momentum.[20]

The *major merits* of criminal prosecution and punishment by an international criminal court can be stated as follows.

(i) The purpose of an impartial tribunal is to determine the *individual* criminal responsibility of individual offenders. Instead of focusing on *collective* guilt, it aims to identify individual responsibility. Thus, it rejects the tendency in times of conflict to blame an entire people for the crimes committed by certain individuals fighting in its name. This individual focus may also have a cathartic or healing effect and may contribute to the creation of peace.

(ii) One of the most important merits of an international tribunal lies in its ability to hold accountable those who violate international humanitarian law and, in so doing, to uphold the rule of international law. As stated by the eminent Dutch international jurist B.V.A. Röling:

> the foremost, essential function of criminal prosecutions [is] to restore confidence in the rule of law. The legal order is the positive inner relation of the people to the recognised values of the community, which relation is disturbed by the commission of crimes. If crimes are not punished, the confidence in the validity of the values of the community is undermined and shaken.[21]

In calling the offenders to account, an international criminal tribunal may serve to fill the vacuum left by national legislation on amnesty, to the extent that a grant of amnesty by a national authority may turn out to have no effect on individual criminal responsibility in international law. An international criminal tribunal may thus do justice where national jurisdictions are unable to do so and where victims would otherwise have no remedy.

(iii) The 'judicial reckoning' of perpetrators of serious violations of international humanitarian law before an independent tribunal, composed of judges of various nations not parties to the conflict and applying impartial justice', can serve to blunt the hatred of the victims and their desire for revenge.

(iv) This easing of tensions through the meting out of impartial justice can, in turn, create the conditions for a return to peaceful relations on the ground.

---

[19] For a review of efforts made with regard to the creation of an international court to try Iraqi leaders for crimes committed during the Iraqi invasion of Kuwait and the ensuing Gulf War, see *The Path to The Hague—Selected Documents on the Origins of the ICTY* (1996).

[20] Recent efforts include the international 'Campaign to indict Iraql War Criminals', see 'All-party Call to Try Saddam', *The Guardian*, 16 January 1997.

[21] Röling, 'Criminal Responsibility for Violations of the Laws of War', 12 *Revue Belge de Droit International* (1976) 8, at 22.

(v) The proceedings of an international criminal tribunal build an impartial and objective *record of events*. This record differs fundamentally from that established by a fact-finding commission (see section 1 above), in that it has passed the rigorous test of judicial scrutiny, that is, the application of a tribunal's strict rules of admissibility of evidence. In this regard, investigations conducted with a view to prosecution before an international criminal tribunal are much more far-reaching and thorough than those undertaken by a fact-finding commission. Thus, the record of an international tribunal is also of crucial value as a historical account of events.

(vi) The holding of trials is a clear statement of the will of the international community to *break with the past* (*rompre avec le passé*) by punishing those who have deviated from acceptable standards of human behaviour. In delivering punishment, the international community's purpose is not so much retribution as stigmatization of the deviant behaviour.

6. The Problems of International Criminal Courts as a Means of Enforcing International Humanitarian Law

The problems faced by the ICTY demonstrate the difficulties in enforcing international humanitarian law through an international mechanism. Among the complaints regularly aired before the General Assembly of the United Nations in the annual speech of the President of the ICTY and in the Annual Report[22] are that:

(i) The ICTY Statute places excessive reliance on state cooperation as the primary means of achieving the mandated objectives of prosecuting persons for violations of international humanitarian law. ICTY, having no police force of its own, must rely on international cooperation in order to effect arrests. It has proved extremely difficult to achieve significant state cooperation in complying with the Tribunal's orders to arrest and deliver indicted persons to The Hague and to provide assistance in evidentiary matters. Impunity is a genuine risk when states and international authorities refuse to arrest indicted individuals.

(ii) There is a crucial need for more arrests of military or political leaders. States, if arresting at all, demonstrate greater willingness to arrest lesser figures, whilst allowing the leaders to remain at large. The process of restoring peace and security to the affected region is thus made all the more difficult.

---

[22] See for example, the Address by the President of the ICTY to the General Assembly on 4 November 1997 and the Fourth Annual Report of the ICTY, 7 August 1997, UN Doc. A/52/375, S/1997/729.

(iii) There are tremendous financial and logistical obstacles in the way of an effective international criminal tribunal. To establish an effective and fully functioning institution from scratch requires enormous funding. ICTY has had to build a courtroom and offices and supply them with all the necessary equipment, hire staff from all around the world, build a detention unit, fund programmes for the protection of victims and witnesses, send teams of investigators into the field, and so on. Yet there remains much to be done. For example, ICTY's Prosecutor, like the rest of the Tribunal's organs, has been severely hampered by lack of funds, and there is a genuine need for more investigators to undertake the many complex and time-consuming inquiries necessary to fulfil the institution's mandate. Witnesses have to be found amongst the Balkan diaspora. They must be interviewed and brought to The Hague to testify and, if necessary, be placed in a witness protection programme. This applies not only to prosecution witnesses, but to defence witnesses as well.

(iv) Finally, the legal régime is not straightforward. Unlike national jurisdictions, which may rely on dozens of codes and hundreds of precedents for guidance, the ICTY has to apply, in addition to its Statute, customary international law, which can only be ascertained by consulting widely-dispersed international law sources. This became particularly clear in the case of *Erdemović*,[23] when the judges of the Appeals Chamber had to determine whether international law recognized the defence of duress, a question on which the Statute remains silent. Furthermore, the work of international tribunals is made all the more problematic by the absence of an international code of criminal procedure, although the Rules of Procedure and Evidence which have been laboriously drafted by the ICTY would provide a blueprint for a future permanent institution.

7. International Criminal Justice v. State Sovereignty

Whilst states continue to shy away from resorting to national penal enforcement (see section 2 above), they are also very reluctant to 'internationalize' the repression of serious violations of international humanitarian law. This proposition remains true, despite the recent moves towards the establishment of a permanent international criminal court, moves which seem to be very close to reaching their goal. The reluctance of states regarding international penal enforcement is hardly surprising, given that international criminal tribunals intrude on one of the most sacred areas of state sovereignty: criminal jurisdiction.

One of the essential features of an international criminal tribunal—whether established ad hoc by the Security Council pursuant to Chapter VII of the UN

---

[23] *Prosecutor v. Drazen Erdemović*, IT-96–23A, AC, Judgment, 7 October 1997.

Charter or whether made permanent through a multilateral treaty—is that it purports to exercise international criminal jurisdiction directly over individuals living in states and subject to the exclusive authority of such states. It thus casts aside the 'shield' of state sovereignty. There is no doubt that the establishment of such tribunals constitutes a major inroad into the traditional omnipotence of sovereign states. However, as I shall now demonstrate by drawing from the experience of the ICTY and from the current proposals for an international criminal court, state sovereignty *resurfaces* when it comes to the day-to-day operations of the Tribunal and its ability to fulfil its mandate. This proves once again the validity of a remark made by a renowned German lawyer, Niemeyer, earlier this century (XXth Century): he pointed out that international law is an edifice built on a *volcano*—state sovereignty.[24] By this he meant that whenever state sovereignty explodes onto the international scene; it may demolish the very bricks and mortar from which the Law of Nations is built. It is for this reason that international law aims to build devices to withstand the seismic activity of states: to prevent or diminish their pernicious effect. This metaphor is particularly apt in relation to an international tribunal. The tribunal must always contend with the violent eruptions of state sovereignty: the effect of states' lack of cooperation is like lava burning away the foundations of the institution.

In order to better understand the effect of state sovereignty on the operation of international criminal tribunals, one must first grasp their constitution and functions. Unlike national courts, which are concerned exclusively with judicial functions and leave investigation and prosecution up to other bodies, the current model for an international criminal court, in fact, provides for *two* organs: (i) a body entrusted with the administration of justice (the Chambers); and (ii) a body responsible for the investigation and prosecution of crimes falling under the Tribunal's jurisdiction. In the ICTY and ICTR, the latter organ is called the 'Office of the Prosecutor'. Under the Draft Statute for a permanent International criminal court, it is designated as 'the Procuracy.[25] As I shall illustrate, the effectiveness of both the judicial arm and the investigation arm of an international criminal tribunal depends heavily on state cooperation and is ultimately impeded by lack of state cooperation under the guise of state sovereignty.

Unlike national courts, an international criminal tribunal has no law enforcement agency akin to a *police judiciaire*. It thus relies primarily on the cooperation of national authorities for the effective investigation and prosecution of persons accused of violations of international humanitarian law. Accordingly, all requests for assistance or orders of the ICTY, for instance, are addressed to and processed by the national system of the relevant state as the first resort. Cooperation is necessary in relation to requests for assistance or orders of the ICTY for the

---

[24] H.G. Niemeyer, *Einstweilige Verfügungen des Weltgerichtchofs, ihr Wesen und ihre Grenzen* (1932), at 3.

[25] Article 12 of the Draft Statute defines the Procuracy as an 'independent organ of the Court responsible for the investigation of complaints'.

identification and location of persons, the taking of testimony and the production of evidence, the service of documents, the arrest or detention of persons, and the surrender or transfer of the accused to the ICTY. States are obliged to cooperate with the ICTY for these purposes pursuant to Article 29 of the ICTY Statute.

However, Rule 59 *bis*[26] of the Rules of Procedure and Evidence of the ICTY provides an alternative procedure to that contemplated by Article 29 (and also Rule 55) concerning arrests by states. A Trial Chamber of the ICTY[27] has held that 'once an arrest warrant has been transmitted to an international authority, an international body, or the Office of the Prosecutor, the accused person named therein may be taken into custody without the involvement of the State in which he or she was located'.[28] Four successful arrests have been made by international authorities in the former Yugoslavia since the adoption of Rule 59 *bis*.[29]

Notwithstanding this development the ICTY remains very much like a giant without arms and legs—it needs artificial limbs to walk and work. And these artificial limbs are state authorities. If the cooperation of states is not forthcoming, the ICTY cannot fulfil its functions. It has no means at its disposal to force states to cooperate with it. This is to be contrasted with the international Military Tribunals at Nuremberg and Tokyo, which investigated and prosecuted war crimes committed in states held under military occupation by the Allied forces.

The obligation of states to cooperate with an international tribunal, whether pursuant to a binding Security Council resolution in the case of ad hoc tribunals or pursuant to their treaty obligations in the case of a permanent international criminal court, requires each state to enact implementing legislation or to amend Its existing legislation for this purpose. A particular problem which arises with respect to most implementing legislation enacted by states to date with regard to the ICTY[30] is the tendency to subsume cooperation with the ICTY under the traditional model of *inter-state* judicial cooperation. For example, many states, in their implementing legislation, apply extradition procedures to requests by the ICTY for the surrender of accused persons, some even referring expressly to 'extradition'

---

[26] 'Transmission of Arrest Warrants:
(A) Notwithstanding Rules 55 to 59, on the order of a Judge, the Registrar shall transmit to an appropriate authority or international body or the Prosecutor a copy of a warrant for the arrest of an accused on such terms as the judge may determine, together with an order that he be taken into custody by that authority or international body or the Prosecutor . . .'.

[27] *Prosecutor v. Zlatko Dokmanovic,* IT-95–13a-PT, TC II, Decision on the Motion for Release by the Accused Zlatko Dokmanovic, 22 October 1997.

[28] *Ibid.* at 18.

[29] Arrests of Milan Kovacevic, Anto Furundija and Goran Jelisic by SFOR and Slavko Dokmanovic by UNTAES respectively. Simo Drijaca was killed in the course of an attempt to arrest him by SFOR.

[30] As at 10 November 1997, the following 20 states have enacted legislation regarding the International Criminal Tribunal for the Former Yugoslavia: Italy, Finland, Netherlands, Germany, Iceland, Spain, Norway, Sweden, Denmark, France, Republic of Bosnia and Herzegovina, Australia, Switzerland, New Zealand, United States, United Kingdom, Belgium, Republic of Croatia, Austria and Hungary. Four countries have indicated that they do not need implementing legislation (Korea, Russia, Singapore and Venezuela).

of accused persons.[31] The application of the law of extradition to cooperation with the ICTY is inappropriate. Extradition to a state and surrender to an international jurisdiction are two totally different and separate mechanisms. The former concerns relations between two sovereign states and is therefore a reflection of the principle of equality of states: it gives rise to a *horizontal* relationship. The latter, instead, concerns the relation between a state and an international judicial body endowed with binding authority; it is therefore the expression of a *vertical* relationship. The Appeals Chamber of the ICTY has recently noted that the relation between national courts of different states is 'horizontal' in nature.[32]

The ICTY is endowed with jurisdiction over individuals living within sovereign states, be they states of the former Yugoslavia or third states, and, in addition, has been conferred with primacy over national courts in its Statute. By the same token, the Statute granted ICTY the power to address to states binding orders concerning a broad variety of judicial matters (including the identification and location of persons, the taking of testimony and the production of evidence, the service of documents, the arrest or detention of persons, and the surrender or transfer of indictees to ICTY). Clearly, a 'vertical' relationship has been established, at least as far as the judicial and injunctory powers of the ICTY are concerned (whereas in the area of enforcement, the ICTY is still dependent upon states and the Security Council). This is borne out by the fact that requests for extradition under the inter-state scheme are subject to the discretionary consent of the state from which extradition is sought or are envisaged in bilateral treaties on extradition; by contrast, the ICTY's requests for surrender are always binding upon states pursuant to ICTY's Statute, to UN Resolution 827 (1993) establishing the ICTY, and to Chapter VII of the UN Charter. Such requests override national legislation. It is worth noting here that Rule 58 of the ICTY's Rules of Procedure and Evidence provides that the duty of cooperation and judicial assistance laid down in Article 29 of the Statute 'shall prevail over any legal impediment to the surrender or transfer of the accused or of a witness to the ICTY which may exist under the national law or extradition treaties of the State concerned'. This Rule effectively codifies the principle of customary international law pursuant to which a state cannot adduce its constitution or its laws as a defence for failure to carry out its international obligations.[33]

---

[31] See, e.g., 'extradition': Article 2 of Denmark's Act on Criminal Proceedings before the International Tribunal for the Prosecution of Persons Responsible for War Crimes Committed in the Territory of Former Yugoslavia: Article 2 of Norway's Act Relating to the Incorporation into Norwegian Law of the United Nations Security Council Resolution on the Establishment of an International Tribunal for Crimes Committed in the Former Yugoslavia: the implicit procedure in Bosnia and Herzegovina's Decree with Force of Law on Deferral upon Request by the International Tribunal, and Article 11 of Italy's Decree Law No. 544 of 28 December 1993.

[32] *Prosecutor v. Tihomir Blaškić*, IT-95-13-AR108 *bis*, AC, Judgement on the Request of the Republic of Croatia for Review of the Decision of Trial Chamber II of 18 July 1997, 29 October 1997.

[33] See *Restatement of the Law—Third, The Foreign Relations Law of the United States.* vol. 1. (1987), para. 115b, at 6d, and *Polish Nationals in Danzig*, 1931 PCIJ, Series A/B, No. 44, at 24.

The importance of state sovereignty as a factor influencing the work of an international tribunal is made glaringly apparent by a recent problem faced by the ICTY with respect to the Office of the Prosecutor's efforts to obtain documents relevant to the case of *Prosecutor v. Tihomir Blaškić*. The problem in that particular instance arose out of two *subpoenae duces tecum* (orders to appear in court for the purpose of handing over documents) issued on 15 January 1997 by a judge of the Trial Chamber, at the request of the Office of the Prosecutor. These *subpoenae* enjoined (i) Bosnia and Herzegovina and 'the Custodian of the Records of the Central Archive of what was formerly the Ministry of Defence of the Croatian Community of Herzeg-Bosna' and (ii) the Republic of Croatia and the Minister of Defence of the Republic of Croatia, to provide the documents listed therein. These subpoenae were not complied with within the allotted time by the Republic of Croatia and were only partially complied with by Bosnia and Herzegovina. In response to the subpoena, the Republic of Croatia argued that the ICTY does not have the competence to issue subpoenae to a sovereign state or to its officials: it added that if the Security Council had intended to depart so drastically from international law (probably intending to refer to those international rules which provide for state immunity as well as the immunity of state agents), it would have stated so plainly in the Statute of the ICTY. It agreed to give its 'full co-operation' to the Office of the Prosecutor with respect to the requested documents, not on the basis of the *subpoena* which it considered unfounded, but rather on the basis of its legislation on cooperation with the ICTY[34] and 'under the terms applicable to all States'. It added, however, that '[l]ike any sovereign State, the Republic of Croatia reserves the right to observe the interests of its national security when assisting the ICTY.'[35] In contrast. Bosnia and Herzegovina stated that it recognized the competence of the ICTY to issue orders against states, such as the *subpoena* in question, and that the Statute allows for the issuance of such orders. It proceeded to argue before the ICTY that it had taken all necessary steps to ensure compliance with the ICTY's order.

The Appeals Chamber[36] ruled that while *subpoenae duces tecum* could not be addressed to states, binding orders could be so addressed: states cannot, by claiming national security interests, withhold documents and other evidentiary material requested by the ICTY. However, it recommended that practical arrangements be adopted by the relevant Trial Chamber to make allowance for legitimate and bona fide concerns of states. The Appeals Chamber also noted that ICTY does not possess any power to take enforcement measures against sovereign states; such powers cannot be regarded as inherent to the functions of an international judicial body. Following the reporting of a judicial finding concerning a state's failure to observe the provisions of the Statute or the Rules, it is for ICTY's parent

---

[34] The Constitutional Act on the Co-operation between the Republic of Croatia and the International Criminal Tribunal, 19 April 1996.

[35] Reply of the Government of the Republic of Croatia to Subpoena Duces Tecum, *Prosecutor v. Tihomir Blaškić*, IT-95–14-T, 10 February 1997, para. 12.

[36] *Supra* note 32.

body, the Security Council, to impose sanctions, if any, against a recalcitrant state, under the conditions provided for in Chapter VII of the United Nations Charter. In addition, subject to certain conditions, each Member State of the United Nations may act upon the communal legal interest in the observance of this international obligation laid down in Article 29 (of the ICTY Statute). A collective response through other intergovernmental organizations may also be envisaged, again 'subject to certain conditions'.

The reluctance of states to give way to international criminal jurisdiction with respect to matters which would otherwise be subject to their exclusive sovereignty becomes even more apparent in light of the way in which the International Law Commission's draft statute on a permanent international criminal court deals with the allocation of jurisdiction between the court and national authorities. In this regard, it is significant that the Preparatory Committee set up by the General Assembly to review the draft found that 'the jurisdictional aspects of the Statute were the object of the most intense and arduous discussions'.[37] The statute of the international criminal court as currently drafted is more restrictive with respect to jurisdiction than that of the existing ad hoc Tribunals. For example:

(i) Like the ICTY and the ICTR, the proposed international criminal court is to have 'complementary' jurisdiction with that of national jurisdiction but, unlike these two ad hoc Tribunals, the proposed court gives *primacy* to *national* jurisdictions.

(ii) The jurisdiction of the proposed international criminal court is triggered by states, and not on the initiative of the Procuracy. The latter does not have the power to investigate ex officio, but only on the basis of the complaint made by a state (although it has sole authority to decide on the issuance of indictments following state complaints).[38]

(iii) In addition, under a proposal currently being discussed, in order for the jurisdiction of the court to 'kick in' in a given case, the complaining state, the state which has custody of the suspect *and* the state on whose territory the crime is alleged to have taken place, must not only have ratified the statute, but must also have 'opted in' with regard to the specific crimes complained of.[39]

It is hoped that these restrictions on the permanent international criminal court's jurisdiction will be tempered so that the court may function effectively.

To sum up, the truth of the matter is that the major concessions that have been made by states over their sovereignty with respect to the establishment of fully

---

[37] Politi, 'The Establishment of an International Criminal Court at a Crossroads: Issues and Prospects after the First Session of the Preparatory Committee', 13 *Nouvelles Etudes Pénales* (1997) 115, at 118.

[38] See ILC Draft Statute. Articles 25 and 26.

[39] An exception is made for the crime of genocide, over which the court has 'inherent jurisdiction' to the extent that ratification of the statute automatically implies acceptance of the court's jurisdiction. See generally Articles 20 through 25 of the ILC Draft Statute for an international criminal court.

functioning international criminal tribunals are nevertheless being negated by an excessive clinging to state sovereignty in the face of requests for cooperation. Having opened the door of state sovereignty, it is all too quickly shut again.

8. Concluding Remarks

The trend towards 'criminalization of international law', through criminal prosecution and punishment of breaches of international humanitarian law by international criminal tribunals, should not blind us to the basic dilemma facing international tribunals: prosecution and punishment or continued respect for state sovereignty? The supremacy of state sovereignty in the form of excessive restrictions on the jurisdiction of international criminal courts can only result in the creation of ineffective institutions.[40]

In addition, the trend towards the institutionalization of international criminal law must not detract from the underlying political realities. Judicial reckoning, while necessary in order to uphold and enforce the international rule of law, should run parallel to steps taken on the political level. The prosecution and punishment of war criminals by an international criminal tribunal (whether ad hoc or permanent) cannot be a substitute for robust action by the United Nations where required to restore international peace and security. As long as the ideological, political and military leaders behind the serious violations of international humanitarian law still remain firmly in power, flaunting with impunity their rendezvous with justice, this can only result in a discrediting of the work of international criminal tribunals. So long as states retain some essential aspects of their sovereignty and fail to set up an effective mechanism to enforce arrest warrants and to execute judgments, international criminal tribunals may have little more than normative impact. Thus, we are once again reminded of the limits posed by international politics on international law.[41]

In spite of these problems, the most effective means of enforcing international humanitarian law remains the prosecution and punishment of offenders within national or international criminal jurisdictions. I will go further and say that the rule of international humanitarian law depends on its enforcement through the prosecution and punishment of its offenders. As Cesare Beccaria stated as long ago as 1764, 'the conviction of finding nowhere a span of earth where real crimes were pardoned might be the most efficacious way of preventing their occurrence',[42] and thus of ensuring respect for the rule of law.

---

[40] Report of the International Law Commission, 46th Session, 1994, at 36.

[41] 'International Law is still limited by international politics, and we must not pretend that either can live and grow without the other.' Stimson, 'The Nuremberg Trial: Landmark in Law', 25 *Foreign Affairs* (1947) 189.

[42] Beccaria, 'Dei delitti e delle pene', *translated in J. Farrar, Crimes & Punishment* (1880), at 193–194.

B. International Crimes of Individuals

21. The International Community, Terrorism and Human Rights*

1. Introductory Remarks

In looking at this intricate and mazy problem area, I perceive four main questions. First, why is terrorism to be condemned from the point of view of the human rights and humanitarian law philosophy? Secondly, under what circumstances can States be called to account for terrorist activities carried out by private groups and organizations? Thirdly, to what extent should terrorists benefit from international and national standards on human rights? Fourthly, is it legitimate to claim that the need to fight terrorism warrants curtailments of or restrictions on the human rights of the whole population?

I shall endeavour to get to grips with each of these issues separately, although of course they are closely interrelated. Before doing so, I should like however to point out that there are admittedly many other problems deserving close attention. One, in particular, stands out: the behaviour of those States which harbour terrorists acting in other countries, or give them training, arms, financial and other forms of assistance. The question here is how to stop States from aiding and abetting such terrorist activities which plainly result in their being strengthened. This and other similar issues I shall however leave aside, although they indubitably impinge upon human rights (the human rights of the victims of terrorism). I submit that the solution here is less complex and tricky than in the case of the four questions mentioned earlier. Indeed the solution might lie in *drafting* and *enforcing* international conventions prohibiting the aforementioned activities, in addition to the application of a few general principles of international law that to some extent could be used to place States under restraint in such matters.

---

* Originally published in *Studi in Onore di Giuseppe Sperduti* (Milano: Giuffrè, 1984) 477.

2. What Assessment of Terrorism Can We Derive from the International Human Rights and Humanitarian Law Doctrine?

All States and organizations are by now agreed on the condemnation of the despicable phenomenon of terrorism—even those which only pay lip service to this condemnation would never admit that they either supported or condoned terrorists. If there exists such broad, albeit loose, consensus on the matter, can we derive a more elaborate and precise appraisal of terrorism from the body of human rights standards and humanitarian law?

We should start from the assumption that terrorists are inspired by political motives and aim at overthrowing the existing legal order or bringing about radical changes in the fabric of society. They are people who rebel against the status quo by resorting to violence and terror. This being so, we should ask two questions: first, to what extent is rebellion legitimized by international law? Secondly, do international standards allow rebels to resort to terrorist methods?

A distinction should be drawn between human rights law and humanitarian law, for these two sets of legal regulations adopt a somewhat different attitude towards rebellion.[1] Humanitarian law does not pronounce on whether people living in a sovereign country have a right to take up arms against the incumbent government. International rules on armed conflict confine themselves to taking account of the fact that insurrections break out and, when rebellion reaches a certain intensity and duration in time, they regulate the conduct of hostilities and how non-combatants should be treated. Only with regard to a limited category of insurrection, i.e. wars of national liberation, does humanitarian law (plus UN law) grant a right of rebellion proper. The bulk of the numerous General Assembly resolutions on self-determination, grant peoples fighting against the oppression of colonial powers, racist régimes or foreign occupants the right to take up arms to achieve self-determination. As international practice has evolved along these lines and was confirmed in 1977 in the Ist Geneva Protocol on the Humanitarian Law of Armed Conflict, we can conclude that those three categories of peoples can legitimately use armed violence to exercise their right of rebellion.[2]

By contrast, human rights standards proclaim a general right of rebellion, albeit implicitly and subject to stringent requirements. If they are met, the right can be used by any group of people, irrespective of the type of régime against which they fight and whatever the intensity and scope of the struggle.

---

[1] In this paper I shall not dwell on treaties on terrorism recently concluded under the auspices of some international organizations, first of all because they have, not yet attained universal application, and secondly because they normally tend to deal with a specific issue only, i.e. international cooperation for the punishment of terrorists (see however *infra*, note 10).

[2] See on the matter SALMON, *Les guerres de libération nationale*, in *The New Humanitarian Law of Armed Conflict*, I, (Cassese ed.), Napoli, 1979, p. 55ff.; ABI-SAAB, *Wars of National Liberation in the Geneva Conventions and Protocols*, in *Recueil des Cours de l'Académie de droit international de La Haye*, 1979-IV, p. 363ff.

It is apparent that on this score human rights standards have a much broader application.

Where and how do international human rights standards lay down the right to rebellion? Attention should be drawn to the third preambular paragraph of the Universal Declaration of Human Rights, which provides that

... [I]t is essential, if man is not to be compelled to have recourse, as a last resort, to rebellion against tyranny and oppression, that human rights should be protected by the rule of law.[3]

It follows that when in a State the basic human rights are grossly trampled upon by the authorities and when no democratic and peaceful means are available to enforce respect for those human rights, rebellion is a legitimate reaction. It should be noted that this right to rebel against tyranny is part and parcel of the Western liberal tradition. It has usually been defined as 'right of resistance' to oppressive Governments. Suffice it to mention the 'Discourse Concerning Unlimited Submission and non-Resistance to the Higher Powers' made in 1750 by the American theologian and liberal political thinker Jonathan Mayhew. He wrote that

[W]hen (the King) ... turns tyrant, and makes his subjects his prey to devour and destroy, instead of his charge to defend and cherish, we are bound to throw off our allegiance to him, and to resist.[4]

The same concept is taken up by some modern Constitutions, such as that of the Federal Republic of Germany, which provides in Article 20 para. 4 that everybody has the right to resist persons seeking to abolish the constitutional order, 'should no other remedy be possible'.

If the right to rebel against oppression is therefore well rooted both at international and national level, how should it be implemented? Should it involve resort to armed violence and if so, within what bounds? Let us first consider the position of liberation movements for, as stated above, they have an international right to use force for their self-determination. Can they also resort to terrorist activities either against the adversary or against other countries, or people or organizations in other countries? For example, can the PLO engage in acts of terrorism in Israel, or in the Federal Republic of Germany, or for that matter, in any other Western country? Humanitarian law, particularly the aforementioned 1977 Geneva Protocol, is sufficiently clear in regulating the relationship between a liberation movement and its counterpart. Civilians must not be the object of indiscriminate attack; in particular, 'acts or threats of violence the primary purpose of which is to spread terror among the civilian population are prohibited' (Art. 51, para. 2 of the Ist Geneva Protocol). Similarly, there is a strict ban on the

---

[3] On the value and importance of the Universal Declaration see the fundamental essay by SPERDUTI, *La Dichiarazione Universale dei diritti dell'Uomo*, in *La Comunità Internazionale*, 1950, p. 216ff.

[4] See the text in VOLKOMMER (ed.), *The Liberal Tradition in American Thought*, New York, 1969, p. 49.

taking of hostages and on inhuman, humiliating or degrading treatment inflicted on civilians or combatants. As for belligerents, they are protected by the prohibition of any form of perfidy, which includes feigning civilian, non-combatant status (see Art. 37 of the Geneva Protocol, which should however be read in conjunction with the rather complicated and puzzling Art. 44 on 'Combatants and Prisoners of War').

The rationale behind these rules is the same as that which motivates all prohibition of terrorism in *any* armed conflict, i.e. 1) the strict distinction drawn between belligerents and civilians for the purpose of sparing the latter from being deliberately involved in armed violence, and 2) the principle derived from the ancient rules of chivalry whereby 'a certain amount of fairness in offence and defence' should be shown and consequently belligerent action should only be permissible to people entitled to combatant status.

It should be noted that a very interesting and significant link between human rights law and humanitarian law is instituted by Art. 12 of the UN Convention Against the Taking of Hostages, of 1979; this provision states that hostage-taking in the course of armed conflict is prohibited by the UN Convention only in so far as it is not already banned by the Conventions of humanitarian law applicable to States parties to the UN Convention. Consequently, the duty to prosecute or hand over hostage-takers who have acted in the course of an armed conflict follows either from the UN Convention itself or from humanitarian law. It is apparent that Art. 12 aims at avoiding any possible gap or loophole, by closely connecting human rights law with humanitarian law.[5]

As for the possible terrorist activities of liberation movements in third countries, their condemnation follows from international instruments on human rights. Thus, the Universal Declaration provides in Art. 3 that 'everyone has the right to life, liberty and security of person' and in Art. 5 that 'No one shall be subjected to torture or to cruel, inhuman or degrading treatment or punishments'. Admittedly, these provisions—that have been elaborated upon and specified in various other international instruments such as the 1966 Covenant on Civil and Political Rights—are mainly intended to impose duties on States or Governments. Nothing, however, prevents both their 'philosophy' and their legal force being extended to other international entities. In other words, it seems proper to derive a general evaluation of terrorism, be it carried out by State authorities or by members of other organized groups having international status. To my mind, among the most important general standards on human rights—which, in the view of the International Court of Justice, have turned into general rules of customary international law[6]—there is included a sweeping ban on terrorist activities. It can be contended that this general ban also applies to international

[5] On this point see VERWEY, *The International Hostages Convention and National Liberation Movements*, in *American Journal of International Law*, 1981, p. 69ff.

[6] See the judgment in the *Barcelona Traction case* (ICJ, *Reports 1970*, p. 32, paras 33–34), the Advisory Opinion in the *Namibia case* (ICJ, *Reports 1971*, p. 57, para. 131) and the judgment in the *Iranian case* (ICJ, *Reports 1980*, p. 42, para. 91).

entities other than States, such as liberation movements having international status. They too are duty-bound to refrain from terrorism and to repress and punish any of their members engaging in terrorist activities.

At this juncture I should like to stress that the rationale behind the human rights standards prohibiting terrorism is somewhat different and broader than that behind humanitarian law. The ban on terrorist activities stemming from human rights standards is based on the concept that the right to life and liberty is one of the most sacred values of mankind; consequently any unlawful action calculated to infringe upon it must be condemned, whether this action be perpetrated by State authorities or by individuals.

So far I have been speaking of the reaction of the international community to one particular category of rebellion against oppression—that of liberation movements. Does the international community take a stand on the extent to which other forms of rebellion against tyranny can go? This is too touchy an issue for States to enact detailed international legislation on the matter. They tend to turn a blind eye to the question, thus leaving each individual State to regulate the phenomenon as it thinks best—normally by criminal legislation. An appraisal of terrorism can however be inferred from international norms. It is an evaluation of strong condemnation.

In case of civil strife on a large scale, terrorism (be it carried out by the lawful authorities or by insurgents) is expressly prohibited if performed against all persons who do not take a direct part or who have ceased to take part in hostilities. Two important international rules should be mentioned: Art. 3 common to the 1949 Geneva Conventions and Art. 4 of the II Geneva Protocol of 1977. The former, as is well known, has a much wider field of application since it applies to all forms of internal armed conflict which reach a certain degree of intensity, whereas the 1977 Protocol provides for a very high 'threshold'.

But what happens in cases of internal disorder and tension such as riots, or isolated and sporadic acts of violence? Even in these cases terrorism is prohibited. Although, as I said before, international custom, treaties and declarations on human rights are mainly intended to impose duties on States, their *general philosophy* should be given full weight and liberally extended to entities other than States. It follows that human dignity must be respected not only by governments but also by individuals and groups. Arbitrary behaviour, inhuman and degrading treatment are to be condemned not only if they are performed by State officials, but also if they are carried out by individuals who do not form organized groups possessed of international standing. From a *strictly legal* point of view, international rules do not directly impose obligations on individuals and private organizations. They are however relevant, at least in the following respect: in cases where individuals and private groups engage in terrorist activities, Government authorities are authorized by international law to meet out harsh treatment to them upon capture. In other words, States are legitimized to treat terrorists more harshly than normal criminal offenders, provided of course they themselves do not overstep the bounds set by international standards on human rights (on the duty of States not to trample upon the human rights of terrorists, see para. 4 below).

However, international standards do not provide a clear-cut answer to all possible questions. There are borderline cases that prove to be open to differing solutions. The following example could be given: A group of people fighting against an undisputedly undemocratic government which denies the most elementary human rights resorts to forms of terrorism (e.g. hostage-taking) against members of the army (or members of the Government at the head of the armed forces) to obtain by force measures designed to ensure greater respect for human rights. Is this action at odds with the doctrine enshrined in such basic international instruments as the Universal Declaration of Human Rights, the Covenant and Article 3 common to the 1949 Conventions? The contention could perhaps be made that the action might be considered permissible so long as certain strict requirements are fulfilled, namely: (1) the incumbent authorities are unquestionably oppressive and do not leave any room for democratic change; (2) the sole purpose of the 'terrorist' action is to achieve some degree of freedom; (3) no innocent civilian is among the victims; (4) no inhuman or degrading treatment is meted out to the people attacked.

3. When Should Governments Be Held Answerable for Violations of Human Rights Committed by Terrorists?

It is well known that in many countries terrorist activities are carried out by private groups or organizations with the tacit support or the acquiescence of Government authorities. The question that crops up here is how can one ensure respect for the right to life and security of the victims of this increasingly menacing form of terrorism? In particular, can one call the Government to account? The solution can easily be found in the traditional principles on State responsibility. It is common knowledge that States bear international responsibility for any failure of their organs to prevent and repress breaches of international law committed by individuals. International standards on human rights enjoin States not only to respect but also *to ensure respect* for human rights: to this end, States undertake to adopt all the necessary measures for implementing international standards on human rights in their municipal systems. It may suffice to quote Art. 2 of the UN Covenant on Civil and Political Rights; in para. 1 it provides that:

Each State party to the present Covenant undertakes to respect and to ensure to all individuals within its territory and subject to its jurisdiction the rights recognized in the present Covenant...

Para. 2 goes on to stipulate that:

Where not already provided for by existing legislation or other measures, each State Party to the present Covenant undertakes to take the necessary steps, in accordance with its constitutional processes and with the provisions of the present Covenant, to adopt such legislative or other measures as may be necessary to give effect to the rights recognized in the present Covenant.

This and similar provisions merely restate and codify a general obligation to respect and ensure respect for those international rules on human rights which are binding upon States. This is clearly proved by international practice and by pronouncements made by States in the UN and other international fora. It follows that States not parties to the UN Covenant or similar treaties are at any rate under an obligation to respect and ensure respect for *general rules* on human rights (e.g. the norm prohibiting gross and systematic violations of human rights, the rule forbidding racial discrimination, that banning genocide, and so forth).

A logical consequence of the above concepts is that whenever a State indirectly aids and abets or even culpably tolerates or condones terrorist activities jeopardizing the life and security of individuals, it can be held legally responsible under international law. This principle has been spelled out with great clarity in the case-law of the European Commission and Court on Human Rights. Professor Giuseppe Sperduti has been one of the most vocal and consistent champions of the principle. The statement he made on behalf of the Commission before the European Court in the *Young, James and Webster* case (so-called closed-shop case) deserves to be quoted here. In strongly advocating that States should bear responsibility even when a national statute simply *allows* behaviour contrary to the European Convention on Human Rights, he pointed out:

Que l'on considère la situation d'insécurité croissante dans laquelle se trouve de nos jours l'individu face aux atteintes qui peuvent provenir d'autres individus, groupes, organisations. Est-ce que l'article 5 de la Convention [on the right of everyone to liberty and security of person], qui commence par reconnaître à chacun les droits à la sécurité de la personne ne saurait être compris pour ce qui est de ce droit que comme visant d'une façon stricte et exclusive, le devoir des autorités publiques de ne pas porter atteinte, elles, à cette sécurité? Est-ce que donc, à l'égard de la Convention un Etat demeurerait à l'abri de toute responsabilité alors même que l'attitude de négligence, voire une attitude permissive des autorités publiques aurait rendu possible que des individus relevant de la juridiction de l'Etat subissent, dans la sphère de cette juridiction, des atteintes graves à leur sûreté de la part d'autres individus groupes, organisations? Il suffit, semble-t-il, de poser ces questions pour que le bon sens même aide à y répondre.[7]

The European Court reasoned along the same lines when it considered whether the British Act authorizing the institution of the closed-shop infringed upon the European Convention on Human Rights. It held that:

Under Art. 1 of the [European] Convention [on Human Rights] each Contracting State 'shall secure to everyone within its jurisdiction the rights and freedoms defined in the Convention'; hence, if a violation of one of those rights and freedoms is the result of non-observance of that obligation in the enactment of domestic legislation, the responsibility of the State for that violation is engaged. Although the proximate cause of the events giving rise to this case was the 1975 agreement between British Rail and the railway union, it was the domestic law in force at the relevant time that made lawful the treatment

---

[7] Text in *Rivista di diritto internazionale*, 1982, p. 65ff., at 69.

of which the applicants complained. The responsibility of the respondent State for any resultant breach of the Convention is thus engaged on this basis.[8]

This ruling is no doubt in keeping with the general principle referred to above. Thus, the contention can be made that the law governing the matter is clear and unquestionable. The fact however remains that in actual practice it proves extremely difficult to ascertain whether Government authorities do in fact culpably tolerate or connive at terrorist activities carried out by private groups. Only in extreme cases can solid evidence become available. In borderline areas—which constitute the rule—the factual situation is so confused that international legal standards turn out to be unworkable. This is where the crux of the matter lies and where law most needs progressive development and, even more, supervisory machinery capable of scrutinizing the actual conduct of States.

4. To what Extent Are Terrorists Entitled to Benefit from Human Rights Standards?

International law does not make any distinction based on the political outlook or the deeds of individuals; it grants rights and freedoms to any human being, irrespective of his criminal record, if any. In particular, international standards on detention and trial are calculated to safeguard the basic human rights of criminal offenders, however heinous their crimes may be. True, international norms do take into account the possibility that some individuals or groups engage in activities designed to undermine the democratic order or to infringe upon the rights and freedoms of others; for this purpose international instruments provide for restrictions on some human rights of those who intend to abuse their own rights and freedoms. I shall dwell on this issue at greater length later on. For the time being it is sufficient to underscore that restrictions are not admitted on such rights as the right not to be arbitrarily deprived of one's own life (Art. 6 of the UN Covenant on Civil and Political Rights), the right not to be tortured or submitted to inhuman and degrading treatment (Art. 7), the right not to be deprived of one's liberty and the right to lawful detention (Art. 9 and 10), and to a fair trial (Art. 14 and 15).

Besides international standards on human rights, all the most important treaties of the humanitarian law of armed conflict spell out the safeguards which should protect people detained by one of the contending parties. These rights and privileges, which are enunciated both in the 1949 Geneva Conventions and in the 1977 Protocols, cannot be subjected to restrictions because of the alleged terrorist activity of the detainees. Terrorist acts, if they are proved, only entail

---

[8] See the European Court's judgment of 13 August 1981, in *Publications of the European Court of Human Rights*, A no. 44, p. 20, para. 49.

that their authors are responsible for war crimes or crimes against humanity, and shall be prosecuted accordingly (in case of civil strife the legal label of war crimes or crimes against humanity shall perhaps be questioned by scholarly authorities; this issue, however, is of such a magnitude that is should be deferred to another occasion).

Turning to situations other than armed conflict, I should also like to quote a dictum of the International Court of Justice in the Iranian case. In its judgment of May 24, 1980, the Court said:

Wrongfully to deprive human beings of their freedom, and to subject them to physical constraint in conditions of hardship is in itself manifestly incompatible with the principles of the Charter of the United Nations, as well as with the fundamental principles enunciated in the Universal Declaration of Human Rights.[9]

Admittedly, this statement refers to victims of State terrorism. *Mutatis mutandis* it can however apply also to people accused of terrorism and held in custody by State authorities.[10]

In short, on the face of it the question as to whether terrorists should enjoy human rights seems of easy solution: nothing can justify any act of a State which aims at depriving terrorists apprehended by police officers or other enforcement agencies of their basic human rights. In practice, however, a host of complex situations arise where one is at a loss to find a safe and clear-cut answer in international standards. Let me give two illustrations. They are taken from two troubled countries (the Federal Republic of Germany and Italy) where terrorism is, or has been, a household occurrence, without, however, reaching the 'threshold' of a 'non-international armed conflict' under Art. 3 common to the 1949 Geneva Conventions.

As for the Federal Republic of Germany, I shall refer to two well-known cases brought before the European Commission of Human Rights. Both cases[11]

---

[9] ICJ, *Reports 1980,* p. 42, para. 91.

[10] It is necessary briefly to mention the multilateral conventions on various forms of terrorism, concluded under the aegis of certain International Organizations. Thus, the UN Convention on the Prevention and Punishment of Crimes against Internationally Protected Persons of 1973 provides in Art. 9 that person accused of terrorism shall enjoy the right to a fair trial—a provision modelled on Art. 4 and 8 *c* of the Washington Convention on terrorism concluded under the auspices of the OAS in 1971. In addition, the European Convention on the Suppression of Terrorism of 1977, like other similar international treaties, allows States to refuse extradition or judicial assistance when a request to this effect has been made 'for the purpose of prosecuting or punishing a person on account of his race, religion, nationality or political opinion' (Art. 5 and 8 para. 2).

[11] See the decision of May 30, 1975 (application no. 6166/73), in *Yearbook of the European Convention on Human Rights,* 1975, p. 132ff.; and the decision of July 8, 1978 (applications nos. 7352/76, 7586/76 and 7587/76), in *Yearbook of the European Convention on Human Rights,* 1978, p. 418ff.

See thereon: BAKKER SCHUT, *Political Justice in the Federal Republic of Germany,* in *Nederlands Juristendblad,* 1975, p. 203ff.; KUNDOCH, *Human Rights in Prison, with Special Reference to the Baader-Meinhof case,* in *Grundrechte,* 1976, p. 54ff.; LANDREVILLE, *Les détenus et les droits de l'homme,* in *Revue de droit pénal et de criminologie,* 1978, p. 387ff.

involved members of the so-called Red Army Faction or Baader-Meinhof Gang (*Rote Armee Faktion*). In both cases the applicants complained that while in detention on remand or serving a sentence imposed on an earlier conviction, the German prison authorities had subjected them to the torture of isolation by cutting them off from all contacts both inside and outside the prison. In the second case, which was decided upon after the three applicants (Gudrun Ensslin, Andreas Baader and Jan Raspe) had committed suicide in prison, the complaints were more numerous. For the purposes of this paper I shall refer mainly to this second case. The applicants argued that they were subjected to exceptional conditions of detention, causing them to undergo considerable physical, psychological and mental suffering, the scale and consequence of which were attested in authoritative medical reports. They also contended that they had not had a fair trial, above all because their defence was systematically annihilated. In particular, they stressed the fact that three of the four principal lawyers to whom they had entrusted their defence had been debarred from defence on the suspicion of belonging to the criminal organization of their clients. In addition, when it had become apparent that the defendants were unable to follow the discussion in the hearings for more than three hours because of their mental and physical conditions, the German Court of Appeal had decided to continue the hearing in their absence, on the ground that the accused had by their own actions (hunger strikes, refusal of any therapy administered by the prison doctors) brought themselves to a state precluding their attendance at the hearings. Furthermore, the applicants claimed that the members of the Court of Appeal and particularly the President of its Chamber in charge of the proceedings were not independent and impartial.

The European Commission of Human Rights dismissed all the applications in both cases. It gave detailed reasons to this effect. As for the exceptional conditions of the defendants' detention, the Commission held that they were justified for security reasons and did not amount to inhuman treatment, for the accused were subjected to short periods of isolation and in addition they were never subjected to 'complete sensory isolation coupled with complete social isolation' (which, in the Commission's view, could no doubt 'destroy the personality' of detainees, thus constituting a form of inhuman treatment). As for the very serious mental and physical conditions of the detainees, the Commission held that emotional disturbance, disturbance in comprehension and ability to think, infantile regressive changes in their mode of life and difficulty in making social contacts were all aspects of a reversible syndrome that can often be found at the end of a period of four to six years' ordinary imprisonment; consequently, the conditions of the applicants did not show that they had been deliberately subjected to a range of physical or mental suffering designed to punish them, to destroy their personality or to break down their resistance.

As for the conduct of the trial, the Commission held that the German authorities had not broken the relevant provisions of the European Convention. In particular, the Commission stressed that the German judge whose impartiality had been called into question by the accused, had been objected to successfully: shortly before the delivery of the judgment, the President of the Court of Appeal's Chamber had been replaced, following his 85th challenge. Regarding the exclusion of three defence lawyers from the case, the Commission pointed out that nonetheless the applicants were still represented by an average of ten lawyers, some of them chosen by the applicants themselves. In addition, the decision to continue the proceedings in the absence of the accused was justified by the need to avoid the proceedings grinding to a halt, without however placing the defence at any disadvantage.

It is apparent from this short summary that the Commission dealt with each particular submission in detail and in a rather satisfactory manner. Nevertheless, one cannot help feeling that the Commission, while it took a long and careful look at each single tree, ultimately lost sight of the forest as a whole. Indeed, in the case at issue each particular complaint was possibly unfounded; however, their *cumulative effect* was striking. The picture of the behaviour of the German prison authorities and courts, resulting from the judgment, is one of gross misbehaviour and biased treatment. Granted that the accused were uniquely dangerous and that there was sound evidence of very grave criminal offences, one may wonder whether this warranted a reaction of the State authorities that was abnormal, to say the least, and therefore either violated the Convention or was on the border-line of doing so.

Let me now very briefly refer to Italy, a country where lately terrorism has been in full bloom. There have been allegations that some of the terrorists detained after a recent spate of arrests have been tortured. Parliamentary questions to this effect were submitted by a few MPs.[12] It is difficult to say whether these allegations are well-founded, although it would seem that both enforcement officers and members of the judiciary tend to behave in accordance with the law (on February 15, 1982, before the House of Deputies the Minister of Interior dismissed the accusations of maltreatment and torture as unfounded, and stressed that at any rate an enquiry had been initiated by the judiciary).[13] It is, however, the law itself that could give rise to some misgivings, at least in some of its provisions. Thus, for example, a recent law on terrorism (Law-Decree of December 15, 1979 no. 625, made law in February 1980, no. 15) provides inter alia in Art. 10 for an extension of the admissible length of pre-trial detention and detention pending appeal. It follows that such detention can be as long as 10 years and 8 months (5 years and 4 months for pre-trial detention, and the same length for detention pending appeal). This provision was challenged before the Constitutional Court,

---

[12] For the text of the various written and oral questions see CAMERA DEI DEPUTATI, *Resoconto sommario no. 460* (seduta di lunedì 15 febbraio 1982), pp. 12–13.

[13] See CAMERA DEI DEPUTATI, *Resoconto sommario* quoted in note 12, pp. 13–15. *Ibidem,* at pp. 15–18, for the replies of the various members of Parliament who had submitted questions or interpellations.

which, however, in a judgment of February 1, 1982 held that the law is legitimate.[14] In the Court's view the great length of detention before the final conviction is justified by reasons of 'public security', by the 'objective difficulty of preliminary investigations and enquiries pending proceedings'. More generally, according to the Court, the 'special characteristics and the gravity of terrorism', which is 'characterized by its design to overthrow the democratic fabric of the State, by violence as a method of political struggle, by the very high technical level of terrorist action, and by the ability of terrorists to enlist recruits in the most disparate social strata', have brought about an 'emergency situation' requiring special legislation.[15]

To be sure, the Court has added a caveat by pointing out that the special measures should come to an end as soon as the emergency situation ceases, and that furthermore the Italian legislature should pass a bill rendering the administration of justice more efficient and rapid. Yet, despite these important qualifications the holding of the Court cannot but arouse apprehension. Under Italian law, as in most countries of the world, 'an accused person shall not be deemed guilty until convicted in a final judgment' (Art. 27 para. 2 of the Constitution). Is it therefore permissible to hold a person in custody for up to ten years and eight months without being entitled to consider him guilty? What if the *final* judgment quashes the previous convictions? The excessive length of criminal proceedings is inadmissible in cases where the accused is out on bail or in any case at liberty; the excessive duration of proceedings becomes *all the more unacceptable* when the accused is being held in custody. The European Commission on Human Rights has rightly held in a number of cases that the excessive length of proceedings is contrary to the European Convention (see e.g. the well-known *Huber* case).[16] Here, however, the European Convention and the case law of the European Commission and Court reveal some astonishing loopholes. Indeed, the two Strasbourg bodies have held in a number of cases that the provision requiring that detention on remand be reasonable in length (Art. 5 para. 3) only covers the period between the beginning of the pre-trial detention and the delivery of the judgment that terminates the trial in the court of first instance (*Wemhoff* case).[17]

In my view, the aforementioned Italian law is contrary both to the Italian Constitution and to the European Convention—if liberally and sensibly construed. Indeed, it stands to reason that it would be inhuman and contrary to all the basic standards on fair trial to hold a person in custody for more than ten years and then possibly conclude that he is not guilty. No satisfactory remedy

---

[14] Decision no. 15 of January 14, 1982 (text in *Publications of the Constitutional Court*, judgment no. 15 of 1982, pp. 1–23).

[15] *Ibidem*, pp. 9–10.

[16] On the *Huber* case see the European Commission's Report (application no, 4517/70), in *Yearbook of the European Convention on Human Rights*, 1975, p. 326ff., as well as the Resolution of the Committee of Ministers of April 15, 1975 (*ibidem*, pp. 324–326).

[17] See the European Court's judgment of June 27, 1968, *Publications of the European Court of Human Rights*, A no. 7, pp. 23–24, para. 9 of 'The Law'.

to this situation can be seen in the recent bill passed by the Italian Council of Ministers for submission to Parliament, with a view to providing compensation (up to 50 million lire) to those held in prison pending trial or appeal and subsequently found innocent. Money cannot easily compensate for long and unwarranted deprivation of liberty.

The Italian legislation referred to above is all the more disconcerting if contrasted with a bill recently passed by the Italian Parliament.[18] It greatly reduces the penalty for those terrorists who cooperate with the police and the courts, so much so that in some cases a terrorist accused of murder can benefit from the complete annulment of his penalty by a court. It seems to me that here the scale is tipped too far in favour of terrorists.

To sum up, it is apparent that are many borderline areas on which the law does not shed much light. It is this penumbra that causes the most serious problems, for it is often unclear how far State authorities can go in repressing acts of terrorism without themselves running the risk of breaking the law.

5. Can the Fight against Terrorism Justify Curtailments of the Human Rights of the Whole Population?

It is common knowledge that in many countries the government claims that as long as terrorism is raging, it cannot but suspend respect for human rights so that its struggle against terrorists may be all the more effective. Similarly, in a few European countries such as Italy and the Federal Republic of Germany, many political groups have urged the government to introduce a state of siege legislation suspending certain basic human rights. In addition, the need to eradicate terrorism in some foreign countries is one of the grounds on which certain great powers such as the United States, have decided to give aid and assistance to those countries, notwithstanding their appalling human rights record.

I submit that here too, international instruments on human rights provide useful suggestions and guidelines for the right path to be followed. On close analysis, it is apparent that *three main guidelines* can be inferred from the corpus of international law.

The *first* one is that restrictions can be placed on some specific human rights, provided however certain conditions are met. The UN Covenant on Civil and Political Rights is the principal international instrument by which one should

---

[18] See the draft bills nos. 1412, 1549 and 1562 in Senato Della Repubblica, VIII Legislatura; *Relazione della 2nda Commissione permanente,* nn. 1412, 1549 e 1562-A, as well as *Relazione di minoranza della 2nda Commissione permanente,* nos. 1412, 1549 e 1562-A bis. See also various statements made thereon by a few MPs, in Senato della Repubblica, VIII Legislatura, *Giunte e Commissioni, Resoconto* (seduta di giovedì 11 marzo 1982) and 395° *Resoconto* (seduta di martedì 16 marzo 1982). The law was enacted on May 29, 1982 (law no. 304, in *Gazzetta Ufficiale* no. 149, of June 2, 1982, p. 4024).

be guided. There, it is provided that 'public safety', 'law and order', 'national security' and the need 'to protect the fundamental rights and duties of others' are conditions that warrant restrictions on some specific rights. The rights on which limitations are permissible include freedom of movement (Art. 12), freedom of expression (Art. 19) and belief (Art. 20), the right of assembly (Art. 21) and freedom of association (Art. 22). Yet another requirement that should be fulfilled for restrictions to be legitimate is that they be provided for by law and not by administrative measures. By contrast, as I have pointed out above, no restrictions are allowed on such basic rights as the right to life (Art. 6), the right not to be subjected to torture (Art. 7), the right to liberty and security of person (Art. 9 and 10), the right to a fair trial (Art. 14 and 15).

The rationale behind this set of provisions is that dangerous social phenomena such as terrorism can warrant limitations on some specific human rights, provided of course they are not capricious and discriminatory. Conversely, those human rights which are intended to safeguard life and limb from the arbitrary interference of public authorities should not be tampered with, for restrictions on those rights might easily lead to abuses: the State authorities might ultimately behave just like those against whom they are fighting, by showing utter disregard for the basic values of human dignity. In other words, the philosophy behind the attitude of the Covenant vis-à-vis individuals and groups likely to endanger the democratic order is that the State should not give up its adherence to those lofty principles which protect the human person, lest it stoop to the same inhuman attitudes and behaviour as terrorists and other similar groups.

The *second* general 'directive' to be drawn from international standards can, again, be found in the UN Covenant. It is laid down in Art. 4, which lists the circumstances under which it is permissible to derogate from a whole set of very important provisions of the Covenant. That Article speaks of 'public emergency which threatens the life of the nation'. When such a situation arises, contracting States can take measures derogating from their obligations under the Covenant. However, 1) the emergency must be officially proclaimed, 2) derogating measures must be 'strictly required by the exigencies of the situation', 3) they must not be inconsistent with other international obligations of the State and 4) they must not be discriminatory.

It is apparent from the above that only when terrorism assumes such proportions and intensity as to threaten the life of the nation, may a state of emergency be declared. Consequently, not just any form of terrorism, however serious or odious it may be, but only those extreme phenomena involving a threat to the very life of the State, can justify a state of siege. The fact that this may *inter alia* involve the suspension of the right not to be subjected to arbitrary arrest or detention and the right to a fair trial, accounts for the need to regard the application of Article 4 as a measure to be taken only as the last resort.

I should like to add that the two aforementioned 'guidelines' that one can derive from international law should be taken into account not only by States which are parties to the UN Covenant, but also by those which are not bound by it. I submit that the general principles of the Covenant should serve as an authoritative source of inspiration for all States regardless of their formal commitments. Thus, for example, third States such as the U.S.A. could use the Covenant as a measuring rod when deciding if and under what conditions to provide assistance to countries beset by terrorism.

Let met add a few remarks on one very important point which deserves close attention. The application of Art. 4 of the UN Covenant normally implies that the State concerned acknowledges the existence of a situation of internal armed conflict under the Geneva II Protocol of 1977, or at least under Art. 3 common to the 1949 Geneva Conventions. It follows that all the safeguards against terrorism enshrined in either of these sets of rules (or even in both of them) shall apply. Thus, as soon as human rights standards are even partially suspended, humanitarian law comes to the aid and helps both to place restraints on terrorism, and to afford safeguards from abuses against terrorists' rights. We are confronted here with a telling illustration of how two different sets of international rules can 'cooperate' in curbing a dangerous phenomenon.

A *third* general 'instruction' that one can derive from international instruments is that the underlying causes of terrorism should never be neglected. As the UN Secretary-General put it in 1972, 'the roots of terrorism and violence in many cases lie in misery, frustration, grievance and despair so deep that men are prepared to sacrifice human lives, including their own, in the attempt to effect radical changes'.[19]

The need to examine the root causes of terrorism (be they social, economic, or political) was stressed both in the General Assembly and in the Special Committee on Terrorism in its Report of 1977[20]—although many States tended to be one-sided on this score, or to over-emphasize some undeniable historical factors such as colonialism, apartheid, international economic inequalities (it stands to reason that these phenomena cannot account for many forms of terrorism in Western Europe).

Despite the gaps and deficiencies of the UN instruments, the important lesson they teach is that States should not confine themselves to combating terrorists by force and violence; they should also endeavour to understand the objective socio-economic and political causes which bring about that distorted and perverted reaction which is terrorism. It is a truism that terrorism flourishes where social and economic inequalities, political instability, or widespread oppression create conditions propitious to indignation and revolt. It follows that in the long run the solution to the problem cannot but lie in curing those ills which gave terrorists their first foothold, and eliminating their *raison d'être*.

---

[19] Note of September 8, 1972, UN doc. A/8791 and Add. 1 Corr. 1, summarized in *Yearbook of the United Nations*, 1972, p. 640.
[20] GAOR, XXXIInd Session, Suppl. no. 37 (A/32/37), para. 10.

6. Conclusions

To sum up, I shall advance the following propositions. First, international stand-ards on human rights permit rebellion to oppression, as a last resort, namely on two conditions, that the target of rebellious acts be an authoritarian government denying the basic human rights, and that no democratic and peaceful means of change be available. However, international standards on human rights as well as humanitarian law do not allow rebels to trespass upon the human rights of innocent people. Even in cases where the goal of their political and military struggle is expressly regarded as legitimate by the international community, i.e. in cases of wars of national liberation, resort to terrorist methods is not permit-ted. International law is strict on the subject. It considers terrorism a *perversion* of the right of rebellion. It should be noted that human rights standards put a ban on terrorism, whatever the circumstances in which it occurs; international humanitarian law, for its part, is specifically directed to strengthen and specify that ban with respect to special circumstances, i.e. internal armed conflict, wars of national liberation and wars between States. Human rights law and humani-tarian law lend each other a hand, as it were, in that they combine to eliminate any possible gap or loophole in the international legal regulation of terrorism.

Secondly, no matter how atrocious and loathsome acts of terrorism may be, their authors must benefit from the basic human rights upon capture; in particu-lar, they should enjoy the right to lawful detention and the right to a fair trial.

Thirdly, terrorism ought not to be used as a pretext for seriously curtailing human rights. Restrictions on human rights for the purpose of a more efficient fight against terrorism can only be warranted under very strict conditions and provided basic human rights (both of the whole population and of terrorists themselves) are not infringed. Large-scale derogations from international under-takings concerning human rights are permissible under exceptional circum-stances, i.e. when a state of siege is formally declared. Again, even in these cases some fundamental safeguards provided for both in human rights standards and in humanitarian law must not be jettisoned, and exceptional measures should be commensurate with the situation of emergency.

In short, international law makes it clear that States must react to terrorism without turning savage themselves; they are always to maintain a humane coun-tenance. To this end, they should endeavour to understand and eliminate the causes of social sickness on which terrorism thrives, and which it aggravates rather than cures.

These propositions reflect, I submit, the status of international law as it now stands and the position that the world community has adopted towards the hein-ous phenomenon under discussion. I have endeavoured to show in this paper that there are however a great many situations where international standards do not prove very helpful. There are borderline areas on which law does not cast much light and where States consequently retain a lot of discretionary power—a power that they of course may easily abuse, albeit for the unquestionably commendable purpose of eradicating terrorism. An attempt has been made in the present essay to show that in these areas either a liberal interpretation or the progressive development of international norms might often prove conducive to solutions that strike a balance between the demands of security and protection of the human rights of victims (or prospective victims) of terrorism, on the one side, and the need for States not to fall into the trap of misbehaving for the sake of fighting the gross misconduct of terrorists, on the other.

22. Terrorism is also Disrupting Some Crucial Legal Categories of International Law*

1. Introduction

The terrorist attack of 11 September has had atrocious effects not only at the human, psychological and political level. It is also having shattering consequences for international law. It is subverting some important legal categories, thereby imposing the need to rethink them, on the one hand, and to lay emphasis on general principles, on the other.

I shall not dwell on the use of the term 'war' by the American President and the whole US administration. It is obvious that in this case 'war' is a misnomer. War is an armed conflict between two or more states. Here we are confronted with an extremely serious terrorist attack by a non-state organization against a state. Admittedly, the use of the term 'war' has a huge psychological impact on public opinion. It is intended to emphasize both that the attack is so serious that it can be equated in its evil effects with a state aggression, and also that the necessary response exacts reliance on all resources and energies, as if in a state of war.

I shall rather discuss two other issues: the legal characterization of the terrorist attack from the viewpoint of international criminal law, and the question of what sort of forcible action international law permits the US to take, and against whom.

2. The Definition of Terrorism: A Crime against Humanity?

So far, terrorist attacks have usually been defined as serious offences, to be punished under national legislation by national courts. The numerous international treaties on the matter oblige the contracting states to engage in judicial cooperation for the repression of those offences. In my opinion, it may be safely contended that, in addition, at least trans-national, state-sponsored or state-condoned terrorism amounts to an international crime, and is already contemplated and prohibited by international customary law as a distinct category of such crimes.

Be that as it may, it is a fact that, when some states, in particular Algeria, India, Sri Lanka and Turkey, proposed that terrorism be considered as one of the international crimes to be subjected to the jurisdiction of the International Criminal

* Originally published as 12 *European Journal of International Law* (2001) 993.

Court (ICC), namely as a crime against humanity,[1] many states including the US opposed such proposal essentially on four grounds: (i) the offence was not well defined; (ii) in their view the inclusion of this crime would politicize the Court; (iii) some acts of terrorism were not sufficiently serious to warrant prosecution by an international tribunal; (iv) generally speaking, prosecution and punishment by national courts were considered more efficient than by international tribunals. Many developing countries also opposed the proposal for they felt that the Statute should distinguish between terrorism and the struggle of peoples under foreign or colonial domination for self-determination and independence. As a result, both that proposal and a later one by India, Sri Lanka and Turkey[2] were rejected. Recent cases are in line with this cautious attitude. In 1984, in *Tel Oren v. Libyan Arab Republic,* the Court of Appeals of the District of Columbia held[3] that since there is no agreement on the definition of terrorism as an international crime under customary international law, this offence does not attract universal jurisdiction. Recently, on 13 March 2001, in a serious case of terrorism allegedly involving Ghaddafi, the French Court of Cassation held that terrorism was not an international crime entailing the lifting of immunity for heads of state; it therefore quashed proceedings initiated against the Libyan leader.[4]

The terrorist attack of 11 September has been defined as a crime against humanity by a prominent French jurist and former Minister of Justice, Robert Badinter, by the UN Secretary-General Kofi Annan, as well as by the UN High Commissioner for Human Rights, Mary Robinson.[5] Distinguished international lawyers have taken the same view.[6] Indeed, that atrocious action exhibits all the hallmarks of crimes against humanity: the magnitude and extreme gravity of the attack as well as the fact that it targeted civilians, is an affront to all humanity, and part of a widespread or systematic practice.

It may happen that states gradually come to share this characterization and consider serious crimes of terrorism as falling under crimes against humanity (in particular, under the subcategories of 'murder' or 'extermination' or 'other inhumane acts' included in Article 7 of the ICC Statute). If this occurs, the notion of crimes against humanity would be broadened. However, the problem would then arise of (i) the specific conditions under which terrorist attacks fall under this notion, and of (ii) whether the future ICC would be authorized also to adjudicate

---

[1] See A/CONF.183/C.I/L 27.

[2] See A/CONF.183/C.1/ L 27/Rev 1.

[3] 726 F.2d 774 (D.C. Cir. 1984).

[4] See the text of the decision in *Bulletin des arrêts de la Cour de Cassation,* Chambre criminelle, March 2001, no. 64. at 218–9. See thereon the comments by Zappalà, in 12 EJIL (2001). 595–612, by Poirat in 105 *RGDIP* (2001), at 47–91 and by Roulot in *Dalloz* (2001) no. 32, 2631–2633.

[5] Badinter and Annan have made statements to the French radio and CNN respectively. For the statement of M. Robinson see *UN Daily Highlights,* 25 September 2001, http://www.un.org/News/dh/20010925.htm

[6] See for instance Alain Pellet, in *Le Monde,* 21 September 2001, at 12. Also the British lawyer G. Robertson, Q.C. had suggested this definition (see *The Times,* 18 September 2001, at 18).

serious cases of terrorism. It is perhaps plausible to contend that large-scale acts of terrorism showing the atrocious features of the attacks of 11 September, or similar to those attacks, fall under the notion of crime against humanity as long as they meet the requirements of that category of crimes (whereas no special account should be taken of one of the specific features of terrorism, namely the intent to spread terror among civilians).

3. Effects on the Law of Self-defence

The impact of the 11 September tragedy on the law of self-defence is more worrisome. Until that date, in spite of legal controversies among both states and scholars, the legal picture was sufficiently clear. In the case of an armed attack by a state on another state, pending action by the Security Council or in the absence of any action by this body, the victim could react in individual *self-defence,* until such time as the Security Council stepped in. The state aggressed could also request assistance of other states, who could thus act in collective self-defence. Resort to force in self-defence was however subject to stringent conditions:

(i) the necessity for forcible reaction had to be 'instant, overwhelming, leaving no choice of means, and no moment for deliberation' (according to the famous formula used by the US Secretary of State Webster in 1842 in the *Caroline* case and taken up by many for post-1945 self-defence);

(ii) the use of force was to be exclusively directed to repel the armed attack of the aggressor state;

(iii) force had to be proportionate to this purpose of driving back aggression;

(iv) the use of force had to be terminated as soon as the aggression had come to an end or the Security Council had taken the necessary measures;

(v) States acting in self-defence had to comply with the fundamental principles of humanitarian law (hence, for instance, respect for the civilian population, refraining from using arms causing unnecessary suffering, etc.).

Intervention of the Security Council was another possible reaction to aggression. The Security Council, being unable to apply Article 42 of the UN Charter for lack of UN armed forces at its disposal, could however *authorize* the victim of aggression as well as other states to use force against the aggressor (this, as is well known, was done in 1950 in the case of Korea, and in 1990, in the case of the Iraqi aggression against Kuwait).

As to the specific question of how to react to *terrorist attacks,* some states (notably Israel, the United States and South Africa) argued in the past that they could use force in self-defence to respond to such attacks, by targeting terrorist bases in the host country. This recourse to self-defence was predicated on the principle that such countries, by harbouring terrorist organizations, in some way promoted or at least tolerated terrorism and were therefore 'accomplices': they were responsible for the so-called indirect armed aggression. However the majority of states did not share let alone approve this view.[7] Furthermore, *armed reprisals* in response to small-scale use of force short of an 'armed attack' proper, have been regarded as unlawful both against states and against terrorist organizations.

The events of 11 September have dramatically altered this legal framework. On 12 September the UN Security Council unanimously passed a resolution on the terrorist strikes (Res. 1368). This resolution is *ambiguous and contradictory*. In its preamble it recognizes the right of individual and collective self-defence: however, in operative para. 1 it defines the terrorist acts of 11 September as a 'threat to the peace', hence not as an 'armed attack' legitimizing self-defence under Article 51 of the UN Charter.[8] In operative para. 5 the resolution expresses the Security Council 'readiness to take all necessary steps to respond to the terrorist attacks . . . in accordance with its responsibilities under the Charter of the United Nations'; in other words, it declares itself to be ready to authorize military and other action, if need be. Thus, by this resolution the Security Council wavers between the desire to take matters into its own hands and resignation to the use of unilateral action by the US. Probably the will of the US to manage the crisis by itself (with the possible assistance of states of its own choice), without having to go through the Security Council and regularly report to it, accounts for the ambiguity of the resolution.

On the same day, the North Atlantic Council unanimously adopted a statement where it relied upon Article 5 of the NATO Statute, which provides for the right of collective self-defence in case of attack on one of the 19 members of the Alliance. By so doing, these 19 states opted for the solution based on Article 51: they preferred this avenue to that of a centralized use of force under the authority of the Security Council.[9]

It would thus seem that in a matter of a few days, practically all states (all members of the Security Council plus members of NATO other than those sitting on the Security Council, plus all states that have not objected to resort to Article 51) have come to *assimilate* a terrorist attack by a terrorist organization to an armed aggression *by a state,* entitling the victim state to resort to individual self-defence and third states to act in collective self-defence (at the request of the former state).

The magnitude of the terrorist attack on New York and Washington may perhaps warrant this *broadening of the notion of self-defence*. I shall leave here in abeyance the question of whether one can speak of 'instant custom', that is of the instantaneous formation of a customary rule widening the scope of self-defence

---

[7] See, among others, Guillaume, 'Terrorisme et droit international', 215 *HR* (1989-III). at 405–406, where the author mentions the judgment of the ICJ in the *Nicaragua* case (ICJ Reports (1986), at paras 191–195, 205, 210–211).

[8] The references to the 'threat to the peace' and 'the right of self-defence' have been reaffirmed in the preamble of the subsequent resolution adopted by the Security Council on 28 September 2001 (res. 1373(2001)).

[9] NATO, press release 124 of 2001 ('The Council agreed that if it is determined that this attack was directed from abroad against the United States, it shall be regarded as an action covered by Article 5 of the Washington Treaty, which states that an armed attack against one or more of the Allies in Europe or North America shall be considered an attack against them all').

as laid down in Article 51 of the UN Charter and in the corresponding rule of customary law. It is too early to take a stand on this difficult matter. Whether we are simply faced with an unsettling 'precedent' or with a conspicuous change in legal rules, the fact remains, however, that this new conception of self-defence poses very serious problems. Let me discuss the principal ones.

So far, self-defence has been justified only *against states*, under the conditions set out above. As a consequence, the target was specified: the aggressor state. The purpose was clear: to repel the aggression. Hence also the duration of the armed action in self-defence was fairly clear: until the end of the aggression. Now, instead, all these conditions become fuzzy. Problems arise with regard to the *target* of self-defence, its *timing*, its *duration*, and the *admissible means*.

The issue of the *target* of the armed action in self-defence raises two serious problems. First, while in 'classic' self-defence the target is of course the state author of the aggression, now it is the terrorist organization that must be targeted: it follows that force may be used against the territory of the state harbouring such organization. This violation of the sovereignty of that state is legally justified by its aiding and abetting terrorism, or in other words by its breach of the international 'duty' laid down in various UN resolutions,[10] and incumbent upon any state, 'to refrain from organizing, instigating, assisting or participating in terrorist acts in another state or acquiescing in organized activities within its territory directed towards the commission of such acts'. Thus, aiding and abetting International terrorism is equated with an 'armed attack' for the purpose of legitimizing the use of force in self-defence. The second problem concerns the range of target states. We know that the entire network of terrorist cells making up the organization that allegedly masterminded and organized the attack of 11 September sprawls across as many as 60 countries. Could all these countries become the target of armed action? Definitely not, otherwise the armed conflict may lead to a third world war. But how can one delimit the number of states against which armed force in self-defence may be legitimately employed? (I shall try to answer this question below.)

In addition, traditional or 'classic' self-defence must be an immediate reaction to aggression; if the victim state allows time to elapse, self-defence must be replaced by action under the authority of the UN Security Council. Nor can the victim state resort to armed reprisals, which, as I said before, are held to be contrary to international law. In the case under discussion states seem instead to have come to accept a *delayed response*.

Furthermore, while it is fairly easy to define when 'traditional' self-defence must come to an end, in this case the *duration* of the action in self-defence may not be established *a priori* for, it has been asserted, the 'war' will take years.

---

[10] See General Assembly res. 2625-XXV, of 24 October 1970 (so-called Declaration on Friendly Relations), as well as Security Council resolutions 1189 (1998) of 13 August 1998 and 1373 (2001), of 28 September 2001.

Things become even more complicated as regards the *means* to be used. 'Classic' self-defence authorized resort to armed force against military objectives, within the bounds set by international humanitarian law. It would seem that now some states tend to legitimize any kind of resort to violence, including a vast range of means and methods that would even encompass extra-judicial assassination of terrorists or even the use of nuclear weapons. This may turn out to be a Pandora's box, setting an extremely serious precedent for the international community.

4. The Need to Rely upon the General Principles of International Law

These dramatic changes make reliance on the *general principles* constituting the foundation of the international community imperative and salutary. These principles, among other things, call upon states:

(i)   to pursue peace and refrain as much as possible from resort to armed violence;

(ii) to respect human rights;

(iii) to spare innocent civilians from belligerent action;

(iv) to settle disputes or resolve crises within a multilateral framework, that is by refraining to act unilaterally, so as to limit arbitrary reactions as much as possible;

(v)   to pursue justice and consequently repress international crimes by bringing the alleged culprits to court.

These principles may serve to restrain the use of force and prevent its spawning violent reactions capable of undermining the very foundations of the international community.

The US initially code-named its action 'infinite justice'. Thus it laid emphasis on making justice rather than taking revenge or engaging in tit-for-tat action. It is suggested that to be consistent and to comply with the existing legal principles of the international community, the action by the US should proceed as much as possible along the following lines:

(i)   It should use unilateral action as little as possible. In the resolutions they have adopted on 12 September 2001, the UN Security Council (Res. 1368) and the General Assembly (Res. 56/1) clearly (and rightly) stressed the need for *concerted and multilateral action*.[11] In the same vein the Security

---

[11] The Security Council called upon 'all States to work together urgently to bring to justice the perpetrators, organizers and sponsors' (operative para. 3), called upon the international community 'to redouble their efforts to prevent and suppress terrorist acts including by increased cooperation' (operative para. 4) and expressed 'its readiness to take all necessary steps to respond to the terrorist acts' (operative para. 5). The General Assembly in paras 3 and 4 urgently called for

Council, in Resolution 1373 unanimously adopted on 28 September 2001, rightly decided on a set of measures all states are obliged to take under Chapter VII to suppress terrorism. The Security Council is thus emphasizing its own authority and the need for collective action. Within this framework, it would seem that, although (subject to the conditions set out below) the US need not require the authorization of the Security Council to take military action, it should at least report to it immediately and, so far as possible, request that body to direct at least some of the military or economic responses to the terrorist attack.

(ii) As has been asserted, there is strong evidence suggesting that the terrorist organization that planned and executed the attacks is headquartered in Afghanistan. Since this state has long tolerated the presence and activities of terrorist organizations on its territory and is not willing to cooperate with the international community for detaining the terrorists, its territory may become a legitimate target.

However, the use of military force must be *proportionate,* not to the massacre caused by the terrorists on 11 September, but to the purpose of such use, which is (i) to detain the persons allegedly responsible for the crimes, and (ii) to destroy military objectives, such as infrastructures, training bases and similar facilities used by the terrorists. Force *may not* be used to wipe out the Afghan leadership or destroy Afghan military installations and other military objectives that have nothing to do with the terrorist organizations, unless the Afghan central authorities show by words or deeds that they approve and endorse the action of terrorist organizations. In this last case one would be confronted with a condition similar to that described by the International Court of Justice in *US Diplomatic and Consular Staff*:[12] the terrorists would have to be treated as state agents and the Afghan state itself would bear international responsibility for their actions, with the consequence that the state's political and military structures could become the legitimate target of US military action in self-defence. In any case, all the fundamental principles of international humanitarian law need to be fully respected. Furthermore, as soon as legitimate military objectives are destroyed, military action must cease.

As for *other* states that allegedly host and protect terrorist organizations linked to the attacks of 11 September, it does not seem legally justified for the US to

---

'international cooperation', respectively to bring to justice the culprits and 'to prevent and eradicate acts of terrorism'.

[12] See ICJ Reports (1980), at 36, para. 74. The Court held that the Iranian militants who had illegally occupied the US embassy and consular premises, once their action was approved and endorsed by the Iranian government, became 'agents' of the Iranian state, which therefore became internationally responsible for their action. As the Special Rapporteur on State Responsibility J. Crawford rightly stated, acknowledgment and approval by a state of conduct 'as its own' may have retroactive effect (International Law Commission, Fiftieth Session (1998), A/CN.4/490/Add. 5, paras 283–4).

decide on its own whether or not to attack them.[13] First, the use of armed force against these states might expand the political and military crisis and eventually lead to a world conflict, contrary to the supreme goal of the UN (and indeed of the whole international community) to preserve peace and security. Second, self-defence is an *exception* to the ban on the threat or use of force laid down in Article 2(4) of the UN Charter, which has by now become a peremptory norm of international law (*jus cogens*). Like any rule laying down exceptions, that on self-defence must be *strictly construed.* It would thus seem that the US is not entitled to further select states as targets of its military action. Such attitude would run contrary to the concept of self-defence and to the aforementioned conditions, to which it is subject. We are not faced here with attack by five or six states on another state, legitimizing the victim immediately to react militarily against all the aggressors, which are states well identified by the fact that they have participated in the aggression. Instead, we are confronted here with attacks emanating from non-state organizations, which may be hosted in various countries possibly not easy to identify and, what is more important, whose degree of 'complicity' may vary. It would be legally unwarranted to grant the state victim of terrorist attacks sweeping discretionary powers that would include the power to decide which states are behind the terrorist organizations and to what degree they have tolerated, or approved or instigated and promoted terrorism. A sober consideration of the general legal principles governing the international community should lead us to a clear conclusion: it would only be for the Security Council to decide whether, and on what conditions, to authorize the use of force against specific states, on the basis of compelling evidence showing that those states, instead of stopping the action of terrorist organizations and detaining its members, harbour, protect, tolerate or promote such organizations, in breach of the general legal duty referred to above.

(iii) In addition to using military force the US should also aim at *bringing the persons accused of the crimes to justice,* by detaining them or inducing the states which host them to hand them over. Although of course the Americans are eager to have their own courts try the alleged culprits, the proposal [...][14] that those alleged perpetrators be handed over to the Hague International Criminal Tribunal for trial, after promptly revising its Statute, has much merit. An international trial would dispel any doubt about a possible bias (as has been noted, a New York jury 'would be too emotionally involved in the crime'[15]). In addition, an international trial would give greater resonance to

---

[13] This would seem instead to be the US position. According to the US Secretary of Defence D.H. Rumsfeld: 'Our response may include firing cruise missiles into military targets somewhere in the world...our opponent is a global network of terrorist organizations and their state sponsors...we may engage militarily against foreign governments' (*The International Herald Tribune,* 28 September 2001, at 6).

[14] See Robertson, *supra* note 6.

[15] *Ibid.*

the prosecution and punishment of the crimes allegedly committed by the accused.

(iv) If the US really wants to pursue justice it must not confine itself to repressive methods. This would be a short-term response. Things must be viewed in *a long-term perspective.* Justice also encompasses social justice, that is, eradication of deep social inequalities such as poverty, economic, social and cultural underdevelopment, ignorance, lack of political pluralism and democracy, and so on. It stands to reason that all these phenomena lie at the root of terrorism and contribute to fuel hatred and bigotry: as Kofi Annan recently stated, 'people who are desperate...become easy recruits for terrorist organizations'.[16] The US could promote a potent multilateral effort, lasting several years, to come to grips with these huge problems. In addition, it could promote the gradual solution of such festering questions as that of the Middle East.

5. Conclusion

In sum, the response to the appalling tragedy of 11 September may lead to acceptable legal change in the international community only if reasonable measures are taken, as much as possible on a collective basis, which do not collide with the generally accepted principles of this community. Otherwise, the road would be open to the setting in of that *anarchy* in the international community so eagerly pursued by terrorists.

[16] Transcript of press conference of President Chirac and Secretary-General Kofi Annan, 19 September 2001, at 4 (http://www.un.org/News/Press/does/2001sgsm7964.doc.htm).

23. Crimes Against Humanity: Comments on Some Problematical Aspects*

1. Introduction

It is well known that the 'laws of humanity' are a catchword widely used in international dealings. Reliance on this expression goes back to time immemorial. Judge Shahabuddeen rightly recalled in his Separate Opinion in *Tadić* (Appeal) that Thucydides mentioned them[1] as far back as 404 BC. To confine myself to the nineteenth century, I shall mention that reference to these laws or, more generally, to considerations of humanity, could be found in important instruments such as the St Petersburg Declaration of 1868 on explosive projectiles inferior to 400 grams.[2]

These references, however, merely constituted homage paid by positive law to natural law. No strictly legal consequence could be assigned to them. They simply amounted to generic and pious exhortations. States admonished themselves not to behave too ruthlessly in international intercourse.

Humanity as a *legal* notion was upheld in international dealings first in 1899 in the celebrated Martens Clause and then in 1915 through the condemnation of 'crimes against humanity'. In both instances the concept of humanity was enshrined in international instruments for political reasons, which were to a large extent extraneous to humanitarian considerations.[3]

In this paper I shall confine myself to the notion of crimes against humanity. After briefly tracing its history, I shall focus on some problematical traits that need to be clarified.

---

* Originally published in L. Boisson de Chazournes and V. Gowlland-Debbas (eds), *The International Legal System in Quest of Equity and Universality, Liber Amicorum G Abi-Saab* (The Hague: Nijhoff, 2001) 429. A very short introduction where the author explains when and where he met Professor G. Abi-Saab has been omitted [Editors' note].

[1] See ICTY, Appeals Chamber, *Tadić (merits)*, Judgment of 15 July 1999, at 150, para. 1.

[2] The last paragraph of the Declaration stated that: 'Les parties contractantes ou accédantes se réservent de s'entendre ultérieurement toutes les fois qu'une proposition précise serait formulée en vue des perfectionnements à venir, que la science pourrait apporter dans l'armement des troupes, afin de maintenir les principes qu'elles out posés et de concilier les nécessités de la guerre avec les lois de l'humanité.'

See also the *Manuel* on the laws of warfare, adopted by the *Institut de Droit International* in 1880. For instance, Art. 32(c) provided that 'des considérations d'humanité' were to restrict the bombardment of enemy fortresses, while Art. 86 stated that resort to reprisals should always be subject to respect for 'les lois de l'humanité et de la morale'.

[3] As for the Martens Clause, I take the liberty of referring to my paper 'The Martens Clause: Half a Loaf or Pie in the Sky?', in 11 *European Journal of International Law* (2000) at 187, also published in this volume, *supra* Ch. 2.

2. The Dubious Birth of the Notion

On 28 May 1915, following the mass killing of Armenians in the Ottoman Empire, the French, British and Russian Governments decided to react strongly. They therefore jointly issued a declaration stating that:

> In view of these new *crimes* of Turkey *against humanity and civilisation,* the Allied governments announce publicly to the *Sublime Porte* that they will hold personally responsible [for] these crimes all members of the Ottoman Government and those of their agents who are implicated in such massacres.[4]

It bears noting that the expression 'crimes against humanity' was not in the original proposal, emanating from the Russian Foreign Minister, Sazonov. He had suggested instead a protest against 'crimes against Christianity and civilisation'. However, the French foreign Minister Delcassé took issue with the reference to crimes against Christianity. He feared that the Moslem populations under French and British colonial domination might take umbrage at that expression, because it excluded them; consequently, they might feel discriminated against.[5] Hence, he proposed, instead of reference to 'crimes against Christianity', mention of 'crimes against humanity'. This proposal was accepted by the Russian and British Foreign Ministers, and passed into the joint Declaration. It would seem that the three states were neither aware of, nor interested in, the general philosophical implications of the phrase they had used. Indeed, they did not ask themselves, nor tried to establish in practice, whether by 'humanity' they meant 'all human beings' or rather 'the feelings of humanity shared by men and women

---

[4] Emphasis added. For the full text of the Note see the dispatch of the United States Ambassador in France, Sharp, to the United States Secretary of State, Bryan, of 28 May 1915, in *Papers Relating to the Foreign Relations of the United States,* 1915, Supplement, Washington (1928), p. 981 (the Foreign Office had requested the United States, in its capacity as a neutral Power, to transmit the Note to the Ottoman Government). For the French text of the Joint Declaration, see the Note of the French Foreign Ministry to the News Agency Havas, of 24 May 1915, drawn from the Archives of the French Foreign Ministry and published in A. Beylerian, *Les Grandes Puissances, l'Empire Ottoman et les Arméniens dans les archives françaises (1914–1918)—Recueil de documents* (Paris, 1983), p. 29 (doc. no. 41).

[5] It is apparent from the diplomatic documents published in the book just mentioned that the note was proposed by the Russian Foreign Minister Sazonov (see the Russian despatch of 11 May 1915, *ibid.,* at 23, doc. no. 29). The Russian draft referred to 'crimes against Christianity and civilisation' (*'crimes de la Turquie contre la chretienté et la civilisation'*); the French Foreign Minister, Delcassé, changed the expression into 'crimes against humanity' (*'crimes contre l'humanité'*), in addition to making another, minor change (*ibid.,* at 23, footnotes with an asterisk). The political reasons for this change, in particular for dropping any reference to Christianity, were set out by the French Ministry in a Note of 20 May 1915 to the British Embassy (*ibid.,* at 26, doc. no. 34: 'L'intérêt qu'il a à ménager le sentiment des populations musulmanes qui vivent sous la souveraineté de la France et de l'Angleterre fera sans doute estimer au gouvenement britannique comme au gouvenement français qu'il convient de s'abstenir de spécifier que l'intérêt des deux puissances paraît ne se porter que du côté des éléments chrétiens'). The two French suggestions were eventually accepted by Great Britain and Russia and the text of the Note was changed accordingly.

of modern nations' or even 'the concept of humanity propounded by ancient and modern philosophy'. They were probably only intent upon solving a short-term political problem, as is shown by the fact that no practical follow-up was given to their joint protest.[6]

Until 1945, this notion did not bear any fruit. It was only by virtue of the London Agreement of 8 August 1945, establishing the Nuremberg International Military Tribunal, that at long last it came to be fleshed out in an international instrument and subsequently in the judgment of the International Military Tribunal.

Thus the concept of crimes against humanity was gradually transformed into a legal notion endowed with all the technical hallmarks of legal constructs, and was increasingly laid down in treaties and other international instruments. Of no lesser importance is the fact that it came to be applied by international and national courts, which articulated and refined all its various legal ramifications and implications.

At present the notion of crimes against humanity is accepted as firmly established in customary international law. It has been restated in the statutes of the International Criminal Tribunals for the former Yugoslavia (ICTY)[7] and for Rwanda (ICTR).[8] It has been laid down in the Statute of the International Criminal Court (ICC)[9] as well. There is also general consensus on the basic content of the notion: crimes against humanity are those gross violations of human rights or humanitarian law that shock our sense of human dignity, and are part of a widespread or systematic practice of inhumanity. Under customary international law these crimes may also be committed in time of peace[10] (although some international instruments such as the Statute of the ICTY take a less broad approach and limit the crimes to time of armed conflict).

3. The Initial Timidity: Nuremberg

As emphasized above, the international prohibition of crimes against humanity proclaimed for the first time in the Charter of the International Military Tribunal of Nuremberg, annexed to the London Agreement of 8 August 1945,

---

[6] The Peace Treaty of Sèvres of 10 August 1920 also provided in Article 230 that the 'Ottoman Government' undertook to hand over to the Allies the persons requested by these Powers as responsible for the massacres perpetrated, during the war, on territories which constituted part of the Ottoman Empire; the Allies reserved the right to 'designate' the tribunal which would try those persons. However, the Treaty was never ratified, and its replacement, the Peace Treaty of Lausanne, 24 July 1923, provided for an amnesty for crimes committed between 1914 and 1922.

[7] See Article 5 of the Statute.

[8] See Article 3 of the Statute.

[9] See Article 7 of the Statute.

[10] See on this point the judgment delivered on 14 January 2000 by Trial Chamber II of the ICTY in *Kupreskić et al.*, para. 577.

Article 6(c) of the Charter, as amended by the Protocol of 6 October 1945, provided as follows:

[The following acts, or any of them, are crimes coming within the jurisdiction of the Tribunal for which there shall be individual responsibility:]
    CRIMES AGAINST HUMANITY: namely, murder, extermination, enslavement, deportation, and other inhumane acts committed against any civilian population, before or during the war, or persecutions on political, racial or religious grounds in execution of or in connection with any crime within the jurisdiction of the Tribunal, whether or not in violation of [the] domestic law of the country where perpetrated.

It has been explicitly or implicitly held by a number of courts and in the legal literature that Article 6(c) of the London Agreement simply crystallized or codified a nascent rule of general international law prohibiting crimes against humanity. It seems more correct to contend that that provision constituted *new* law. This explains both the *limitations* to which the new notion was subjected and the extreme caution and indeed *reticence* of the International Military Tribunal (IMT).

    As for *limitations,* suffice it to mention that crimes against humanity were only punishable if they were somehow linked to war: Article 6(c) indeed required, for crimes against humanity to come under the jurisdiction of the IMT, that they be perpetrated 'in execution of or in connection with' war crimes or crimes against peace. This link was not spelled out, but it was clear that it was only within the context of a war or of the unleashing of unlawful aggression that these crimes could be prosecuted and punished.

    The extremely cautious attitude of the IMT on the matter is striking. Six points should in particular be stressed. First, the IMT tackled the issue of *ex post facto* law only with regard to crimes against peace (in particular aggression) whereas it did not pronounce at all upon the no less delicate question of whether or not crimes against humanity constituted a new category.[11] Second, when dealing with *ex*

---

[11] However, probably, this was also due to the fact that in their joint Motion of 19 November 1945, Defense Counsel only invoked the prohibition of *ex post facto* law with regard to 'crimes against peace' (see *Trial of the Major War Ciminals before the international Military Tribunal, Nuremberg,* 14 November 1945–1 October 1946, (Nuremberg 1947) vol. 1, 168–170.
    Interestingly, the question was dealt with, with specific regard to crimes against humanity, by the German Supreme Court in the British Occupied Zone. According to this court:
[R]etroactive punishment is unjust when the action, at the time of its commission, falls foul not only of a positive rule of criminal law, but also of the moral law (*Sittengesetz*). This is not the case for crimes against humanity. In the view of any morally oriented person, serious injustice (*schweres Unrecht*) was perpetrated, the punishment of which would have been a legal obligation of the state. The subsequent cure of such dereliction of a duty through retroactive punishment is in keeping with justice. This also does not entail any violation of legal security (*Rechtssicherheit*) but rather the re-establishment of its basis and presuppositions. (Judgment of 4 May 1948, case against *Bl.,* in *Entscheidungen des Obersten Gerichtshofes für die Britische Zone in Strafsachen,* Berlin 1950, vol. 1, at 5 (author's translation).)
    See also the following judgments: 15 February 1949, *B and A* case, *ibid.,* at 297; 18 October 1949, *H* case, *ibid.,* vol. 2, at 232–233; 12 July 1949, *N* case, *ibid.,* vol. 2, at 335; 11 September 1950, *ibid.,* vol. 3, at 135.

post facto law, the IMT was rather reticent and indeed vague, as is apparent from, *inter alia,* the glaring discrepancy between the English and the French text of the judgment,[12] both being authoritative. Third, probably because of the awareness of the novelty of that class of crimes, the IMT tended to find that some defendants accused of various classes of crimes were guilty both of war crimes and of crimes against humanity (this was the case with 14 defendants). In other words, the Tribunal tended not to identify clearly the distinction between the two classes but preferred instead to find that in many cases the defendant was answerable for both. Fourth, the IMT held that no evidence had been produced to the effect that crimes against humanity had been committed *before* the war, in execution of or in connection with German aggression.[13] The IMT thus markedly narrowed the scope, *in casu,* of the category of crimes against humanity, although it asserted that it did so on grounds linked to the evidence produced. Fifth, in the only two cases where the Tribunal found defendants guilty exclusively of crimes against humanity (Streicher and von Schirach), it did not specify the nature, content and scope of the link between crimes against humanity and war crimes (in the case of Streicher) or crimes against humanity and aggression (in the case of von Schirach). Rather, the Tribunal confined itself to a generic reference to the connection between the various classes of crimes, without any further elaboration. Finally, it is striking that in the part of the judgment referring to Streicher, the English text is markedly different from the French. In the English text it is stated that 'Streicher's incitement to murder and extermination at the time when Jews in the East were being killed under the most horrible conditions clearly constitutes *persecution on political and racial grounds in connection with War Crimes, as defined in the Charter, and constitutes a crime against humanity*'.[14] By contrast, in the French text it is stated that Streicher's persecution of Jews *was itself a war crime as well*

Other judgments include elaborate reasoning concerning the distinction to be drawn between law enacted by the Occupying Powers and German law: see for example 21 March 1950, *G* case, *ibid.,* vol. 2. at 362–364; 21 March 1950, *M et al.* case, *ibid.,* vol. 2, at 378–381 (this judgment contains important reasoning in support of the view that crimes against humanity could be punished retroactively, at 380–381).

[12] In the English text, the IMT stated that 'the maxim *nullum crimen sine lege* is not a limitation of sovereignty, *but is in general a principle of justice*' (*Trial of the Major War Criminals before the International Military Tribunal, supra,* note 11, vol. 1, at 219; emphasis added), while in the French text it is stated that *'Nullum crimen sine lege* ne limite pas la souveraineté des États; *elle ne formule qu'une regle généralement suivie*' (at 231; emphasis added). Furthermore, the phrase in the English text 'On this view of the case alone, it would appear that the maxim has no application to the present facts' (at 219) does not appear in the French text.

[13] The Tribunal stated the following: 'To constitute crimes against humanity, the acts relied on before the outbreak of war must have been in execution of, or in connection with, any crime within the jurisdiction of the Tribunal. The Tribunal is of the opinion that revolting and horrible as many of these crimes were, it has not been satisfactorily proved that they were done in execution of, or in connection with, any such crime. The Tribunal therefore cannot make a general declaration that the acts before 1939 were crimes against humanity within the meaning of the Charter' (*ibid.,* at 254).

[14] *Ibid.,* at 304 (emphasis added).

as a crime against humanity.[15] Clearly, this wording reflects the position of the French Chief Prosecutor, François de Menthon, as well as the reservations and misgivings of the French Judge, Donnedieu de Vabres. These were set forth in 1947 in several scholarly papers in which the distinguished criminal lawyer argued that crimes against humanity simultaneously constituted war crimes and hence, the Tribunal did not breach the *nullum crimen, nulla poena sine lege* principle.[16]

4. Problematical Features of the Customary Rule

A. The Possible Authors of the Crime

A crucial question arises concerning the nature and implications of the link between an offence and a large-scale or systematic practice of abuses necessary in order for the offence to be characterized as a crime against humanity. The question can be framed as follows: normally crimes against humanity are perpetrated by state organs, i.e. individuals acting in an official capacity, such as military commanders, servicemen, etc. Is this a necessary element of crimes against humanity, that is, *must* the offence be perpetrated by organs or agents of a state or a governmental authority or on behalf of such bodies, or may it be committed by individuals not acting in an official capacity? In the latter case, must the offence be approved or at least condoned or countenanced by a governmental body for it to amount to a crime against humanity?

The available case law seems to indicate that crimes against humanity may be committed by individuals acting in their private capacity, provided they act in unison, as it were, with a general state policy and find support in their misdeeds in such policy. This is clearly shown by the numerous cases brought after 1945 before the German Supreme Court in the British Occupied Zone and concerning denunciations to the German authorities of Jews or political opponents by private German individuals.[17]

An interesting problem that may arise is whether crimes against humanity may be committed by state officials acting in a private capacity and without formal approval of their superior authorities. It would seem that in such cases some sort of explicit or implicit approval or endorsement by state or governmental

---

[15] 'Le fait que Streicher poussait au meurtre et à l'extermination, à l'époque même où, dans l'Est, les juifs étaient massacrés dans les conditions les plus horribles, réalise "la persécution pour des motifs politques et raciaux" prévue parmi les crimes de guerre définis par le Statut, et constitue également un crime contre l'Humanité' (at 324).

[16] See H. Donnedieu de Vabres, 'Le Jugement de Nuremberg et le principe de légalité des délits et des peines', in (1946–1947) 27 *Revue de droit pénal et de criminologie* at 826–827. See also his Hague Academy lectures: 'Le procès de Nuremberg devant les principes modernes du droit pénal international', *RCADI* (1947–1), pp. 525–527 (see in particular note 1 at 526).

[17] See the German cases cited in *Kupreskić et al., supra* note 10, para. 550.

authorities is required, or else that it is necessary for the offence to be clearly encouraged by a general governmental policy or to fit clearly within such a policy. This is best illustrated by the *Weller* case. This case, which seems to be unknown until it was cited by the International Criminal Tribunal for the former Yugoslavia in *Kupreškić*,[18] gave rise to six different judgments by German courts after World War II.[19] Given its significance, it may be useful to dwell on it at some length.

The facts, as set out in almost all the six judgments,[20] are as follows. In early 1940, in the small German town of Mönchengladbach (near Düsseldorf) various Jewish families were obliged to move together into one house; eventually 16 persons lived there. One night, in May 1940, three persons broke into the house. One of them was the accused Weller, a member of the *SS,* who was in civilian clothing; another wore the *SA* uniform and the third wore the blue uniform of the German Navy. They obliged all the sixteen inhabitants to assemble in the basement, then went to the kitchen, where they summoned, one by one, the 16 persons. There, the inhabitants of the house were ill treated.[21] The next day the injured parties reported to the Jewish community (*Jüdische Gemeinde*), which turned to the local Gestapo. The head of the Gestapo informed the wronged Jews that Weller's actions were an isolated event, which would in no way be approved. Thereafter Weller was summoned by the Gestapo and strongly taken to task by the district leader (*Kreisleiter*) of the NSDAP (the national-socialist party). It is not clear (nor was it established by the various German courts dealing with the case after 1945) whether in 1940 Weller had in fact been fined 20 RM for bodily harm, as alleged, instead of imprisonment for not less than two months (being the penalty which was usually imposed by German law for bodily harm). After the war, the case was brought before the District Court (*Landgericht*) of

---

[18] *Ibid.*

[19] See the decision of the *Landgericht* of Mönchengladbach of 16 June 1948 (unpublished), the decision of the *Oberlandesgericht* of Düsseldorf of 21 October 1948 (unpublished) and the decision of the German Supreme Court in the British Occupied Zone, of 21 December 1948 (in *Entscheidungen des Obersten Gerichtshofes für die Britische Zone in Strafsachen, supra* note 11, at 203–208), the decision of the *Schwurgericht* of Mönchengladbach of 20 April 1949 (unpublished), that of the German Supreme Court in the British Occupied Zone, of 10 October 1949 (unpublished) and the decision of the *Schwurgericht* of Mönchengladbach of 21 June 1950 (unpublished). The aforementioned decisions are on the ICTY files. It should be pointed out that, except for the three decisions that will be quoted in this article, the others deal mainly with procedural matters or issues of German law.

[20] This paper will, however, rely primarily on the *Landgericht*'s decision of 16 June 1948, at 1–6 of the typewritten text, for this is the judgment that most fully sets forth the facts.

[21] In particular, the judgment recalls that Weller questioned them on their particulars; after that the 16 persons were requested by Weller to reveal their buttocks and lie on a table. Eleven of them were then hit by one of the two uniformed men with a heavy leather whip, at Weller's command. The five persons not physically ill treated were among the oldest men or women. One of them, an old lady who had doggedly refused to lie on the table, was sent out of the kitchen by Weller, who shouted at her, calling her a 'Jewish bitch' (*Judensau*) (*ibid.*).

Mönchengladbach.[22] The court found Weller guilty of grievous bodily harm and sentenced him to 18 months' imprisonment. While admitting that he had acted out of racist motives, the court ruled that his action could nevertheless not be regarded as a crime against humanity. In this connection the court held that three requirements were to be met for such a crime to exist: (i) a significant breach of human dignity (this the court held to have been established in the case at issue, and lay in the ill treatment of Jews); (ii) the racial motivation of the offence (this could also be found in this case) and (iii) the action (*Tat*) must be perpetrated 'by abusing the authority of the state or of the police' (*unter Missbrauch staatlicher oder polizeilicher Macht*). The court found that this third element was lacking. It held that a crime against humanity must be 'either systematically organized by the government or carried out with its approval'. In the case at issue, one was faced with the 'occasional persecution of various persons by one person', not with abuses perpetrated by the 'holder of political power or at least by a person acting under the protection of or with the approval of [those holding] political power.' In short, the necessary 'link between crimes against humanity and state authority' was lacking.[23]

On appeal, the case was submitted by the Court of Appeal in Düsseldorf to the Supreme Court for the British Occupied Zone, which overturned the decision of the District Court and held that the offence did indeed constitute a crime against humanity. According to the Supreme Court, it was sufficient for the attack on human dignity to be *connected* to the national-socialist system of power and hegemony.[24]

---

[22] According to the judgment of the *Landgericht* (at 2), in December 1945 Weller was put in an internment camp because of his membership of the SS. On 21 March 1948 he was then transferred to prison as a result of a judicial arrest warrant issued on 22 September 1947 in connection with the indictment charging him with grievous bodily harm. On 12 May 1948 he was sentenced by the Court of Assizes (*Spruchgericht*) of Stade to six months' imprisonment for his membership of the SS.

[23] See the typewritten text of the decision, at 7–12.

[24] The court stated the following: 'Actions which seemingly or actually originated from quite personal decisions were also often and readily put by the national-socialist leadership at the service of its criminal goals and plans. This held true even for actions which outwardly were even disapproved of. The link, in this sense, with the national-socialist system of power and tyranny does in the case at issue manifestly exist. The state and the party had long before the action at issue made Jews out to be sub-humans (*Untermenschen*). Also the actions of the accused fitted into the numerous persecutory measures which were then imposed against the Jews in Germany or could at any time be imposed against them. *The link with the national-socialist system of power and tyranny does not exist only in the case of those actions which are ordered and approved by the holders of hegemony; that link exists also when those actions can only be explained by the atmosphere and conditions (Stimmung und Lage) created by the authorities in power.* The trial court was wrong when it attached decisive value to the fact that the accused after his action was 'rebuked' and that even the Gestapo disapproved of the excess as an isolated infringement (*Einzelübergriff*). Nevertheless *this action fitted into the persecution of Jews effected by the state and the party.* This is proved in and of itself by the fact that the accused, admitting that he was the subject of an order of summary punishment (*Strafbefehl*) or a criminal measure (*Strafverfügung*) for the payment of 20 RM, was not held criminally accountable in a manner commensurate to the gravity of his guilt. Given the gravity of the abuse (*Ausschreitung*), the harm caused to the victims produced consequences going beyond the isolated individuals and affecting the whole of humanity (*überindividuelle Wirkungen für the*

B. The Victims of the Crime

Another problematical aspect of the notion under discussion concerns the question of who may be the victim of crimes against humanity.

Article 6(c) of the London Agreement clearly prohibited two distinct categories of crimes: (1) inhumane acts such as murder, extermination, enslavement and deportation of *any* civilian population, i.e. *any group of civilians* whatever their nationality, and (2) persecutions on political, racial or religious grounds. Since the customary international law that has emerged in the world community is largely based on Article 6(c), it is fitting to look into the fundamental elements of that provision.

It is apparent from the wording of Article 6(c) that the *actus reus* is different for the two classes mentioned above. In the case of murder, extermination and other 'inhumane acts', they first constitute to a large extent offences already covered by all national legal systems and, secondly, are committed against civilians. As for 'persecutions', these embrace actions that may not be prohibited by national legal systems. In other words, such actions take the form of acts other than murder, extermination, enslavement or deportation.[25] Furthermore, since no mention is made of the possible victims of persecutions, or rather, as it is not specified that such persecutions should target 'any civilian population', the inference is warranted that not only any civilian group but also members of the armed forces may be the victims of this class of crimes.

For the purposes of our investigation, it proves useful to deal distinctly with each of the two classes of crimes against humanity, namely first with murder-type crimes and then crimes consisting of persecution.

i. 'Murder-type' crimes against humanity

This class embraces crimes that are perpetrated 'against *any civilian* population'. The words 'any' and 'civilian' need careful interpretation. As for 'any', it is apparent, both from the text of the provision and from the legislative history of Article 6(c),[26] that it was intended to cover civilians other than those belonging to the

---

menschheit)'. See *Entscheidungen, supra* note 11, vol. 1, at 206–207 (author's translation; emphasis added.).

The Supreme Court for the British Occupied Zone returned to this matter, albeit only fleetingly, in its decision of 10 October 1949 (unpublished), where it restated its position on the issue of crimes against humanity (see 4–5 of the typescript).

[25] For an elaborate definition of persecution as a crime against humanity, see *Kupreskić et al., supra* note 10, paras 567–636.

[26] See, in addition to the works of the Drafting Committee which worked out Article 6 (in *Report of R.H. Jackson, U.S. Representative to the international Conference on Military Trials,* US Department of State (Washington, 1949), pp. 22–211), the more enlightening notes and memoranda prepared by various United States organs, in B.F. Smith (ed.), *The American Road to Nuremberg—The Documentary Record: 1944–45* (Stanford, 1982), pp. 33–47, 113–117, 144.

enemy, who were already protected by the traditional rules of the law of warfare. In other words, by using 'any', the draftsmen intended to protect the civilian population of the state committing crimes against humanity, as well as civilians of its allied countries or of countries under its control, although formally under no military occupation.

As for the word 'civilian', it is apparent that it was intended to refer to persons other than lawful combatants, *whether or not* such persons were civilians fighting alongside enemy military forces. In other words, this phrase does not cover the categories of lawful belligerents envisaged in the Regulations annexed to the IVth Hague Convention of 1899/1907 (subsequently supplemented by Article 4 of the IIIrd Geneva Convention of 1949 and Articles 43–44 of the 1st Additional Protocol of 1977). The rationale for this relatively limited scope of Article 6(c) is that *enemy* combatants were already protected by the traditional laws of warfare, while it was deemed unlikely that a belligerent might commit atrocities against *its own* servicemen or those of *allied* countries. In any event, such atrocities, if any, would come under the jurisdiction of the courts-martial of the country concerned; in other words, they would fall under the province of *national* legislation.

ii. 'Persecution type' crimes

As stated above, it is apparent from Article 6(c) that in the case of *persecution*, the victims of crimes against humanity need not necessarily be civilians; they may also include military personnel. This was stated implicitly in the *Pilz* case by the Dutch Special Court of Cassation[27] and explicitly by French courts in the *Barbie* and *Touvier* cases.[28]

---

[27] In the *Pilz* case, a German medical doctor having the rank of *Hauptstüurmführer* in the German army occupying the Netherlands had been accused of having (i) ordered or allowed a subordinate to shoot at and wound *a soldier* of the German occupying army (who happened to be a Dutch national by birth) and (ii) prevented medical assistance being given by a doctor and hospital orderly to the wounded soldier, thus causing his death. The Dutch Court of Cassation, to which appeal had been made, after finding that this offence could not be regarded as a war crime, but rather a crime within the province of the internal laws of Germany, pointed out that 'a doctor's refusing medical help and causing the killing of a wounded person, if proved, are appalling crimes, in violation of all humanitarian principles'. It then held that the offences at issue could not constitute crimes against humanity either, 'because the victim was not part of the civilian population of an occupied territory, nor [could] the acts with which he [was] charged be seen as forming part of a system of persecution on political, racial, or religious grounds' (Judgment of 5 July 1950, in *Nederlandse Jurisprudentie* 1950, No. 681, at 1210–1211; a very short summary can be found in *International Law Reports* (1950), at 391–392). Note that by emphasizing the non-civilian character of the soldier, this case seems to take a more restrictive approach to the permissible categories of victims than is mandated by customary international law and to that taken in the *Barbie* and *Touvier* cases. Nevertheless, it appears that had those acts taken the form of persecution on one of the grounds mentioned by the court, the offence might have been regarded as a crime against humanity.

[28] In the *Barbie* decision, rendered on 20 December 1985, the French Court of Cassation held that crimes against humanity in the form of persecution had been perpetrated against members of the French resistance movements (in *Gazette du Palais* (1986) 271–274, and 74 *International*

A perusal of the relevant case law relating to the notion of 'civilian' population, shows that two trends have emerged, one *restrictive* and the other *liberal*. The *restrictive trend* does not concern the question of whether the victims of the crimes at issue should embrace not only civilians but also military personnel. Rather, it relates to the issue of whether those victims may be nationals of the state concerned, or must be foreigners. In this connection mention may be made of a few cases brought before the United States Military Tribunals sitting at Nuremberg. In these cases some defendants had been accused of crimes against humanity for participating in euthanasia programmes for the chronically disabled or terminally ill. The Tribunals held that euthanasia amounted to a crime against humanity only if carried out against *foreigners,* i.e. non-nationals of the state practising euthanasia.

In the *Karl Brandt* case, the Tribunal found that the defendant had participated in a programme for the extermination of disabled persons, and that this programme had quickly been extended to Jews and then to concentration camp inmates (those inmates deemed to be unfit for labour were ruthlessly weeded out and sent to extermination camps in great numbers). The Tribunal stressed that it was difficult to believe Brandt's assertion that he was not implicated in the extermination of Jews or of concentration camp inmates; however, even if it were true, 'the evidence [was] conclusive that almost at the outset of the programme *non-German nationals* were selected for euthanasia and extermination.'[29] This restrictive view was also taken by the same Tribunal in the *Hildebrandt* case.[30]

Law Reports, at 136). The same view was adopted by the *Chambre d'accusation* of the Court of Appeal of Paris in a judgment of 9 July 1986 in the same case (*ibid.*) and confirmed by the *Chambre d'accusation* of the Court of Appeal of Paris in a judgment of 13 April 1992 in the *Touvier* case (74 *International Law Reports,* 139–140). It should be stressed that in both cases, the crimes at issue were held to constitute persecution.

[29] See *Trials of War Criminals before the Nuremberg Military Tribunals under Control Council Law no.* 10 (Washington, 1951), vol. 2, at 197. The Tribunal added that it had no doubt that Karl Brandt was 'a sincere believer in the administration of euthanasia to persons hopelessly ill, whose lives are burdensome to themselves and an expense to the state or to their families'. It then went on to state that: 'The abstract proposition of whether or not euthanasia is justified in certain cases of the class referred to is no concern of this Tribunal. Whether or not a state may validly enact legislation which imposes euthanasia upon certain classes of its citizens is likewise *a question which does not enter into the issue.* Assuming that it may do so, the Family of Nations is not obliged to give recognition to such legislation *when it manifestly gives legality to plain murder and torture of defenceless and powerless human beings of other nations.* The evidence is conclusive that persons are included in the program who *were non-German nationals.* The dereliction of the defendant Brandt contributed to their extermination. That is enough to require this Tribunal to find that he is criminally responsible for the program.' (*ibid.,* at 197–198; emphasis added).

[30] The lead defendant, Richard Hildebrandt, a high-ranking SS and police chief in Danzig-West Prussia, had been deeply implicated in many measures put into effect in the furtherance of the so-called 'Germanization programme'.

The Tribunal found that he was responsible for the kidnapping of *alien* children, forcing Eastern workers to have abortions; removal of infants from Eastern workers; the illegal and unjust punishment of *foreign* nationals for sexual intercourse with Germans; hampering the reproduction of

By contrast, a broad interpretation of Article 6(c) was propounded by the Supreme Court of Germany in the British Occupied Zone. This court held in at least three cases that military persons could be the victims of crimes against humanity even in situations where the crime did not take the form of persecution. In other words, the court held that the crime at issue could be perpetrated against military personnel even if the offence was not one of those envisaged in the second part of Article 6(c) or in the corresponding second part of Article II (1) (c) of Control Council Law No. 10. As a consequence, the notion of 'any civilian population' included in the first part of the provisions just mentioned was substantially broadened by the court. These three cases will be briefly summarized.

In a decision of 27 July 1948, the court pronounced upon the guilt of a member of the NSDAP[31] and the NSKK[32] who had in 1944 denounced another member of the NSDAP and of the SA[33] for insulting the leadership of the NSDAP. As a result of this denunciation, the victim had been brought to trial three times and eventually sentenced to death (the sentence had not been carried out because in the interim the Russians had occupied Germany). The court held that the denunciation could constitute a crime against humanity if it could be proved that the agent had intended to hand over the victim to the 'uncontrollable power structure of the [Nazi] party and state', knowing that as a consequence of his denunciation, the victim was likely to be caught up in an arbitrary and violent system.[34]

In the 1948 *P et al.* case, the same court applied the notion of crimes against humanity to members of the military. In the night following Germany's partial capitulation (5 May 1945), four German marines had tried to escape from Denmark back to Germany. The next day they were caught by Danes and delivered to the German troops, who court-martialled and sentenced three of them to death for desertion; on the very day of the general capitulation of Germany (10 May 1945), the three were executed. The German Supreme Court found that the five members of the court-martial were guilty of complicity in a crime against humanity. According to the Supreme Court, the glaring discrepancy between the offence and the punishment proved that the execution of the three marines had constituted a clear manifestation of the Nazis' brutal and intimidatory justice, which denied the very essence of humanity in blind deference to the superior exigencies of the Nazi state. In this case as well, there had taken place 'an

enemy nationals; the forced evacuation and resettlement of populations; the forced Germanization of *enemy* nationals and the utilization of *enemy* nationals as slave labour.

[31] *Nationalsozialistische Deutsche Arbeiterpartei.*
[32] *Nationalsozialistische Kommando Korps.*
[33] The *Sturmabteilungen* was a formation of the Nazi Party organized on military lines and under the immediate jurisdiction of Hitler. Its membership 'was composed of volunteers serving as political soldiers of the Party' (*IMT Indictment*, in *Trial of the Major War Criminals, supra* note 12, vol. 1, at 83).
[34] Decision in the *R* case, in *Entscheidungen; supra* note 11, vol. 1, at 45–49. The Supreme Court remitted the case to the trial court, because the requisite *mens rea* had not been sufficiently proved.

intolerable degradation of the victims to mere means for the pursuit of a goal, hence the depersonalisation and reification of human beings';[35] consequently, by sentencing to death those marines, the members of the court-martial had also injured humanity as a whole.[36] With regard to the wording of the relevant provision on crimes against humanity (namely, Article II(1)(c) of Control Council Law No. 10, which referred only to offences 'against civilian populations'), the court observed the following:

> However, whoever notes the expressly emphasized illustrative character of the instances and classes of instance mentioned there, cannot come to the conclusion that action between soldiers may not constitute crimes against humanity. [Admittedly], a single and isolated excess would not constitute a crime against humanity pursuant to the legal notion of such crimes. [However], it has already been shown [in the judgment] that the action at issue *can* belong to the criminal system and criminal tendency of the Nazi era. For the offence to be a crime against humanity, it is not necessary that the action should support or keep up Nazi tyranny, or that the accused should intend so to act.[37]

Finally, in its decision of 18 October 1949 in *H.,* the court dealt with a case in which a German presiding judge (*Verhandlungleiter*) had presided over two trials by a naval court-martial (*Bordkriegsgericlu*) against two officers of the German Navy: one against a commander of submarines (*U-Bootkommandant*) who had been charged with criticizing Hitler in 1944, the other against a lieutenant-commander (*Kapitänleutnant*) of the German naval forces, charged with procuring two foreign identity cards for himself and his wife in 1944. The judge had initially sentenced both officers to death (the first had been executed, while the sentence against the second had been commuted by Hitler to ten years imprisonment). The Supreme Court held that the judge could be held guilty of crimes against humanity to the extent that his action was undertaken deliberately in connection with the Nazi system of violence and terror.[38]

It should be added that the French Court of Cassation in *Barbie* held that the victims of crimes against humanity may include 'the opponents of [...] [a] policy [of ideological supremacy, manifesting itself in inhumane acts and persecution committed in a systematic manner], whatever the form of their "opposition" '.[39] In addition, the ICTY has placed a liberal interpretation on the narrow notion of victims of crimes against humanity upheld in Article 5 of its Statute (according to which those crimes can only be committed against 'any civilian population'). In its decision in *Prosecutor v. Mrksic et al.* (taken on the strength of Rule 61 of the Rules of Procedure and Evidence), Trial Chamber I held that crimes against

---

[35] See *ibid.,* vol. 1, at 220.
[36] *Ibid.*
[37] *Ibid.,* at 228–229.
[38] *Entscheidungen, supra* note 11, vol. 2, at 231–246.
[39] See the decision of 20 December 1985, in 78 *International Law Reports,* at 125.

humanity may be committed even where the victims at one time bore arms.[40] In *Kupreskic et al.* Trial Chamber II held that 'the presence of those actively involved in the conflict should not prevent the characterization of a population as civilian and those actively involved in a resistance movement can qualify as victims of crimes against humanity'.[41]

It is submitted that as a result of the gradual disappearance in customary international law of the nexus between crimes against humanity and armed conflict, so too has the emphasis on civilians as the exclusive class of victims of such crimes disappeared. For, if crimes against humanity may be committed *in time of peace* as well, it no longer makes sense to require that such crimes be perpetrated against civilians alone. Why should members of military forces be excluded, since they in any case would not be protected by international humanitarian law in the absence of any armed conflict? Plainly in times of peace military personnel too may become the object of crimes against humanity at the hand of their own authorities. By the same token, *in time of armed hostilities,* there is no longer any reason for excluding servicemen *hors de combat* (wounded, sick or prisoners of war) from protection against crimes against humanity (chiefly persecution), whether committed by their own authorities, by allied forces, or by the enemy.

This broadening of the category of persons safeguarded by the relevant rules of customary international law is consonant with the overall trend in international humanitarian law toward expanding the scope of protection of the basic values of human dignity, regardless of the legal status of those entitled to such protection. This trend has manifested itself in, *inter alia,* the adoption of international treaties protecting human rights and treaties prohibiting crimes such as genocide, apartheid, or torture, in the adoption of some significant resolutions by the United Nations General Assembly, and in certain pronouncements of the International Court of Justice. Nowadays, international human rights standards also clearly protect individuals against abuses and misdeeds of *their own* governmental authorities. It follows that there no longer exists any substantial reason for refusing to apply the notion of crimes against humanity to vicious and inhumane actions undertaken on a large scale by governments against the human dignity of their own military or the military personnel of allies or other non-enemy countries (or even of the enemy). It is worth noting that, had this expansion of the notion of crimes against humanity not occurred, a strict interpretation of the notion of civilians would lead in times of armed conflict to a questionable result. Some categories of combatants who, in modern armed conflicts (particularly in internal conflicts) often find themselves in a twilight area, would remain unprotected—or scantily protected—against serious atrocities. Consider, for example,

---

[40] Decision of 3 April 1996, para. 29.
[41] See *Kupreskić et al., supra* note 10, para. 549.

members of paramilitary forces or members of police forces who occasionally or sporadically take part in hostilities, etc. These are persons whose legal status may be uncertain, as one may not be sure whether they are to be regarded as combatants or civilians. It could therefore follow that, under a strict and traditional interpretation of the crimes at issue, and assuming that these persons were at the same time regarded as combatants, they would ultimately be unprotected by the prohibition against such crimes.

By way of conclusion on this point, the proposition is warranted that the scope of the customary rule on crimes against humanity is much broader than normally admitted. Those crimes may also be perpetrated by private individuals (provided the governmental authorities approve of or condone their action or this action fits into a general pattern of official misconduct). Furthermore, the victims of those crimes may embrace both civilians and combatants. In addition, such victims need not have the nationality of an enemy country but may belong to the country whose authorities order, or approve or condone the pattern of misbehaviour amounting to crimes against humanity.

It should be added that, however, the statutes of the ICTY, the ICTR and the ICC take a narrow notion of crimes against humanity, in that they restrict the victims of such crimes to 'any civilian population', thus excluding crimes committed against military personnel. This is a questionable development, particularly in the case of the ICC: this court does not deal only with crimes perpetrated in armed conflict; it is also endowed with jurisdiction over, among other things, crimes against humanity committed in time of peace. Legally speaking, the provisions of these statutes do not affect the status and content of customary law on the matter.[42] Nevertheless, in the long run the case law of these courts, together with the application of national legislation,[43] might end up having an adverse effect on customary law, by gradually bringing about a narrowing of the notion at issue. Hopefully the three courts, as well as national courts, will place a liberal interpretation on the relevant provisions, by construing them in the light of general international law.

---

[42] In the case of the ICC this is expressly provided for. Article 10 provides that 'Nothing in this Part shall be interpreted as limiting or prejudicing in any way existing or developing rules of international law for purposes other than this Statute'.

[43] A narrow notion of the victims of crimes against humanity is also taken in the French legislation. Art. 212–1 of the Criminal Code (enacted by Law No. 92–1336 of 16 December 1992, modified by Law No. 93–913 of 19 July 1993, entered into force on 1 March 1994) restricts the target of the crime to '*un groupe de population civile*'.

By contrast, para. 7 (3.76) of the Canadian Criminal Code provides that 'crimes against humanity' means murder, extermination, enslavement, deportation, persecution or any other inhumane act or omission that is committed against any civilian population *or any identifiable group of persons*, whether or not it constitutes a contravention of the law in force at the time and in the place of its commission, and that, at that time and in that place, constitutes a contravention of customary international law or conventional international law or is criminal according to the general principles of law recognized by the community of nations (emphasis added).

C. Whether There Exists a Power or Even an Obligation for National Courts to Try Alleged Authors of These Crimes under the Universality of Jurisdiction Principle

Let us now briefly consider another problematical aspect, relating to the question of *national* prosecution and punishment of crimes against humanity. The question can be framed as follows: does there exist an international rule conferring on states the power to prosecute and try such crimes, or even imposing upon them an obligation to do so?

As for the power to bring to trial persons allegedly responsible for those crimes, state practice shows that this power is not contested whenever proof is given of the usual links based on territoriality (the alleged crime has been committed on the territory of the prosecuting state) or on active or passive nationality (i.e. the perpetrator or the victim has the nationality of the prosecuting state). The question arises when such links are lacking and the universality of jurisdiction principle or, to put it more correctly, the *forum deprehensionis* principle is invoked; that is, jurisdiction is based on the presence of the alleged perpetrator on the territory of a given state.

State practice does not provide much assistance on this matter. So far crimes against humanity have been tried by national courts of states on whose territory the crime had been committed, under the territoriality and possibly the passive or passive and active) nationality principles (think, for example, of the *Barbie, Touvier, Papon* cases). Or these crimes have been tried under special national legislation, as that passed in the United Kingdom, Canada or Australia, relating a specific set of crimes, namely those committed during World War II by Nazis, or else they have been tried under legislation enacted to implement such international treaties as the 1984 UN Convention on Torture. It would appear that the only case where a person has been tried for crimes against humanity in a state with which he had no links is *Eichmann*. Although this seems to be an isolated case, it is extremely significant that no state concerned protested against the trial: neither the Federal Republic of Germany nor the German Democratic Republic, nor the countries on whose territory the acts of genocide planned or organized by Eichmann had been committed, nor the states of which the victims of genocide had nationality. It would thus seem that states did not challenge the principle enunciated by the Supreme Court of Israel whereby 'the peculiarly universal character of these crimes [against humanity] vests in every state the authority to and punish anyone who participated in their commission'.[44]

---

[44] Judgement of 29 May 1962, in 36 *International law Reports,* at 287. See also at 298–304. The court concluded as follows: 'Not only do all the crimes attributed to the appellant bear an international character, but their harmful and murderous effects were so embracing and widespread as to shake the international community to its very foundations. The state of Israel

It should be added that the acceptance by states of the exercise of 'universal' jurisdiction by Israel is in line with the general principle enunciated back in 1927 by the Permanent Court of International Justice in the *Lotus* case: states are free to exercise their criminal jurisdiction over acts performed outside their territory, whenever there do not exist specific international limitations (provided for either in treaties or in customary rules) upon such freedom.[45] Indeed, one fails to discern any customary or treaty limitation on the power of states to try and punish crimes against humanity perpetrated abroad by foreigners against other foreigners.

More difficult is the question whether international rules impose on states an obligation to prosecute and try the authors of alleged crimes against humanity. An affirmative answer to this query has been given by some commentators.[46] It must, however, be objected, with respect, that their arguments do not seem to be compelling. To be sure, there exist a few international treaties providing for so-called universal jurisdiction: suffice it to mention the 1984 UN Convention against Torture, or the various treaties on terrorism (assuming terrorist acts may be regarded as crimes against humanity). By contrast, it seems difficult to prove the emergence of a customary rule imposing on states an obligation to punish

---

therefore was entitled, pursuant to the principle of universality of jurisdiction and in the capacity of a guardian of international law and an agent for its enforcement, to try the appellant' (*ibid.,* at 304).

[45] The court held that: 'Far from laying down a general prohibition to the effect that states may not extend the application of their laws and the jurisdiction of their courts to persons, property and acts outside their territory, it [international law] leaves them in this respect a wide measure of discretion which is only limited in certain cases by prohibitive rules; as regards other cases, every state remains free to adopt the principles which it regards as best and most suitable' (PCIJ, Judgment of 7 September 1927, Series A, No. 10, at 19).

[46] See for instance Condorelli, 'Il sistema della repressione dei crimini di guerrn nelle Convenzioni di Ginevra del 1949 e nel Primo Protocollo addizionale del 1977' in P. Lamberti Zanardi and G. Venturini (eds), *Crimini di guerra e competenza delle giurisdizioni nazionali* (Milan, 1998), pp. 28, 30, 36–37, 42; *ibid.,* 'La Cour Pénale Internationale: un pas de géant (pourvu qu'il soit accompli', (1999) *Revue générale de droit international public* at 19–21. It would seem that in the former paper this distinguished author derives the general obligation of states to prosecute and punish (or extradite) alleged authors of crimes against humanity and genocide (as well as war crimes other than grave breaches of the Geneva Conventions and Protocol I of 1997) not only from Article 89 of Protocol I of 1977 (in situations of serious violations of the Conventions or this Protocol, the High Contracting Parties undertake to act, jointly or individually, in cooperation with the United Nations and in conformity with the United Nations Charter), that he considers, in the wake of the ICJ Advisory Opinion on *Legality of Nuclear Weapons,* as part of customary international law, but also from the 'Nuremberg principles' adopted by the UN General Assembly as well as the UN Convention on Genocide.

In the latter paper Condorelli insists on the sixth preambular paragraph of the Rome Statute of the International Criminal Court ('*Recalling* that it is the duty of every state to exercise its criminal jurisdiction over those responsible for international crimes'). In his view this paragraph confirms 'the principle of universality of jurisdiction', that is the general obligation to prosecute and try (or extradite) alleged authors of international crimes who happen to be on the territory of a state.

this category of crimes. State practice supporting a contention to this effect is lacking. Similarly, no widespread *opinio iuris* or *opinio necessitatis* can be found. In addition, it would seem that no general international principle might be relied upon to warrant the proposition that such an obligation has materialized in the international community. At most, one could argue that in those areas where treaties provide for such an obligation, a corresponding customary rule may have emerged, or may be in the process of formation.

C. *Respondeat Superior* v. Subordinates' Liability

24. Abraham and Antigone: Two Conflicting Imperatives*

To the two German soldiers, shot because they refused to join in the massacre at Marzabotto.[1]

1. Abraham and Antigone: Two Archetypes

In the *Book of Genesis* we are told that God called Abraham and ordered him to take his son, Isaac, and go with him into the land of Moriah and offer him there as a burnt sacrifice. Abraham obeyed: he saddled his ass, called Isaac and two young servants, gathered wood for the sacrifice and went unto the place God had commanded him. When, after three days, they came to the mountain, he told the young men to wait, loaded Isaac with the wood, took torch and knife and together they walked up towards the appointed place. Isaac then asked where the sacrificial lamb was; Abraham answered that God would provide the lamb. When they came to the place, Abraham built an altar, laid the wood for the pyre, bound Isaac and set him on the altar and took the knife to slay him. Then, and only then, did the Angel of the Lord stay his hand ('Now I know that thou fearest God, seeing thou hast not withheld thy son, thine only son from me'). So runs the story in Genesis.[2]

Commentators dwell on how cruel a test God expects Abraham to pass to prove his faith. But there is something even more striking in this biblical tale. After receiving God's command, Abraham shows no hesitation in carrying it out: the most cruel command imaginable, one that contravenes all the laws of humanity and ethics: to kill his own son, his 'only' son. Yet Abraham never rebels, never

---

* Originally published as Ch. 8 of A. Cassese, *Violence and Law in the Modern Age* (Oxford: Polity Press, 1988) 119.

[1] In 1944, German troops commanded by Colonel Walter Reder massacred all the inhabitants of the small Italian village of Marzabotto, in the province of Bologne. Most of the 1,836 killed were women and children. The military action was carried out by way of reprisal for the attacks of partisans in the area. According to some eyewitness accounts, two members of the German troops refused to take part in the shooting of harmless civilians, and were executed by order of Colonel Reder.

[2] Genesis 22:1–12.

wonders whether the command is just, never berates a God who has forced him to commit such a wicked act. Except that he lacks the courage to tell Isaac he is himself the sacrificial victim and answers his query with a linguistic wile, avoiding the question and concealing the truth. Indeed, Abraham is the archetype of the man who 'obeys authority blindly', as the saying goes, who never for a moment questions the order imparted; he is the archetypal yes-man.

At the opposite extreme is Antigone. Two of her brothers have killed one another; one, Polynices, had led the assault on Thebes; the other, Eteocles, had defended the city. Creon, king of Thebes, forbids the burial of the former because he had tried to 'burn and destroy his fatherland' and rebelled against the power that held sway in the city where he was born. Creon wishes to inflict a punishment such as will be remembered by all those who spread 'anarchy' and try to 'demolish the houses', because 'great honour is given to him who upholdeth his country's laws'. As the sister of the two dead men, Antigone decides to disobey Creon's command: her love for her brothers, as well as the 'unchangeable' and 'eternal' laws that require us to bury the dead, she feels, override the orders of the authorities. Creon then condemns her to life imprisonment and Antigone kills herself. This, in essence, is the heart of one of Sophocles' most beautiful tragedies, one in which Antigone stands for all those who break the laws of the establishment to obey more humane imperatives. Antigone is the archetype of those who, caught in the dichotomy between an order from the powers that be and respect for higher values, choose the latter, knowing full well that they will be made to pay for their choice. It is no accident that Antigone is a woman. At the beginning of the tragedy, her sister Ismene refuses to connive in breaking the 'laws of the sovereign' and reminds Antigone: 'we are women; it is not for us to fight against men; our rulers are stronger than we, and we must obey in this, or in worse than this.' However, Antigone is firmly resolved to commit 'a holy crime'. Whosoever has to bear oppression day by day, but does so with moral strength and fighting spirit, is more easily led to revolt against a single injurious act, the last of a host of iniquities.

Abraham and Antigone are the mythic emblems of two possible 'answers' to 'superior orders'. Myth and poetry show, in sublimated and dramatic idiom, two kinds of reaction, both of them 'human', to the injunctions of rulers; they illustrate the alternatives 'invented' by mankind to solve a conflict that, in either case, must end in tragedy. But are these the only possible 'answers', or have people in their daily lives contrived other solutions? And has law perhaps proposed other ways to solve the terrible dilemma? We all know that during the last world war orders were given that were contrary to the most elementary respect for human dignity and that, later on, those who had carried them out, on being required to account for their actions before the tribunals (of their ex-enemies), excused their acts by claiming to have obeyed superior 'orders'. What did the tribunals ordain? Whom did they uphold, Abraham or Antigone? And how should we judge them today? Above all, how are we to behave if we receive an order (from a political ruler or a military superior) which we feel is contrary to moral tenets and to the highest legal imperatives?

2. Obedience in a Democratic State: Milgram's Experiments

Before taking a look at how 'law' responds to these questions, let us glance at how things work in effect, in our day-to-day lives. From this point of view, the experiments of an American psychologist Stanley Milgram, carried out between 1960 and 1963 on adults in the New Haven area of Connecticut,[3] are extremely helpful. Bearing in mind how during the Second World War numerous Nazis, on orders from their superiors, took part in wholesale persecution and slaughter, Milgram wanted to test, in rigorous experiment, the mechanism that induces individuals to inflict pain on others and discover to what extent we are conditioned by the 'commands' of our superiors. The technique he used in the experiments was quite simple: adults taken from different social classes and of differing cultural backgrounds were invited to the Yale laboratory to take part in a study on 'memory and learning'. The test, it was explained, was meant to ascertain the effects of punishment on learning. A 'learner' (an actor, though the person taking part in the experiment did not know this) was seated with his hands tied and electrodes attached to his wrists. His task was to memorize a list of verbal associations. The real subject of the experiment, the 'teacher', was taken into the room where the 'learner' was sitting and seated in front of an enormous generator with push buttons. His task was to make sure the 'learner' made the correct answers to his questions on verbal associations. For every wrong answer he had to administer an electric shock, starting with the lowest voltage and increasing steadily. The 'instructor' (one of the psychologists taking part in the experiment), dressed in a white coat, gave orders to the 'teacher' whenever the latter hesitated or refused to push the button to give the 'learner' a shock after a wrong answer. Naturally, the 'learner's' ability to memorize was a pretext; the real object of the test was to see to what extent the 'teacher' would inflict pain on the 'learner' obeying the 'instructor's' order.

Milgram's experiments proved beyond doubt that, despite the atrocious pain the 'learner' felt (or pretended to feel), in over half the cases the subject of the experiment continued to administer the shocks. As Milgram remarked:

The results, as seen and felt in the laboratory, are...disturbing. They raise the possibility that human nature, or—more specifically—the kind of character produced in American democratic society, cannot be counted on to insulate its citizens from brutality and inhumane treatment at the direction of malevolent authority. A substantial proportion of people do what they are told to do, irrespective of the content of the act and without limitations of conscience, so long as they perceive that the command comes from a legitimate authority.[4]

How can these results be accounted for? Milgram and other psychologists have underscored the essentially authoritarian role of the family, the school, the Church

---

[3] S. Milgram, *Obedience to Authority* (Yale University Press, New Haven, 1974).
[4] S. Milgram, 'Some conditions of obedience and disobedience to authority', *Human Relations* 18 (1965), p.75.

and the place of work; all these 'communities' instil in the individual respect for authority, the duty to bow to 'superior' orders, relieving his conscience from any sense of responsibility (from the earliest age when a father tells his child not to beat up children of his own age, not only is he teaching him the duty to respect others, but transmitting another 'hidden' message: a father must be obeyed by his child; this message becomes even more imperious, though more contradictory, when the father beats his child because it has beaten up other children). The interiorization of the hierarchical structure of the social groups in which we live helps us to accept orders even in 'conflictual situations', such as when we discover that by carrying out an order we inflict pain on others.

This socio-psychological context, with its serious consequences for national communities that are otherwise democratic, is obviously exasperated in authoritarian structures, such as the *armed forces* and, on a larger scale, in autocratic states.

These rapid observations should be borne in mind now that I am about to examine the 'response' of law, to inquire how realistic it is and, therefore, to what extent it is capable of guiding human conduct *effectively*.

3. Military Structures and the Question of Subordinates

In the international community the question of 'superior orders' has often been posed, but only or almost exclusively in relation to *military structures* and in case of *war:* when military commanders have told their subordinates to perform acts that were in fact criminal. What was the subordinate to do? He was faced with an awful dilemma: military discipline is based on obedience and on a scrupulous respect for orders from one's superiors; if a subordinate were to question and dispute an order, what would happen to discipline and relations between superiors and inferiors and to the military structure itself? On the other hand, may a soldier carry out an order passively, even though it obviously contradicts not only the most elementary moral tenets, but also the legal rules that regulate social relations? The subordinate is, therefore, trapped between dramatic alternatives—all the more serious because he is at war and, by carrying out an obviously criminal order, he may be punished by the enemy. In more general terms, the great English constitutionalist, A.V. Dicey,[5] observed that a soldier is obviously caught in a grievously conflictual situation:

The position of a soldier is in theory and may be in practice a difficult one. He may, as it has been well said, be liable to be shot by a court-martial if he disobeys an order, and to be hanged by a judge and jury if he obeys it.

The problem becomes even more complex with the addition of other circumstances: for instance, what should be done if an officer tells a soldier to shoot some

---

[5] A.V. Dicey, *Introduction to the Study of Law of the Constitution*, 10th edn (Macmillian, London, 1959), p. 303.

prisoners of war and, when his subordinate hesitates, draws a pistol and threatens to shoot him if he does not obey? To such instances of physical or 'moral' coercion one may add cases of 'ignorance of the facts' by an inferior. For example, an officer tells a soldier to shoot an enemy civilian and, when the latter wavers, explains that the civilian had illegally taken part in belligerent activities, thereby committing the war crimes for which he had been regularly tried; after the execution it is revealed that the officer had lied; in such circumstances can one hold that the soldier is also guilty?

These cases—none of them invented, because they all happened in fact—are further complicated by others. But it serves no purpose to add to the list. Let us now see how law 'responded'. Since it is formed by people under the impulse of both practical needs and the dictates of morality, let us see how law reacted to these two sources.

4. The 'Old' Law Begins to Crack

For centuries the principle of obedience to hierarchical superiors has held sway. Eichmann, speaking before the District Court of Jerusalem, called it 'the cadaver's obedience' (*Kadavergehorsam*), using an expression that echoed the well-known dictum of the Jesuits. The reason why obedience went unquestioned for so much of history was that people believed army discipline and passive obedience were intrinsic to military life. The corrosive acid of the doctrine of human rights had not yet eaten into these principles, suggesting the virtue of insubordination to orders that seem contrary to human dignity. For centuries, therefore, whenever responsibility for criminal acts had been detected and punished, this responsibility had belonged entirely to the *officers* who imparted the criminal order: the executors were protected by the maxim *respondeat superior*.

Leafing through legal decisions and the practice of states, the first example we find of a flaw in the principle of passive obedience comes from the United States. During the Civil War (1861–5), Captain Henry Wirz, a Swiss doctor who had emigrated to Louisiana and, 'carried away by the maelstrom of excitement' (as he was to write later), had joined the Confederate army of the Southern states, was given the command of a prison camp in Andersonville (Georgia). Here he contravened the current laws of war and maltreated the prisoners, keeping tens of thousands of Unionist soldiers in inhuman conditions; some of these were even tortured and killed (the statements of the 'survivors' and the eye-witness accounts given at Wirz's trial remind one of an *ante litteram* Rudolf Hoess—though, Hoess obviously had far more 'refined' means at his disposal in Auschwitz, as well as extremely efficient medical, bureaucratic and military assistance). In 1865, when the war was over, Wirz was tried by a military commission in Washington; he defended himself by saying he had acted on superior orders, because he had been merely 'a medium, or better; a tool in the hands of his superiors'. At this point the judge advocate objected that when an order is illegal, both the superior officer and his subordinate are guilty. His exact words were:

I know that it is urged [by the defense] that during all this time he was acting under General Winder's orders, and for the purpose of argument I will concede that he was so acting. A superior officer cannot order a subordinate to do an illegal act, and if a subordinate obey such an order and disastrous consequences result, both the superior and the subordinate must answer for it. General Winder could no more command the prisoner to violate the laws of war than could the prisoner do so without orders. The conclusion is plain, that where such orders exist both are guilty, and *a fortiori* where the prisoner at the bar acted upon his own motion he was guilty.

The commission accepted this argument and condemned Wirz to death by hanging. The execution, confirmed by President Johnson, took place on 11 November 1865.[6]

For a full understanding of the reasons behind this early breach in the solid edifice of military requirements one should remember that the trial was held by the victors against the vanquished, as well as the nature of the crimes attributed to Wirz. I feel it is apposite here to recall the distinction B.V.A. Röling, the great Dutch jurist, drew between two categories of war crimes. There is 'individual criminality', that is crimes committed by a single man (killing old people and children, rape, plunder, and so on); and 'system criminality', that is crimes of a collective nature: these are the unlawful acts of soldiers or officers, performed at the instigation or on the orders of the whole military structure and, if not of the political establishment itself, at least with the wholehearted approval of the state authorities, acts that include the use of forbidden weapons, the systematic bombing of a civilian population, large-scale maltreatment of prisoners, and so on. In the first case, the criminal act is the expression of the violent impulses of one man, seen by the army to which he belongs as a dishonourable act that discredits the whole armed forces; he is then punished without delay by the courts of his native country. On the other hand, 'system criminality', that is the actions of one man, dictated or approved by the whole collectivity, is punished—if ever—only by the *enemy* and only when the latter has *won* the war.[7]

Now, if we apply this essential distinction in the light of the historical facts at our disposal, it would appear that the case of Captain Wirz was one of 'system criminality'. The military commission in Washington only broke with the traditional principle *respondeat superior* because, as I have already noted, Wirz was a *former enemy*.

The next breach in the traditional respect for superior orders takes us right up to the First World War. In 1915 Fryatt, the British commander of the merchant

---

[6] The decision in the *Wirz* case is reprinted in L. Friedman, *The Law of War*, vol. I (Random House, New York, 1972), p. 783ff. The passage reported in my text is at p. 796. On the appalling conditions of prisoners at Andersonville, see J. McElroy, *Andersonville: A Story of Rebel Military Prisons* (1895), (Fawcett, New York, 1962).

[7] B.V.A. Röling, 'The Significance of the Laws of War', in A. Cassese (ed.), *Current Problems of International Law* (Milan: Giuffrè, 1975), p. 133, at 137.

vessel *Brussels,* flying the Union Jack, crossed the path of a German submarine, which ordered him to heave to and identify himself. Instead of obeying, Fryatt, on orders from the Admiralty to all merchant vessels in similar circumstances, bore down at full speed on the enemy submarine and tried to ram it. The submarine moved off to avoid collision and Fryatt got away. On another voyage, however, the *Brussels* was captured and Fryatt tried and condemned for war crimes (he was regarded as a *franc tireur,* that is an unlawful combatant) even though he had merely been carrying out superior orders.[8] The British commander's criminal action belonged to the category of 'system criminality'. His obvious violation of the laws of war (which only allowed members of the armed forces and a few other circumscribed categories of combatants to take part in the hostilities) and the fact that Fryatt was tried *by the enemy,* explains why the Germans ignored the circumstances that he had obeyed instructions from the British Admiralty.

However, after the war the Germans continued along the same lines, taking no notice of superior orders in a series of trials against German soldiers held before the Supreme Court in Leipzig (the Allies had wanted to try the Germans who had violated the laws of war, but for various political reasons the importance of these trials deflated and the job was handed over to a German tribunal, the Leipzig Court).

Of the Leipzig trials let me recall briefly those that are outstanding from our present point of view: the 'Dover Castle' and 'Llandovery Castle' cases.[9]

Underlying both cases was the Allied practice of using hospital ships for belligerent purposes (that is to transport munitions and troops), contrary to the laws of war. In 1917, to put an end to this practice, the German Admiralty had officially requested the Allied commanders of hospital ships to comply with the regulations, if they wished the Germans to respect their immunity. As it had not obeyed the German directives, the British hospital ship 'Dover Castle' was attacked and sunk by a German submarine whose commander, Karl Neumann, assured the Court in Leipzig that he had acted on orders from the German Admiralty. The Court decided—quite rightly—that Neumann had every right to believe those orders had been legitimate and that his actions were merely a reprisal against the British. Thus, Neumann could not be condemned, because article 47 of the German military penal code of 1872 only foresaw the punishment of a subordinate who carried out an order when that order was illegal, or when he overstepped the limits of that order. Although the Court did not declare the accused guilty, it did rule on the general principle that a subordinate is responsible for his acts if these are criminal, even when he is acting on the orders from his superiors.

In applying the same domestic law and the same general principle, the Court reached a different conclusion in the 'Llandovery Castle' case. This was also a British hospital ship, but it was illegally sunk because it was not in the area

---

[8] On the *Brussels* case, see J.W. Garner, *International Law and the World War,* vol. 1 (Longmens, Green, London, 1920), pp. 407–13.

[9] For the English text of the decisions in the *Dover Castle* and *Llandovery Castle* cases, *see American Journal of International Law* 16 (1922), pp. 704–8 and 708–24, respectively.

covered by the instructions of the German Admiralty. In this case Patzig, the commander of the German submarine, first sunk the ship and then ordered three of his officers to fire on the three lifeboats the English had launched, to remove all trace of the illegal sinking. Patzig disappeared after the war, but two of the three officers (Dithmar and Boldt) were arrested and tried. Naturally, they told the Leipzig court that they had merely carried out Patzig's orders. However, the Court turned down their plea and stated that the orders had clearly been unlawful because they contravened the laws of war. The Court stressed among other things that, so as not to have witnesses, Patzig had made his crew go below deck before he started to shoot the survivors; besides, the day after the sinking, he summoned his crew and asked them not to mention the shelling of the lifeboats, for which 'he, alone, would answer before God and his own conscience'; he did not enter the events in his log book; and, unluckily for him, the survivors on one of the lifeboats had been picked up and had denounced him.

The importance of this decision (for the first time a state court had condemned its *own nationals* for obeying an unjust order) is however reduced by three facts. First, the Leipzig trials were to a certain extent 'forced' on Germany by the victorious Allies. Second, Dithmar's and Boldt's offences were clear examples of 'individual criminality'. Third, the Leipzig trials were, in general, far from exemplary on the practical plane (the few offenders whose guilt was recognized were given ridiculously light sentences and almost all escaped from their respective prisons, apparently with the complicity, or at least under the blind eye, of the German authorities). However, in our particular case the fact remains that the sentence rejected the principle *respondeat superior*. If we are to appreciate its importance, we must remember that in the past the prevailing rule had always been that of *passive obedience:* this decision, together with the others I have briefly summarized, are all happy exceptions, the first signs of a tendency that was just beginning to emerge. We must remember that the rules applying to the British and American armed forces at that time punished *only the superior officers* who had given the criminal orders; they completely exonerated their subordinates from any responsibility. Thus, two such civilized countries as Britain and the United States, together with the rest of the international community, still allowed the exigencies of military discipline to prevail.

5. Nuremberg: A Turning Point

Things changed drastically during the Second World War. The massacre of civilians and prisoners of war, the persecution of the Jews, the gypsies and political opponents, had become a large-scale phenomenon. Above all, this was a *'policy' pursued by the highest Nazi echelons* (and on a lesser scale by the Italian fascists and the Japanese) with predetermination and perseverance, and applied by the whole military and bureaucratic apparatus. (One of the most ruthless Nazi criminals, Hans

Frank, responsible for persecutions and massacres in Poland, and subsequently justly condemned to death, declared, with a sudden flash of guilt to the Tribunal in Nuremberg: 'We have fought against Jewry; we have fought against it for years. And we have allowed ourselves to make utterances—and my own diary has become a witness against me in this connection—utterances which are terrible... A thousand years will pass and this guilt of Germany will not be erased'.)[10]

Collective criminality became possible because there existed an efficient bureaucratic structure, founded on a scrupulous respect for 'superior orders' and thus on order and discipline. It was the very existence of this modern administrative machinery that made the 'banality of evil' (H. Arendt)[11] possible, with the most inhuman directives being carried out promptly and efficiently. Thus we had the rapid, 'perfect' construction of concentration camps; the impeccable transport by rail of civilians and prisoners of war to forced labour camps; the meticulous bureaucratic slaughter of thousands and thousands of Jews. The whole military and bureaucratic apparatus, as well as the German population itself, obeyed and kept silent (fortunately there were exceptions: among these the bishop M. Niemöller and the 'White Rose' group). All the directives came from above and everyone obeyed them: it is the *Führerprinzip,* a monstrous hypertrophy of the maxim *respondeat superior,* which was made possible by the pyramidal structure of the totalitarian state and by the systematic elimination of any pocket of political and moral resistance. The crimes requested by the directives of the dictator and the Nazi leaders naturally belong to 'collective or system criminality': such was their nature that it would have been impossible to punish them by using the courts of the state to which the perpetrators belonged. Only an adversary could have made sure that justice was done, after first winning the war, that is.

Thus the Allies felt duty bound to find a new remedy. Since the criminal actions had spilled over from the traditional offences (war crimes) into an area that had previously been protected by the tenets of morality and respect for human dignity (or at least diplomatic prudence), there was now the unhappy need to 'invent' *new juridical categories:* those of 'crimes against humanity' (racial, religious or political persecution; the extermination or deportation of non-enemy populations, for example the populations of allies) and of 'crimes against peace' (wars of aggression; criminal plans to attack peace-abiding states).

But this was not enough. The *Führerprinzip* and the postulate that every order must be carried out without fail (*Befehl ist Befehl,* or an order is an order: what a sinister tautology!), can create an *unsurmountable barrier,* protecting the thousands of politicians, industrialists, bureaucrats and military men who at all levels applied to varying effect, but almost always with zeal, the Führer's inhuman directives. It was essential to shatter this barrier. The colossal scale at which

---

[10] *Trial of Major War Criminals before the International Military Tribunal,* Nuremberg 14 November 1945–1 October 1946 (Nuremberg, 1947), vol. 1, p. 248.

[11] H. Arendt, *Eichmann in Jerusalem: A Report on the Banality of Evil* (Penguin Books, London, 1976), p. 253ff.

systematically criminal political directives were *passively* carried out, *en masse,* required that the Allies adopt radical measures, tailored to the enormity of what had gone on. Great Britain, and then the United States, both modified their military regulations in 1944, substituting the rule *respondeat superior* with another: if an order is illegal, both the superior officer who gave it and its executor are responsible. However, the decisive step had to be taken at an international level. Thus, between 1943 and 1945, the United Nations War Crimes Commission, made up of seventeen Allied countries, laid down a specific norm (among other rules) based on the American and Soviet suggestions. Later, this rule became the famous article 8 of the Statute of the International Military Tribunal of Nuremberg (1945), which provides as follows: 'The fact that the defendant acted pursuant to order of his Government or of a superior shall not free him from responsibility, but may be considered in mitigation of punishment if the Tribunal determine that justice so requires'.

Not unexpectedly, during the trial before the International Tribunal in Nuremberg, the Nazi defence invoked the *Führerprinzip* and pleaded that the accused had always acted on orders from the supreme head of state. As Nelte, one of the counsels for the defence, stated, the accused had been 'merely mouthpieces or tools of an overwhelming will'.[12] But the Tribunal rejected these explanations. In referring to the *Führerprinzip,* it noted:

Hitler could not make aggressive war by himself. He had to have the co-operation of statesmen, military leaders, diplomats, and businessmen. When they, with knowledge of his aims, gave him their co-operation, they made themselves parties to the plan he had initiated. They are not to be deemed innocent because Hitler made use of them, if they knew what they were doing. That they were assigned to their tasks by a dictator does not absolve them from responsibility for their acts. The relation of leader and follower does not preclude responsibility here any more than it does in the comparable tyranny of organized domestic crime.[13]

The Tribunal also dismissed another objection: that the defendants had acted on orders that conformed to the *laws* of the *whole* German military and bureaucratic structure—in other words, the *whole German legal system* required such conduct and they had felt duty bound to obey. On this point the Tribunal remarked that: 'the very essence of the Charter [of the Tribunal] is that individuals have international duties which transcend the national obligations of obedience imposed by the individual state'.[14]

To be more specific, the Tribunal applied the rigorous precepts contained in article 8 of its Statute, adding, however, one qualification that in which a subordinate did not have 'moral choice'.[15] According to the most plausible interpretation,

---

[12] *Trial of the Major War Criminals,* vol. 18, p. 6 (final plea of defendent Keitel, by Nelte).
[13] *Trial of the Major War Criminals,* vol. 1, p. 226.
[14] *Ibid.,* p. 223.
[15] *Ibid.,* p. 224.

the Tribunal intended this somewhat unclear concept to emphasize the fact that the judges must always bear in mind not only the superior orders, but other circumstances too; for example, duress (the commanding officer forces a subordinate to carry out an order at pistol point), or errors of fact (think of the case I mentioned earlier, where a civilian is shot by a soldier who had been told by his officer that the man had had a regular trial and had been sentenced).

However, the important point is that the International Tribunal—in general and also in the specific cases of Keitel and Jodl, when it ruled on the plea of superior orders—clearly rejected the exceptions advanced by the defence and declared it the duty of a subordinate to refuse to carry out a criminal order (except in the circumstances I have just mentioned).

The judgement of the Nuremberg Tribunal, later reiterated by the International Tribunal in Tokyo, is one of the highest points ever reached by the new juridical conscience. Until that moment, individuals had to obey the imperatives of their own national laws and, more specifically, they had to obey the orders of their superior officers, even when these were contrary to the most elementary moral tenets and to the humanitarian rules that had crystallized in international law. Up to that time the *exceptions* (already mentioned earlier) had been very few and far between. Not only did the Nuremberg Tribunal proclaim that a 'superior order' must be disregarded if it is contrary to national law, it also laid down that—for the first time in history—when the *international rules* that protect humanitarian values are in conflict with *state laws* that contravene those values, *every individual must transgress the state laws* (except where there is no room for 'moral choice'). This was a veritable revolution, both in the field of law and of ethics. But what was its effect thereafter? Was its impact limited by the fact that the verdict had been given by the victors against the vanquished? How many other states and peoples took up the torch, and how many remained anchored to old principles of state sovereignty?

6. Decisions of National Courts

If we take a look at the post-war judgements of the American Tribunal in Nuremberg (not to be confused with the International Tribunal), which operated in the American military zone from 1946 to 1949, as well as the decisions of the victorious (or almost victorious) nations such as Britain, France, the Netherlands, Norway, Italy, not to mention the Eastern European countries (the USSR and Poland, for example), it becomes clear that the principles applied in Nuremberg by the International Tribunal were never questioned but reiterated, spelt out and broadened. In fact, the courts asserted unequivocally that a subordinate must refuse to carry out an illegal order, the only possible justification being that he was forced to do so (or was misinformed by errors of fact). In reasserting the principle of what the French call 'intelligent bayonets', the courts wavered, however, between two different interpretations. In some cases the 'objective' criterion of the *obviously criminal* nature of the superior order was applied; in other cases a more 'subjective' criterion was preferred: the subordinate was guilty if he *was* (*or should have been*) *aware* of the criminal nature of the order. But these variations were inessential and left the substance of the principle unchanged.

Out of a stack of cases I shall mention only a few, choosing those I feel are most significant.

One of the cases brought before the American Tribunal in Nuremberg was the *Einsatzgruppen* case.[16] These were 'action groups' created in 1941 by two sinister Nazi organizations, the *Sicherheitsdienst* (security services) and the *Sicherheitspolizei* (security police), to carry out a double job in territories occupied by the German army: police functions (especially in the anti-partisan war), and the 'liquidation' of Jews, gypsies and political opponents. Most of all the *Einsatzgruppen* distinguished themselves by their pitiless extermination of Jews. However, in the Nuremberg Court the accused, who were all members of these 'groups', were so brazen as to invoke 'superior orders'.

The Court remarked that admittedly, to be efficient, all military structures must insist on military discipline, which means that soldiers are duty-bound to obey. But this obedience must not be blind:

> It is a fallacy of widespread consumption that a soldier is required to do everything his superior officer orders him to do. A very simple illustration will show to what absurd extreme such a theory could be carried. If every military person were required, regardless of the nature of the command, to obey unconditionally, a sergeant could order the corporal to shoot the lieutenant, the lieutenant could order the sergeant to shoot the captain, the captain could order the lieutenant to shoot the colonel, and in each instance the executioner would be absolved of blame. The mere statement of such a proposition is its own commentary... The obedience of a soldier is not the obedience of an automaton. A soldier is a reasoning agent. He does not respond, and is not expected to respond, like a piece of machinery.

My other case concerns the *High Command*.[17] Among the defendants were high-ranking officers in the German army accused of having taken part in various ways in war crimes, crimes against humanity or against peace. They had either ordered criminal acts, or they had taken an active part in devising and planning these actions, or they had endorsed or even passively transmitted Hitler's orders and those of other top Nazi leaders. Among other pleas, the defendants pointed out that Hitler became the High Commander of the German armed forces in 1938 and, therefore, his orders had to be obeyed by his subordinates, especially by those of highest military rank such as the accused. Among the orders given by Hitler, or by his closest collaborators, they mentioned the 1941 directive on the execution without trial of Soviet political commissars; the infamous 'Barbarossa'

---

[16] For the text of the decision in the *Einsatzgruppen* case, see *Annual Digest and Reports of Public International Law Cases* 15 (1948) (London, 1953), pp. 656–68.

[17] For the text of the decision see L. Friedman, *The Law of War*, vol. II, p. 1421ff. (the passage quoted above is at p. 1431).

order given by Keitel, also in 1941, on shooting without trial partisans and other enemy civilians fighting the invading German troops; also the subsequent 1941 decree, issued by Hitler with Keitel's signature, called 'Night and Fog' (*Nacht und Nebel*), on the summary execution of 'non-German civilians' who had committed offences against the German forces of occupation; Hitler's 1942 order for the summary execution of sabotage commandos, and so on.

The Court rejected the defence's pleas, though it did take note that some of the defendants (Wilhelm von Leeb among others) had somehow opposed Hitler's orders, or had put off or circumscribed their execution. However, the Court was very firm in applying the principle, adding new reasons to those adduced in previous cases. It stated it would have been absurd to declare Hitler alone to be guilty of all the misdeeds. It added that the directives and orders quoted by the defence were all contrary to international law (which, among other points, insists that there always be a trial against civilians or soldiers accused of crimes against the occupying forces). The Court went on as follows:

The defendants in this case who received obviously criminal orders were placed in a difficult position, but servile compliance with orders clearly criminal for fear of some disadvantage or punishment not immediately threatened cannot be recognized as a defense. To establish the defense of coercion or necessity in the face of danger there must be a demonstration of circumstances such that a reasonable man would apprehend that he was in such imminent physical peril as to deprive him of freedom to choose the right and refrain from the wrong. No such situation has been shown in this case.

It further buttressed its view by remarking that not only did article 47 of the German military criminal code (which I have already had occasion to mention) punish those who carried out illegal orders, but in 1940 this rule had been modified such that the duty of a subordinate not to carry out a criminal order had been strengthened. Ironically, in 1944, Goebbels (then minister for propaganda), speaking of Allied pilots, had taken the opportunity to write the following on military duties: 'No law of war provides that a soldier will remain unpunished for a hateful crime by referring to the orders of his superiors, if their orders are in striking opposition to all human ethics, to all international customs in the conduct of war.'[18]

Another famous case is the *'Peleus'*, adjudicated by a British military court in Hamburg (in the British military zone) in 1945.[19] The facts resembled those of the 'Llandovery Castle' case. The *'Peleus'*, a Greek merchant vessel serving the British, had been torpedoed by a German submarine under the command of Captain Eck. The ship did not sink at once and various members of the crew

---

[18] These words were written by Goebbels on 28 May 1944 in an article in the German periodical *Völkischer Beobachter*. The article was intended to justify the murder of Allied pilots by German mobs. Goebbels contended that 'the pilots cannot validly claim that as soldiers they obeyed orders', and then went on to write the words quoted above in my text. The whole passage of Goebbels' article was quoted at Nuremberg by the French Chief Prosecutor François de Menthon: see, *Trial of the Major War Criminals*, vol. 5, p. 418.
[19] See *Law Reports of Trials of War Criminals selected and prepared by the UN War Crimes Commission* (1947–9), vol. I, p. 1ff. (The passage I have quoted is at p. 12).

were able to cling to two rafts and to the shipwrecked vessel. The submarine surfaced and the commander and four officers shot at the shipwrecked sailors, killing many of them. At the trial, the counsel for the defence of the four officers said they were not responsible because they had been carrying out Eck's orders. Turning to the Court the judge advocate rebutted this plea as follows:

It is quite obvious that no sailor and no soldier can carry with him a library of International Law, or have immediate access to a professor in that subject who can tell him whether or not a particular command is a lawful one. If this were a case which involved the careful consideration of questions of International Law as to whether or not the command to fire at helpless survivors struggling in the water was unlawful, you might well think it would not be fair to hold any of the subordinates accused in this case responsible for what they are alleged to have done; but is it not fairly obvious to you that if in fact the carrying out of Eck's command involved the killing of these helpless survivors, it was not a lawful command, and it must have been obvious to the most rudimentary intelligence that it was not a lawful command, and that those who did that shooting are not to be excused for doing it upon the ground of superior orders?

The Court accepted his arguments and sentenced all five of the defendants.

Finally, let me deal with a more recent case: Eichmann, who was tried and sentenced [to death] (1961–2) by the District Court of Jerusalem and by the Supreme Court of Israel for having organized the 'final solution' for the Jews.[20] Eichmann claimed he was a 'mere cog' in the monstrous machinery of Nazism.

However, at a certain stage, in answer to a question put by the District Court he admitted to having known about the criminal nature of his actions:

I already realized at the time that this solution [to the Jewish question] by the use of force was something unlawful, something terrible, but to my regret I was obliged to deal with it in matters of transportation, because of my oath of loyalty [to the Führer] from which I was not released.

Both courts rejected his plea. The Supreme Court argued that, in fact, Eichmann had acted with complete independence:

In point of fact, the appellant did not receive orders 'from above' at all; he was the high and mighty one, the commander of all that pertained to Jewish affairs...He was possessed by the concept of the 'final solution' and...did far more than was demanded or expected of him by his superiors in the chain of command.

The Court added that, even if it were agreed that Eichmann was 'carrying out orders', he could not hide behind the principle *respondeat superior*. Indeed, he was well aware, and it could not have been otherwise, of the highly criminal nature of his actions. Besides, there was no question of threats to his life had he not carried out the directives. It was quite untenable to say that he had acted out of necessity, or had been subjected to coercion. As we know, Eichmann was hanged.

[20] See *International Law Reports*, vol. 36, pp. 277–342. The passages quoted are at pp. 315 and 339, respectively.

This brief survey of post-war rulings shows that, in all the countries which held trials of Nazi war criminals, the courts upheld the principle of the *responsibility of subordinates*. I should add that after the war various states, which either drew up or rewrote their military manuals, all made explicit reference to superior orders and followed the new approach. I have already mentioned the American and British military manuals. These were both redrafted: the former in 1956 and the latter in 1958. Other nations to follow suit were the Federal Republic of Germany (1961), Israel and Switzerland (1963), Austria (1965) and the Netherlands (1974). As for other states, I can say nothing (except that the German Democratic Republic drafted its military manual in 1968, with an explicit rule on this subject)[21] because they either have no laws or manuals covering war, or because they are not accessible.

7. A More Recent Case: Lieutenant Calley

Thus, after the 1950s, the courts, the laws and military manuals unanimously (or almost unanimously) rejected the Nazi theory of passive obedience. However, it might be objected that these courts (and legislators) all belonged to the victorious powers and were judging soldiers and high-powered civil servants of defeated states. To what extent, one might ask, were the principles of a 'new international law', formulated between 1945 and 1950, considered binding by those same victorious powers? The question is a fair one because, as we all know, none of the courts I have referred to tried any of the very serious crimes committed by the Allies themselves (the indiscriminate bombing of many German and Japanese towns and the use of the atomic bomb).

In part I have already answered this query by quoting the numerous military manuals newly drafted, or updated, by many Western states (and the German Democratic Republic) from the 1950s onwards. But one case—particularly important because it concerns one of the two superpowers—proves that, as far as public opinion and certain sectors of the American Administration are concerned, the principles of Nuremberg are not dead and buried. This was the Calley case.[22] The facts are well known: on 16 May 1968 Lieutenant William L. Calley led a unit in an assault on My Lai, a village in South Vietnam, and killed about one hundred civilians. The massacre was kept secret. But, later, a

---

[21] See *Handbuch Militärisches Grundwissen*, 5th edn (Militärverlag der DDR, Berlin, 1972), p. 61 (section 5.3.4).

[22] For the statement of the US Judge advocate in the *Calley* case see L. Friedman, *The Law of War*, vol. II, p. 1703ff. The statement in the *Medina* case is pp. 1279ff. The decision handed down by the Court of Military Appeals in the *Calley* case is reprinted in *International Lawyer* 8 (1974), p. 523ff.

An account of the trial before the Court Martial is given by R. Hammer, *The Court-Martial of Lt. Calley* (Coward and McCann, New York, 1971). On the follow-up to the trial, see *International Herald Tribune*, 22–3 December 1973; *New York Times*, 26 September 1974.

courageous American soldier, Ronald Ridenhour, on learning by chance what had happened from some members of the 'expedition', felt duty bound to inform the Department of Defense so that an inquiry could be held. A short while later, Seymour M. Hersh, an American journalist who had heard rumours of the massacre, ferreted out the truth and soon My Lai was spread across the pages of the newspapers. The US Army decided to court-martial both Calley and some of his subordinate officers (who were immediately acquitted for reasons that are not at all clear) and Calley's commanding officer, Captain Medina. At the trial, among other things, Calley said that he had merely carried out Medina's orders: the latter had told him to consider all those he found in the village enemies and, therefore, to 'waste the people'. Medina denied having given these orders; when asked whether women and children were also to be killed, he apparently said common sense should be used, adding that it was admissible to shoot women and children if they had taken part in the hostilities or had tried to attack the American troops. Whatever the truth of the facts, the military judge whose 'job' it was to tell the members of the court martial what laws they were to apply, rejected the plea of superior orders, reiterating the main ideas that inspired the Nuremberg trials.

These concepts underlay the court martial's decision to consider Calley guilty: he was sentenced to life imprisonment. Naturally, he appealed. But the sentence was confirmed both by the Army Court of Military Review and by the Court of Military Appeals, although it was reduced to twenty years at the first appeal. The judgement of the second court of appeal was particularly interesting. Calley's defence had objected that, in weighing the responsibility of a soldier who had carried out an order, one should not adopt the criterion (followed by the court martial) that one must ascertain whether a man of 'ordinary sense and understanding' would have realized that the order was unlawful. Calley's counsel felt this criterion penalized the less intelligent soldiers, as well as those who were uninformed or inexperienced. They therefore suggested another criterion: that an order is unlawful when it is seen as such by 'a person of the commonest understanding'. They added that, since Calley was not particularly intelligent, he had not realized that the order to kill Vietnamese civilians was against the current laws. The majority of the Court rejected the plea. The judge who read out the majority opinion (R.E. Quinn) remarked that, even if it were possible to accept the plea, the final decision would remain unaffected: even a soldier of the lowest intellect, totally uninformed on points of military law, could not ignore the fact that to kill children and defenceless civilians was contrary to the most elementary principles of the laws of war.

Thus, the American judges applied the main ideas introduced in Nuremberg. The fact that, before the first appeal, President Nixon immediately ordered that Calley should be put on house arrest and not imprisoned, and that later, after the appeals and the reduction of his sentence, the President pardoned the lieutenant, casts an unfavourable light on the US Administration at that time. However, it does not detract from the importance of the judges' decisions. The judgement of the Calley case was all the more important since the My Lai massacre was one instance of the 'collective or system criminality' I mentioned earlier. This is proved among other things by the fact that the US Army tried to smother the 'episode'. It is important to remember (as the American general, Telford Taylor, himself asserted) that at the time the United States was pursuing a 'repressive' policy, leading to acts such as that for which Calley was justly condemned. (Indirect proof of this, among other points, was that in 1972, when the New York Bar requested Nixon to set up a 'national commission' to guard against the recurrence of another My Lai, the request was turned down in the President's name by one of his advisers. He explained that to accept the request would only have divided American public opinion further and, besides, an inquiry would have made public the 'rules governing the conduct of hostilities' for the American operations in Indo-China, which were and should remain a military secret. Telford Taylor's comment on this last justification was that orders and directives given to ensure a proper respect for the rules of war are effective only if the troops know and understand them; this was quite incompatible with military secrecy which, according to the President, should cover these orders and directives.)[23]

That the My Lai slaughter was a case of 'system criminality' makes the trial and sentence of an American officer by American military courts all the more significant. Furthermore, it is worth remembering here that quite a few American soldiers refused to take part in certain military operations to avoid becoming involved in criminal acts. A case in point was that of Captain Donald Dawson of the US Air Force. He was arrested for having refused to obey an order to undertake a mission with a B–52 bomber in Cambodia on 5 June 1973 (he said he was morally opposed to bombing Cambodia after the Paris agreements on Vietnam had been signed).[24] It is worth noting that in 1974 Dawson was released, after his right to be a conscientious objector had been recognized.

8. The Upshot of All Post-War Case Law

What can be deduced from my brief survey? The easiest conclusion, and one which many have already drawn, is that after the Second World War the profound indignation felt by the victorious nations at the *enormity* of what had been perpetrated, as well as the trials these countries did well to hold, led to a definite result on a legal plane: a general rule of international law emerged that was binding on all states. This was that subordinates are now held to be as responsible as their superiors when they carry out an obviously criminal act, that is one that is contrary to the essential rules of international law.

Let us pause a moment to examine this rule and ask ourselves if it is not too 'exacting' and therefore unrealistic. To demand that an inferior rebel against an

[23] T. Taylor, in L. Friedman, *The Law of War*, vol. I, p. XXIV.
[24] See *International Herald Tribune*, 2–3 February 1974.

illegal order—that is to demand that he not only is able to express his opinion on that order, but that he disobey, thereby taking a step that might cost him dear—may seem too much to ask, given the nature of military structures. Take, for example, Dicey's human dilemma, mentioned earlier. Can a subordinate be expected to sacrifice his career, his interests, perhaps his life as well, rather than obey an unlawful order? By so providing does the law demand that soldiers behave as heroes? I feel the 'answer' law gives to this question is less far-fetched and unrealistic than would seem at first glance. The rule on superior orders should be taken together with that on physical or 'moral' coercion, and that on errors of fact, mentioned earlier. If an officer obliges me, at gunpoint, to shoot a prisoner of war, I am not answerable for my act precisely because, in this case, the unlawful order was carried out under duress. I no longer have that 'moral choice' of which the International Tribunal of Nuremberg spoke; nor can I be expected to sacrifice my life rather than carry out an unjust order. As you see, law does remember that men are what they are and does not punish anyone who, forced to choose between his own life and that of another, prefers to save his own skin. Law does not expect us to behave as saints, martyrs or heroes, but it can demand that we risk a court martial, imprisonment and the sacrifice of a career, rather than carry out an obviously unlawful order.

These rules have marked an *extremely significant change of direction* in the international community. To a certain extent they have subverted military discipline. The imperatives of international law have seeped into the military structures of states, forcing soldiers to *disobey* their orders if they are contrary to international law and to the rulings that have been 'incorporated' into domestic law. Thus, the armour plating of state sovereignty has been torn at one of its most sensitive points: the hierarchical relations within a military structure. A man who carries out an obviously criminal order knows that he can be tried, sentenced and even put to death, either by court martial in his own country, or by a foreign court. At least in this area—but it is at the very 'heart' of the state—the humanitarian and progressive values contained in so many international rules have prevailed over the traditional 'impermeability' of military structures to the claims of the outside world. And that is a great step forward.

Yet, something is not quite right. This is not so much the gap, or even the strident difference, between this great advance along the road to civilization and the traditional closed structure of many states. Quite a different factor leaves us perplexed. If we take another look at the decisions and rules of the military manuals I mentioned, one fact stands out. They all belong to Western states, or to Eastern European states (as well as Yugoslavia). The Third World is absent, for obvious reasons. The majority of African and Asian states that now make up—at least from a numerical point of view—the backbone of the international community, were not yet independent immediately after the Second World War. Therefore, they could not express their views. For various historical reasons, the Latin American countries either did not have occasion, or did not wish, to hold trials against war criminals. After perusing the collections of decisions and the various military manuals, we have no idea of what their attitude is. In the absence of official statements from the Third World, can we say it considers itself bound by the general international rule on superior orders? We know well that the trauma of the crimes committed during the Second World War affected the consciences of all Western and socialist countries and led to their solemn pledge never to commit such horrors again and to the removal of that convenient loophole of 'superior orders'. Did it also affect Third World leaders?

This is not a strictly legal problem, but one of substance. Let me rephrase the question in other terms: can it be said that the Third World has also freed itself from an obsession with the *absolute principle* of *military discipline?* In the dichotomy between state sovereignty and international and humanitarian values, has it opted for the latter?

Alas, there is a whole pile of evidence that it hasn't, culled from debates in international organizations or at diplomatic conferences: in New York in 1948, and in Geneva in 1949 and then again in 1974–7.

9. The Third World Challenges the Right to Disobey Criminal Orders

A. Negotiations for the Convention on Genocide

The first opportunity states had to express their opinion on the new rule was the preparatory work on the Convention on Genocide, which began in 1947 at the instigation of the United Nations.[25] In an *ad hoc* committee set up by the United Nations Economic and Social Council to make a draft of the Convention, the Soviet delegate suggested the introduction of a rule that reiterated the text proposed by the UN secretariat ('Command of the law or superior orders shall be no defence for crimes set out in this Convention, but may be considered in mitigation of punishment'). Of the other six members of the committee only the Pole gave his unconditional support to the Soviet proposal. The delegates from (Nationalist) China and Venezuela vigorously opposed it; their main reason for doing so was given by the Venezuelan as follows:

that principle is a danger to the stability of the institutions of the state. The Charter of the Military Tribunal of Nuremberg admitted that principle having in mind the crimes of war; but to accept it in time of peace is to invite the armed forces to disobedience, when they are in themselves a non-political body, bound to obedience, and non-deliberative.[26]

---

[25] For the drafting documents of the Genocide Convention on the question at issue, see *Ad Hoc Committee on Genocide, Summary Records*, UN doc. E/AC.25/SR. 18. See also *General Assembly Official Records*, 3rd Session, part. I, VIth Committee, pp. 302–14.

[26] UN doc. E/AC.25/SR. 28 (10 May 1948), p. 9.

There is no point in insisting here—as an Israeli scholar, Yoram Dinstein, did quite rightly a few years ago—that, in drawing a distinction between times of war and times of peace, the reasoning is fallacious (if there is a period of tension in which the exceptional nature of the moment could, to some extent, justify the requirements of military discipline, that is war; in times of peace 'there is no justification for sacrificing the supremacy of the law on the altar of military discipline').[27] Apart from these considerations, the significant point to be drawn from the Venezuelan argument is that a Third World country should have, for the first time, expressed its perplexities and reservations on how the principle would affect the stability of state institutions. As we shall see, these are motives that later induced most developing countries to oppose the idea that a subordinate can legitimately disobey criminal orders.

However, the Soviet proposal was rejected, both at the committee level and, later, by the General Assembly of the United Nations, one of the reasons being that several Western countries (with the US to the forefront) added to the Latin American reservations (which dealt with general points and matters of principle) a whole set of marginal objections (for example, that the proposed rule was too 'rigid'; that the times were not ripe for a debate on superior orders; that the inclusion of the rule might impede the ratification of the Convention by some states, and so on). In any case, it was clear that the majority of states, especially Latin American and some Western countries, lacked the political will to accept a principle proposed and upheld by the same Western countries (and the Soviet Union) a few years earlier. The new Convention on Genocide, so important in some aspects and so weak and ambiguous in others, was born without one of its essential limbs: since acts of genocide are usually perpetrated by government authorities, or with their tacit support or connivance, genocide is a particularly fertile terrain for the principle *respondeat superior*.

Lawyers and diplomats who interpret the Convention are faced with a serious dilemma: in the absence of a specific rule on superior orders, is it possible, in suitable circumstances, to apply the general principle which several jurists felt had crystallized immediately after the Second World War? Or, does the rejection of the Soviet proposal mean that most of the states present in New York wished to rule out the responsibility of the subordinate in cases of genocide? This is still an open question.

B. Negotiations for Updating the Laws of War

What took place in New York in 1948 was repeated in Geneva in 1949 when the four famous Conventions on War Victims were discussed and approved; then again in 1974–7, when the two additional Protocols to these Conventions were

---

[27] Y. Dinstein, *The Defense of 'Obedience to Superior Orders' in International Law* (Sijthoff, Leyden, 1965), p. 219.

drafted. Of these two occasions I feel the most significant was the second: it is closer to us in time and, above all, many more countries, especially non-Western ones, took part in the second lap of Geneva debates.[28] These debates give us a particularly revealing cross-section of the attitudes of various states, or groups of states, as well as their political and diplomatic motivations. Let us therefore take a look at the 1974–7 conference.

Once again a proposal had been made at the conference to insert a rule on superior orders into the First Additional Protocol (the one on international armed conflict, either between states or between states and national liberation movements). This time the proposal had been made not by a state, but by the International Committee of the Red Cross, which had drafted the basic texts on which the delegations were to express their views. The rule (article 77) was wisely worded and introduced the question of superior orders into the wider context of a soldier's obedience to the hierarchy. It went as follows:

1) No person shall be punished for refusing to obey an order of his government or of a superior which, if carried out, would constitute a grave breach of the provisions of the Conventions or of the present Protocol.
2) The fact of having acted pursuant to an order of his government or of a superior does not absolve an accused person from penal responsibility if it be established that, in the circumstances at the time, he should have reasonably known that he was committing a grave breach of the Convention or of the present Protocol and that he had the possibility of refusing to obey the order.

Clearly, the rule sanctioned the *idea of superior orders* only for 'grave breaches' and did not extend it to 'ordinary' ones. Although this limitation was open to criticism, it was motivated by the fear that, otherwise, article 77 would not have been accepted by many countries. Despite the intentional lacuna, the rule was well drafted because it stated in clear terms the *logical premise* to the 'theory of superior orders', that is the *duty and right of the subordinate to refuse to obey*. What had always been *implicit* was now spelt out. But, precisely because the unsuppressible premise to the 'doctrine' was made patent, numerous governments rejected it firmly, in the belief that military discipline is one of the mainstays of the state and, consequently, it is one of the duties of a soldier to obey his orders without questioning them.

The proposal was the subject of lengthy and even bitter debate and, in the end, it foundered. But it is worth casting a rapid glance at the positions of states. For the sake of brevity, I shall ignore those that seem the least significant (either because they were isolated, or because they were based on ideas that were not shared by other delegations), as well as intermediate positions. In a nutshell, two main attitudes emerged: the one favourable to and the other against the rule.

[28] See Diplomatic Conference on Humanitarian Law, *Official Records*, vol. IX, p. 27pff.

The group of states that supported the rule, and in several cases suggested improvements to broaden its scope, included Western nations (Australia, Finland, the United States, Belgium, Norway, Canada, the Netherlands, Israel, Sweden, France, Japan, Ireland) and the Holy See, together with various socialist states (Poland, Ukraine, Yugoslavia, Cuba, the Socialist Republic of Vietnam) and a small group of Third World countries (Tunisia, the Philippines, Mexico).

Within this group, wholehearted support for article 77 came from the United States which, in 1976, suggested amendments to improve the rule. In particular, the rule should be applicable to 'ordinary crimes' as well as 'grave breaches'— an extremely important suggestion, which eliminated one possible loophole and made article 77 even more consistent. Obviously, by 1976, the United States had changed its attitude and become one of the most ardent supporters of 'intelligent bayonets'.

The group of states that were substantially opposed to the principle of superior orders included various Arab states (Syria, Libya, Oman, United Arab Emirates, Kuwait, Yemen), as well as other developing nations (India, Ghana, the Republic of Korea). Briefly, to various extents and with varying attitudes, these countries felt extremely dubious, above all because they feared the rule would *lend legitimacy to insubordination*. This fear was expressed very adroitly by the Syrian and Indian delegates. In particular, the latter declared,

Article 77 . . . amounted to encouraging subordinates to disobey orders which they deemed contrary to the provisions of the Geneva Convention and Protocol I. The assumption was that Governments or superior officers would in some cases commit deliberate breaches of Protocol I. In such cases, whatever provisions might be inserted would remain inoperative.[29]

The war of words between the two groups ended in victory for the group that was opposed. Among other reasons, this was because some governments in the first group (such as the United States), preferred to vote against it after witnessing repeated attempts to water down article 77 and deprive it of its strength, believing that it was better to go home empty-handed than with an ill-conceived rule. Besides, they believed the Protocol would in no way impinge upon the general principle on superior orders, which they felt had crystallized after the Second World War.

What can be said of this final result? Certainly, the victors were state sovereignty and one of its mainstays, military discipline.

The countries to emerge victorious were those that feared that the 'free will' of subordinates was a powerful acid that would erode the efficiency of their military machines.

'In times no less than in regions there are wastes and deserts', as Bacon wrote in 1621.[30] From the beginning of the cold war to the present day, the supreme

---

[29] *Official Records*, vol. IX, p. 143 (doc. CDDH/I/SR. 52, para. 38).

[30] F. Bacon, *Novum Organum* 1, 78 ('*Sunt enim non minus temporum quam regionum eremi et vastitates*').

principles developed between 1945 and 1947 are desert bound. This has come about in spite of the birth of a new doctrine, foreshadowed by 'Nuremberg law': the 'doctrine of human rights', which has translated the natural law concept of 'human dignity' into positive legal rules and also underlies the concept of making subordinates 'responsible' for their actions. But, on closer inspection, even the acceptance of human rights by the Third World has been slow, it has come up against reticence, reservations and opposition and has often been accepted only begrudgingly. Military and political necessity in these countries, their need for strong, centralized administrations—a need that derives, in part, from their recent history—their respect for authoritarian ideologies and an excessive impermeability to values that, in the long run, would benefit the more backward societies, are all factors that help to explain the hostility of developing countries to any disruption of military discipline.

The deep rift in this area, as in others, would encourage a pessimist to think that we are witnessing the development of a 'two speed' law.

10. Conclusion

It is now time to haul our nets back into the boat and see how international law, that is states and their courts of law, has solved—if at all—the dilemma that first upset Abraham and Antigone, as well as thousands of men before, during and after the Second World War.

In these pages I have tried to show how, after that great conflagration, a conviction slowly crystallized in the international community that the duty to obey cannot cover the guilt of a soldier when essential values, such as respect for the life and dignity of a human being, are at stake. However, on closer examination, we discovered that an important sector of the international community had not contributed to that process of crystallization. Later, the Third World countries were able to express their opinion—true, not on the rule (or putative rule) directly, but on whether or not to draft provisions on limited issues that would reflect that rule.

It is for jurists *emunctae naris*—for exegetes and commentators—to discuss whether the attitude of developing countries proves that the rule never crystallized in fact; or that it did do so but, later, the hostility of a vast number of states splintered and weakened it; or, again, that the rule itself is hale and hearty, but some states are dubious about its applicability to certain areas. I, for one, feel it is important to highlight the *actual* behaviour of 'traditional' and emerging states on various occasions. Despite 'resistances' that, as Milgram's experiments showed, exist even in democratic states, where obedience to authority is no less eradicated than in authoritarian states, immediately after the Second World War the victorious nations managed to introduce the principle that a soldier must not obey orders like a robot. Furthermore, they also proclaimed a 'concept' that I should like to emphasize once again: a soldier must disobey not only an order that transgresses the legislative dictates of his mother country, but—when the *whole texture of state laws has been infected*—he must even disregard orders that conflict with *extra-state commands,* that is the humanitarian values embodied in international law. Thus, *international law* has made a gigantic stride forwards compared to the psychosocial life of states, including democratic states. In spite of momentary hesitations, almost all Western and socialist states have stood firmly by those principles. Conversely, the majority of newly independent states have turned in the opposite direction; obsessed as they are with military necessity and security, they reject the idea that a soldier can challenge the orders of his superiors. In the end, these countries sacrifice to the requirements of authority the individual's independent judgement and his sense of personal responsibility. As far as they are concerned, there must be no Antigone.

The concepts that emerged from Nuremberg—one of the high points in our march towards legal civilization and an awareness of human dignity—are in danger of being silted up. What can be done? Should we wait until the authoritarian structure of many Latin American and Afro-Asian countries, based as they are on the force of arms and on the loyalty of troops, slowly open their portals to the canons of democracy? This process is likely to take years. Rather, public opinion should apply pressure, as from now, on the more enlightened sectors of the Third World to encourage these countries to realize that, in the long run, authoritarianism and oppression are always on the losing side. Indeed, however strong his imagery, Jean-Jacques Rousseau was wrong when he wrote in his *Discours sur l'origine et les fondements de l'inégalité parmi les hommes* that 'it is with liberty as it is with those solid and succulent foods, or with those generous wines, which are well adapted to nourish and fortify robust constitutions that are used to them, but ruin and intoxicate weak and delicate constitutions to which they are not suited.'[31] Perhaps jurists, as well as diplomats, could be of use by inventing in the various international fora better formulas that will lessen the diffidence of developing nations without diluting the essence of the principles that Antigone was the first to embody, paying for having transgressed Creon's orders with her life.

---

[31] J.J. Rousseau, *Discours sur l'origine et les fondements de l'inégalité parmi les hommes* (Gallimard, Paris, 1965), p. 19.

D. Developments in International Criminal Justice

25. The Statute of the International Criminal Court: Some Preliminary Reflections*

1. Introduction

It is easy to find fault in any new legal institution. In the case of the International Criminal Court (ICC), whose Statute was adopted in Rome on 17 July 1998, however, one should be mindful of the fact that, firstly, this is a revolutionary institution that intrudes into state sovereignty by subjecting states' nationals to an international criminal jurisdiction. Consequently, if and when it becomes an operational and effective judicial mechanism, the ICC could mark a real turning point in the world community. Secondly, as happened in the case of the International Court of Justice (ICJ), and subsequently the International Criminal Tribunal for the former Yugoslavia (ICTY) and the International Criminal Tribunal for Rwanda (ICTR), only gradually and over a fairly long period of time can the ICC become vital and credible. A thorough and sound appraisal of this new institution must therefore wait some time.

Subject to this caveat, however, by and large one cannot but welcome the institution of the ICC as a significant building block in the construction of a truly international legal community. Although it is premature to make an in-depth assessment of a complex treaty and the merits and flaws of the legal institution it is designed to set up, I shall nevertheless attempt in this article to set out some initial and tentative comments on some of the salient traits of the future ICC.

2. General Remarks

The Statute of the ICC can be examined from various angles. In particular, it may be considered from the viewpoint of treaty law, *qua* a multilateral international treaty, or it can be viewed from the perspective of its contribution to international criminal law, both substantive and procedural.

* Originally published in 10 *European Journal of International Law* (1999) 144–171.

Considered as a contribution to international treaty law, the Statute strikes the commentator as a text that is markedly different from other modern multilateral treaties. It bears the mark of strong political and diplomatic differences over certain major issues, and shows the difficulty of ironing them out. The existence of these differences and of their partial solution manifests itself in many ways, some of which may be pinpointed briefly as follows.

First of all, unlike most multilateral treaties concluded under the auspices of the United Nations, in the case of the Rome Statute there hardly exist preparatory works reflecting the debates and negotations that took place at the Rome Diplomatic Conference. The need for informal off-the-record discussions clearly arose out of the necessity to overcome major rifts in a smooth manner and in such a way as to avoid states losing face by changing their position. Secondly, it is striking that the text was drafted in one language (English) and that for months after its adoption no official text was available in the other five languages which, pursuant to Article 128, are 'equally authentic'. Thirdly, one must emphasize the fact that on some crucial issues the Rome Conference failed to take action and simply put off any decision until amendments to the Statute are adopted: this holds true for the definition of the crime of aggression (Article 5), for the articulation of the elements of crimes (Article 9(1)) and for the determination of weapons whose use is contrary to the prohibition on weapons that cause superfluous suffering or are inherently indiscriminate (Article 8(2)(b)(xx)). Fourthly, it is surprising that while Article 120 provides that no reservations may be made to the Statute, Article 124 entitled 'Transitional Provision' in fact provides for reservations narrowing the jurisdiction of the Court. Pursuant to this provision, on becoming a party to the Statute a state 'may declare that, for a period of seven years after the entry into force of this Statute for the State concerned, It does not accept the jurisdiction of the Court with respect to [war crimes] when [such a] crime is alleged to have been committed by its nationals or on its territory'. Admittedly, these are reservations whose purpose and contents, as well as duration in time, are predetermined by the Treaty. The fact remains, however, that, on account of their object and scope, they cannot but be regarded as reservations proper.

Turning to consider the Rome Statute from the perspective of its contribution to international criminal law, the balance sheet is more positive. In brief, it can be said that the Statute has made a notable contribution to the development of *substantive* international criminal law, in that it has defined three of the classes of crimes it envisages in addition to setting out the most important among the general principles of international criminal law. Clearly, though, its major contribution lies in the field of *procedural* international criminal law: the Statute has set up a complex judicial body with detailed regulations governing all the stages in the adjudication of international crimes.

In this paper I shall endeavour to appraise in some detail how the Rome Statute has contributed to both substantive and procedural criminal law.

3. The Scope of the Court's Jurisdiction; Or the Rome Statute's Contribution to Substantive Criminal Law

A. Subject-matter Jurisdiction

i. *The question of aggression as a crime under the court's jurisdiction*

The Court's jurisdiction embraces four categories of crimes: genocide, crimes against humanity, war crimes and aggression.[1]

While it was wise to exclude such crimes as terrorism and drug trafficking, which at the present stage of international relations are best investigated and prosecuted at the national level, doubts can be expressed about the inclusion of aggression. Aggression is in some sense the arch-crime which most menaces international society. Once war is unleashed, all the horrors and miseries of war are let loose. At Nuremberg it was therefore regarded as the 'supreme international crime differing only from other war crimes in that it contains within itself the accumulated evil of the whole'.[2] It has been suggested that one ought to beware the tendency of the Security Council to be treated as 'the mouth of the oracle' for the determination of whether aggression has taken place, with the consequence that none of the Permanent Members has ever been accused by the United Nations of aggression. On the other hand, it may be argued that only a political organ such as the Security Council can ascertain whether aggression has occurred and that it would be difficult for a judicial body to do so, the more so because the evidence may prove difficult to obtain. In fact, it is fair to say that such evidence is likely to be obtained only or primarily when the aggressor state has been defeated, militarily or politically.

Another factor is that aggression is a crime for which a definition (in its form as a state's wrongful act) has not yet been achieved, despite United Nations discussions lasting many decades and culminating in the disappointing General Assembly Resolution 3314 (xxix) adopted by consensus on 14 December 1974. As is well known, the definition laid down in that resolution is not exhaustive, as stated in Article 4 of the resolution, which adds that 'the Security Council may determine that other acts [than those listed in Articles 2 and 3 as amounting to aggression] constitute aggression under the provisions of the Charter'. That the definition was deliberately left incomplete is quite understandable: to define aggression also means, among other things, to decide whether so-called pre-emptive self-defence is lawful under the Charter or must instead be regarded as a form of

---

[1] Article 5(1)(d) states that the crime of aggression is within the jurisdiction of the Court, although Article 5(2) provides that such jurisdiction will not exist until a definition and conditions for exercising jurisdiction are adopted in accordance with Articles 121 and 123. Those articles concern 'amending' the Statute.

[2] See *Trial of the Major War Criminals before the International Criminal Tribunal,* Nuremberg 1947, vol. 1, at 186.

aggression. There may be other reasons. Arguably, an enumerative list of cases of aggression might contain gaps which would encourage the aggressor to exploit the definition. It was most likely felt that any definition of aggression had to contain a margin of discretion and that therefore an exhaustive definition was impossible.

It thus seems most probable that the definition of this crime, to be adopted under Article 5(2) of the Statute in accordance with Articles 121 and 123, will not be agreed upon, at least not in the near future. If this is so, the ICC is likely to start out on the wrong footing, for lack of definition of one of the four classes of crimes over which it has been granted jurisdiction.

Nevertheless, the fact that Article 5(1)(d) provides that the crime of aggression is within the jurisdiction of the Court does create, at least, the *expectation* that the states parties will strive to find an acceptable definition, creating an impetus which would be altogether absent if Article 5(2) did not exist. It is also import-ant that *if* a definition of aggression is ever agreed upon, the 'conditions under which the Court shall exercise jurisdiction with respect to this crime' remain to be agreed, and the Statute does not exclude the possibility that, in addition to the Security Council, the Prosecutor or states might one day be allowed to initiate investigations into whether aggression has been committed. This eventu-ality would be a welcome development inasmuch as it would break the Security Council's stranglehold on the notion of aggression. Judicial review of aggression might prove a useful counterbalance to the monopolizing power of the Security Council.

ii. *Main traits of the regulation of classes of crimes defined by the statute*

It is well known that the current rules of international law on individual criminal responsibility make up a body of law that is still rudimentary and fairly unsophisti-cated. These rules, among other things, suffer from a major defect. Unlike national law, where the principle of *specificity* of criminal law (*Bestimmtheitsgrundsatz, tassatività delle norme penali, nullum crimen sine lege stricta*) is prevalent, inter-national criminal law includes many provisions that do not determine the essen-tial elements of the crime in detail. To this extent, international criminal law departs from the fundamental principle of specificity, which requires that a crim-inal rule be detailed and indicate in clear terms the various elements of the crime. This principle constitutes a fundamental guarantee for the potential accused and any indicted person, because it lays down in well-defined terms the confines of the prohibited conduct, thus giving him notice of what he stands accused. By the same token, that principle greatly restricts the courts' latitude (*arbitrium judicis*).

This striking feature of international criminal rules—lack of specificity—pri-marily manifests itself in three ways.

First, and more generally, unlike the corresponding national rules, most inter-national rules do not prohibit a certain conduct (say, murder, rape, etc.) by provid-ing a specific detailed description of such conduct. They instead embrace a broad set of offences (say, war crimes or crimes against humanity), without individual identification by a delineation of the prohibited behaviour.[3] A typical example of this approach can be found in some provisions of the Statute of the ICTY: Article 2 (on grave breaches of the Geneva Conventions), Article 3 (on violations of the laws or customs of war) and Article 5 (on crimes against humanity). It follows that, when applying these rules, one must first of all identify the *general* ingredients proper to each category of crime (say, crimes against humanity) and then the *specific* ingredients of the sub-class one may have to deal with (say, rape or persecution). Often, while the general ingredients may be inferred from the international rule (for instance, a widespread or systematic context for crimes against humanity), the specific ingredients are not identifiable (for instance, the precise definition of rape), let alone spelt out in the rule. The interpreter must therefore draw on comparative analysis of national criminal law.[4]

Secondly, some international criminal rules are quite loose and do not specify the prohibited conduct, not even by indirect reference to national rules. The most conspicuous illustration is the provision on crimes against humanity laid down in the London Agreement of 8 August 1945 (Article 6(c)) and taken up in Control Council Law no. 10 (Article II(l)(c)) and in the Statutes of the ICTY (Article 5(i)) and ICTR (Article 3), whereby 'other inhumane acts' are prohibited and therefore fall under the jurisdiction of those courts. 'Other inhumane acts' are not further defined in those instruments.

Thirdly, current international criminal law does not define accurately and in incontrovertible terms the *mental* element (*mens rea*) of the various international crimes.

The Rome Statute has to a large extent obviated most of these flaws, thus making a notable contribution to the evolution of *substantive* criminal law. However, we will see below that this contribution may be faulted in some respects. Let us first focus on the meritorious side of the Rome Statute.

First of all, the Statute sets out in Article 8 the various instances of war crimes and defines each war crime in a specific and detailed manner. Furthermore, it is commendable that Article 8 lays emphasis on war crimes which are 'committed as part of a plan or policy or as part of a large-scale commission of such crimes'. At both the ICTY and ICTR, this would have been a useful qualification to avoid

---

[3] To the best of my knowledge, this feature of international criminal rules has only been emphasized by the German Supreme Court in the German zone occupied by Britain, in its judgment of 20 May 1948 in the *P.* case. See *Entscheidungen des Obersten Gerichtshofes für die Britische Zone in Strafsachen,* vol. 1 (1949), at 12–14.

[4] In the *Akayesu* Judgment of 2 September 1998, Trial Chamber I of the ICTR defined rape, murder, torture and extermination for the purposes of determining whether or not the accused had committed crimes against humanity (see paras 589 (definition of murder), 592 (definition of extermination), 594 (definition of torture), and 598 (definition of rape)). The ICTY Judgment in *Delalić et al.* of 16 November 1998 has likewise furnished detailed definitions of murder, rape, torture and other war crimes. On the definition of rape and torture as war crimes see now the judgment delivered by Trial Chamber II of the ICTY in *Furundžija* (Judgment of 10 December 1998, para. 131 ff).

prosecutions of isolated atrocities, which do not pose a threat to international order as much as atrocities which are committed as part of a plan or policy or on a large scale.[5] It should, however, be noted that the requirement that war crimes be committed as part of a plan or policy or a large-scale practice only relates to the Court's jurisdiction and must not affect the existing notion of war crimes. In other words, the fact that the Court shall only pronounce upon war crimes that form part of a plan or policy does not mean that the definition of war crimes under international law is thereby narrowed so as only to cover such large-scale war crimes. It should be added that another commendable feature of the Rome Statute lies in its extending the class of war crimes to serious violations of international humanitarian law perpetrated in internal armed conflicts. This is in line with the pronouncement of the ICTY in the *Tadić (Interlocutory Appeal on Jurisdiction) Decision*,[6] and subsequent ICTY judgments, notably in *Delalić et al.*[7] However, as argued below, an even better approach would be simply to establish one body of law applicable to *all* armed conflicts—internal or international—without distinction.

Secondly, Article 7 gives a fairly precise definition of crimes against humanity ('any of the foregoing acts when committed as part of a widespread or systematic attack against any civilian population, with knowledge of the act'), followed by the enumeration of the various sub-classes of acts amounting to such a crime. It is worth noting, incidentally, that, unlike the charter provisions of the Nuremberg Tribunal and the ICTY relating to crimes against humanity, but like the relevant article of the ICTR Statute, Article 7 of the ICC Statute does *not* require that crimes against humanity be committed in connection with an armed conflict. This seems to reflect current international law.

As regards the classes of crimes against humanity enumerated in the ICC Statute, such offences as enforced prostitution, forced pregnancy and enforced disappearance of persons are now explicitly included. These practices, often associated with 'ethnic cleansing' and, in the case of disappearances, the pursuit of power by terror and elimination of political opposition, properly belong in any modern description of crimes against humanity by virtue of the role they play

---

[5] It is mainly the leaders and organizers of such plans or policies who threaten international public order and who should therefore be prosecuted by an international court. See the ICTY *Martić* Rule 61 of 6 March 1996, para. 21: 'The Tribunal has particularly valid grounds for exercising its jurisdiction over persons who, through their position of political or military authority, are able to order the commission of crimes falling within its competence *ratione materiae* or who knowingly refrain from preventing or punishing the perpetrators of such crimes. In a Decision of 16 May 1995, this Trial Chamber considered that such persons "more so than those just carrying out orders (...) would thus undermine international public order" (Karadžić, Mladić and Stanisić, IT-95-5-D, official request for deferral, para. 25). Since the criminal intent is formulated at a high level of the administrative hierarchy, the violation of the norm of international humanitarian law is part of a system of criminality specifically justifying the intervention of the Tribunal.'

[6] See Decision of 2 October 1995, at 68–71, paras 128–137.

[7] *Judgment,* 16 November 1998, paras 202 and 314.

in policies of repression against civilian populations. Examples of each of these practices readily spring to mind.

Emphasis on the principle of specificity is also evident in the sub-class of crimes against humanity termed 'other inhuman acts'. This broad class is narrowed down in the ICC Statute because it is specified that they must be 'of a similar character [to that of the other subclasses and] intentionally causing great suffering, or serious injury to body or to mental or physical health'.

iii. Flaws in the definitions of crimes

A number of flaws can be discerned in the norms concerning the various categories of crimes. I shall confine myself to war crimes (Article 8).

(A) Insofar as Article 8 separates the law applicable to international armed conflict from that applicable to internal armed conflict, it is somewhat *retrograde*, as the current trend has been to abolish this distinction and to have simply one *corpus* of law applicable to *all* conflicts. It can be confusing—and unjust—to have one law for international armed conflict and another for internal armed conflict.

(B) Two provisions of the general article on war crimes are worded in such a way as to give rise to serious problems of interpretation. On the face of it, they markedly differentiate the various classes of war crimes they envisage from all the other war crimes provided for in the Statute as well as genocide and crimes against humanity. I am referring to Article 8(2)(b) and (e), which deal respectively with war crimes in international armed conflicts and war crimes in non-international war crimes. These two provisions are worded as follows:

[For the purposes of this Statute 'war crimes' means] Other serious violations of the laws and customs applicable in international armed conflict [in armed conflicts not of an international character: litt (e)], *within the established framework of international law,* namely, any of the following acts . . . (emphasis added)

Strikingly, neither in the other provisions of Article 8 concerning war crimes nor in the Statute's provisions on genocide and crimes against humanity is reference made to 'the established framework of international law'. A plausible explanation for this odd phrase could be that for the purposes of the Statute the offences listed in the two aforementioned provisions are to be considered as war crimes only if they are so classified by *customary international law.* In other words, while in respect of the other classes of war crimes (or, for that matter, crimes against humanity and genocide) the Statute confines itself to setting out the content of the prohibited conduct, and the relevant provision can thus be directly and immediately applied by the Court, it would be otherwise in the case of the two provisions under consideration. The Court might find that the conduct envisaged in these provisions amounted to a war crime *only if and to the extent that* general international law already regarded the offence as a war crime. Under this interpretation, 'declaring that no quarter be given' (Article 8(2)(b)(xii)), for example, would no doubt be taken to amount to a war crime, because denial of quarter is indisputably prohibited by customary international law and, if it should be declared that no quarter be given (i.e. that no prisoners be taken), a war crime would thereby have been committed. By contrast, an offence such as 'the transfer, directly or indirectly, by the Occupying Power of parts of its own civilian population into the territory it occupies...' (Article 8(2)(b)(viii)) could not be *ipso facto* regarded as a war crime. The Court would first have to establish (i) whether under general international law such transfer or deportation is considered a breach of international humanitarian law of armed conflict, and in addition, (ii) whether under customary international law such a breach would amount to a war crime.

To support the above explanation one could stress that for the two other classes of war crimes envisaged in Article 8 no reference to the 'established framework of international law' is made. These two classes, provided for in Article 8(2)(a) and (c), respectively, embrace two categories of crimes undoubtedly covered by international customary law: grave breaches of the Geneva Conventions and serious violations of common Article 3 of the Geneva Conventions. It would follow from this interpretation of Article 8 that, as regards two broad categories of war crimes, the Statute would not provide a self-contained legal regime, but would rather presuppose a mandatory examination by the Court, on a case by case basis, of the current status of general international law.

However, this interpretation should not be entertained. First of all, it would loosen the net of international prohibitions to which combatants are subject. What is even more important, it would result in a deviation from the legal regime envisaged by the framers of the Rome Statute which, as I have pointed out above, is designed to implement the principle of specificity, i.e. to set out in detail all the classes of crimes falling under the jurisdiction of the Court, so as to have a *lex scripta* laying down the substantive criminal rules to be applied by the ICC. On the other hand, one cannot simply read out of Article 8 the expression 'within the established framework of international law' *tamquam non esset;* this would run counter to basic principles of treaty interpretation. Perhaps the following construction could commend itself: the expression at issue is intended to convey the notion that for the authors of the Statute the various classes of war crimes specified in Article 8(2)(b) and (e) are already part of the 'established framework of international law'. In other words, by the use of that expression the draughtsmen aimed at making it clear that these two provisions were declaratory of customary international law, as much as the provisions of Article 8(2)(a), concerning 'grave breaches', and Article 8(2)(c), concerning common Article 3. Since no one contests that these two last provisions refer to war crimes already firmly established in customary law, whereas for the other two categories doubts might arise, the framers of the Rome Statute aimed at dispelling such doubts by making reference to the 'established framework of international law'.

(C) The Statute does not classify as crimes falling under the ICC jurisdiction the use in international armed conflict of modern weapons that are contrary to the two basic principles prohibiting weapons which (a) cause superfluous injury or unnecessary suffering or (b) are inherently indiscriminate. Under Article 8(2) (b)(xx) the use of weapons, projectiles, materials or methods of warfare contrary to one of those two principles amounts to a war crime if the weapon, projectile, etc. 'are the subject of a comprehensive prohibition and are included in an Annex to this Statute, by an amendment' to the Statute made pursuant to Articles 121 and 123. In practice, given the extreme unlikelihood that such amendment will ever be agreed upon, the use of those weapons, projectiles, etc. may eventually not amount to a war crime within the jurisdiction of the Court. Thus, ultimately the two principles are deprived of their overarching legal value. This seems all the more questionable because even bacteriological weapons, which are undoubtedly prohibited by general international law, might be used without entailing the commission of a crime falling under the jurisdiction of the Court. The same would hold true for the use of nuclear weapons, to the extent that such weapons prove to be indiscriminate and to cause unnecessary suffering (it would seem that by contrast the use of chemical weapons is covered by the ban on 'asphyxiating, poisonous or other gases and all analogous liquids, materials or devices', contained in Article 8(b)(xviii)).

(D) The prohibited use of weapons in internal armed conflicts is not regarded as a war crime under the ICC Statute. This regulation does not reflect the current status of general international law. As the Appeals Chamber of the ICTY stressed in the *Tadić (Interlocutory Appeal on Jurisdiction) Decision,* it no longer makes sense in modern warfare to distinguish between international and internal armed conflicts:

> Why protect civilians from belligerent violence, or ban rape, torture or the wanton destruction of hospitals, churches, museums or private property, *as well as proscribe weapons causing unnecessary suffering when two sovereign States are engaged in war, and yet refrain from enacting the same bans or providing the same protection when armed violence has erupted 'only' within the territory of a sovereign State?*[8]

The Appeals Chamber rightly answered this question by finding that the prohibition of weapons causing unnecessary suffering, as well as the specific ban on chemical weapons, also applies to internal armed conflicts.[9]

(E) While children may be conscripted or enlisted from the age of 15 (Article 8(2)(b)(xxvi), and (e)(vii)), the Court has no jurisdiction over persons *under* the age of 18 at the commission of the crime (Article 26). Thus, a person between 15 and 17 is regarded as a lawful combatant and may commit a crime without being brought to court and punished. A commander could therefore recruit minors into his army expressly for the purpose of forming terrorist units whose members would be immune from prosecution. Moreover, in modern warfare, particularly in developing countries, young persons are more and more involved in armed

---

[8] At 54, para. 97, emphasis added.
[9] See *ibid*, at 64–67, paras 119–124.

hostilities and thus increasingly placed to commit war crimes and crimes against humanity.

B. General Principles of Criminal Law

One of the merits of the Rome Statute is that it sets out in detail the most important principles of criminal law: the ban on analogy, the principle of *favor rei*, the *nullum crimen* and *nulla poena* principles, the principle of non-retroactivity of criminal law, the various forms of international criminal responsibility (for commission of crimes, aiding and abetting, etc.), the responsibility of military commanders and other superiors, the notion of *mens rea*, the grounds for excluding criminal responsibility, the rule of speciality, and so forth. Although most of these principles are familiar to national criminal lawyers, they had never until this time been specified in international treaties or at any rate been spelt out in detail. Hence, this section of the Rome Statute undoubtedly constitutes a major advance in international criminal law and, in addition, contributes to making this branch of law more congruent with the basic requirement of 'specificity'.

Nevertheless, some provisions of the Statute give rise to serious misgivings. I shall confine myself to commenting on only a few provisions.

i. Mens Rea

Article 30 of the Rome Statute defines the mental element of crimes as consisting of intent and knowledge.[10] While it is no doubt meritorious to have defined these two notions, it appears questionable to have excluded recklessness as a culpable *mens rea* under the Statute. One fails to see why, at least in the case of war crimes, this last mental element may not suffice for criminal responsibility to arise. Admittedly, in the case of genocide, crimes against humanity and aggression, the extreme gravity of the offence presupposes that it may only be perpetrated when intent and knowledge are present. However, for less serious crimes, such as war crimes, current international law must be taken to allow for recklessness: for example, it is admissible to convict a person who, when shelling a town, takes a high and unjustifiable risk that civilians will be killed—without, however, *intending,* that they be killed—with the result that the civilians are, in fact, thereby killed.

---

[10] Article 30 ('Mental element') reads: '1. Unless otherwise provided, a person shall be criminally responsible and liable for punishment for a crime within the jurisdiction of the Court only if the material elements are committed with intent and knowledge. 2. For the purposes of this article, a person has intent where: (a) In relation to conduct, that person means to engage in the conduct; (b) In relation to a consequence, that person means to cause that consequence or is aware that it will occur in the ordinary course of events. 3. For the purposes of this article, "knowledge" means awareness that a circumstance exists or a consequence will occur in the ordinary course of events. "Know" and "knowingly" shall be construed accordingly.'

Hence, on this score the Rome Statute marks a step backwards with respect to *lex lata,* and possibly creates a loophole: persons responsible for war crimes, when they acted recklessly, may be brought to trial and convicted before national courts, while they would be acquitted by the ICC. It would seem that the draughtsmen have unduly expanded the shield they intended to provide to the military.

ii. Self-defence

Article 31(1)(c) of the ICC Statute addresses the subject of self-defence.[11] The notion of self-defence as a ground for excusing criminal responsibility laid down in this provision seems to be excessively broad and at variance with existing international criminal law.

While it seems admissible to extend self-defence to the protection of another person or to property essential to the survival of the person or of another person (this may be regarded as implicit in the current notion of self-defence in international criminal law), it is highly questionable to extend the notion at issue to the need to protect 'property which is essential for accomplishing a military mission'. This extension is manifestly outside *lex lata,* and may generate quite a few misgivings. Firstly, via international criminal law a norm of international humanitarian law has been created whereby a serviceman may now lawfully commit an international crime for the purpose of defending any 'property essential for accomplishing a military mission' against an imminent and unlawful use of force. So far such unlawful use of force against the 'property' at issue has not entitled the military to commit war crimes. They could only react by using lawful means or methods of combat or, *ex post facto,* by resorting to lawful reprisals against enemy belligerents. Secondly, the notion of 'property essential for accomplishing a military mission' is very loose and may be difficult to interpret.

iii. Mistake of law

Under Article 32(2) a mistake of law may constitute a ground for excluding criminal responsibility 'if it negates the mental element required for such a crime, or as provided for in Article 33 [on superior orders]'. Thus, a serviceman may be relieved of his responsibility if he can prove that he was not aware that what he was doing was prohibited by international law as a crime and that therefore

---

[11] Article 31 ('Grounds for Excluding Criminal Responsibility') reads in pertinent part: '1. In addition to other grounds for excluding criminal responsibility provided for in this Statute, a person shall not be criminally responsible if, at the time of that person's conduct: ... (c) The person acts reasonably to defend himself or herself or another person or, in the case of war crimes, property which is essential for the survival of the person or another person or property which is essential for accomplishing a military mission, against an imminent and unlawful use of force in a manner proportionate to the degree of danger to the person or the other person or property protected. The fact that the person was involved in a defensive operation conducted by forces shall not in itself constitute a ground for excluding criminal responsibility under this subparagraph.'

he lacked the requisite intent and knowledge or that he was not aware that the superior order he executed was contrary to international criminal law.[12]

First, this rule seems to diverge from current international criminal law, which rules out mistake of law as an excuse, in accordance with the principle upheld in the criminal law of most countries that *ignorantia legis non excusat.* International case law (the *Scuttled U-boats,*[13] the *Flick*[14] and the *Wilhelm Jung*[15] cases) seems to bear out this principle.[16] Admittedly, there are areas of international criminal law which may still be regarded as shrouded in uncertainty and therefore open to conflicting interpretations. Nevertheless, it should be recalled that the broad categories of crimes against humanity, war crimes and genocide embrace offences (such as murder, extermination, enslavement, torture, rape, persecution, deportation, etc.) that are punished by all criminal codes of the world, regardless of whether or not those offences are perpetrated during an armed conflict. It would therefore be to no avail to claim that while individuals are expected and required to know the criminal laws of their own country, they cannot be required to know international criminal law. In short, mistake of law—at least as regards general international law on international crimes[17]—cannot be regarded as an excuse but may be urged in mitigation.

My second remark is that Article 32(2) is all the more questionable within the context of the Rome Statute, for it refers to criminal offences that are enumerated in a specific and detailed manner in the relevant provisions of the Statute: Articles 6 (genocide), 7 (crimes against humanity) and 8 (war crimes). As I have emphasized above, these provisions do not confine themselves to indicating in a summary fashion the classes of offences that they do not define; rather, they provide a detailed description of the main elements of the crimes envisaged therein. This being so,

---

[12] Interestingly, the Rome Statute thus takes up the argument put forward by a defence counsel in the *Flick* case, before a United States Military Court sitting at Nuremberg ('This statute... cannot mean and concern... the act of a human being who acted free from guilt, because he neither was aware of the criminal nature, that he was not conscious of its illegality, or because he had acted under physical compulsion'. Closing statement by defence counsel Dix, in Law Reports of Trials of War Criminals, vol. VI, at 1153).

[13] See *Law Reports of Trials of War Criminals*, vol. XV, at 182–183.

[14] See *Law Reports of Trials of War Criminals*, vol. IX, at 23 and *Law Reports of Trials of War Criminals*, vol. VI, at 1208: 'It was stated in the beginning that responsibility of an individual for infractions of international law is not open to question. In dealing with property located outside his own state, he must be expected to ascertain and keep within applicable law. *Ignorance thereof will not excuse guilt but may mitigate punishment'* (emphasis added).

[15] See Record of Proceedings of the Trial by Canadian Military Court of Wilhelm Jung and Johann Georg Schumacher, held at Aurich (Germany, 15–25 March 1946 (unpublished typescript), at 221).

[16] See, however, the decision delivered by the German *Bundesgerichtshof* on 14 October 1952, in 6 *Neue Juristische Wochenschrift* (1953), at 112.

[17] In the light of the *Scuttled U-Boats* case, where the question revolved around the issue of whether or not the accused was required to know the act of German surrender which laid down law binding upon him, it would seem appropriate to exclude from the proposition set out in the text those pieces of special legislation which are not of a general nature and are not part of the general corpus of international criminal law. This issue could also be construed as a mistake of fact—the fact of German surrender and its consequences—rather than an issue of mistake of law.

there seems to be no justification for relieving persons of criminal responsibility whenever, by ignoring the fact that certain conduct amounts to a crime under the Statute, they lacked the requisite *mens rea* or were unaware that a superior order was unlawful. At the least, it is to be hoped that armies will furnish soldiers with a copy of Article 8 (war crimes) of the Statute and teach them its commandments. It follows that Article 32(2) amounts to a serious loophole in the whole system of international criminal law and may eventually be misused for the purpose of justifying the perpetration of crimes clearly prohibited by international law.

Thirdly, Article 32(2) may constitute a disincentive to the dissemination and implementation of international humanitarian law (why bother learning this branch of law if one can be relieved of criminal responsibility for one's acts by proving that one was ignorant of the fact that they were prohibited under international humanitarian law?).

iv. Superior orders

As pointed out in the paper by Gaeta [. . .][17bis] the correct position under customary international law would seem to be that superior orders are *never* a defence to serious violations of international humanitarian law, be they crimes of genocide, crimes against humanity or war crimes, but may only be urged in mitigation. The Rome Statute provides in Article 33 for a different regulation. Under this provision, superior orders shall not relieve a person of criminal responsibility *unless* the person (a) was legally bound to obey the order, and (b) did not know that the order was unlawful, and (c) the order was not manifestly unlawful. The Article adds, however, that orders to commit genocide or crimes against humanity are always manifestly unlawful. It follows that under Article 33 a superior order may only be urged as a defence for *war crimes* when the order was not *manifestly illegal*. The order would itself remain illegal, and the superior issuing the order liable to punishment, but the subordinate who executed the order in good-faith reliance on its legality, and in circumstances in which it was not 'manifestly unlawful', would have a complete defence entitling him to an acquittal. This conclusion is first of all at odds with *lex lata,* under which any order to commit an international crime—regardless of its classification—is illegal and therefore may not be urged in defence by the subordinate who obeys the order. Secondly, it is all the more surprising because Article 8 of the Rome Statute is intended to specify and enumerate through an exhaustive list the war crimes falling under the ICC jurisdiction. Given this specificity of Article 8, one fails to see under what circumstances the order to commit one of the crimes listed therein may be regarded as being not manifestly unlawful, i.e. if nothing else, it would be 'manifest' in the text of the Rome Statute itself. Therefore, if the subordinate knew the Rome Statute's provisions, then the illegality of any order to commit a war crime as defined in the Statute would *ipso facto* be manifest to him.

[17bis] 'The Defence of Superior Orders: The Statute of International Criminal Court *versus* Customary International Law', in 10 *EJIL* (1999) 172.

Of course, the issue may be clouded by a mistake of fact, but the Statute already provides for defences based on this principle.

On this score, therefore, Article 33 must be faulted as marking a retrogression with respect to existing customary law.

C. Could Retrogressions in the Rome Statute Jeopardize Existing International Law?

If the above propositions are correct, it follows that in various areas of substantive international criminal law the Rome Statute constitutes a retrogression. Will this affect current international law?

The draughtsmen of the Statute seem to have been alert to this danger, for they formulated a few provisions designed to leave existing law unaffected. First of all, Article 10 provides that: 'Nothing in this Part [Part II, on Jurisdiction, Admissibility and Applicable Law] shall be interpreted as limiting or prejudicing in any way existing or developing rules of international law for purposes other than this Statute.' Secondly, Article 22 (on *nullum crimen sine lege*), provides in paragraph 3 that: 'This Article shall not affect the characterization of any conduct as criminal under international law independently of this Statute.' Thus, the Statute itself seems to postulate the future existence of *two possible regimes or corpora of international criminal law,* one established by the Statute and the other laid down in general international criminal law. The Statute also seems to presuppose the partial coincidence of these two bodies of law: they will probably be similar or identical to a very large extent, but there will be areas of discrepancy.

Is there a way of creating a bridge between the two regimes? Clearly, the Court will have to give pride of place to the Statute, as is provided in Article 21, which states that only 'in the second place' can the Court apply 'where appropriate, applicable treaties and principles and rules of international law, including the established principles of international law of armed conflict'. Hence, in case of discrepancy, the Court is bound to give precedence to the rules of criminal law established in the Statute.

While no doubt in some grey areas where the Statute is not explicit or does not regulate matters, general international law will be relied upon by the Court, it remains true that the restrictive attitude taken at Rome in many provisions of substantive criminal law might have adverse consequences on general international law. The gradual development of a Court's case law based on that restrictive attitude might in the long run be conducive to a gradual narrowing of the scope of general principles and rules. This, no doubt, would constitute a serious setback. Moreover, national courts—as well as the ICTY and ICTR—might be tempted to rely on the ICC's restrictive provisions as codifying existing international law.

4. Procedural Law

A. Complementarity

Preambular paragraph 10 of the Statute as well as Articles 1, 17 and 18 lay down the principle that the ICC is complementary to national criminal courts. These provisions create a presumption in favour of action at the level of states. In other words, the ICC does not enjoy primacy over national courts but should only step in when the competent domestic prosecutors or courts fail, or are unwilling or unable to act. The Rome Statute makes it clear that states' judicial authorities have the primary responsibility of prosecuting and punishing international crimes. This should be their normal task, and the ICC can only deal with cases where national judicial systems do not prove to be up to this assignment.

To have provided for this sort of complementarity is in many respects a positive step. Plainly, it falls primarily to national prosecutors and courts to investigate, prosecute and try the numerous international crimes being perpetrated in many parts of the world. First of all, those national institutions are in the best position to do justice, for they normally constitute the *forum conveniens,* where both the evidence and the alleged culprit are to be found. Secondly, under international law, national or territorial states have the right to prosecute and try international crimes, and often even a duty to do so. Thirdly, national jurisdiction over those crimes is normally very broad, and embraces even lesser international crimes, such as sporadic and isolated crimes, which do not make up, nor are part of, a pattern of criminal behaviour. Were the ICC also to deal with all sorts of international crimes, including those of lesser gravity, it would soon be flooded with cases and become ineffective as a result of an excessive and disproportionate workload. To a certain extent, this has already occurred at the ICTY and has necessitated the *withdrawal* of indictments of minor individuals in the political-military hierarchy.[18]

It is therefore quite appropriate that the ICC should intervene only when national institutions fail to do so.

However, complementarity might lend itself to abuse. It might amount to a shield used by states to thwart international justice. This might happen with regard to those crimes (genocide, crimes against humanity) which are normally perpetrated with the help and assistance, or the connivance or acquiescence, of national authorities. In these cases, state authorities may pretend to investigate

---

[18] See, for example, the *Order granting leave for withdrawal of charges against Govedarica, Gruban, Janjić, Kostić, Paspalj, Pavlić, Popović, Predojević, Savić, Bablć and Spaonja* issued by Judge Riad on 8 May 1998: '...Considering the submission of the Prosecutor that the increase in the number of arrests and surrenders of accused to the custody of the International Tribunal has compelled her to re-evaluate all outstanding indictments *vis-à-vis* the overall investigative and prosecutorial strategies of the Office of the Prosecutor...Considering that the named accused could appropriately be tried in another forum, such as a State forum...'

and try crimes, and may even conduct proceedings, but only for the purpose of actually protecting the allegedly responsible persons.

This danger is all the more serious because the principle of complementarity also applies to *third states, i.e. states that are not parties to the Statute.* Under Article 18(1) all states parties, as well as 'those States which, taking into account the information available, would normally exercise jurisdiction over the crimes concerned', must be notified by the Prosecutor that he intends to initiate an investigation upon referral of a state or intends to proceed with an investigation initiated *proprio motu.* Furthermore, although no notification is necessary in case of referral by the Security Council under Article 13(b), any state having jurisdiction over the crimes which form the object of the referral is entitled to inform the Prosecutor that it is investigating or prosecuting the case (this proposition can be logically inferred from Article 17). All this entails that any third state having jurisdiction over the crimes may invoke the principle of complementarity, thus obliging the Prosecutor to defer to the state's authorities. True, for all these cases Article 17 of the Court's Statute envisages a range of safeguards designed to quash any attempt made by national authorities *de facto* to shield the alleged culprits. One may however wonder whether the monitoring by the ICC of such state attempts to escape its jurisdiction will be sufficiently effective and thorough to ensure that international justice is done.

By the same token, one might wonder whether the ICC may act efficiently to preserve the evidence whenever it might appear that national authorities are trying to evade international justice: are the provisions of Article 18(6)[19] sufficient when one is faced with a state bent on shunning international jurisdiction and therefore unwilling to cooperate in the search for and collection of evidence, or even willing to destroy such evidence to evade justice?

B. Preconditions to the Exercise of Jurisdiction

The preconditions to the exercise of the jurisdiction of the ICC are laid down in Article 12(2) of the Rome Statute.[20] This article—like so much else, the product

---

[19] Article 18(6) provides: 'Pending a ruling by the Pre-Trial Chamber, or at any time when the Prosecutor has deferred an investigation under this article, the Prosecutor may, on an exceptional basis, seek authority from the Pre-Trial Chamber to pursue necessary investigative steps for the purpose of preserving evidence where there is a unique opportunity to obtain important evidence or there is a significant risk that such evidence may not be subsequently available.'

[20] Article 12 ('Preconditions to the exercise of Jurisdiction') reads:

1. A State which becomes a Party to this Statute thereby accepts the jurisdiction of the Court with respect to the crimes referred to in article 5.
2. In the case of article 13, para. (a) or (c), the Court may exercise its jurisdiction if one or more of the following States are Parties to this Statute or have accepted the jurisdiction of the Court in accordance with para. 3:
    (a) The State on the territory of which the conduct in question occurred or, if the crime was committed on board a vessel or aircraft, the State of registration of that vessel or aircraft;
    (b) The State of which the person accused of the crime is a national.

of intense negotiations and compromise—has its pros and cons. On the one hand, it is meritorious in allowing that the nationals of a state which did not sign the treaty may be internationally prosecuted for crimes committed on foreign soil. An important class of persons falling under this category would be soldiers serving abroad; for instance, troops of one country committing atrocities in another country. It is right that they should be prosecutable under the Statute.

It would be fallacious to consider that in this way the Rome Statute imposes obligations upon states not parties (for example, the United States, if—as anticipated—it never signs and ratifies the treaty). Nationals of third states perpetrating crimes at home are, of course, not subject to the ICC's jurisdiction. Admittedly, if they commit crimes abroad, they may become amenable to the Court's jurisdiction if the territorial state has accepted the Court's jurisdiction. However, the territorial state would have jurisdiction over the crimes in any event—territorial jurisdiction over crimes is firmly established in international law, alongside the active and passive personality principles. The ICC would simply exercise its jurisdiction in lieu of the territorial state. Hence, the Rome Statute does not impose obligations upon third states. It simply authorizes the Court to exercise its jurisdiction with regard to nationals of third states, whenever these nationals may have committed crimes in the territory of a state party (or of a state accepting *ad hoc* the exercise of the Court's jurisdiction). Thus the Rome Statute authorizes the ICC to substitute itself for a consenting state, which would thus waive its right to exercise its criminal jurisdiction. This does not appear to be contrary to international law.

However, a serious problem may arise whenever a third state has made a treaty with a state party or a state accepting *ad hoc* the Court's jurisdiction, whereby the latter state either waives its criminal jurisdiction over crimes committed on its territory by nationals of the former state or undertakes to extradite those nationals to the other state. In such cases there obviously arises for the state party to the Rome Statute (or a state having accepted *ad hoc* the Court's jurisdiction) a conflict between inconsistent international obligations. The Rome Statute only partially takes into account and makes provision for such conflicts. In Article 90(4–6) it envisages the possibility that extradition may be requested, under an international treaty, by a state not party to a state party, and this request for extradition may be in conflict with a request for surrender from the ICC. For such cases the Rome Statute does not impose upon states parties the obligation to give priority to the Court's request for surrender from the Court: Article 90(6) simply lists a set of factors that the requested state must take into account when deciding on the matter. This regulation would seem to be questionable on three

---

3. If the acceptance of a State which is not a Party to this Statute is required under para. 2, that State may, by declaration lodged with the Registrar, accept the exercise of jurisdiction by the Court with respect to the crime in question.

The accepting State shall cooperate with the Court without any delay or exception in accordance with Part 9.

counts: first, it does not take into account the possibility that under its national legislation the requested state may be obliged to waive its jurisdiction without even triggering the extradition process; secondly, it does not envisage the case of a requested state that, while not a party to the Rome Statute, has accepted the Court's jurisdiction *ad hoc:* thirdly, it does not impose upon the requested state the obligation to give priority to the Court's request for surrender.

Let us now move to an even more questionable side of the rule on the preconditions to the exercise of jurisdiction, namely Article 12(2). The major flaw of this provision appears whenever one is faced with crimes such as genocide, war crimes in a civil war, or crimes against humanity, that are normally committed at the instigation or with the support or acquiescence of the national authorities. If a state on whose territory such crimes are perpetrated by its own nationals has not accepted the Court's jurisdiction at the time the crimes are committed, the ICC will be impotent to act. There is however an exception: this is when the Security Council decides to refer the 'situation' to the Prosecutor pursuant to Article 13(b), in which case the state's acceptance of the Court's jurisdiction is not required. This is the 'sledgehammer' of the ICC. In effect, the mechanism by which the Security Council established the ICTY and ICTR is imported into the ICC. This mechanism may prove to be the most effective to seize the Court whenever situations similar to those in the former Yugoslavia and Rwanda occur.

C. The Trigger Mechanisms and in Particular the Role of the Prosecutor

It is well known that two tendencies clashed at the Rome Conference: some states (including the United States, China and others) insisted on granting the power to set investigations and prosecutions in motion to states and the Security Council only; other states (the group of the so-called like-minded countries) were bent on advocating the institution of an independent Prosecutor capable of initiating *proprio motu* investigations and prosecutions. The clash was between sovereignty-oriented countries and states eager to implement the rule of law in the world community.

The final result was a compromise. First of all the right to carry out investigations and prosecute was not left to the authorities of individual states or entrusted to a commission of inquiry or similar bodies; this option, which was undoubtedly open to the Rome conference, was discarded. Instead, a Prosecutor was envisaged.

Once they decided to set up a Prosecutor, states had two options: (i) the Nuremberg model, whereby the Prosecutor is an official of the state that has initiated the investigation and prosecution, and is therefore designated by that state and remains throughout under its control; (ii) the ICTY and ICTR model, whereby the Prosecutor is a totally independent body. Fortunately the latter option was chosen. As an independent and impartial body, the Prosecutor was granted the power to investigate and prosecute *ex officio,* although subject to significant restrictions.

Secondly, the power to initiate investigations was conferred both on the Prosecutor (subject to judicial scrutiny) and on states, as well as the Security Council. In short, a three-pronged system was envisaged:

(a) investigations may be initiated at the request of a state, but then the Prosecutor must immediately notify all other states, so as to enable those which intend to exercise their jurisdiction to rely upon the principle of complementarity;

(b) investigations may be initiated by the Prosecutor, but only subject to two conditions: (i) a Pre-trial Chamber must authorize them and (ii) they must be notified to all states;

(c) investigations may be initiated at the request of the Security Council, and in this case the intervention of the Pre-trial Chamber is not required, nor is notification to all states.

Clearly, this is a balanced system, which takes into account both the interests of states and the demands of international justice. In addition, as has been rightly pointed out,[21] the Prosecutor acts both as an 'administrator of justice' (in that he acts in the interest of international justice by pursuing the goal of identifying, investigating and prosecuting the most serious international crimes) and, as in common law legal orders, as a party in an adversarial system.

The best safeguard for the proper administration of international justice can be seen in a key provision of the Statute: Article 53(2). On the strength of this provision, the Prosecutor enjoys broad powers in sifting through cases initiated either by entities that may be politically motivated (states) or by a political organ (the Security Council). By virtue of Article 53(2) the Prosecutor may decide that there is not a sufficient basis for a prosecution even when the case has been initiated by a state or by the Security Council. It should be noted that under this provision the Prosecutor may conclude that a prosecution is not warranted not only because (i) there is no legal or factual basis for a warrant of arrest or a summons to issue, but also because (ii) the case is inadmissible under Article 17, as a state which has jurisdiction over the crimes is investigating or prosecuting it, and—what is even more important—if (iii) 'a prosecution is not in the interests of justice, taking into account all the circumstances, including the gravity of the crime, the interests of the victims and the age or infirmity of the alleged perpetrator, and his or her role in the alleged crime'.

This rule is of crucial importance, for it assigns to the Prosecutor the role of an independent and impartial organ responsible for seeing to it that the interests of justice and the rule of law prevail. The Prosecutor may thus bar any initiative of states or even any deferral by the Security Council which may prove politically

---

[21] See on this point the apposite remarks of Zappalà, 'Il procuratore della Corte Penale Internazionale: luci ed ombre', 82 *Rivista di diritto internazionale* (1999) 39 *et seq.*

motivated and contrary to the interests of justice. In short, 'prosecutorial discretion' has been enshrined in the Statute (subject to review by the state making a referral and by the Pre-trial Chamber); an important principle, since not every crime which technically falls within the ICC's jurisdiction should be prosecuted before the Court.

One might object that this balanced and well-justified relation between political entities (states and the Security Council) and an 'administrator of justice' such as the Prosecutor may be thwarted whenever the Security Council decides, under Article 16 of the Rome Statute, to request the Prosecutor to defer any investigation or prosecution for a period of 12 months (or a shorter period). At first sight this provision seems to allow a political body to interfere grossly with a judicial body. However, a sound interpretation of this provision leads to the conclusion that the powers of the Security Council are not unfettered. The request may only be made by a resolution adopted under Chapter VII of the United Nations Charter. Hence, the Security Council may request the Prosecutor to defer his activity only if it explicitly decides that continuation of his investigation or prosecution may amount to a threat to the peace. The Prosecutor is undoubtedly bound by that request, but the whole context of the Statute and the reference in Article 16 to Chapter VII of the United Nations Charter seem to rule out the possibility that that request be arbitrary.[22] Moreover, the Security Council must 'show its hand' if it wishes to stay an ICC proceeding—and continue to show its hand every 12 months—and this visibility creates accountability.

D. The Role of the Judges

The Rome Conference has rightly opted for a system that ensures that the 18 Judges making up the Court be and remain independent of any state: under Article 36(9)(a) they are elected for nine years and may not be re-elected.

Nevertheless, the Statute seems to evince a certain mistrust in the Judges, despite the safeguard that, to qualify for that position, they must not only be professionally competent but also of high moral character, impartiality and integrity (Article 36(3)(a)). First of all, the Statute includes provisions that are unusual in a basic text and are normally laid down in sub-statutory provisions (e.g. the Rules of Procedure): (i) detailed provisions envisage the disqualification of Judges (Article 41); (ii) similarly, the Statute regulates in detail the removal of Judges from office (Article 46); and (iii) disciplinary measures are provided for (Article 47).

Secondly, the Rules of Procedure and Evidence may only be proposed by Judges and must be adopted by the Assembly of the states parties (Article 51). It appears likely that this was a reaction against the ICTY and ICTR precedents, where the Judges were, in a sense, both rule-makers and decision-makers. There were good reasons, however, for allocating this role to the Judges of the *ad hoc*

---

[22] *Ibid.*

tribunals and for the extensive amendments they made in discharging this role. The ICTY's and ICTR's Rules of Procedure and Evidence constituted the first international criminal procedural and evidentiary codes ever adopted and they had to be amended gradually to deal with a panoply of contingencies which were not anticipated by the framers of their Statutes.

Under the ICC Statute, such judicial rule-making is impossible, or at least only marginally possible; under Article 51(3):

After the adoption of the Rules of Procedure and Evidence, in urgent cases where the Rules do not provide for a specific situation before the Court, the judges may, by a two-thirds majority, draw up provisional Rules to be applied until adopted, amended or rejected at the next ordinary or special session of the Assembly of States Parties.

Nevertheless, what the Statute does not rule out—and indeed cannot rule out—is the emergence of a doctrine of precedent (*stare decisis*) among the Judges of the Court, whereby they follow each others decisions and practice in the interests of a coherent jurisprudence. This is likely to emerge, as occurred at the ICTY and ICTR, and should be welcomed. In this respect, attention should be drawn to Article 21(2), which provides that 'the Court may apply principles and rules of law as interpreted in its previous decisions', and which clearly favours this development of precedent.

E. Cooperation of States

i. General

Plainly, in the case of the ICC as in that of the ICTY and ICTR, state cooperation is crucial to the effectiveness of judicial process. The decisions, orders and requests of international criminal courts can only be enforced by others, namely national authorities (or international organizations). Unlike domestic criminal courts, international tribunals have no enforcement agencies at their disposal: without the intermediary of national authorities, they cannot execute arrest warrants; they cannot seize evidentiary material, nor compel witnesses to give testimony, nor search the scenes where crimes have allegedly been committed. For all these purposes, international courts must turn to state authorities and request them to take action to assist the courts' officers and investigators. Without the help of these authorities, international courts cannot operate. Admittedly, this holds true for all international institutions, which need the support of states to be able to operate. However international criminal courts need the support of states more, and more urgently, than any other international institution, because their actions have a direct impact on individuals who live on the territory of sovereign states and are subject to their jurisdiction. Trials must be expeditious; evidence must be collected before it becomes stale and the court must be able to summon witnesses to testify at short notice.

I shall make a second general point. In deciding upon how to regulate the cooperation of states with an international criminal court, the framers of the Court's Statute had to choose between two possible models. First, the inter-state model, whereby the relations between states and the international court are shaped on the pattern of inter-state judicial cooperation in criminal matters. Under this model the Court has no superior authority over states except for the legal power to adjudicate crimes perpetrated by individuals subject to state sovereignty. Apart from this power, the Court cannot in any way force states to lend their cooperation, let alone exercise coercive powers within the territory of sovereign states.

The second model could be termed 'supra-state'. It departs from the traditional setting of state to state judicial cooperation, where by definition all cooperating states are on an equal footing. This more progressive model presupposes that the international judicial body is vested with sweeping powers not only *vis-à-vis* individuals subject to the sovereign authority of states, but also towards states themselves. Under this model the international court is empowered to issue binding orders to states and, in case of non-compliance, may set in motion enforcement mechanisms. What is no less important, the international court is given the final say on evidentiary matters: states are not allowed to withhold evidence on grounds of self-defined national interests or to refuse to execute arrest warrants or other courts' orders. In short, the international court is endowed with an authority over states that markedly differentiates it from other international institutions. The ICTY and ICTR—with the Chapter VII authority of the Security Council behind them—follow this coercive, 'supra-state' model.

It is interesting to note, as a third general point, that there exists a marked difference between the ICC and the two *ad hoc* tribunals. The law of the *ad hoc* international tribunals as it concerns state cooperation is largely judge-made. Article 29 of the ICTY Statute—and the corresponding article, Article 28 of the ICTR Statute—simply provide in a general way that 'States shall cooperate with the International Tribunal' and 'shall comply without undue delay with any request for assistance or an order issued by a Trial Chamber'. However, the specific practice as it relates to arrest warrants and orders for transfer of an accused, requests for assistance, *subpoenas*—to whom they may be addressed, the required breadth and specificity—the penalties available for a non-cooperative state, and many related questions, were left to the Judges to define. This happened in due course in the *Blaškić* case when a Trial Chamber issued *subpoenas* to Croatia and one of its senior ministers; a decision which was later overturned on appeal, confining *subpoenas* to individuals acting in a private capacity, while allowing binding orders to be directed to states.[23]

In contrast to the ICTY and ICTR, which are creatures of the Security Council moulded into their present shape in large part by the Judges, states have had the opportunity, in drawing up the ICC Statute, to express themselves, in no uncer-

---

[23] [ICTY] *Judgment on the Request of the Republic of Croatia for Review of the Decision of Trial Chamber II of 18 July 1997*, 29 October 1997, Appeals Chamber.

tain terms, about how they wish international justice to work, and they have adopted a mostly state-oriented approach.

ii. *The largely state-oriented approach taken in the Rome statute*

Four points are relevant in this regard.

First, the Statute does not specify whether the taking of evidence, execution of summonses and warrants, etc. is to be undertaken by officials of the Prosecutor with the assistance, when needed, of state authorities, or whether instead it will be for state enforcement or judicial authorities to execute those acts at the request of the Prosecutor. Judging from the insistence in the Statute on the need to comply with the requirements of national legislation, however, the conclusion would seem to be warranted that the framers of the Statute intended the latter.

Secondly, in the event of failure of states to cooperate, Article 87(7) provides for the means substantially enunciated by the ICTY in the Appeals Chamber decision in *Blaškić (subpoena)*, namely, 'the Court may make a finding to that effect and refer the matter to the Assembly of States Parties or, where the Security Council referred the matter to the Court, to the Security Council'. However, the ICC could arguably have gone further and articulated the consequences of a Court's finding of non-cooperation by a state. The Statute could have specified that the Assembly of States Parties might agree upon countermeasures, or authorize contracting states to adopt such countermeasures, or, in the event of disagreement, that each contracting state might take such countermeasures. In addition, it would have been appropriate to provide for the possibility of the Security Council stepping in and adopting sanctions even in cases where the matter had not been previously referred by this body to the Court: one fails to see why the Security Council should not act upon Chapter VII if a state refuses to cooperate and such refusal amounts to a threat to the peace, even in cases previously referred to the Court by a state or initiated by the Prosecutor *proprio motu*. Of course, this possibility is not *excluded* by the ICC Statute, but it also would have been a good idea expressly to include it.

Thirdly, in case of competing requests for surrender or extradition, i.e. a request for arrest and surrender of a person, emanating from the Court, and a request for extradition from a state not party, the request from the Court does not automatically prevail. As I have already pointed out above, under Article 90(6) and (7), a state party may decide between compliance with the request from the Court and compliance with the request from a non-party state with which the state party is bound by an extradition treaty. This seems odd, for one would have thought that the obligations stemming from the Rome Statute should have taken precedence over those flowing from other treaties. Arguably, this priority would follow both from the primacy of a Statute establishing a *universal* criminal court over bilateral treaties (or multilateral treaties binding on a group of states) and from the very purpose of the Statute—to administer international justice in the interest of peace. It seems instead that the Statute, faced with the dilemma of international justice versus national justice, has left the option to the relevant states.

Fourthly, as regards the protection of national security information, the Statute substantially caters to state concerns by creating a national security exception to requests for assistance. Article 93(4) provides that 'a State Party may deny a request for assistance, in whole or in part, only if the request concerns the production of any documents or disclosure of evidence which relates to its national security'. Admittedly, Article 72, to which this provision refers, does envisage a complex mechanism designed to induce a state invoking national security concerns to disclose as much as possible the information it wishes to withhold. This mechanism is largely based on the *Blaškić* decision of the ICTY Appeals Chamber. However, the various stages of this mechanism are turned in the Statute into formal modalities that will be cumbersome and time-consuming.[24] In addition, in *Blaškić* the emphasis was on the obligation of states to disclose information; only in exceptional circumstances were states allowed to resort to special steps for the purpose of shielding that information from undue disclosure to entities other than the Court. In Article 72 emphasis is instead laid on the right of states to deny the Court's request for assistance.

F. The Role Assigned to the Victim

One of the merits of the ICC Statute is the role assigned to the victims of atrocities. Article 15(3) (The Prosecutor) provides that, 'Victims may *make representations* to the Pre-Trial Chamber, in accordance with the Rules of Procedure and Evidence' regarding the reasonableness or otherwise of proceeding with an investigation (emphasis added). Under Article 19, victims may also make submissions in proceedings with respect to jurisdiction or admissibility. What is even more important, the victims may take part in the trial proceedings. They may do so in two ways. First of all, they may set out in court their 'views' and 'concerns' on matters of fact and law. Pursuant to Article 68(3):

Where the personal interests of the victims are affected, the Court shall permit *their views and concerns* to be presented and considered at stages of the proceedings determined to be appropriate by the Court and in a manner which is not prejudicial to or inconsistent with

---

[24] Article 72 ('Protection of national security information') establishes a three-step procedure when a State—or individual—invokes national security. Article 72 is triggered when a state is of the opinion that 'disclosure of information [requested by the Court or Prosecutor] would prejudice its national security interests'. First, cooperative means are employed to reach an amicable settlement, e.g. modification of the request, a determination by the Court of the relevance of the information sought or agreement of conditions under which the assistance could be provided. Second, if cooperative means fail, and the state decides against disclosure, it must notify the Court or Prosecutor 'of the specific reasons for its decision, unless a specific description of the reasons would itself necessarily result in such prejudice to the State's national security interests'. The Court may then hold further consultations on the matter, if need be *ex parte* and/or in camera. The third step in the event that the state is found to be not complying with its obligations is for the Court to refer the matter to the Assembly of States Parties or, if the Security Council originally referred the matter to the Court, to the Security Council.

the rights of the accused and a fair and impartial trial. Such views and concerns may be presented by the legal representatives of the victims where the Court considers it appropriate, in accordance with the Rules of Procedure and Evidence. (Emphasis added.)

This provision is of great significance. For the first time in international criminal proceedings the victims are allowed to take part in such proceedings by expounding in court their 'views and concerns', either in person or through their legal counsel, on matters relevant to the proceedings. Although it will be for the Assembly of States Parties to define and specify the standing of the victims in the Rules of Procedure and Evidence, there is no gainsaying that this Article marks a great advance in international criminal procedure.

The second modality of victims' participation in the trial proceedings concerns the possibility for the victims to seek reparation, restitution, compensation or rehabilitation. This possibility is envisaged in Article 75(1) and (3), albeit in a rather contorted or convoluted manner. Once again, it is to be hoped that the Rules of Procedure and Evidence will duly elaborate upon this matter and adequately spell out the procedural rights of victims.[25]

These provisions allowing victims to have a role in the administration of justice before the Court are highly innovative in the context of international tribunals. No such allowance was made at Nuremberg, Tokyo, the ICTY or the ICTR. In continental civil law systems, the concept of *partie civile* is, of course, well known, but in adversarial systems—of whose procedure the four above-mentioned tribunals overwhelmingly partake—justice is administered in the form of a contest between the State, or the executive, in the shape of the Prosecutor, and the defendant, with the Judge acting as arbiter between them, and played out before the jury as trier of fact. Victims, in this system, utterly lack *locus standi*. However, the ICC differs from national, adversarial systems, in which the law courts are the permanent, indispensable components of a civilized and ordered society; the ICC, by contrast, was created in response to the fact that 'during this century millions of children, women and men have been victims of unimaginable atrocities that deeply shock the conscience of humanity' (Preamble). The victims of these atrocities are thus central to the notion of international criminal justice. It is therefore appropriate that their needs and demands be given voice in the ICC Statute.

G. The Attempt to Weld Elements of the Inquisitorial Model into the Adversarial System

The points just made with regard to the role of victims lead me to deal, albeit briefly, with the more general question of the type of proceedings chosen at

---

[25] See also Article 65(4) stating that a Trial Chamber may request additional evidence if this is required 'in the interest of the victims'. It should also be noted that Article 43(6) provides for the establishment of a Victims and Witnesses Unit, in common with the ICTR and ICTY.

Rome, i.e. whether the trial before the ICC must follow the civil law model (the inquisitorial system) or rather the common law model (the adversarial approach).

It is clear from even a cursory examination of the Rome Statute that states have basically opted for the common law approach. No investigating judge or chamber has been instituted, and the investigations and prosecution are entrusted to the Prosecutor, to whom it falls to search for and collect the evidence and prosecute the case before the Court. In addition, one can discern in the Statute the typical feature of adversarial proceedings, namely the fact that the evidence, instead of being submitted to the court by an investigating judge, is presented in oral proceedings and exhibits tendered by each party to the trial are admitted into evidence if and when it is so decided by the Court.

Although the common law system has been basically adopted, a number of fundamental elements typical of the civil law approach have been incorporated. I shall list those which I consider the principal ones.

First of all, it is clear from the Statute that the Prosecutor is not simply, or not only, an instrument of executive justice, a party to the proceedings whose exclusive interest is to present the facts and evidence as seen by him or her in order to accuse and to secure the indictee's conviction. The Prosecutor is rather conceived of as both a party to the proceedings and also an impartial truth-seeker or organ of justice. This is, among other things, evinced by Article 54(1)(a) whereby:

In order to establish the truth [the Prosecutor] shall extend the investigation to cover all facts and evidence relevant to an assessment of whether there is criminal responsibility under this Statute and, in doing so. *investigate incriminating and exonerating circumstances equally.* (Emphasis added.)

Secondly, at the pre-trial stage, the Prosecutor normally acts under the scrutiny of a Pre-trial Chamber, which to a large extent resembles the *Giudice per le indagini preliminari* (Judge dealing with preliminary matters) provided for in the 1989 Italian Code of Criminal Procedure (that basically opts for the adversarial system, subject however to some major concessions to the inquisitorial approach). If the Prosecutor decides to initiate investigations *proprio motu,* pursuant to Article 15(3), he needs the Chamber's authorization to conduct such investigation. Furthermore, any time a state having jurisdiction over a crime requests the Prosecutor to defer to the state jurisdiction, a Pre-trial Chamber may nevertheless, upon request of the Prosecutor, authorize the investigation (Article 18(2)). Similarly, the Chamber may authorize the Prosecutor to take steps for the purpose of preserving evidence when the Prosecutor has deferred an investigation to a state (Article 18(6)). The Pre-trial Chamber is also responsible for deciding upon challenges to the admissibility of a case or to the jurisdiction of the Court, prior to the confirmation of the charges (Article 19(6)).

Thirdly, as pointed out above, victims may take part in the proceedings, even at the pre-trial stage, and seek compensation or reparation. Thus, as in civil law systems, civil proceedings designed to claim reparation for the injuries caused by a crime are made part and parcel of criminal proceedings (designed to establish whether the accused is liable for the crime).

Fourthly, at the trial stage the Trial Chambers are entrusted with a pro-active role—typical of civil law systems—with regard to evidence. Pursuant to Article 64(5)(d), a Chamber may 'order the production of evidence in addition to that already collected prior to the trial or presented during the trial by the parties'.

Fifthly, the accused has the right, during trial, 'to make an unsworn oral or written statement in his or her defence' (Article 67(1)(h)). This, again, is a departure from the common law system and from the ICTY and ICTR Statutes and Rules of Procedure and Evidence (where no provision is made for the accused to be confronted by the witnesses; the accused may take part in the proceedings only *qua* witness in his own behalf and only if he decides to testify during the defence case, after all the prosecution evidence has been heard). This regulation of the Rome Statute seems to be a move towards the civil law system.

Having stressed the points of convergence between the two systems, I should add that in many areas the Statute does not provide any clue as to whether the proceedings will be adversarial or inquisitorial. Thus, for instance, it does not indicate whether the order of presentation of evidence will be that typical of common law systems (examination-in-chief, cross-examination and re-examination). Nor does the Statute indicate whether appeals will follow the continental or the common law system, i.e. whether appellate proceedings will entail a complete rehearing on facts and law, or cassation on a point of law, or will be confined to the judicial review of specifically alleged grave errors of act or law.

5. Concluding Remarks

As a multilateral treaty,[26] the Rome Statute, in spite of its unique features as well as its flaws, marks an indisputable advance in international *procedural* criminal law. It establishes a permanent and complex mechanism for international justice which by and large seems well balanced. In particular, the three-pronged system set up in Rome for triggering the Court's action, if somewhat cumbersome, strikes a fairly satisfactory balance between states' concerns and the demands of international criminal justice. In addition, the role assigned to victims in international criminal proceedings before the Court is extremely innovative; it is indicative of the meritorious acceptance of a fundamental feature of civil law systems within a procedure basically grounded in the adversarial system typical of common law countries. By contrast, the framers of the Rome Statute were not sufficiently bold to jettison the sovereignty-oriented approach to state cooperation with the Court and opt for a 'supra-national' approach. Instead of granting the Court greater

---

[26] See Section 2 *supra*.

authority over states, the draughtsmen have left too many loopholes permitting states to delay or even thwart the Court's proceedings.

The Rome Statute appears to be less commendable as far as *substantive criminal* law is concerned. True, many crimes have been defined with the required degree of specificity, and the general principles of criminal liability have been set out in detail. Furthermore, the notion of war crimes has rightly been extended to offences committed in times of internal armed conflict. In addition, much progress has been made in the field of penalties, for capital punishment has been excluded.[27] However, in many areas of substantive criminal law the Statute marks a retrogression with respect to existing international law. This applies in particular to war crimes (in spite of the progress just underlined). Among the various means of restricting jurisdiction over such crimes, the following appear in the Statute: (i) the exclusion of the use of modern weapons that are inherently indiscriminate or cause unnecessary suffering from this category of crimes; (ii) the fact that allowance has been made for superior orders to relieve subordinates of their responsibility for the execution of orders involving the commission of war crimes; (iii) the exclusion of liability for reckless commission of international crimes (as pointed put above, in practice this exclusion is only relevant with respect to war crimes); (iv) the fact that Article 124 allows states to declare, upon becoming parties to the Statute, that the Court's jurisdiction over war crimes committed by their nationals or on their territory shall not become operative for a period of seven years.[28] One is therefore left with the impression that the framers have been eager to shield their servicemen as much as possible from being brought to trial for, and possibly convicted of, war crimes.

In sum, a tentative appraisal of the Rome Statute cannot but be chequered: in many respects the Statute marks a great advance in international criminal law, in others it proves instead faulty; in particular, it is marred by being too obsequious to state sovereignty.

The diplomat and historian C.J. Burckhardt once stated that the 1899 Hague Conventions constituted a 'mis-print in world history'. Certainly, he was wrong. It is equally certain that, for all its flaws, the Rome Statute, far from amounting to a 'mis-print', represents a luminous page in world history.

---

[27] It is worth noting that the ICC Statute provides for a maximum penalty of life imprisonment of a person convicted of offences under the Statute: the death sentence is not envisaged. This represents an advance, in humanitarian terms, on the Nuremberg and Tokyo Tribunals' imposition of the death penalty and is in line with the Statutes of the ICTY and ICTR and current international human rights law, which does not endorse capital punishment (see. e.g. Article 6(2),(4) and (5) of the International Covenant on Civil and Political Rights).

[28] Article 124 (Transitional Provision) reads: 'Notwithstanding article 12 para. 1, a State, on becoming a party to this Statute, may declare that, for a period of seven years after the entry into force of this Statute for the State concerned, it does not accept the jurisdiction of the Court with respect to the category of crimes referred to in article 8 when a crime is alleged to have been committed by its nationals or on its territory....'

It is to be hoped that the ICC will be established as soon as possible. One of the keys to its success, it is submitted, lies in the choice and election of highly professional and absolutely independent persons for the positions of Prosecutor and Judges. The election of persons of great competence and integrity may ensure that the ICC will become an efficient body, capable of administering international criminal justice in such a manner as to attract the trust and respect of states, while fully realizing the demands of justice. Furthermore, it will be crucial for the Court to be provided with adequate financial means so as to be able to work efficiently. Thirdly, the provisions on state cooperation with the Court should be clarified and strengthened so as to leave no loopholes available to those states which are unwilling to allow the Court to exercise criminal jurisdiction over persons under their control. Fourthly, the Rules of Procedure and Evidence to be drafted should enhance certain significant elements of civil law systems so as to weld into a fundamentally adversarial system the best features of the inquisitorial model.

In short, it is imperative that all states and individuals concerned strive not only to make the ICC a living reality, but also to improve its profile as much as possible. Now more than ever is a permanent international criminal court needed to curb man's tendency to annihilate his neighbour, mistaking him for his own shadow.[29]

[29] C. G. Jung, describing a person's shadow as 'his own worst danger', wrote: 'It is everybody's allotted fate to become conscious of and learn to deal with this shadow...If, for instance, the French Swiss should assume that the German Swiss were all devils, we in Switzerland could have the grandest civil war in no time...', 'The Fight with the Shadow' in *Essays on Contemporary Events* (1946), at 6–7.

Index

dum-dum bullets 196, 199–200
general principle 199–201
length of wars 198
preparatory works 195
proposed interpretation 195–8
'suffering' 195
'unnecessary suffering' 197–8
hypervelocity rifles 192–3
incendiary weapons 192
increasing use in modern wars 192–3
negative stand as to normative value of
    Article 23(e) 208–11
neo-conventional weapons 208–11
practice of States in relation to Article
    23(e) 201–7

atomic bomb 202
comparison test 206–7
irregular-shaped bullets 202
military imperativeness test 206
military manuals 203–6
proportionality test 206
saw-edged bayonets 202
shotguns 201–2
prohibited, whether 192–217
significance of Article 23(e) 214
specific-ban approach 214–15
specific bans 193–4
suggested general principle 216–17
ut res magis valeat quam pereat 212–13
vagueness of Article 23(e) 211–12